Contents

4   Fiction   95

INTEGRATING LITERATURE

IN THE CONTENT AREAS

*Enhancing
Adolescent Learning
& Literacy*

SHARON KANE

STATE UNIVERSITY OF NEW YORK AT OSWEGO

Holcomb Hathaway, Publishers
Scottsdale, Arizona

Library of Congress Cataloging-in-Publication Data

Kane, Sharon.
    Integrating literature in the content areas : enhancing adolescent
learning and literacy / Sharon Kane. — 1st ed.
        p. cm.
    Includes bibliographical references and index.
    ISBN 978-1-890871-80-2
    1. Content area reading.   2. Interdisciplinary approach in education.   3.
Literature—Study and teaching (Secondary)   4. Teenagers—Books and reading.
I. Title.
    LB1050.455.K363 2008
    428.4071′2—dc22

                                    2007037397

I dedicate this book to Molly Keating Kane

Holcomb Hathaway, Publishers, Inc.
6207 North Cattletrack Road
Scottsdale, Arizona 85250
(480) 991-7881
www.hh-pub.com

10 9 8 7 6 5 4 3 2 1

ISBN 13: 978-1-890871-80-2

7 How-To and Hands-On Books   261

8 Concluding Thoughts   301

I've received requests from some readers to give information about myself and to talk a bit about what audiences I envision for this text. I'll do both here.

I earned my B.A. from LeMoyne College, my M.S. from the State University of New York at Oswego, and my Ph.D. from Syracuse University. I taught reading in middle schools and high schools for nine years, then taught college writing courses for six. Since then, I have been in the Curriculum & Instruction Department at SUNY Oswego, where I teach a variety of courses, including Literacy in the Content Areas; Literature, Arts, and Media; English Methods; and Teaching with Young Adult Literature.

It won't surprise you to hear that I spend a good deal of my time reading and writing for pleasure, and that I belong to both a writing group and a book discussion club. I also enjoy travel. In 2004 I went on a pilgrimage, walking a major part of the Camino de Santiago across northern Spain. In 2006 I traveled to West Africa, where I had the privilege of working with teachers in Benin.

I believe this book will be useful to teachers, librarians, literacy coaches, administrators, college faculty, and parents. You who are teachers often tell me that you'd love to read more trade books related to your content area, for pleasure as well as for the purposes of keeping current and incorporating interesting information into your lessons. You also want to recommend books to students who show interest in certain topics within their courses, or who need to be motivated. But teachers are busy, and you don't always know where to turn to discover what literature is out there for you. The annotated bibliographies in this book can guide you. The strategies that are explained and modeled show how you can use literary texts representing all genres to address content standards, enhance students' skills and knowledge, and help your classes make connections between the course material and what practitioners in the fields of math, art, science, and so on actually do.

I also believe this book will be a useful resource for those of you who are literacy coaches and librarians and who work closely with teachers in all content areas. For example, as a literacy coach or librarian, you may use the Author Studies (Part 3 in each genre chapter) to show how author centers can lead to independent and collaborative exploration within classrooms and schools; teachers can then use the same structure to investigate the works of other authors who write books relating to relevant curricular topics. You may also use the annotated bibliographies as you make decisions relating to acquisitions for resource centers and libraries. As a staff developer, you may have your audiences participate in those activities from Part 2 of each chapter that will assist them in meeting their professional development goals. I use parts of the book in my own work with practicing teachers. They think of ways particular classes and students can benefit from the literature introduced, and they adapt the strategies to make them their own.

I mention in the first chapter that my mission is getting trade books into the hands of content area teachers and their students. I'll end with an example showing how this is working. I recently received the following e-mail from a teacher I have never met:

> I am a Global 10 teacher here at Watertown High School. I was told during one of my workshops here in the district that you were the person to come to with literacy questions. I am trying to fit a couple picture books into my curriculum this year and cannot seem to find a picture book covering the Industrial Revolution in Europe. I am looking for something that just covers the basics in about 15 minutes as an intro to the larger unit. If you know of any picture books like this that would work well for a read-aloud, please let me know. Thanks so much.
>
> Patrick

I sent him the book *The Industrial Revolution,* by Andrew Langley (see the Booktalk on p. 89) and received the following feedback:

> The Industrial Revolution book is perfect for class. It was just what I was looking for and I plan to use it next week in my lesson. Thanks again.
>
> Patrick

I was happy.

—*Sharon Kane*

Using Literature in Content Area Classrooms

WHY? AND HOW?

"Nothing happens unless first a dream."

CARL SANDBURG

Introduction

Dream . . .

A dream—noun . . .

To dream—verb.

Such an important word. Poet Langston Hughes speaks of a dream deferred. Memoirists often use a dream motif, sometimes even using the word *dream* in their titles. Similarly, texts about education often employ a dream image (e.g., "The American Dream and Public Schools" [Lugg, 2005]; "Charter Schools: Delivering a Dream" [Mathes, 2005]; "School of Dreams" [McMahon & Kaven, 2005]; "The Persistent Dream: A Principal's Promising Reform of an At-Risk Elementary Urban School" [Mullen & Patrick, 2000]). A common—and fitting—assignment while teaching about the passionate social justice leader Martin Luther King Jr. is to have students write their own speech or essay starting with his inspirational opening line, "I have a dream." As teachers, we want to encourage students' personal dreams, as well as their dreams to make the world a better place. Based on their oral/written answers to the prompt, teachers can mentor and lead them to resources and actions, thereby empowering them in their pursuit of worthy goals.

In response to a similar prompt several years ago, I told a group of pre-service teachers about my own dream. My hope is that one day every intermediate and secondary teacher in our country will have a classroom library where students can learn curricular content, improve their literacy, and enjoy wonderful texts. Once I had voiced this mission, I began to take the steps that would make it a reality, at least in my corner of the world. I order from book clubs and explore warehouse sales, library sales, and garage sales for bargains, then sell the books at cost to my college students so that they can build their own curriculum libraries. I begin each of my education classes with time for students (i.e., teachers or future teachers) to tell their peers about the great discipline-specific books they've found and about how they might use these books to further knowledge, motivate students, and stimulate thinking and action.

This book is the result of the path I have taken to pursue my dream. I decided to do some legwork so that you, as a busy teacher, can use what I've found as a resource to find books that fit with what you're teaching. Use and adapt the strategies and sample reading guides as you plan literature-based lessons that address your specific content standards. This chapter will give a rationale for, and discuss what the research says about, the benefits of literature-based teaching and learning, no matter what your subject area.

The Current State of Adolescent Literacy

Around 8 million young people in grades 4 through 12 struggle to read at grade level (NCES, 2003), and 40 percent of high school graduates lack literacy skills employers seek (Achieve, 2005). As a result of these and other startling statistics about the current state of adolescent literacy, such professional organizations as the National Council of Teachers of English, as well as educators, researchers, and school administrators, have recognized the need to address the problem and improve adolescent literacy. Allington (2007) argues for intervention all day long for struggling readers in order for them to reach goals set for adequate yearly progress. Such intervention will require teachers to use methods other than whole-class lessons and readers to have access to content-related books that are at a level they can comprehend and read fluently. Materials that are too difficult do not help students read better or learn the content. Allington offers the following advice:

Districts simply cannot purchase grade-level sets of materials—literature anthologies, science books, social studies books—and hope to accelerate the academic development of students who struggle with schooling. There is no scientific evidence that distributing 25 copies of a grade-level text to all students will result in anything other than many students being left behind. . . . All-day-long-intervention designs begin by focusing on the match between the student and the curriculum material . . . all day long. (pp. 8–9)

Integrating Literature in the Content Areas offers ways in which general education teachers—subject area teachers—can begin to understand the benefits of the more differentiated sets of curriculum materials Allington calls for. The books in the following chapters are interesting and informative, yet many are written on an easier level than those usually found in a traditional middle or high school classroom. Others target an adult audience, and can challenge students who are very skilled readers or who possess the background knowledge and passion that call for more advanced texts than those typically recommended for secondary classrooms.

Current research shows "that effective literacy programs move students to deeper understandings of texts and increase their ability to generate ideas and knowledge for their own uses (Newmann, King, & Rigdon, 1997). This text also includes strategies and resources that will enable teachers, while addressing standards for their content areas, to incorporate some of the key elements *Reading Next* identifies and proposes for effective literacy instruction, including the following:

- *Effective instructional practices embedded in content*: language arts teachers using content area texts and content area teachers providing instruction and practice in reading and writing skills specific to their subject area
- *Motivation and self-directed learning*: building motivation to read and learn and providing students with the instruction and supports needed for independent learning tasks they will face after graduation
- *Text-based collaborative learning*: students interacting with one another around a variety of texts
- *Diverse texts*: texts at a variety of difficulty levels and on a variety of topics (Biancarosa & Snow, 2004, p. 4)

Integrating Literature in the Content Areas will enable teachers to incorporate the above effective literacy practices in their classrooms while still addressing standards for their content areas. It is my hope that teachers who use the principles and types of literature espoused in this text will see far-reaching effects of their instruction, including evidence of students

- acquiring the passion for learning
- seeking the literacy skills needed to succeed after graduation in jobs
- participating as caring, thinking members of communities ranging from local to global.

Reasons to Use Literature and Give Literacy Instruction in Content Area Classes

It's a given that an educator's goal is to increase students' learning and knowledge. To accomplish this feat, many things must first be in place. One purpose of this book is to give teachers not only ideas and resources for their own reading for pleasure and intellectual enhancement but also a range of book choices for their students. Often when I need to brush up on a topic or need new information for my teaching, I head to the children's section of a library. I usually find what I need, and if I need more, I have some background to help my comprehension of adult level, sometimes technical and advanced, books. If you read voluminously yourself, your students will benefit. Books offer stories, tidbits to make lectures more captivating, poetry to add beauty and wonder to the topics in a curriculum, and ideas about books to recommend to students.

Farmer (2003) demonstrates that "the research evidence is overwhelming that students read better when they read more, and they read more when they can choose from a wide range of reading material that are developmentally appropriate and engaging" (p. 128). She stresses the importance of providing informational literature in addition to other genres for our students to read for pleasure and for their own purposes as well as for school purposes. Saunders (2007) quotes literacy expert Judith Langer, who told teachers collaborating on a research project, "'I keep hearing about the (choice) between instilling a love of literature versus preparing kids for tests, but the research shows they don't have to be separate'" (p. 5).

In addition, the following reasons also support using literature in content area classrooms, which I will discuss in the next sections:

- to enhance the learning of content;
- to create opportunities for challenging discussions;
- to enable the teaching of content from multiple perspectives and sources; and
- to stimulate interest and motivation to read and learn.

TO ENHANCE THE LEARNING OF CONTENT

Pratt and Pratt (2004) discuss the integration of the disciplines of literacy and science, making it clear that the ultimate goal of this integration must be the learning of content. Noting evidence that difficult concepts are comprehended better by students who are taught scientific content through the use of literature, they present a research-based model that integrates science inquiry and strategies for a variety of texts. The model's phases, which are applicable to the integration of literacy with any content area, include engagement, exploration, explanation, elaboration, and evaluation. It's an application of the popular *K-W-L Plus strategy* (Carr & Ogle, 1987), and it involves

- vocabulary instruction;
- the use of word walls;
- activities enabling students to have direct experience with objects, phenomena, and organisms;
- providing appropriate texts; and
- opportunities for students to organize their thinking and use what they have learned in new situations.

The points the authors make about the benefits of using trade books in the content areas can similarly apply to other content areas. Hong (1996) studied kindergarten students, finding that those using math-related children's literature at reading and discussion time did significantly better in shape tasks, classification, and number combination. They also spent more time in the mathematics corner during free play time.

Fallin (1995) found that children's literature can reinforce music knowledge and skills, encourage creativity, expand multicultural awareness, and enhance listening. Calogero (2002) combined music and literature using a thematic approach, concluding, "Integrating music instruction with children's books enhances the ideas and themes implicit in both, while improving basic understandings of language and story" (p. 23). She notes that showing relationships between music and other disciplines, and between music and history and culture, addresses the goals of the National Standards for Music Education in terms of content. In addition, she found:

> Adding literature to a music lesson helps music seem less abstract or intangible to children, clarifies musical concepts, and demonstrates how different forms of expression—words, art, and music—can represent the same ideas through different mediums, making the ideas more real and immediate. (p. 24)

In history/social studies, teachers who have used trade books and analyzed the data collected from student work make a strong argument for the amount of learning that can occur. D'Acosta (2002), for example, has found that students will indeed read if the teacher allows them to choose their own books:

> Students choose topics as varied as the California Gold Rush, the Mexican War, the Civil War, the last Indian wars, Westward expansion, and industrial development. Books on these topics include biographies, journals, historical fiction such as Michael Shaara's *Killer Angels*, Louisa May Alcott's *Little Women*, and Alex Haley's *Roots*. Students may read books by Mark Twain or a Twain biography. (p. 170)

D'Acosta has had success requiring his students to keep a personal, dialectical journal, in which they react to passages they select, relating it to something else, pondering its meaning, or expressing their like or dislike of the excerpt; at the completion of the project students hand in a polished reaction paper. He notes that the reading and writing project meets two of the National Early Adolescence/Social Studies-History Standards for teachers: "Valuing diversity: Accomplished teachers understand that each student brings diverse perspectives to any experience," and "Assessment: Accomplished teachers employ a variety of assessment methods" (p. 172).

In *Caldecott Connections to Science*, Glandon (2000) uses picture books that have won the prestigious Caldecott Award to introduce and reinforce science concepts and skills. "The science connections increase students' abilities to observe and classify, hypothesize, experiment, draw conclusions, and communicate results" (p. xiv). She applies various books to a wide range of topics in the fields of life science, geology, and physics. Her curricular connections for Karen Ackerman's *Song and Dance Man* (1988) read as follows:

> Human body, with emphasis on this science idea: The systems of the human body work together to give us energy from foods we eat and the air we breathe; to provide protection from injury, to supply movement, coordination, and control; and to help us reproduce. (p. 133)

The author presents several activities, linking them to Gardner's Multiple Intelligences such as Bodily/Kinesthetic, Verbal/Linguistic, Visual/Spatial, and Interpersonal. Students write in science journals, construct graphic organizers, and explore the movement of their own bodies as they simultaneously engage with the work of literature.

In *Teaching Art with Books Kids Love*, Frohardt (1999) provides a rationale for teaching art appreciation, art elements, and design through award-winning children's literature, including:

- The artists who create the illustrations use the same elements of art, principles of design, and artistic styles of fine artists.
- The subject matter of the artwork is appropriate for children.
- The artwork is of high quality.
- The books are easy to find in most public libraries and schools. (p. xiii)

Teachers may use Frohardt's examples of fine art and those of children's literature given in the chapters to have students compare the works of art. For example, in the chapter on realism, the author recommends famous paintings by

Gustave Courbet (*The Corn Sifters*), Jean Francois Millet (*The Gleaners*), and Winslow Homer (*Snap the Whip*), as well as picture books including John Steptoe's *Mufaro's Beautiful Daughters: An African Tale* (1987), Allen Say's *Grandfather's Journey* (1993), and Jane Yolen's *Owl Moon* (1987), illustrated by John Schoenherr.

Edgington (1998) presents a review of the research on using children's literature and textbooks in the social studies curriculum. He found that some studies showed the literature approach to be more effective in mastering material; others found that students preferred the literature approach, and others did not confirm these findings. Therefore, he suggests that using a combination of a textbook and trade books may be best. Similarly, Royce and Wiley (1996) say much of the research literature on content teaching and learning through literature in all disciplines is based on research-in-action. Because quantitative data is scarce, they stress the importance of teachers selecting books carefully, avoiding material that isn't accurate or that may contain stereotypes, and using graphic organizers to clarify content. Royce and Wiley conclude that teaching through children's literature holds promise, but only if teachers are well trained in research-based content area teaching methodology.

TO CREATE OPPORTUNITIES FOR CHALLENGING DISCUSSIONS

Carroll and Gregg (2003) recommend giving readers opportunities to increase critical literacy through literature-based instruction:

> We must teach adolescents to use reading skills and broader literacies in order to differentiate between important and unimportant ideas, helpful and harmful information, reasonable and unreasonable conclusions, humane and inhumane recommendations, and uplifting and damaging credos. (p. 63)

The researchers recommend that teachers stock a "Good Books Box" in middle school classrooms, become acquainted with popular contemporary authors, and allow students to read without interference, just as readers do outside the classroom. This practice will increase student fluency and promote positive attitudes in addition to developing their critical literacy skills. Carroll and Gregg found that teachers need not fear that students will select only simple books about uncomplicated subjects. The authors surveyed secondary school students and analyzed 2,070 responses to questions about the kinds of books adolescents like to read. Their findings led them to question several of their previously held assumptions, including one having to do with what books adolescents will freely choose. "We were surprised to find that their choices included long books with challenging levels of detail. . . . We were surprised, too, with the sophistication in subject matter and themes for which many young readers indicated a preference" (p. 61).

Although some educators may consider picture books as too simple for adolescent readers, other experts recommend using picture books specifically with the middle school audience. Tiedt (2000) provides a rationale for doing so:

- they can present part of our literary heritage,
- provide information about various cultures,
- stimulate thinking about provocative topics, and
- promote writing and learning about grammar and style. (p. 6)

In a chapter on thematic studies, she shows how picture books can be used to explore themes such as immigration, the settling of the western United States, death and grieving, gods and goddesses, changing stereotyped thinking, and the contributions of women, among others. Throughout the chapters are connections to art, math, science, and social studies. According to Tiedt, picture books can benefit teachers as well as students by enabling them to address such themes after only a short amount of reading.

Polette and Ebbesmeyer (2002) attempt to dispel the myth that picture books are intended solely for a young audience by giving examples that challenge the thinking of young adults and address their concerns:

> Picture books with mature themes, absorbing illustrations, and playful text can stimulate every critical thinking skill. Imagine, for example, that cows can type. Although this may seem ridiculous, Doreen Cronin's *Click, Clack, Moo Cows That Type* is a thought-provoking introduction to the power of collective bargaining. Using such a clever story to introduce *The Pushcart War*, a novel by Jean Merrill, provides students with a winning combination that presents a painless course in economics. (p. xv)

The authors show how teachers can use picture books to help students use "story strategies to learn and recall ideas" (p. xvii) with curricular topics such as civil disobedience, the Holocaust, Native American identity, creativity, perception, the power of nature, witchcraft, the pioneer spirit, suicide, and homelessness. They connect each picture book introduced to one or more novels dealing with the same issues, and include discussion questions and writing prompts. For example, there's an entire section teachers could use to teach parody. It includes many examples of published children's books (e.g., *The Inner City Mother Goose*, by Eve Merriam [1996]; *The Thinker's Mother Goose*, by Nancy Polette [1990]; *Whatever Happened to Humpty Dumpty?: And Other Surprising Sequels to Mother Goose Rhymes*, by David Greenberg [1999]) with annotations, followed by writing suggestions along with creative examples of how the prompts could be reacted to.

In *Picture This!: Using Picture Story Books for Character Education in the Classroom* (Stephens, 2004), the author's primary purpose is to promote positive values such as citizenship, patriotism, courage, responsibility, and commitment through the use of picture books. Moreover, Stephens chooses books that can also teach curricular content and gives ways to use the books to increase literacy skills and connect to various disciplines. For example, in the chapter devoted to the principle of self-control, she focuses on *Baseball Saved Us*, by Ken Mochizuki, illustrated by Dom Lee (1993), which portrays life in a Japanese American internment camp during World War II. She provides questions that promote comprehension and discussion of values and offers connections to art, language arts, science, math, and geography, as well as additional books and websites to explore the topic of this sad chapter in American history. Physical education teachers could use a book presented in the "Perseverance and Patience" chapter, *America's Champion Swimmer: Gertrude Ederle*, by David Adler, illustrated by Terry Widener (2000). The story is rich in vocabulary and biographical details; readers learn about the English Channel and the Olympic Games as they root for the swimmer.

TO ENABLE THE TEACHING OF CONTENT FROM MULTIPLE PERSPECTIVES AND SOURCES

Daniels and Zemelman (2004) provide the following rationale for using multiple texts, including literature, in content area instruction to introduce multiple perspectives in the content area classroom:

> As we move away from dependence on a single textbook, one of the wonderful possibilities is to show students the range of views, the variety of theories, the different schools of thought that make intellectual life in our subject interesting, controversial—dare we say, exciting. . . . Does evolution proceed at a steady pace or by divine design? Should we revere Jefferson as a philosopher of human freedom or revile him as a hypocritical slave-owner? How important was Fibonnacci's contribution to mathematics compared to other innovators'? Which is the finest of Shakespeare's tragedies? None of these questions can be intelligently addressed unless we consult multiple authorities. As you gather nonfiction articles, it is

especially useful to gradually create sets of pieces that take different angles on the same topic. (p. 62)

In *Multicultural American History Through Children's Literature*, Ellermeyer and Chick (2003) concur that teaching content through stories in multiple genres encourages consideration of multiple perspectives. They found that picture books provide alternative perspectives on events and reveal history through the eyes of fictional or real people who lived through the historical events being studied, the details adding depth to topics. The authors connect each book and lesson they present to the National History Standards. They provide follow-up activities that cross disciplinary boundaries; for example, after reading three books that take place during the Civil War era, students can sing both a Confederate version and a Union version of a song called "The Battle Cry of Freedom" (p. 66). After reading books on the Civil Rights Movement, they can choose one of the Jim Crow laws written in the book, then make a diorama of the law being played out in a restaurant, a theater, a church, a school, a circus, a bus.

It might be useful to stop at this point and begin a list of questions like the examples in the quote above that connect with your curriculum. These questions will serve as aids for organizing text sets and setting up curriculum bins or classroom library shelves.

TO STIMULATE INTEREST AND MOTIVATION TO READ AND LEARN

Rosalie Fink (2006) studied more than 60 adults who were successful in their careers, yet who had struggled with reading throughout their school years. The common theme among their stories was their passionate interest and willingness to go to great lengths to learn about the topic they loved. Most eventually taught themselves to read so that they could pursue their interest. Based on her findings, Fink developed what she calls the interest-based model of reading to promote success with striving readers, consisting of the following key elements:

- A passionate, personal interest that spurs sustained reading.
- Avid, topic-specific reading.
- Deep schema knowledge.
- Contextual reading strategies.
- Mentoring support. (p. 17)

Fink gives several compelling reasons for using this model:

Students who read about a topic of personal interest are likely to become deeply engaged and read more frequently. The sheer volume of this increased reading can supply the requisite repetition and practice that enhances fluency and comprehension of increasingly sophisticated texts. Consequently, reading about a topic of passionate, personal interest can promote reading at higher and higher levels. (p. 17)

Granted, content area teachers do not have the luxury of allowing students to pursue any areas they happen to be passionate about. For example, a social studies teacher can't allow individual students who love butterfly collecting, car racing, cartoon drawing, or snowboarding to read about their passions for 180 days in class, even if the teacher wanted to and thought it would be good for the students. These students would not have the time to achieve the state and national content standards the teacher is responsible for teaching. However, teachers can adapt an interest-based model that will work. Fink found that reading speed and fluency are content area–dependent. Some students read science and math texts with more fluency than they do English or social studies material, and others might demonstrate the reverse of that.

So, your job is two-pronged: Stimulate interest in the designated topics (most of which you are probably passionate about, thankfully), and provide interesting, accessible texts on those topics so that students can read widely and deeply, thus building their background knowledge and ability to comprehend the course content. The strategies, and especially the reading resources across genres that this book provides, are intended to help you do just that. After a school year in a biology class with a teacher who uses the interest-based model of reading and who provides a classroom library filled with books representing all genres, students who entered with virtually no interest in what they considered a boring school subject might eagerly anticipate a summer reading about new genetic engineering research, preservation of America's wild buffalo population, new viruses, conservation of the rainforests, and promising new cancer treatments. Your goal can be to share your personal passion for your subject area as well as the passion shown by authors of trade books relating to your curriculum.

Various theories of motivation recognize how social interaction can foster learning (Bowen, 2000; McCombs, 1989; Oldfather, 1993; Stevens, 2003; Vaughan, 2002). Research indicates that collaboration promotes higher-level cognition, desire to read, and achievement (Almasi, 1995). When students have a sense of belonging in the classroom, along with a caring teacher, they are more likely to be motivated to read (Wentzel, 1997). From a body of research, Gambrell (1996) concludes that opportunities for talking with others about books are an important factor in developing motivated readers and supports the contention that social interactions, as well as teachers who explicitly model reading behavior and provide appropriate reading incentives, have a positive influence on reading achievement.

A Look Ahead

The next chapter highlights several pedagogical structures and methods that many individual teachers and school faculties have found helpful as they teach their curricular content; teach literacy skills within disciplinary contexts; and, most important, teach the students they are privileged to have in their classes. Subsequent chapters are categorized by genres to help you expand your repertoire of ways to encourage your students to read widely in your field for pleasure and profit. I chose to organize the book chapters by genres rather than disciplines to encourage cross-disciplinary collaboration and to open new ways of thinking about the content areas. Separate chapters address informational books, fiction, biography, poetry, and how-to or hands-on texts, and each chapter consists of four parts. In Part 1, I discuss the genre and explore how content area teachers are using books within the genre to further content learning and enhance literacy skills in their students. Part 2 of the chapter describes instructional strategies involving the use of literature. Each strategy includes at least one learning standard based on a standard from a national organization representing a specific discipline (see Figure 1.1). These standards serve as examples of how content area standards can be used to integrate content, literature, and literacy skills in an activity.

For each instructional strategy, I provide steps in the procedure and/or a walk-through modeling the strategy in a certain context using specific books. (Sometimes these sections are combined because procedural steps are not necessary or

| FIGURE | 1.1 | Sources for the learning standards accompanying this book's activities and strategies. |

American Alliance of Health, Physical Education, Recreation, and Dance. National Health Education Standards. Available: www.aahperd.org/aahe/pdf_files/standards.pdf

Consortium of National Arts Education Associations. National Standards for Arts Education. Available: http://artsedge.kennedy-center.org/teach/standards.cfm?subjectId=VAR&gradeBandId=&sortColumn=&x=11&y=9

National Business Education Association. The National Standards for Business Education. Available: www.nbea.org/curriculum/bes.html

National Center for History in the Schools. National Standards for History Basic Edition, 1996. Available: http://nchs.ucla.edu/standards/toc.html

National Council for Geographic Education. National Geography Standards. Available: www.ncge.org/

publications/tutorial/standards/ee2/standard4.html

National Council of Teachers of English/International Reading Association. Standards for the English Language Arts. Available: www.ncte.org/about/over/standards/110846.htm

National Council for the Social Studies. Curriculum Standards for Social Studies. Available: http://cnets.iste.org/currstands/index.html

National Council of Teachers of Mathematics. Principles and Standards for School Mathematics. Available: http://standards.nctm.org/document/chapter3/index.htm

National Sciences Teachers Association. National Science Education Standards. Available: www.nap.edu/readingroom/books/nses/6a.html.

appropriate.) (*Note: All books discussed in this section are either annotated in Part 4 of the chapter or are included in the "Literature Cited" list at chapter end.*) You'll be able to think of ways to adapt the strategies and reading guides described here to best suit your particular students, available texts, and/or curriculum, in order to help your students gain rich knowledge through the reading of trade books connected to your curriculum.

In Part 3 of each chapter, I highlight several authors who write texts in that genre related to various content areas, and I explain how you might use their books to help students explore issues within your curriculum and gain a depth of knowledge about topics in your discipline. The books represent a range in difficulty level, making the combination appropriate for differentiated instruction. Students can get to know the authors, their styles, their beliefs, and the experiences that led to their passion for various subjects.

Part 4 of each chapter consists of an annotated bibliography of books organized by various disciplines that could be part of a classroom library. These lists are in no way meant to be exhaustive; rather, they are representative of the types of literature available to you as you teach your curriculum. In most cases, I use a booktalk format for the annotation, speaking directly to you as a teacher (or future teacher). I include suggestions for teaching from the book and ponder instructional implications. Some of the booktalks are written using the voice of a character within the book to introduce the story; others include an excerpt taken from a real reader's response to the book (usually a pre-service teacher from my own classes). Many of the book annotations contain cross-references to the teaching strategies with which they may be used in case you become intrigued by a book and want to know how you can use it with your class to teach content as well as to improve your students' literacy skills.

Throughout *Integrating Literature in the Content Areas*, I often associate books with a specific discipline or disciplines. These associations are intended only as suggestions—I believe that many of these books can be used in multiple disciplines for multiple purposes, depending upon your ideas and objectives.

Finally, each chapter concludes with a complete list of references and a "Literature Cited" list. As mentioned earlier, if a book is already discussed/annotated in Part 4 of the chapter, it will not be included in the citations.

Conclusion

As Wilhelm (2007) reminds us in an article aptly titled "Personalizing Our Teaching: No Specific Human Being Left Behind," all teachers, no matter what their grade level or discipline, instruct "individual human beings who are wonderfully various in their interests and issues," and so:

> We must engage each of our multifarious young charges personally and provide them with appropriate challenges. We cannot do this through traditional forms of information-transmission teaching; rather, we must accomplish this through apprenticeship and inquiry settings. (p. 40)

The trade book recommendations and strategies discussed in *Integrating Literature in the Content Areas* are geared toward helping teachers differentiate instruction, relative to Wilhelm's call to action. A variety of resources at different levels and with different formats can be used simultaneously to meet standards and lead to achievement based on curricular guidelines. In addition, these resources can work toward Wilhelm's goal of situating instruction in real or simulated contexts that result in authentic learning:

> Learning is the induction of the novice learner into the possibility of being, behaving, thinking, and performing like a real practitioner. Becoming a better writer or reader (or mathematician, ethicist, or social scientist) requires the learner to imagine and rehearse being a particular and new kind of person. (pp. 40–41)

Freedman and Carver (2007) underscore the importance of "secondary teacher candidates' understandings of the integrated nature of literacy and learning" (p. 654) as well as an appreciation for "students' acquisition of content knowledge through the use of multiple print materials" (p. 655). So, using trade books like the ones annotated in this book, far from taking time away from instruction in the discipline, can enhance teachers' lessons so that they are intellectually more rigorous, and both content area literacy skills and content learning improve. As students become immersed in nonfiction and fiction texts that involve practitioners in various disciplines, they may understand and appreciate content at a deeper level, and might envision themselves somehow involved in those fields after they leave high school.

REFERENCES

Achieve, Inc. (2005). Rising to the challenge: Are high school graduates prepared for college and work? Washington, DC: Author.

Allington, R. L. (2007). Intervention all day long: New hope for struggling readers. *Voices from the Middle,* 14 (4), 7–14.

Almasi, J. F. (1995). The nature of fourth-graders' sociocognitive conflicts in peer-led and teacher-led discussions of literature. *Reading Research Quarterly,* 30, 314–351.

Biancarosa, G., & Snow, C. E. (2004). *Reading next—A vision for action and research in middle and high school literacy: A report to Carnegie Corporation of New York.* Washington, DC: Alliance for Excellent Education.

Bowen, C. W. (2000). A quantitative literature review of cooperative learning effects on high school and college chemistry environment. *Journal of Chemical Education,* 77 (1), 116–119.

Calogero, J. M. (2002). Integrating music and children's literature. *Music Educators Journal,* 88 (5), 23–30.

Carr, E., & Ogle, D. (1987). K-W-L Plus: A strategy for comprehension and summarization. *Journal of Reading,* 30, 626–631.

Carroll, P. S., & Gregg, G. P. (2003). Literature-based instruction for middle school readers: Harry Potter and more. *ALAN Review,* 30 (3), 60–64.

D'Acosta, J. W. (2002). Reading books instead of book reviews. In R. Stone (Ed), *Best practices for high school classrooms: What award-winning secondary teachers do* (pp. 169–173). Thousand Oaks, CA: Corwin Press.

Daniels, H., & Zemelman, S. (2004). *Subjects matter: Every teacher's guide to content-area reading.* Portsmouth, NH: Heinemann.

Edgington, W. D. (1998). The use of children's literature in middle school social studies: What research does and does not show. *Clearing House,* 72 (2), 121–125.

Ellermeyer, D. A., & Chick, K. A. (2003). *Multicultural American history through children's literature.* Portsmouth, NH: Teacher Ideas Press.

Fallin, J. R. (1995). Children's literature as a springboard for music. *Music Educators Journal, 81* (5), 24–27.

Farmer, L. S. J. (2003). *Student success and library media programs: A systems approach to research and best practice.* Westport, CT: Libraries Unlimited.

Fink, R. (2006). *Why Jane and John couldn't read—and how they learned: A new look at striving readers.* Newark, DE: International Reading Association.

Freedman, L., & Carver, C. (2007). Preservice teacher understandings of adolescent literacy development: Naïve wonder to dawning realization to intellectual rigor. *Journal of Adolescent and Adult Literacy, 50* (8), 654–665.

Frohardt, D. C. (1999). *Teaching art with books kids love.* Golden, CO: Fulcrum Publishing.

Gambrell, L. B. (1996). Creating classroom cultures that foster reading motivation. *The Reading Teacher, 50,* 14–25.

Gardner, H. (1983/2004). *Frames of mind: The theory of multiple intelligences.* New York: Basic Books.

Glandon, S. (2000). *Caldecott connections to science.* Englewood, CO: Libraries Unlimited.

Hong, H. (1996). Effects of mathematics learning through children's literature on math achievement and dispositional outcomes. *Early Childhood Research Quarterly, 11,* 477–494.

Lugg, C. A. (2005). The American dream and public schools. *American Journal of Education, 111* (3), 421–424.

Mathes, J. (2005). Charter schools: Delivering a dream. *School Construction News, 8* (5), 18.

McCombs, B. L. (1989). Self-regulated learning and academic achievement: A phenomenological view. In B. J. Zimmerman & D. H. Schunk (Eds.), *Self-regulated learning and achievement: Theory, research, and practice* (pp. 51–82). New York: Springer-Verlag.

McMahon, M., & Kaven, G. (2005). School of dreams. *Issues in Teacher Education, 14* (1), 109–112.

Mullen, C. A., & Patrick, R. L. (2000). The persistent dream: A principal's promising reform of an at-risk elementary urban school. *Journal of Education for Students Placed at Risk, 5* (3), 229–250.

National Center for Education Statistics (NCES). (2003). *Nation's report card: Reading 2002.* Washington, DC: U. S. Government Printing Office.

Newmann, F., King, B., & Rigdon, M. (1997). Accountability and school performance: Implications from restructuring schools. *Harvard Educational Review, 67,* 41–74.

Oldfather, P. (1993). What students say about motivating experiences in a whole language classroom. *The Reading Teacher, 46* (8), 672–681.

Polette, N. J., & Ebbesmeyer, J. (2002). *Literature lures: Using picture books and novels to motivate middle school readers.* Greenwood Village, CO: Teacher Ideas Press.

Pratt, H., & Pratt, N. (2004). Integrating science and literacy instruction with a common goal of learning science content. In W. Saul (Ed.), *Crossing borders in literacy and science instruction: Perspectives on theory and practice* (pp. 395–406). Newark, DE: International Reading Association and Arlington, VA: National Science Teachers Association.

Royce, C. A., & Wiley, D. A. (1996). Children's literature and the teaching of science: Possibilities and cautions. *Clearing House, 70* (1), 18–20.

Saunders, S. (2007). Building a minds-on classroom. *New York Teacher* (March 1), 5, 7.

Stephens, C. G. (2004). *Picture this!: Using picture story books for character education in the classroom.* Westport, CT: Libraries Unlimited.

Stevens, R. J. (2003). Student team reading and writing: A cooperative learning approach to middle school literature instruction. *Educational Research and Evaluation, 9* (2), 137–160.

Tiedt, I. M. (2000). *Teaching with picture books in the middle school.* Newark, DE: International Reading Association.

Vaughan, W. (2002). Effects of cooperative learning on achievement and attitude among students of color. *Journal of Educational Research, 95* (6), 364–369.

Wentzel, K. R. (1997). Student motivation in middle school: The role of perceived pedagogical caring. *Journal of Educational Psychology, 89* (3), 411–419.

Wilhelm, J. (2007). Personalizing our teaching: No specific human being left behind. *Voices from the Middle, 14* (4), 40–41.

LITERATURE CITED

Ackerman, K. (1988). *Song and dance man.* Illus. S. Gammell. New York: Knopf.

Adler, D. (2000). *America's champion swimmer: Gertrude Ederle.* Illus T. Widener. San Diego: Harcourt.

Mochizuki, K. (1993). *Baseball saved us.* Illus. D. Lee. New York: Lee & Low.

Say, A. (1993). *Grandfather's journey.* Boston: Houghton Mifflin.

Steptoe, J. (1987). *Mufaro's beautiful daughters: An African tale.* New York: Lothrop, Lee & Shepard.

Yolen, J. (1987). *Owl moon.* Illus. J. Schoenherr. New York: Philomel Books.

Ways to Incorporate Literature into Content Area Teaching and Learning

"When I look back, I am so impressed again with the life-giving power of literature. If I were a young person today, trying to gain a sense of myself in the world, I would do that again by reading, just as I did when I was young."

MAYA ANGELOU

Middle and high school teachers, even English teachers, are sometimes nervous about how to fit literature into their tight schedules. Daniels and Zemelman (2004) sympathize with teachers who are concerned about the time involved in doing ambitious inquiry projects involving multiple reading sources. It's true that the material most high school and middle school teachers have to cover is extensive, and the days throughout the school years are packed, with teachers and students feeling rushed and pressured. But they insist such projects are necessary:

> It boils down to a trade-off. We can "cover" all the material, with most of our students passing a test and immediately forgetting most of what was taught; or we can let a bit of it go . . . and fit these valuable experiences in, so that more of our students deeply understand some topics, and come to value the subjects we teach. (p. 230)

The authors point out that project work is especially essential for students who are struggling academically, and also that it's consistent with what national standards documents call for: giving students opportunities to ask meaningful questions, think critically, and delve into topics of interest rather than skim over endless facts.

The following sections provide various suggestions about ways content area teachers can incorporate literature into their curriculum. The discussion will begin with guidance for helping students select books that will promote their wide reading in your subject area.

Helping Students Select Books

We can't assume that just because we have acquired a good variety of content area–related books for our classroom libraries that students will automatically know how to choose the books that are best for them. Especially if they have been given little choice in previous grades, and/or if they have not very often visited libraries with family members or friends, they might feel uncomfortable or anxious about choosing for themselves; or they might pick books that are either not challenging enough or too difficult. They truly might not have learned that it is okay to abandon a book that is not working toward their pleasure or purpose, and that skimming is often a legitimate and efficient strategy. So booktalks are in order, as well as mini-lessons on choosing appropriate books for independent exploration.

Chandler-Olcott (2001) offers a framework for when and how to help students select books. Based on a similar strategy developed by Mooney (1990) for the primary grades, Chandler-Olcott purports that secondary teachers need to use a range of instructional approaches, stating "there will be times when it's best for us to choose texts FOR students; times when we will choose texts WITH them, or support them in choosing them WITH others; and times when they will choose texts BY themselves" (p. 20).

She highlights the second phase of the continuum, choosing books WITH students, since this happens least often in practice, yet it's where students and teachers are most "likely to meet, metaphorically speaking, within Vygotsky's (1986) zone of proximal development, or the difference between what a learner can do independently and what she or he can do with the assistance of a more capable person" (p. 23). She shows that teachers can use

- interest inventories to learn about students' reading preferences and habits,
- written reading plans and guided choice sheets to individualize the advice given to students based on their needs and interests, and
- field trips to bookstores and public libraries where joint exploration and modeling can happen.

From these shared experiences, teachers can make available books that will bring enjoyment and meaning to students and that are of interest to particular readers. In addition, teachers should look for the following characteristics in the books they offer students in their classroom library or suggest for assignments (DeVries, 2008):

- Make sure the books present accurate information.
- Choose books with accurate and diverse multicultural representations.
- Use books from a range of genres.
- Provide books at many reading levels.
- Choose books with high-quality illustrations.
- Choose books with complementary text and illustrations.
- Select books at a length appropriate for the desired reading level.
- Use instructional level books that are challenging but not discouraging.
- Include easy reading level books to build fluency and allow readers to build comprehension rather than focusing on deciphering words.

Teachers can also ask themselves the following questions (Kane, 2007):

- Do I like this book?
- Does it connect to one or more of my curricular topics?
- Does it have potential to build background knowledge for the topics in my course? Does it assume background knowledge my students might not possess?
- Is it accurate and up-to-date? Do I detect any biases or stereotypical treatment of people? Are issues relating to diversity represented well?
- Will my students find it attractive and appealing?
- How easy or difficult will it be for various students?
- What do I think of the book's style and tone? How will my students react to these?
- What do I know about the author or publisher?

Make Your Reading Processes Visible

hris Tovani, author of *I Read It, But I Don't Get It: Comprehension Strategies for Adolescent Readers* (2000), offers two tips for teachers—non-reading specialists—who wish to improve their students' comprehension of discipline-specific materials. The first is:

> 1. *Become a passionate reader of what you teach.* . . . I guarantee that if you don't like the material you're assigning, your students won't either. Search for interesting text and get it into the hands of your students. Rediscover why you fell in love with the subject you teach and why you wanted to teach it to others. Take time to read. Weed out the dull, poorly written text. Give your students the gift of something wonderful to read. (pp. 20–21)

The annotated lists of books in Part 4 of each of the succeeding chapters are aimed at helping teachers do exactly this. I've provided the booktalks for teachers as the audience, who can then decide which books to pursue and how to use which book parts in their instruction, and/or how to entice their students to take a peek.

Tovani's second suggestion for enhancing students' comprehension of content area concepts follows:

> 2. *Model how good readers read.* Think about what you as a reader do to construct meaning and share this information with your students. Different types of reading

require different strategies. Don't feel pressured to teach all your students how to read everything well. Just show them how you read the material you assign. (p. 21)

Part 2 of each of the next five chapters in this book offers suggestions of teaching strategies and reading strategies, many of which you can model, as Tovani suggests.

Many content area teachers lament their students' poor reading skills, but feel somewhat powerless to change the situation. After all, these teachers have not been trained as literacy specialists. Yet Schoenbach et al. (2003) insist, "Clearly, the best mentors for student apprentices learning discipline-based literacy practices are those teachers who have mastered these very practices—subject area teachers" (p. x). Think about that—*you* are the teachers who choose to read professional journals in your field, as well as books related to the discipline you loved enough to want to teach it to young minds. So, the authors have developed an instructional framework, similar to a studio approach, that is embedded in the actual process of teaching content. It is not an add-on to the curriculum. That's good news! The system advocates engaging students in more reading and involves a cognitive dimension where teachers make explicit the processes they use while reading various types of material themselves. They make their thinking visible to their students, who are apprentice scientists, historians, mathematicians, or analyzers of literature. They might do a "cold" think-aloud reading, where they take a text they've never read before, and read it out loud, stopping frequently to let students in on their thoughts as they attempt to construct meaning from the author's words. In classrooms where the apprenticeship model is in place:

> The metacognitive conversation is the central dynamic. . . . teacher and students discuss their personal relationships to reading in the discipline, the cognitive strategies they use to solve comprehension problems, the structure and language of particular types of texts, and the kinds of knowledge required to make sense of reading materials. . . . The routines stress metacognition—thinking about one's thinking—and collaborative meaning-making. (p. x)

Teacher Jeffrey Wilhelm devotes a whole book to *Improving Comprehension with Think-Aloud Strategies* (2001). His premise is as follows:

> To help our students to become expert readers, we must model the strategies of expert readers using authentic texts—novels, short stories, nonfiction books, newspaper articles, arguments, and Internet sites—and then support students in taking on these expert stances for themselves as they read independently. (p. 7)

In every subject, students need teachers who make their own strategies for comprehending materials visible. Have you ever tried to verbally state what's going on in your head as you read a science article, a poem, a movie review, a court decision? In order to let you in on what this might look like, I tried it myself. I hope you'll try it out, too, with a text you're reading for the first time. The following is part of a script I created for a history lesson when reading a YA (young adult) historical novel to model a teacher think-aloud:

> *I'm about to read* Doomed Queen Anne, *by Carolyn Meyer. I'm eager to start, because I've already read* Mary, Bloody Mary, *by the same author, and I remember how young Mary, Catherine of Aragon's daughter, was banished from the palace, and had to hear about how her father (Henry VIII) had taken up with the young Anne Boleyn, who had been one of her mother's handmaids! Mary, of course, did not think highly of Anne, so now I want to hear Anne's side of the story.*
>
> *There's a chart or timeline of the Tudors before the story starts. I see the dates of Anne's life, 1507?–1536. Hmmm—What's that question mark mean? Guess she wasn't important enough at birth for historians to have a record of the exact year. I do some subtraction, and my heart sinks to realize that she was not even thirty when she died.*
>
> *Ok, I turn to the Prologue. It takes place in 1536—ah, I know from the timeline that's right at the end of her life—in the Tower of London. Oh, I've been there on a sightseeing*

trip, and it was really eerie to think about all the royalty imprisoned and executed there. Anne says she's afraid. Well, I guess so! She prays throughout the night and thinks of the people responsible for her being in this predicament. And she misses her little daughter— Hmm, let's see, who would that be? Elizabeth? Yes, the child of Anne and Henry who grew up to be Queen Elizabeth I—and Anne wonders if her child will ever know the truth about her mother, "the doomed Queen Anne." Oh, that's where the title comes from. I notice the next chapter is labeled with a date to let the reader know the story's moving back to 1520. Ok, that would make Anne 13 at this point. I skim to see other chapters—looks like the rest of the chapters will be Anne's recalling of how she came to the throne, and then, obviously, lost favor. So, here I go, along for the ride.

Read-Alouds

One way to use trade books in the classroom is to read them aloud to the class. More important, this should not be a one-way activity, with the teacher just transmitting information to a passive student audience. Pappas and Varelas (2004) describe how they use information book read-alouds to promote dialogic inquiry with urban elementary grade students. Rather than the teacher controlling discussion, and merely evaluating children's responses to questions to check comprehension, they allow for voices of students as well as teachers to be heard; the books stimulate thinking, "so students and teacher together propose, negotiate, debate, and develop scientific understandings" (p. 164). The authors pay particular attention to the intertextual connections the children made while talking, referring to other materials they had read, or rhymes or experiences they knew of as they developed the ability to partake in scientific talk.

Drawing on a study of teachers' various ways of reading Joanna Cole's *Magic School Bus* books to students, Smolkin and Donovan (2004) recommend that teachers prepare for reading Cole's books aloud by going over the book carefully beforehand; bring objects to the classroom that relate to the science content if appropriate; read running text first, then speech balloons, then any student reports on the pages. They highlight one teacher who "brought a sense of wonder to the scientific aspects of her read-aloud," encouraged scientific speculation; helped students transfer the book's science content to other situations; stressed scientific terms; and "encouraged a deeper processing of the way the world works around us" (p. 310). That's quite a pay-off for the investment of reading aloud in class.

Following are some suggestions for reading aloud to students adapted from the recommendations of Jim Trelease (2001).

- Read a variety of books but only share those you enjoy that will generate interest and enthusiasm.
- Practice reading the book before class and consider shortening or deleting parts of the text if it seems appropriate.
- Provide variety in the materials you read, including nonfiction, magazine articles, factual newspaper accounts, poetry, and fiction. Also include books that reflect authors from many cultures. Sometimes use an audiobook or filmstrip for the session.
- When reading aloud, make sure everyone can see you.
- Read slowly, clearly, and with expression.
- When possible use props, as Smolkin and Donovan recommended.
- Allow time for student questions and comments.

No matter what age, level of sophistication, or background knowledge of students, there will be appropriate books, instructional strategies, and reading guides that can promote scientific thought and talk. The following chapters explore these in more detail. For a deeper understanding of and more suggestions for using the strategy of reading aloud in your courses, check out Judy Richardson's (2000) *Read It Aloud! Using Literature in the Secondary Content Classroom.*

Readers Theatre

H ere's a definition from a student: "'Readers theatre is a very fun way of learning things by acting them out'" (Black & Stave, 2007, p. 10). Readers theatre can be a continuing part of your course throughout the year; it works particularly well as a means of reviewing topics. It involves students (and/or teachers) creating a script, often based on a book they've read, and then performing from the written script, which is visible to the audience. There's no need to memorize lines, though rehearsal is advisable so that students with speaking parts work well together and read with fluency and expression. As a content area teacher, you may require that the created script contain concepts and vocabulary terms from your curriculum. Students can add props or costumes, but don't compromise the very ease and simplicity of readers theatre with too many extras; part of the method's beauty is that it is far less time consuming than actually putting on a play.

Two professional books are very helpful for teachers wanting to incorporate readers' theatre into their courses. *Dramatizing the Content with Curriculum-Based Readers Theatre, Grades 6–12* (Flynn, 2007) offers a framework for content area teachers to use as students write scripts, practice, and perform in a way that emphasizes the content they've learned. The book includes reproducible scripts and templates; teachers can also go to the author's website (www.rosalindflynn.com) for dozens of scripts related to topics in several content areas. *A Comprehensive Guide to Readers Theatre: Enhancing Fluency and Comprehension in Middle School and Beyond* (Black & Stave, 2007) provides a theoretical and research base, rationale, instructions for implementation, and suggestions for adaptations of readers theatre for gifted students, struggling readers, content area classrooms, and English learners.

Following is an example of a readers theatre script created by a group of students who had just read *The Yellow Star: The Legend of King Christian X of Denmark,* by Carmen Agra Deedy (2000). Students could rehearse and perform the script for those members of the class who read different books relating to World War II, and who would also perform readers theatre from scripts they composed to teach others what they learned.

Narrator: Welcome to Denmark. The year is 1940. The times are bleak and scary.

Speakers 1, 2, and 3: We love and respect our leader, King Christian. But war is spreading across Europe, and Nazi soldiers have arrived.

King Christian: I have sent a soldier to remove the Nazi flag that was raised at the palace in Copenhagen.

Nazi officer: If you do that again, I will have that soldier shot!

King Christian: Then be prepared to shoot me. I will be the man.

Narrator: The Nazi flag did not go back up. But something awful happened next. All Jews were ordered to wear a yellow star.

Speakers 1, 2, and 3: We have heard stories from neighboring countries. First Jews had to wear the yellow star. And then they disappeared.

King Christian: I don't want our Jewish people to be singled out this way. I want them to look like any other Danes. We are alike, all Danes who worship God in different ways. I must model how I want my people to respond to this threat.

Narrator: The king called his tailor and gave him some instructions. The next day, he rode alone on his horse through the streets.

Speaker 1: Our king is wearing his finest clothes.

Speaker 2: Look what else he is wearing—a yellow star!

Speaker 3: You know what we all have to go home and do.

Narrator: Unlike in other countries, no Jews within Denmark were forced to wear the yellow star. And unlike other countries, Denmark rescued most of its Jews. If you want to read more, we recommend Carmen Agra Deedy's *The Yellow Star.*

Reading Workshop

Your students may already be familiar with the reading workshop model because they may have participated in it regularly in the elementary grades, when "Reading" was a daily subject, and/or in English classrooms. But this approach can work quite well to further content learning and to motivate students to look elsewhere for more information on topics that have piqued their interest through the independent reading opportunities and choice of materials you have offered.

A few elements common to most workshops include the following (Kane, 2007):

Student choice. A classroom workshop is student centered. The teacher knows the students as individuals, so can suggest particular books and materials to fit their needs and match their learning styles. Seldom will you walk into the room to find all of the students reading the same thing at the same time. A classroom library containing a variety of genres of trade books, as well as reference materials and magazines, is arranged invitingly, because there is a relatively high association between the size of a classroom library and student reading achievement (Elley, 1992). Harste and Leland (2007) note, "Choice is central to the learning process. It is the element of choice that allows students and teachers the opportunity to make curriculum critical as well as culturally responsive" (p. 8).

Talking and listening. Talk is valued and necessary in a workshop. Individual conferences between student and teacher are common, as are small group conferences among students. Students share information they've discovered, read drafts of their work to classmates, question each other, formulate projects, and talk out ideas. Literature circles, explained later in more detail, are a familiar occurrence in workshop classrooms. Social interaction is encouraged as a way for learners to develop.

Writing. The language components of reading, writing, talking, and listening are interrelated—good literacy education does not separate them or treat them in an isolated manner; neither is writing confined to English class. Other teachers incorporate more writing than reading, or vice versa, which may be appropriate for their particular teaching situation. In any event, many types of writing occur for many purposes in a workshop classroom.

Structure. It might appear to an outsider that the structure of a workshop classroom is quite loose because some students might be walking around or talking, while others are writing, reading, listening to the teacher, or exploring the Internet. Actually, there must be consistency and an organization that matches the goals of the class. Students have to know what to expect from the teacher and their classmates and what is expected of them. Time blocks for various responsibilities and a list of rules are likely to be posted in the room; routines can be depended upon. The following represents a typical workshop routine:

1. *Opening/teacher share time.* During this period, a teacher may read a book aloud or give a booktalk.

2. *Mini-lesson.* In this period, a teacher might teach a specific skill or specific concepts or vocabulary. For example, in a science lesson, a teacher might review the scientific method, pointing out text about this topic in the class textbook, and then ask students to apply this knowledge by putting sticky notes on pages in the biographies they're reading during workshop time to note places where the subject of their book is using, or deviating from, the scientific method.

3. *Student-selected reading/writing and response.* This period should be the major part of the workshop. During this time, students should be reading and writing while a teacher conferences with individual students.

4. *Closing/student share time.* During this period, students share the books they have been reading as well as their written work.

Daniels and Zemelman (2004) describe how a high school chemistry teacher has used the independent reading workshop format successfully, devoting about 45 minutes a week to it. During a unit on body chemistry, Mr. Cannon took sections of the book *Chemcom: Chemistry in the Community* (American Chemical Society, 1998) and also printed articles from websites on teenagers' diets. He began the workshop period with a five-minute mini-lesson reviewing some basic chemistry principles and vocabulary relating to the readings. During the next five minutes, he summarized the focus of the articles available, then gave instructions on writing journal responses; he asked students to write something they learned, their feelings and thoughts, and something they might do differently as a result of their new knowledge. Students chose articles and read silently; Mr. Cannon circulated among them, holding brief conferences with students who had indicated questions or a need for clarification or help. During the last 15 minutes of class, students shared what they learned and discussed the new issues raised.

The authors list many benefits of using the workshop approach in a content area course, along with tips on assuring the smooth operation of the workshop and advice on conducting mini-lessons within the workshop setting, keeping students on task, and conducting one-on-one conferences. They tell how to record observations and assess student learning. For example, they show Mr. Cannon stopping after a conference, writing a note on a sticky pad, and placing the sticky note next to the student's name on a class list, which he carries around on his clipboard. (The list has a rectangle next to each name just the right size for the notes.)

Literature Circles

Like reading workshops, literature circles are popular in elementary and intermediate grade classrooms, as well as in English classrooms at the middle and high school levels, using novels and other narrative texts. But they can be productive and beneficial in other subject area classes, too. Daniels and Bizar (1998) list 12 "defining ingredients" of genuine literature circles:

1. Students *choose* their own reading materials.

2. *Small temporary groups* are formed, based on book choice.

3. Different groups read *different books.*

4. Groups meet on a *regular, predictable schedule* to discuss their reading.

5. Students use writing or drawn *notes* to guide both their reading and discussion.

6. Discussion *topics come from the students.*

7. Group meetings aim to be *open, natural conversations about books,* so personal connections, digressions, and open-ended questions are welcome.

8. In newly forming groups, students play a rotating assortment of *task roles.*

9. The teacher serves as a *facilitator,* not a group member or instructor.

10. Evaluation is by *teacher observation and student self-evaluation.*

11. A spirit of *playfulness and fun* pervade the room.

12. When books are finished, *readers share with their classmates,* and then *new groups form* around new reading choices. (pp. 75–76)

Literature circles, which can be part of a workshop approach or used on their own, give students the opportunity to share responses to what they read as they learn from classmates' insights and reactions. The teacher might or might not participate, and there may or may not be guide questions, depending on the purposes and needs of the participants. Questions about and suggestions for discussion topics can be very helpful to get the talk going in certain groups, especially for students who are new to learning via sharing and listening, but may be totally unnecessary or even impede the progress of veteran discussion group participants. Teacher decision making in terms of how much and what kinds of facilitation and guidance to provide is crucial.

The size of literature circles can vary, from the whole class to small groups of students. Usually the circle consists of people who have read and responded to the same work of literature, and sometimes the group may then share its knowledge with the whole class.

It's natural that content area teachers, working within the constraints of their particular discipline standards and curricular requirements, will need to make some adaptations to fit the requirement of their contexts. Following are some guidelines for teaching with content area literature circles (Kane, 2007):

PREREADING

1. Prepare a text set of books, magazines, newspapers, Internet sites, or other sources on one topic or theme.

2. Prepare a study or discussion guide for the materials (optional).

3. Give booktalks to introduce each of the reading selections and important content concepts and to arouse interest in the readings.

4. Allow students to choose from the texts. Sometimes a student will have to make a second choice if no one else chooses the same text. Groups should optimally have four or five members to ensure different perspectives and responses.

DURING READING

5. Have students read independently and record their responses in learning logs, listing important page numbers, drawing pictures, noting unknown words and concepts, making connections with their own lives, and noting questions they have about the material.

POSTREADING

6. Have students meet with the others reading the same selection. Meetings should be scheduled regularly, daily or weekly and should last at least 30 to 45 minutes. Students should take turns leading the discussion, but all students should be involved.

Johnson and Freedman (2001) show how literature circles using informational trade books encourage students to talk about content knowledge. In a fifth-grade science classroom, groups read a variety of books on the subject of rainforests. Pairs of students within the groups read aloud to each other and stopped to talk with other group members when they found something interesting. The researchers noted that the students liked reading informational picture books and did indeed obtain relevant information from them. Also, they "became more open in their discussions, and the atmosphere was charged with excitement as the students learned about the flora and fauna of the rainforest" (p. 57).

An eighth-grade social studies class used literature circles in a unit on explorers. After some reading, individuals within groups chose roles as suggested by Daniels (1994, 2001), and then met with students from other groups that had the same responsibilities. So, those labeled "discussion directors" collaborated to create questions to pursue in the literature circles, while the "word wizard" group found ways to explore, highlight, and apply relevant vocabulary, such as *conquistador* and *inhabitants.* There was an illustrator group, a connector group, and a summary group as well. Their teacher found that her students "openly wrestled with the information presented in a more complex manner, and they made deeper connections" (p. 58) than they had done with information from the textbook. In addition, students asked follow-up questions. In short, Johnson and Freedman concluded that, "Given a variety of materials coupled with adequate scaffolding of student knowledge in relation to the subject, literature circles produce amazing results" (p. 60). (It's interesting that Harvey Daniels has changed his position on assigning task roles to students, and now recommends not using them since the roles themselves can become the focus of a group's interaction rather than the rich material and ideas they are reading about [Daniels, 2006]. Try out the roles and see how they work for your students, but use them cautiously and sparingly, perhaps phasing them out as students get more used to talking with peers about what they've read.)

Modify how your literature circles are conducted depending on the students you have, the resources that are available, and the topics you're teaching. Use a combination of fiction and nonfiction, picture books and audio books, magazines and newspapers. One pleasant side effect of literature circles is that students often go on to read the books they've heard their classmates discuss. So keep the books readily available for independent pursuit after you've moved on to something else in the curriculum. What was learned from one book can be reinforced as students continue reading on their own.

Independent Reading

Independent reading is also referred to as "drop everything and read" (DEAR) and sustained silent reading (SSR). This practice, which has been around for decades, often falls out of vogue due to the pressures teachers experience related to time constraints and the amount of material to be covered in order to prepare students for testing. What is independent reading? Its name pretty much says it all. It involves supplying the time in school for students to read what they want to read. Teachers using the approach advocate it as a way to motivate students; increase interest; improve vocabulary, fluency, and comprehension skills; and reinforce and enhance content knowledge. Research points to numerous benefits of independent reading (e.g., Akmal, 2002; Ivey & Broaddus, 2001; Krashen, 1993). However, Hasbrouck (2006) urges caution: "What about those students who struggle with basic reading skills and who may not use their silent reading time well—either wasting time by doing little to no reading or writing, or trying to read materials that cause frustration because they are too difficult?" (p. 22).

Of course, independent reading cannot replace actual reading instruction and other methods designed to improve fluency, especially for readers who struggle.

Teachers need to monitor what happens during silent reading time and note the students who look bored, sleepy, off-task, or frustrated. Ask them what problems they're encountering and figure out ways to make their experience more fruitful and satisfying. Perhaps we need a wider range of texts in terms of difficulty levels, or we could bring in books with more visuals. Clausen-Grace and Kelley (2007) use an interest inventory to match students to books, explaining, "There are great books out there, but often kids do not know where they are or that they even exist. Our job (though not an easy one) is to find the right book for the right reader, and then to teach students to fully engage every time they read" (p. 43).

DeBenedictus (2007) provides a literature review showing how independent reading programs have evolved over 70 years, and provides a list of resources for implementing SSR, including Steve Gardiner's (2005) *Building Student Literacy Through Sustained Silent Reading*, and *Are They Really Reading?: Expanding SSR in the Middle Grades*, by Jodi Crum Marshall (2002).

Independent reading can be an organized school effort, where a period of time each day—perhaps 30 minutes—is designated when all other activities stop and everyone reads. Administrators, secretaries, students, custodians, teachers, cafeteria workers, and teacher assistants participate, reading a book or other text of choice. Fisher (2004) documents how the SSR program was resuscitated in an urban high school, noting effects as perceived by students and teachers. It can also be done in an individual teacher's class; students might know that in Mr. Ondrako's science class, the first hour is spent taking notes from a lecture or doing lab work or group work, but the second part of the 90-minute block is devoted to reading any book or magazine from the classroom library.

Consider the following steps for implementing SSR in your class:

- Put together a classroom library that includes a wide variety of topics and reading levels.
- To introduce students to silent reading time, explain that the whole class will all be reading something for a specified number of minutes at the same time each day. "Talk up" a few selections from the classroom library. Have students make one or two selections ahead of time that they will be browsing or reading during the first session.
- Explain the rules for SSR:

  Everyone is silent.

  Everyone is reading or looking at a book.

  Students remain in their seats.

- Remember, your role as an actively reading role model is essential.
- Start with a brief exposure and gradually extend the time.

You'll decide how to adapt SSR to best meet your curriculum standards and your students' needs. You'll also determine if mini-lessons regarding selecting and keeping track of books, figuring out if a book is too easy or too hard, or how to know when to abandon a book, are necessary. Here's a sample scenario that will help you visualize the activity at work.

Pre-SSR. Ms. Spies, a ninth-grade global studies teacher, has been collecting trade books for her classroom library for a couple of years, and has a few dozen nonfiction texts about countries all over the globe and representing all time periods, which she keeps on a shelf labeled SSR Possibilities. Each month she works with the school's librarian to gather and sign out about 20 informational books from the school library. She tells students the titles of the borrowed books, gives a few quick booktalks, and puts them on the SSR shelf with her own books.

Ms. Spies: As usual, we'll begin class with twenty minutes of sustained silent reading. I see you've all either brought your books or picked out something from the SSR shelf. When the timer signals the end of SSR, you have one minute to record the pages you've read in your SSR logs, along with a sentence or a couple of key phrases about what you learned. I'll call on a few people to give us their status when time's up.

Post-SSR. *Ms. Spies:* Okay, before you put your logs away, let's listen to a few readers. You might hear something that will help you as we piece together this big picture we call world history, and you might discover what book you want to read next. Mia, what's your status?

Mia: I just started a new book, *Three Wishes: Palestinian and Israeli Children Speak.* The author, Deborah Ellis, interviewed children and asked them to tell her what made them happy, sad, angry—stuff like that. There are pictures of the kids. I can't wait to read more.

Ms. Spies: Thanks, Mia. Ramón, how about you?

Ramón: I'm finishing up the book on Fiji my aunt brought me from her vacation. I'm going to live there some day!

Ms. Spies: Ah, sounds like a plan. Dorota?

Dorota: I'm in the middle of *Hitler Youth: Growing Up in Hitler's Shadow,* by Susan Campbell Bartoletti. My family is from Poland, so I'm interested in this topic. The photographs are amazing.

Ramón: I want that book next!

Ms. Spies: Thanks for sharing today. I'm continuing *Walking the Camino de Santiago,* by Bethan Davies, getting prepared for *my* vacation this summer by reading about this route across northern Spain. On your way out, I'd like the people who reported today to place a sticky note on our world map, pinpointing the place you read about. Now, please put your logs away and get your notebooks out. Remember that we've been talking about Africa in post-colonial times. . . .

Combining Genres

T hough this book is organized into chapters by genre for practical purposes, I highly recommend that as you study particular curricular topics, you provide books from a variety of genres, as well as those that cross genres or represent more than one genre. You might read from an informational text, then read a poem that connects or makes the same point in a different way. Combine a memoir with a fiction story, a nonfiction narrative with a how-to book, a picture book with a non-illustrated biography.

Imagine introducing a middle school social studies unit on labor with a read-aloud of the novel *Iqbal*, by Francesco D'Adamo (2003). Students will hear an awe-inspiring story from Fatima, the narrator who was taken from her family as a young child and is chained to a loom in a carpet factory in Pakistan all day, every day. She meets a fellow bonded worker, Iqbal, who offers hope and encouragement; who runs away; who wins an award and travels to America; and who returns to help labor leaders free more children. Listeners will be heartbroken as Fatima reads the letter telling of Iqbal's murder at around age 13. Through this story, they will learn about human nature and about character development, but they will also learn historical facts and concepts related to labor and social justice. Important vocabulary related to the social studies curriculum is introduced; for example, in the Introduction, the author explains:

Today, more than two hundred million children between the ages of five and seventeen are "economically active" in the world. About seventy-three million of these are under ten years of age, and almost six million children are working in conditions of "forced and bonded labor." Bonded labor is a system in which a person works for a preestablished period of time to pay off a debt. Many of America's early colonists started out as indentured servants, receiving their passage to the colonies in return for a number of years of labor, after which they acquired their liberty and a grant of land. (pp. v–vi)

In the story, Fatima learns from Iqbal that, in reality, she and the other bonded children are slaves. Their debt never disappears, they are under the complete control of their masters, and they are invisible to the outside world. Students vicariously feel what bonded labor is like for its victims; they are not likely to forget the concept, or think of it only as something they must remember for a quiz on Friday or a final exam.

After students have had the opportunity to discuss their reactions to the story, and to ask questions they'd now like answers to, you can produce the nonfiction book by Susan Kuklin, *Iqbal Masih and the Crusaders Against Child Slavery* (1998). The photographs and chapters show the remarkable influence this young boy had around the world as well as in his native Pakistan. Students will see Iqbal accepting the Reebok Human Rights Award; discover details of his murder on Easter Sunday, 1995; and learn how the children from Broad Meadows Middle School in Quincy, Massachusetts—where Iqbal had visited—reacted to news of his death by circulating a petition asking for an independent investigation into his murder, and initiated the Kids' Campaign to Build a School for Iqbal. Imagine, now, what ideas your students might share to further the cause for justice for the enslaved children of the world.

You can use multiple genres within your schools and classrooms in many ways, especially if you like to collaborate with teachers in other disciplines. Students could simultaneously read Chris Crowe's novel, *Mississippi Trial, 1955* (2002) in English class and the same author's *Getting Away with Murder: The True Story of the Emmett Till Case* (2003) in social studies. They'll learn much about a shameful aspect of American history in early Civil Rights Movement days from the literature, and perhaps talk about their responses in both classes. The teachers could then guide the students to perform the 15 interconnected sonnets in Marilyn Nelson's *A Wreath for Emmett Till* (2005).

Science, social studies, and English teachers could work together with a pairing of Laurie Halse Anderson's novel *Fever 1793* (2000) with *An American Plague: The True and Terrifying Story of the Yellow Fever Epidemic of 1793*, by Jim Murphy (2003). Both are set in our young nation's capital, Philadelphia. Both talk about the controversy over the best medical treatment for the disease. Was Dr. Benjamin Rush's prescription for the administering of heavy doses of toxic poisons, including mercury, combined with bloodletting, more harmful than helpful? (He didn't hesitate to subject himself to the same remedies when stricken with the illness.) Students will learn how devastating yellow fever was to the whole city, with thousands succumbing, in Murphy's book; they'll learn how devastating it was on a personal and family level through the story of 14-year-old Mattie in the novel.

You'll be able to pair or group many more books representing various genres using annotations in the coming chapters—books that will help your curriculum and your discipline come alive for your fortunate students. And you can keep abreast of new children's, young adult, and adult titles as they are published through databases, reference sources, and your school and public librarians. There has never been a time so rich in terms of resources.

Book Clubs and Discussion Clubs

You might think about starting a book club in your school, or at least in your classroom, that would function much like the hundreds of weekly or monthly book clubs in which adults choose to participate outside of schools. There could be a teacher book club and a student book club, and sometimes they could choose to read the same selection. Daniels and Zemelman (2004) define book clubs as "small, peer-led discussion groups whose members have chosen to read the same article, chapter, or book. These groups can be organized in a wide variety of ways." (p. 201). They give an example of a history book club in progress, where each group has chosen a historical novel set during the Depression, World War II, or the Cold War. The authors give tips on setting up the groups, providing students with ways to organize their responses, and assessing the process and results.

Begin by going through the chapters of your textbook or sections of your state or district curriculum, then find titles of books or articles that could accompany them. Sometimes textbook companies provide lists of supplemental materials, so a lot of the exploratory work might be done already.

Frank Smith (1985) coined the term *joining the literacy club* to explain young children's desire to read and write in terms of their desire for belonging, and many teachers have initiated a variety of types of clubs to entice their students into literacy. *The Book Club Connection: Literacy Learning and Classroom Talk* (McMahon & Raphael, 1997) includes chapters by teachers and researchers who have implemented a book club approach that is founded on theoretical principles of learning as a sociocultural activity and that is research based. Furthermore, the book details results and implications of ongoing classroom research conducted over several years of using McMahon and Raphael's model. This model involves community sharing in a whole class setting: reading, writing, and small, student-led discussion groups. In order to assure successful group discussions, teachers employ explicit instruction, modeling, and scaffolding. They teach the processes involved in discussion; they give instruction in how to participate. McMahon gives the example of how adults—teachers and researchers—modeled different kinds of discussion for a fifth-grade classroom, exemplifying both good, facilitative practices and practices to avoid, such as round-robin reading of journal responses with no interaction, and rudely interrupting a speaker.

Goatley (1997) found that the book club approach enhanced opportunities for students in special education classes to talk and interact with text and peers, who valued and encouraged them; language use facilitated their literacy growth. She found that the needs of the special education students and the others in the class were quite similar; *all* students required various forms of instructional support, and when she identified students needing more in the way of explicit instruction or scaffolding, she was able to supply it. Brock (1997) explored the use of book clubs for English learners in mainstreamed classrooms, and reported on three research studies examining these students' participation through a case study approach. She concludes from her analysis of the data:

> First, second-language learners are capable of engaging in complex thinking and reasoning *while they are in the process of acquiring English.* Second, teachers must realize that second-language learners have important and valuable ideas and experiences to contribute to the class. The unique contributions they have to offer the classroom community can be capitalized on for the benefit of all students in the classroom. (p. 154)

Boyd (1997) studied the use of the book club model in a cross-aged literacy program that was designed to help adolescent readers who are struggling. She found that the older students who participated, all of whom were members of ethnic minorities and considered to be readers and writers with poor skill development and low motivation, showed increased interest in oral reading, learned to raise questions around text-based issues for a variety of purposes, shared personal stories related to text-based issues, and assumed responsibility for their contributions to the program. Boyd contrasts this alternative literacy experience with the more typical reading instruction in which the students were not thriving, and with the common deficit perspective of literacy instruction so often adopted with struggling or resistant readers. The cross-aged book club experience allowed the teacher and the students themselves to look at their strengths rather than their weaknesses.

In other types of academic clubs, books may not be primary, but certainly can play a part. Posamentier and Stepelman (1999) give suggestions for organizing and moderating a mathematics club, along with ideas for what such a club might get involved in, such as forming competitive teams, joining area mathematics contests, holding a mathematics fair for the school and/or community, inviting guest speakers, taking class trips of mathematical significance, establishing a school math magazine, or conducting a peer teaching program. Imagine how all these things would involve a great deal of discussion and collaborative problem solving. The authors also list dozens of topics for mathematics projects, including cryptography, crystallography, dynamic symmetry, game theory, paper folding, map projections, mathematics and art, unsolved problems, fractals, the geometry of bubbles, prime numbers, mathematics and music, and tessellations. No matter what your content area specialty, consider creating a similar list of fascinating topics and related books for your students to pursue in a formal discussion club situation or in informal book discussion groups in your classroom.

Chandler (1997) tells of the Beach Book Club she conducted over three summers in an effort to change her students who "were card-carrying members of Smith's metaphorical 'literacy club'—they had learned to read—but they weren't using their membership privileges very often" (p. 104). She tells of soliciting volunteer members of her summer book club through a written invitation and through booktalks given in class. The discussions were informal, relaxed, and collaborative, and were combined with games and other social activities (which the students eventually asked be reduced so there would be more time to discuss the literature). Rather than ask leading questions, Chandler learned to "share my wonderings" (p. 112). The Beach Book Club was a success on many levels, as is demonstrated by this message written to her by a former club participant:

> I think that the most important thing I got from book club was to be able to listen to others' ideas and see their point of view. When doing this I had to let my feelings and position go to see theirs. Discussing books made me see that not everyone gets the same ideas from reading the material. Everyone is going to interpret a different meaning. The meaning is worthwhile only when you are able to back it up with material from the book. . . . Discussing books is not about trying to persuade someone's point of view, but to make it able for everyone to see all sides of a certain issue. (p. 112)

Teacher Laura Pardo (1997) applied the book club model to her social studies curriculum. She combined each of her unit topics with book club literature and themes and issues. For example, her September unit was on Native Americans. She chose *Sing Down the Moon*, by Scott O'Dell (1973), for students to read and discuss in book club, and selected the issues of prejudice, slavery, and cultural heritage awareness to highlight during discussions.

The above examples should reinforce the many potential benefits of applying a book club approach in your content area classroom. You can find further ideas that might help you think about how to make your book discussions as authentic as possible in Michael W. Smith's "Conversations About Literature Outside Classrooms: How Adults Talk About Books in Their Book Clubs" (1996). He found that men and women valued the social aspect of book clubs as well as the spirit of cooperation and equality that prevailed. Readers read differently when they knew they'd be discussing the texts and listening to others' reactions; they began imagining what the others would be thinking about as they read, thus adding to their own strategies.

Young (1998) reports on the speech genre created by a group of students belonging to a Thursday afternoon gathering called the Read and Talk Club. Students resisted reading and talking about the same book, as is so often done in school; instead, they chose individual selections and shared reactions with their peers in a way that showed they had temporarily disbanded the rules typically associated with school talk and replaced them with their own rules:

> The conversations moved quickly from one subject to another and back again. Their voices tended to blend together. There were side conversations, interruptions, and laughter and fun. They were loud! . . . They had indeed talked about

all kinds of texts—books or magazines they had read, computer programs, or movies they had seen. They also had focused their discussions around a prese-lected theme (e.g., people against nature, personal conflict) or they had done a comparative analysis of different texts. (p. 252)

No matter what form your book club takes, teacher assessment and student self-assessment must play an integral part. Fountas and Pinnell (2006) recommend assessing both process and content:

> Process includes the desired interactions and conversational routines. But remember that students can be having a discussion that looks very good from a process point of view but is still empty in terms of content . . . you will want to assess the depth of your students' thinking, the degree to which they can summarize the text and think beyond it, and their ability to ground the talk in the texts and in their own experience. (p. 301)

Figure 2.1 gives an example of what might transpire in an interdisciplinary book club.

| FIGURE | 2.1 | An example of an interdisciplinary book club meeting. |

SETTING

Madeleine L'Engle High School, which prides itself on having an interdisciplinary focus, has a book club that meets twice a month after school; a couple of dozen usually attend. Each semester focuses on a particular theme or genre, decided on by the consensus of group members. This semester the group has been reading fantasy books, and at the last meeting, the topic was the Harry Potter books and movies. The club advisor has agreed to bring in materials related to the Harry Potter phenomenon for today's follow-up reading workshop day.

READING WORKSHOP GUIDE

"We agreed at the last meeting that we'd like to explore the interdisciplinary connections relative to the Harry Potter books and movies. I've got five readings available; decide from the titles which you'd like to read independently today. Choose one, go to a comfortable spot to read, and take notes about your reactions and thoughts if you want. Then come back in a half hour for discussion, first with others who have read the same material, then with the whole group. At the conclusion of today's meeting, you may sign out any of the articles to enjoy and to share with family, teachers, and friends. Also, I've acquired companion reference texts by Rowling that I've added to our Harry Potter bin, which you can sign out to take home for three days. Check out *Fantastic Beasts and Where to Find Them* (2001) and *Quidditch Through the Ages* (2001)."

TEXT CHOICES

1. "Hunting Down Harry Potter: An Exploration of Religious Concerns About Children's Literature," by Kimbra Wilder Gish, *The Horn Book Magazine* (May/June, 2000, pp. 262–271).
2. Excerpt from *The science of Harry Potter: How magic really works*, by Roger Highfield (New York: Viking, 2002).
3. Excerpt from *The magical worlds of Harry Potter: A treasury of myths, legends, and fascinating facts*, by David Colbert (New York: Berkley Books, 2002).
4. *New York Times* reviews of the movies.
5. Chapter 6, "Controversies and Criticism," of *J. K. Rowling: A biography*, by Connie Ann Kirk (Westport, CT: Greenwood Press, 2003).

AN EXAMPLE OF A WEEK-LONG SCHOOL-WIDE INTERDISCIPLINARY UNIT

My decision to organize the chapters of this book by genres does not mean I think of genres as mutually exclusive. Likewise, dividing the bibliographies by subject area does not indicate that the books are appropriate only for a single curriculum. On the contrary, I envision teachers breaking down artificial subject area walls as they collaborate with other teachers and help students explore in an interdisciplinary fashion. To exemplify what I mean, I provide the following example of how a school might combine resources and teacher brainpower to create a schoolwide learning experience.

SCENARIO

The faculty at Lewis and Clark Middle School has decided to devote a week in the spring to an interdisciplinary, whole-school exploration of the school's namesakes and their legendary expedition. Teachers in grades 5 through 8 have been working, with the extensive assistance of the school librarian, throughout the fall semester to plan activities that will both celebrate the theme and meet their curricular standards and goals. They've done their own exploring via the Internet to obtain ideas, resources, and lesson plans. Let's listen in as they present a progress report at a faculty meeting.

SOCIAL STUDIES TEACHERS

We'll have our students read biographies of Lewis, Clark, York, Sacajawea, and Thomas Jefferson, as well as some informational texts about the expedition and about the Native American tribes they met along the way. We'll study some primary documents, and create some document-based questions based on those resources. We'll study maps and learn about the geography of the territory the explorers covered. Here are some books that will be available for use in our classrooms:

Ambrose, S. (1996). *Undaunted Courage.* New York: Simon & Schuster.

Blumberg, R. (2004). *York's Adventures with Lewis and Clark: An African-American's Part in the Great Expedition.* New York: HarperCollins.

Blumberg, R. (2003). *The Incredible Journey of Lewis and Clark.* New York: HarperTrophy.

Blumberg, R. (1999). *What's the Deal?: Jefferson, Napoleon, and the Louisiana Purchase.* Washington, DC: National Geographic.

Botkin, D. B. (1995). *Our Natural History: The Lessons of Lewis and Clark.* New York: G. P. Putnam's Sons.

Fifer, B., & Soderberg, V. (2002). *Along the Trail with Lewis and Clark.* Helena, MT: Montana Magazine/Farcountry Press.

Kimmel, E. C. (2003). *As Far as the Eye Can See: Lewis and Clark's Westward Quest.* New York: Random House Books for Young Readers.

Molzahn, A. B. (2003). *Lewis and Clark: American Explorers.* Berkeley Heights, NJ: Enslow.

Orr, T. (2004). *The Lewis and Clark Expedition: A Primary Source History of the Journey of the Corps of Discovery.* New York: The Rosen Publishing Group.

ENGLISH LANGUAGE ARTS

Like our social studies colleagues, we'll have biographies available. But we'll also have fiction books. Students can have fun with point of view as they read novels narrated by Seaman, the dog on the journey; reflect on the alternating views of Sacajawea and William Clark in Bruchac's novel; and imagine the expedition as told from a 12-year-old's point of view as they read the novel by Lasky. As students work on research reports for other subject areas, we'll help them with the writing aspects, including organization and editing. Students can do some creative writing in our classes, taking on the roles of the people involved, creating a newspaper or magazine, or compiling a collection of short stories they've written for the theme week. Some groups will compose a play to be performed for parents and the community on the last day of the celebration. They'll also read some of the explorers' journal entries and model some of their own journal entries after them. They'll get to listen to a sound recording of the journals, and watch the Ken Burns video. Here are some books we'll have in our rooms:

Ambrose, S. E. (2003). *This Vast Land: A Young Man's Journal of the Lewis and Clark Expedition.* New York: Simon & Schuster.

Bruchac, J. (2000). *Sacajawea: The Story of Bird Woman and the Lewis and Clark Expedition.* San Diego: Silver Whistle.

DeVoto, B. (1997). *The Journals of Lewis and Clark.* New York: Mariner Books.

Edwards, J. (2003). *The Great Expedition of Lewis and Clark, by Private Reubin Field, Member of the Corps of Discovery.* Illus. S. W. Comport. New York: Farrar Straus Giroux.

Erdrich, L. (2003). *Sacagawea.* Illus. J. Buffalohead. Minneapolis, MN: Carolrhoda Books.

(continued)

A WEEK-LONG SCHOOL-WIDE INTERDISCIPLINARY UNIT, *continued*

Hall, B. (2003). *I Should Be Extremely Happy in Your Company: A Novel of Lewis and Clark.* New York: Viking.

Hunsaker, J. B. (2001). *Sacajawea Speaks: Beyond the Shiny Mountains with Lewis and Clark.* Guilford, CT: Two Dot Books.

Johmann, C. A. (2003). *The Lewis & Clark Expedition.* Charlotte, VT: Williamson Publishing.

Karwaski, G., & Watling, J. (1999). *Seaman: The Dog Who Explored the West with Lewis and Clark.* Atlanta, GA: Peachtree.

Lasky, K. (2000). *The Journal of Augustus Pelletier: The Lewis and Clark Expedition.* My Name Is America Series. New York: Scholastic.

Myers, L. (2002). *Lewis and Clark and Me: A Dog's Tale.* Illus. M. Dooling. New York: Henry Holt & Co.

Nevin, D. (2004). *Meriwether: A Novel of Meriwether Lewis and the Lewis and Clark Expedition.* New York: Forge.

Pringle, L. (2002). *Dog of Discovery: A Newfoundland's Adventures with Lewis and Clark.* Honesdale, PA: Boyds Mills Press.

Scieszka, J. (2006). *The Time Warp Trio: Lewis and Clark and . . . Jodie, Freddie and Samantha.* New York: HarperTrophy.

Smith, R. (2000). *The Captain's Dog: My Journey with the Lewis and Clark Tribe.* San Diego: Harcourt Brace.

Wheeler, R. S. (2002). *Eclipse: A Novel of Lewis and Clark.* New York: Tor, Forge.

Wolf, A. (2004). *New Found Land: A Novel.* Cambridge, MA: Candlewick Press.

SCIENCE

We've found some great resources. We'll divide our students into teams of zoologists, botanists, and geologists; they'll research the animals, plants, and land formations that the explorers encountered. We'll take a virtual field trip to the Lewis and Clark Herbarium through www.life.umd.edu/emeritus/reveal/pbio/LnC/LnCpublic.html. Here are books with which our students can start their explorations:

Cutright, P. R. (1989). *Lewis and Clark: Pioneering Naturalists.* Lincoln, NE: University of Nebraska Press.

Patent, D. H. (2003). *Plants on the Trail with Lewis and Clark.* New York: Clarion Books.

Patent, D. H. (2002). *Animals on the Trail with Lewis and Clark.* New York: Clarion Books.

Phillips, H. W. (2003). *Plants of the Lewis and Clark Expedition.* Missoula, MT: Mountain Press.

Schullery, P. (2002). *Lewis and Clark Among the Grizzlies: Legend and Legacy in the American West.* Guilford, CT: Falcon.

ART

We can't wait for this project to begin; our students are going to transform the school building. We'll paint murals on the walls of the hallways depicting scenes from the expedition, and the main hall will be transformed into a giant map of the trail. We plan to study Native American art and the crafts that were popular at the time, such as ceramics, quilting and mask-making. And of course, we'll be responsible for the sets and costumes for the school play. We'll study and critique the illustrations in children's books such as the following:

Adler, D., & Himler, R. (2003). *A Picture Book of Lewis and Clark.* New York: Holiday House.

Gunderson, J. (2007). *The Lewis & Clark Expedition.* Illus. S. Irwin, K. Williams, & C. Barnett III. Graphic Library: Graphic History. Mankato, MN: Capstone Press.

Mussulman, J. A. (2004). *Discovering Lewis & Clark from the Air.* Photography by Jim Wark. Sevierville, TN: Mountain Press.

Redmond, S. R. (2003). *Lewis and Clark: A Prairie Dog for the President.* Illus. J. Manders. New York: Scholastic.

PHYSICAL EDUCATION

We're going to concentrate on the outdoors. We'll turn the path through the woods on the school property into a replica of the trail, complete with markers. Then we'll serve as guides to classes from the elementary school who will come over for field trips, as well as parents and community members who want to hike our trail after the school play. We'll all get our exercise! Here are some of the books we'll have available to our students:

Grossman, C. (2003). *Adventuring Along the Lewis and Clark Trail.* San Francisco: Sierra Club Books.

Long, B. (2000). *Backtracking by Foot, Canoe, and Subaru Along the Lewis and Clark Trail.* Seattle, WA: Sasquatch Books.

Lourie, P. (2001). *On the Trail of Sacagawea.* Honesdale, PA: Caroline House.

Schmidt, T. (2002). *The Lewis and Clark Trail.* Washington, DC: National Geographic Society.

(continued)

A WEEK-LONG SCHOOL-WIDE INTERDISCIPLINARY UNIT, *continued*

MATH

We're definitely up for this challenge. There are loads of ways mathematical principles can be involved in a study of Lewis and Clark. We'll do a land survey and measure distances; our students will build models of keelboats. They'll pore through books looking for numbers: mileage, percentages, populations, etc. We'll create word problems for ourselves and others to solve. Get ready for our puzzles and conundrums! Herbert's book, *Lewis and Clark for Kids: Their Journey of Discovery with 21 Activities* (2000) teaches how to figure out latitude and longitude, which will connect to the geometry we've been studying.

MUSIC

Well, of course our students will research the music of the time period, and then learn and sing the songs. Count on us to provide the music and choreography for the school play. In *Lewis and Clark for Kids: Their Journey of Discovery with 21 Activities*, by Janis Herbert (2000), there are instructions for making drums and dance rattles; we'll be using that book also to learn how to do the Whooping Crane Waltz and the Sharp-Tailed Shake.

HOME AND CAREERS

We'll be cooking up ideas—literally. We found the book *Cooking on the Lewis and Clark Expedition*, by M. Gunderson (2000). Students will learn about the kinds of food the explorers ate, and will try out some of the recipes provided. We'll prepare refreshments for the reception after the school play. Also, we've found recipes for fruit leather and for Great Plains Stew in *Lewis and Clark for Kids: Their Journey of Discovery with 21 Activities*, by Janis Herbert (2000). The same book has instructions for making baskets, moccasins, and beeswax candles. We'll be busy!

Conclusion

While the focus of this book will be on literature and strategies that can result in gains in content knowledge, achievement in curricular goals, and enhancement of skills necessary for the practice of the disciplines, remember: the same materials and practices can increase the literacy levels of your students. For example, Fisher (2001) reports on a study showing how a school-wide effort at incorporating some of the strategies exemplified in this book, including writing to learn, K-W-L, reciprocal teaching, concept mapping, daily independent reading, and read-alouds, resulted in significant gains in reading scores as measured by a standardized achievement test. Of course, it's not hard to imagine that these better readers will be better able to complete the classroom tasks that could result in achievement in terms of content acquisition. Everybody wins!

REFERENCES

Akmal, T. T. (2002). Ecological approaches to sustained silent reading: Confirming, contracting, and relating to middle school students. *Clearing House, 75* (3), 154–157.

Black, A., & Stave, A. (2007). *A comprehensive guide to readers theatre: Enhancing fluency and comprehension in middle school and beyond.* Newark, DE: International Reading Association.

Boyd, F. B. (1997). The cross-aged literacy program: Preparing struggling adolescents for book club discussions. In S. I. McMahon & T. E. Raphael (Eds.), *The book club connection* (pp. 162–181). New York: Teachers College Press.

Brock, C. H. (1997). Second-language learners in mainstream classrooms. In S. I. McMahon & T. E. Raphael (Eds.), *The book club connection* (pp. 141–158). New York: Teachers College Press.

Chandler, K. (1997). The beach book club: Literacy in the "lazy days of summer." *Journal of Adolescent and Adult Literacy, 41* (2), 104–115.

Chandler-Olcott, K. (2001). Scaffolding love: A framework for choosing books for, with, and by adolescents. *The Language and Literacy Spectrum, 2,* 18–32.

Clausen-Grace, N., & Kelley, M. (2007). You can't hide in R5: Restructuring independent reading to be more strategic and engaging. *Voices from the Middle, 14* (3), 38–42.

Daniels, H. (2006). What's the next big thing with literature circles? *Voices from the Middle, 13* (4), 10–15.

Daniels, H. (2001). *Literature circles: Voice and choice in the student-centered classroom.* York, ME: Stenhouse.

Daniels, H. (1994). *Literature circles: Voice and choice in the student-centered classroom* (2nd ed). York, ME: Stenhouse.

Daniels, H., & Bizar, M. (1998). *Methods that matter: Six structures for best practice classrooms.* York, ME: Stenhouse.

Daniels, H., & Zemelman, S. (2004). *Subjects matter: Every teacher's guide to content-area reading.* Portsmouth, NH: Heinemann.

DeBenedictus, D. (2007). Sustained silent reading: Making adaptations. *Voices from the Middle, 14* (3), 29–37.

DeVries, B. (2008). *Literacy assessment and intervention for K–6 classrooms* (2nd ed.). Scottsdale, AZ: Holcomb Hathaway.

Elley, W. B. (1992). *How in the world do students read?* Newark, DE: International Reading Association.

Fisher, D. (2004). Setting the "opportunity to read" standard: Resuscitating the SSR program in an urban high school. *Journal of Adolescent and Adult Literacy, 48* (2), 138–150.

Fisher, D. (2001). "We're moving on up": Creating a school-wide literacy effort in an urban high school. *Journal of Adolescent and Adult Literacy, 45* (2), 92–101.

Flynn, R. M. (2007). *Dramatizing the content with curriculum-based readers theatre, grades 6–12.* Newark, DE: International Reading Association.

Fountas, I. C., & Pinnell, G. S. (2006). *Teaching for comprehension and fluency: Thinking, talking, and writing about reading, K–8.* Portsmouth, NH: Heinemann.

Gardiner, S. (2005). *Building student literacy through sustained silent reading.* Alexandria, VA: Association for Supervision and Curriculum Development.

Goatley, V. J. (1997). Talk about text among special education students. In S. I. McMahon & T. E. Raphael (Eds.), *The book club connection* (pp. 119–137). New York: Teachers College Press.

Harste, J. C., & Leland, C. (2007). On getting lost, finding one's direction, and teacher research. *Voices from the Middle, 14* (3), 7–11.

Hasbrouck, J. (2006). Drop everything and read—But how? *American Educator, 30* (2), 22–27, 30–31, 46–47.

Herbert, J. (2000). *Lewis and Clark for kids: Their journey of discovery with 21 activities.* Chicago: Chicago Review Press.

Ivey, G., & Broaddus, K. (2001). "Just plain reading": A survey of what makes students want to read in middle school classrooms. *Reading Research Quarterly, 36* (4), 350–377.

Johnson, H., & Freedman, L. (2001). Talking about content knowledge at the middle level: Using informational trade books in content-area literature circles. *The Language and Literacy Spectrum, 2,* 52–62.

Kane, S. (2007). *Literacy and learning in the content areas* (2nd ed.). Scottsdale, AZ: Holcomb Hathaway.

Krashen, S. (1993). *The power of reading: Insights from the research.* Englewood, CO: Libraries Unlimited.

Marshall, J. C. (2002). *Are they really reading?: Expanding SSR in the middle grades.* Portland, ME: Stenhouse.

McMahon, S. I., & Raphael, T. (Eds.). (1997). *The book club connection: Literacy learning and classroom talk.* New York: Teachers College Press.

Mooney, M. (1990). *Reading to, with, and by children.* Katonah, NY: Richard C. Owen.

Pappas, C. C., & Varelas, M., with Barry, A., & Rife, A. (2004). Promoting dialogic inquiry in information book read-alouds: Young urban children's ways of making sense in science. In W. Saul (Ed.), *Crossing borders in literacy and science instruction: Perspectives on theory and practice* (pp. 161–189). Newark, DE: International Reading Association and Arlington, VA: National Science Teachers Association.

Pardo, L. (1997). Reflective teaching for continuing development of book club. In S. I. McMahon & T. E. Raphael (Eds.), *The book club connection* (pp. 162–181). New York: Teachers College Press.

Posamentier, A. S., & Stepelman, J. (1999). *Teaching secondary mathematics: Techniques and enrichment units* (5th ed.). Upper Saddle River, NJ: Merrill.

Richardson, J. (2000). *Read it aloud!: Using literature in the secondary content classroom.* Newark, DE: International Reading Association.

Schoenbach, R., Braunger, J., Greenleaf, C., et al. (2003). Apprenticing adolescents to reading in subject-area classrooms. *Phi Delta Kappan, 85* (2), 133–138.

Smith, F. (1985). *Reading without nonsense.* New York: Teachers College Press.

Smith, M. W. (1996). Conversations about literature outside classrooms: How adults talk about books in their book clubs. *Journal of Adolescent & Adult Literacy, 40* (3), 180–186.

Smolkin, L. B., & Donovan, C. A. (2004). How not to get lost on *The Magic School Bus:* What makes high science content read-alouds? In W. Saul (Ed.), *Crossing borders in literacy and science instruction: Perspectives on theory and practice* (pp. 291–313). Newark, DE: International Reading Association and Arlington, VA: National Science Teachers Association.

Tovani, C. (2000). *I read it, but I don't get it: Comprehension strategies for adolescent readers.* Portland, ME: Stenhouse.

Trelease, J. (2001). *The read-aloud handbook* (5th ed.). New York: Penguin Books.

Vygotsky, L. (1986). *Mind in society: The development of higher psychological processes.* Cambridge, MA: Massachusetts Institute of Technology Press.

Wilhelm, J. (2001). *Improving comprehension with think-aloud strategies.* New York: Professional Books.

Young, J. P. (1998). Discussion as a practice of carnival. In D. E. Alvermann, K. A. Hinchman, D. W. Moore, S. F. Phelps, & D. R. Waff (Eds.), *Reconceptualizing the literacies in adolescents' lives* (pp. 247–264). Mahwah, NJ: Lawrence Erlbaum Associates.

LITERATURE CITED

American Chemical Society. (1998). *Chemcom: Chemistry in the community.* Dubuque, IO: Kendall/Hunt Pub. Co.

Anderson, L. H. (2000). *Fever 1793.* New York: Simon & Schuster.

Bartoletti, S. C. (2005). *Hitler youth: Growing up in Hitler's shadow.* New York: Scholastic.

Crowe, C. (2003). *Getting away with murder: The true story of the Emmett Till case.* New York: Phyllis Fogelman Books.

Crowe, C. (2002). *Mississippi trial, 1955.* New York: Speak.

D'Adamo, F. (2003). *Iqbal: A novel.* Trans. A. Leorori. New York: Atheneum.

Davies, B. (2003). *Walking the Camino de Santiago.* Vancouver: Pili Pala Press.

Deedy, C. A. (2000). *The yellow star: The legend of King Christian X of Denmark.* Illus. H. Sørensen. Atlanta, GA: Peachtree.

Ellis, D. (2004). *Three wishes: Palestinian and Israeli children speak.* Toronto: Groundwood Books.

Gunderson, M. (2000). *Cooking on the Lewis & Clark expedition.* Mankato, MN: Blue Earth Books.

Kuklin, S. (1998). *Iqbal Masih and the crusaders against child slavery.* New York: Henry Holt & Co.

Meyer, C. (2001). *Beware, Princess Elizabeth!* San Diego: Harcourt.

Meyer, C. (2002). *Doomed Queen Anne.* San Diego: Harcourt.

Meyer, C. (2001). *Mary, Bloody Mary.* San Diego: Harcourt.

Murphy, J. (2003). *An American plague: The true and terrifying story of the yellow fever epidemic of 1793.* New York: Clarion Books.

Nelson, M. (2005). *A wreath for Emmett Till.* Illus. P. Lardy. Boston: Houghton.

O'Dell, S. (1973). *Sing down the moon.* New York: Dell.

Rowling, J. K. (2001). *Quidditch through the ages.* New York: Arthur A. Levine Books.

Rowling, J. K. (2001). *Fantastic beasts and where to find them.* New York: Arthur A. Levine Books.

Informational Books

3

"There are wonderfully rich and evocative non-fiction books available for readers at all levels that stimulate interest and provoke aesthetic response."

KURKJIAN & LIVINGSTON, 2005, p. 582

the why and how

OF USING INFORMATIONAL BOOKS

We've lived in the Information Age for some time now and recognize that there is more information than ever before and that information is changing faster all the time. Why, then, especially with the multiple and rapid ways of obtaining information at our fingertips, should we have shelves in our classrooms filled with informational trade books?

Informational books can promote scientific and health literacy, aesthetic literacy, and understanding of many different cultures and people within all professions and walks of life. These books will support curricula throughout a child's school day. For example, students might be introduced to the scientific method through informational books. Norton (2003) explains:

> Through firsthand experience and reading about the work of scientists, children discover how scientists observe, compare, formulate and test hypotheses, and draw conclusions or withhold them until they discover more evidence. Children also become familiar with the instruments used by scientists. As children learn about the scientific method, they gain appreciation for the attitudes of people who use this method. Children discover the importance of careful observations over long periods of time, the need for gathering data from many sources, and the requirement that scientists, whatever their field, make no conclusions before all the data have been collected. (p. 547)

Similar points can be made about what students can learn in the fields of music, health, art, language study, and history. Informational books can provide great enjoyment as they extend the curriculum for students who need a challenge or have a special interest. Nilsen and Donelson (2001) tell of added benefits:

> They also serve as models for research, and they go beyond the obvious facts to present information that is too complicated, too detailed, too obscure, or too controversial to be included in textbooks. (p. 283)

Most of what adults read is informational text (Duke, 2003). Different strategies are required for these texts as opposed to fictional ones, so you will need an abundance of informational materials and tactics for how to best use and comprehend them. In addition, standardized tests use informational text far more than fictional text (Calkins, Montgomery, Santman, & Falk, 1998). For this reason, also, we must prepare our students so that they are comfortable with and knowledgeable about engaging with the genre.

James Cross Giblin, himself a noted writer of informational children's books, discusses the potential value of books that deal with topics that used to be considered taboo for children:

> ... nonfiction writers have explored in a frank, thoroughgoing manner such subjects as child abuse, teenage sex and pregnancy, abortion, homosexuality, and substance abuse.... Sensitively handled, these explorations can be an effective counterbalance to all the exploitative programming that is readily available to young people today via television and the internet. (2000, p. 423)

As in the case of fiction, students don't have to read informational books in their entirety. Teachers can help them to identify their purposes and to use the index and Table of Contents efficiently to get what they need. Of course, readers may start with a limited purpose and then become so absorbed that they stay with the text for an extended visit. That happens to me quite often.

Hoyt (2002) assures teachers that they can use informational texts for two goals simultaneously, teaching content knowledge and teaching reading strategies. She gives several tips for reading informational texts, which we can pass along and model for our students. These include

- thinking about what you already know about the topic of the book;
- previewing the text before reading by looking at charts, words in bold, and pictures;
- noticing the author's style;
- stopping often to ask about what you have learned and what questions you have;
- finding the big idea; and
- making connections. (p. 4)

Palmer and Stewart (2005) offer a model for using informational books with children in early elementary grades (which can be adapted for middle and high school). They include teacher-directed instruction, then scaffolded student investigation, and finally independent student investigation. These stages are explained in Figure 3.1.

Yet another reason to use informational books in the content area classroom is that we tend to remember things we learn by way of story, and many nonfiction books contain true and fascinating stories relative to our curricular content. Galda and Cullinan (2002) recommend incorporating both fiction and nonfiction genres as math is taught:

> Mathematics programs today reflect a philosophy in which fiction and nonfiction literature fit naturally. Earlier mathematics instruction involved practicing isolated skills endlessly, calculating answers, memorizing combinations of numerals, and watching for a place to apply memorized routines. Today, we present mathe-

Model for using informational books with children (based on Palmer & Stewart, 2005).	FIGURE	3.1

Teacher-directed instruction. In the first stage, teachers read aloud, supply background knowledge, and teach students how to navigate the text and extract information strategically:

> For example, students should understand they can search for specific facts about a topic rather than read from cover to cover as in fiction. Organizational features such as headings, index and glossary are comprehension tools; visuals (e.g., photos, diagrams, charts) supply additional information. (p. 428)

Scaffolded student investigation. In the scaffolded student investigation stage, students get some choice of books, and complete structured guides teachers have created. There's lots of interaction among students, and the teacher monitors behavior and performance.

Independent student investigation. In the independent student investigation, students explore topics of choice, either within a class unit or with no constraints. The teacher supplies books and helps generate meaningful questions along with the student researchers.

matical problems in context, draw upon children's background knowledge to solve them, and model strategies for alternate ways to solve problems.

Today, many mathematics lessons begin with a story—a story with a problem that can be solved through a mathematical process. Teachers invite children to propose as many different strategies as possible to try to solve the problem. Together, they apply each strategy and evaluate its accuracy and efficiency. (p. 261)

Informational trade books can be used effectively to help students understand multiple points of view. The books also help students understand that issues are most often not clear-cut, and that reasonable people can be on opposite sides of a debate. Some books actually set out with the purpose of showing

contrast. For example, *George vs. George: The American Revolution as Seen from Both Sides*, by Rosalyn Schanzer (2004), begins by speaking of all the similarities between King George III of England and George Washington. Many factors, some involving taxes, led to their becoming enemies. The author contrasts daily life, government, and military organization on both sides of the Atlantic. Readers begin to understand that the American Revolution cannot neatly be wrapped up as a story of "good guy vs. bad guy."

Another book that shows contrasting perceptions and understandings is Anne Fadiman's *The Spirit Catches You and You Fall Down: A Hmong Child, her American Doctors, and the Collision of Two Cultures* (1997). This story recounts a loving family's attempt to raise a baby with severe epilepsy, as well as the dedication of the hospital staff who tried to save the baby's life. They are two very different stories, and the researcher does not try to turn them into one simple story with heroes and villains. Through extensive interviews both with people in the Hmong community and with doctors, Fadiman learned how neither culture understood the other, and her analysis shows the reader how very complex medical, ethical, spiritual, governmental, and societal issues can be.

Sometimes people change opinions and sides over time, realizing that their earlier beliefs were immature, misguided, or wrong. Diane McWhorter, author of *A Dream of Freedom: The Civil Rights Movement from 1954 to 1968* (2004), does a great job of explaining this happening in her own life. In the introduction, "The Mysterious Ways of History," she talks of growing up in Birmingham, Alabama. She was in sixth grade when Martin Luther King Jr. led the landmark 1963 march there. McWhorter recalls:

> Black children my age marched in protest of segregation. City officials sicced police dogs and turned fire hoses on them. . . . I didn't see those pictures or grasp the significance of what they revealed. . . . From my point of view, as a white child of privilege . . . here's how things looked from my side of the civil rights revolution:
>
> . . . I thought Martin Luther King was an "outside agitator" and that he had come to Birmingham to stir up our black people so that he could get rich. . . .
>
> I couldn't tell you then what *civil rights* meant, but grown-ups sounded so disgusted when they mentioned them that I figured they had to be bad words. (pp. 8–9)

McWhorter certainly changed and regretted her earlier stance, as attested by her decades of work researching and writing about the era. Because she identifies herself as a person who had been on the wrong side, her teaching through text is powerful. As a teacher, you can draw on books like hers to help students understand the complexities of society and of history. McWhorter's personal story is the story of a generation.

Using a number of books coming at a topic from different angles or with different purposes can be helpful to students as they think through curricular material. For example, *Dred Scott: Person or Property?*, by Corinne J. Naden and Rose Blue (2005), is part of the Supreme Court Milestones series published by Benchmark Books. Its focus is on the judicial process and the legalities of this famous case. In Chapter 4, "The Worst Decision," readers are taken through the session of the Supreme Court on February 11, 1856, when the opening arguments in the *Scott v. Sandford* case were heard, and then told of subsequent court discussions, rearguments, and finally, the decision, on March 6, 1857, that ". . . by a vote of seven to two, kept Dred Scott in the status of a slave" (p. 78). Readers have taken part in a very important courtroom drama. They might be surprised at the picture from the time period, with the caption underneath, "Violence over slavery spilled over onto the Senate floor. Senator Charles Sumner was beaten so badly by a fellow Congressman over a speech he gave against slavery that he didn't recover for three years" (Naden & Blue, p. 73).

By contrast, *Dred and Harriet Scott: A Family's Struggle for Freedom*, by Gwenyth Swain (2004), concentrates on the personal story of the couple. The Introduction begins:

> Children are precious. Every parent knows that. Yet slaves in America were never really free to hold onto their children. They couldn't keep their babies close to them. Slave babies belonged not to their parents, but to Master. (p. 3)

Readers are told of how the couple met, and how the decision to fight the system legally was fueled by the love the parents had for their children:

> They had lost two babies already. Those little boys died from the harshness of slavery. Dred and Harriet couldn't bear to think of losing their girls, too. Eliza was close to the age of the children who stood on auction blocks in St. Louis— the ones slave traders called "young and likely." The ones who brought top dollar. (p. 41)

The book gives much information about the Supreme Court case, and includes photographs, a glossary, a chronology, and a bibliography. Which book is the better for teaching your students? We needn't even ask that question. Used together, the books can help deepen your students' understanding of the horrors of slavery and of our government system at work during this time in history when society was so split about the crucial issue of what freedom meant and who was entitled to it. As students peruse the books, they'll see the document that the son of Dred's original owner signed in May of 1857, giving freedom at last to Dred Scott, Harriet, and daughters Lizzie and Eliza (Swain, 2004, p. 78).

By using a variety of books presenting multiple perspectives on a topic, students have the opportunity to take positions on issues, support their conclusions, draw analogies, and see issues from various viewpoints. As a result, they may well desire to research the topic further.

instructional
STRATEGIES AND ACTIVITIES

Involving Informational Books

▶▶▶ **CHECKING INFORMATIONAL BOOKS FOR ACCURACY AND CONSISTENCY**

Standards Addressed

Science: All students should develop an understanding of the abilities necessary to do scientific inquiry. All students should develop an understanding of evolution and equilibrium.

History: Students compare and contrast differing sets of ideas, values, personalities, behaviors, and institutions.

English/Language Arts: Students read a wide range of literature from many periods in many genres to build an understanding of the many dimensions (e.g., philosophical, ethical, aesthetic) of human experience.

Context/Rationale

In "Nonfiction Matters, Too: Books About People, Places, and Things," Lesesne (2001) offers criteria for selecting and evaluating informational books. Relevant questions include

- What are the qualifications of the author?
- What are the scope and purpose of the book?
- Is the information accurate?
- Does the author use primary sources?
- Is the information presented in an interesting and unusual way?
- How well does the book organize the information to be presented? (pp. 79–82)

The author includes commentary on recent nonfiction that exemplifies positive traits, then describes the following activity for students to examine books for accuracy.

Procedure

- Compile a set or sets of nonfiction books about the same subject (see Figure 3.2). Part 4 of this chapter contains many suggestions for informational books on a variety of subjects in various disciplines.
- Divide your class into small groups.
- Have students read a book, noting the basic facts presented on the topic on a chart (see Figure 3.3).

- Continue to have students read the remaining books in the set, noting on the chart where there is agreement in the books about the facts, as well as where there is disagreement.
- Ask students to conduct library and/or online research to find at least two sources that might clarify each fact under dispute.
- Finally, have the groups decide which of the books in their set is the most accurate and write a report explaining their findings.

Figure 3.2 contains a sample text set for the topic of evolution. Figure 3.3 shows a sample chart that could be used with this activity.

Sample text set of books on evolution.   FIGURE **3.2**

Braun, E. (ed.). (2006). *Creationism vs. evolution.* San Diego: Greenhaven Press.

Jenkins, S. (2002). *Life on earth: The story of evolution.* Boston: Houghton Mifflin.

Lawson, K. (2003). *Darwin and evolution for kids: His life and ideas, with 21 activities.* Chicago: Chicago Review Press.

Olson, S. P. (2004). *The trial of John T. Scopes: A primary source account.* New York: Rosen Publishing Group.

Sloan, C. (2004). *The human story: Our evolution from pre-historic ancestors to today.* Washington, DC: National Geographic Society.

Walker, R. (2003). *Genes and DNA.* Boston: Kingfisher.

Sample chart for checking factual accuracy or consistency in a text set.   FIGURE **3.3**

Authors: ○ Braun   ⊗ Jenkins   ⊗ Lawson   ○ Olson   ⊗ Sloan   ⊗ Walker

Topic 1: Natural Selection

JENKINS: "After many generations, variations and mutations can make a species larger, or more colorful, or different in some other way. Each difference is tested by natural selection: either a change makes a plant or animal better able to survive and pass on new features to its offspring, or it makes survival less likely . . ." (unpaged)

LAWSON: ". . . natural selection works on variations to bring about transmutation of species over long periods of time . . ." (p. 84). "Those animals with some features that helped them avoid predators, get food, or find mates more successfully tended to survive longer than their brothers and sisters who lacked those features." (p. 95)

SLOAN: "Natural selection is the process that influences whether or not an organism repro-duces. If a mutation creates a variant of an animal or plant that makes it healthier and stronger, this might improve its ability to survive in an environment and reproduce. It would then have a chance to pass on its genes—perhaps including the mutation—to its offspring." (p. 10)

WALKER: "This process—called natural selection—is the driving force of evolution. Over many gen-erations natural selection can produce changes that result in a new species. . . . Scientists have found that mutations are caused by accidental changes in DNA . . . the fact that living things use the same genetic code suggest they have all, humans included, evolved from a common ancestor . . ." (p. 37)

Topic 2: . . .

Topic 3: . . .

Walk-Through

Following is an example of how one instructor used this strategy in a social studies class.

> The major pattern of organization in *George vs. George: The American Revolution as Seen from Both Sides,* as you've noticed, is that of comparison/contrast. You can also see the chronological order as the story unfolds from the pre-revolution years through the years of the actual war. Another informational book is *Countdown to Independence: A Revolution of Ideas in England and Her American Colonies: 1760–1776,* by Natalie S. Bober. It's also arranged using both chronological order and comparison/contrast. A chart in the beginning pages tells the major events of each year from 1760 to 1776. It's followed by two pages listing the main characters in the colonies and the main characters in England.
>
> Your task now is to explore Bober's book, and do some comparing and contrasting of your own. Note similarities between *George vs. George,* and *Countdown to Independence* and check out how they're different. What information is there about which both books concur? Are there some things focused on in one book and not the other? Are there discrepancies, areas where the authors contradict each other? Make a Venn diagram or graphic organizer to show your findings.
>
> Now write a personal response, stating which book you like better and why. Think about the organization, layout, author's tone, pictures and captions, and interest level.

▶ ▶ ▶ ## JIGSAW II: A COOPERATIVE LEARNING ACTIVITY

Standards Addressed

History: Students consider multiple perspectives.

English/Language Arts: Students read a wide range of literature from many periods in many genres to build an understanding of the many dimensions (e.g., philosophical, ethical, aesthetic) of human experience.

Context/Rationale

The Jigsaw Classroom (Aronson, Blaney, Stephan, et al., 1978) and *Jigsaw II* (Slavin, 1986) are types of cooperative learning, which has been linked to improved academic achievement, self-esteem, and motivation (Vermette, 1998). Many students enjoy working with others on projects and assignments, and teachers can monitor groups and learn much about the learning strategies of students as they observe and listen to interactions among peers.

Procedure

- Select an informational text related to a topic in your curriculum. In my courses I have used the *Jigsaw II* cooperative learning strategy with Penny Colman's book *Girls: A History of Growing Up Female in America* (2000).
- Divide the class into groups. Figure the number of students in a group so that each student can read an equal number of chapters, excluding the first and last one (e.g., Colman's book has 10 chapters, so groups should consist of four students, each reading two chapters).
- Assign the book for homework in the following way.
    - Ask all students to read the Introduction, Chapter 1, and the final chapter. They should also read the pictures and captions throughout the book.
    - In addition, have each member of a group be responsible for carefully reading and summarizing the main points of a specified number of consecutive chapters from the middle. For example each person is assigned two chapters; one person takes Chapters 2 and 3, another 4 and 5, etc.

- In the next class meeting, ask the people who read the same middle chapters (e.g., all students who read Chapters 2 and 3) to meet in "Expert Groups" to compare what they selected as main points.

- Have the Expert Groups decide how they can best teach the important information from their chapters to the members of their base groups who did not read them.

- Finally, assemble the base groups again and have the students teach and learn from each other. The base groups might also make a wall chart with panels depicting text and graphic representations of the main points of this history book.

Walk-Through

During a unit on world religions, Ms. Putala uses the *Sacred Text* series (see Figure 3.4), which offers similarly structured books about the focal texts of six of the world's major religions. Quotations and colorful pictures add a dimension. With the help of the school librarian, Ms. Putala locates four copies of each book. She organizes her class into base groups of six and assigns each student within a group to read a different book in the series. The reader's job is to take notes and prepare to teach the others in his or her base group about the sacred text of a particular religion, focusing on the origins of the text; its structure and content; and its message and teachings. After a few days, expert groups consisting of the four students who have read about Judaism, those who have read about Islam, etc., meet to compare notes and share ideas about how best to teach the highlights of the book to others who have not read it but need to understand the main tenets of the sacred texts. Finally, base groups meet, listening to and learning from each other. Together, these books and the discussions within the cooperative learning groups offered students insight into the big picture of the importance of religion and religious texts throughout the world's history and continuing today.

Sacred Text series.   FIGURE   3.4

Brown, A. (2003). *The Bible and Christianity*. North Mankato, MN: Smart Apple Media.

Cato, V. (2003). *The Torah and Judaism*. North Mankato, MN: Smart Apple Media.

Ganeri, A. (2003). *The Guru Granth Sahib and Sikism*. North Mankato, MN: Smart Apple Media.

Ganeri, A. (2003). *The Qur'an and Islam*. North Mankato, MN: Smart Apple Media.

Ganeri, A. (2003). *The Ramayana and Hinduism*. North Mankato, MN: Smart Apple Media.

Ganeri, A. (2003). *The Tipitaka and Buddhism*. North Mankato, MN: Smart Apple Media.

COMBINING NONFICTION AWARD WINNERS WITH AUTHORS' ACCEPTANCE SPEECHES

Standards Addressed

Science: All students should develop an understanding of historical perspectives of the history and nature of science. All students should develop understandings about scientific inquiry.

English/Language Arts: Students read a wide range of literature from many periods in many genres to build an understanding of the many dimensions (e.g., philosophical, ethical, aesthetic) of human experience.

Context/Rationale

There's nothing like being an insider, no matter what our age. In award acceptance speeches, writers bring us into the inside world of their creative process. We can read speeches to our students, or simply make them available. I usually use them after my students have read the nonfiction book, but at times they, in their entirety or through excerpts, can be used as a sort of booktalk, enticing students to enter the worlds of the books themselves.

Walk-Through

An American Plague: The True and Terrifying Story of the Yellow Fever Epidemic of 1793 (Murphy, 2003) was the winner of at least five major literary awards. Many a teen can identify with author Jim Murphy's (2005) confession, "Now, I like a good plague, especially from a safe distance. . . ." (p. 27). Our students will learn much about the city of Philadelphia, the nation's capital in 1793, and about social conditions, the economy, and the spread of an infectious disease. Layers of stories reside within the main story of yellow fever and its victims. There are stories of heroes, such as the members of the free African Society, the only ones to volunteer to bury the dead and care for the suffering. Those stories could be connected with the archetype of hero in English class, or with schools' efforts to promote character education. Biology is involved, as the gruesome details of how the disease acted on the human body are provided; and the medical procedures used to try to cure patients, such as bloodletting, which all too often hastened their end, tell an interesting sub-story of a particular point in the history of medicine. The copies of primary documents in the book, as well as the sources cited at the end, can keep social studies teachers and students productively engaged for a long time.

As much as I appreciated *An American Plague*, I loved Jim Murphy's acceptance speech for the 2004 Boston Globe-Horn Book Award even more. Science and English teachers will delight in the story he tells of himself as a five-year-old in his school auditorium, firing a nail into a socket to see if the electricity is on, as an analogy for:

> . . . what a writer goes through when putting a project together. A chance encounter with a new topic; a strange, irresistible attraction; the encouragement from friends, editors and creditors—countered by the possibility of failure and public humiliation. (p. 27)

If the title of Murphy's book isn't enough to intrigue students in a social studies or science class to explore the contents, maybe this excerpt from Murphy's speech about the book he found that got him started writing on this topic will be. J. H. Powell, the author of *Bring Out Your Dead* (1949), warned readers not to read it before eating or during a sleepless night, since it was revolting, filled with true but disgusting details. Murphy comments (teaching history even here):

> And what he described after this was delicious. A mysterious disease charmingly nicknamed the "Black Vomit" enters the city and begins infecting and killing folk in a gooey, gruesome way. The rich and famous flee. Even such familiar luminaries as George Washington, Thomas Jefferson, James Madison, and James Monroe ran for the pure, fresh air of the hills. The sick, the dying, and the poor were left behind to fend for themselves. (p. 27)

The speech continues to fill readers in on Murphy's methods of research as he quested for the inside stories so that he could transport readers back in time.

Students and teachers who get hooked on listening to authors tell about their own research and writing voyages will be happy to know there are many more speeches and articles published by writers of nonfiction. To get you started on your explorations, check out Mordicai Gerstein's *The Man Who Walked Between the Towers* (2003) along with his 2004 Caldecott Acceptance Speech, which can be found in the

July/August 2004 issue of *The Horn Book* magazine. In the speech, Gerstein talks about Philippe Petit's memoir, *To Reach the Clouds: My High Wire Walk Between the Twin Towers* (2002). Some students will go rushing to find this account from the walker himself, which also discusses other daring feats. Both books are multidisciplinary, connecting to art, physical education, language arts, science, and social studies.

RETELLING

Standards Addressed

Art: Students reflect on how artworks differ visually, spatially, temporally, and functionally, and describe how these are related to history and culture. Students analyze contemporary and historic meanings in specific artworks through cultural and aesthetic inquiry.

English/Language Arts: Students adjust their own use of spoken, written, and visual language (e.g., conventions, style, vocabulary) to communicate effectively with a variety of audiences for a variety of purposes.

Context/Rationale

In order to retell a passage they've read, students have to comprehend it, choose and organize main points, summarize, and put ideas into their own words. Those are all good skills that will serve students well in virtually all subject areas, as well as outside of school.

Procedure

Hoyt (2002) recommends giving students a list of connectives, such as "first," "then," "also," "finally," and "after" if the main pattern of organization is sequence; "however" and "on the other hand" for contrasting ideas; and "because" and "as a result of" for cause and effect (p. 57). She advocates a specific strategy, "Read, Cover, Remember, Tell," involving the steps of

- finding a partner,
- reading as much as you can cover with one hand,
- quietly remembering what you've just read,
- telling your partner, and then
- repeating those steps.

Walk-Through

Here's a script of how this might play out in an art classroom. Mr. Ahle wants his students to get an overview of the major classifications of painting and the eras in history most associated with particular styles. He has instructed the students to read selected excerpts from *Sister Wendy's Story of Painting* (Beckett, 1994) and use the retelling strategy with a partner.

> *Anna:* I just read about the Renaissance concept of perspective. It brought science and art together. Painters knew that we see the world, oh, you know, like objects appear smaller as they go off into the distance, like lines of trees seem to converge as you look out into the distance. So they painted their pictures being aware of a "vanishing point," a fixed, single point. Sometimes we see it, or sometimes we imagine it based on the rest of what we see. The painting *The Hunt in the Forest,* by Uccello, was used as an example. Hunters are coming from both directions, and dogs are (or seem to be) in front of them, and in the center (the vanishing point), very tiny, is this stag running away. Okay, your turn.

Winthrop: You won't believe how different mine is. I read about the beginning of Impressionism. There was no talk of science in my section. Anyway, the term "Impressionism" started as a derogatory one, by someone making a sarcastic remark about one of Monet's paintings. And the painters took on the label themselves and ran with it, kind of as a rebellion against the status quo! They wanted to achieve more of a natural feel in their paintings, to show the movement of wind, the motion of people, the light playing on objects. Monet sometimes put unmixed paints right onto his canvas over a white coating, enhancing the sort of disharmony in the picture. He used sketchy brushwork to quickly capture a scene, and captured optical effects—hey, I guess we are talking about some of the same things even though our types of painting are centuries apart! Anyway, back to the retelling. Sister Wendy uses several of Monet's paintings, including one of a cathedral and one of his waterlily pond, to illustrate (ha ha, no pun intended) what she says about the characteristics of the Impressionist style.

So, which kind of art do you like better?

Anna: We don't have to make judgments; we just have to use the retelling strategy.

Winthrop: I know. So which kind of art do you like better?

After listening to a student, you can determine if he or she has been able to pick out central ideas and support them with details; whether more instruction or modeling is needed; or if the student is perhaps ready to pursue more challenging texts.

▶ ▶ ▶ REFLECTIVE LISTENING DURING READING OR IN A POST-READING SETTING

Standards Addressed

Science: All students should develop an understanding of science as a human endeavor. All students should develop an understanding of science and technology in local, national, and global challenges.

English/Language Arts: Students adjust their own use of spoken, written, and visual language (e.g., conventions, style, vocabulary) to communicate effectively with a variety of audiences for a variety of purposes.

Context/Rationale

Reflective listening is good for teachers and students, whether they're in the role of listener or speaker. As its name implies, it involves listening carefully and then reflecting the speaker's words with a slightly different wording. Jentz and Murphy (2005) explain that reflective listening differs from normal listening, which usually automatically involves making judgments as one listens. Reflective listening involves putting oneself in the speaker's (or author's) shoes, then testing what has been heard by reflecting the essence of the other person's words in different words. This type of listening is an acquired skill, and it takes practice to learn how to apply it to actual situations. In addition, according to Jentz and Murphy,

> . . . reflective listening is especially difficult when you most need to do it—in situations where new information threatens to undercut your cherished assumptions. . . . Yet, as hard as reflective listening may be, it is an essential tool for checking the depth and accuracy of your understanding. . . . Reflective listening also ensures that . . . people feel that they have been heard and understood, thus increasing their inclination to trust and collaborate with you. By mastering and using this skill, you produce conditions for joint inquiry rather than confrontation. (pp. 364–365)

Hoyt (2002) has found the strategy to be especially helpful with students whose first language is one other than English:

> Reflective listening seems to have a number of benefits to ELL [English language learners] students. (1) They feel that they have been respected and really heard when they hear someone reflect their ideas back to them. (2) If the message wasn't clear, they have an opportunity to clarify. (3) They listen more carefully to the language interactions of the group if they know they may need to reflect the content back in their own words. (p. 58)

Procedure

To incorporate reflective listening in your class, follow these steps, which involve you modeling the procedure with a student and then your students practicing it with each other.

- Listen to a student explain a principle in your subject area.
- Using direct eye contact, repeat the thought beginning with, "So what I'm hearing you say is . . ." or something to that effect.
- Have the listener confirm that you have received his or her intended message or clarify the thought to clear up any misunderstanding.
- Let your students know they can do the same with you after you have explained or read something aloud.
- Have them practice using the strategy in pairs with each other, one person being the speaker and the other the reflective listener and then changing roles.

This skill can serve them well throughout their lives, far beyond academic settings.

Walk-Through

Here's what reflective listening might sound like between partners in a senior Participation in Government class reading the essay "Bombs and Potatoes" (pp. 73–77), a book review from Freeman Dyson's *The Scientist as Rebel* (2006):

Ursula (speaker): I read the first two and a half pages. The author doesn't even mention the book he's supposed to be reviewing. He begins with a speech of J. Robert Oppenheimer given after he received a certificate in 1945 stating the government's appreciation of the work of the Los Alamos Laboratory. After Oppenheimer expresses his thanks, he launches into his concerns about how the nuclear age is going to affect humanity. He says all peoples must unite or perish. But then Dyson talks about how people in England were feeling in 1939, at the beginning of the war. A huge number of casualties was anticipated, and everyone was expecting the worst. Some people thought the war had to be fought anyway, because surrender to Hitler was out of the question. Others tried to follow the teaching of Gandhi, and formed the English pacifist movement.

Damien (listener): Okay, I hear you saying . . . hmmm . . . first, that Oppenheimer was one of these rebel scientists Dyson's book is about. Instead of saying, Thanks for the award, rah-rah USA, we dropped the bomb first, he talked about a new way of connecting to people, not based on nationality.

Ursula (speaker): Exactly!

Damien (listener): Okay, after that I think I heard you say that people in England were pretty pessimistic when they entered the war. But there wasn't agreement about the best way to go about fighting Hitler.

Ursula (speaker): Bingo! Right on, again! Okay, now you tell me about the part of the essay you read.

Damien (speaker): Well, I started where you left off, and Dyson does talk about the book *Nuclear Disaster,* by Tom Stonier. He seems to like the fact that Stonier is a biologist, so can give a different view from the physicists, who I guess are usually the ones who give their predictions about the effects of nuclear war. Stonier states pretty strongly that the United States would not survive in its present form after nuclear warfare. Dyson says Stonier knows what he's talking about in terms of both the biological and physical effects of nuclear explosions. BUT—then he says that Stonier's predictions of the social and polit- ical consequences of nuclear warfare are necessarily conjecture. Here's where Dyson brings in Oppenheimer and the predictions in England of the outcome of World War II again. He says it's hard to predict things like the long-range recovery of civilization. So Stonier, and his book, might be wrong. The end.

Ursula (listener): Wow, that's a lot to take in. I hear you saying that Dyson admires, or respects, Stonier, whose book he's reviewing. But that doesn't mean he buys the whole thing. The author is a biologist, but that doesn't mean he has some crystal ball. Am I right?

Damien (speaker): Pretty much. By the way, at the very end Dyson calls Stonier's book a good reminder of possible danger, and he calls his book ". . . sober, thoughtful, and elo- quent" (p. 77).

Ursula (listener): I hear that as a pretty good review. I wouldn't mind a book of mine being described that way!

The discussion goes on as Ursula continues to rephrase Damien's comments and ask questions for clarification.

▶ ▶ ▶ RECIPROCAL TEACHING

Standards Addressed

Mathematics: Students communicate their mathematical thinking coherently and clearly to peers, teachers, and others. Students analyze and evaluate the mathe- matical thinking and strategies of others.

English/Language Arts: Students apply a wide range of strategies to comprehend, interpret, evaluate, and appreciate texts.

Context/Rationale

Reciprocal teaching (Palincsar & Brown, 1984) is a way to guide and assure com- prehension of a text. This method involves the steps of predicting, questioning, summarizing, and clarifying, and is useful when students are partner reading or reading in small groups. Reciprocal teaching also may involve the students ques- tioning the teacher, thus reversing traditional roles. This alternative way of mak- ing students conscious of what good readers do when engaging with a text brings thinking about the process of reading to the metacognitive level. Hoyt (2002) sug- gests typing the steps of the reciprocal teaching strategy onto cards for students to refer to when they are working independently. She finds that the cards increase engagement because students can follow the process easily, and that students with reading difficulties, with this added support, can participate to a greater degree when a group is using the strategy (p. 235).

Procedure

As stated previously, reciprocal teaching involves four steps:

- *Predicting:* students are asked to make predictions based on the book title, illustrations, and previous passage read, then the teacher records the pre- dictions.

- *Questioning*: students compose questions to establish a purpose for their reading. Teachers should encourage students to ask questions beyond the literal level.
- *Summarizing*: students compose a summary of the passage, focusing on the main ideas.
- *Clarifying*: students and teachers discuss areas of confusion with the passage, including unfamiliar vocabulary and content and complex organization. The teacher suggests some strategies to use for understanding.

Teachers should begin by modeling the process for students. Once they have modeled the process several times, students should work in pairs or small groups with one of them assuming the role of teacher. Students should switch roles so that every student has the opportunity to assume the role of teacher.

Walk-Through

The following scenario (Kane, 2007) will exemplify the reciprocal teaching strategy at work. In a high school math class, students have been divided into groups of four and assigned five pages from the book *Real-Life Math: Everyday Use of Mathematical Concepts* (Glazer & McConnell, 2002). The four stages of reciprocal teaching have been modeled by the teacher and practiced by the students several times during the semester. Now the teacher is circulating among the groups, facilitating as needed.

Elbia: I'm the summarizer, so I'll start, okay? Ms. Kilpatrick says it doesn't matter what order we go in. We read the section called "Exponential Growth, on pages thirty through thirty-four. I think the main point is that exponential growth is based on repeated multiplication, and that there are examples of it all around us. One example is that of the population explosion that occurred when rabbits were introduced into Australia, where they had no natural enemies. There are also situations involving money that show exponential growth, like earning compound interest. It's important to understand exponential growth, and to recognize that it's the basis of scams, like chain letters. Don't believe those empty promises of getting rich just by passing along a letter to some friends and sending your hard-earned money to the first person on the list!

Giulia: Thanks, Elbia. Since I've been assigned the role of questioner, I'll ask you three a few questions to see if you've understood the passage. Okay, here goes. Number one: The text says some scientists say that carbon dioxide is increasing in the upper atmosphere exponentially. Why is that a problem?

Rudolph: It's not bad in the early stages, just like a few rabbits were no big deal in Australia. But as the carbon monoxide increases exponentially, global warming can result. Not good!

Giulia: Exactly. Good connection of examples, Rude. Okay, how about this? Who runs a bigger risk, people who buy into franchises at an early stage or a late stage?

Olivia: If it's a fraud, where franchises sell further franchises, the originators can make millions and the latecomers lose their money. So I'll buy in early, please!

Giulia: Very funny, Liv. But you made your point. Let's hear more from you now, our esteemed "Clarifier."

Olivia: Well, I'm in charge of pointing out difficult or potentially troublesome parts, and figuring out how we can go about, well, *clarifying* those confusing parts. I thought I was following the examples of the concept of exponential growth pretty well, and I found the graphs helpful. But then I came to the sentence "When the growth factor is less than one, the curve will decrease" (p. 31). And I went, "Huh?" Luckily, the authors gave a hint right after that, so I followed their advice and looked back at the section called "Exponential Decay," and I saw graphs with curves going the opposite direction, and saw the example of the exponential decay of a radioactive substance. We learned about that in chemistry. So, does everyone get it?

Rudolph: Yeah. We're running out of time, so I'd better play the role of predictor, and if we have time we'll come back for more clarifying and questioning. Okay, the next part gives online sources for learning more about exponential growth. What do I see in my crystal ball? I think we'll get more examples of both legitimate uses of the concept, and more schemes that we'd better beware of. The headings tell us what to expect. I'm going to check out the one for pricing diamond rings. One of you can go to the one on the U.S. national debt. I predict I'll have more fun than you!

▷ ▷ ▷   JOB SHADOWING THROUGH INFORMATIONAL BOOKS

Standards Addressed

Science: All students should develop an understanding of science as a human endeavor. All students should develop an understanding of the abilities necessary to do scientific inquiry.

English/Language Arts: Students read a wide range of print and nonprint texts to build an understanding of texts, of themselves, and of the cultures of the United States and the world; to acquire new information; to respond to the needs and demands of society and the workplace; and for personal fulfillment.

Context/Rationale

The practice of having students shadow people, following them around at their jobs, is a popular one. Some schools and communities designate a calendar date as "Take Your Child to Work Day." The use of practicum experiences, internships, and apprenticeships recognizes the value of fledglings in a field (or those pondering career choices) learning through observation of and discussion with workers while they are on the job. Through trade books, your students can "shadow" an expert in your discipline.

Procedure

- Select an informational book related to a curricular topic that also shows one or more practitioners working in your field. Examples include:

  All in a Day's Work: Careers Using Science by M. Sullivan (2007) (science)

  Opportunities in Visual Arts Careers by M. Salmon (2001) (art)

  Career Opportunities in Photography by G. Gilbert and P. Fehl (2006) (art)

  Letters to a Young Mathematician by I. Stewart (2006) (math)

  How Jane Won: 35 Successful Women Share How They Grew from Ordinary Girls to Extraordinary Women by S. Rimm (2001) (health, science, art)

  More examples are included in Part 4 of this chapter. And see Part 4 of Chapter 7 for the following books, which would also be appropriate for this activity:

  So, You Wanna Be a Comic Book Artist?: How to Break into Comics! by P. Amara (2001) (art)

  Career Ideas for Kids Who Like Writing by D. L. Reeves (1998) (English)

  The Musician's Handbook: A Practical Guide to Understanding the Music Business by B. Borg (2003) (music)

- Introduce students to the book, providing some background and indicating the profession of the person who wrote the book or about whom the book is written.
- Divide students into small groups.

- Have them brainstorm to predict what a day on the job for someone in the profession might involve.
- Ask them to research at the library or on the Internet the kind of education, experience, and skills a person would need to have to enter the profession.
- Finally, ask them to compile a list of questions they would like to ask a person in the profession about his or her profession.
- Bring the class together and discuss the findings of the small groups.
- As a class, create a poster with the questions students have about the profession. Questions can be added to the poster as students continue reading the book.

Walk-Through

The following example presents a scenario you might encounter in a seventh-grade life science course using this activity.

Ms. Michel: Last month we went to sea with Jacques Cousteau. Starting today, we're traveling in a different direction. We've been invited to join scientific researcher Sophie Webb as she works for a month as a seabird observer in Alaska, along the Aleutian Island chain. Let's locate where we'll be going on our wall map.

Now, before we read the journal entries of Sophie recorded in this book, *Looking for Seabirds: Journal from an Alaskan Voyage,* which was published in 2004, let's think about what her job might be like. How would one begin to do research on seabirds? Wait, let's back up even further. What do you already know about seabirds? Risi, would you please write a list on this poster as your classmates tell what they know and make hypotheses about what the researcher might do?

Okay, get ready to shadow this scientist as she conducts her fieldwork. Imagine you're following secretly behind her, seeing the things she sees, hearing the things she hears. I'll be reading a couple of entries from Sophie's journal each day this month. She'll be telling us about the trip itself, the equipment aboard ship, and what the crew does to amuse themselves when they're not working. She'll also explain things about the seabirds she finds and studies. We'll keep the poster Risi started up on the wall, and as we job shadowers travel, when you think of questions you can put them on the poster. Maybe Sophie will answer them in later entries, or we might need to do some research ourselves to get the answers. All aboard? Let's begin with her entry on May 14. "I leave San Francisco at 9:00 A.M., flying to Seattle and then on to Anchorage, where I spend the night in a hotel . . ." (p. 4)

LITERARY FIELD TRIP

Standards Addressed

Art: Students analyze relationships of works of art to one another in terms of history, aesthetics, and culture, justifying conclusions made in the analysis and using such conclusions to inform their own art making.

English/Language Arts: Students read a wide range of print and nonprint texts to build an understanding of texts, of themselves, and of the cultures of the United States and the world; to acquire new information . . . and for personal fulfillment.

Context/Rationale

You probably can't take your students on too many field trips—you'll be constrained by geography, time, and finances. But you can go anywhere in place or time with the help of literature, primary documents, and a strategy I call *literary field trips.* Following are guidelines for preparing a literary field trip for a content area.

Procedure (Kane, 2007)

- Choose a place or location relevant to a content area lesson you are preparing.
- Select book(s), websites, and/or other materials relevant to the lesson; for example:

  The Big "M" by C. Rothman (2002) (art)

  The Young Person's Guide to the Opera by A. Ganeri and N. Barber (2001) (music)

  Our Documents: 100 Milestone Documents from the National Archives edited by C. Compston and R. F. Seidman (2004) (social studies)

- Together with your students, brainstorm what they might expect to find on the tour.
- Divide students into groups and have them prepare questions for their "tour guide."
- Have the groups "tour" the location by reading and visiting the Internet sites.
- Ask students to prepare a summary of tour highlights, telling what they learned about the location and its related content area subject.
- Have students plot their journeys on a map and/or timeline.
- Discuss where the students' inquiry can go from here, and what other resources they might "tour" next to learn about the topic in more depth and answer any remaining or new questions.

Walk-Through

Mr. Lassec wants his art students to get to know famous artists as real people, people with families, flaws, personalities, and friends and enemies, as well as with varying styles and artistic processes. So he takes them on literary field trips to places where artists lived and worked. We join him now as he guides his students on a tour of Susan Goldman Rubin's *The Yellow House: Vincent van Gogh & Paul Gauguin Side by Side* (2001).

Mr. Lassec: We're going across the ocean today to visit a yellow house. It's in the south of France, in Arles. For nine weeks, this house was shared by two geniuses of the art world, Paul Gauguin and Vincent van Gogh. From your background knowledge about either or both of these artists, tell me what you'll expect to find:

Patrice: Paintings of sunflowers and starry nights drying on easels.

Anna Elizabeth: Probably some discussion at night about what they've been painting that day.

Craig: An ear on the floor!

Mr. Lassec: Actually, Craig, you'll find that the ear does come off during these nine weeks. I'll bet that makes you anxious to get started on this tour! But, before we go, I want you to formulate some questions you might ask the two artists who will be our hosts. Mohammed, will you please record our questions on our chart paper up here at the easel?

Sylvia: I'd like to know if they liked each other's works, if they inspired each other, and maybe was there any jealousy between them?

Richard: I wonder how their ways of going about getting ideas and then actually painting were different from each other.

Mr. Lassec: Those are good questions to ask these men. Let's go; I think the sun should be setting when we arrive and they can tell us about their day. Jot down some interesting things you learn from them, and write at least one new question that has entered your mind as a result of your visit. And for those of you who didn't get as many details as you wanted from this short picture book, I recommend *The Yellow House: Van Gogh, Gauguin, and Nine Turbulent Weeks in Arles,* by Martin Gayford (2006). This book won't just be a quick class field trip; you'll live with the artists for a while! I loved it.

READING AND WRITING TRAVEL JOURNALS

Standards Addressed

Science: All students should develop an understanding of interdependence of organisms. All students should develop an understanding of origin and evolution of the earth.

Social Studies: Students understand how culture and experience influence people's perceptions of places and regions. Students understand how to use mental maps to organize information about people, places, and environments in a spatial context.

English/Language Arts: Students read a wide range of print and nonprint texts to build an understanding of texts, of themselves, and of the cultures of the United States and the world; to acquire new information; to respond to the needs and demands of society and the workplace; and for personal fulfillment.

Context/Rationale

This strategy is a variation of the literary field trip described above; use the same procedure, but add the elements of reading and writing travel journals. Lead your students through a literary field trip by reading aloud from a travel journal about a rainforest, a desert, a space camp, a bridge construction site, an art museum, a synagogue, a symphony hall. You can also promote the reading of travel journals by having books available and by playing the role of travel agent, enticing students to go on literary field trips by advertising through booktalks. After students are familiar with the genre and hooked on this type of travel literature, they'll recognize features they like in their favorites. They may then be encouraged to write their own travel journals, whether they're spending a semester abroad or visiting an aunt in a neighboring town. They can even write about their own village or city, targeting an audience of people who might be interested in coming to where they live.

Walk-Through

Listen as one middle school teacher introduces Oliver Sacks's journal of his travels in Mexico to her students.

> It's clear that Oliver Sacks advocates passionate exploration and learning. Why else would he dedicate his *Oaxaca Journal* (2002) "For the American Fern Society and for plant hunters, birders, divers, stargazers, rock hounds, fossickers, amateur naturalists the world over"? (p. vii). Sacks gives an authentic rendering of the value of keeping a journal while traveling, and can serve as a mentor as to how to go about it:
>
> > . . . all journeys incite me to keep journals. Indeed, I have been keeping them since the age of fourteen. . . . None of these journals has any pretension to comprehensiveness or authority; they are light, fragmentary, impressionistic, and, above all, personal. . . .
> >
> > Why do I keep journals? I do not know. Perhaps primarily to clarify my thoughts, to organize my impressions into a sort of narrative or story, and to do this in "real time," and not in retrospect. . . . (pp. xiv–xv)
>
> *Oaxaca Journal,* part of the National Geographic Society's "Literary Travel Series," covers a span of 10 days, as Sacks travels to Mexico to explore one of his many passions,

ferns. Readers learn a great deal about ferns, of course, as Sacks makes his discoveries; but they also learn about his fellow fern enthusiasts, the culture and some history of Oaxaca, stories of people and places and emotions, and the trials and joys of travel. A sampling of subsections of Chapter Nine, "Saturday," show the diversity of topics: Divine mathematics . . . an encounter with the police . . . passionflowers and hummingbirds . . . a museum and library of pre-Hispanic artifacts. . . .

Here's what a student's travel journal might look like in an earth science course:

October 25, 2007/October 25, 1842: I thought the pictures Ms. Rule showed us about Mammoth Cave were cool, so I checked out *Journey to the Bottomless Pit,* by Elizabeth Mitchell, from the library. Man, did I go on some trip!!! I was whisked back in time and given a private tour of the cave by the coolest guide ever. Stephen Bishop was an African American slave, who discovered a lot of the stuff that had been previously unknown. The tour was spooky and scary, especially knowing there were bats around, but I felt perfectly safe with Stephen. He showed me artifacts that Indians (the first people to explore the cave) left behind. He dropped a rock into the Bottomless Pit, and I never heard it land. He pointed out stalactites and lots of other stuff we learned about in our geology unit. We traveled on rivers and saw fish that had no eyes 'cause they had evolved that way. Stephen even showed me a hospital that had been built in the cave for patients with consumption. (By the way, that experiment failed.) My whole trip was amazing; I'm in total awe of my guide and this natural wonder. Mammoth Cave rocks! (Get it?)

Figure 3.5 gives suggestions of travel journals your students might read to vicariously visit places beyond their home states. Have them begin keeping a travel journal, making entries during school vacations, and including a list of places they hope to visit in the future. To help them plan, encourage them to read travel guidebooks, which you might stock your shelves with. A good book to start with is Patricia Schultz's *1,000 Places to See Before You Die: A Traveler's Life List* (2003).

Now, here's what a student might write who is using the travel journal strategy while reading *Wrong About Japan* (2005), by Peter Carey.

Dear Journal,

As you know, I'm traveling through Japan with the author Peter Carey and his son Charley. I'm seeing the Japan we want to learn about, not the ordinary tourist's Japan. No temples or museums for us! We're meeting people associated with manga and anime, which are

---

FIGURE 3.5 Sample bibliography of travel journals.

Bryson, B. (1998). *A walk in the woods: Rediscovering America on the Appalachian Trail.* New York: Broadway Books. (science, social studies)

Carey, P. (2005). *Wrong about Japan: A father's journey with his son.* New York: Alfred A. Knopf. (culture, art, social studies)

The da Vinci Code travel journal: Based on the novel by Dan Brown. (2006). New York: Potter Style. (English, art)

Harrison, K. (2003). *The road to Santiago.* Washington, DC: National Geographic. (culture, social studies, English)

Hartmann, W. K. (2003). *A traveler's guide to Mars: The mysterious landscapes of the Red Planet.* New York: Workman Publishing. (science)

Michaux, H. (2001). *Ecuador: A travel journal.* Evanston, IL: Marlboro Press/Northwestern, Northwestern University Press. (culture, social studies)

Mondloch, K. (2005). *Flight of the osprey: A journal of renewal: An absorbing travel memoir exploring love, loss, and spiritual discovery.* Lincoln, NE: iUniverse. (science)

So, S. (2006). *Shanyi goes to China.* London: Francis Lincoln Children's Books. (culture, social studies)

Steinbach, A. (2004). *Educating Alice: Adventures of a curious woman.* Waterville, ME: Thorndike Press. (English)

huge in this country. So, I'll tell you where we went today—a place called Sega World at Akihabara, or Electric Town. It was one cool place. Listen to this description:

> We wandered from floor to floor. Stuffu (sic) everywhere—plasma screens, cell phones as thin as credit cards with guerilla war playing on their screens, those crazy science fiction toilets. . . . There was plenty of noise, but nothing like the barrage that awaited us in Sega World: five floors devoted to terrifying arcade games where kids with guns shoot men like fish in a bucket. (pp. 57–58)

In case you couldn't tell, that was the father talking; I'm sure Charley was experiencing it differently. Anyway, gotta go get some rest. Tomorrow Charley and I are being dragged to experience Kabuki—I'll let you know what it is after I read the next chapter. Good night.

DOUBLE-ENTRY JOURNALS

Standards Addressed

History: Students identify in historical narratives the temporal structure of a historical narrative or story. Students interrogate historical data.

English/Language Arts: Students employ a wide range of strategies as they write and use different writing process elements appropriately to communicate with different audiences for a variety of purposes.

Context/Rationale

When I assign learning logs, asking students to engage and interact with a text and write a response, sometimes students are puzzled as to what I "really want." Do I want a summary? Should they be trying to prove that they indeed read the selection? Is there a right, or a wrong, way to write a response? I suggest trying the double-entry diary approach, where, as Tovani (2000) points out, "You get to choose how you want students to structure their thinking, while students get to show you what they are thinking" (p. 30).

Procedure

- Before a reading assignment of an information book related to a particular curriculum topic, have your students fold a piece of paper in half lengthwise, or draw a line down the middle of the page.
- Tell them to record key words and phrases, main points, important sentences, or summarize the passage in their own words in the left-hand column.
- In the right-hand column, have them write inferences, thoughts, evaluations, critical questions, places of confusion, connections to other texts, or issues they disagree with and so would like the teacher's or classmates' opinions on.
- After the reading assignments, collect the papers and provide feedback to the student or divide the students in pairs and have them provide feedback to each other.

Walk-Through

The following example shows a teacher modeling the strategy in a social studies class.

Mr. Goughary: Since we're studying the Vietnam War, and its aftereffects in both Vietnam and the United States, I've brought in a book I found called *Escape from Saigon: How a Vietnam War Orphan Became an American Boy,* published in 2004. It's by Andrea Warren, who adopted a baby girl who was rescued in Operation Babylift, which we talked about yesterday. I'm going to read the Prologue, then make entries in my Double-Entry Diary. In the first column, I'll jot down facts that I'll be able to refer to later if I need to. In the second, I'll get down my thoughts. Then I'll read the first page or so and write entries again. When I'm done, you can ask me about the procedure, then we'll try a bit of the text together. For your homework tonight, I've copied the beginning of Chapter Two. Come in tomorrow with a double-entry diary, and we'll base our class discussion on what you've noted and thought out. We'll pay special attention to questions you have.

[Teacher reads Prologue, then writes on transparency in first column (see Figure 3.6).]

Mr. Goughary: Any questions or comments so far? Spud?

Spud: Do we have to go back and answer the questions we write?

Mr. Goughary: No, though you could. I'm more interested at this point in looking to see if my questions will be answered later in the book. Ok, let's start Chapter One, "A Little Boy All Alone."

[Teacher reads first two pages, then writes the information shown in Figure 3.7.]

FIGURE 3.6   Sample double-entry journal for the prologue of *Escape from Saigon*.

— Vietnam is on eastern coast of Southeast Asia

— rich in natural resources

— conquered many times

— China ruled Vietnam for a thousand years

— French ruled from 1859–1954, defeated

— 1954—Vietnam split—North was Communist, South tried an independent republic

— Ah, resources—no wonder there's always war—sounds like oil in the Middle East today. I wonder what their natural resources are?

— I haven't seen anything yet telling me why or when the United States got involved. When did that happen?

FIGURE 3.7   Sample double-entry journal for Chapter One of *Escape from Saigon*.

— little boy named Long

— his father is American, mother Vietnamese

— father gone when Long is 2; mother unhappy

— they move to Saigon, capital of South Vietnam

— U.S. has soldiers there since 1961 to support struggle against North Vietnamese communists

— 1968—Communists attack, almost take over U.S. Embassy

— Vietcong—short for Vietnamese Communists—"guerrilla fighters who sided with North"

— Vietcong—no uniforms—so they looked like South Vietnamese villagers

— U.S. called Vietcong "Charlie"—American soldiers known to terrorize villages or use bombs to find Vietcong

— I know that babies of American fathers were often shunned by everyone. So I predict Long is going to be in trouble. Maybe no one will want him.

— I sure don't like hearing about American troops terrorizing villages—they're kind of caught in the middle, not knowing who's the enemy. But what about ethics? What about not harming civilians? And what about the innocent kids?

Mr. Goughary: Is this making sense to you? Do you understand why I have two sides going in my "double-sided journal"?

Carmen: Yeah, I see the difference. We get to jot down key words and points from the reading to help us remember, but we also get to give our opinion.

Mr. Goughary: Exactly. With this strategy, the reader has a voice.

CREATIVE WRITING INSPIRED BY INFORMATIONAL TEXTS

Standards Addressed

History: Students consider multiple perspectives. Students challenge arguments of historical inevitability. Students compare and contrast differing sets of ideas, values, personalities, behaviors, and institutions.

English/Language Arts: Students employ a wide range of strategies as they write and use different writing process elements appropriately to communicate with different audiences for a variety of purposes.

Context/Rationale

Some of your students might be intimidated by poetry, both of reading it and writing it. They might also think poetry belongs strictly in English class. Yet poetry can help students in many disciplines engage with topics and remember concepts, facts, and procedures (e.g., Kane & Rule, 2004). Strive to confront, and ultimately lessen, their fear by sharing some examples of poems people have written in response to nonfiction texts in your subject area. Make available to them such resources as *Rhyme, Meter, and Other Word Music* by J. Fandel (2006) or other works by this author (see the English section in Part 4 of this chapter). Provide tips on forms their poems might take. Also encourage them to try other forms of creative expression, such as newspaper articles, board games, graphics, cartoons, and songs.

Walk-Through

Here's a poem written by one of my former students to get you started. It was written in response to *We Were There, Too* by P. Hoose (2001), a collection of essays about young people who played a role in significant events in American history. I hope you'll add one or two of your own creations, so students can view you as a role model, and a poetic muse.

American Child

American child, your future so bright
How will you change the world?
Will you go to war?
Fight for women's rights?
Lead the way North to freedom?
Create alphabets and art?

Or will you be buried in coal mines?
Strike against unfair labor laws?
Will you go exploring on the high seas
      or the wild west?
Will your poetry change the world?
Will you be at the center of a crisis?

Will you stand up for the rights of others
As you stand up for your own?

Speak out against war
Or be victimized by it?
Will you be feared or ridiculed?
Will you be brilliant?

American child, this land is yours
To build and shape and grow
So change your world
And show for all time
That age doesn't matter.

—Jennifer Gianetto

Post students' creative products on the wall, or keep them in a file on your library shelves, so classmates can read each other's creations and get new ideas and motivation for future responsive creations. The following post-reading assignments relating to *George vs. George: The American Revolution as Seen from Both Sides*, by Rosalyn Schanzer (2004) and created by teacher Jennifer Connor, exemplify how teachers can encourage students to allow their creative juices to flow after reading informational texts.

ORIGINAL PATRIOTIC/BRITISH POEM OR SONG ACTIVITY

Task: You will create your own poem based on information from *George vs. George: The American Revolution as Seen from Both Sides* (2004) by Rosalyn Schanzer. You must first decide whether your poem will be patriotic (Colonially speaking) or pro-British. You may pick any aspect of the book, including battles, taxes, the end of King George, etc. You will recite your poem to the class. *Optional:* If you know how to read and write music, you may create a simple score for your poem, turning it into a song. You may use the classroom keyboard and blank sheet music from our music corner and you will be singing your poem to the class.

Here is a model poem based on information on pages 8 and 9:

"Britain's King"

Of their George the British did sing
A horseman and a farmer
A tall man, well-liked
But the colonists said,
"Not our king!"

NEWSPAPER FRONT PAGE ACTIVITY

Task: You have already been divided into two groups. Half of you will write out an entire front page from a London newspaper, and the other group will write the same from the perspective of a Philadelphia or Boston newspaper. Both front pages will be written on a date that falls sometime during the American Revolution. (The date will be mutually decided upon.) Ideas should be based on material from the book.

Use scrap paper to write drafts of articles. Divide up the topics, and give feedback on each other's work. Cut and paste onto the wrong side of the poster board for your draft. When you are satisfied with your front page, print it out on the computer, using an authentic-looking font. Glue final copies to the right side of the poster board for your finished product. Remember to give your newspaper a name, and show the date. Be ready to compare your perspective of the day's news with that of the group representing the opposite side of the Atlantic.

POLITICAL CARTOON ACTIVITY

Task: You will draw a political cartoon based on something you learned from reading *George vs. George*. Your cartoon can be from either perspective, the British or American. Caricatures are acceptable. Be sure to give your cartoon an appropriate title and/or caption.

GRAPHIC ACTIVITY USING COMPUTER

Task: Based on information from the book, create an informational graphic of your choice, using the computer with a "draw" or "paint" option. Choose a format from among the following:

- pie graph
- bar graph
- pictograph
- line graph
- any other similar form of representing information.

One example is to represent the numbers of British and rebel forces at a particular time.

Label your graph accurately and in such a way that the reader will be able to interpret the information displayed. Give your graph a title.

CREATE A BOARD GAME

Task: You will work in groups of three, and may choose your own partners. You'll make a board game that reflects some aspects of the American Revolution as depicted in *George vs. George*. Your game will include the following:

1. A playing board with your own chosen scene from the American Revolution drawn on it. Tempera paints and brushes will be provided.

2. Strategy game pieces and player game pieces. Your choice of pieces will depend on the strategy of your game. You might want to make a spinner out of a brass tack and light cardboard, or use dice, etc. You can make your own pieces or borrow items to use, such as buttons, jax, or even pieces of uncooked macaroni in keeping with the theme.

2. Twelve 3 x 5 cards on which you have written original questions based on information taken from the book.

3. Twelve 3 x 5 cards that provide correct answers to these questions.

4. A set of well-written instructions that clearly state the strategy and goal of the game. Write your instructions in the second person.

DOCUMENT-BASED QUESTIONS (Adapted from Kane, 2007)

Standards Addressed

History: Students analyze cause-and-effect relationships and multiple causation, including the importance of the individual, the influence of ideas, and the role of chance. Students compare competing historical narratives.

English/Language Arts: Students gather, evaluate, and synthesize data from a variety of sources (e.g., print and nonprint texts, artifacts, people) to communicate their discoveries in ways that suit their purpose and audience.

Context/Rationale

A prevalent type of writing in social studies classrooms and some standardized tests uses document-based questions (DBQs). As the name suggests, the questions call for students to comprehend, interpret, and analyze documents or other data the teacher provides. Then, the students synthesize information from two or more sources related to a theme, issue, or problem in order to craft an essay noting patterns or contrasting information found in various data.

Procedure

- Gather a group of resources related to a curricular topic or theme. Include poetry, excerpts from original documents in archives, quotations from philosophers, eyewitness accounts, letters, memoirs, cartoons, maps, charts, tables, paintings, diary entries, official memos, and Internet sites. For younger students, you need only provide two or three resources. For advanced high school students, use as many as eight. Example books to use for this activity from Part 4 of this chapter include:

    Our Documents: 100 Milestone Documents from the National Archives (2004) edited by C. Compston and R. F. Seidman (social studies)

    Into the Land of Freedom: African Americans in Reconstruction by M. Greene (2004) (social studies)

    Catherine the Great by C. Hatt (2004) (social studies)

- Model the thinking involved in examining and reflecting on several documents from your group. Have your students watch as you work with the documents using an overhead projector or computer and LCD projector.
- Allow students to ask questions and discuss the process.
- Then, introduce a question leading to a DBQ essay.
- Facilitate a discussion of how students might organize their ideas, connect the pieces of data, and use the data to support their points.
- Either you or a student can outline the essay based on the discussion. Students can then either flesh out the essay for homework or follow the process based on the following steps to write a different DBQ essay.
    - Read the question carefully to determine the required task, underlining key words, names, places, and issues.
    - Write down what you already know about the topic.
    - Identify each document's type, author, time written, and point of view.
    - Group documents according to relationships (e.g., data that support a position, data that do not).
    - Outline the essay.
    - Construct an introduction, a thesis statement, body paragraphs, and a concluding paragraph explaining evidence from the data.

Walk-Through

Ms. Petrowicz is teaching a unit on World War II. She begins class one day by asking, "What made Nazism possible? How was Hitler able to wield such power to do such evil?" The class brainstorms to list reasons they know and to offer hypotheses; Ms. Petrowicz is able to ascertain their background knowledge. She then projects several documents on the screen that she has acquired from *Hitler and the Nazis: A History in Documents*, by David F. Crew (2005). They include a photo of trench warfare in World War I, a 1930 election poster, an anti-Communist poster, a 1928 picture of Hitler wearing the Iron Cross he was awarded for his military service in World War I, the cover of *Mein Kampf*, a 1933 quote about businessmen's desire for a strong leader who would form a long-lasting government, photographs of a schoolroom and a Mercedes showroom, both with Hitler's image prominently displayed, and a German postcard celebrating the 1938 conference where France and England gave Germany the Sudetenland.

Together the class discusses connections between and among the documents, offering themes and synthesizing the information. Ms. Petrowicz asks them to outline an essay that will answer the questions that initiated the class, using details from the documents to back up the points they make.

INSIDE–OUTSIDE CIRCLE ACTIVITY

Standards Addressed

History: Students hypothesize the influence of the past.

English/Language Arts: Students adjust their use of spoken, written, and visual language (e.g., conventions, style, vocabulary) to communicate effectively with a variety of audiences and for different purposes.

Context/Rationale

Using the inside–outside circle (Kagan, 1989) ensures lively discussion in a comfortable atmosphere. As the name suggests, two circles form, then the inside circle members face those on the outside, and discuss whatever issue the teacher has raised, or a work of literature or some other text. Example books to use for this activity from Part 4 of this chapter include:

Latino Arts and Their Influence on the United States by R. Makosz (1998) (art, culture, music)

The History of Rap Music by C. Lommel (2001) (music, history)

The Scientist as Rebel by F. Dyson (2006) (science)

Drawing the Line: Science and the Case for Animal Rights by S. M. Wise (2002) (science)

A Kid's Guide to the Bill of Rights: Curfews, Censorship, and the 100-Pound Giant by K. Krull (1999) (social studies)

After a short period of time, the teacher can give a signal and members of one circle move to the right a couple of people, so new partners are facing each other. Have the students continue to discuss the issues they began with, hearing new opinions and thoughts, or offer a new prompt. Students who are reluctant to speak in a large group often feel more secure about talking one-on-one with a peer. And no one gets left out of a conversation.

Walk-Through

INSIDE–OUTSIDE CIRCLE ACTIVITY

Created by Angela Bussiere

Text: *Incidents in the Life of a Slave Girl,* by Harriet Jacobs

We've read several books about pre–Civil War times, including *Christmas in the Big House, Christmas in the Quarters,* by Patricia C. McKissack and Frederick L. McKissack (1994). I want everybody to take out a sheet of paper. For the next five minutes I want you to imagine you are either a slave or a plantation owner, and describe what your life is like. If you are a slave, talk about what you do every day, your hardships, how you live, how your owner treats you, what your family is like, your dreams, and so forth. If you are the owner of slaves, talk about your views of your slaves, how you think they fit in society and the economy, what your job and responsibilities are, how well (or poorly) you treat your slaves (and why), and why you have slaves. You might be explaining your position to a northern abolitionist.

Now I'd like the plantation owners to make a circle facing inward, and the slaves to form an inner circle facing outward. I want you to share what your life is like with the person across from you. You have three minutes to do this.

Then move three people to the right, and share your life experiences and your positions again. Now we are going to have a discussion on slavery, keeping the roles of plantation owners and slaves. Get into your two groups; choose a recorder, and list three to five reasons for your positions, and be ready to discuss them. Anticipate some of your opponents' views and prepare to refute them.

Post activity:

You took on the perspectives of your assigned roles very well. Sometimes it's particularly hard to express views we now know are unacceptable, such as the position that slavery can ever be morally or socially acceptable. Yet it's important that we try to understand how and why many people who considered themselves upright did indeed accept slavery as a tenable system. Now you're ready for our next book, *Incidents in the Life of a Slave Girl,* by Harriet Jacobs. You're going to love it.

USING READING GUIDES TO REINFORCE ORGANIZATION PATTERNS

Standards Addressed

Science: All students should develop an understanding of historical perspectives. All students should develop an understanding of science as a human endeavor. All students should develop an understanding of science and technology in local, national, and global challenges.

Mathematics: Students understand numbers, ways of representing numbers, relationships among numbers, and number systems. Students understand how mathematical ideas interconnect and build on one another to produce a coherent whole.

English/Language Arts: Students conduct research on issues and interests by generating ideas and questions, and by posing problems. They gather, evaluate, and synthesize data from a variety of sources (e.g., print and nonprint texts, artifacts, people) to communicate their discoveries in ways that suit their purpose and audience. Students apply a wide range of strategies to comprehend, interpret, evaluate, and appreciate texts. They draw on their prior knowledge [and] their interactions with other readers and writers.

Context/Rationale

A reading guide is, as its name implies, a structure to aid students in the comprehension of a text. Whereas worksheets sometimes do little more than assess whether students have comprehended material, a reading guide's aim is always to provide help along the way. You may encounter numerous types of reading guides, for different texts will call for different amounts and kinds of scaffolding; and you know your students and their needs. Anticipation guides, given before a text is read, and graphic organizers, structures that help students make connections and understand the patterns of organization of a text, are examples of reading guides.

Figures 3.8 through 3.11 present example reading guides used for each of the following organizational patterns:

- *Sequence:* The timeline in Figure 3.8 is based on D. Adler's *A Picture Book of Benjamin Franklin* (1990).

- *Comparison/contrast:* Various organizers can be used to depict comparison and contrast. Figure 3.9 is one example based on M. Cerullo's *Dolphins: What They Can Teach Us* (1999).
- *Cause/effect:* Figure 3.10 depicts the acts of nature that cause a volcano. The information is based on F. Watt's *Earthquakes and Volcanoes* (1993).
- *Problem/solution:* The problem/solution timeline in Figure 3.11 is based on E. Partridge's *Restless Spirit: The Life and Work of Dorothea Lange* (2002).

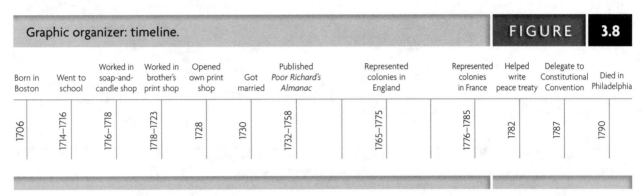

Graphic organizer: timeline. FIGURE **3.8**

Source: DeVries, 2008. Timeline based on Adler, D. (1990). *A Picture Book of Benjamin Franklin.* New York: Trumpet Club.

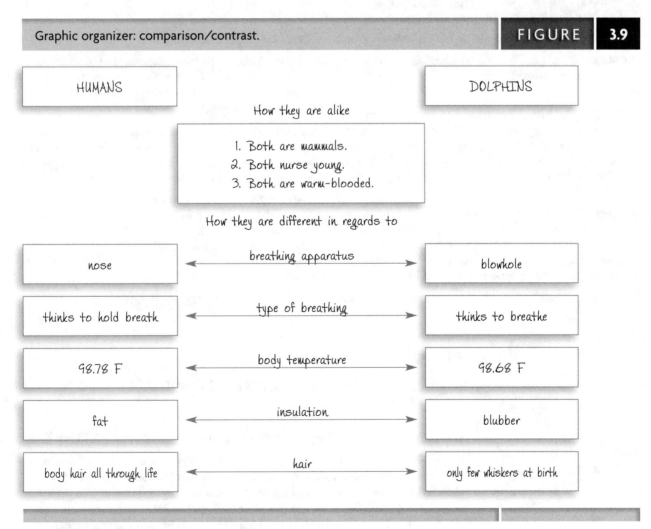

Graphic organizer: comparison/contrast. FIGURE **3.9**

Source: DeVries, 2008. Organizer based on Cerullo, M. (1999). *Dolphins: What They Can Teach Us.* New York: Scholastic.

| FIGURE | 3.10 | Graphic organizer: cause/effect. |

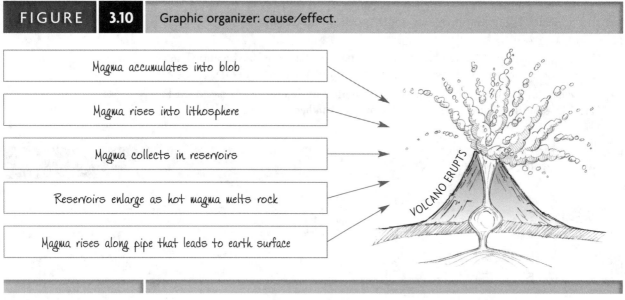

Magma accumulates into blob

Magma rises into lithosphere

Magma collects in reservoirs

Reservoirs enlarge as hot magma melts rock

Magma rises along pipe that leads to earth surface

VOLCANO ERUPTS

Source: DeVries, 2008. Organizer based on Watt, F. (1993). *Earthquakes and Volcanoes.* New York: Scholastic.

| FIGURE | 3.11 | A problem/solution timeline. |

Timeline based on *Restless Spirit: The Life and Work of Dorothea Lange* by Elizabeth Partridge (2002).

PROBLEM: 1936. Dorothea knows she has to help the starving migrant workers at the pea-pickers' camp at Nipoma, California.

SOLUTION: She brings her photos to the *San Francisco News,* and they are published. "Seeing the desperate, helpless mother unable to feed her children shocked Americans. . . . The federal government acted immediately, shipping twenty thousand pounds of food to the California fields" (p. 5).

PROBLEM: 1942. Dorothea is conflicted about working for the War Relocation Authority, since she disagrees with Executive Order 9066, which calls for the forcible removal of people of Japanese descent living on the West Coast, taking away basic freedoms guaranteed by the Bill of Rights.

SOLUTION: Though she hasn't the power to provide a real solution, she decides, "The best she could do was to photograph the process, so there would be a clear record of what was actually happening" (pp. 83–84).

PROBLEM: 1964. Dorothea is diagnosed with incurable cancer of the esophagus. She longs for the peace and care that her doctor recommends, and must decide how to spend her final months of life.

SOLUTION: She chooses to do a retrospective show at the Museum of Modern Art in New York, covering her lifetime of photography. "In this show, I would like to be speaking to others in the sound of my own voice, poor though it may be . . . I don't care how wide I lay myself open, this time" (p. 108).

Source: Kane, 2007.

Walk-Through

SEQUENTIAL READING GUIDE

Created by Helen Kemper

Text: *What a Great Idea: Inventions That Changed the World,* by Stephen M. Tomecek

Take a look around you. Notice the materials used to make the desk at which you sit. Think about the clothing you wear, and the natural or artificial substances needed to make up the woven threads. Where did you buy your clothing, and how do you think it ended up on the shelves in the clothing store? Do you remember when you were first able to access the Internet, and how the information could be accessed at the touch of a finger? Think of the time you save doing research with the help of the Internet. Now

Chart of inventions.			FIGURE **3.12**
ITEM	NATURAL RESOURCES	IMPACT ON SOCIETY	TIME PERIOD INVENTED
Clothing			
Money			
Microscope			
Steam engine			
Plastics			
Chemical fertilizers			
Incandescent lightbulb			
X-rays			
Antibiotics			
Nuclear reactor			
Computer			

think about windows you look out of and the natural resources beyond the windows that existed "naturally" at the time our founding fathers came to this country.

All of these thoughts must be connected somehow. With every new invention, an impact is made on society. Take a few minutes before you read Stephen Tomecek's book, *What a Great Idea: Inventions That Changed the World,* and try to connect the natural resources of our environment that make up items we use today and the impact these modern inventions had on society. Try to make educated guesses, using your knowledge of history, as to when these items were invented. Record your responses in Figure 3.12.

ANTICIPATION GUIDE

Created by Mary Schiraldi

Text: *Piece of Pi: Wit-Sharpening, Brain-Bruising, Number-Crunching Activities with Pi,* by Naila Bokhari

Directions: Before reading *Piece of Pi,* by Naila Bokhari, answer the following questions. You may work with a partner and may consult your math textbook, the dictionary, and the Internet as you answer.

1. What are some approximate values of pi that are commonly used?
2. What does it mean for someone to be irrational? How about an irrational number? Is there anything in common between the two?
3. List as many digits of pi as you can. Is there a pattern? Should there be a pattern?
4. How many different formulas can you find that have pi in them? What do they all have in common?
5. Do you think the value of pi is special? Why or why not?

Now you are ready to learn more about pi. After you have read the book, we will discuss how your answers compare with those of your classmates and to the book. On the back of this paper, you'll write the three most interesting things you have learned about pi. Again, you may work with a partner.

P A R T 3

author STUDIES

PENNY COLMAN

Use this author's books in **English, science, social studies,** *and other disciplines.*

Figure 3.13 is a bibliography of some of Penny Coleman's works.

Do you, or do you expect to, have reluctant readers in your classes? The titles of many of Penny Colman's informational books might draw them in: *Toilets, Bathtubs, Sinks, and Sewers: A History of the Bathroom* (1994), for example, or *Corpses, Coffins, and Crypts: A History of Burial* (1997). Readers interested in true war stories will appreciate *Spies! Women in the Civil War* (1992), and *Where the Action Was: Women War Correspondents in World War II* (2002). *Rosie the Riveter: Women Working on the Home Front in World War II* (1995) won the Orbis Pictus Honor Award. Colman has several other books about social justice issues, often highlighting women who led crusades against injustice. History classrooms will be enriched with titles such as *Strike! The Bitter Struggle of American Workers from Colonial Time to the Present* (1995) and *Mother Jones and the March of the Mill Children* (1994).

A perfect companion to a middle school history textbook would be Colman's *Girls: A History of Growing Up Female in America* (2000). In the Author's Note at the beginning, she shares how the idea for the book came to her; while she was standing at a corner in New York City, the words that became the title ". . . suddenly popped up in my brain like a jack-in-the-box. . . . The words . . . electrified me" (p. 9). She goes on to describe how she conducted research through reading letters, memoirs, diaries, and journals written by girls living at different times. After reading this book, some students will be eager to take *Adventurous Women: Eight True Stories About Women Who Made a Difference* (2006) out of the classroom library.

Colman writes what one editor calls "hard-core nonfiction" (Editors, 2002, p. 59); "I do not make up dialogue, use composite characters, invent scenes, attribute thoughts or feelings, imagine motives, or in any way cross the line between fact and fiction" (Editors, 2002, p. 60). She loves writing nonfiction because "Kids care deeply about whether something really happened, whether it is *really* a true story" (p. 60), and because:

| FIGURE | **3.13** | Selected works by Penny Colman. |

Colman, P. (2006). *Adventurous women: Eight true stories about women who made a difference.* New York: Henry Holt.

Colman, P. (2002). *Where the action was: Women war correspondents in World War II.* New York: Crown Publishers.

Colman, P. (2000). *Girls: A history of growing up female in America.* New York: Scholastic.

Colman, P. (1997). *Corpses, coffins, and crypts: A history of burial.* New York: Henry Holt.

Colman, P. (1995). *Rosie the riveter: Women working on the home front in World War II.* New York: Crown Publishers.

Colman, P. (1995). *Strike!: The bitter struggle of American workers from colonial times to the present.* Brookfield, CT: Millbrook Press.

Colman, P. (1994). *Madam C. J. Walker: Building a business empire.* Brookfield, CT: Millbrook Press.

Colman, P. (1994). *Mother Jones and the march of the mill children.* Brookfield, CT: Millbrook Press.

Colman, P. (1994). *Toilets, bathtubs, sinks, and sewers: A history of the bathroom.* New York: Atheneum Books for Young People.

Colman, P., & Bogan, P. (1994). *101 ways to do better in school.* Mahwah, NJ: Troll Associates.

Colman, P. (1993). *A woman unafraid: The achievements of Frances Perkins.* New York: Atheneum.

Colman, P. (1993). *Fannie Lou Hamer and the fight for the vote.* Brookfield, CT: Millbrook Press.

Colman, P. (1992). *Breaking the chains: The crusade of Dorothea Lynde Dix.* White Hall, VA: Shoe Tree Press.

Colman, P. (1992). *Spies!: Women in the Civil War.* White Hall, VA: Shoe Tree Press.

Nonfiction is the currency with which public policies and legislation are made, societal needs are discussed, cultural aesthetics are defined, life lessons are conveyed, historical narratives are transmitted, and matters of war and peace are decided. Nonfiction is about life itself, and that is why I am passionate about it. (p. 60)

Classroom activities for different subject areas based on Penny Colman's books can be found at www.pennycolman.com. The site also has biographical information on Colman, as well as a list of awards, speeches, essays, and articles. Readers can check her blog to see what she's currently working on.

TONYA BOLDEN

Use this author's books in **English, physical education, social studies,** *and other disciplines.*

Figure 3.14 is a bibliography of some of Tonya Bolden's works.

When you enter the world of Tonya Bolden's books, you'll emerge wiser and full of appreciation for the people and institutions you've met while there. Some of your new friends will be artists featured in *Wake Up Our Souls: A Celebration of Black American Artists* (2004). Others will be the same ages as your students, encountered in *Tell All the Children Our Story: Memories and Mementos of Being Young and Black in America* (2001), designed and presented as a scrapbook—a perfect book to include in the Scrapbook Biography activity described in Chapter 5, Part 2. You'll meet courageous people in *And Not Afraid to Dare: The Stories of Ten African-American Women* (2003). And you'll get good, and lively, advice in a book she edited, *33 Things Every Girl Should Know: Stories, Songs, Poems, and Smart Talk by 33 Extraordinary Women* (1998), and another, *33 Things Every Girl Should Know About Women's History: From Suffragettes to Skirt Lengths to the ERA* (2002). You'll experience the fellowship and spirituality Bolden knew as a girl in her informational book told through poetry, *Rock of Ages: A Tribute to the Black Church* (2003).

You'll find out how Tonya Bolden views heroism in *Portraits of African-American Heroes* (2003) and *American Patriots: The Story of Blacks in the Military from the Revolution to Desert Storm* (2003). In *The Champ: The Story of Muhammad Ali* (2004), you'll experience victories, defeats, and comebacks with the inspirational athlete and human being whose story is told using nonconventional text. A less well-known hero is *Maritcha Remond Lyons*, the first Black person to graduate from Providence High School, who then spent the next half-century as an educator. In the Author's Note at the end of *Maritcha: A Nineteenth American Century Girl*, Bolden (2005) tells us that her subject "... remained, to borrow from

---

Selected works by Tonya Bolden.   FIGURE   **3.14**

Bolden, T. (2007). *M.L.K.: Journey of a king.* New York: Abrams Books for Young Readers.

Bolden, T. (2005). *Cause: Reconstruction America 1863–1877.* New York: Knopf.

Bolden, T. (2005). *Maritcha: A nineteenth-century American girl.* New York: Harry N. Abrams.

Bolden, T. (2004). *The book of African-American women: 150 crusaders, creators, and uplifters.* Avon, MA: Adams Media.

Bolden, T. (2004). *The champ: The story of Muhammad Ali.* Illus. G. Christie. New York: A.A. Knopf.

Bolden, T. (2004). *Wake up our souls: A celebration of African American artists.* New York: Harry N. Abrams; Washington, DC: Published in association with the Smithsonian American Art Museum.

Bolden, T. (2003). *And not afraid to dare: The stories of ten African-American women.* New York: Scholastic.

Bolden, T. (2003). *Portraits of African-American heroes.* New York: Scholastic.

Bolden, T. (2003). *Rock of ages: A tribute to the Black church.* Illus. G. Christie. New York: Dell Dragonfly.

Bolden, T., & Buckley, G. L. (2003). *American patriots: The story of Blacks in the military from the Revolution to Desert Storm.* New York: Crown.

Bolden, T. (2002). *33 things every girl should know about women's history: From suffragettes to skirt lengths to the ERA.* New York: Crown Publishers.

Bolden, T. (2001). *Tell all the children our story: Memories and mementos of being young and Black in America.* New York: Abrams.

Khan, C., & Bolden, T. (2003). *Chaka!: Through the fire.* Emmaus, PA: Rodale; New York: Distributed by St. Martin's Press.

Mother Love, & Bolden, T. (2002). *Forgive or forget: Never underestimate the power of forgiveness.* Los Angeles: Milligan Books.

Bolden, T. (1998). *33 things every girl should know: Stories, songs, poems and smart talk by 33 extraordinary women.* New York: Crown.

Toni Morrison, 'a friend of mine' over the years" (p. 41). Maritcha can be our friend, too, since Tonya Bolden has shared her with us. And she can serve as a teacher's assistant, as the curricular theme of girls and women in American history is explored. You can find out more about Bolden's life, current writing and speaking projects, and resources for teaching at www.TonyaBolden.com.

JAMES CROSS GIBLIN

Use this author's books in **English, science, social studies,** *and other disciplines.*

Figure 3.15 is a selected bibliography of James Cross Giblin's works.

James Cross Giblin's books cover a wide range of topics. He answers many questions, some of which you probably never thought to ask—but maybe some students have—in *Be Seated: A Book About Chairs* (1993). If the courses you teach involve the teaching of symbolism, *Fireworks, Picnics, and Flags: The Story of Fourth of July Symbols* (2001) can help you teach the concept with style. Your fledgling historians and archaeologists can discover the *Secrets of the Sphinx* (2004), thanks to Giblin's research. Meanwhile, your students with ambitions relating to the medical field can explore *When Plague Strikes: The Black Death, Smallpox, AIDS* (1995). And future politicians

can enjoy *Edith Wilson: The Woman Who Ran the White House* (1992).

James Cross Giblin is not timid about tackling tough subjects. In *Charles A. Lindbergh: A Human Hero* (1997), he does not omit or gloss over Lindbergh's anti-Semitism and pro-Nazi leanings, as so many other biographies for children do. And he helps students think critically through his presentation of *The Life and Death of Adolf Hitler* (2002). The author explains, "I've always been curious about people and events in history, and writing about them enables me to satisfy my own curiosity first of all. I often say that every one of my nonfiction books for children has been like an adult-education course for me!" (Robb, 2004, p. 12). Giblin is an avid reader, which informs his writing. He notes: "I read a broad assortment of things, non-fiction and fiction, newspaper articles and columns, magazine pieces, and books. Recently, I've been delving into a collection of classic examples of journalism from the World War II years" (Robb, 2004, p. 38).

Giblin doesn't limit himself to writing nonfiction. He has contributed stories to Michael Cart's *Tomorrowland: 10 Stories about the Future* (1999) and Marion Dane Bauer's *Am I Blue?: Coming Out from the Silence* (1994). In 1996, *The Dwarf, the Giant, and the Unicorn: A Tale of King Arthur*, was published. An author center can highlight his versatility. James Cross Giblin has something for everyone.

FIGURE	3.15	Selected works by James Cross Giblin.

Giblin, J. C. (2005). *Good brother, bad brother: The story of Edwin Booth and John Wilkes Booth*. New York: Clarion Books.

Giblin, J. C. (2004). *Secrets of the Sphinx*. Illus. B. Ibatoulline. New York: Scholastic.

Giblin, J. C. (2002). *The life and death of Adolf Hitler*. New York: Clarion Books.

Giblin, J. C. (2000). *The amazing life of Benjamin Franklin*. New York: Scholastic.

Giblin, J. C. (2000). *The century that was: Reflections on the last one hundred years*. New York: Atheneum Books For Young Readers.

Giblin, J. C. (2000). *The mystery of the mammoth bones: And how it was solved*. New York: Scholastic.

Giblin, J. C. (1999). Night of the plague. In Cart, M. (ed.), *Tomorrowland: 10 stories about the future*. New York: Scholastic, pp. 157–168.

Giblin, J. C. (1998). *Writing books for young people*. Boston: Writer, Inc.

Giblin, J. C. (1997). *Charles A. Lindbergh: A human hero*. New York: Clarion Books.

Giblin, J. C., & Frampton, D. (1997). *When plague strikes: The Black Death, Smallpox, AIDS*. New York: HarperCollins.

Giblin, J. C. (1996). *The dwarf, the giant, and the unicorn: A tale of King Arthur*. New York: Clarion Books.

Giblin, J. C. (1996). *Thomas Jefferson: A picture book biography*. Illus. M. Dooling. New York: Scholastic.

Giblin, J. C. (1995). *When plague strikes: The Black Death, Smallpox, AIDS*. New York: HarperCollins.

Giblin, J. C. (1994). Three Mondays in July. In Bauer, M. D. (ed.), *Am I Blue?: Coming Out from the Silence*. Illus. B. Underwood. New York: HarperCollins, pp. 105–124.

Giblin, J. C. (1993). *Be seated: A book about chairs*. New York: HarperCollins.

Giblin, J. C. (1992). *Edith Wilson: The woman who ran the United States*. Illus. M. LaPorte. New York: Viking.

P A R T | 4

A N N O T A T E D **books and booktalks**

CODE: E = Elementary, **I** = Intermediate, **M** = Middle school, **H** = High School

The following annotations are grouped by discipline. Although I have had to place each book in one category, please keep in mind that many of the books can be used creatively in other disciplines, too; in fact, from time to time I will make suggestions, and when I do, we will **boldface** the other discipline.

The following annotations vary in format. Most of them I have directed to an audience of teachers and future teachers (you!). A few are "character booktalks," written from a book character's point of view; these will be labeled "Character Booktalk" (see p. 126). Still others are excerpts from my own pre-service students' reader response logs. You may adapt any of these annotations to create booktalks tailored to *your* audience and appropriately connected to your curriculum.

ART

Anderson, D. (2005). *Ancient China: History in Art.* Chicago: Raintree. **(I, M, H)**

The premise of this book is that readers can learn much about ancient China from the artifacts and works of art that have been uncovered by archaeologists. The chapters are organized so that your students will see photographs of objects and read explanations relating to them in terms of technology, government, daily life, and philosophies. After poring through the colorful and informative pages of this book, your students will understand the great civilization that existed between 5000 BCE and 220 CE.

Burnham, B. (2003). *Cave of Lascaux: The Cave of Prehistoric Wall Paintings.* New York: PowerKids Press. **(E, I, M, H)**

It's amazing to learn that the cave was discovered so recently—1940—considering the paintings were done over 17,000 years ago. The author uses student-friendly comparisons to help readers envision the work. For example, he describes the ceiling of the Hall of Bulls as 23 feet wide and 20 feet high, or ". . . as tall as three basketball players standing on top of one another!" (p. 9). He also explains how archaeologists have used clues to determine how the Magdalenians created the art. The colors of paints came from minerals; the artists built and stood on scaffolds to paint the ceilings. This is a terrific book to begin a lesson or unit on the history of art.

Finley, C. (1998). *Art of the Far North: Inuit Sculpture, Drawing, and Printmaking.* Minneapolis: Lerner. **(I, M, H)**

Like many informational art books, this one teaches about the history and culture of a people as it explains and gives background for the works themselves. Several chapters are devoted to Inuit life as viewed through sculptures and prints. The artwork represents the people's dreams, storytelling, modern life, hunting, and dancing. We learn about shamans, and the changing seasons. Pictures and biographical information about modern Inuit artists are included. Art teachers strive to broaden students' awareness of and appreciation for multicultural forms of art; this book can help do that.

Gilbert, G., with Fehl, P. (2006). *Career Opportunities in Photography.* New York: Checkmark Books. **(H)**

This is an excellent resource to have in a classroom library. Students may peruse it leisurely and ponder some of the 62 job descriptions, or can research information about particular types of photography they wish to pursue. Categories of careers include cinematography and videography; business and industrial photography; event and travel photography; commercial photography, advertising, and publicity; portrait photography; and medical and scientific photography. Each article provides information about salaries, employment prospects, required training, tips for entry, and more. You may have a group of students reading this book while others explore similar career reference books about other types of art, or a more general career opportunity resource such as *Career Ideas for Kids Who Like Art*, by Reeves, D. L. (1998, illus. N. Bond. New York: Facts on File). Both books are excellent resources for the job shadowing strategy discussed in Part 2 of this chapter.

Makosz, R. (2006). *Latino Arts and Their Influence on the United States: Songs, Dreams, and Dances.* Philadelphia: Mason Crest Publishers. **(M, H)**

This book is perfect for interdisciplinary study because the arts are defined broadly to include **music** and the performing arts as well as visual arts, and the connection between the **arts** and **culture** are central to the text. The standards for all curricular areas call for students to be able to think critically, and this book can help address those goals; the author gives examples of controversial issues related to murals, city ordinances, and censorship of art; he poses questions that teachers may use to stimulate debate, such as, "What is the difference between graffiti (generally considered undesirable) and urban art (highly esteemed)?" (p. 87).

Martin, R. (2002). *Picasso's War: The Destruction of Guernica and the Masterpiece That Changed the World.* New York: Plume. **(H)**

The relationship of art and **history** is made very clear in this book, which gives the background against which and the purposes for which Picasso painted *Guernica*, the large painting that had a large impact. I was equally struck by Russell Martin's own story of relating to this particular piece of art; it reinforced the idea of art being alive and changing as times and people change. In the Prologue, the American author tells of studying in Spain as a youth and learning from his art and culture professor of the tragedies brought on by the Spanish Civil War. The teacher then introduced the class to the painting itself, the original of which was then in New York City. More than three decades later, Martin visited the museum in Madrid that now held Picasso's response to war to view it for the first time. It was September 11, 2001. As he stood in front of the painting:

> . . . the city of New York fell under an utterly new kind of attack, yet one that also eerily echoed the April attack on *Gernika* sixty-four years before. In both instances, the targets were symbolic; the aim of both attacks was to incite terror from out of the otherwise sheltering sky, and to destroy thousands of people who had no inkling of their supposed crimes. (pp. 6–7)

Martin continues this thread of his personal story in the Epilogue, telling of his learning about the attack from others in the museum, and of later attending a requiem mass in Barcelona for those who had died in New York City. He ends his book with a quote from the artist himself:

> "I stand for life against death," Picasso had claimed a quarter-century before his demise, in the midst of a fear-wracked era when *Guernica* had hung in a bold but far more innocent New York City. "I stand for peace against war." (p. 269)

Art teachers may show a copy of *Guernica* to the class and ask for initial reactions. They may compare student reactions to those of the initial viewers of the painting (described on pp. 100–101), and see if their reactions to the masterpiece are different after

learning about Picasso's purpose and the many changes made during its creation, which are documented by photographs and described in the book.

Metropolitan Museum of Art. (2002). *Museum ABC.* Boston: Little, Brown and Company. **(E, I, M, H)**

If you read only the text of this book, it sounds like many other alphabet books: A is for Apple, B is for Boat. But the pages facing the text are divided into quarters, each showing a work of art or a detail from an artwork that pictures the object chosen for each letter. So, H is for Hair, and we see four very different renderings of hair: George Washington's wig in a Gilbert Stuart painting, a close-up from Kitagawa Utamaro's *Woman of the Pleasure District at Shinagawa*, part of *Portrait of a Woman with a Dog* by French artist Jean Honoré Fragonard, and an Egyptian work, *Ipuy and His Wife Receiving Offerings from Their Children*. Student artists can study and compare the pictures, turn to the back to see what art works they're from, and then do further research to find out more about their favorites.

Rothman, C. (2002). *The Big "M."* New York: Scholastic. **(E, I, M)**

The text is simple, yet the photographs of the treasures located in the Metropolitan Museum of Art make this book appealing to all ages. A grandmother takes her grandchildren on a tour; at various points she shows them cards and encourages them to look for the matching work of art. Consider using this system when you and your students visit a local museum. Have your students use this book as a model when they create books based on the favorite things they find on a museum tour, even if the tour is a virtual one using school computers. I use this book with English learners, since it's easy but sophisticated. Have them create books to introduce their classmates to works of art in museums from their countries or cultures.

Rubin, S. G. (2004). *Art Against the Odds: From Slave Quilts to Prison Paintings.* New York: Crown Publishers. **(H)**

The first chapter defines "outsider art," a term coined by art historian Roger Cardinal in 1972, to categorize artwork created by criminals, psychiatric patients, spiritualists, prisoners of war, and other types of people excluded from mainstream society. This book is filled with photographs of artwork and fascinating stories of talented artists, most self-taught, who produced great works under terrible constraints. The Foreword is transcribed from an interview Rubin had in 2003 with Helga Weissová, who explained that drawing helped her escape from the terrible reality of the Terezin concentration camp when she was a child during World War II.

Readers will learn about the quilts made by slaves to give directions regarding the Underground Railroad, and about the art produced in a Japanese American internment camp.

The book includes stories of artists who suffered from schizophrenia, and examples of folk art created by artists growing up in hard times and situations. One chapter highlights special education teacher Tim Rollins, who worked with a group of poor South Bronx students who called themselves K.O.S. (Kids of Survival). Here's how their art began:

> Rollins wanted to introduce the kids to classic literature, a seemingly impossible task. "For kids, books were the enemy," he said. When he handed out copies of George Orwell's *1984* and asked them to draw while he read aloud, they misunderstood and started drawing directly on the pages of their books. The kids got excited about what they had done, and so did Rollins. Rather than scolding them for defacing books, he realized that they had hit on an innovative new art form. Together they applied the pages of the text to canvas and began working collectively on a large-scale composition . . . "our classroom, Room 318, had been transformed into a working studio for young artists." . . . (pp. 35–36)

As an art teacher, you may connect this book to your curriculum in numerous ways; for instance, use examples from the book to inspire students to create their own art against the odds, or use the book as an aid in teaching about materials, processes, and the power of art to make both personal and political statements.

Rubin, S. G. (2001). *The Yellow House: Vincent van Gogh & Paul Gauguin Side by Side.* **Illus. J. A. Smith.** New York: Harry N. Abrams. **(E, I, M)**

This short book is a great example of how an author uses comparison and contrast to help readers access information. Vincent painted quickly, and he painted what he saw in front of him. Paul took his time and painted from his imagination. Contrasting illustrations, too, show how the two artists depicted the same subject. The story of the nine weeks these artistic geniuses shared, learning from each other, fighting, and producing great works, is a fascinating read. Part 2 of this chapter shows how this book can be used with the Literary Field Trip strategy.

Sayre, H. (2004). *Cave Paintings to Picasso: The Inside Scoop on 50 Art Masterpieces.* San Francisco: Chronicle Books. **(I, M, H)**

Besides the huge time span indicated in the title, this book is truly global in its reach, and offers tremendous variety in terms of types of art. In addition to some classic European paintings, your students will discover a woodblock print, *The Great Wave off Kanagawa*, by Japanese artist Katsushika Hokusai; the *Toreador Fresco* from about 1500 BCE from an island in Greece; the modern fresco *Sugar Cane* of the great muralist from Mexico, Diego Rivera; the *Book of Kells* made and illustrated by Irish monks; the Easter Island Ancestor figures made from volcanic stone; and many other unique masterpieces. Along with a timeline on every page, the author provides a context to the work of art and some information about the medium used. The photos of the art combined with the explanatory text inspire awe.

ENGLISH/LANGUAGE ARTS

Baker, R. (2003). *In a Word: 750 Words and Their Fascinating Stories and Origins.* **Illus. T. Lopes.** Peterborough, NH: Cobblestone Publishing. **(I, M, H)**

The author's enthusiasm for language is clear from the first paragraph of the Introduction:

> . . . since my first week in 9th-grade Latin class, I have enjoyed dissecting words. I enjoyed learning just what words really mean and how these meanings had evolved. I already spoke English and Portuguese, so Latin seemed to fill a "gap" of understanding. . . . As I studied French, German, and Greek, each again broadened my perception of language and how words reflect a people's beliefs and customs. (p. viii)

Those words reminded me of my son Patrick in ninth grade, who similarly fell in love with Latin, and subsequently sent his girlfriend a love poem praising her pulchritude and talking about her ubiquitous presence. (He sent along a glossary.) Like the author, Patrick pursued other languages, becoming excited over the connections he found. Many students will love exploring the words in this book, categorized by chapter titles including "Awesome Archaeology," "Military Madness," "Glorious Gizmos & Great Grub," and "Math Magic and Science Synergies."

Fandel, J. (2006). *Rhyme, Meter, and Other Word Music.* Mankato, MN: Creative Education. **(M, H)**

The comparison of terms and concepts inherent in poetry instruction with similar concepts in music will appeal to many of our youth. Fandel begins with a bit of history about minstrels singing poetry, and other aspects of poetry's oral tradition. Each mini-lesson on a curricular concept, such as meter, form, rhyme, beat, and free verse, is accompanied by a poem that exemplifies the idea. Students may use this resource, as well as other books in the *Understanding Poetry* series such as Fandel's *Puns, Allusions, and Other Word Secrets* (2006), as they both read and write poetry in class or at home. Have these books available for the creative writing strategy described in Part 2 of this chapter or if sponsoring an after-school poetry club.

Flexner, S. B., & Soukhanov, A. H. (1997). *Speaking Freely: A Guided Tour of American English from Plymouth Rock to Silicon Valley.* New York: Oxford University Press. (H)

Your students can open this book to any page and learn dozens of bits of information about how, when, and why language changes. Or have them pick out a topic that interests them from the Table of Contents, and turn to the sections about pop culture, gender gaps, fashions, religion, sports, sex, environmental studies, or crime as those themes relate to American English. Depending on your curricular needs, you might direct your students to chapters with names like "Cyberspace: I Hear America Clicking," "The Word of the Law and the Law of the Land," "Geography: It's on the Map," or "Genetic Engineering . . . And Linguistic Reengineering." This is a great reference tool, but also a fun book to just peruse.

Greenblatt, S. (2004). *Will in the World: How Shakespeare Became Shakespeare.* New York: W.W. Norton & Company. (H)

This biography goes beyond relaying the facts of a person's life. Greenblatt tells the reader his purpose right away, which is to ponder causes and connections that might help us understand how Shakespeare was able to write his masterpieces and become so successful and famous during his lifetime. *Genius* is just not enough to explain his phenomenal accomplishments. The author also demonstrates repeatedly how scholars have had to speculate and make inferences while putting the pieces of Shakespeare's life together from the data that exist. He invites the reader along on an important and exciting quest:

> . . . this artist was unusually open to the world and discovered the means to allow this world into his works. To understand how he did this so effectively, it is important to look carefully at his verbal artistry—his command of rhetoric, his uncanny ventriloquism, his virtual obsession with language . . . and to understand how Shakespeare used his imagination to transform his life into his art, it is important to use our own imagination. (p. 14)

High school literature curricula call for not only the reading of Shakespeare's work, but the understanding of the Bard's life and times. This book, along with other materials about the Globe Theatre, Elizabethan times, and Shakespeare's contemporaries, can help students context the plays and poems of Shakespeare.

O'Conner, P. (2003). *Woe Is I: The Grammarphobe's Guide to Better English in Plain English,* 2nd edition. New York: Riverhead Books. (H)

Who's the target audience for this book? Who should read it? Our students? Sure. Ourselves? Sure. The author explains that

> *Woe Is I* is a survival guide for intelligent people who probably never have diagrammed a sentence and never will. Most of us don't know a gerund from a gerbil and don't care, but we'd like to speak and write as though we did. (p. xv)

Well, I have diagrammed my share of sentences, but I still learned a lot and laughed a lot as I read O'Conner's helpful explanations and examples of grammar principles of the ever-changing English language. The book is anything but intimidating, with chapter titles such as: "Comma Sutra: The Joy of Punctuation," "The Living Dead: Let Bygone Rules Be Gone," "Yours Truly: The Possessives and the Possessed," and "Woe Is I: Therapy for Pronoun Anxiety." A new chapter in this edition gives friendly advice regarding grammatical issues related to e-mail writing. This book belongs in an English teacher's toolbox for making language issues relevant and interesting. When students ask for more like it, offer O'Conner's *Words Fail Me: What Everyone Who Writes Should Know About Writing* (2000, New York: Harcourt Brace).

O'Reilly, G. (2004). *Slangalicious: Where We Got that Crazy Lingo.* Illus. K. Johnson. New York: Annick Press. (I, M, H)

Readers are invited in this story to join the narrator as he writes a research paper on slang. We learn, along with him, two definitions of slang, along with many examples and stories of their origins. There are some mini–history lessons as we learn about the Beat Generation, railroad workers, sports teams, the Jazz Age, wartime slang, the advent and development of television and computers, and diner slang. Readers will build vocabulary of the non-slang variety as well. English teachers can use this book to introduce the topic of etymology and encourage students to research the origins of words. The author lists resources for doing this (pp. 79–80), and recommends several language-related websites, including www.etymonline.com and www.wordorigins.org (p. 79).

Truss, L. (2003). *Eats, Shoots and Leaves: The Zero Tolerance Approach to Punctuation.* New York: Gotham Books. (H)

I can't offer a better rationale for using this book than that provided by memoirist Frank McCourt in the Foreword, so I'll borrow his words:

The book is so spirited, so scholarly . . . English teachers will sweep all other topics aside to get to, you guessed it, punctuation. Parents and children will gather by the fire many an evening to read passages on the history of the semicolon and the terrible things being done to the apostrophe. . . . Oh, to be an English teacher in the Age of Truss. (pp. xi–xiv)

For even more fun, or to differentiate instruction for students at different levels of understanding punctuation, add the picture book version, illustrated by Bonnie Timmons: *Eats, Shoots & Leaves: Why, Commas Really Do Make a Difference!* (2006, New York, G.P. Putnam's Sons). Each double-page spread has the same sentence, but punctuated differently, and the pictures show how the meaning changes accordingly. For example, one spread has "Look at that huge hot dog!" opposite "Look at that huge, hot dog!" (unpaged). After students experience Truss's books, be prepared for punctuation projects and punctuation parties.

Wulffson, D., & Sulffson, P. (2003). *Abracadabra to Zombie: More Than 300 Whacky Word Origins.* **Illus. J. Lee. New York: Dutton Children's Books. (I, M, H)**

Forget chapter titles for this one—after an Introduction that explains the concept of etymology and an example from a dictionary definition of the word *diaper*, the rest is an alphabetical listing of words along with the stories of how they came to be. Readers learn about brand names, names of popular musical bands, and sports teams' nicknames, but they'll also encounter words that are part of our school curricula, such as sarcophagus, placebo, lobbyist, utopia, and Bunker Hill. This book provides a painless and amusing way for students to enhance their vocabulary.

LANGUAGES AND CULTURE

Amis, N. (2003). *The Orphans of Normandy: A True Story of World War II Told Through Drawings by Children.* **New York: Athenium. (E, I, M)**

Talk about authentic learning! Each right-hand page illustrates a full page drawing by one of the orphans who walked 150 miles through a war, along with the French text they wrote. The 100 girls were in danger both from the Germans and the Allies who had invaded Normandy. On the opposite pages your students can read the English translation of the girls' words. Here are a few:

> "The night of June 5 and 6, 1944, at the Clos, began well. Everybody went quietly to sleep as usual, but soon we were startled awake by unusual noises . . . with a sigh

of relief, they shouted, 'It's the invasion!'"—Rose Marie Vail, 12

> "Crossing the Cinglais forest, the girls passed German tanks in flames and dead Germans. The brave little girls of the Clos followed other evacuees. All the while waving their white flags at the approaching planes."—Odette Daigromont, 13

> "August 11. A few days after their arrival at Beaufort, the little girls of the Clos were happy to see American tanks. That consoled them for all that they had lost."—Artist unknown (unpaged)

French students can discuss their reactions to the styles of art, translate the French text accompanying the drawings, and learn about the role of France during World War II.

Carey, P. (2005). *Wrong About Japan: A Father's Journey with His Son.* **New York: Alfred A. Knopf. (M, H)**

Novelist Peter Carey was introduced to the Japanese art forms of manga and anime by his 12-year-old son, and their joint exploration eventually led them to visit Tokyo to learn more. The author presents himself as a learner, one who makes mistakes; needs to rely on mentors, even if those more knowledgeable others are children; and delights in the wonders of discovering new and radically different ways of thinking, living, and expressing artistic ideas. Readers come away feeling like they've been on a life-changing trip. This book would provide an enticing introduction to an **art** or **social studies** unit on Japan. It also is a good stimulus for travel journal writing as discussed in Part 2 of this chapter.

Perez, A. I. (2002). *My Diary from Here to There/Mi Diario de Aqui hasta Allá.* **Illus. M. C. Gonzalez. San Francisco: Children's Book Press. (E, I, M, H)**

This recounting of the author's immigration will interest students who have experienced moving or who enjoy reflecting in diary form. In addition students can read in Spanish and English, since the entries appear in both languages on the same page. This makes it great for high school Spanish classrooms as well as ESL (English as a second language) classrooms and any other rooms where teachers are promoting good reading and broadening horizons.

MATH AND TECHNOLOGY

Aczel, A. D. (2006). *The Artist and the Mathematician: The Story of Nicholas Bourbaki, the Genius Mathematician Who Never Existed.* **New York: Thunders' Mouth Press. (H)**

Use this book to entice students at the beginning of a lesson or unit on the history of mathematics, a topic students might at first perceive as rather dry and irrelevant to their lives. The author brings in many developments of the twentieth century, including Einstein's theory of special relativity, the cubist art of Braque and Picasso, Claude Levi-Strauss and structuralism, linguistics, economics, psychology, and the mathematical legacy of Nicolas Bourbaki. What does the mysterious subtitle allude to? I'm sorry, I can't spoil a good ending.

Albert, J., & Bennett, J. (2001). *Curve Ball: Baseball, Statistics, and the Role of Chance in the Game.* New York: Copernicus Books. **(H)**

As a teacher of a statistics course, you may take examples and explanations from this book to teach many of the required curricular topics, such as probability and data analysis, and then add other authentic examples from the world beyond baseball and sports for further clarification, application, and reinforcement. The authors state the primary goal of their text: ". . . to provide insights that can be gleaned when statistical models are applied to Major League Baseball data" (p. xvi). In the first chapter, they show how tabletop games can be used to simulate the interactions of batters and pitchers. Subsequent chapters explain techniques used by statisticians along with pitching and hitting patterns they reveal; provide an explanation of chance variation using the topic of hot streaks and cold streaks; propose a statistical model that demonstrates that ". . . run production is a curved, not a linear, phenomenon" (p. iv); discuss the means of and reliability of prediction; and end with a review entitled "Post-Game Comments" (p. 343). The book is a wealth of information that will (I predict) result in readers having better understanding of the statistics and commentary on sports channels and in newspapers, as well as the interest and ability to apply what they've learned in other contexts.

Bodanis, D. (2000). *E=mc2: A Biography of the World's Most Famous Equation.* New York: Walker & Company. **(H)**

Bodanis's voice is reassuring from the start; he explains his purpose of trying to make Einstein's earth-shattering equation understandable to a lay audience, while sharing the interesting stories of many scientists before and after the 1905 "birth" of the equation who are related to it in some way. He shares his decision to craft his book according to a familiar genre: "Everyone knows that a biography entails stories of the ancestors, childhood, adolescence, and adulthood of your subject. It's the same with the equation." Along the way, he invokes the poetry of Robert Frost, gives much relevant historical information about World War II, tells of the impact the equation has on modern-day medical and household devices, and predicts how our world will end. (Don't worry, the year had so many zeroes

in it I chose not to use the space to copy them all.) If your students think the math you teach and the lives they lead are mutually exclusive, this is the book to offer them.

Borden, L. (2004). *Sea Clocks: The Story of Longitude.* **Illus. E. Blegvad.** New York: Simon & Schuster. **(E, I, M)**

Borden spends part of this book explaining why finding an instrument that could calculate longitude was so important and how bits of the puzzle were discovered by various scientists, including Isaac Newton and Edmond Halley, who independently tried to solve the problem. This information is interspersed with biographical stories involving John Harrison, the mechanical genius who, after more than 40 years of work, invents a clock that works at sea. Will he win the 20,000-pound reward offered for the solution to the great mathematical dilemma? Harrison himself waits a long time to find out; surely your students will be willing to read to the end of this adventure to see if perseverance and talent are rewarded. Use this book to help students understand how crucial mathematical calculations can be, and how math theory and practical applications come together.

Derbyshire, J. (2003). *Prime Obsession: Bernard Riemann and the Greatest Unsolved Problem in Mathematics.* Washington, DC: Joseph Henry Press. **(H)**

This genre-combining book is part biography, part informational. The study of prime numbers is a fascinating part of the high school curriculum; many articles and websites offer games, puzzles, and challenges galore. With this book, your students can add true stories about prime numbers to the mix. Derbyshire recounts the century-and-a-half-long quest to find out whether a hypothesis made by 32-year-old Bernhard Riemann to a group of assembled mathematicians is true or false. Students may be surprised to find that so many people actually are obsessed with math, and are willing to devote their entire lives—inside and outside schools, inside and outside jobs—to pondering conundrums. Maybe one of your students will join the journey so many others have undertaken. Recommend this book also to students who have read Mark Haddon's novel, *The Curious Incident of the Dog in the Night-time* (2003, New York: Doubleday), whose narrator is also passionate about primes.

Eastaway, R., & Wyndham, J. (1998). *Why Do Buses Come in Threes?: The Hidden Mathematics of Everyday Life.* New York: John Wiley & Sons. **(I, M, H)**

I'll start my booktalk with the authors' final words to us about an important practical use for math:

... which is to make life more fun. And fun doesn't have to come from a surprise or unexpected result in the end. A lot of the stimulation of this subject comes from observing a pattern and asking, "Why?" That was the inspiration behind most of the chapters in this book. . . . Next time someone asks you what math is, don't say it is about learning your times tables. Math is the study of pretty patterns. And we all love pretty patterns. (p. 151)

The chapters will intrigue your students, at least those whom you can get interested in the mathematics behind sports rankings, or coincidences, or betting, or nature, or code-making and breaking, or cutting cake, or explaining bad luck, or in murder mysteries, or in political statistics—the list goes on. Curricular connections can be made when teaching topics of geometry, trigonometry, probability, logic, factorials, and exponents.

Glazer, E. M., & McConnell, J. W. (2002). *Real-Life Math: Everyday Use of Mathematical Concepts.* Westport, CT: Greenwood Press. (M, H)

If I were a math teacher, I'd have this book on my desk at all times. Dozens of mathematical concepts are listed in alphabetical order; for each, the authors have provided a practical application based on nature, careers, or everyday life. Despite the fact that the Principles and Standards for School Mathematics provided by NCTM (2000) call for the exploration of realistic applications that result in meaningful learning, the authors know that "Thousands of American students still work from textbooks that limit applications to age problems and the mixture of nuts" (p. ix). Glazer and McConnell believe ". . . students should have an opportunity to see a broad expanse of math applications so they can find links between their interests and aspirations and their mathematics coursework" (p. x). You undoubtedly will welcome the examples in this book that offer practical uses for concepts such as complex numbers, symmetry, polynomial functions, square roots, Cartesian coordinates, and the Fibonacci sequence.

Gonnick, L., & Smith, W. (2005). *The Cartoon Guide to Statistics.* New York: CollinsReference. (H)

Consider gathering your own statistics before introducing this book. For example, how many of your students think learning statistics will be easy? fun? challenging? impossible? doable? What are the chances that everyone will pass the end-of-unit exam? Students' anxiety will lessen as they enjoy the cartoons and read the captions, speech bubbles, and surrounding text that explain terms and concepts such as distributions, variables, hypothesis testing, experimental design, sampling, confidence intervals, and regression.

Hartston, W. (2000). *The Book of Numbers: The Ultimate Compendium of Facts and Figures.* London: Metro. (H)

This book will be great to have on your library shelf for those students who have just a minute or two to spare, and for those who get hooked on the numerically ordered compilation of number-related facts. The author explains the book's purpose:

As a work of reference, it is designed to answer any question beginning with the words "How Many . . . ?", particularly questions that you would never have thought of asking in the first place. (Preface, unpaged)

I opened the book at random, to number 49. I found a verse from a folk song; a definition of a "forty-niner"; lists of films and books with the number in their titles; and facts, such as that 49 is the number of:

- instant lottery tickets sold every second in Britain,
- phonetic symbols of the zhuyin zimu pronunciation alphabet, officially promulgated in 1918 by the Chinese government,
- professional fights fought and won by Rocky Marciano,
- years of age at which your mind is in its prime [according to Aristotle] . . . (unpaged)

You get the idea of the breadth of this work. Use this text when teaching curricular topics relating to number theory.

Kuhn, H. W., & Nasar, S. (2002). *The Essential John Nash.* Princeton, NJ: Princeton University Press. (H)

I recommend placing this in your class library right next to Nasar's *A Beautiful Mind* (1998). Have your students read the biography first; many may have seen the movie of the same title. Some students will then be eager to read Kuhn and Nasar's follow-up, which uses John Nash's own words to describe his contributions to the field of mathematics. This book includes the text of nine of his papers, and presents a photo essay of the years covering his career. A fascinating life story (complete with his remarriage to Alecia in 2001), and stimulating math—what a great combination for our learners. Your students who need a challenge and who can go beyond the minimum curricular expectations can explore this book along with T. Siegfried's (2006) *A Beautiful Math: John Nash, Game Theory, and the Modern Quest for a Code of Nature* (Washington, DC: Joseph Henry Press).

MATH

Odifreddi, P. (2004). *The Mathematical Century: The 30 Greatest Problems of the Last 100 Years.* Trans. A. Sangalli. Princeton, NJ: Princeton University Press. **(H)**

Sometimes our students have the idea that literature changes, science develops, history continues to happen, but math—well, math is just there. The author counteracts that inaccurate perception. This book offers a lively tale of the development of math over the past century, with some open-ended problems presented for twenty-first-century mathematicians (i.e., your students) to try.

Posamentier, A. S. (2003). *Math Charmers: Tantalizing Tidbits for the Mind.* Amherst, NY: Prometheus Books. **(M, H)**

In 2002, the author wrote an article in the *New York Times* that ". . . called for the need to inspire people by the beauty of mathematics and not necessarily its usefulness, as is most often the case when trying to motivate youngsters to the subject" (p. 19). After receiving more than 500 e-mails and letters in response, he decided to write this book. And it is full of beauty. For example, the author takes the year number 2002, a palindrome (reads the same backward or forward). He gives some selected products of 2002: (2,002 3 4 5 8,008; 2,002 3 98 5 196,196; 2,002 3 444 5 888,888; etc.). He alludes to the "beautiful relationships (or quirks) of our number system" (p. 20). Even the chapter titles, including "Some Arithmetic Marvels," "Algebraic Entertainment," "Geometric Wonders," "Mathematical Potpourri," are inviting. And the subsections, such as "The Pigeonhole Principle," "The Amazing Number 1,089," "Some Mind-bogglers on P," "The Fabulous Fibonacci Numbers," are equally enticing. Students can learn about numerous math concepts, including polyhedrons, invariants, proofs, logic, concentric circles, successive averages, percentages, and number patterns, all while pondering beauty.

Salsburg, D. (2001). *The Lady Tasting Tea: How Statistics Revolutionized Science in the Twentieth Century.* New York: W.H. Freeman. **(H)**

Statistics and probability theory through story— what a fascinating way to teach. The author's purpose is to help the nonmathematician catch up, because, "By the end of the twentieth century, almost all of science had shifted to using statistical models. Popular culture has failed to keep up with this scientific revolution" (p. viii). After reading chapters like "The Dose That Kills," "The Mozart of Mathematics," "When Part Is Better Than the Whole," "The Picasso of Statistics," "The Computer Turns Upon Itself," and "Advice from the Lady in Black," Your students will be ready to see where the revolution will go from here. Use the examples and explanations in this book to teach many statistical concepts and terms, such as experimental design, analysis of variance, correlation coefficient, normal distribution, resampling, regression to the mean, and fuzzy approximation.

Seife, C. (2000). *Zero: The Biography of a Dangerous Idea.* New York: Viking. **(H)**

I didn't have to look farther than the Table of Contents for my booktalk. The chapter titles are intriguing; there's Chapter 4, "The Infinite God of Nothing: The Theology of Zero," and Chapter 5, "Infinite Zeros and Infidel Mathematicians: Zero and the Scientific Revolution." The book will surprise students to find there was a time when the concept of zero was unknown, and times when its existence had to be argued for, sometimes at great personal cost. They'll want to read Chapter 8, "Zero Hour at Ground Zero: Zero at the Edge of Space and Time," and continue on to the final chapter, which is labeled with an infinity symbol rather than a number: "Zero's Final Victory: End Time." Sounds like a winner at the finish (or unfinished?) line! Turn to this book as you teach base systems, binary numbers, equations, imaginary numbers, and other curricular topics.

Shaffner, G. (1999). *The Arithmetic of Life.* New York: Ballantine Books. **(H)**

For students who might think math is unimportant, try pointing them to this book. The author illustrates that, in this Information Age, ". . . Now is not a good time to be a Math Refugee" (p. xii). Who fits this category? Shaffner includes

> . . . tailgaters who cause one-sixth of all traffic accidents in return for getting to work about two seconds sooner . . . teenagers who leave high school just before their senior year, when a diploma could be worth half a million dollars more to them in future income . . . that coworker . . . who apparently feels no personal obligations to perform actual work . . . (p. xiii)

Chapters highlight these subjects, among many others. Have your students follow along as he uses math to calculate the chances of there being life after death! This book can serve to motivate and build background knowledge in curricular areas involving statistics and probability.

Sossinsky, A. (2002). *Knots: Mathematics with a Twist.* Cambridge, MA: Harvard University Press. **(H)**

The author, recognized mathematician and expert on knot theory, points out that mathematical theories of knots are of concern to physicists, chemists, and biologists. He speculates on the audience for this book:

> . . . those with a solid scientific background, young people who like mathematics, and others, more numerous, who feel they have no aptitude for math as a result of their experiences in school but whose natural curiosity remains intact. (p. viii)

We may have students in each of the latter two categories; however, give them books like this one and some might end up in the first. There are also curricular connections for **science** as well as math to topics including atoms, polynomials, and finite-order invariants.

Stewart, I. (2006). *Letters to a Young Mathematician.* New York: Basic Books. **(H)**

The title sold me. It's so important for your students to take on the identity of mathematicians as they explore your curricula. The book consists of a series of letters to Meg, who starts out as a high school student contemplating a career in math. Some of the chapter titles ask questions: "Hasn't It All Been Done?", "Can't Computers Solve Everything?", "Pure or Applied?", "Where Do You Get Those Crazy Ideas?", and "Is God a Mathematician?" Having this book in your classroom library as a resource lets your students know that you recognize they have the potential to pursue mathematics as a career or an avocation, and that you support them 100 percent. It would also be a good resource for the job shadowing strategy presented earlier in this chapter.

Wainer, H. (2005). *Graphic Discovery: A Trout in the Milk and Other Visual Adventures.* Princeton, NJ: Princeton University Press. **(H)**

How can one resist an author who begins his Introduction with, "Let me begin with a few kind words about the bubonic plague" (p. 1)? Wainer begins his history of the use of graphs here, and takes us up to the "Graphical Displays of the Twenty-First Century" (p. 115). The book abounds with examples of real graphs from a variety of sources, along with clear explanations and intriguing stories. **Language arts** as well as math teachers can use this book to help students appreciate how ubiquitous graphs are for visually displaying information in virtually every area of academics and everyday life. Students will learn to be critical consumers who can recognize when graphs have been used to distort or misrepresent data and/or lead to faulty conclusions. In a chapter titled "Sex, Smoking and Life Insurance: A Graphical View," the author gives a practical example of how statistics are graphed and used to make decisions or defend policies.

Wells, D. G. (2005). *Prime Numbers: The Most Mysterious Figures in Math.* Hoboken, NJ: Wiley. **(H)**

In case your students think math is static, unchanging, and that there's nothing new to discover, this book provides an A–Z guide to the primes, including not-yet-solved conjectures, and stories of mathematicians, living as well as long gone, who have worked on prime-related puzzles. There are suggestions for websites and more books at the end. The author's Note at the beginning should impress your class:

> As this book went to press, the record for the largest known prime number was broken by Dr. Martin Nowak, a German eye specialist who is a member of the worldwide GIMPS (Great Internet Mersenne Prime Search) project, after fifty days of searching on his 2.4GHZ Pentium 4 personal computer. His record prime is $2^{25,964,951}-1$ and has 7,816,230 digits. (p. 5)

Ask your students to see if that record has been broken. By searching, they might learn about a new club they can join!

MUSIC

Ganeri, A., & Barber, N. (2001). *The Young Person's Guide to the Opera.* New York: Harcourt. **(I, M, H)**

This book was written and published in association with the Royal Opera House and the San Diego Opera. Text and pictures explain various types of opera, such as classical, grand, and modern. The authors provide story lines from operas, feature famous opera houses and stars, and entice readers to imagine designing sets and costumes. The book comes with a CD, and the 11 songs are introduced and discussed in a separate chapter. Use this terrific book as part of a literary field trip to one of the great opera houses you've planned for your students (see the activity in Part 2 of this chapter).

Getzinger, D., & Felsenfeld, D. (2004). *Johann Sebastian Bach and the Art of Baroque Music.* Greensboro, NC: Morgan Reynolds. **(M, H)**

This book is part biography, but goes beyond to introduce musical terms and concepts, as well as the historical context of Bach's work. Readers learn, for example, that in northern Germany in the early eighteenth century, a Protestant sect known as the Pietists considered Bach's ornate compositions to be ". . . self-indulgent and therefore disrespectful to God. This was difficult for Bach to understand, for he considered his music to be his highest form of tribute to God" (p. 60). The photographs of organs, church interiors, a Bach composition, and a receipt for his salary as organist are awe-inspiring. See the

Glossary of Musical Terms for teaching vocabulary and concepts related to the music curriculum.

Handyside, C. (2006). *Folk.* Chicago: Heinemann Library. **(I, M)**

The text explains the evolution of the folk music genre throughout the decades; connects it to social movements and key historical events and people; and discusses the sounds, techniques, and musical instruments that characterize folk music. The photographs depict icons such as Bob Dylan; Woody Guthrie; Joan Baez; Pete Seeger; Simon and Garfunkel; and Peter, Paul, & Mary, as well as musicians who represent the present and future of folk music, such as Ani DiFranco and Beck. The timeline at the back weaves historical events and key moments in the history of folk music. As students in music classes sing and listen to classic folk tunes, they'll be participating in a great tradition. **Social studies** as well as music teachers can use this along with other books in the "A History of American Music" series, including books about blues, rock, country, jazz, and soul, to help students appreciate how music changes as it's influenced by happenings in society, and how music has been a part of social movements that have impacted the history of our country.

Krull, K. (2003). *M Is for Music.* **Illus. S. Innerst.** New York: Harcourt. **(M, H)**

What would life be without music? This book begins with an answer from philosopher Friedrich Nietzsche, "Without music, life would be a mistake." Then Helen Keller speaks to us, "Hear the music of voices, the song of the bird, the mighty strains of an orchestra, as if you would be stricken deaf tomorrow" (unpaged).

M Is for Music will help you follow this advice as you view music vocabulary, accompanied by pictures, from A to Z. You might wonder at pages that celebrate H for Hildegarde, k for klezmer, and z for zydeco and zither, zapateade, and zarzuela, but the endnotes help with explanations. Use this book to introduce students to musical terminology that they'll need for future lessons.

Lesh, P. (2005). *Searching for the Sound: My Life with The Grateful Dead.* Boston: Little, Brown & Company. **(H)**

As a former member of The Grateful Dead, Phil Lesh gives an insider's perspective on the decades-long run of the legendary rock band that still interests both young and old. He believes that "Music can define life itself, and it has indeed defined my life" (p. 3). The author explains how a group collaborates to produce something new, powerful, and inspiring.

Some of our present-day students also live for their music, and make music an integral part of their lives. Consider using this book as a springboard to other books about musicians and music movements. For example, guide students to find comparisons and contrasts using this book and Getzinger's and Felsenfeld's *Johann Sebastian Bach and the Art of Baroque Music* (2004), introduced above.

Levitin, D. J. (2006). *This Is Your Brain on Music: The Science of a Human Obsession.* New York: Dutton. **(H)**

As is evident from the title of the book, as well as that of the author's Introduction ("I Love Music and I Love Science—Why Would I Want to Mix the Two?"), **science** teachers and music teachers in a school could use this book to break down the artificial boundaries of academic disciplines. Daniel Levitin defines and explains various aspects of music, discusses how we categorize music, "dissects" expertise to explore what makes a musician, and helps readers investigate emotional responses to music. Start by surveying your students about their favorite types of music, then use this book to deepen their understanding and appreciation of the rich combination of **art** and **science** that is embodied in music.

Lommel, C. (2001). *The History of Rap Music.* Philadelphia: Chelsea House Publishers. **(M, H)**

The chapters do provide a chronological history of rap and hip-hop music. Students might be surprised to find that rap has its roots in the stories and culture brought to America long ago by African slaves. But teachers can also use the book to provoke thought and debate about many political issues of today. A chapter titled "Politics of an Art Form" discusses and gives examples of censorship and First Amendment issues, lawsuits over copyright infringement due to sampling, ". . . the electronic copying of snippets from another artist's recordings" (p. 75), and the ongoing discussion as to what constitutes pornography. Have students add information about this genre of music in the years following this book's publication to continue discussion of these issues.

With this book both music teachers and **history** teachers can help students cross disciplinary boundaries. Encourage students to create rap songs with political messages and their opinions about current events.

Rappaport, D. (2004). *Free at Last: Stories and Songs of Emancipation.* **Illus. S. W. Evans.** Cambridge, MA: Candlewick Press. **(I, M, H)**

The author takes readers from 1863, the year of the Emancipation Proclamation, to 1954, the year of the Supreme Court decision that declared school segregation illegal. The artist, Shane W. Evans, gives good advice for how to read this book:

... it is easy to lose sight of the fact that we continue to be divided by boundaries of our own making. We continually fail to realize that we are all simply human. So as you read the words and gaze at the images in this "our story," put yourself in the shoes of these people who fought and loved so hard, for they are all of us. (p. 59)

Interspersed among the stories of the leaders and the lesser-known, but no less brave, citizens who lived through these troubled times are the words and music to songs that were integral to a people who had great pride despite their oppression. They include "Free at Last" (p. 12), "John Henry" whose subject "symbolizes the strength and resilience of all African Americans who helped build the nation" (p. 31), and "Lift Ev'ry Voice and Sing" (p. 39), which became known as the Negro National Anthem. As they sing these songs, students in music classes can learn about the power of music during social movements. The author tells us, "I followed the thread of slave spirituals, work songs, anthems, and blues. . . . I saw the special place of music and song in articulating feelings and in fortifying and unifying people" (p. 3).

Rappaport, D. (2002). *No More!: Stories and Songs of Slave Resistance.* Illus. S. W. Evans. Cambridge, MA: Candlewick Press. **(I, M, H)**

Social studies classes as well as music classes can delve into the historical account provided here through the true stories of courageous individuals and the music of enslaved Africans who, as they learned a strange language, ". . . created new songs to describe their new lives. They counted up the wrongs inflicted on them and vented their outrage" (p. 20). Moreover, they figured out ways to use music to communicate secret messages, as in "Gospel Train" (p. 43), that would lead fellow slaves to freedom via the Underground Railroad. Have students sing these spirited, meaningful, emotion-evoking songs as a group, and discuss the power and implications of music used in subversive ways. From there, students can explore songs of protest from other eras, including our own.

PHYSICAL EDUCATION, HEALTH, AND WELLNESS

Davis, S., Jenkins, G., & Hunt, R., with S. Draper. (2005). *We Beat the Street: How a Friendship Pact Led to Success.* New York: Dutton Children's Books. **(M, H)**

Did you ever set a joint goal with a friend? Sometimes it's easier to achieve something if there's positive peer pressure, and this true story is a testament to that. The authors were childhood friends living in a tough neighborhood. They had their share of troubles, some brought on by poor decisions they made, but they made one excellent decision together—to support each other through college and become doctors. Dr. George Jenkins reflects:

We also had no idea that day that we were forming a pact that would last a lifetime. We just knew that somehow each of us individually might fail, but the strength of the three of us together just might be enough to succeed. (p. 99)

Succeed they did, and now "The Three Doctors," as they call themselves, work in their old community. Looking for role models? Here are three. Looking for materials for character education lessons? Here's the book. Health teachers and others will relish the authors' narratives about positive and negative peer pressure.

Haduch, B. (2004). *Go Fly a Bike!: The Ultimate Book About Bicycle Fun, Freedom & Science.* Illus. C. Murphy. New York: Dutton Children's Books. **(I, M, H)**

The 83 easy-to-read pages in this book include hundreds of fascinating details and helpful suggestions. Science principles are embedded in real-life stories within chapters carrying enticing titles like "The Problem at the Center of the Earth: It's Called Gravity," "There's Something in the Air: Aerodynamics and Your Bike," and "The Bicycle Balancing Act: How and Why Your Bike Stays Up." The author gives the history of the bicycle and reports on many "Extremely Cool Bike Events." This excellent book will help your students learn about Olympic events and champions, the Tour de France, competition opportunities for a variety of bike types, and the choice of biking as a lifetime physical activity. The cartoons throughout add to the fun. Health and physical education teachers can use this book as they teach about safety and exercise. (See booktalk section in Chapter 7 also.)

Levenson, G. (2004). *Bread Comes to Life: A Garden of Wheat and a Loaf to Eat.* Photography by S. Thaler. Berkeley, CA: Tricycle Press. **(E, I, M)**

Don't use this book before lunch; students will get so hungry when they look at these appetizing photos of bagels, black bread, pizza, and pita bread that they won't be able to pay attention. The author guides readers through the process of growing, harvesting and grinding grains, blending ingredients and kneading the dough, and baking variations of "the staff of life" (unpaged). Endnotes give tips for readers who want to grow a plot of wheat, or make wheat chewing gum. The book provides a recipe

MUSIC

PE/HEALTH

along with the author's blessing, "May all be fed" (unpaged). Use this book when instructing about nutrition and food groups, and encourage students to find out more at the companion Internet site, www.breadcomestolife.com.

Rimm, S., with S. Rimm-Kaufman. (2001). *How Jane Won: 55 Successful Women Share How They Grew from Ordinary Girls to Extraordinary Women.* New York: Crown Publishers. **(M, H)**

Our students wonder what their futures hold, they dream dreams, they worry. This book helps readers understand that there are many definitions of success, that many paths can lead to fulfilling careers and vocations, that present obstacles don't have to keep young people from achieving high goals. Sections of the book share stories of women involved in law careers, women who have shattered the glass ceiling in corporations, women in health and science professions, nurturers, and artists, among others. Students can look through the list of job titles and choose the ones that most closely match their own hopes. Or they can just turn to chapters whose titles appeal to them. The first one I turned to was "Harry Potter Flew into Her Life," the story of illustrator Mary GrandPré. Maybe someone else would start with "Selling Jelly-Beans at Recess Was Her First Marketing Experience," which tells of Tamara Minick-Scokalo, a marketing director for Procter & Gamble.

Use this book in conjunction with the Job Shadowing activity in Part 2 of this chapter. It would serve health teachers, and indeed all teachers, who are working within their curricula to enhance the self-esteem of their students and help them to choose positive values and to set goals for their futures.

Rosen, M. (2004). *Michael Rosen's Sad Book.* Illus. Quentin Blake. Cambridge, MA: Candlewick Press. **(E, I, M, H)**

This book would be an excellent opening to a unit about grieving. Rosen shares his sadness over the death of his son Eddie. He admits to feelings of anger, even at Eddie for dying. He explains that sometimes he finds someone to talk to about his sadness. But that's not always what he needs:

> Sometimes I don't want to talk about it.
> Not to anyone. No one. No one at all.
> I just want to think about it on my own.
> Because it's mine. And no one else's. (unpaged)

Rosen goes on to share some of the ways he has figured out to have the sadness not hurt quite as much, such as trying to accomplish one thing each day he can be proud of, or writing about the sadness. He also thinks of happy memories of those who have died.

Readers will react to this book in different ways at different times, depending on whether they're experiencing deep sadness themselves, or trying to figure out how to help a friend who is grieving. The book works on many levels. Health teachers often deal with sensitive issues, including depression and death, in their curriculum. This book will help them introduce students to a real person who is coping with both.

Wideman, J. E. (2001). *Hoop Roots: Playground Basketball, Love, and Race.* Boston: Houghton Mifflin. **(H)**

This is a hard book to categorize, but your students won't mind. There are seven essays, and the author doesn't mind if we read them out of order. "Different pieces coming from different places—read them in sequence or improvise," he suggests in the Table of Contents. He confesses that he wrote this text for himself first, as a way to both hold on and let go. "Telling playground basketball stories, and if I tell them well they will be more about basketball than about me. Because the game rules. The game will assert its primacy" (pp. 3–4). Students love to tell what's so great about the sport or hobby they're passionate about; they can talk back to John Edgar Wideman. Include this book in your classroom library and encourage students to read about all aspects of sports as they get experiences on the school courts and fields.

SCIENCE

Colbert, G. (2005). *Ashes and Snow: Photographs.* New York: Flying Elephant Press. **(M, H)**

Is it possible to dissolve boundaries between humans and other species, between art and nature, between now and forever? That's what photographer Gregory Colbert has done. He combines the letters of an anonymous voyager to his wife with sepia-toned pictures of children serenely collaborating with elephants, eagles, and cheetahs. Through the photographs and letters, students will be transported to Egypt, Myanmar, and Namibia, where they might actively experience a shared understanding with Colbert's beasts. [Booktalk by Mary Harrell.]

Teachers can invite students to express their thoughts as they study the photographs, then share the article "Animal Magnetism," by Cathleen McGuigan (2005), which contains some of Colbert's photos and also tells of some of the negative criticism they have drawn. This might cause students to exercise their critical-thinking skills as they join the conversation.

PE/HEALTH

SCIENCE

Conniff, R. (2002). *Rats!: The Good, the Bad, and the Ugly.*
New York: Crown Publishers. **(I, M)**

I learned many facts through this book, maybe even more than I wanted to know! Some of the pictures are eerie, such as rats piled on top of one another, or Darwin, a hairless rat. The author tells of the role rats have played in times of plague and other diseases. But he also exposes common myths, such as that rats are dirty, and replaces misinformation with accurate facts. Throughout the book, chapters tell of the scientific and medical uses of rats, and discuss rats as pets. A 12-year-old rat owner has discovered that "They're smart.... I can teach them their names and they'll come when I call" (p. 32). Scientific experiments confirm that rats are intelligent:

> Rats will remember a winning scent even weeks later, and they can make logical deductions about what they've learned. For instance: If Sample A (the oregano) always contains the reward when it's paired with sample B (the cinnamon), but B always contains the reward when paired with C, rats are always smart enough to choose B over C, and C over D, and so on. What's the right choice when B is paired with D? Can't figure it out? A rat can. (p. 18)

Have students compare and contrast information found in this book with that in Albert Marren's (2006) *Oh, Rats!: The Story of Rats and People* (Illus. C. B. Mordan. New York: Dutton Children's Books). Neither book will collect dust on the shelf. Your students will go home with interesting answers for that "What'd you learn in school today?" ritual.

Davidson, S., & Morgan, B. (2002). *Human Body Revealed.*
New York: DK Publishing. **(I, M, H)**

Readers of this book are amazed at the computer images depicting the inside of the human body. Right away the authors introduce "a vertical slice through a nine-year-old boy, made by ... an MRI scanner" (p. 6). Close-ups show everything from bone cells to chromosomes, from lungs secreting mucus to kidneys sending wastes to the bladder. The images display muscles of the small intestine as they contract to push food along its way. Plastic overlays allow readers to see several layers within the body; parts are labeled and defined. The colors of the images and photographs are vibrant; the text is fascinating. No doubt, visual learners will benefit from the enlarged pictures of tiny things. And children who delight in details and numbers can recount to others that goose bumps are caused by tiny muscles pulling the base of hairs and producing lumps under nose hairs; fingernails grow at the rate of two inches per year; each of us has three mil-

lion sweat pores ... the list goes on. You will find this book a terrific aid as you teach about body systems and organs.

Dyson, F. (2006). *The Scientist as Rebel.* New York: New York Review Books. **(H)**

Many students will find the title of this book enticing, and the essays and stories within can help them understand science, as the author does, as a subversive activity, or as "... an alliance of free spirits in all cultures rebelling against the local tyranny that each culture imposes on its children" (p. 4). Guide your students to think critically as they read the chapters whose titles ask, "Can Science be Ethical?" and "Is God in the Lab?"

Dyson, F. J. (2004). *Infinite in All Directions.* New York: Perennial. **(H)**

This revised edition of a renowned theoretical physicist's essays on nuclear weapons, the beginning of life, space and black holes, string theory, the end of life, and butterflies will give your students much to think about. Freeman J. Dyson helps readers to understand that the debate raging among those who pit science against religion is based on a false dichotomy:

> I see science as a way of exploring the universe with a limited set of tools, and religion as another way of exploring with a different set of tools. Science uses telescopes and computers and differential equations. Religion uses music and painting and meditation and ritual and worship.... The two views are not in conflict, but they cannot both be seen at the same time. (p. xiv)

Use this book to help students make connections between various branches of science, including biology, physics, and astronomy.

Feynman, M. (Ed.). (2005). *Perfectly Reasonable Deviations from the Beaten Path: The Letters of Richard P. Feynman.* **(H)**

The letters of renowned physicist Richard Feynman are edited and introduced by his daughter, who also gives a glimpse of what it was like growing up with a father who was recognized as one of the smartest people in the world. Maria Feynman notes that scientists who knew her father were surprised that there even *was* a collection of existing letters, ranging from 1937 to 1987, to publish. "... he had a reputation in the physics community for not writing letters. Why had he spent so much time corresponding with the general public and not with his fellow scientists?" His daughter's hypothesis—that the reason he did so was that he loved to teach, and so when ordinary

SCIENCE

people wrote to him asking questions, he answered—is good news for science teachers today. For these letters will keep on teaching science topics, including nuclear power, the Challenger disaster, gravity, quarks, time and space dimensions, and astrophysics, if we make them available to our students.

Students will also be inspired by letters from people telling Richard Feynman how he influenced their lives. Frank Potter, for example, was an undergraduate when he met Feynman; he subsequently changed his career objective and earned a Ph.D. in physics. He writes, "That spirit which I saw you display continues to infect me in my career as a Lecturer in Physics here at UC Irvine" (p. 370).

Hartmann, W. K. (2003). *A Traveler's Guide to Mars: The Mysterious Landscapes of the Red Planet.* New York: Workman Publishing. (H)

The author guides readers through many types of travel in this book. The pages begin with a brightly colored foldout "Topographical Map of the Major Features of Mars, Derived from Mars Global Surveyor Laser Altimetry in 1997–2000" (unpaged). Hartmann invites us to visit the 40 hottest cold spots on Mars, to view volcanoes, rock formations, moons, mountains, and ice caps. But we can also travel back through geological time to think about the history of the red planet. The scientist/author explains how discoveries were made by various space missions. Many of the subsections are titled with questions that are then answered or pondered, such as, "Ancient Greenhouse Warming?" (p. 110), "Radar Maps a Coastline?" (p. 143), "Slow Flow or Sudden Flood?" (p. 222), "Where Do We Come From?" (p. 413).

Our tour guide discusses many theories, showing how scientists conjecture, dispute, come to consensus, and create new questions. In the conclusion, Hartmann notes that Mars beckons, and reminds us that while we know how to get there, in terms of spacecraft technology, ". . . the question is whether we humans have the will and resources to carry on, and whether we can agree on the benefits" (p. 434). He suggests that the readers of this book may be the first to make footsteps on Mars. That means our students might some day be thanking us for introducing them to the dream via books like this dreamer's guide! Use this excellent resource with the Reading and Writing Travel Journals activity in Part 2 of this chapter. Based on this book, have your students research and write their own travel journal to a planet or star of their choice as you continue your unit on space.

Highfield, R. (2002). *The Science of Harry Potter: How Magic Really Works.* New York: Viking. (M, H)

This book will fly off your shelves as fast as Harry's broomstick, but there will be a logical explanation for it, as there is for all the examples of magic discussed in the book. Highfield promises

> Harry's magical world can help illuminate rather than undermine science, casting a fascinating light on some of the most interesting issues that researchers struggle with today. Similarly, what we have learned from our scientific investigations in many fields can help explain many extraordinary and seemingly magical phenomena. (pp. xv–xvi)

After reading this book, your students will be teaching each other scientific principles explaining time travel, potions, invisibility, owl intelligence, mutated bodies, and clothes with cleaning bugs within the fabric. A chapter that will especially challenge students' minds is "The Mathematics of Evil," which explains game theory and its relationship to the languages Harry encounters during his adventures. It might lead students to other books, such as T. Siegfried's (2006) *A Beautiful Math: John Nash, Game Theory, and the Modern Quest for a Code of Nature* (Washington, DC: Joseph Henry Press).

Hoose, P. (2004). *The Race to Save the Lord God Bird.* New York: Farrar, Straus and Giroux. (M, H)

This book contains two emotion-evoking and thought-provoking stories. One contains the history of the ivory-billed woodpecker, and the story of its demise over the past 100 years from a flourishing species to a possibly extinct one. The author tells of hopeful birdwatchers for three decades before the publication of this book who would hear a report that the bird's call had been identified:

> Again and again, even the slimmest of rumors sends hopeful birdwatchers lunging for their boots, smearing mosquito repellent onto their arms, and bolting out the door to look for it. Year after year they return with soggy boots, bug-bitten arms, and no evidence. (pp. 4–5)

Your students will learn a larger story from Hoose's book—about the fight in general to save species from extinction caused by human consumption of resources. It's a fight to save natural habitats, and it involves politics and economics as well as science. He quotes ornithologist William Beebe to help readers understand the enormity of the concept of extinction: "When the last individual of a race of living things breathes no more, another heaven and earth must pass before such a one can be again" (p. 3).

Delight your students by helping them research developments since the actual sighting of the ivory-billed woodpecker in the spring of 2005. Hopeful news!

Le Couteur, P., & Burreson, J. (2003). *Napoleon's Buttons: How 17 Molecules Changed History.* New York: Jeremy P. Tarcher/Putnam. **(H)**

In the Introduction, the authors explain that this is not a book about the history of chemistry, but rather a collection of stories about chemistry *in* history:

> We will explain why we believe certain molecules were the impetus for geographic exploration, while others made possible the ensuing voyages of discovery. We will describe molecules . . . that were responsible for human migrations and colonization, and that led to slavery. . . . We will look at molecules that spurred advances in medicine. . . . We will explore how many changes in gender roles, in human cultures and society, in law, and in the environment can be attributed to the chemical structures of a small number of crucial molecules. (p. 6)

Consider reading excerpts from this book at the beginning of a chemistry course, for it sets the stage nicely for a year of making connections that will cause students to think scientifically, to be open to new cause–effect relationships. But I recommend skipping the story that explains the title of the book. Instead, encourage your students to open the book themselves during Independent Reading (see Chapter 2) to see if the book can convince them that little tin buttons led to the defeat of Napoleon.

Pass this gem along to your colleagues in the **history** department, too.

Miles, V. (2004). *Wild Science: Amazing Encounters Between Animals and the People Who Study Them.* Vancouver: Raincoast Books. **(I, M, H)**

Use the words of the author's dedication as you send your students into this book: "To Emily, may your heart lead and your head follow." Each chapter is organized into four parts. The first, "From the Field," introduces your students to a particular case involving wild animals. Part II, "The Scientist," supplies biographical information, along with a photograph and a quote, about a present-day biologist. The third part teaches relevant scientific information, and finally we're treated to "Animal Notes," facts and figures about the featured animal, whether it be the leatherback sea turtle, the silver-haired bat, the gray wolf, or the grizzly bear. Assign teams of scientists from your class one of the 10 chapters to study, and have them follow up with a presentation for their colleagues who have been off studying different wild life with other experts. (See the Jigsaw activity in Part 2 of this chapter.)

Parker, B. (2003). *The Isaac Newton School of Driving: Physics and Your Car.* Baltimore: The Johns Hopkins University Press. **(H)**

Some of your students would rather be driving around or working on their cars than be in science class. This book entertains and teaches as it explains the physics principles involved in driving and in car design and maintenance. Students might especially enjoy Chapter 8, "A Crash Course: The Physics of Collisions"; and racing fans will enjoy Chapter 9, "Checkered Flags: the Physics of Auto Racing." Those with car-owning plans in their dreams will turn to Chapter 11, "The Road Ahead: Cars of the Future." Many students will find tests easier to study for once they read these authentic applications of curricular concepts such as force, momentum, friction, energy, thermodynamics, and chaos theory. Helpful diagrams are interspersed throughout.

Pert, C. B. (1997). *Molecules of Emotion: Why You Feel How You Feel.* New York: Scribner. **(H)**

Studying for a chemistry test might seem worlds away from real life to many students. To read a book that connects chemistry to emotions, which they most certainly are interested in, can bridge a gap. Besides giving lots of explanations about the causes of certain good and not so good feelings, the author offers recommendations, "Prevention-Oriented Tips for Healthful, Blissful Living" (p. 321). Your students will have lots to talk about. Many terms they have encountered in biology and or chemistry classes, including *paradigm, psychosomatic, receptors, placebo effect, neurons, ribosomes, biomolecular,* and *neurochemistry,* are used in authentic contexts. In addition, students get to know about the life of a research scientist, as Candice Pert shares stories both in and out of the lab.

Platt, R. (2003). *Eureka!: Great Inventions and How They Happened.* Boston: Kingfisher. **(I, M, H)**

Photographs and text work together to aid readers in experiencing many "eureka moments" (p. 9) in the history of science, including the invention of the pendulum, nylon, DNA fingerprinting, the Polaroid camera, video games, and the Internet. The book explains how scientists and others construct and then test theories. For example, Edward Jenner, a doctor during the time when smallpox killed one-tenth of all children in Great Britain, experienced his eureka moment when he heard a dairymaid brag that she could not get smallpox because she had once caught cowpox from cows. After that, he noticed that his patients who had caught cowpox didn't get smallpox, so he tested the theory by infecting a healthy person with cowpox, then repeating

SCIENCE

the experiment on the boy with puss from a small-pox victim. He called his way of immunizing someone *vaccination*. Thanks to his courage and insight, smallpox was wiped out. Your classroom might become filled with a new generation of inventors as a result of introducing this book. They'll learn facts related to curricular topics involving light, electricity, and disease, while being inspired by the perseverance and insightfulness of the inventors presented in these pages.

Pringle, L. (1997). *An Extraordinary Life: The Story of a Monarch Butterfly.* Illus. B. Marshall. New York: Orchard Books. (E, I, M)

When your students picture the size and fragility of a single butterfly and then look at the opening map depicting its journey from a field in Massachusetts to its landing in the southern part of Mexico, they'll be ready for the adventure detailed in the text of this book. After explaining the beginnings of a caterpillar's life, Pringle proposes, "Let's call this caterpillar, the one that emerged from her mother's last egg, Danaus" (p. 13). We're privy to a very detailed account of Danaus's transition from caterpillar to butterfly, complete with pictures of stages as pupa and chrysalis. Then, "Without thought, without practice, Danaus gave her wings a powerful down-stroke. Her feet lifted off of the stem. She was moving up, up through the air. She began to explore the world as a butterfly" (p. 20). In the following chapters, we travel across the continent with Danaus at a rate of 80 miles per day, experiencing threats from predators and weather. Final chapters give information on saving the monarchs' winter refuges and on raising monarch butterflies.

Use this book as a model when your students research other animals; they can create a story about one creature they have named, giving facts throughout the story about the animal's habitat and habits.

Ridley, M. (1999). *Genome: The Autobiography of a Species in 23 Chapters.* New York: HarperCollins. (H)

The author cleverly uses a book analogy to teach his scientific topic. If the genome is a book, then the chromosomes are chapters, and the genes, stories. He extends the metaphor: "The genome is a very clever book, because in the right conditions it can both photocopy itself and read itself. The photocopying is known as REPLICATION, and the reading as TRANS-LATION" (p. 7). Ridley's chapters focus on genetics-related topics ranging from fate to free will, and including death, stress, personality, politics, intelligence, instinct, and sex.

Students will learn an enormous amount from this readable book, and will be able to ponder and debate statements such as the one at the end of the chapter on eugenics:

> Many modern accounts of the history of eugenics present it as an example of the dangers of letting science, genetics especially, out of control. It is much more an example of the danger of letting government out of control. (p. 300)

For an appropriate post-reading activity, have your students explore the advances that have occurred since the publication of this book, perhaps looking for things Ridley himself has written.

Stonehouse, B. (2000). *Partners.* Illus. J. Francis. New York: Tangerine Press. (I, M, H)

Talk about cooperation! This text explains the relationships between animals that form partnerships with another species, often with mutual benefits. Readers learn about striped remoras, fish with suckers by which they clamp onto the undersides of sharks, thus assured that predators will stay away. Challenge your students to compile a chart about whom they think benefits more and why from such pairings as black garden ants and rose aphids, gray hornbills and green monkeys, Galapagos red crabs and marine iguanas, ostriches and zebras. There are "barber fish" who obtain nutrition by cleaning the mouths of large, dangerous fish. Their hosts benefit because this grooming keeps them free from parasites and disease-causing organisms. The last page stimulates thinking and discussion about the relationships between animals and humans.

Watson, J., with A. Berry. (2003). *DNA: The Secret of Life.* New York: Alfred A. Knopf. (H)

The 159 photographs in this history of genetics as recounted by the scientist who, at age 24, discovered the double helix configuration of DNA tell a story of their own. Enlarged pictures depict normal and deformed fruit fly faces; a couple of pair-bonded prairie voles seemingly reading and ". . . pondering the DNA sequence of the gene that makes them so lovey-dovey" (p. 386); a child whose immune system disorder made it necessary for him to live in a plastic bubble; a portrait of James Watson drawn by a nine-year-old gene-therapy patient; protesters carrying signs against eugenics and cloning; a beautiful colored picture of "The cell's protein factory, the ribosome, in all its 3-D glory as revealed by X-ray analysis" (p. 62). The text includes stories about real people's dilemmas and how they relate to genetics: If parents learn through pre-natal testing that their child will have Down syndrome, what are the options? How are gene mappers tackling the genetic components of mental illnesses such as schizophre-

SCIENCE

nia and bipolar disease? "Germ-line gene therapy has the potential for making humans resistant to the ravages of HIV. . . . But should this be pursued?" (p. 399). This book is full of information, explanations of concepts, and opportunities for critical thinking. You will not hear students asking, "Why do we have to learn this stuff?" if you use excerpts from this book when you teach about DNA.

Winchester, S. (2003). *Krakatoa: The Day the World Exploded, August 27, 1888.* New York: HarperCollins. **(H)**

The author opens with a quote from one of my favorite fantasy books, Antoine de Saint-Exupery's *The Little Prince* (1943), which is fitting, because the quote is about volcanoes, and because Simon Winchester tells the story of the Krakatoa's eruption with a tone of amazement and awe that we sometimes reserve for the supernatural. He shows a geologist's respect for the cataclysmic event, and tells his own stories of visiting the site of the eruption, learning about it, and also pondering its meaning and relevance. He explains:

> . . . in learning of these places and of the terrible events that occurred there, so the world's people suddenly became part of a new brotherhood of knowledge—in a sense it was that day in August 1883 that the modern phenomenon known as "the global village" was born . . . the disaster left a trail of practical consequences— political, religious, social, economic, psychological, and scientific. . . . (p. 6)

Use this book to teach about tsunamis, volcanoes, and geology-related terminology, as well as how scientists track the effects and ramifications of natural disasters. Students will incidentally learn a lot of geography from the maps, illustrations, and text.

Wise, S. M. (2002). *Drawing the Line: Science and the Case for Animal Rights.* Cambridge, MA: Perseus Books. **(H)**

This is a great interdisciplinary book, since the author teaches animal rights law at Harvard Law School and works in legal arguments throughout. He uses a similar structure in each chapter. In one chapter, he introduces Alex, who has been taught to communicate, to mentally represent, and to count. Then he poses the question, "Does Alex Have a Self?" (p. 109). Alex is a bird. In another chapter, we meet Phoenix and Ake. They have grammar, they can make sense of nonsense, they use words to symbolize the world, they have self-awareness, but do they have practical autonomy? Phoenix and Ake are dolphins. Wise shows through numerous examples how gorillas and orangutans meet the criteria for personhood, and argues that for this reason they are entitled to

legal rights. Students may use this book as a starting place as they think through some tough issues and decide their position on the case for animal rights.

SOCIAL STUDIES/HISTORY

Aronson, M. (2005). *The Real Revolution: The Global Story of American Independence.* New York: Clarion Books. **(M, H)**

For many students of American history, there's an "us" and a "them." They've learned in the elementary grades about the British policies and practices that caused the Patriots to rebel. They know the phrase "Taxation without Representation." But have they ever wondered what British schools teach about the American Revolution? And about what was happening in other parts of the world at the same time? Aronson's book will help teachers provide insight about the big picture of the late eighteenth century. Perhaps as important, at the end of the book the author speaks to his readers, explaining that, while the revolution was fought because the people in America no longer wanted to be part of an empire, the United States now has a turn at handling global leadership:

> We have become the even more potent successor of the empire we overthrew. That is both our danger and our challenge. Can we learn from our own past . . . ? In large part, that is up to readers of books like this. . . . The danger of empire is arrogance, the assumption that a nation is better because it is stronger. It was that outlook that cost England first America, then India, then all its colonies." (pp. 189–190)

Aronson believes that his readers will have a part in determining the role of our country in the future. Consider this a very good place to begin a class discussion.

Bausum, A. (2004). *With Courage and Cloth: Winning the Fight for a Woman's Right to Vote.* Washington, DC: National Geographic. **(M, H)**

I was hooked from the author's opening sentences:

> Once Alice Paul and I stood head to head and eye to eye. I was 13 years old; she was eighty-six. . . . My father, who introduced us, explained at the time how this wizened old woman had fought years earlier for my right to vote. I didn't doubt it. Plenty of flame remained in her eyes. (p. 7)

This book gives background in one chapter devoted to the years 1848 through 1906, but most of the chapters focus on the years from 1906 to 1920, the years Alice Paul was most active in shaping history with her fellow suffragists.

SCIENCE

SS/HIS

I was intrigued by the title, and soon found an explanation. Bausum explained that fighters for the cause of voting rights for women:

> . . . instead of taking up guns and swords, armed themselves with courage and cloth.
>
> Cloth was a fitting choice. It was a substance all women knew intimately, having woven, sewn, cleaned, and mended it for generations. . . . Women turned it into sashes, made it into signs, and sewed it into flags. Just choosing to wear clothing of a certain color—the signature choice was white—put a woman into uniform for the fight. (pp. 8–9)

After the final chapter, "Victory: 1919–1920," there are photographs and profiles of key women, a Chronology beginning with the adoption of the U.S. Constitution in 1788, and a Resource guide with information about places to visit, either actually or virtually. This book makes the curricular topic of the long fight for women's right to vote come alive.

Bial, R. (2002). *Tenement: Immigrant Life on the Lower East Side.* Boston: Houghton Mifflin. **(M, H)**

Can there be a beautiful book about poverty? Your students will see photographs and read stories of beautiful people in surroundings that are anything but beautiful. They will appreciate the circumstances that trapped so many immigrants who, though extremely hardworking, struggled because of low wages, prejudice, and other seemingly overwhelming obstacles. They'll see hope refusing to be squelched, and they'll read of some ways that the immigrants eventually survived, sometimes even thrived, making tremendous contributions to our society. This book makes the important curricular topic of immigration become real for students. Use this book along with historical fiction such as Kathryn Lasky's (1998) *Dreams in the Golden Country: The Diary of Zipporah Feldman, a Jewish Immigrant Girl* (New York: Scholastic), which is set in the lower East Side of New York City in 1903–1904.

Brennan, L. C. (2004). *The Black Regiment of the American Revolution.* Illus. C. K. Noll. North Kingston, RI: Moon Mountain Publishing. **(I, M)**

In 1777, the Rhode Island legislature passed a law saying that slaves who enlisted in a designated regiment would be freed and compensated at the same rate as white soldiers. This book chronicles the battles involving the regiment, as well as historians' analyses of the effects and importance of their role. Sidebars give details of such topics as weapons, leaders, battles, and uniforms. You can help your students see the parallels in types of freedom being sought during the American Revolution: freedom from British rule, and personal freedom within the colonial society. Students will be moved by a poem written by young Lemuel Hayes of the regiment:

> For liberty, each freeman strives
> as it's a gift of God
> and for it yield their lives
> much better there in death confin'd
> than surviving as a slave. (p. 26)

Buckley, S., & Leacock, E. (2006). *Kids Make History: A New Look at America's Story.* Illus. R. Jones. Boston: Houghton Mifflin. **(I, M, H)**

American history is not just the story of what adults accomplished and perpetrated over the past several centuries, though our students might get that idea if the classroom textbook is all they have to go by. This book tells of significant events and time periods from the perspectives and actions of youths. Readers learn about the part 12-year-old Ann Putnam had in initiating the Salem witch trials in 1692. They meet Susie Baker, a 13-year-old freed slave rejoicing at Abraham Lincoln's Emancipation Proclamation in 1863. They vicariously experience the bombing of Pearl Harbor in 1941 along with nine-year-old Joan Zuber, and travel the migrant worker circuit with sixth grader Francisco Jiminez in 1955. They can join teenager Malcolm Hooks in Birmingham in 1963 as he marches for freedom and endures arrest and imprisonment, as well as Stuyvesant High School student Jukay Hsu as he works as a Red Cross volunteer on September 11, 2001. This book would work well as part of the "Analyzing Attributes of Fiction and Nonfiction Texts" strategy described in Chapter 4, since the authors note, "We use double quotation marks when we know exactly what someone said or thought. We use single quotation marks when we have invented statements based on historical evidence" (p. 2).

Cohn, S. (2004). *Liberty's Children: Stories of Eleven Revolutionary War Children.* Guilford, CT: Globe Pequot Press. **(M, H)**

I have found that students are fascinated by historical lessons and materials that highlight people their own age. Scotti Cohn offers an alternative or supplement to the standard school fare. "History books usually do not describe how a nine-year-old Massachusetts boy might have felt when his friend was killed in the Boston Massacre or what went through the mind of a teenage Quaker girl when her family fled Philadelphia" (Introduction, unpaged). The author presents stories involving African Americans and Native Americans. This book enhances the curriculum relating to the American Revolution, by providing ". . . a clear picture of what life was like for the average person during the years before, during, and immediately after the war" (Introduction).

Compston, C., & Seidman, R. F. (Eds.). (2004). *Our Documents: 100 Milestone Documents from the National Archives.* New York: Oxford University Press. **(M, H)**

Take your students on a literary field trip (see Part 2 of this chapter) to the National Archives; the collections in this archive can help them see just how real history is and can serve as a great resource as their year of American history progresses. In the Foreword, Michael Beschloss gives a hint of the thrill of the National Archives when he describes ". . . the hermetically sealed cases filled with inert helium gas, the device that would plunge the documents into an underground vault at the first hint of impending vandalism, fire, or nuclear war" (p. 7).

Students can use the documents here to create their own document-based questions (see activity in Part 2 of this chapter). Have your students work at making relationships and connections, and I believe they'll come to an appreciation similar to Beschloss's for the Constitution and other writings. "For twenty-one decades, we had protected those pieces of parchment, and for twenty-one decades, the basic ideas they embodied had protected all of us" (p. 7).

Crew, D. F. (2005). *Hitler and the Nazis: A History in Documents.* New York: Oxford University Press. **(M, H)**

The book begins with a definition and explanation of what a document is, followed by instructions on how to read a document. Relevant documents are found on virtually every one of the 157 pages, along with reader-friendly text. The title of the first chapter asks the question, "What Made Nazism Possible?" and the rest of the book answers that question and many more about the years of Nazi power. Teachers will appreciate this book as a great resource for document-based questions (see the strategy in Part 2 of this chapter). Students will find the photographs, posters, political cartoons, quotes, and stories fascinating.

Edwards, J. (2003). *The Great Expedition of Lewis and Clark, by Private Reubin Field, Member of the Corps of Discovery.* **Illus. S. W. Comport.** New York: Farrar Straus Giroux. **(I, M)**

The facts are the same as in other books on the topic of the expedition, but the voice the author chooses to use is that of a lesser known member of the company—Reubin. He's telling of the adventure after it's over, and he sounds like even he is amazed at the crew's survival and success. He asks the reader questions that help one imagine the daily trials, like, "Ever tried to swallow dried, boiled elk without any salt? That was our New Year's Day dinner, January 1, 1806" (unpaged). He recaps the journey to the Pacific:

> We had, by Captain Clark's reckoning, traveled 4,164 miles. He worked on a map of the country we'd crossed, and Captain Lewis wrote in his journal about all the amazing new plants and animals we'd seen. Animals such as bighorn sheep, grizzly bears, antelope, mule deer, jackrabbits, badgers . . . I could go on. Captain Lewis tallied that we'd seen, all new to us, thirty-three species of mammals, thirty species of land birds, and twenty-six species of waterbirds. (unpaged)

Students might use Reubin as a model as they write reports of other historical events. Have them choose one person involved and tell the story from that person's perspective, using their imagination to get into the person's mind and heart.

Feiler, B. (2004). *Walking the Bible: An Illustrated Journey for Kids Through the Greatest Stories Ever Told.* New York: HarperCollins. **(I, M, H)**

In preparation for his walk through Middle Eastern countries, Bruce Feiler spent a year reading over a hundred books about the Bible, ". . . its history, archaeology, geography, botany. . . . The homework itself became part of the adventure" (p. 6). He takes readers along on his journey to Egypt, Israel, and other places where the events of Genesis and the other four books that together comprise the Torah occurred. Take your students along as the author climbs Mount Sinai, where the Bible says Moses received the Ten Commandments.

The author and his archaeologist companion have visited the Western Wall, or Wailing Wall, in Jerusalem. Then they walk to the peak where tradition says that Abraham came to sacrifice his son:

> We sat down and opened our Bibles. In Genesis 22, Abraham and Isaac arrive on the mountaintop. Abraham prepares a fire and ties his son to the altar. Then he raises his arms and prepares to kill his son. Will he? Will the great father of humanity . . . actually destroy the son he waited his whole life to have? . . . I turned to [Avner]. "So would you have done it?" (pp. 57–58)

Have your students use this as a model for participating in "You Are There" reading experiences as they read texts about other world religions. (See activity described in Part 2, Chapter 4.)

Gaskins, P. F. (2004). *I Believe in . . . : Christian, Jewish, and Muslim Young People Speak About Their Faith.* Chicago: Cricket Books. **(H)**

I can't think of a better way of teaching world religions than by reading from this book. Students will listen to the dozens of teenagers and 20-somethings who share their religious upbringings; present beliefs and practices; ways of relating to others within their religion and those belonging to religions

SS/HIS

with different, sometimes opposing views; and doubts, concerns, and questions. Vocabulary is explained in context, and much information about the various religions throughout the personal stories related here. There are photographs of the interviewees, as well as intriguing subtitles such as "Being Christian Does Not Top the Cool List" (p. 73), "It Takes a Lot of Courage to Wear a Kippah" (p. 12), "The Qur'an Is What Saved Me" (p. 108), "You Always Know That There Are People Out There That Hate You" (p. 88), and "How Can You Be Both?" (p. 34). After reading this book, students can research to find how young people who practice Hinduism, Buddhism, and other religions speak about their faiths. Ask your students to put their own stories and spiritual searches in writing to add to the collections.

Greene, M. (2004). *Into the Land of Freedom: African Americans in Reconstruction.* Minneapolis: Lerner Publications Company. (M, H)

This book tells much about the new freedoms African Americans enjoyed after the Emancipation Proclamation and the end of the Civil War; pictures and text depict marriages, people learning to read, the owning of land. It also details the continuing hardships and dangers: Black Codes, the rise of the Ku Klux Klan, the sharecropping life that offered little more than slavery. The author includes photographs; quotes from leaders such as Frederick Douglass, Sojourner Truth, and W. E. B. Du Bois; the texts of the Emancipation Proclamation and the Civil Rights Act of 1875; as well as political cartoons. This great resource can help you design document-based questions (see Part 2 of this chapter), and offers a very interesting read to include in units on the history of Reconstruction.

Hansen, D. D. (2003). *The Dream: Martin Luther King, Jr. and the Speech That Inspired a Nation.* New York: HarperCollins. (H)

A reader could make a great graphic organizer focusing on the cause/effect pattern of organization after reading this book (see Figure 3.10). Hansen gives background on the time of the speech that can help students contextualize it. Your students can visualize the "racial caste system" (p. 1) he describes when they read, "Not a single black child in South Carolina, Alabama, or Mississippi attended an integrated public school during the 1962–63 school year" (p. 1). The author describes how the speech was composed, and analyzes it in terms of its literary merit and political power, making the book appropriate for **language arts** as well as social studies. Readers will feel that they're among the 250,000 marchers in Washington on the day King delivered the speech. The author then goes on to discuss the effects of the speech, both

immediately after, and through the years. Students will have a great appreciation for the leaders and participants of the Civil Rights Movement after being exposed to this powerful book about a powerful speech by a powerful man.

Hatt, C. (2004). *Catherine the Great.* Milwaukee, WI: World Almanac Library. (M, H)

Part of the "Judge for Yourself" series, this book provides nine biographical chapters that also context Catherine's life in light of Russian society at the time, and then proceeds to chapters whose titles ask questions, such as "Enlightenment Empress or Old-fashioned Autocrat?", "The Serf's Friend or the Serf's Enemy?", and "Education Policy—Success or Failure?" In the two-page chapter, "Was Catherine a Murderer?", five excerpts from sources such as manifestos, reports, and letters are provided so that readers can weigh the evidence and come to a decision. The other chapters follow a similar format. Consider using this book with the document-based questions strategy in Part 2 of this chapter as a good way to help your students prepare for exams requiring document-based essays. At the same time, you will immerse them in the messy times and fascinating personal life of a controversial monarch.

Hoffman, L. A., & Wolfson, R. (2004). *What You Will See Inside a Synagogue.* Photographs by B. Aron. Woodstock, VT: Skylight Paths Publishing. (E, I, M)

Rabbi Hoffman is the tour guide, who explains not only what the things are in a synagogue, but why they're there and what they mean. Readers will come to understand how, when, where, and to whom Jews pray; in what ongoing ways they "fix the world" (p. 18); details about bar and bat mitzvahs, as well as Jewish weddings; how the High Holy Days are celebrated; and how they remember the horrors of the Holocaust. Students learn the pronunciation and meanings of Hebrew terms, and see the Torah Scroll and a page from the Talmud.

Other books in this series will introduce students to what's inside a mosque, a Catholic church, and a Hindu Temple, offering opportunities for pondering similarities and differences, as well as encouraging respect for people of all religions. Use this series in a variation of the Jigsaw activity discussed in Part 2 of this chapter by having expert groups focus on one book and one religion in order to teach it to the rest of the class.

Hunter, R. A. (2003). *Into the Air: An Illustrated History of Flight.* Illus. Y. Nascimbene. Washington, DC: National Geographic. (E, I, M, H)

This author celebrates the imagination of those responsible for the achievements in aviation; his

SS/HIS

imaginations and the illustrator's are evident as well. The timeline starts 360 million years ago, as some insects began to fly. Readers visit 12,000 BCE, when stone-age people sailed the first boomerangs through the air; 1500 BCE, when a Persian king supposedly trained four eagles to carry his throne into the heavenly kingdom; 1200 BCE, when legend tells us Icarus flew too close to the sun with his waxen wings. Readers see the designs for flying machines of Leonardo da Vinci in 1490, watch Jeanne Labrosse as the first woman to pilot a balloon, take part in the historic 1903 flight of the Wright brothers, observe airplanes used for the first time in combat during World War I. They'll fly with Charles Lindbergh and with Amelia Earhart over the Atlantic, and with Richard E. Byrd over the North Pole. They'll see some designs for possible flights of the future, perhaps adding their own dreams and designs to those in the book. The Endnote is written by former NASA astronaut Dr. Kathryn Sullivan, who gives a timeline of her career:

> My own path "into the air" as a pilot—and later into space as an astronaut—started simply. As a child, I envied the birds and wondered what it would be like to fly something myself. Step by step, I followed my curiosity and built my skills. Flying in space was my greatest adventure and reward. (unpaged)

In short, this book will help your students' knowledge and imaginations soar as they learn about the history of flight, an important curricular topic in social studies classes.

Krull, K. (1999). *A Kid's Guide to the Bill of Rights: Curfews, Censorship, and the 100-Pound Giant.* Illus A. DiVito. New York: Avon Books. (M, H)

I tried to skim this book, but found myself engrossed in the stories exemplifying the concepts of each of the amendments. If you read a few samples to your class, many students might want to continue on their own. The cartoon-like illustrations are accompanied by quotes from relevant people or thought-provoking questions such as, "Can Bible verses be broadcast in school?" (p. 30), "Should the Ku Klux Klan be allowed to broadcast on public TV?" (p. 51), "Can the government tell librarians what to say?" (p. 54), "Can kids in school print anything they want in school newspapers?" (p. 69), "What about metal detectors at school?" (p. 110), "Will cameras in the courtrooms affect the Bill of Rights?" (p. 211). The topic of the Bill of Rights is an important one in American history courses, and has great relevance for citizens today. Use this book to help students appreciate how the Bill of

Rights has influenced our history and continues to operate in our country.

Kurlansky, M. (2004). *1968: The Year That Rocked the World.* New York: Ballantine Books. (H)

When I ask my students what happened in 1492, they can name one thing. After they're introduced to the book co-authored by several noted children's authors, *The World in 1492* (Fritz et al., 1992), they can name things that simultaneously happened in Asia, Africa, Europe, and the Americas. Similarly, readers of *1968* will come away with a broad understanding of world events and a deep understanding of how a crucial year can change the world forever; there's no going back. Kurlansky will take your students through the seasons in the four major parts of this book: "The Winter of Our Discontent," "Prague Spring," "The Summer Olympics," and "The Fall of Nixon." Along the way they'll learn facts about the assassinations of Martin Luther King Jr. and Robert Kennedy; Vietnam and the antiwar movement; the Women's Movement; Black Power; and political disruptions in the Middle East. They will finish their journey wiser and more thoughtful, perhaps with more questions than they entered with. Challenge students to research other crucial years, for example 2001, 1945, 1776, as well as the events of the year they are currently living through.

Langley, A. (1994). The Industrial Revolution. New York: Viking. (M, H)

Part of the See-Through History series, this book offers a wealth of information about the Industrial Revolution as well as see-through cutaways that allow the reader to view the outsides of a coal miner's home, a railroad station, and a cotton factory, then lift the plastic pages to get a look at the insides. The author fits numerous pictures and a remarkable amount of information into the two-page chapters, covering topics such as machinery, spinning and weaving, health and disease, social reform, steam power, immigrants, architecture and art, railroads and canals, and a host of inventions. Social studies teachers can use the Jigsaw 2 strategy to have students explore various facets of the Industrial Revolution, discuss the main points in their expert groups, and then teach members of their base groups about what they learned.

Macaulay, D. (2003). *Mosque.* Boston: Houghton Mifflin. (I, M, H)

The author places you there with the architects, with the stonecutters, with the ceiling painters, as they create this sixteenth-century Ottoman mosque. Readers can ponder the mathematics involved, the money and politics involved, the Muslim religion, the rich history of the times. Use this book after

SS/HIS

your students have read Demi's picture book biography of Muhammed, and before teaching about present-day Muslim houses of prayer and life in the Middle East.

McPherson, J. M. (2002). *Fields of Fury: The American Civil War.* New York: Atheneum. **(I, M, H)**

It took me a while to get past the end pages, which contain a detailed timeline from 1854 to 1865. In fact, every page was a slow one for me, since every picture or photograph is enticing, each map tells a story for those who will follow it, and the "Quick Facts" in the margins beg to be read. The Glossary, a guide to Civil War websites, and text all combine to give a full picture of the war, including the roles of women, slaves, and children. Your students will come away from this book with an appreciation that war is not glorious or pretty, but I think they will return again and again to this book to ponder the era.

McWhorter, D. (2004). *A Dream of Freedom: The Civil Rights Movement from 1954 to 1968.* New York: Scholastic. **(I, M, H)**

This chapter of American history is organized chronologically, and readers get the big picture as they view photos and hear from participants of the major events of 1955, 1963, 1966, and so on. The Prologue, "The World Unmade by the Movement," gives a great overview of the pre–civil rights era. And the Epilogue, "The Unfinished Work," tells stories from the lives of civil rights leaders in the decades following 1968. For example, Bob Moses protested the Vietnam War by moving to Africa. But he came back in 1976 and began teaching algebra to poor blacks in Mississippi. McWhorter ends with an inspiring message to young readers:

> I hope that the civil rights movement has also made you wonder how your life may be intersecting with the grand plan of the present era. . . . Have no doubt: History is going on around you right now. You can either make it or it will make you. No one knows while it's happening how it will turn out. But everything counts. (p. 156)

After reading this book, have your students research current civil rights issues and leaders.

Miller, B. M. (2003). *Good Women of a Well-Blessed Land: Women's Lives in Colonial America.* Minneapolis, MN: Lerner Publications. **(I, M, H)**

Would you have liked to experience the adventures of life as a colonial woman? What do you think were the pros and cons of her existence? You might say it depends on her individual circumstances, and you would be right. Miller gives us details about the lives of Native Americans, African Americans, and

European Americans during the seventeenth and eighteenth centuries, using primary resources, telling quotes, and offering great photographs. We meet poets Phillis Wheatley and Anne Bradstreet, banished Puritan Anne Hutchinson, peacemaker Pocahontas, and numerous unnamed women as they go about daily life in those harsh times. The author feels a personal connection to the lives she relates, since an ancestor of hers who refused to marry a man whose marriage proposal she had earlier accepted was sued in Virginia's first breach of promise case. This book helps fill a gap evident in some history textbooks, which often tend to emphasize the lives and actions of men.

Myers, W. D. (2004). *USS Constellation: Pride of the American Navy.* New York: Holiday House. **(I, M, H)**

Countries have histories; people have histories; buildings and ships have histories, too. Reading the history of the ship the USS *Constellation* enables the reader to gain an understanding of important people and events. The ship was involved in a perhaps surprising, certainly heroic way in the sorry chapter of the African slave trade. The ship played a role in the Civil War. The ship has a role to play, even today.

In the Author's Note, Myers shares a bit of his research and the pleasure it gives him:

> History books . . . may not tell us about blacks who served in the Union navy during the Civil War, but photographs do. . . . In researching the *Constellation*, I was lucky enough to find photographs once owned by the captain of that ship. . . . Magazines from the naval training station in Rhode Island gave me an idea of what life was like for young sailors nearly a hundred years ago. A thin chapter in a training manual spoke volumes about the dangers aboard ship. (p. 80)

Bring out this book periodically as you proceed chronologically through an American History course, since the ship has such a long, rich history itself.

Preston, D. (2003). *Remember the Lusitania!* New York: Walker Publishing. **(M, H)**

This dramatic telling of the torpedoing and sinking of the Lusitania is from the viewpoints of three people who were children on the boat. The author interviewed the survivors, researched historical documents, and selected photographs to produce this work that invites readers aboard to experience the event. Whether your students study the pictures and captions, or read all the detail, they will learn a lot, and also feel a lot as they read about the loss of 785 passengers and 413 crew members (a diagram of human figures of various sizes on a page helps readers to visualize the number). The Epilogue compares the shock the world felt to one many readers will

SS/HIS

remember, the terrorist attacks of September 11, 2001, and then explains that the reactions ranged from a newspaper headline, GERMANY SURELY MUST HAVE GONE MAD, to newspaper stories that said a pirate would apologize for such an outrage, and that, ". . . unlike the German Navy, even a rattlesnake used its rattle to give a warning before attacking." There's President Woodrow Wilson's tearful question, "'How could any nation calling itself civilized [do] such a terrible thing?'" (p. 87). This book will help your students understand how the event was a leading cause of the United States' entry into World War I.

Schultz, P. (2003). *1,000 Places to See Before You Die: A Traveler's Life List.* New York: Workman Publishing. **(M, H)**

Teaching geography through literature in the travel genre is the way to go! Instruct your students as to how to behave in the role of travel agents or guides, have them choose a place from this book that matches a piece of your curriculum, and let them travel! Global Studies students can make a literary visit to the world's largest Buddhist monument in Java, Indonesia. Classmates can vicariously skate on the Rideau Canal in Canada's capital city of Ottawa, tour the Anne Frank House in Amsterdam, stay at the Jean-Michel Cousteau Fiji Islands Resort, explore Peru's Upper Amazon Basin, dive with Tobago's manta rays. Use the book as a starting point for the Reading and Writing Travel Journals activity discussed in Part 2 of this chapter. Be sure to ask your students to promise to send you a postcard from places they end up really visiting in years to come as a result of this book's introduction and appeal.

Waldman, S. (2003). *We Asked for Nothing: The Remarkable Journey of Cabeza de Vaca.* Illus. T. McNeely. New York: Mikaya Press. **(I, M, H)**

This story deserves to be told whenever students are learning about explorers of the "New World." De Vaca, a Spanish conquistador who was shipwrecked in 1528 off the coast of Texas, got a whole different kind of exploration than he had bargained for. Clearly your students will react to the text telling of the kindness of the Indians who rescued the starving men, and explore the words from de Vaca's journal placed in the margins of the book, which detail his discoveries about these people he had formerly viewed as savages. For example, he notes in an entry titled "The Karankawa":

> Of all the people in the world they are the ones who love their children most and treat them best; and should the child of one of them die, the parents and kinfolk and the whole tribe weeps for him, and their lamentation lasts for a full year, day after day. . . . (p. 20)

The Epilogue notes that, centuries after de Vaca's death, his book about his eight years among the Indians is still considered an important work from the Age of Exploration, especially his ". . . rich and detailed descriptions of the daily life of the native people of the Southwest: their customs, rituals, celebrations, what they ate, where they lived, how they hunted, traveled, married, raised children, fought, and died" (p. 45). Through Waldman's picture book, your students will feel like they are along on the journey through uncharted territory and into the minds and hearts of a people as they learn the history of this period and region.

Wolney, P. (2004). *The Underground Railroad: A Primary Source History of the Journey to Freedom.* New York: The Rosen Publishing Group. **(I, M, H)**

The visuals in this book are powerful; they include pages from various editions of Harriet Beecher Stowe's *Uncle Tom's Cabin*, a photograph of a slave who had himself shipped to freedom in a box, patterns from quilts containing coded messages to help fugitives, hiding places, and the words of radical abolitionist John Brown after he was sentenced to death. The text also draws readers into the terrible drama that was being played out during this period of history. Other titles in the "Primary Sources in American History" series have to do with Ellis Island, The Louisiana Purchase, and The Trail of Tears.

Zinn, H., & Arnove, A. (2004). *Voices of a People's History of the United States.* New York: Seven Stories Press. **(H)**

In the Introduction, historian Howard Zinn makes no claims of being objective or of keeping his point of view to himself. "I knew that a historian (or a journalist, or anyone telling a story) was forced to choose, from an infinite number of facts, what to present, what to omit" (p. 25). He explains that behind every fact presented by a writer, or teacher, there is a judgment, at least that the fact is important. He shares his own thinking and imagination with his readers: "I wondered how the foreign policies of the United States would look if we wiped out the national boundaries of the world, at least in our minds, and thought of children everywhere as our own" (p. 27).

This book is filled with excerpts from actual documents, introduced and contexted by the authors. Students can read these as they read their regular history textbooks and then question their teachers or look further on their own to reconcile differences, check for accuracy, investigate additional voices, and think critically about issues, people, and events such as the Civil Rights Movement and the Vietnam War. All this adds up to the potential for very lively, very effective, history lessons.

SS/HIS

REFERENCES

Aronson, E., Blaney, N., Stephan, C., Sikes, J., & Snapp, M. (1978). *The jigsaw classroom*. Beverly Hills, CA: Sage.

Calkins, L., Montgomery, K., Santman, D., & Falk, B. (1998). *A teacher's guide to standardized reading tests: Knowledge is power*. Portsmouth, NH: Heinemann.

DeVries, B. (2008). *Literacy assessment and intervention for K-6 classrooms (2nd ed.)*. Scottsdale, AZ: Holcomb Hathaway.

Duke, N. K. (2003). *Informational text? The research says, "Yes!"* In L. Hoyt, M. Mooney, & B. Parkes (Eds.), *Exploring informational texts: From theory to practice* (pp. 2–7). Portsmouth, NH: Heinemann.

Editors. (2002). Adventures in nonfiction: Talking with Penny Colman. *Journal of Children's Literature, 28* (2), 58–61.

Fisher, D. (2004). Setting the "opportunity to read" standard: Resuscitating the SSR program in an urban high school. *Journal of Adolescent and Adult Literacy, 48* (2), 138–150.

Galda, L., & Cullinan, B. E. (2002). *Literature and the child* (5th ed.). Belmont, CA: Wadsworth.

Gerstein, M. (2004). Caldecott Medal acceptance. *The Horn Book Magazine, 80* (4), 395–399.

Giblin, J. C. (2000). More than just the facts: A hundred years of children's nonfiction. *The Horn Book Magazine* (July/August), 413–424.

Hoyt, L. (2002). *Make it real: Strategies for success with informational texts*. Portsmouth, NH: Heinemann.

Jentz, B. C., & Murphy, J. T. (2005). Embracing confusion: What leaders do when they don't know what to do. *Phi Delta Kappan, 86* (5), 358–366.

Kagan, S. (1989). *Cooperative learning resources for teachers*. San Juan Capistrano, CA: Resources for Teachers.

Kane, S. (2007). *Literacy and learning in the content areas* (2nd ed.). Scottsdale, AZ: Holcomb Hathaway.

Kane, S., & Rule, A. C. (2004). Poetry connections can enhance content area learning. *Journal of Adolescent and Adult Literacy, 47* (8), 658–669.

Kurkjian, C., & Livingston, N. (2005). Learning to read and reading to learn: Informational Series Books. *The Reading Teacher, 58*(6), 592–600.

Lesesne, T. S. (2001). Nonfiction matters, too: Books about people, places, and things. *Journal of Children's Literature, 27* (2), 79–84.

McGuigan, C. (2005). Animal magnetism. Photographs by Gregory Colbert. *Smithsonian, 36* (3), 72–79.

Murphy, J. (2005). Nonfiction award winner. *The Horn Book Magazine, 81* (1), 25–29.

NCTM. (2000). *Principles and standards for school mathematics*. Reston, VA: National Council of Teachers of Mathematics.

Nilsen, A. P., & Donelson, K. L. (2001). *Literature for today's young adults* (6th ed.). New York: Longman.

Norton, D. (2003). *Through the eyes of a child: An introduction to children's literature*. Upper Saddle River, NJ: Merrill.

Palincsar, A. S., & Brown, A. L. (1984). Reciprocal teaching of comprehension-fostering and comprehension-monitoring activities. *Cognition and Instruction, 1,* 117–175.

Palmer, R. G., & Stewart, R. A. (2005). Models for using nonfiction in the primary grades. *The Reading Teacher, 58* (5), 426–434.

Robb, L. (2004). *Nonfiction writing: From the inside out*. New York: Scholastic.

Slavin, R. E. (1986). *Jigsaw II: Using student team learning* (3rd ed.). Johns Hopkins University, Center for Research on Elementary and Middle Schools.

Tovani, C. (2000). *I read it but I don't get it: Comprehension strategies for adolescent readers*. Portland, ME: Stenhouse Publishers.

Vermette, P. J. (1998.) *Making cooperative learning work*. Upper Saddle River, NJ: Prentice Hall.

LITERATURE CITED

If you don't find a book listed here, it is included in Part 4, Annotated Books and Booktalks.

Adler, D. (1990). *A picture book of Benjamin Franklin*. New York: Trumpet Club.

Bartoletti, S. C. (2005). *Hitler youth: Growing up in Hitler's shadow*. New York: Scholastic.

Beckett, W. (1994). *Sister Wendy's story of painting*. New York: DK Publishing.

Blumberg, R. (2003). *York's adventures with Lewis and Clark: An African-American's part in the Great Expedition*. New York: HarperCollins.

Bober, N. (2001). *Countdown to independence: A revolution of ideas in England and her American colonies: 1760-1776*. New York: Atheneum Books for Young Readers.

Bokhari, N. (2001). *Piece of pi: Wit-sharpening, brain-bruising, number-crunching activities with pi*. Illus. S.

O'Shaughnessy. San Louis Obispo, CA: Dandy Lion Publications.

Cerullo, M. (1999). *Dolphins: What they can teach us.* New York: Scholastic.

Colman, P. (2000). *Girls: A history of growing up female in America.* New York: Scholastic.

Crew, D. F. (2005). *Hitler and the Nazis: A history in documents.* New York: Oxford University Press.

de Saint-Exupery, A. (1943). *The little prince.* Trans. K. Woods. Harcourt, Brace & World.

Ellis, D. (2004). *Three wishes: Palestinian and Israeli children speak.* Toronto: Douglas & McIntyre.

Fadiman, A. (1997). *The spirit catches you and you fall down: A Hmong child, her American doctors, and the collision of two cultures.* New York: Farrar, Straus and Giroux.

Fandel, J. (2006). *Puns, allusions, and other word secrets.* Mankato, MN: Creative Education.

Fritz, J., Paterson, K., McKissack, P., McKissack, F., Mahy, M., & Highwater, J. (1992). *The world in 1492.* New York: Henry Holt.

Gayford, M. (2006). *The yellow house: Van Gogh, Gauguin, and nine turbulent weeks in Arles.* Boston: Little, Brown and Company.

Gerstein, M. (2003). *The man who walked between the towers.* Brookfield, CT: Roaring Brook Press.

Hoose, P. (2001). *We were there, too: Young people in U.S. history.* New York: Melanie Kroupa Books.

Jacobs, H. (2001). *Incidents in the life of a slave girl.* Mineola, NY: Dover Publications.

McKissack, P. C., & McKissack, F. L. (1994). *Christmas in the big house, Christmas in the quarters.* Illus. J. Thompson. New York: Scholastic.

McWhorter, D. (2004). *A dream of freedom: The Civil Rights Movement from 1954 to 1968.* New York: Scholastic.

Mitchell, E. (2004). *Journey to the bottomless pit: The story of Stephen Bishop & Mammoth Cave.* Illus. K. Alder. New York: Viking.

Murphy, J. (2003). *An American plague: The true and terrifying story of the yellow fever epidemic of 1793.* New York: Clarion Books.

Naden, C. J., & Blue, R. (2005). *Dred Scott: Person or property?* New York: Benchmark Books.

Nasar, S. (1998). *A beautiful mind: A biography of John Forbes Nash, winner of the Nobel Prize in economics.* New York: Simon & Schuster.

O'Connor, P. T. (2003). *Woe is I: The grammarphobe's guide to better English in plain English.* New York: Penguin Putnam.

Partridge, E. (2002). *Restless spirit: The life and work of Dorothea Lange.* New York: Scholastic.

Petit, P. (2002). *To reach the clouds: My high wire walk between the twin towers.* New York: North Point Press.

Powell, J. H. (1949). *Bring out your dead: The great plague of yellow fever in Philadelphia in 1793.* New York: Arno Press.

Sacks, O. (2002). *Oaxaca journal.* Washington, DC: National Geographic.

Salmon, M. (2001). *Opportunities in visual arts careers.* Chicago: VGM Career Books.

Schanzer, R. (2004). *George vs. George: The American Revolution as seen from both sides.* Washington, DC: National Geographic.

Schultz, P. (2003). *1,000 places to see before you die: A traveler's life list.* New York: Workman Pub.

Stonier, T. (1964). *Nuclear disaster.* Cleveland: World Pub.

Swain, G. (2004). *Dred and Harriet Scott: A family's struggle for freedom.* St. Paul, MN: Borealis Books.

Tomecek, S. M. (2003). *What a great idea: Inventions that changed the world.* Illus. D. Stuckenschneider. New York: Scholastic.

Warren, A. (2004). *Escape from Saigon: How a Vietnam War orphan became an American boy.* New York: Farrar, Straus and Giroux.

Watt, F. (1993). *Earthquakes and volcanoes.* New York: Scholastic.

Webb, S. (2004). *Looking for seabirds: Journal from an Alaskan voyage.* Boston: Houghton Mifflin.

Fiction

4

We first looked up at the stars and saw stories of ourselves and the gods and heroes. Now we begin to see the stars themselves, and they tell us stories we've never heard before about how everything began: the stars, the planets, space, and, maybe someday, the origin of stories.

MORDICAI GERSTEIN, 2005, P. 21

the why and how
OF USING FICTION IN CONTENT AREAS

Although everyone loves a good story, you may think that in the content areas stories are something extra, supplemental, perhaps to be shared and enjoyed as a reward after the hard work of learning the curriculum has been accomplished. Katherine Paterson (1989), storyteller extraordinaire, exhorts teachers:

> I want to encourage you to feel that stories are at the center, not at the edge, of that process [education]. They are the center not only because stories help us shape our lives and our society but because they have the power to lure us into learning. (p. 139)

Azar Nafisi, in *Reading Lolita in Tehran: A Memoir in Books* (2003), tells of the considerable risks she (who had lost her job as professor of literature at the University of Tehran) and her former students took to continue reading and discussing works of fiction that had been banned in the Islamic Republic of Iran. I attended a lecture by Nafisi in which she expressed her belief that, given the present political climate and national and world events, we need literature more than ever. "It is exactly now that we need works of imagination, that we need thought, that we need reflection" (Rosamond Gifford Lecture, Syracuse, NY, 4/12/07).

This chapter's aim is to demonstrate how discipline-specific information and subject-related concepts can be learned *through* story. Paterson says stories "allow us a vision or a partial vision of what in scientific or even literary terms is unknowable" (p. 133), and I've found that to be true in my own reading. For example, I recently read Mark Haddon's *The Curious Incident of the Dog in the Night-Time* (2003). This fascinating mystery has intrigued many teen and adult readers. Along the way, the narrator, Christopher Boone, shares a wealth of information that he carries around his head. As he relates his search for a dog's killer in novel form, his love for prime numbers leads him to number his chapters with only primes. He has lost his mother recently, and he shares his knowledge of aneurisms and embolism as he tells of the probable cause of her death. He models his criminal investigation after the techniques of his hero, Sherlock Holmes. In addition, Christopher explains how he thinks and relates to people in a different way due to his autism; he is extremely self-aware. For example, he calms himself down by solving algorithms. So the time spent reading this book was a good investment. I came away from it with new facts about topics ranging from black holes to animal behavior, as well as a better understanding of how some people with autism come to negotiate their lives, learning, and emotions.

A good fiction book can build background knowledge about a subject. While I was reading Nancy Werlin's *Double Helix* (2004), I felt like an involved intern as the narrator, Luke, unraveled the mystery of his origins. When he was sneaking through a scientist's files on eggs that had been extracted from Luke's mother, he recognized the significance of a repetition of a gene on the fourth chromosome of one of the eggs. "The notation for the map of Kayla's chromosome four . . . C-A-G, it said. *Repeats: 59*" (p. 228). He, and hence the reader, learned that his sister will contract Huntington's disease. I was totally involved in the story and its emotional impact. Later, as I was reading a chapter from Matt Ridley's *Genome: The Autobiography of a Species in 23 Chapters* (1999), I came across this explanation:

... we now know in excruciating detail how and why and where [the gene connected with Huntington's chorea] can go wrong and what the consequence for the body is. The gene contains a single 'word', repeated over and over again: CAG, CAG, CAG, CAG. . . . The repetition continues sometimes just six times, sometimes thirty, sometimes more than a hundred times. Your destiny, your sanity, and your life hang by the thread of this repetition. If the 'word' is repeated thirty-five times or fewer, you will be fine. . . . If the 'word' is repeated thirty-nine times or more, you will in mid-life slowly start to lose your balance, grow steadily more incapable of looking after yourself and die prematurely. (p. 55)

I recognized this description because Luke had been previously watching his own mother from the onset of her disease to her death. The work of fiction had prepared me in a way that made comprehension of the expository material easier and deeper.

Reading workshop, or a book club format (see Chapter 2), is common in many language arts classes, but seen less often in content area classes. Yet it can be very beneficial to activate book discussion groups relative to any discipline. Have available multiple copies of several novels that offer information, concepts, or procedures relevant to the curriculum you teach. Allow students to choose which book they want to pursue and then talk with others about their personal reactions as well as what science, or music, or history lessons they've learned. Reading the books may also help them formulate new questions that lead them to future research, perhaps with your help or the help of parents or community members.

It's important to remember, too, that for classroom purposes, books do not have to be taught or read in their entirety. Many times I read excerpts from literature to get across a point I'm teaching, then leave it up to my audience to decide whether they'll pursue the book further. You may post a quote, chart, or list; you may read some dialogue, or whatever works to make the content area concepts come alive through the literature.

Books in two particular genres of fiction, science fiction and historical fiction, are filled with natural curricular connections for use with specific disciplines. The following two sections will demonstrate how you may use fictional texts to motivate students to think in ways that will help them in science, math, and social studies classes, as well as to learn specific course content.

SCIENCE FICTION

In "Taming the Alien Genre: Bringing Science Fiction into the Classroom" (2001), authors Bucher and Manning give sound reasons for teaching science concepts through and with stories in this genre. Reading about the future and about alternate worlds helps students ponder their own time and surroundings, and possibly build the future they want. There are many potential curricular connections, since:

No longer just "the good versus the bad," current science fiction reflects many topics such as future worlds, super-intelligent mechanical and human beings, time travel and altered historical events, robots, DNA experiments, nuclear holocaust and survival, toxic wastes, and germ warfare. In fact, a strength of science fiction is its diversity. . . . (p. 42)

The authors give suggestions for selecting pertinent and quality science fiction literature, noting that teachers should pay attention to the context in which the genre will be used and the purpose for introducing the stories. "Certainly, a novel which is taught for its literary concepts is judged differently than one which is taught for other concepts such as ecological or social awareness" (p. 43).

Teach content and watch students learn through the use of science fiction trade books. Scientific principles that can be difficult to understand in the abstract sometimes make sense when explained as part of a story. Many scientists, including Carl Sagan, have credited science fiction with bringing them into the field. You will find that both girls and boys enjoy this genre. Janice M. Bogstad (2004) recalls how her interest in science was nurtured by her science fiction reading throughout childhood and adolescence. ". . . [Alice Mary] Norton's novels were my first introduction to the possibility of a matriarchal society and to the horrors of nuclear war. And Robert Heinlein provided me with my first introduction to women scientists, starship captains, or heroes" (p. vi). Robert Goddard dreamed of spaceflight after reading H. G. Wells's *War of the Worlds*, and went on to become one of the first rocket scientists (Haven & Clark, 1999, as described in Raham, p. 24).

Gary Raham, author of *Teaching Science Fact with Science Fiction* (2004), provides a rationale for teaching with science fiction:

> . . . science has utterly altered our view of the world and so rapidly increased our collective capacity to change the world that everyone needs to understand how it works and what it can and cannot do. That's where science fiction comes in. . . . Human beings respond to stories as a way to learn. Good science fiction starts with a universe consistent with scientific discoveries and operating under natural laws as we understand them at the time. . . . Most students will not become scientists, but all students will live their lives in a world where boundaries are defined by science . . . it is an amazingly powerful tool that, when used carefully and with some insight, can greatly enrich our lives. (p. ix)

Raham argues that science fiction can be used to teach not only science content but also math concepts. He notes that a theme in much science fiction is that math is a universal language. He shares ideas and mathematical activities using science fiction books as springboards. For example, he recommends Edwin Abbott's *Flatland* (1952) as a resource for teaching about multiple space dimensions and relativity, as well as multidimensional forms such as hyperspheres and tesseracts. He gives a visual that helps readers understand the concept of tesseract, along with a definition: "An unfolded hypercube in 3-d space" (p. 99). He gives instructions so that students can make a model of Flatland, turn it into a mathematical game board, and design buildings for it.

The national standards of several disciplines stress the importance of students being able to care for their world and think well enough to anticipate future consequences of our actions today. Science fiction, along with the related genre of utopian/dystopian literature, addresses these concerns, often in an interdisciplinary manner, involving the areas of social studies and language arts in addition to science. Nilsen and Donelson (2001) explain:

> Science fiction presents real heroes to readers who find their own world often devoid of anyone worth admiring, of heroes doing something brave, going to the ultimate frontiers, even pushing these frontiers further back, all important at a time when many young people wonder if any new frontiers exist. (pp. 222–223)

Let's at this point take a look at a particular topic. The concept and reality of cloning are much in the news and connect to the science curriculum. National standards in both science and English language arts advocate critical thinking among student learners. And the benefits, applications of, and worries about cloning are popular themes in children's trade books. Crew (2004) shows how young adult books, such as Nancy Farmer's *The House of the Scorpion* (2002), Mildred Ames's *Anna to the Infinite Power* (1981), and Kathryn Lasky's *Star Split* (2001), connect to current nonfiction texts such as *The Second Creation: Dolly and the Age of Biological Control* (Wilmut, Campbell, & Tudge, 2000), *Human Cloning and Human Dignity: The Report of the President's Council on Bioethics* (Kass, 2002), and *Cloning* (Nardo, 2005). Teachers may use fictional plots to help students think critically about the value issues being argued in scientific, religious, medical, and political circles. Crew notes, "The moral and ethical reasons against

Science fiction books involving ethical issues.   FIGURE   4.1

Anderson, M. T. (2002). *Feed*. Cambridge, MA: Candlewick Press.

Brockmeier, K. (2006). *Grooves: A kind of mystery*. New York: Katherine Tegen Books.

Choyce, L. (2006). *Deconstructing Dylan*. Toronto: Boardwalk Book/Dundurn Press.

Haddix, M. P. (2000). *Turnabout*. New York: Simon & Schuster.

Krossing, K. (2005). *Pure*. Toronto: Second Story Press.

Matas, C. (1999). *Cloning Miranda*. Toronto: Scholastic Canada.

Thompson, K. (2006). *Only human*. New York: Bloomsbury.

cloning-to-produce-children are made clear in Farmer's story, including the unjustified dehumanization of life by viewing and treating a child as a product to be used, the violation of a child's most basic rights, and a child's lack of biological parents" (p. 207). What a great impetus for student research when they read texts for the purpose of discovering the field of cloning. They will engage with Matt, the main character in *The House of the Scorpion*, as he learns that he was created—cloned—for the purpose of supplying his uncle with body parts. Figure 4.1 contains a list of science fiction books that give scientific information while providing scenarios that stimulate critical thinking about the ethics of scientific developments.

Make these and many other science fiction texts available to your students and help them make connections between these stimulating stories and the course material. Next we'll see how social studies teachers may use fictional trade books as they meet the demands of their curricular standards.

HISTORICAL FICTION

Historical fiction is alive and well, capable of helping history come alive through story for your social studies students. Readers find out how authors do research and immerse themselves in other times and places in order to accurately portray their characters and events. For example, when Avi was asked by an interviewer about how much research his novel *Crispin: The Cross of Lead* (2002) required, and whether it was done beforehand or as he went along, he replied:

> I read or used more than 200 books about the period. John Ball, of course, is real, and his speech is a paraphrase of one he gave during the Peasants' Rebellion of 1381—which was extraordinarily violent—both the uprising and the suppression. It was during this rebellion that the idea, "All men are created equal," was first expressed in English. . . . (Blasingame, 2003, p. 39)

In a few words, Avi has offered much historical information and lots to think about. It would only take a moment for a teacher to share this author's wisdom with a class.

An interview with Korean American author Linda Sue Park (2001) reveals her process:

> I spend months doing research before I begin writing. . . . Some of the books I have used are more than one hundred years old! . . . I keep a pad of sticky notes handy. I put a note on the page whenever I come across something that might be useful . . . but overall I try to make the research a part of me. I think the story is best when it comes from "inside" the writer. (unpaged, at end of *A Single Shard*)

Newbery Acceptance speeches, found in the July issues of *The Horn Book Magazine*, are an easy place to start looking for anecdotes that will help students connect story and history. For example, Karen Hesse had this to say when she received the medal in 1998 for *Out of the Dust* (1997):

> I love research, love dipping into another time and place, and asking the tough questions in a way that helps me see both question and answer with a clearer perspective.... In *Out of the Dust*, when Billie Jo's mother reaches for the pail, she ... doesn't realize her mistake, that she is pouring kerosene, until the flames rise up from the stove.
>
> Readers ask, could such a terrible mistake really happen? Yes. It happened often. I based the accident on a series of articles appearing in the 1934 Boise City News. That particular family tragedy planted the seed for *Out of the Dust*, as much as the dust storms did.
>
> Let me tell you. I never make up any of the bad things that happen to my characters. I love them too much to hurt them deliberately.... (pp. 422–423)

Students might be inspired after reading or hearing Hesse's speech to do their own research of an era and create a tale representing their favorite part of history. They'll also be primed to read more award acceptance speeches by their favorite authors, and more historical fiction.

Numerous well-written stories at all levels help readers understand people's thinking and actions in different times and places, so they are perfect for the classroom. History may be taught either chronologically or thematically; either way, historical fiction is there for us as a supplement and complement to the textbooks, primary sources, media, and other materials we use. Consider the large topic of war, since often our curricula seem to be organized around wars. Our students should know the causes and the results of the wars they study, but they also need to understand how, where, and when the wars were fought, what countries or factions were involved, who the leaders were. In addition, as Nilsen and Donelson (2001) point out:

> Young adults are conscious of the nearness of war though they likely know little of the realities of war and even less about the details of past wars. Reading literature about war, fiction or not, acquaints young people with the ambiguous nature of war, on one hand illustrating humanity's evil and horror, on the other hand revealing humanity's decency and heroism. (p. 248)

Have your whole class read a single novel about each war that occurred during the time period your curriculum covers. Or perhaps introduce and have available a number of books, not necessarily limited to one genre, from which to choose as they engage with the subject. Figure 4.2 lists fictional works about the Vietnam War. A variety of difficulty levels are represented, making differentiated instruction easier. Help students choose books that are right for them; they'll share what they learned with others, and learn from readers of different books as well. These books contain well-researched information about the war woven into stories that involve characters struggling with values, decisions, and relationships.

Nilsen and Donelson offer criteria that can help teachers identify quality historical fiction. Among the characteristics of a good historical novel are "An authentic rendition of the time, place, and people being featured.... Evidence that even

Fiction about the Vietnam War.   FIGURE   **4.2**

Antle, N. (1998). *Lost in the war.* New York: Dial Books for Young Readers.

Antle, N. (1993). *Tough choices: A story about the Vietnam War.* New York: Viking.

Armstrong, J. (Ed.). (2002). *Shattered: Stories of children and war.* New York: Knopf.

Couloumbis, A. (2005). *Summer's end.* New York: G.P. Putnam's Sons.

Crist-Evans, C. (2003). *Amaryllis.* Cambridge, MA: Candlewick Press.

Hobbes, V. (2002). *Sonny's war.* New York: Farrar, Straus and Giroux.

McDaniel, L. (2003). *Garden of angels.* New York: Bantam Books.

Myers, W. D. (2001). *Patrol: An American soldier in Vietnam.* Collages by A. Grifalconi. New York: HarperCollins.

O'Brien, T. (1998). *The things they carried.* New York: Broadway.

Pevsner, S., & Tang, F. (1997). *Sing for your father, Su Phan.* New York: Clarion Books.

Sherlock, P. (2004). *Letters from Wolfie.* New York: Viking.

Testa, M. (2003). *Almost forever.* Cambridge, MA: Candlewick Press.

White, E. E. (2002). *The journal of Patrick Seamus Flaherty, United States Marine Corps.* New York: Scholastic.

White, E. E. (2002). *Where have all the flowers gone?: The diary of Molly Mackenzie Flaherty.* New York: Scholastic.

Woodworth, C. (2006). *Georgie's moon.* New York: Farrar, Straus and Giroux.

across great time spans people share similar emotions. . . . [and] references to well-known events or people or other clues through which the reader can place the happenings in their correct historic framework" (p. 239). Students may offer their insights about what makes some of their chosen historical fiction selections particularly good reads.

Beck, Nelson-Faulkner, and Pierce (2000) report, "Teachers are relying increasingly on novels as part of classroom inquiries into historical periods" (p. 546). They interviewed Karen Hesse, author of *Out of the Dust,* a story set in the Dust Bowl during 1934, who explained:

> "No one can recreate history with perfect authenticity. But an author can do a fairly accurate representation of the period or of an historical figure based on documentable material. If the writer is creating historical fiction which is going to ultimately end up in the classroom as a supplement to curriculum, that writer is responsible for portraying that period as close to the facts as is humanly possible." (p. 548)

FICTION CONNECTED TO OTHER DISCIPLINES

No matter what your subject area, you can find and promote works of fiction in order to help students understand content, see real-life applications of what they're learning, and meet the standards of your discipline. The strategies and activities that follow will show how stories relating to art, geography, and physical education can be used effectively.

The books annotated in Part 4 represent only a small fraction of the possible fiction resources for our students as they study and explore various curricula during their school days and years.

YOU-ARE-THERE READING

Standards Addressed

Social Studies: Students understand the physical and human characteristics of places. Students understand how culture and experience influence people's perceptions of places and regions.

English/Language Arts: Students read a wide range of print and nonprint texts to build an understanding of texts, or themselves, and of the cultures of the United States and the world. . . .

Context/Rationale

Anne Fadiman (1998) espouses what she has coined ". . . You-Are-There reading, the practice of reading books in the places they describe" (p. 63). Fadiman gives personal examples:

> . . . I have read Yeats in Sligo, Isak Dinesen in Kenya, and John Muir in the Sierras. By far my finest You-Are-There hour, however, was spent reading the journals of John Wesley Powell, the one-armed Civil War veteran who led the first expedition down the Colorado River, while I was camped at Grand Rapids in the bottom of the Grand Canyon. (p. 67)

We cannot bring our students to most of the physical places mentioned in our courses. So how about adapting Fadiman's approach to one we'll call "We-Are-There-In-Our-Textbook"? With the help of a good wall map or with Google Earth, we can mark our journey, and read books set in those places as we proceed through the year's curriculum. Let's say you're responsible for teaching about the Middle East and Africa since World War II. Figure 4.3 contains a list of fictional trade books students may read to become immersed in the places and the lives of the people who live there.

Encourage your students to simultaneously explore nonfiction books, such as Satrapi's (2003) *Persepolis: The Story of a Childhood*, a memoir of girl growing up in Iran during the Islamic Revolution, written in graphic form; and *The Storyteller's Daughter: One Woman's Return to Her Lost Homeland*, by Saira Shah (2003). There's also *Reading Lolita in Tehran: A Memoir in Books*, by Azar Nafisi (2003). Have your students compare the settings and historical information presented in the class textbook, as well as the fiction and nonfiction pairings.

Walk-Through

An assignment using the You-Are-There strategy might look like this:

> You've learned about the Middle East through in-class lessons; through reading Chapter Six in our textbook; and through your explorations using the Internet, magazines, television news, and newspapers. I've also asked you to practice the "You-Are-There" strategy by

Fiction appropriate for the "You-Are-There" reading strategy.	FIGURE	4.3

Achebe, C. (1994). *Things fall apart.* New York: Anchor. (Nigeria)

Adichie, C. N. (2003). *Purple hibiscus.* New York: Anchor. (modern Nigeria)

Carmi, D., & Lotan, Y. (2000). *Samir and Yonatan.* New York: Arthur A. Levine. (Israel)

Galgut, D. (2003). *The good doctor, A novel.* New York: Grove. (South Africa after Apartheid)

Kingsolver, B. (1998). *The poisonwood Bible.* New York: HarperCollins. (the Congo/Zaire)

Nye, N. S. (1997). *Habibi.* New York: Simon & Schuster. (Jerusalem)

Staples, S. F. (2005). *Under the persimmon tree.* New York: Farrar, Straus and Giroux. (Afghanistan, Pakistan)

Stein, T. (2005). *Light years.* New York: Knopf. (modern-day Israel)

Stratton, A. (2004). *Chanda's secrets.* New York: Annick Press. (present day sub-Saharan Africa)

reading at least three stories from Elsa Marston's *Figs and Fate: Stories About Growing Up in the Arab World Today* (2005) and at least three chapters of the nonfiction book *Three Wishes: Palestinian and Israeli Children Speak,* by Deborah Ellis (2004) to immerse your- selves in the Middle East. Please get together in your base groups to share your "travel diaries," with your responses to these texts that show how you imagined being in these settings and what you might be thinking, feeling, and learning in these places. Compile a list of things you've learned (in these places) about the land, the people, the government, the religions, the culture, and the current challenges.

FANFICTION

Standards Addressed

History: Students should be able to hypothesize the influence of the past. All stu- dents should be able to compare competing historical narratives.

Health: Students will analyze the influence of family, peers, culture, media, tech- nology, and other factors on health behaviors.

English/Language Arts: Students develop an understanding of and respect for diver- sity in language use, patterns and dialects across cultures, ethnic groups, geo- graphic regions, and social roles.

Context/Rationale

Fanfiction is a popular hobby of Internet-savvy young people that involves using a media text as a jumping-off place for one's own creative writing. By adapting the method of fanfiction, your students will bring characters from different books together, resulting in a lot of fun as well as a rich knowledge of historical settings. Chandler-Olcott and Mahar (2003) studied students' use of fanfiction and other out-of-school literacy practices in order to help ". . . devise new ways to make school literacy more meaningful and engaging" (p. 563). Fanfiction sites on the Internet show how people of all ages are playing with ideas by bringing together characters from different soap operas, movies, and comics. A writer of fanfiction is in control of time, place, and scenario.

Walk-Through

The following example shows how fanfiction might work in a middle school classroom.

1934–1935: What was happening in the United States? You may have multiple answers, depending upon which areas of the country you think of. I ask about 1934 because there are several children's novels I know of that are set in that year. In Karen Hesse's *Out of the Dust* (1997), Billy Jo's diary entries from the year she is 14 years old give vivid descriptions of the Dust Bowl. Cassie Logan narrates Mildred Taylor's *Roll of Thunder, Hear My Cry* (2001), providing the perspective of an African American child living in the Deep South. And in *Meet Kit: An American Girl,* by Valerie Tripp (2000), Kit is a child who loves to write news stories, and much of the news involves how the depression is affecting her family and others in Cincinnati. *Hannah, Divided,* by A. Griffin (2002), tells of a teen's experience as a boarder and a struggling student in Philadelphia during the same year. *Al Capone Does My Shirts* (Choldenko, 2004), narrated by an adolescent boy, is set in 1935 on the island of Alcatraz off the Pacific coast. *The Trial,* by Jen Bryant (2004), takes place in New Jersey during the 1934 trial of the man accused of kidnapping Charles Lindbergh's baby. Marian Hale's (2004) *The Truth About Sparrows* takes the main character, and the reader, from Missouri to Texas in the same year. What would these characters have to say to each other? Find out by imagining these characters as pen pals. Write letters or figure out a way to bring instant messaging back in time so all these characters can talk together at once.

Anything is possible if you combine imagination and the concept of fanfiction. Form several groups of students who choose one of the books to read, or have students read all the books. They might create a timeline based on other books they're reading; they'll find ways to group other novels by era and geography. The variations are endless. However, as Chandler-Olcott and Mahar recognize, "... 'importing' adolescents' personal literacies and preferred texts into school is far from simple" (p. 565). Guide your students during a fanfiction exercise to assure they are focusing on content rather than getting carried away with their stories. For instance, a chemistry teacher might invite students to create an imagined meeting between Kate in Laurie Halse Anderson's chemistry-based novel *Catalyst* (2002) and the authors of current journal articles she has taught with in class. The teacher could stipulate that the conversation be chemistry-centered and that certain chemistry concepts or terms be included.

You might want to take a minute now to think of other characters you and your classes could bring together to elaborate on themes or information relative to your disciplines. Figure 4.4 presents a partial list from the brainstorming my students have done.

| FIGURE | 4.4 | Suggested titles for fanfiction projects in various content areas. |

- Milo, from *The Phantom Tollbooth* (Juster, 2001) could converse with Meg Murry, from *A Wrinkle in Time* (L'Engle, 1962). (math)
- The teen characters from *Hoot* (Hiaasen, 2002), who were trying to protect baby owls in Florida from a construction company's building, could dialogue with the seventh-grade science group from *Tangerine* (Bloor, 1997), who were trying to solve a mystery involving the environment in another part of the state. (science)
- Harry Potter, from *Harry Potter and the Half-Blood Prince* (Rowling, 2005), could team up with Lila from Philip Pullman's *The Amber Spyglass* (2000). (English)

- Esperanza, from *Esperanza Rising* (Ryan, 2000), could meet Naomi Léon, a character from *Becoming Naomi Léon*, by the same author (2004). (Spanish)
- The narrator of *Where Have All the Flowers Gone?: The Diary of Molly Mackenzie Flaherty* (2002) could converse with her brother, narrator of *The Journal of Patrick Seamus Flaherty* (2002). Both are by Ellen Emerson White; both take place during the Vietnam War, though Molly is in Boston and Patrick is in Vietnam; both reflect on moral and political issues as well as individual responsibility; both are great resources for classes studying this era. (history)

Figure 4.5 shows a reading guide for a health/character education class that calls for students to create fanfiction.

A reading guide exemplifying fanfiction, adapted by Sean McKean. **FIGURE 4.5**

POST-READING RESPONSE GUIDE FOR LITERATURE CIRCLE MEMBERS

Directions: After reading *Stargirl*, by Jerry Spinelli, please respond by writing a letter to any character in the book. Oh, by the way, you must put *yourself* in the place of any character in the book, also. Here are suggestions of things you might include:

- What you thought about the character's treatment of Stargirl at certain places in the story
- What you think the character might have done differently, and how an alternative action could result in a different consequence
- How you felt about major events in the book, such as the hot seat episode or the basketball playoffs
- What you might have done if faced with the same choices as the character you're writing to
- What lessons you learned from one or more episodes in the story, and lessons you think the character you're writing to has learned (or could learn) that will result in future behavior and choices.

Be sure to remain in character as you write your letter.

TEACHER READ-ALOUD

◄ ◄ ◄

Standards Addressed

Math: Students understand patterns, relations, and functions by being able to represent, analyze, and generalize a variety of patterns with tables, graphs, words, and, when possible, symbolic rules.

English/Language Arts: Students apply a wide range of strategies to comprehend, interpret, evaluate, and appreciate texts.

Context/Rationale

Teacher read-alouds may add a valuable dimension to our class day. Use them for motivation, building background knowledge, and exemplifying concepts and themes. When done well, they are most enjoyable for all. Erickson (1996) points out the benefits of reading aloud from a variety of genres to reluctant readers. Lesesne (2006), drawing on several decades of research showing the value of reading aloud, also recommends daily read-aloud activities to introduce new topics, explain concepts, and improve skills. Teachers who read with enthusiasm and expression model fluency for students. This can be especially helpful to English learners.

Walk-Through

I start this activity by asking a student if I can borrow a penny. When I have it in hand, I say, "I need this today, but tomorrow I'll be able to give you back double, and every day after that for the next month I'll double what I gave you the day before. Deal? I'm usually met with rolling of eyes, communicating that if the students think it's a deal, it's certainly not a big one. They call out things the recipient might be able to buy—a movie ticket? a new CD? a sweater? a snowboard? That half-minute interchange sets the audience up for the hearing of *One Grain of Rice: A Mathematical Folktale*, by Demi (1997).

I use my storytelling voice to read the tale of the selfish raja who gathered rice from his people and put it in storehouses, but then would not give the poor any to eat during a famine. One day, when a village girl picked up a grain of rice that fell and returned it to the raja, he offered to reward her. She asked for a single grain of rice. "'Then, each day for thirty days you will give me double the rice you gave me the day before'" (unpaged). I continue reading, and by the time I read that on the ninth day, Rani was presented with 256 grains of rice, and on the twelfth she got 2,048 grains, the wheels are spinning in my students' heads—and they're thinking about pennies in addition to grains of rice! They're astounded as they hear, "On the twenty-seventh day, thirty-two Brahma bulls were needed to deliver sixty-four baskets of rice. . . . On the twenty-ninth day, Rani was presented with the contents of two royal storehouses." Foldout pages show 256 elephants delivering the final day's rice payment (536,870,912). Rani uses her billion plus grains of rice to feed the poor, the raja has learned a lesson in kindness, my students have enjoyed a folktale from India, and the read-aloud strategy has taught a mathematical principle that the members of the class will not soon forget. They're ready for lessons on exponents, factorials, and other concepts related to patterns, functions, and relations.

▶ ▶ ▶ ## SYMBOLISM CIRCLE

Standards Addressed

History: All students should be able to draw upon visual, literary, and musical scores.

English/Language Arts: Students apply knowledge of language structure, language conventions . . . figurative language, and genre to create, critique, and discuss print and nonprint texts.

Context/Rationale

Understanding symbolic representation is a skill that's necessary and pervasive throughout the disciplines. Yet students often find the concept of one thing standing in for or representing another to be abstract and hard to explain or comprehend. Symbolism, especially in literature classes, is often taught in a way that seems intangible to learners, and in a way that sometimes leads to the false conclusion that there is a single answer that is somehow the *right* answer. I wanted a way that would demystify the subject of symbolism, and I have one of my former students, Laura, to thank for helping me. She came into class with real objects that could represent symbols. I have since gathered dozens of toys and miniature objects that I keep in my Symbolism Box.

Procedure

- Collect a group of artifacts used as symbols in the literature you have read during a semester and place them in a box.
- Near the end of the semester, after your students have read the books, have students form a circle.
- Have each person choose an object from the box, and take it back to their seat.
- Going around the circle, ask students to hold up their object, tell what book they're connecting it to, and explain why the object qualifies as a symbol, how it represents something beyond its literal meaning.

An adaptation of this activity involves having a shoebox on your shelf for some of the titles in your classroom library. As students read a particular book, have them bring in objects to add to the appropriate symbol box that previous readers who have appreciated the book have decorated. As students put objects in, perhaps with a note as to what the object symbolizes, ask them to examine the items already in the box, perhaps reflecting on some possible symbolic happenings or material things mentioned in the book that they had not yet thought about.

Walk-Through

In my class, I model by holding up a wooden apple and musing:

> The apple has been a symbol for temptation for about as long as literature has existed. In the Hebrew story of the Garden of Eden, Adam and Eve were warned not to eat the fruit from the tree of the knowledge of good and evil, and this fruit has traditionally been pictured as an apple. Snow White is tempted by the apple the witch offers, and you know what happens when she takes a bite. More recently, in Lois Lowry's *The Giver* (1993), when Jonas is first beginning to understand that he is different and will receive knowledge the rest of the community is not privy to, he sees the color red as he is tossing an apple in a game. Is this temptation, to enter a world that is not safe but is full of knowledge, and life? See, we can interpret symbols differently as readers. That's okay; the possibilities are endless.

I can attest to the numerous possibilities of symbolic interpretation, because each time I play this game in my class I hear new connections that I had not thought of. Here are a few examples my students have come up with:

> *Lynne (holding up a plastic triangle of cheese):* This reminds me of Adam in *I Am the Cheese*, by Robert Cormier. He remembers from his distant past his parents singing him the nursery rhyme, "The Farmer in the Dell," which contains the line "The cheese stands alone." Adam is utterly alone in this story, and it's the story also of so many of other adolescents we teach. This cheese is the symbol of isolation.

> *Jason (showing a baseball):* My symbol is kind of the opposite of the one Lynne just talked about. This is the baseball that Moose, in Gennifer Choldenko's *Al Capone Does My Shirts*, finds on the island of Alcatraz, where he has felt isolated since his family moved there so his father could be a prison guard. He has finally found something familiar, something from his past life, something that promises that here, too, he can become connected to friends through the sport he loves.

> *Leigh (displays an empty picture frame):* This represents the absence of a loved one. It could represent how Sal feels after her mother has died in Sharon Creech's *Walk Two Moons*. Or, oh, I just thought of this—it could be a visual of Miracle, in *Dancing on the Edge*, by Han Nolan—someone who has lost her sense of self, doesn't even know if she's real. If Miracle looked in a mirror, this is what she'd see—an empty frame!

> *Mark (extending a rubber rat, which elicits groans and shudders from his classmates):* I read *Eva*, by Peter Dickerson. Even though Eva is part of an experiment where her mind has been put into a host body of a chimpanzee, she can identify with this lab rat, 'cause that's how she feels. She's lost her freedom; she feels a lack of control. Lab rats aren't asked how they feel about what's being done to them, for the good of humanity.

This exercise also may help students transfer their knowledge of the importance and prevalence of symbolism to other academic subjects. Symbolism is vital in the fields of music, art, math, social studies, and science. The concept of symbolic representation would make a wonderful focus for an interdisciplinary exploration or a theme week in a middle or high school.

USING MULTIMEDIA TO TEACH DECODING AND FLUENCY

Standards Addressed

English/Language Arts: Students apply a wide range of strategies to comprehend, interpret, evaluate, and appreciate texts. They draw on their prior experience, their interactions with other readers and writers, their knowledge of word meaning and of other texts, their word identification strategies, and their understanding of textual features (e.g., sound–letter correspondence, sentence structure, context, graphics).

Context/Rationale

We've all had students who struggle with reading not because of problems at the word level or with fluency, but because they cannot comprehend the text. However, some students at the middle and high school level cannot decode text beyond a rudimentary level. It's difficult to find appropriate text to use to teach (or reteach) phonics principles and word analysis skills, because most text written at the beginning level will seem too babyish, so self-respecting adolescents will resist reading them. But most texts written specifically for instruction in decoding are artificial, and thus unappealing. What to do? Try a multimedia approach. Combine text with pictures, music, film, dance, and/or recorded voices. The students will be having such a good time, they might not even realize how much they're learning.

Walk-Through

Show clips from the video of The Beatles' "Yellow Submarine," then play the song separately, with the words charted out so that all can see and sing along. The verses and lines are repetitive, and most of the words are phonetically regular. Give mini-lessons on word parts, breaking the word *submarine* into its parts, for example. Next, introduce the picture book *The Beatles: Yellow Submarine* (Gardner, 2004). Charlie Gardner adapted the story from the screenplay. Readers may work together to decode, then compare the book and its illustrations to the movie version. Since they'll already be familiar with the storyline (strange as it is), they'll be able to bring meaning to the text, which should help as they're reading the words.

Students may then use this picture book idea as a model. Have them pick their favorite movies, and retell the stories, perhaps with a younger audience in mind. You might script what the students compose, and get it down in a written form they can then reread themselves, revising if they wish. They'll be getting lots of practice with all aspects of literacy, including fluency.

This strategy may also be used effectively with English learners.

"WHAT IF?"

Standards Addressed

History: Students should be able to hypothesize the influence of the past. Students should be able to analyze cause/effect relationships and multiple causation, including the importance of the individual, the influence of ideas, and the role of chance.

English/Language Arts: Students read a wide range of literature from many periods in many genres to build an understanding of the many dimensions (e.g., philosophical, ethical, aesthetic) of human experience.

Context/Rationale

A common pattern of thinking involves asking questions involving the word *if* and then making decisions based on variations of a scenario. If certain conditions pre-

What-If anticipation guide for *Fallen Angels,* by Walter Dean Myers, created by Lynn Halloran.

FIGURE   **4.6**

Directions: Before beginning the novel, react to the following what-if questions in your journal. Think about how you would feel and how you would act.

1. WHAT IF you were a 17-year-old soldier sent to fight in your first combat overseas?
2. WHAT IF you saw a man killed right in front of your eyes on your first day in the country, on your way to your base?
3. WHAT IF you had to write a letter to the wife of your commander after he died while protecting you and the other men in your platoon in battle?
4. WHAT IF you were fighting a war for your country that you knew people at home were protesting and that many didn't support?
5. WHAT IF you couldn't tell the enemy from the civilians you were trying to protect?
6. WHAT IF some of the people who were in charge of your unit were racist, and you were an African American fighting side by side with them?

vail, we will do one thing; if something else occurs, our tactics will change. Problems in every subject area can be thought about in terms of the question "What if?" What happens if these two chemicals combine? What if we apply this statistical procedure to our data? What if this character had reacted with forgiveness instead of revenge? What if a larger percentage of voters had turned out for that presidential election? Teach students to be aware of this structure in texts that they read by using the what-if strategy to brainstorm solutions to problems and to set their imaginations free as they write creatively. Encourage your students to focus on premises and possibilities by modeling the strategy, perhaps through a think-aloud, and by creating reading guides providing the structure for this conditional thinking.

Walk-Through

A social studies teacher is introducing the topic of the Vietnam War; in addition to the course textbook and several primary source documents, she has secured a class set of Walter Dean Myers's novel *Fallen Angels* (1988), which she knows from previous experience will help history come alive for her students. She gives students the "What-If?" anticipation guide (Figure 4.6) before she passes out the books, telling students:

> In the book *Fallen Angels,* Richie Perry encounters each of these situations and much, much more. After answering these questions, think about what you already know about the Vietnam War and the effects it had on Americans—civilians, soldiers, and politicians alike. This reading guide and the book it pertains to are attempts to further your understanding of the war and what it was like for the soldiers who fought for a very controversial cause in our nation's history. When you complete the book, I would like you to write a brief reaction to it, reflecting on how it may have changed your perceptions, and how the what-if questions affected your interpretation of the text.

VOCABULARY GUIDES

Standards Addressed

Social Studies: Students understand the search for community, stability, and peace in an interdependent world. All students should be able to consider multiple perspectives. Students understand how . . . colonial empires broke up.

English/Language Arts: Students apply a wide range of strategies to comprehend, interpret, evaluate, and appreciate texts. They draw on their prior experiences, their interactions with other readers and writers, their knowledge of word meaning and of other texts, their word identification strategies, and their understanding of textual features (e.g., sound–letter correspondence, sentence structure, context, graphics).

Context/Rationale

Teaching vocabulary in the content area you teach is critical, and the terms and concepts tend to build background knowledge for future lessons. Sometimes a vocabulary lesson can make the difference between students comprehending a text or not understanding it. As a teacher, you must decide when to let students figure words out on their own, when to teach terms directly, when to have them look up words, and when to teach vocabulary by example. Strategies for enhancing vocabulary include breaking words up to show how morphemes (prefixes, suffixes, and roots) affect meaning; discussing the denotation and connotation of words; having students keep vocabulary journals where they record words and definitions teachers give them as well as words they come across in their outside reading; and creating and posting word walls in the classroom. If you show enthusiasm and respect for words, your students will be more apt to pay attention to content-related terms as they read.

Procedure

- Preview the book your class will be reading next for any vocabulary words with which your students may not be familiar.
- Prepare a vocabulary guide with the words listed.
- Before reading: Ask students to either look up the words in a dictionary and write the definition or view the words in a sentence and write the definitions from the context. For the latter option, make sure the sentence contains directive context clues.
- During reading: Have students keep a vocabulary journal. Ask them to record in it any words from their reading about which they think they know the definition but are not totally sure. After they write their guesses, have them check the dictionary to determine their definition's accuracy.
- After reading: Ask students to use the new vocabulary in some authentic task (e.g., ask them to respond to questions about the reading assignment that require them to understand and use the new words).

Walk-Through

English teacher Meghan O'Brien chooses historical fiction throughout the year that connects to her students' social studies curriculum. Explicit about her purpose, she encourages students to tell the class what they learn in social studies that relates to their novels, and what they learn by reading stories that helps make the history lessons clearer or more meaningful. When she asks students to work with vocabulary, she gives her reasons for doing so. Figure 4.7 presents a guide she created exemplifying how teachers can aid reading by using vocabulary guides.

▶ ▶ ▶ **THREE-LEVEL COMPREHENSION GUIDE**

Standards Addressed

Health: Students will analyze the influence of family, peers, culture, media, technology, and other factors on health behaviors.

English/Language Arts: Students apply a wide range of strategies to comprehend, interpret, evaluate, and appreciate texts.

Vocabulary guide for *Fallen Angels,* created by Meghan O'Brien.	FIGURE	4.7

On Wednesday, we will begin the book *Fallen Angels,* by Walter Dean Myers. With any book you read, there may be words that you do not know the meaning of, or may not be sure of. This guide is provided to help you in developing a strategy you can use every time you begin a new book. Complete Steps 1 and 2 before the reading, Step 3 during the reading, and Step 4 after finishing the book.

BEFORE READING

Step 1. Look up the following words in a dictionary; this will help you with the reading.

    Casualty: _____

    Platoon: _____

    Pacification: _____

Step 2. The next two vocabulary words are used in a sentence. After reading the sentences, write down the meaning of the words based on the context in which they are used.

    "The medevacs risked their lives every time they went out to rescue more soldiers."

        Medevac: _____

    "If there is ever a fire in the building, be sure to follow the evacuation guidelines we practiced."

        Evacuation: _____

DURING READING

Step 3. While reading the novel, be sure to keep a **vocabulary journal.** Try to figure out the meaning of any words you are not positive of but think you might have an idea about. After you make a guess, check in the dictionary to see just how close you were. Also, be sure to underline and look up any words that you are clueless about. By completing this step, you will better understand the material you are reading, while expanding your vocabulary at the same time!

AFTER READING

Step 4. Please answer the following questions.

1. Do you feel that Perry and the other men in his platoon were looking out for one another? Was it because of each person's individual strength that they did not experience as many *casualties* as other platoons did? Explain.

2. How did the vocabulary strategies provided in this guide assist you with your reading?

3. Write several words you added to your vocabulary other than the ones in this guide. How might you teach the meaning of these words to your classmates?

Context/Rationale

Sometimes students don't differentiate between and among the types of questions on worksheets or tests. This can get them in trouble. They might spend considerable time looking in a passage for an answer to a question that requires them to make an inference or bring in background knowledge. Teachers may give instruction in and model how to identify levels of questions and go about answering them. It's important that teachers vary the types of questions they ask, also. If their quizzes always consist of questions at the literal level, students won't get practice combining bits of information to form conclusions, and thinking critically about their subject matter. Creating guides that are structured according to different levels of comprehension helps students as they tackle texts and use the information in them to build their overall knowledge and skills in a content area (Herber, 1978). A typical three-level comprehension guide consists of questions at

1. the *literal* level, which can be answered directly from the text;
2. the *interpretive* level, which requires the reader to draw inferences based on what the author implies; and
3. the *applied* level, which involves the reader going beyond the text, perhaps applying the idea to a new context, or making connections between what the author says and information from experience or other sources.

The categories are not always discrete, so a question might be thought by one person to be interpretive, and another to be applied. This is fine. The important thing is for students to recognize that questions may call for different types of comprehension and thinking, and apply the skills to answer the various kinds of questions.

Walk-Through

Ms. Gianetto teaches health in a middle school where the faculty and administration are making a concerted effort to stop bullying, increase tolerance, and assure that no students feel excluded or ridiculed for being different. She has chosen Jerry Spinelli's novel *Stargirl* (2000) to reach these goals as well as the school's goal of improving the students' literacy skills by incorporating literature across the curriculum. Figure 4.8 is the guide she gives her students to complete during the week the class is reading and discussing the story.

▶ ▶ ▶ ANALYZING ATTRIBUTES OF FICTION AND NONFICTION TEXTS

Standards Addressed

History: Students read historical narratives imaginatively. Students appreciate historical perspectives. Students interrogate historical data. Students identify the gaps in the available records, marshal contextual knowledge and perspectives of the time and place, and construct a sound historical interpretation.

English/Language Arts: Students apply a wide range of strategies to comprehend, interpret, evaluate, and appreciate texts.

Context/Rationale

The boundaries between fiction and nonfiction texts are blurring more and more; some novels are well-researched and contain a wealth of accurate information, and other books are primarily informational but contain fictional characters or dialogue. Students might reflect on the characteristics they find in both genres, as well as in hybrid texts. Penny Colman, an author highlighted in the previous chapter, has devised a visual model for analyzing books using nine elements ". . . that reflect decisions writers make as part of the writing process" (2007, p. 261). She believes her strategy:

> . . . can offer a new way to understand and assess literature, a way for teachers to make sure that the reading material they offer students represents the full range of high-quality literature, a way for teachers and students to compare and discuss their visual profiles of specific texts, a way for teachers and students to assess their own reading and writing, and a way to explore the breadth and depth of literature. (p. 267)

The strategy uses a template Colman designed to help readers plot a text in a way that creates a visual profile, which represents an analysis of the book according to the nine criteria she established. For example, a book can be 100 percent made up,

| Three-level comprehension guide for *Stargirl*, by Jerry Spinelli, created by Jennifer Gianetto. | FIGURE 4.8 |

BEFORE YOU READ

Think for a few minutes about the school you attend. Think of some of the things people do or say that are considered "normal" for your school. Is there a certain way that is "normal" for people to dress? A normal way to act? A normal way to talk?

Now think about what it would mean to be "different" in your school. On the web below, write down some examples of personality traits or behaviors that would characterize someone as being "different." Draw additional lines if you need to.

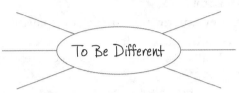

Very briefly, explain how you would feel and what you would do if a person in your school who is considered "different" decided to become your friend.

AFTER YOU READ

Once you have finished reading *Stargirl*, answer the following questions. For the first part, the answers to the questions are stated directly in the story. For the second part, the answers are in the story, but you will have to think about the question and search for the answers, maybe putting pieces of information together to make inferences. For the third part, use your prior knowledge, your personal philosophy, and the insight you gained from the story and apply them to the situations framed in the questions.

On the Outside

1. What does Stargirl do on every student's birthday?
2. What animal does Stargirl carry with her wherever she goes?
3. Where does Stargirl take Leo to show him her "enchanted place"?

On the Inside

1. Why is Leo hesitant to ask Stargirl to be on Hot Seat?
2. Why does Stargirl cheer for the other team at football and basketball games?
3. Why has Stargirl changed her name so many times during her life?

Among the Stars

1. If you were going to change your name to better reflect the person you have become, what name would you give yourself? Why?
2. Stargirl tries to change who she is and act "normal." Why doesn't the change work? In your school, do you think it's more important for people to be themselves or to conform to what is "normal"? Why?

AN ENCHANTED PLACE

To further apply the knowledge you gained from reading *Stargirl*, pair up with a partner and read Jerry Spinelli's *Loser* together. As you read and after you read, have a discussion about the differences and similarities between Stargirl and Donald Zinkoff, as well as the schools they attend. Then, experiment with some fanfiction. Work with your partner to either write a short story (with dialogue) or draw a picture that tells about a meeting between Stargirl and Donald Zinkoff after they have each graduated from high school. What do you think they would be like? What would they talk about? What would they be doing with their lives? What are their future plans?

or it could have no made-up parts at all, or it could be anywhere in between. The reader, based on her impressions while reading, fills in a bar on the continuum to the point that represents the book she has read. Following is Colman's explanation of the nine criteria (compiled from Colman, 2007, pp. 261–266):

1. Made-up material is material that is fictionalized or unverifiable.
2. Information includes fact, events, biographical accounts, etc. that are real, actual, and verifiable. This element refers to the quantity of the information.
3. Structure is how the material is organized, e.g., chronological, thematic, episodic, etc. Simple structures have one layer of organization. Complex structures have multiple layers.
4. Narrative text tells a story.
5. Expository text conveys information or explains something.
6. Literary devices are techniques such as diction or word choice, metaphors, repetition, telling details, etc., that are used to create a particular effect or evoke a particular response.
7. Author's voice is when the reader senses the presence of a distinct author by style and/or voice in the text. It can be both visible—the author uses personal pronouns and/or relates personal stories—and invisible—the reader senses the presence of an actual and distinctive author in the text.
8. Front matter appears before the main text and comprises such entries as the title page, table of contents, and preface. Back matter appears after it and may include the appendix, a glossary, and/or an index.
9. Visual material includes illustrations, maps, graphs, diagrams, etc.

Walk-Through

For extensive explanations and examples of Colman's categories, I urge you to read her article, "A New Way to Look at Literature: A Visual Model for Analyzing Fiction and Nonfiction Texts." For now, you can see my application of her model after reading the picture book *The Great Expedition of Lewis and Clark, by Private Reubin Field, Member of the Corps of Discovery*, as recorded by Edwards and Comport (2003) (see Figure 4.9). One reason I chose this book was that I have found

FIGURE 4.9 Visual model for analyzing fiction and nonfiction texts, applied to *The Great Expedition of Lewis and Clark . . .* by Edwards and Comport.

Instructions: Assess the text for each element. Starting at the left side, fill in the bar to show the extent to which each element is present in the text. If an element is not present, leave the bar blank (p. 261).

No Made-Up Material — All Made-Up Material

Minimal Information — Lots of Information

Simple Structure — Complex Structure

No Narrative Text — All Narrative Text

No Expository Text — All Expository Text

No Literary Devices — Many Literary Devices

Minimal Author's Voice — Intense Author's Voice

No Front/Back Matter — Copious Front/Back Matter

No Visual Material — Copious Visual Material

Source: Colman, P. (2007). A new way to look at literature: A visual model for analyzing fiction and nonfiction texts. *Language Arts, 84*(3), 257–268. Copyright 2007 by the National Council of Teachers of English. Reprinted and used with permission.

| Books appropriate for analyzing attributes of fiction and nonfiction. | FIGURE 4.10 |

D'Amato, F. (2003). *Iqbal: A novel*. Trans. A. Leorori. New York: Atheneum.

Darrow, S. (2003). *Through the tempests dark and wild: A story of Mary Shelley, creator of Frankenstein*. Illus. A. Barrett. Cambridge, MA: Candlewick Press.

Ellis, J. (2004). *What's your angle, Pythagoras?: A math adventure*. Illus. P. Hornung. Watertown, MA: Charlesbridge.

Greenberg, J., Jordan, S., & Parker, R. A. (2005). *Action Jackson*. London: Francis Lincoln.

Gerstein, M. (2003). *The man who walked between the towers*. Brookfield, CT: Roaring Brook Press.

Hausman, G., & Hausman, L. (2006). *A mind with wings: The story of Henry David Thoreau*. Boston: Trumpeter.

Keating, S., & Tartarotti, S. (2003). *Archimedes: Ancient Greek mathematician*. Philadelphia: Mason Crest Publishers.

Latham, J. L. (2003). *Carry on, Mr. Bowditch*. Illus. J. O'Hara. Cosgrave, IL: Houghton Mifflin.

Meyer, C. (2006). *Loving Will Shakespeare*. New York: Harcourt.

Pettenati, J. K. (2006). *Galileo's journal, 1609–1610*. Illus. P. Rui. Watertown, MA: Charlesbridge.

Rinaldi, A. (2003). *Or give me death: A novel of Patrick Henry's family*. Orlando, FL: Harcourt.

it in some libraries catalogued as nonfiction, and in other libraries shelved as fiction. In Figure 4.9 I used Colman's directions and template, and have filled in the bars based on my own judgments.

Applying Colman's model actually did help me to think about this book in ways I might not have otherwise. The text has much information that I know to be accurate, thanks to other texts I've read. But the story is told in Reubin Field's voice, and I don't see anything in the six titles in the bibliography that leads me to believe the words were taken from any journal Field kept. As a reader, I find myself doubting that Field actually said things like, "So what were a bunch of grown men doing putting up with mud, mosquitoes, and midnight visits from large wild animals? You can blame President Thomas Jefferson." Other than the half-page of biographical information on Reubin Field on the last page, I would consider this a fictional account of the expedition of the Corps of Discovery. It would be interesting to compare the chart I made with those made by other readers; if there were discrepancies, we could talk about why we filled in the bars as we did.

Figure 4.10 contains a list of books that may work well with this strategy.

ANTICIPATION GUIDES

Standards Addressed

History: All students should be able to hypothesize the influence of the past. All students should be able to formulate historical questions.

English/Language Arts: Students read a wide range of literature from many periods in many genres to build an understanding of the many dimensions (e.g., philosophical, ethical, aesthetic) of human experience.

Context/Rationale

Teachers know that what they do before a lesson and how they introduce a topic or a text can determine how successful the lesson will be. Anticipation guides can activate students' schema, motivate them to want to investigate a topic, and aid them as they make hypotheses and create questions they want to find answers to. Select a text for students to read, then ask yourself what kinds of questions or instructions will best help students get ready for, and anticipate, the assigned text.

Alvermann, Phelps, and Ridgeway (2007) provide the following concrete steps to help teachers create and use anticipation guides:

1. Analyze the reading assignment to identify key ideas and information.
2. Think of points of congruence between text ideas and students' prior knowledge.
3. Anticipate ideas that may be counterintuitive or controversial, especially any misconceptions that students may have about the material.
4. Devise written statements that address students' existing schemata.
5. Write a brief background or introduction to the reading assignment.
6. Write directions for students. Be sure to provide a bridge between the reader and the author. Direct students to read the text with reference to their own ideas.
7. Have students work on the guide after a brief introduction to the topic.
8. Small-group discussion of the guide, both before and after reading, is an effective means for generating student involvement. (p. 176)

Walk-Through

Ms. Rudd is a social studies teacher responsible for teaching English history. She concentrates on helping her students get to know the key figures; she doesn't want them merely learning names for a test. She has a great time while teaching about the reign of Henry VIII; this king gave her so much to work with as she tells his story, and the stories of those over whom he had power. Figure 4.11 provides the guide she created to prepare her students for one of the novels set during the time period the class is studying, as well as for the unit as a whole.

CREATING A MARKETING PLAN (Created by Leah Deasy)

Standards Addressed

Business: Students know unique characteristics of an entrepreneur. Students know characteristics and features of viable business opportunities. Students understand components and strategies of effective marketing plans (e.g., product development, pricing, distribution processes and methods, forms of promotion).

English/Language Arts: Students employ a wide range of strategies as they write and use different writing process elements appropriately to communicate with different audiences for a variety of purposes.

Context/Rationale

Comprehension of material is a primary goal in content classes, but certainly not the only one. Teachers can find ways to help students take what they've learned and apply it to their lives, to other knowledge they already have, and to new thinking related to the subject they're taking.

Procedure

- Divide students into groups of two.
- Have them create a product or merchandise they want to sell. It can be a pre-existing product or it can be made up. If it's pre-existing, they will have to think of a new way to market the product.
- Tell students that the product they choose or create must be family-oriented and should not hurt or make anyone else feel bad.

Anticipation guide for *Doomed Queen Anne,* by Carolyn Meyer, created by Chelsea Rudd (adapted).

FIGURE **4.11**

You will complete three different activities that will prepare you for learning about Anne Boleyn.

I. In the boxes, write phrases and words you associate with England or English History.

England	English History

II. In this section, you will reflect on sibling relationships, because Anne had a sister with whom she had a very complicated relationship.

- What are your relationships like with your brothers or sisters? Do you think birth order influences how siblings act toward one another? If you are an "only child," what do you think are the advantages, and what do you think you might be missing? As an alternative, you can reflect on siblings in a family you know well.

- What do you think the relationships of siblings in royal families has been like throughout history? Did (does) birth order make a difference? If you know of any brothers or sisters within royal families, mention them.

III. TEST YOUR PSYCHIC POWERS! Look at the front and back cover of the book, and make predictions about what kind of person Anne Boleyn is. Then, write any questions that come to mind that you hope this work of historical fiction will answer.

Now, you're ready to read. Be ready for lots of ups and downs! After you've gotten into the head and heart of King Henry VIII's second wife, you'll want to read some nonfiction about the king and his "doomed queen."

- Suggest that they use the computer, art, and other materials that will be appropriate to sell the product to the public.

- Have them decide on an audience for the report, e.g., their boss at the marketing firm at which they work or the CEO of the company producing the product.

- Within the report, have students address the following points:

  - What is the *product?* Describe it.

  - How is it made?

  - How will they sell *consumers* their product, either by a speech or with added materials?

- How much will the product *cost* to *produce?*
- How much would they sell the *product* for?
- What is their *profit margin* if they sell one?
- Who is their *target consumer?* Be specific.
- Include a visual.

- After the groups have prepared their marketing plans, have them give a class presentation on the plan, allowing 10 minutes per group: a five-minute description of the plan and a five-minute question and answer period after each presentation.

Walk-Through

Picture a business marketing course in a high school. Ms. Deasy wants her students to immerse themselves in her subject and actually think like marketers, taking on a certain identity other than that of student. To accomplish this objective, she has assigned students to create a marketing plan after reading Joan Bauer's novel *Rules of the Road* (1998). The novel's main character, Jenna, is an enterprising teenager who has a love of and knack for selling shoes, and the story exemplifies many of the crucial concepts of Ms. Deasy's business course, including pricing, advertising, sales, consumerism, and production costs. For example, Jenna talks about how she takes a product and immerses it in its environment to make it more appealing to potential buyers. When she displays work boots, she puts them on a brick and makes them look tough because that represents the environment where a person would wear them.

The students in Ms. Deasy's class came up with many creative products and ways to market them. Megan and Kim thought of a binder with built-in dividers and pockets, to be used for organizing notes and handouts. Renée, Jodi, and Michele invented a Robo-maid that goes up and down stairs and uses extendable limbs to clean dishes, laundry, floors, and pets. Ashley, Ray, and Sarah created a product that fits around a door frame and cleans children as they come through the doorway. "Think Kid Car Wash!" their ad says to consumers. Trina, Malinda, and Sara invented a literary trivia game, with game pieces constructed as various book characters and questions relating to various genres of children's literature. All the groups were able to show their understanding that the cost of production had to be well under the cost the product would sell for. After the sharing of ideas, Ms. Deasy directed them to the website www.peoplesdesignaward.org, which invites readers to submit ideas for inventions to lighten the load of the 2.8 billion people who subsist on less than $2 per day. The students could see an authentic application of the principles embodied in the activity and the course curriculum. Then as a reward for all their hard work, Ms. Deasy ordered the sequel to *Rules of the Road* for the classroom library. By the time the students' plans were finished, they were able to check out Joan Bauer's *Best Foot Forward* (2005).

See Figure 4.12 for a sample marketing plan from Ms. Deasy's class.

▶ ▶ ▶ **DURING-READING AND POST-READING CREATIVE ACTIVITY**

Standards Addressed

History: Students compare and contrast differing sets of ideas, values, personalities, behaviors, and institutions.

English/Language Arts: Students employ a wide range of strategies as they write and use different writing process elements appropriately to communicate with different audiences for a variety of purposes.

| Marketing report for food re-hydration device. | FIGURE | 4.12 |

**HYDROWAVE
MARKETING REPORT**

1. **Product description:** A small, pill-shaped single serving of food—place in re-hydration device and allow to re-hydrate and cook for instructed amount of time. The re-hydration device is our design.

2. **How it is made:** Dehydrate the food and compress it into the small pills that are shaped like the food they turn into. The re-hydration device is similar to a microwave, except it hydrates the food using an even warm mist at designated intervals during the cooking process.

3. **Target audience:** Busy, middle-class families

4. **Advertisement:** Television ads, infomercials

5. **Cost of production:** Food to dehydrate—depending on selected amount:

   Machine—$2,500 for original (developing included). Since we own all stages of production it should be cheaper than if we had to buy from other companies.

   Food—$300 per month.

6. **Selling/going price:**

   Machine—$500

   Food—$1.75 per pill
   (1 pill = 1 serving)

Group members: Rebekah, Rob, and Cody

Context/Rationale

Creating post-reading assignments and project suggestions can be one of the most important tools available to teachers. Texts students have read stay alive as students use them to pursue new avenues of learning.

Walk-Through

Mr. Hawthorne is using creative activities such as writing and illustrating poetry to connect to a novel that he hopes will engage his students in the theme of world religions and philosophies, a major part of his global studies curriculum. Figure 4.13 shows what he gives his students.

FIGURE   4.13   Reading guide for *Godless*, by Pete Hautman, created by Jason Hawthorne.

PART ONE: Belief Systems Chart

Directions: You are going to complete a Beliefs System Chart while you are reading the novel. The template is provided below. As you come across information on a religion we have studied in global studies this year, put it on your chart and fill in the details about it. You should read about four or five religions by the time you finish the book.

Name of Religion	Founder	Holy Place(s)	Place of Worship	Major Tenets

PART TWO: Connections with the Protestant Reformation

During the novel *Godless*, the main characters break from the religion they were raised in and create their own. They make several references to a specific time period we study in world history.

Task:

A. Create a graphic organizer (any format you like) showing comparisons to the Protestant Reformation in 1517 that you find in the novel.

B. Using this graphic organizer, write an essay explaining the significance of the Protestant Reformation in the story, and then the effects the Reformation had on world history.

PART THREE:

A. Read the poem below, which I created after reading the novel.

B. Discuss the poem in terms of how each verse relates to the novel.

C. Search the Internet for relevant images that can form a border around the poem. Or, draw some symbols and pictures to decorate the page.

D. Write a poem about some aspects of the story, or about the Protestant Reformation, or about the role of religion in general in terms of history, or about a related topic of your choice. Then add some artwork to the text. Illustrate your page in some way.

E. Read at least two of your peers' poems, and respond to them in writing.

Response Poem:

Godless

The leader of the group, Jason Bock
With his size you would not mock

Bock and his group worship the water tower
He's happier now with Magda his flower

Problems now with Shin and heights
Breaking the group up with bad fights

Divided they fall with no cooperation
Much like Luther and the Reformation

Bock grounded now for the rest of the summer
Reading theology books, man what a bummer

The Chutengodians have all left the flock
Except for the founder, Jason Bock

P A R T 3

author STUDIES

CHRIS CRUTCHER

Use this author's books in **English, health, physical education,** *and other disciplines.*

Figure 4.14 contains a selected bibliography of Chris Crutcher's works.

Chris Crutcher's books will be an easy sell, even to reluctant readers. His stories are captivating; the author covers lots of topics and makes many points without getting preachy. Most of his books involve athletics in some way, and thus are naturals for physical education classes as students learn about the dedication, determination, and training they need to succeed in competition, plus the benefits of these things to the individual. But the stories go way beyond, enticing even readers who don't usually like sports-related stories. Crutcher is by trade a family therapist, and his understanding of and compassion for flawed human beings of all ages shines through. I especially like how he conveys family relationships and school dynamics.

In *Ironman* (2004), Bo Brewster is an angry young man (which explains his forced attendance in a school-based anger management group); though he has called his English teacher a name we wouldn't want to hear from our students, we are in Bo's court all the way. This is good, since his own father betrays him as he competes in a triathlon. Bo addresses his journal entries to Larry King, and this might make your English students think about new audiences for their informal writing. Use this book in a health class to talk about child abuse, controlling anger, and family counseling.

Staying Fat for Sarah Byrnes (2003) tells the story of two misfits who have formed a deep and lasting bond. A teacher plays a role in a young girl's healing from physical and emotional abuse; Ms. Lemry also offers a model way of dealing with class discussions about sensitive topics. Readers might choose to further explore issues related to swimming, burn injuries, abortion, adoption, selective mutism, and/or children's legal rights after savoring this excellent story of true friendship.

Athletic Shorts (2002) consists of six short stories involving characters from Crutcher's novels. (The author is dabbling with fanfiction here.) These stories might help class discussions about issues ranging from sexual orientation to death: they embody the principles of tolerance and acceptance; they are sad, humorous, exciting, thought-provoking. And they're quick and easy to read.

The Sledding Hill (2005) is narrated by a teenager who has recently died but is sticking around a bit to help his best friend cope. The story might lead to a good debate about censorship, since there's a raging debate going on in the story over guess whose work—Chris Crutcher's!

Crutcher shares memories of his growing-up years and relates events that directly or indirectly played a part in his becoming a writer in *King of the Mild Frontier: An Ill-Advised Autobiography* (2004). He pokes fun at his younger self in this series of vignettes; he tells about his relationship with his

---

Selected works by Chris Crutcher.

FIGURE 4.14

Crutcher, C. (2005). *The sledding hill.* New York : Greenwillow Books.

Crutcher, C. (2004). *Chinese handcuffs.* New York: HarperTempest.

Crutcher, C. (2004). *Ironman.* New York: HarperTempest.

Crutcher, C. (2004). *King of the mild frontier: An ill-advised autobiography. New York: HarperTempest.*

Crutcher, C. (2003). *The Crazy Horse electric game.* New York: HarperTempest.

Crutcher, C. (2003). *Running loose.* New York: HarperTempest.

Crutcher, C. (2003). *Staying fat for Sarah Byrnes.* New York: HarperTempest.

Crutcher, C. (2003). *Stotan!* New York: HarperTempest.

Crutcher, C. (2002). *Athletic shorts: Six short stories.* New York: HarperTempest.

Crutcher, C. (2002). *Whale talk.* Waterville, ME: Thorndike Press.

parents, who had their share of weaknesses and problems, and with his siblings and his teachers. He gives ample evidence to convince readers that he was far from a model student. He didn't fit the norm for much of anything, which is maybe why he can write so convincingly of the "losers" who form a swim team in *Whale Talk* (2002) as well as those in his other novels. Students might find themselves inspired to write their own life chapters, perhaps to tuck away to reread during their adult years. In any event, they'll consider Chris Crutcher a friend.

Crutcher (2005) shows in books, speeches, and articles that he understands teachers, too, as well as the constraints under which they work:

> Our educational system is caught in a crippling place right now . . . an environment where the intangible that powers the learning engines—*creativity*—is missing. Creativity is what teachers use to foster a love of knowledge, and creativity is what students use as a receptor. (p. 7)

Crutcher can recognize a good teacher by his or her effects on students. He spoke to a 17-year-old who had demonstrated a pattern of doing well in some teachers' classes and poorly in others based on how he felt in their classrooms. Crutcher asked what the boy's favorite subject was, and got this reply:

> "Doesn't matter. I hate history but I love Mr. Hodges' [history] class. He gets so excited about the war of 1812, and Reconstruction and the stock market going bust that you get caught up in it. He's real funny. And he knows what it's like to be me." (p. 7)

In Chris Crutcher's stories, his knowing what it's like to be a teenager shines through, and readers respond by getting caught up in them. He's a good teacher himself. His homepage, www.chriscrutcher.com, contains many pictures and links to articles and resources, examples of student projects that have been sent to him, and pictures from movies made from his books, as well as a Guide to Teaching Challenged and Banned Books: Featuring the Novels of Chris Crutcher. There are lesson plans available at www.webenglishteacher.com/ya1.htm, and www.falcon.jmu.edu/~ramseyil/crutcher.htm.

JULIA ALVAREZ

Use this author's books in **English, English language, social studies, Spanish,** *and other disciplines.*

Figure 4.15 lists selected titles by Julia Alvarez. Figure 4.16 lists resources teachers and students might seek out to further study Alvarez and her body of works. Also visit www.juliaalvarez.com.

> "You go where your life takes you and the song comes out of that adventure."
>
> —*Julia Alvarez*

Some beautiful books have come out of Julia Alvarez's adventures. In 1960, when she was 10, her family fled the Dominican Republic. Her father had been involved in an underground movement begun by the Mirabel sisters, who were murdered by the dictatorship three months after the Alvarez family escaped. Later, Alvarez wrote a historical novel, *In the Time of the Butterflies* (1994), about these martyrs. One reason Alvarez gave for this book's existence: ". . . being a survivor placed a responsibility on me to tell the story of these brave young women who did not survive the dictatorship" (www.julia alvarez.com/about). Her books, including her first novel *How the Garcia Girls Lost their Accents* (1991), are

---

FIGURE | 4.15   Selected works by Julia Alvarez.

Alvarez, J. (2006). *Saving the world.* Chapel Hill, NC: Algonquin Books.

Alvarez, J. (2005). *A gift of gracias: The legend of Altagracia.* New York: Knopf Books for Young Readers.

Alvarez, J. (2004). *Finding miracles.* New York: Knopf Books for Young Readers.

Alvarez, J. (2004). *The woman I kept to myself.* Chapel Hill, NC: Algonquin Books.

Alvarez, J. (2002). *Before we were free.* New York: Knopf Books for Young Readers.

Alvarez, J. (2001). *A cafecito story.* White River Junction, VT: Chelsea Green Publishers, woodcuts by Belkis Ramirez.

Alvarez, J. (2001). *How Tia Lola came to visit stay.* New York: Knopf Books for Young Readers.

Alvarez, J. (1998). *Something to declare.* Chapel Hill, NC: Algonquin Books.

Alvarez, J. (1996). *Homecoming: New and collected poems.* New York: Plume.

Alvarez, J. (1994). *In the time of the butterflies.* Chapel Hill, NC: Algonquin Books.

Alvarez, J. (1991). *How the Garcia girls lost their accents.* Chapel Hill, NC: Algonquin Books.

| Selected resources relating to Julia Alvarez and her works. | FIGURE | 4.16 |

Alvarez, J. (2006). *Doing the write thing.* Sojourners Magazine, 35 (10).

Bess, J. (2007). Imploding the Miranda Complex in Julia Alvarez's *How the Garcia girls lost their accents. College Literature,* 34 (1), 78–105.

Bing, J. (1996). Julia Alvarez: Books that cross borders. *Publishers Weekly,* 243 (51), 38–39.

Henao, E. B. (2003). *The colonial subject's search for nation, culture, and identity in the works of Julia*

Alvarez, *Rosario Ferré, and Ana Lydia Vega.* Lewiston, NY: E. Mellon Press.

Johnston, J. (2006). Julia Alvarez: Writing a new place on the map. *Multicultural Review,* 15 (2), 71.

Puelo, G. (1998). Remembering and reconstructing the Mirabel sisters in Julia Alvarez's *In the time of the butterflies. Bilingual Review,* 23 (1), #00945366.

Sirias, S. (2001). *Julia Alvarez: A critical companion.* Westport, CT: Greenwood Press.

filled with issues relating to language, not surprising since she came to the United States not knowing English, and thus paying great attention to words as she learned a new language, as well as culture.

A study of Alvarez would be valuable in many classrooms. English teachers, besides using the stories themselves, may lead students to her book of essays, *Something to Declare* (1998), many of which deal with her writing process and writing life. (She is a writer-in-residence at Middlebury College in Vermont, so she often combines writing and teaching.) Students also discover poetry through her collections, *The Woman I Kept to Myself* (2004) and *Homecoming: New and Collected Poems* (1996).

Social studies teachers may use the essays about her life as well as her historical fiction to help students understand political systems and unrest, about the geography and people of the Dominican Republic, and about the challenges immigrants face as well as the contributions they make. Help your students understand current trends through Alvarez's writing about her sustainable farm-literacy center in the Dominican Republic. Her fable *A Cafecito Story* (2001) was inspired by the project. The website www.cafealtagracia.com will give students information and ideas about how they can get involved.

Spanish teachers and ESL teachers will find Alvarez useful, since most of her works are published in both Spanish and English.

WALTER DEAN MYERS

Use this author's books in **English, social studies,** *and other disciplines.*

Figure 4.17 contains a selected bibliography of Walter Dean Myers' works.

> "I give a voice to certain people. I give voice to the urban experience, to poor people, working-class people."
> *Walter Dean Myers, in Ryan, 2005, p. 5*

Several genres are represented in the work of prolific author Walter Dean Myers, and young fans will find that as they grow into more sophisticated readers, they'll be able to find books by Myers that are still right and that break new territory.

Myers is well known for his fiction. His innovative *Monster* (1999) won the first Printz Award in 2000, given by the American Library Association for the work considered to be the best book for young adults published the previous year; the award parallels their prestigious Newbery Medal given to an author of children's literature. *Monster* combines the narrator's journaling and scriptwriting as he tries to figure out how he landed in jail on trial for murder, and just how guilty he really is. Several novels with a sports theme will keep discriminating readers happy: *Hoops* (1983) and *Slam!* (1996), among others. *Fallen Angels* (1988), a work of historical fiction, explores young soldiers' roles in Vietnam. *The Beast* (2005) deals with the reality and ramifications of drug abuse, and *Shooter* (2005) with the tragically relevant topic of school shootings.

Biography is a strong suit for Myers as well. *The Greatest: Mohammed Ali* (2001) is both informative and thought provoking; his memoir *Bad Boy* (2005) explores his own youth and the influences that played into the person and writer he has become.

Myers's poetry has the ability to enhance many units of study at several grade levels. In *Brown Angels: An Album of Pictures and Verse* (1993), the author's beginning letter explains how he collected the pictures of African American children at flea markets, auction houses, and antique shops. As for the poems he shares, they ". . . were inspired sometimes by the pictures, sometimes by the memory of children I have known, and sometimes just by the joy of a summer day" (unpaged). He followed with *Glorious Angels* (1995) combining antique pictures of children from various heritages around the world with new poems that celebrate childhood. In his let-

| FIGURE | 4.17 | Selected works by Walter Dean Myers. |

Myers, W. D. (2006). *Jazz.* Illus C. Myers. New York: Holiday House.

Myers, W. D. (2006). *Street love.* New York: Amistad.

Myers, W. D., & Miles, W. (2006). *The Harlem Hellfighters: When pride met courage.* New York: Amistad.

Myers, W. D. (2005). *Autobiography of my dead brother.* Illus. C. Myers. New York: HarperTempest/Amistad.

Myers, W. D. (2005). *Bad boy: A memoir.* Waterville, ME: Thorndike Press.

Myers, W. D. (2005). *The beast.* New York: Scholastic.

Myers, W. D. (2005). *Patrol: An American soldier in Vietnam.* New York: HarperTrophy.

Myers, W. D. (2005). *Shooter.* New York: Amistad/Harper Tempest.

Myers, W. D. (2004) *Antarctica: Journeys to the South Pole.* New York: Scholastic.

Myers, W. D. (2004). *Here in Harlem: Poems in many voices.* New York: Holiday House.

Myers, W. D. (2004). *USS Constellation: Pride of the American Navy.* New York: Holiday House.

Myers, W. D., & Jenkins, L. (2004). *I've seen the promised land: The life of Dr. Martin Luther King, Jr.* New York: HarperCollins.

Myers, W. D. (2003). *Blues journey.* Illus. C. Myers. New York: Holiday House.

Myers, W. D. (2003). *A time to love: Stories from the Old Testament.* Illus. C. Myers. New York: Scholastic.

Myers, W. D. (2001). *The greatest: Mohammed Ali.* New York: Scholastic.

Myers, W. D. (2001). *The journal of Buddy Owens: The Negro League.* New York: Scholastic.

Myers. W. D. (1999). *The journal of Joshua Loper: A Black cowboy: The Chisolm Trail.* New York: Scholastic.

Myers, W. D. (1999). *The journal of Scott Pendleton Collins: A World War II soldier.* New York: Scholastic.

Myers, W. D. (1999). *Monster.* Illus. C. Myers. New York: HarperCollins.

Myers, W. D. (1996). *Slam!* New York: Scholastic.

Myers, W. D. (1988). *Fallen angels.* New York: Scholastic.

Myers, W. D. (1983). *Hoops.* New York: Dell.

---

ter introducing *Angel to Angel: A Mother's Gift of Love* (1998), Myers recognizes that he's probably always wanted to create this book, since "Thumbing through my collection of photographs, I'm always bowled over by pictures of mothers and children" (unpaged). Maybe even more important:

> The woman who gave me birth died when I was not quite two. I don't have an undisputed image of her, and no picture of me with her. I look at these pictures, pictures of children leaning against their mothers, standing in the shadows of their strengths, of their love, and I am made whole. (unpaged)

This book demonstrates the power of combining poetic text with evocative pictures. Your students will want to try the strategy. Yet another book that can be used as an inspiration and a model for student writing and performing is Myers's *Here in Harlem* (2004).

Students will enjoy exploring the books that combine Walter Dean Myers's poems with his son Christopher's illustrations. Caldecott Honor–winning *Harlem* (1997) celebrates the many aspects of life and culture in the city; and *Blues Journey* (2003) honors the history of a special kind of music, from slavery to freedom, from the rural South to urban areas. Myers concludes, "From an encounter between two cultures, an encounter not without its tragic overtones, a truly American music, the blues, has been created" (unpaged). A timeline and a blues glossary are included at the end. *Jazz* (2006) is aptly dedicated to the children of New Orleans. It includes an introductory essay, more than a dozen poems, and a Jazz timeline.

Numerous websites contain resources and lesson plans teachers have used to teach works of Walter Dean Myers, including www.webenglish teacher.com/myers.htm.

ALLEN SAY

Use this author's books in **art, Japanese, English, social studies, music, English language arts,** *and other disciplines.*

Figure 4.18 contains a bibliography of selected works by this talented author/illustrator.

Allen Say is well known and respected as both an illustrator and writer. His writing and artistic work are intertwined during his creative process:

> Usually, my books start with a very vague notion or idea. Then I begin to draw things that come into my mind. Eventually, I see a pattern within the pictures. It is this pattern that develops into a tentative plot. My next step is to complete all my paintings for the book. After they are fin-

| Selected works by Allen Say. | FIGURE | **4.18** |

Say, A. (2006). *The ink-keeper's apprentice*. Boston: Walter Lorraine Books/Houghton Mifflin.

Say, A. (2005). *Kamishibai man*. Boston: Houghton Mifflin.

Say, A. (2005). *Under the cherry blossom tree: An old Japanese tale*. Boston: Walter Lorraine Books/ Houghton Mifflin.

Say, A. (2004). *Music for Alice*. Boston: Houghton Mifflin.

Say, A. (2002). *Home of the brave*. Boston: Houghton Mifflin.

Say, A. (2000). *The sign painter*. Boston: Houghton Mifflin.

Say, A. (1999). *Stranger in the mirror*. Boston: Houghton Mifflin.

Say, A. (1993). *Grandfather's journey*. Boston: Houghton Mifflin.

Say, A. (1991). *Tree of cranes*. Boston: Houghton Mifflin.

Snyder, D. (1988). *The boy of the three-year nap*. Illus. A. Say. Boston: Houghton Mifflin.

ished, I write the story. This may seem like the reverse of what appears to be the natural storytelling process, but for me, the plot of the story develops through the pictures. (http://houhgton-mifflinbooks.com/authors/allensay/questions.shtml. Retrieved 3/23/2007)

Many of Say's books are autobiographical, based on his experiences of going back and forth between Japanese and American cultures. He discusses this topic, as well as a recurring theme of various levels of dreams, in his Caldecott acceptance speech:

> I am striving to give shape to my dreams—the old business of making myths—the fundamental force of art. And so, *Grandfather's Journey* is essentially a dream book, for the life's journey is an endless dreaming of the places we have left behind and the places we have yet to reach. (1994, p. 431)

Say tackles some challenging topics in his picture books, such as the internment of Japanese Americans during World War II in *Home of the Brave* (2002) and ageism in *Stranger in the Mirror* (1999). His folktales, including *The Boy of the Three-Year Nap* (1988) and *Under the Cherry Blossom Tree* (2005) would work well in a unit on multicultural folktales in an English language arts or a social studies classroom. His autobiographical novel *The Ink-Keeper's Apprentice* (2006) explores the relationship between an adolescent aspiring artist and his mentor. This, along with other stories based on his childhood, such as *Tree of Cranes* (1991) can serve as authentic models of memoir writing and short story writing in a writers' workshop setting. Art teachers could have students study the evolution of his style over two decades of his publications. Allen Say's body of work lends itself to an interdisciplinary study at the intermediate or middle school levels.

| P A R T | 4 | |

A N N O T A T E D **books and booktalks**

CODE: E = Elementary, **I** = Intermediate, **M** = Middle school, **H** = High School

The following annotations will vary in format. Most will be annotations I wrote directed at a teacher audience. Some will be character booktalks, which are brought to listeners via some character's point of view, and these will be labeled "Character Booktalk." Still others will be excerpts from my students' reader response logs. You can adapt any of them to make the booktalk just right for your audience and appropriately connected to your curricular topics.

ART

Anderson, L. H. (1999). *Speak.* New York: Farrar, Straus & Giroux. **(H)**

Lots of high school English students are being introduced to this book, featuring a ninth-grade girl who has been traumatized and is now experiencing exclusion from her peer group. Or, teens are finding it on their own, and spreading the good news by word of mouth. But it also offers great possibilities for an art course. After she is raped, Melinda's healing process only begins as a result of a caring art teacher and a project that allows her to deal with and express her emotions. Her drawing of a tree is significant, so teachers could have students drawing various kinds of trees to express meaning, as well as exploring trees in the artwork of famous artists. In your art class, have one group examine Monet's trees, another Cezanne's or van Gogh's. Have students research trees done by sculptors, or ways of depicting trees in modern art. What might trees symbolize? How important is the context surrounding the trees? How do trees in art relate to trees in poetry? You can ask an infinite number of questions, and students might surprise you with some unique answers and the creation of innovative artistic representations of the trees of their dreams.

Balliett, B. (2004). *Chasing Vermeer.* **Illus. B. Helquist.** New York: Scholastic. **(M)**

This clever mystery builds readers' knowledge of art while also teaching about **math** concepts. An explanation and a drawing of pentominoes, which play a part in the mystery, precede Chapter 1. Clues also are worked into the illustrations, so readers, like the young protagonists, have to put many pieces together to save the stolen Vermeer painting, *A Lady Writing*. Use this book as a literature circle choice among other art mysteries; it could lead students to a study of Vermeer's works and/or an exploration of famous art crimes and how (if) they were solved.

Bowler, T. (2002). *River Boy.* New York: Simon Pulse. **(M, H)**

This is the story of a painting, *River Boy*, made by Jess's grandfather after a heart attack. As she struggles to find its meaning and relevance, readers learn how necessary art is for some people's lives. This book depicts life, death, coming of age, rivers, and beauty—both natural and that created by artists. Use this book when talking about the concept of perceptions of art. Students tend to think that a famous work of art has a particular meaning, which they must discover or learn. A painting titled *River Boy* is central to this book, but the characters are unable to see a boy in the painting of a river until the main character has a life experience that enables

her to see and appreciate the work of art on a new level. Have students look at various paintings and discuss what they see and how they react, recognizing that unique interpretations are acceptable.

Creech, S. (2004). *Heartbeat.* New York: Joanna Cotler/HarperCollins. **(M)**

> *character booktalk*
>
> Hi, nice to meet you, my name is Annie. Lots of changes are going on around me. My mom is pregnant. My grandfather is getting weak and forgetful. My friend is trying to push me into running on my school track team. And my art teacher has given us the strangest assignment—to draw the same apple every day for one hundred days. Can you imagine? What's the purpose? What's her point? Hey, I have an idea—how about joining me and my life for a hundred days or so? Together we can maybe figure out how to make sense of all the changes in my life right now.

Lead your students to the study of artists who used this technique of painting the same subject over and over, depicting seasonal changes or light changes due to time of day. Monet and his water lilies come to mind immediately. Consider this book also as a stimulus to a similar class activity. Ask students to choose something else that is or has been alive, and draw it at regular intervals throughout the year, reflecting on changes in the object, the self as artist, the creative process, and surprises that occur during the completion of the project. Possible subjects to draw or paint include a tree, a baby brother, a family garden plot, a kitten, a snake, a house plant such as an African violet, a Chia Pet, a guinea pig, a beaver lodge, and a pet rat.

Cummings, P. (2001). *A Face First.* New York: Dutton's Children's Books. **(M, H)**

> *character booktalk*
>
> It's easier for me to talk to you, Reader, than to my own friends. That's because you can't see me. My face was badly burned in a car accident, and I've had to wear a plastic mask for months. I've refused to see people; I've thrown their cards unopened into the garbage. I had decided not to go back to school in the fall, but now I'm having second thoughts. I let my sister take me to an art museum today. You see, I've discovered that I can draw, and I want to take art lessons. That will mean venturing beyond my house. Anyway, in the museum today, Leah showed me paintings by the impressionists. When we were close, we could see brush strokes, unusual colors, but the big pictures were sort of unrecognizable. From farther away, the pictures as a whole were so beautiful. The colors blend. I found myself wishing people could do that for me—step back and see me for who I am, instead of focusing on the brush strokes of my scars. If you'll read this book, you can join my journey to figure out where in the world I now belong.

Teachers may use this book as they teach about the therapeutic uses of art. The informational book *Opportunities in Visual Arts Careers*, by Mark Salmon (2001, Chicago: VGM Career Books) has a chapter devoted to art therapy; some students might be drawn to a field they didn't know existed.

Giff, P. R. (2002). *Pictures of Hollis Woods.* New York: Scholastic. (I, M, H)

I have to confess that I like heartwarming tales, and this fits the category. Hollis is a foster child who deals with events and emotions of sadness and loss through drawing pictures. Each chapter is preceded by an italicized section describing a picture: the "W" picture she drew as a six-year-old to convey what she wanted and wished for; the pictures trying to catch the image of Stephen Regan, who was like a real brother; pictures she had drawn of and for her former foster parents in the Regan family, and so on. Hollis looks at her pictures as she remembers good and bad times; they help her reflect and wonder. For example, when she's at her current foster home with old Josie, who is losing her memory but not her ability to love, Hollis examines a scene she drew after a happy day with the Regans:

> Later I drew it all, and whenever I look at the picture I remember the taste of the fish that night, grilled on the coals, my feet bare under the porch table, and in front of us, the river. I remember Izzy touching my shoulder as she stood up to get something from the kitchen.
>
> Why did I have to mess everything up? (p. 29)

As the story unfolds, readers will find out exactly how Hollis "messed up" and why she is no longer with the family who loved her and was preparing to adopt her. Watch her mature into a person who can return love, and who can even save a life. She's an artist, and she's much more. Like the previous book, this one lends itself to the topic of art therapy, a possible career choice for your students. In addition, consider asking students to use Hollis's story as a model as they create their own memoir of a portion of their childhood using pictures rather than words.

Heuston, K. (2003). *Dante's Daughter.* Asheville, NC: Front Street. (H)

Dante's daughter? Did our history textbook mention a daughter? Heuston takes the little historical information available on Antonia and weaves a tale of a talented artist who has the advantage of working with painters Giotto and Duccio; who has deep conversations with her father, as he struggles spiritually, financially, politically, and maritally while penning *The Divine Comedy*; and who is ultimately constrained by the choices of her time: marriage or life in a cloistered convent. The journey motif is strong, and students will have lots to talk about in terms of life circumstances and nurturing talent as well as the historical relationship between Church and State. This book would make a great companion to the biographical *Galileo's Daughter: A Historical Memoir of Science, Faith, and Love*, by Dana Sobel (1999) as well as the novels *Hitler's Daughter*, by Jackie French (2003) and *Shakespeare's Daughter*, by P. W. Hassinger (2004). As a writing extension, have your students write creatively about and/or research children of other famous people, imagining what it might be like to have a genius, or someone who greatly impacted the world, for a parent. Susan Vreeland does this in her short story collection, *Life Studies* (2005). Or, in art history class, they might look up the families of great artists and see if family members shared the artistic talent, or explore how their lives were impacted by being related to and living with the artist. If your class studies Giotto, read the excerpt from this novel that shows Antonia helping Giotto with his frescoes, learning about his artistic processes as she does so.

Holmes. B. W. (2002). *Following Fake Man.* New York: Dell Yearling. (I, M, H)

character booktalk

Hi, I'm Homer. I'm an artist. And I'm mad. Wouldn't YOU be mad if your mother was a linguist but couldn't find the words to talk about your dead father? I've tried to be the good boy she wants, but it seems that *good* has to mean *unquestioning*, and when I *question* I trigger one of her horrendous headaches. Well, I'm about to be a not-so-good son. I'm in a village on the coast of Maine that I think will reveal the mystery of my father, who died when I was only two. My new weird friend Roger is going to help. Come along on this art-fueled quest, and let me know what you think of the Fake Man we're following. I know he's connected to my father—but how?

Consider this a good book to connect to art history lessons involving artists who needed to go into isolation in order to continue working once they became famous. Why? Because the character Owen Castle is just such an artist. You might use the father–son artist connection in the novel to discuss to what extent and in what ways talent can be inherited; then it's a short step to lead students to the fascinating real-life stories of artists in families.

Koja, K. (2003). *Buddha Boy.* New York: Frances Foster Books. (M, H)

Several gifted artists feature in this story, including the title character, whose art teacher had helped him use art as therapy during grieving and, combined with a spiritual journey, as a way to change his behavior. But you can use this book in a number of broader school settings, since it involves conflict between different social groups within a high school, nonviolent ways to respond to cruelty and injustice, a narrator struggling with his own identity and decisions, and much more. It's a door into talking about the principles of Buddhism and the Four Noble Truths that **social studies** teachers might lead their students through. It also deals with the concept of beauty, and all that is good and worthy in art. Readers will have lots to talk about after finishing this short novel.

Does art therapy really exist? How does it connect to grief therapy? Have students research these topics and find other works of fiction where characters are helped through a grieving time by using art in some way. *Speak*, by Laurie Halse Anderson (1999); *Rachel Rude Rowdy*, by Ginny Kalish (2001); and *The Tiger Rising*, by Kate di Camillo (2001) are good places to start.

Konigsburg, E. L. (2004). *The Outcasts of 19 Schuyler Place.* New York: Atheneum. **(I, M, H)**

This book offers a combination summer camp story and lesson in folk art (or outsider art, as the art historian in the story calls it). It also teaches a lesson in resisting evil. Margaret's behavior typifies passive resistance as she responds (or rather doesn't respond, "I prefer not to . . .") to ill treatment by her cabinmates and the camp administrator. But she uses active resistance when she climbs a tower and camps out on it rather than let it be demolished by court order. This story is a good companion to Julia Butterfly Hill's memoir, *The Legacy of Luna: The Story of a Tree, a Woman, and the Struggle to Save the Redwoods* (2000). Art students may explore examples of American outsider art and examine some basic questions: "What makes art art?" "Who decides whether works of art are good, and what criteria do they use?" **Social studies** students may research to find other examples of young people applying the principles of passive resistance.

In addition to some mention of artists in the characters' conversations are a quote from Tennyson and references to Melville's "Bartleby, the Scrivener." Use this book in **English** class as a companion to Konigsburg's *Silent to the Bone* (2000). The main character, Margaret Rose Kane, is a 12-year-old here in *The Outcasts*, and a grown-up sister to Connor, one of the main characters in *Silent to the Bone*. Watch how this will lead to interesting discussions about decisions writers make about their characters.

Mack, T. (2000). *Drawing Lessons.* New York: Scholastic. **(I, M)**

I'm Rori. I used to like being an artist who was the daughter of an artist. My dad painted at home, and he'd mentor and encourage me. That is, until I opened his studio door and found him kissing a strange woman. I wouldn't speak to him, I treated him like he was a creep, I wouldn't forgive him. My dad left home; I'm sure it's because of me! Now I can't paint, and I'm about to disappoint my art teacher by not entering a contest he thinks I can win. My friend Nicky says, "You're not you if you don't draw" (p. 114). So who am I? I don't know why you'd want to enter my world when it's so falling apart, but you're welcome to join me as I try to figure out my family, my art, and myself.

Readers get tips from Rori's father about perspective and color; but, more important, you may use this book to help them understand the relationship of emotions and art. What artists, like Rori, responded to tragedy or trauma by stopping their work? How did Picasso respond to the carnage of World War I? What effect did love, or heartbreak, have on various artists? You'll find a rich field to mine here.

Park, L. S. (2001). *A Single Shard.* New York: Dell Yearling. **(I, M, H)**

This Newbery winner might actually serve teachers in a number of content area courses at the same time it intrigues readers. This coming-of-age story takes place in a Korean potters' village in the twelfth century. Tree-Ear embarks on a dangerous journey and shows by his courage and caring that he has left his childhood behind. Teachers may use the description of the pottery of the time, of the procedures used to create certain types of pottery, and the story of the potters' lives in an art class, perhaps in conjunction with books about today's potters around the world. The historical period is vividly portrayed, and the Author's Note gives further background about Korea at that time. Park points out that the pieces she describes in the novel still exist in museums or private collections, and that the focal piece of the story, the "Thousand Cranes Vase," can be visited at the Kansong Museum of Art in Seoul, Korea.

Paulsen, G. (1991). *The Monument.* New York: Delacorte. **(I, M, H)**

A child artist follows and observes an adult artist who has been commissioned to create a monument to the town's fallen war heroes. The sketches meet with resistance from the residents. Lead your students to research through this book. Have them look for the designs and decisions and stories relating to the Vietnam Memorial and more recent memorials in Washington, D.C., as well as the Women's Rights Memorial in Seneca Falls and various 9/11 memorial sites.

Plummer, L. (1991). *My Name Is Sus5an Smith, the 5 Is Silent.* New York: Delacorte. **(M, H)**

As readers absorb themselves in the artistic dreams and coming-of-age experiences of the narrator, they'll also encounter information about Leonardo da Vinci, Titian, and other painters. Sus5an passes along advice from her art teacher about finding one's own way of viewing the world. "'Try to find a new way of seeing.' . . . He's always talking about Picasso finding a new way to see. 'Pablo was an original.' He calls Picasso by his first name like they were cousins or something" (p. 27). Sus5an leaves her Utah home, where her disturbing paintings cause her parents discomfort, and makes some mistakes in Boston as she follows her teacher's advice to find a new way. Your art students who wonder about their own post–high school plans will identify with Sus5an.

ENGLISH/LANGUAGE ARTS

Avi. (1991). *Nothing But the Truth.* New York: Orchard Books. **(M, H)**

What is truth? It's something different from every character's perspective in this documentary novel, told through journal entries, newspaper clippings, letters, telephone conversations, and memos. What begins as a confrontation between a teenager and his English teacher grows to a national issue regarding patriotism, students' rights, and the power of the press. Classes might present this story as a readers' theatre production, inviting parents and community members to add their voices to that of the cast.

Bennett, C., & Gottesfeld, J. (2004). *A Heart Divided.* New York: Delacorte. **(M, H)**

Kate has wanted to be a playwright since she was 12, but received the experience she needed to follow the standard advice "write what you know about" when she fought her school's team name (Rebels) and flying of the Confederate flag, causing a war to break out in the Tennessee town. The resulting play, which the authors give permission to be performed in classrooms, is based on the format of Anna Deveare Smith's *Fires in the Mirror* (1993), in which the author performs transcribed interviews with people after the civil disturbances in Crown Heights, Brooklyn, in 1991. Kate interviewed students and adults, then formatted the scripts into poetry that was performed by two classmates. Teachers may use *A Heart Divided* in a **social studies** class or **theatre** class as well as within a creative writing unit in an **English** class.

Donnelly, J. (2003). *A Northern Light.* New York: Harcourt. **(M, H)**

Mattie is a word collector. Her prospects of higher education look dim, given her isolation in the Adirondacks in 1906, her family responsibilities after her mother's death, and her father's lack of support. Yet she collects words from the dictionary, she has friendly word duels with her classmate Weaver, she even makes up words appropriate for her feelings and situations. Readers may add to their own vocabulary as Mattie uses the words in sentences and will learn about the classics that she studies in school, and that she gets from the Fulton Chain Floating Library, including Alexander Dumas's *The Count of Monte Cristo* (1996) and Edith Wharton's *House of Mirth* (1964). Mattie has some letters that a woman gave her just before she was drowned, and thus becomes involved in the solving of a murder mystery. This book is based on the famous trial of Chester Gilette for the murder of Grace Brown, the same case upon which Theodore Dreiser wrote *An American Tragedy* (1978). Pair the young adult novel with the earlier classic, and use the sources listed in the back of *A Northern Light* to find out more about the real trial.

Fiedler, L. (2002). *Dating Hamlet.* New York: Henry Holt and Company. **(M, H)**

If you had the power to change the ending of Hamlet, would you? How about a happy ending? or at least fewer deaths? The book jacket tells us that Lisa Fiedler felt ". . . female characters like Ophelia always got a raw deal . . ." so she wrote this novel (which actually began as a poem in a college writing workshop) with Ophelia as a narrator, and a powerful one at that. She changed Hamlet's destiny as well as her own. Consider this book as a follow-up to reading Shakespeare's play; use it as a model of the fanfiction genre. Students might write their own versions from another character's viewpoint, or create Hamlet and Ophelia's next adventure, which was hinted at in the last chapter of the novel. Have students read this book before studying some of the literary criticism regarding Shakespeare's Ophelia.

Fleischman, P. (2003). *Breakout.* Chicago: Cricket Books. **(H)**

Do some of your students dream of writing plays? If so, they might enjoy the two alternating sections in this book. One story chronicles the afternoon 17-year-old Del faked her own death and ran away from the Los Angeles foster care system, only to be stuck in a traffic jam on the freeway. Here she had plenty of time to reflect on her past, observe the behavior of other frustrated drivers, and plan her future with a new name in a new state.

The alternating sections are in italics; eight years have passed, and Del (now Elena) is performing a one-woman play that is based on that traffic jam, which she has turned into a metaphor for life itself. The character offers some wisdom our students might ponder:

It's not just other people we have to accept. It's Otherness. Things we have no control over, didn't ask for, don't deserve. History. Earthquakes. Cancer. Family. Traffic jams. . . . It's a lifetime trek, a destination you never reach. Anger comes so much more easily than acceptance. Dragging an eighteen-wheeler off the road is easier than open-hearted acceptance. The jam was just a beginner's exercise in giving up control, in receiving with good grace everything given us at birth and everything that comes after. In eating everything on our plates. (pp. 122–123)

Include this book in a mini-lesson on writing from our own experience. Elena tells an interviewer that all the characters in the show are really based on herself, and calls fiction "autobiography seen through weird, wavy glass" (p. 7). She compares her writing process to the series of haystack paintings Monet did at different times. Her play is based on a traffic jam she was actually in, ". . . but altered, disguised, given to different characters. Changed. From life into art. . . . That's what writers do" (p. 8).

Grifalconi, A. (2002). *The Village That Vanished.* Illus. K. Nelson. New York: Dial Books for Young Readers.   **(I, M, H)**

This African folktale depicts a group of people who decided to disappear. They had witnessed the surrounding villages being attacked; their people were being taken away to be sold as slaves. To outwit the captors, they disassembled their village, buried everything, crossed the river, and moved deep into the forest. Their bravery shines through, but students will also understand the terrible magnitude of the practice of enslaving innocent people. You might follow up this book with Tom Feelings's wordless picture book, *Middle Passage* (1995) so that students see what it was like to travel across the ocean. Continue with fictional and nonfiction accounts of slaves' lives in America.

Use this book in a unit on African folktales or multicultural folktales. As with most folktales, there is a moral or message that goes beyond the story itself, which students might discuss and apply to their own lives. Courage is a theme of this story, and there is guidance provided as the ancestor spirits show the way.

Henkes, K. (2003). *Olive's Ocean.* New York: Greenwillow Books.   **(M)**

Hello. I'm Martha. I'm twelve, and I've begun to keep some secrets from my family. But if you come with me to my grandmother's house at the ocean, I'll let you in on some of them. There was this girl in my class—Olive—who was killed by a car, and her mother came and gave me Olive's journal, where she wrote

I was the nicest girl in our whole class. What made her write that?

Oh, speaking of writing, that's my second secret. I want to be a writer. I'm *going* to be a writer. Don't tell my father. He's trying to write a novel, and I don't want him to think I'm just copying him. Just come along to the beach.

You may use this book along with others that have teen characters who write in various genres, such as *Sleeping Freshmen Never Lie*, by David Lubar (2005, New York: Dutton Books) and Sheila Greenwald's *Rosie Cole's Memoir Explosion* (2006, New York: Farrar, Straus, and Giroux). Fictional characters will provide great motivation and inspiration to real fledgling writers who are experimenting with form and content, and wondering where ideas come from.

Koertge, R. (2003). *Shakespeare Bats Clean Up.* Cambridge, MA: Candlewick Press.   **(M, H)**

Kevin loves baseball, NOT poetry. Oh, they're not mutually exclusive? He learns a lot when his bout with mono forces him to endure bed rest. He plays around with reading and writing various forms of poetry, often with a baseball theme, but sometimes exploring his conflicted feelings about his deceased mother. Readers will enjoy his "How Do You Do, Haiku," "Why I Watch the History Channel," "Pantoum for Mom," "But Baseball and Sex?" "And a Half-Order of Sestina, Please," "Contemporary Elegy," "Secret Couplets," and others. In the last entry, "A Poem for Poetry," Kevin actually addresses poetry, admitting that he's glad he got sick, because otherwise:

> I wouldn't know you like I do now. I would
> have missed the way you pour down the
> middle of the page like a river compared
> to your pal, Prose, who takes up all
> the room like a fat kid on the school bus. (p. 115)

Students might take courage from Kevin's offerings and try some couplets of their own.

Lisle, J. T. (2002). *How I Became a Writer and Oggie Learned to Drive.* New York: Philomel.   **(I, M)**

"Suddenly, a door flew open in my head. The Mysterious Mole People story burst in. WHAM-MO! There it was, SCREAMING to be told. . . . I remembered an old spiral notebook left over from fourth grade science that was in the bottom drawer of my desk. . . ." (p. 35)

Well, everyone's writing process is a little different. Twelve-year-old Archie is happy to share his experience and advice with would-be writers, from the brainstorming stage to the publication stage. He includes warnings; after refusing his father's request to see his story, he explains:

> One of the problems writers have . . . is people always asking what you're writing about. Then they want to read it, which is not a good idea. Nobody ever likes anything that somebody they know wrote. . . . I read someplace that Edgar Allan Poe's family hated his stuff at first. They thought his mind was polluted. Hans Christian Andersen was considered a freak until he finally got published. (pp. 61–62)

But the rewards of writing are great; students who might not believe that the hard work is worth it if they hear it from teachers might trust this narrator who is their peer. "You remember how you sat down and wrote something amazing, far beyond what you ever thought you could, and you're hoping like mad you can do it again" (p. 2).

You can probably tell from these quotes that this book would make a great read-aloud. The main story and the story-within-a-story exemplify all the conventions of a good story: initiating action, conflict, character development, climax, resolution.

Lowry, L. (2004). *Messenger.* Boston: Houghton Mifflin. (M, H)

The third in Lowry's utopian/dystopian trilogy, this story brings together characters from *The Giver* (1993) and *Gathering Blue* (2000). It's a good example of the genre, involving a society that is trying to live out noble ideals, a temptation to trade away the good parts of the self for possessions and temporary pleasures, a cohort of characters fighting evil, and a hero's sacrifice for a great cause. There's plenty of symbolism, and students might continue the story by writing what they think will happen after Forest has been saved and the characters who survived return to Village. All three of the books will stimulate conversation about comparative governmental structures, and would be appropriate for a **social studies** class on this topic.

Martin, R. (2005). *Birdwing.* New York: Arthur A. Levine. (M, H)

character booktalk

Have you ever felt different from everyone else, sort of like you don't fit in anywhere? I have. I was a prince; then, due to a curse, I was a swan. My sister broke the curse and rescued my brothers and me, but I was left with one wing instead of an arm. Now part of me wants the freedom to soar through the air; part of me wants to be normal and have a girlfriend. I'm sick of being excluded, tired of being ridiculed. But if I could be all of one species, which should I choose? Maybe you can help me decide as you read *Birdwing*, Rafe

Martin's continuation of a fairytale by the Brothers Grimm.

Birdwing is one of many reconstructed or extended fairy tales published in recent years and aimed at middle grade readers. Try combining this book with *Just Ella*, by Margaret Peterson Haddix (1999), *The Goose Girl*, by Shannon Hale (2003), and others in a unit. Have students follow up their reading with rewriting a fairy tale of their choice. They'll come to see the sophistication in fairy tales and realize the stories are appropriate for mature audiences as well as children.

McLaren, C. (2000). *Waiting for Odysseus.* New York: Atheneum. (M, H)

> As a child hooked on the myths, I was both fascinated and frustrated by *The Odyssey*, especially when the women characters left their endless weaving to make brief, intriguing appearances in the men's hall. I always wanted to know how they felt about what was going on. Did Helen enjoy having the world's most beautiful face? Did Penelope blame her for the great war? And why did Circe keep changing men into pigs? So many stories left untold. (p. 141)

McLaren, in these words from her Author's Epilogue, gives the purpose for her writing this novel, which tells the story of four women whose jobs seemed to be that of *waiting* during the decades of Odysseus's voyage home after the Trojan War. We get to listen to episodes of the epic from the point of view of his wife Penelope, the sorceress Circe, the goddess Athena, and Odysseus's childhood nanny Eurycleia. The experience might open up whole new worlds to explore, and create, as students write fanfiction versions of myths and classic stories from new vantage points. Other examples of the genre for students to consider include *My Mother's Daughter: Four Greek Goddesses Speak*, by Doris Orgel (2003); *I Am Morgan le Fay*, by Nancy Springer (2001); and McLaren's *Inside the Walls of Troy: A Novel of the Women Who Lived the Trojan War* (1996).

Moses, K. (2003). *Wintering: A Novel of Sylvia Plath.* New York: St. Martin's Press. (H)

The life story of Sylvia Plath continues to fascinate and mystify generations of readers. Moses imagines what Sylvia's last few weeks were like, adjusting to a new house and changes in relationships after the breakup of her marriage with fellow poet Ted Hughes. The daily caring for her babies provides both comfort and stress; she is prolific though sometimes blocked in terms of her writing; her autobiographical novel, *The Bell Jar*, is awaiting imminent publication. The Author's Note at the end explains that

Wintering closely follows documented events, with rare exceptions that she notes. She created the dialogue and the thoughts of Sylvia as she dealt with her situation and her feelings. Ask your students to discuss how true to life the story seems or might be, and have them try their hand at doing the same kind of imagining in terms of her husband's thoughts. A classroom library or text set might include Hughes's *Birthday Letters* (1998), a series of poems about the couple's relationship published a long time after Sylvia's 1962 death, along with Plath's work and biographical sources, many of which are listed at the end of *Wintering*.

Nelson, T. (2003). *Ruby Electric.* New York: Atheneum. (M, H)

Ruby is a screenwriter, so it makes sense that some of this story is in the format of a screenplay, where we read stage directions as well as dialogue. The main character uses her writing to create a world where she has some control, and where she can work out feelings and conflicts in her own life. This book is a great companion to Walter Dean Myers's *Monster*, which has a male screenwriter exploring crucial issues of identity and ethics. Ruby prepares her scripts for Steven Spielberg; it's possible your students have movies inside of them, too, waiting to be developed and sent out to the world.

Paulsen, G. (2003). *The Glass Cafe: Or the Stripper and the State; How My Mother Started a War with the System That Made Us Rich and a Little Bit Famous.* New York: Random House. (M, H)

I moved this book around a lot within my discipline categories. The main character, Tony, is a talented artist with big aspirations, which is why he drew nudes at the club where his mother dances, which started the trouble. But by the end, he's branching out:

> As for me, well, I'm studying art more and Mrs. Klein says I'm getting better and I think I am except that I read an article about how math, pure math, might be an art and so I started to look at it that way instead of something just to get through alive and I must admit that it has interest for me because I always thought math was silly unless you could apply it some way to life and if I can make it an art that will break down barriers and allow me True Math Freedom. (p. 99)

Although it could have been included in the **math** or **art** sections, I finally decided to include it with the English curriculum books, for two reasons. First, as Tony writes the story of his life, he carries on a running commentary about which literary conventions and story parts he's portraying: conflict and resolution, character arc, plot development, epilogue, etc. The second, as you can see from the sentence I quoted above, is that the book is chock full of run-on sentences, making it ideal for a grammar mini-lesson. Does Gary Paulsen, after writing over 200 books, not know about the mortal sin of run-on sentences? Or might he be deliberately choosing this style for a rhetorical purpose?

Philbrick, R. (2004). *The Young Man and the Sea.* New York: Scholastic. (M, H)

Narrator Skiff Beaman is on a quest. His mother has died, and his father is drowning his grief through alcohol, so Skiff decides it's up to him to raise up their sunken boat, the *Mary Rose*, and make it seaworthy again. To earn money, he goes out to sea in search of a giant tuna. This adventure story has the archetypal obstacles and enemies; descent to the underworld; and hero's return, which makes it ideal to teach the quest genre. It's also a great way to get students ready to tackle Hemingway's classic, *The Old Man and the Sea* (1987). Students might enjoy observing parallels and debating which is the better tale.

Schwartz, L. S. (2002). *Moby Dick: Based on the Novel by Herman Melville.* Illus. D. Giordano. Boston: Houghton Mifflin. (M, H)

Students who like comic books will be enthralled with this retelling of Melville's classic in graphic format. Dialogue accompanies the pictures, and informational frames are interspersed with the story. For example, on a page when the boat is about to meet up with a whale, a frame depicts a cartoon drawing of a sperm whale, with eight or so facts listed in boxes within the frame (p. 19). As with all good adventure comics, there are large-print exclamations, such as "THAR SHE BLOWS!" (p. 33). In addition to getting to see and know Ishmael, Queequeg, Ahab, and the other crew members of the Pequod, readers will enjoy the short biographical piece about Herman Melville and informational sections at the end about whales and whaling, and about the city of New Bedford, Massachusetts. Some may be ready and eager for the unabridged text of the original novel.

Stevenson, R. L. (2003). *Treasure Island.* Illus. N. C. Wyeth. New York: Atheneum. (I, M, H)

This abridged, illustrated version of the classic tale of adventure and pirates might serve as a gateway to the original, or as a satisfying tale in itself. There are many ethical dilemmas to discuss, lots of dialogue, and a strong narrator's voice. Listen to how Jim Hawkins begins his story: "I had nightmares about the one-legged man long before I had ever laid eyes on him" (p. 1). Who could keep from reading on?

Tiffany, G. (2003). *My Father Had a Daughter: Judith Shakespeare's Tale.* New York: Berkley/Penguin. **(H)**

Imagine being very young, having a father you seldom see and whom you know as "the scribbling one." That was Shakespeare's daughter's introduction to the Bard. Judith came to understand some of her father's genius; and he also admitted, on his deathbed, that she was a talented actor. She also shows herself at the end to be a philosopher, for she takes some of her father's words, and asks, "If our lives are lent to us, does that mean when they leave us they go off to where they began?" (p. 289). Her father's dying promise was "I . . . will . . . find . . . out" (p. 289), and this is where Judith becomes a literary critic worthy of our own twenty-first century:

> I have toyed with it, and can find in it different shapes of meaning. Perhaps it was, "I will find out," or perhaps again it was, "I—Will, find out!"—less hopeful and more determined. Or maybe he meant that he, Will, was finding an out, an exit from our worldly stage. But being himself, he probably meant all three of those things at once, and possibly more besides. (p. 290)

Students who have seen the movie *Shakespeare in Love* will appreciate this added story that makes Shakespeare seem more real by placing him in the context of his family. Students will be able to take a vicarious tour of the Globe Theatre, seeing it (as well as the playwright) through the daughter's eyes. Take them on a virtual tour of the theatre via the Internet so they can compare what they learn with the impression they got from the story.

Vande Velde, V. (2001). *The Rumplestiltskin Problem.* New York: Scholastic. **(I, M, H)**

The author offers six alternative versions of the fairy tale she thinks makes no sense in its classic form. She lays out the problems in the introductory Author's Note:

> Why would a man tell the king his daughter could spin straw into gold when he knew she couldn't? Why would a little man who could spin any amount of straw into gold need the princess's little gold ring? Why would he make the deal that if she guesses his name he won't take her first-born after all? Why does he get so mad when she does guess it that he tears himself in two? What do you think your teacher would say if you handed in a story like that? I think you'd be lucky to get a D–. And that's assuming your spelling was good. (p. xii)

The author plays with a feminist interpretation, among others. Students might analyze other fairy tales for logic problems, and have great fun fracturing the tales for peer audiences. You'll need a special section of the classroom library for their whacky creations, as well as a corner for performances of the new versions.

Vaupel, R. (2003). *My Contract with Henry.* New York: Holiday House. **(M, H)**

Thoreau is a big part of the American Literature curriculum, and Beth, sitting in her English class with her textbook open, can introduce him to your students:

> I'd already skimmed enough to realize that this was not your typical dead writer. Scattered throughout the chapter were sketches of forests, lakes, insects, and woodchucks. There was even the picture of the jail cell where Henry spent the night to protest slavery. . . . Henry David Thoreau, with his serious, deep-set eyes, was going to rescue me from my life. (p. 2)

This story exemplifies hands-on learning. Beth and her friends build a cabin in the woods and model their new self-sufficient lives on that of Thoreau. They get the opportunity to follow their role model in the area of political protest, also. Stimulating Thoreau quotes introduce every chapter. After reading this book, students will no longer wonder how a nineteenth-century writer could possibly have anything to say to them in the twenty-first. Maybe they'll ask for the opportunity to live a Walden-like existence (as Beth did) as part of their English course. Or they'll look around to see what injustices they might protest in writing, speech, and/or action.

Good companion books include Jim Murphy's biographical account *Into the Deep Forest with Henry David Thoreau* (1995, New York: Clarion) and Gerald and Loretta Hausman's fictionalized biography *A Mind with Wings: The Story of Henry David Thoreau* (2006, Boston: Trumpeter).

Willard, N. (2004). *The Tale of Paradise Lost.* Illus. J. Daly. New York: Atheneum. **(M, H)**

Newbery Award–winner Nancy Willard takes on the retelling of John Milton's famous, but to some unaided readers somewhat inaccessible, poem. Her purpose is to "invite readers into the tale" (p. viii) and her hope is that readers will have the pleasure of discovering the actual poem. This would be most teachers' hope, also. In addition to heading to the epic poem, and discussing deep issues involving good and evil, students might well wish to add their artistic additions to the beautiful illustrations in this book.

Yumoto, K. (2002). *The Letters.* New York: Farrar Straus Giroux. **(H)**

> *"The landlady told me ... it is by entrusting [a] letter to a carrier, whether the postman or a bottle floating in the sea, that the heart of the writer is truly freed. Although it sounds like a childish trick, oddly enough, when she said it, I could feel the tightness that has gripped my heart loosen its hold, whether I willed it or not."* (p. 157)

These words are contained in a letter written by a widow of a man who committed suicide. Do they represent a truth? Is there a healing power in writing? Even if the person a letter is addressed to is dead? Readers may debate these questions as they follow the letters written by Chiaki to her deceased father. After they enjoy the story, ask students to write their own letters to people important in their lives, or to historical figures or characters in their favorite books. They also might explore the letters written by famous people to each other. Good example include *Famous Letters: Messages and Thoughts That Shaped Our World* (McLynn, 1993), and *Letters of a Nation: A Collection of Extraordinary American Letters* (1997), as well as *Famous Love Letters* (Tamplin, 1995).

LANGUAGES AND CULTURE

Brown, J. (2004). *Little Cricket.* New York: Hyperion. **(I, M)**

Little Cricket begins in Laos in the 1970s, a tragic time for Kia's family and village. Her father has been killed, Communist forces have taken away all the men from the village by force, and the family has to evacuate and live in a refugee camp in Thailand. Kia, her brother, and her grandfather are sponsored by a church organization and brought to Minnesota, but her mother and grandmother are not cleared to go with them. Readers will learn how these immigrants struggled to learn English and learn American customs, while not giving up their own language and culture. The book ends with a guide to pronouncing Hmong words and teaches a lot about this tonal language. Lead your students to the website recommended in the book, www.saturn. stpaul.k12.mn.us/hmong/pronunciation.html, so that they can hear Hmong speakers.

Cheng, A. (2004). *Honeysuckle House.* Asheville, NC: Front Street. **(I, M)**

It's easy and common for people to think that people sharing race or ethnicity will have a common bond, something that links them. Sarah, a Chinese American, resents this. She doesn't even know Chinese, but when a new girl arrives from China, the teacher puts her near Sarah, and the other kids think they look like sisters. Readers will get to know both girls as they narrate alternating chapters; they encounter issues like those above that will enable them to examine their own assumptions, prejudices, and beliefs about cultures and about friendship. Pair this book with the Printz Award winner *American Born Chinese*, by Gene Luen Yang (2006), a graphic novel having a similar theme. (See p. 138 for booktalk.)

Cofer, J. O. (2004). *Call Me Maria.* New York: Orchard Books. **(M, H)**

Readers who have been introduced to Cofer's dual worlds of New Jersey and Puerto Rico through the stories in *An Island Like You* (see below) will enjoy reading this extended story of one girl who leaves Puerto Rico for New York City, leaving her mother behind. She meets a new way of life in the apartment building where her father is the super, in the barrio itself, in school, and in the big city. She struggles with her very identity through stories and poems about the strangeness of her new world and about her language, or languages. Students will ponder language-related issues as they read chapters with titles such as "Spanglish for You and Maybe for Me," "English Declaration: I Am the Subject of a Sentence," and "Confessions of a Non-Native Speaker."

Cofer, J. O. (1996). *An Island Like You: Stories of the Barrio.* New York: Puffin/Penguin. **(M, H)**

Introduce this short story collection by reading aloud Cofer's introductory poem, "Day in the Barrio," then share a couple of enticing sentences from introductory paragraphs of other stories. "Arturo's Flight" begins, "Sometimes I just have to get out and walk. It's a real need with me. ... What I am is impatient. Sometimes I feel trapped, trapped in a school that's like an insane asylum, a trapped rat in this city that's a maze ... (p. 27). In another story, Arturo starts by telling us:

> My grandfather is in a nursing home in Brooklyn, and my mother wants me to spend some time with him, since the doctors say he doesn't have too long to go now. I don't have much time left of my summer vacation, and there's a stack of books next to my bed I've got to read if I'm going to get into the AP English class I want. (p. 66)

Here's the opening of another:

> "You made me feel like a zero, like a nothing," she says in Spanish, un cero, nada. She is trembling, an angry little old woman lost in a heavy winter coat that belongs to my mother. And I end up being sent to my room, like I was a child, to think about my grandmother's idea of math. (p. 107)

Whether the stories take place in New Jersey or Puerto Rico, the teen characters deal with issues and relationships that all readers, regardless of backgrounds, will recognize as universal and will be able to appreciate. Students in Spanish class will learn a bit about various aspects and varieties of Hispanic culture, and see some Spanish words and phrases used in the context of these stories.

Conover, S., & Crane, F. (2004). *Ayat Jamilah: Beautiful Signs: A Treasury of Islamic Wisdom for Children and Parents.* Korea: Codra. (I, M, H)

Your students will learn much from this collection of folk tales, writings about historical Muslims, stories from the Qur'an, and stories from the revelations of the Prophet Muhammed. Sayings are interspersed throughout, including this definition of life: "sometimes the man on the saddle, sometimes the saddle on the man" (p. 2). The stories illustrate some of the advice our students may contemplate with regard to their own lives, such as "If you would be rich, choose only contentment, for it is the only true richness," (p. 106) and "Truth brings peace to the heart" (p. 113). Have students add their own stories, as well as create, decorate, and display posters with these and other wise sayings. Perhaps the stories in this book, combined with your guidance and facilitation of discussion, will result in your class subscribing to the tenet: "The human race is created from one source. If one man feels pain, the others, from the same source, cannot be indifferent to it" (p. 16).

Ferris, J. (2001). *Of Sound Mind.* New York: Farrar, Straus Giroux. (H)

This story also belongs in the **math** category, since Theo is passionate about math, and Ivy, his new girlfriend, lets him know, "I love it when you talk mathematics to me" (p. 148). His mom is a talented sculptor, so the novel relates to **art,** too; and Ivy has culinary skills that she'll increase in college. But much of the story revolves around language. Theo's parents and brother are deaf, so American Sign Language is the language used in his home. The story explores the roles and responsibilities Theo has being the only hearing person in the family. He makes phone calls; he interprets. Is his mother taking advantage of him? Is she being too selfish? Does he have the right to pursue his dreams at MIT, or would a good son stay home?

Jimenez, F. (2001). *Breaking Through.* Boston: Houghton Mifflin. (M, H)

This book is the sequel to Jimenez's *The Circuit: Stories from the Life of a Migrant Child* (1999, Boston: Houghton Mifflin). He also has a book for younger readers, *La Mariposa* (1998, illus. Silva. Boston: Houghton Mifflin). All three books will help students understand the life of migrant workers, especially the children in the families. They'll also come to appreciate the important roles that language barriers and language learning can play in people's lives.

Le, T. D. T. (2003). *The Gangster We Are All Looking For, a Novel.* New York: Alfred A. Knopf. (H)

The story goes back and forth in time, as well as back and forth from Vietnam to America. Readers see glimpses of what it was like for people who escaped Vietnam in boats and eventually resettled in the United States. The narrator was six years old when she and her father arrived; she misses her mother, who had not escaped with them as she had planned. The narrator also thinks often of her older brother, who drowned in Vietnam. She tells of her early school experiences, and various stories of her coming-of-age. But she also watches her father, struggling to learn English, forced to work as a welder and a gardener, drinking alcohol more and more. After her mother finally joins the family, the narrator observes her working as a seamstress, adjusting to a whole new culture. Use this book in conjunction with other immigrant stories, which have so much to teach us about language, customs, politics, and the human condition.

Marston, E. (2005). *Figs and Fate: Stories About Growing Up in the Arab World Today.* New York: George Braziller. (M, H)

Readers of these stories will learn much about the land and people of modern countries of the Middle East, while simultaneously realizing how universal are the hopes, fears, and interests among teens everywhere. Have your students locate the countries representing the settings of the characters' adventures: Egypt, Lebanon, Syria, Iraq, and a Palestinian refugee camp within Lebanon. Readers may also note similarities between the happenings in these fictional lives and the lives of those described in nonfiction about Arab countries, such as *Reading Lolita in Tehran: A Memoir in Books,* by Azar Nafisi (2003).

Martinez, V. (1996). *Parrot in the Oven: Mi Vida.* New York: HarperTrophy. (H)

Manny Hernandez, the narrator, is growing up in the barrio. Life isn't easy, and thinking about his identity and his future is hard. For one thing,

> [Mom] thought schooling could graduate me into places that would make her eyes gleam. Dad thought I should cut school altogether and get a dishwashing job. *Start at the bottom and work your*

way up, that's what he'd say. Only most of the people he knew started on the bottom and worked their way sideways." (p. 38)

Manny matter-of-factly recounts episodes of his father's drunkenness, his father's going after his mother with a rifle and subsequently being taken away by the police, his sister's ill treatment in an emergency room after a miscarriage, beatings endured at the hands of neighborhood boys, temptations to join forces with gang members and thieves. Spanish phrases are woven through this coming-of-age story, as well as social justice issues for students to ponder as they root for Manny despite all the obstacles he faces.

Na, A. (2001). *A Step from Heaven.* Asheville, NC: Front Street. (M, H)

Young Ju's family comes to America from Korea when she is four. Readers glimpse what it's like inside her head as she grows up and constructs her own identity. School is strange, the English language is strange, her parents' behavior seems really strange. Life is far from the heaven she had dreamed about. This novel is terrific for helping students understand the process—and the pluses and minuses—of acculturation. Use in conjunction with other stories of immigration; students will see similarities in the struggles, yet realize that every family is unique in how its members handle the obstacles, opportunities, new relationships, and the changing dream. Read aloud An Na's Acceptance Speech for the Printz Award. Have students then talk about the autobiographical aspects of the writing, and perhaps play with a fictionalized account of their own early years.

Namioka, L. (2002). *An Ocean Apart, A World Away.* New York: Delacorte. (M, H)

It's 1911, and Yanyan has ambitions; she's interested in both traditional Chinese medicine and Western medicine. She finds she must make a choice between marrying Liang Baoshu, who wants her to share his idea of an adventurous life, and studying to become a doctor. She leaves for Cornell University in Ithaca, New York, only to hear from her advisor that, "Female students generally take home economics when they enter the university . . . you learn the most efficient ways to cook, sew, and clean house. . . . Here at Cornell, we teach young ladies all the womanly arts in order to make them proper wives and mothers'" (p. 110). Not exactly what Yanyan had come to the other side of the world to experience!

Besides portraying how Yanyan overcomes these obstacles, the story deals with language and cultural issues. Yanyan makes mistakes with English idioms, as when she tells people that she has to struggle in her physics course, ". . . but if I pull my guts together, I think I can pass it" (p. 144). One day a guest in the home where she is boarding mistakes her for a maid, and asks the owner if the Chinese girl's English was adequate so that she could understand orders. Yanyan bursts out, "'I can muster up enough English to follow orders and mop up your spilled drink'" (p. 145), but tries to behave better during dinner. "I fought down a temptation to show off my command of English by quoting *Beowulf.* I didn't think it would be appreciated" (p. 145).

Your students might also like the companion story, *Ties That Bind, Ties That Break* (1999), by the same author.

Osa, N. (2003). *Cuba 15.* New York: Delacorte. (M, H)

This book opens as Violet Paz turns 15. Her Abuela explains that this is the age in Cuba when a girl is given a party, is recognized as a woman, and is expected to accept the responsibilities thereof. Violet feels American—after all, she has grown up in Illinois—but agrees to learn more about her Cuban roots. She begins to understand what the politics of the Castro regime has meant for her relatives, her people, while she simultaneously negotiates her school life and dating. She learns that when her own ways of getting information don't match her parents', there's conflict and they treat her like a child again. Readers will learn what the quinceañera entails, and they'll learn how one person comes of age in this age of diversity.

In the Acknowledgments, the author offers "Millón de gracias" to several individuals, and also to ". . . speech and Spanish teachers everywhere" (unpaged).

Rodriguez, L. J. (1999). *It Doesn't Have to Be This Way: A Barrio Story/No Tiene Que Ser Asi: Una Historia del barrio.* Illus. D. Galvez. San Francisco: Children's Book Press. (E, I, M, H)

This bilingual story places English and Spanish side by side on each page, making it valuable to those who are learning either language. The book has credibility because the author tells us in the Introduction that he was involved in gangs between the ages of 11 and 18, and that many friends from those years are no longer alive. He is not at all judgmental. "I know why young people join gangs: to belong, to be cared for, to be embraced" (p. 3). He offers this story of a young boy who learns what can happen to loved ones as the result of gang violence in an effort to help readers think through the important choices they must make while growing up.

Ryan, P. M. (2004). *Becoming Naomi Léon.* New York: Scholastic. **(M, H)**

What do you think your life would be like at school if your last name was *Outlaw*? You don't even want to go there, I'm sure, but I had no choice. That's my Gram's name, and since my mom abandoned my brother and me, we landed in Gram's trailer, with Gram's values, Gram's love, and Gram's name. So I get pretty tired of hearing "'Have you robbed any banks lately?'" every day at school. But when we're not in school, we have a pretty good time with Gram and her kooky neighbors, and she encourages my hobby—soap carving. I'm pretty good.

If you read my story, you'll learn about my mom reappearing after seven years, and Gram's flight with us to Mexico. I learned about my roots, my heritage, the art of carving, and my dad. You can learn stuff, too. Come on!

Teachers will have to do very little extra in terms of instruction; students will learn language and information about culture as they take the trip to Mexico via these pages. Have your students find the specific places mentioned on your classroom map or on Google Earth (www.earth.google.com), and compare what they learn about the holidays and customs with what their textbooks have provided. Ask them to search the Internet for more facets that might interest them.

Ryan, P. M. (2000). *Esperanza Rising.* New York: Scholastic. **(I, M)**

The novel begins with two Mexican proverbs in both Spanish and English, including the seemingly paradoxical, "The rich person is richer when he becomes poor, than the poor person when he becomes rich" (unpaged). Students might not believe the wisdom presented at first, but Esperanza's story proves that theme, for her life is richer in many ways by the end of her hard journey from the former life of a spoiled rich daughter of a Mexican landowner, through many American fields as a migrant worker in the 1930s, to a resolution where she can feel the happiness she thought was gone forever, and can actually tell another, "Do not ever be afraid to start over" (p. 253). The chapters are labeled according to what the characters are picking: onions, figs, guavas, papayas, etc. The Author's Note tells of the real-life grandmother, Esperanza Ortega, whose life was the stimulus and model for the fictional story.

Pair this work with Steinbeck's (1939) *Grapes of Wrath*, Gary Paulsen's (2000) *The Beet Fields*, and other stories of migrant workers. Esperanza and her family certainly will help your students to attach faces to the concepts of illegal immigrants, political and economic refugees, and migrant workers, which also make the books relevant for **social studies.**

Saldana, R. (2003). *Finding Our Way: Stories.* New York: Wendy Lamb Books. **(M, H)**

Each story tells a different aspect of Chicano culture, while also bringing out the universals of teenage life. Kids are having problems with parents, with school, with friends. We're invited inside the minds of two students in special education, as well as one of their classmates; we're with a boy in the principal's office, saying whatever is necessary to keep from being sent to the alternative school; then we read the autobiography of someone who is actually attending the alternative school. It begins, "For this to work, you've got to back off, give me a little bit of storytelling room, especially when you start thinking what I'm telling you isn't making so much sense, like a story should you'd read in a book" (p. 49). Spanish phrases are laced through the dialogue, helping the characters express what's deep in their hearts.

Shea, P. D. (2003). *Tangled Threads: A Hmong Girl's Story.* New York: Clarion Books. **(M, H)**

Begin your booktalk of *Tangled Threads* by showing the cover, perhaps on a large screen. It depicts a storycloth, which is appropriate considering 13-year-old Mai Yang and her grandmother lived in a Thailand refugee camp for virtually her whole life, stitching storyquilts. If you place the open book down, the back becomes the left-hand side, and shows an embroidered picture of Hmong people pursued by soldiers with guns. On the bottom are those who are in the water, leaving, and on the front cover the "story" continues with a scene of vehicles, and more, unidentified, guards. The photograph of a girl's face graces the front cover, looking toward the right-hand side of the picture, presumably the future. At this point, students will have to delve inside the book to have their curiosity satisfied. They'll come to understand the obstacles Mai has to overcome in Providence, Rhode Island, a culture literally a world away from what she knew. Her grandmother, like so many older immigrants, could not adjust to American life, and so became dependent on the girl. Meanwhile, letters from the homeland inform Mai, and the reader, about the situation in Laos under the Communists.

The story can help students discuss the complex issues of acculturation and celebrating diversity. Near the end, Mai finds her cousin, who had come to America before her, at a New Year's Hmong celebration. She greeted Lisa with, "I thought you outgrew all this Hmong stuff" (p. 216). Lisa's shrugging answer is telling. "I guess I grew back into it" (p. 216).

Glossaries of Hmong words and Thai words are included at the end.

Sheth, K. (2004). *Blue Jasmine.* **New York: Hyperion. (I, M, H)**

An important concept is inherent in this story. A person does not, or should not, have to choose between two cultures. The story begins in India; the main character moves to Iowa City due to her microbiologist father's career. She makes the transition to life in America, then must go back to India when her grandmother falls ill. Many writers, including Allen Say, Katherine Paterson, Amy Tan, Richard Rodriguez, and Azar Nafisi, tackle the topics of the tension immigrants may feel between a former identity and a new identity; the integration of the seemingly separate selves is told through story. The Glossary of Indian terms will enhance your students' understanding and knowledge.

Soto, G. (2005). *Help Wanted: Stories.* **New York: Harcourt. (M, H)**

Soto provides 10 stories involving Mexican American teens living in Fresno, California. They deal with issues of identity, as most young adult literature does. Students will learn things about various aspects of Hispanic culture as well as some Spanish that is used in dialogue. A list of Spanish words and phrases is supplied at the end; ask students to see if they can figure out the meanings in context, and then check their inferences with the definitions supplied. For native Spanish speakers, the words will already be familiar and comfortable, of course, so will most likely be welcome.

Yang, G. L. (2006). *American Born Chinese.* **Coloring by L. Pien. New York: First Second. (M, H)**

This graphic novel, winner of the 2007 Printz Award, should have wide appeal. Three stories are going on simultaneously, including the Chinese fable of the Monkey King; the story of a Chinese American teen trying to fit in at his school and negotiate first love; and the story of two cousins, one a popular athlete, the other a yearly visitor from China whose seeming purpose in life is to ruin his cousin's. By the end, the three stories converge and show a common theme involving identity.

Invite discussions about the artistic value of the cartoon panels, about language and culture, about negative stereotypes, and about acceptance of self and others. Students might choose to jump into Jin Wang's, Chin-Kee's, and the Monkey King's stories through writing some fanfiction, perhaps in graphic novel form, making the book appropriate for **art** or **English** classes as well.

MATH AND TECHNOLOGY

Abbott, E. A. (1992). *Flatland.* **New York: Dover Publications. (H)**

This book was first published in 1884, and has fascinated readers who are interested in perspective, dimensions, time travel, mathematical principles, and social satire ever since. I ask my students to perform the experiment the narrator recommends to get an idea of the nature of Flatland, where he lives:

> Place a penny on the middle of one of your tables in Space; and leaning over it, look down upon it. It will appear a circle.
>
> But now, drawing back to the edge of the table, gradually lower your eye (thus bringing yourself more and more into the condition of the inhabitants of Flatland), and at last when you have placed your eye exactly on the edge of the table (so that you are, as it were, actually a Flatlander) the penny will then have ceased to appear oval at all, and will have become, so far as you can see, a straight line. (p. 3)

Readers will travel with A. Square through several dimensions and have their imaginations and math knowledge expanded with every adventure. Some will sign up for further travel with Ian Stewart's *Flatterland* (2001). (See booktalk on p. 141.)

Brown, D. (2003). *The Da Vinci Code.* **New York: Doubleday. (H)**

This book has proven to be popular not just because of its intrigue, **art** history, and religious speculation, but also because of the mathematical codes integral to the solving of the mystery. After enjoying the story, students may look up some of the dozens of articles written about the mathematical principles in this story. They'll be off on an Internet hunt that may have as many twists and turns as the storyline itself as they research the number pi, Fibonacci sequences, etc. They'll find ways they hadn't thought of that math and life intersect. And, as adults have done, they'll run for the prequel, *Angels and Demons* (Brown, 2000).

Ellis, J. (2004). *What's Your Angle, Pythagoras?: A Math Adventure.* **Illus. P. Hornung. Watertown, MA: Charlesbridge. (I, M)**

Most of us know approximately one thing about the ancient Greek mathematician Pythagoras: he discovered what we now know as the Pythagorean theorem, which we need in order to pass math class. The author's daughter questioned the practical applications of the theorem, as do so many of our students. Julie Ellis's imagination took over, and so she gives us many examples in this book about the principle's uses, including charting a course across the sea, building a ladder the right height for a reaching the roof of a temple, and fixing crooked bases of the temple's columns. What's more, she gives us a fictional story of the childhood of Pythagoras (history does not provide us with facts), pondering how he might have used his inquisitiveness and the knowledge of the time to experiment with the formula.

Enzensberger, J. M. (1998). *The Number Devil*. Illus. R. S. Berner. New York: Metropolitan Books. **(M, H)**

Every night Robert is visited in his dreams by the number devil, who explains mathematical principles and demonstrates them through examples, projects, and charts. Your students will come away with a deeper conceptual understanding of *mathematics*, which Robert comes to realize is much different from plain old *computation*. At the ends of the chapters, the author addresses the reader directly, with openings such as "Are any of you curious about what kind of pattern we get when we light up all the numbers that can be divided by four?" (p. 145), or "If you still don't believe that nature acts as if it knew how numbers work, turn to the tree on the next page" (p. 121). He adds further hands-on experiments that your students may try to reinforce or extend the knowledge they've gained within Robert's dream. Every secondary math classroom should have a copy of this stimulating adventure.

Fox, H. (2004). *Eager*. New York: Lamb/Random. **(I, M)**

This is a wonderful book to use in a course involving **technology**. EGR3, or Eager, as his family calls him, is a household robot that has been programmed to learn as well as to feel emotions. The family members, existing in the not-too-distant future setting of this story, confront questions about the boundary between machines and humans. Have students investigate topics relating to artificial intelligence and the learning and emotional capacities of present-day robotic devices, as well as mathematicians' and engineers' visions of the next generation of robots. Start with Ray Kurzweil's *The Age of Spiritual Machines: When Computers Exceed Human Intelligence* (1999).

Freymann-Wehr, G. (2003). *The Kings Are Already Here*. Boston: Houghton Mifflin. **(M, H)**

This truly interdisciplinary book deals with both **dance** and chess, tied together by a focus on passion—or is it obsession? Phoebe has spent most of her 15 years training to be a world-class ballerina. Nikolai is an international chess champion at 16. They meet, then share a job of organizing Phoebe's grandfather's extensive book collection, books that can be categorized in a near-infinite number of ways. Phoebe notes, "It will be twenty-five or thirty years before I have any time free for reading" (p. 38). That gives us a hint of what an unbalanced life a top ballerina would have. Whether the rewards will be worth the sacrifice is the dilemma she faces now. She listens as Nikolai tells her of his choosing not to move with his mother at the age of about 10, since ". . . she thought chess would confine me" (p. 147). Phoebe understood. "His mother would not empower his game. His mother would free him to choose a life full of options. This is why we have mothers. To help us look at that choice. To force us to confront it" (p. 147). Readers learn much more than chess moves in this story.

As a math teacher, help students see the connections between playing chess and doing math: both require concentration, both involve making and revising hypotheses, both involve spatial and sequential operations, etc. Books about real chess champions and about strategies for playing chess should be part of a math classroom library.

Friedman, A. (1994). *The King's Commissioner*. Illus. S. Guevara. New York: Scholastic. **(E, I, M)**

In this fairy tale, the king is having trouble organizing the many commissioners he has put in charge of the kingdom's problems. His system of counting them individually proves unwieldy, and each of his advisors tallies them in a different way, confusing him more. As the story unfolds, your students will come to understand the concept of grouping large numbers, and also the concept of place value. This book might provide the key that has puzzled some struggling middle grade students. Ask them to explain their understanding of other mathematical principles by creating a fairy tale, using this one as a model. Do I see a class book in the near future for you?

Green, J. (2006). *An Abundance of Katherines*. New York: Dutton Books. **(H)**

When should you give a booktalk on this novel? The first time you hear a student ask, "Why do we have to learn these theorems? What good are they? When will we ever need them? And who makes them up anyway?" The protagonist, Colin, has always been identified as a child prodigy, but now he's out of high school and has just been dumped by the nineteenth Katherine he has dated. He's struggling to find an identity, something that will make him matter. While on a road trip, he devises, adapts, and tests out a theorem that can use data about two people in a relationship and predict who will end it and at what point in the relationship. Do students believe such a theorem could work?

MATH

Would they use it if they had it? Invite them to read the book to find out Colin's fate with his newest girlfriend, and to study the graphs along the way.

In an Author's Note, John Green confesses that he was not a good math student, though as a young adult:

> I became—and I know this is weird—kind of *into* math. Unfortunately, I still suck at it. I'm into math the way my nine-year-old self was into skateboarding. I talk about it a lot, and I think about it a lot, but I can't actually, like, *do* it. (p. 219)

Green credits his friend Daniel Bliss, a young, world-famous mathematician, with creating Colin's dumper-dumpee formula, which is "...real math that really works within the context of the book" (p. 219). Bliss provides an appendix explaining the math in this clever, entertaining, thought-provoking story.

Griffin, A. (2002). *Hannah, Divided.* New York: Hyperion Books for Children. **(I, M)**

This novel relays the story of a teenager in 1934 who has a reading disability but is very talented in math. She's a boarder in Philadelphia who is preparing for a scholarship exam. When confronted with problems or sadness or rejection, she does math:

> ...Hannah knew that math itself was her one pure enjoyment.... She constructed bases, built areas, balanced equations, and memorized the laws of right angles and the hypotenuse. The answer was there, its question a lock to be picked and pried. Natural, integer, rational, real. The answer was always waiting and perfect and standing alone. (p. 235)

Through this book, your students will realize that there are kids who (perhaps like them) see the world through a mathematical lens. Provide sticky notes so students can track the scenes in which Hannah uses math to help her think or solve problems.

Hirsch, O. (2003). *Hazel Green.* New York: Bloomsbury. **(I, M)**

Yakov is a new boy in the apartment building. The Yak, as Hazel has dubbed him, is a mathematician. What do mathematicians do? Are they always as serious as Yak acts, or is it possible for mathematicians to have fun? He shows her a proof he's worked out showing that the tower a group is building for a parade will fall over in the wind. But when she asks if he could work out how high it *should* be, he responds, "Do you think a mathematician's mind would concern itself with this? Do you think there would be any great mathematics in the world if this were all we thought about?" (p. 82). As the story progresses, Hazel begins to understand this boy who loves order, who thinks

proofs by subtraction are the most elegant, who stays in his room looking for an answer to Fermat's last theorem. A tentative friendship forms. Listen in as they express to each other through metaphor what the world means to them:

> "The world is based on order," said the Yak. "The physical forces that make things happen, the logic of thought, the sequence of—"
>
> "No, it isn't!" said Hazel. "I've never heard such nonsense. The world is a great big soup and everything is mixed up in it.".... [to herself] And not a very clear soup.... A thick, rich, chunky, swirly, mixed up soup with a great big dollop of cream added just to confuse everything even more.
>
> "... No. I'll tell you what it is: a drop of honey.... A perfectly formed drop. With a fine tip and an absolutely spherical body. Completely symmetrical. Perfectly smooth. And absolutely translucent, so you can see through to its very centre from every side without a single disruption." (pp. 176–177).

Use this book to help students understand the many ways in which math and **science** are connected. Instruct students to tackle the problems brought up in the novel and keep a list of the various types of math required; they'll come to understand that mathematicians ask these kinds of questions in real life.

Latham, J. L. (2003). *Carry on, Mr. Bowditch.* Boston: Houghton Mifflin. **(M)**

While middle school students are learning about the early days of our country in **social studies** classes, they can simultaneously be learning about Nathaniel Bowditch, a self-taught mathematician of that era, through this fictionalized biography. Readers will be inspired by the story of the poor boy who worked tirelessly as an apprentice to a ship chandler, yet taught himself Latin and calculus so that he could read Newton's famous *Principia*. He learned to navigate ships using mathematics and gained recognition due to his feats of guiding ships into harbor in bad weather. Continue the story from where the novel leaves off. Bowditch wrote of his discoveries, eventually becoming internationally renowned. He was offered positions teaching mathematics at Harvard University and others. This historical novel belongs on your bookshelf along with biographies of past and present contributors to the practical applications of math.

Neville, K. (1990). *The Eight.* New York: Ballantine Books. **(H)**

This mystery story combines elements of math, chess, **art,** computer science, **history,** and philosophy. Your students will ponder issues relating to infinity, number theory, and life-and-death. It's perfect for your students who are ready for an intellectual challenge.

Stewart, I. (2001). *Flatterland: Like Flatland Only More So.* Cambridge, MA: Perseus Publishing. **(H)**

Take a journey through the 10 dimensions of the Mathiverse with Victoria Line. With chapter titles like "The Topologist's Tea-Party," "Grape Theory," "The Paradox Twins," and "Down the Wormhole," there will be something for everyone: word lovers, number lovers, problem solvers, doubters, cat lovers, quark lovers, etc. Diary keepers will appreciate Victoria's figuring things out as she addresses her diary. For example, she contemplates a scheme for unifying the forces of nature:

> . . . a plausible route to a Theory of Everything. All you have to do is set up a really symmetric version of physics, appropriate to the time of the Big Bang, and then break the symmetry in the right way.
>
> Not easy. But symmetry, Dear Diary, is the key. (p. 275)

Math teachers: introduce the term *geometry* by reading aloud excerpts from the chapter, "What Is a Geometry?" (pp. 131–144), as the narrator attempts to answer the title question. She has been shown examples through her travels of plane Euclidean geometry, fractal geometry, finite geometry, projective geometry, and topological geometry, but now she's looking for an organizing principle that will help her capture the essence of the concept of *geometry*. From there, give the definition of geometry that will work for your course.

MUSIC

Armstrong, J. (Ed.). (2004). *What a Song Can Do: 12 Riffs on the Power of Music.* New York: Alfred A. Knopf. **(M, H)**

The 12 short stories presented here in different formats by diverse authors represent a variety of ways teens make music a part of their lives. Many instruments, including piano, guitar, and violin, play a part; several stories involve singing. Jennifer Armstrong, in her "Prelude—Overture—Intro," expresses her belief that music can be a bridge, and can inspire, which ". . . can communicate subtleties that words cannot express" (p. 2). Similarly, I believe that literature such as this collection can motivate in a way no classroom pep talk or instruction can. The stories will complement our instruction, letting students get to know others for whom music is a central force. Readers will sympathize with the characters as they make sacrifices and devote hours to practice; they might identify with someone who

uses music as a comfort and solace in times of sorrow. Students may make a more serious commitment to learning about music and growing as musicians as a result of reading this book.

Bowler, T. (2004). *Firmament.* New York: McElderry Books. **(M, H)**

Luke is extremely gifted in music but equally confused about life. He's grieving his father's death; he's resentful of the man with whom his mother has fallen in love; he's succumbing to peer pressure by gang members; he's skipping school to play the piano for a mysterious old lady and a troubled, blind child. This action-packed story invites readers into a world where the wonders of heaven and earth are represented by music and sound. Listen to a bit of the lyrical prose coming from Luke's music teacher:

> "All matter . . . is in a state of constant vibration . . . each individual atom and each individual molecule has its own unique vibratory fingerprint . . . every single thing—whether it's a stick, a stone, a cloud, an animal, a human being, whatever—has its own unique song . . . thoughts have vibrations, feelings have vibrations, desires have vibrations . . . [your father] said there's a harmony to the cosmos and if you listen carefully enough, you can hear it." (pp. 181–183)

The teacher goes on to talk about the connection between sound and color that scientists are exploring. This is a great book to bring together principles of music and physics, making it appropriate for **science** as well as **math.**

Cowell, S. (2004). *Marrying Mozart.* New York: Viking. **(H)**

Play music by Mozart in the background as you give this booktalk. The novel involves four sisters, all of whom were important to the musician, one of whom became his wife. The story is set in various German and Austrian cities, based on historical events and authentic letters, and full of information about music. The beginning and end are narrated by Sophie, the youngest Weber sister, now an old woman reminiscing in 1842, long after the death of Mozart. In answer to a biographer who was interviewing her and wanted to know if Mozart and Constanze had been happily married, she tried to explain:

> There was passion, oh yes, that. There was a lot of gaiety, and then other times there were troubles because our beloved Mozart was not quite suited to this world. (p. 349)

Mozart's life, unique talents, and personality remain interesting to people today; the popularity of the movie *Amadeus*, the plethora of recent biographies,

MATH

MUSIC

and the celebrations that took place all over the world in 2006 to commemorate the 250th anniversary of his birth confirm this. Having historical fiction and biographical information about classical musicians available for teen musicians will add to their knowledge of the world of music.

Gardner, C., Andreanelli, F., & Edelmann, H. (2004). *Yellow Submarine.* Cambridge, MA: Candlewick Press. (E, I, M, H)

Young children will love the zany story; middle-age kids will love the corny jokes; high school students will enjoy the references to various Beatles songs. This book provides all sorts of opportunities for observing visual effects, connecting this text with the movie, replaying the Beatles' *Revolver* album, identifying satire, determining the theme relating to war, illustrating the words to other songs. If you run out of ideas as to where to go next, just ask your students. (A multimedia activity using this book is described in Part 2.) The book is appropriate for **art** as well as music classes.

Ingold, J. (2003). *Mountain Solo.* New York: Harcourt. (M, H)

Use Robert Frost's poem, "The Road Not Taken" to introduce students to this book, since there are several characters who must make hard decisions that will affect their futures. There are gains and losses resulting from even the best of choices, Tess learns. Should she live with her father in Montana, or her mother in New York? Should she continue studying the violin, which she has played since age three, even though in order to be excellent she'd have to sacrifice so much else? Can one be both gifted and normal? When she asks her new stepmother, an ardent archaeologist, "'Why do you care so much . . . about things that happened so long ago?'" the wise response is, "'Why do you care about music? Or for that matter, why does anyone become passionate about a particular thing?'" (p. 222).

Have students debate to what extent prodigies in any field should be pushed, perhaps starting with a book the author recommends, *Musical Prodigies: Perilous Journeys, Remarkable Lives,* by Claude Kenneson (1998, Portland, OR: Amadeus Press). Ask them to write about tough choices they've made or are likely to make in their own lives, pondering where the road not taken might have led.

Lasky, K. (2005). *Broken Song.* New York: Viking. (M, H)

Hi, my name is Rachel. I'm not the star of this story. That would be my brother Reuven, who was absolutely passionate about music, and his violin; Reuven, who saved my life. When I was a baby, the rest of our family was killed in a pogram that wiped out our Russian village in 1897. Reuven could have escaped a lot easier without me, but he carried me on his back in a grain basket! Later, he allowed us to be separated so that I could have a life in the United States. It would be many years before I would see my brother again. You can find out what happened to him—and his violin—during those years, by reading this book. I think you will love Reuven as much as I do.

Read aloud from this book to help students realize the value of music, even (or maybe especially) in desperate times.

Proulx, E. A. (1996). *Accordion Crimes.* New York: Scribner. (H)

The musical instrument of the title is the stable feature of this book that spans many years and has a large cast of characters, mainly immigrants. This book will delight teachers who have an interdisciplinary focus; students will learn much about the crafting of a story (**English**) as well as about the fates and challenges of immigrant populations (**social studies**), and the power of music.

As with the book above, this book emphasizes, through story, the value music can have throughout a person's life, and the role it can play during difficult times. By having a number of stories like this available, teachers help students realize that music is not just a subject they take in school; they can appreciate and stay involved with music of many types as they enter adulthood.

Vagin, V. (2000). *Peter and the Wolf: From the Symphony by Sergei Prokofiev.* New York: Scholastic. (E, I, M, H)

This wonderful book helps students understand the relationship of story and music. Vladimir Vagin's lively illustrations and retelling of the story comprise most of the book, then they're followed by a bit of information about the symphony itself, with lines of music for the violin (representing Peter), the bassoon (Grandfather), the oboe (Duck), the clarinet (Cat), french horns (Wolf), kettle drum (Hunters), and flute (Bird). The last page provides a short biography of the composer, Sergei Prokofiev.

Consider playing a CD of the symphony as background music while your class enjoys this book.

Wolff, V. E. (1991). *The Mozart Season.* New York: Holt. (M, H)

By joining Allegra during her twelfth summer as she prepares to compete in a violin competition, readers will learn, along with her, about the combination of passion and perseverance; about the Holocaust; about family; about growing up and finding—or composing—an identity.

This excellent book will motivate students who must commit themselves to hours of practice, whether it be for a voice competition, or for marching band, or another music-related endeavor. Yes, they must make sacrifices in terms of social oppor-

MUSIC

character booktalk

tunities and other activities that would consume their time, but this story shows that the rewards, especially the intangible ones, are well worth it.

PHYSICAL EDUCATION, HEALTH, AND WELLNESS

Cadnum, M. (1998). *Heat.* New York: Viking. **(M, H)**

I learned about both physical and emotional aspects of diving as I read this book. Teachers may use it as they give instruction about diving safety, since Bonnie is injured during competition. Ask students to read excerpts about particular techniques of diving that reinforce lessons in class. Recommend this story as one of inspiration, determination, and persistence, relaying how hard Bonnie works to regain the level of excellence she demonstrated before her accident. My favorite part is the author's sharing his thoughts on his own reading and writing processes after the conclusion of the story:

> I sit down to write every morning, and I don't know what will happen. I don't plan my novels in great detail. I have the feeling the world of my characters is waiting to be discovered, if I garden carefully enough, and clear away the weeds. . . . I think one of the things I love about reading is that it is a quietly joyful act, the writer and reader in a conspiracy together. . . . (unpaged)

Perhaps students could use this book as a model as they take the sport they play or the hobby they're passionate about, and use it as a central metaphor as they enter, through writing, a world of characters and events waiting to be discovered.

Draper, S. M. (2004). *Double Dutch.* New York: Aladdin. **(I, M, H)**

Some students think of sports only in terms of the traditional teams most schools or communities sponsor, but we should be encouraging students to think broadly when it comes to physical fitness. This novel is based on jumping rope, a great form of exercise. And I learned from the narrator that there is an official American Double Dutch League, which "... has official rules, standards, and regulations, with teams for kids as young as third grade, and even a senior division for adults. . . ." (p. 31). Delia learns much about competition, friendship, and exercise through her double dutch activities. The sport also gives her language to use when she finally works up the courage to tell her mother that she has a reading disability. "'I've been hiding it, Mom, and I'm tired of pretending. . . . You gotta find me some help so the words quit jumping on the page like they're jumping double dutch'" (p. 171).

After jumping into this story, where there's another character hiding a secret also, students might want to research more about the rules of jumping rope, and practice the activity themselves.

Feinstein, J. (2005). *Last Shot: A Final Four Mystery.* New York: Alfred A. Knopf. **(M, H)**

Sports fans, mystery buffs, and budding writers will be drawn to this book. It begins with a dream come true for Stevie Thomas; he has won a writing contest and gets to go to the college basketball championship as a working journalist. What he hasn't planned on is overhearing someone blackmailing and threatening a player, instructing him to make sure his team loses the final game. What's the right thing for Stevie to do? After readers take this journey into the world of excitement and ethics, they'll be ready to read Feinstein's nonfiction books, essays, and newspaper and magazine columns relating to sports and the larger arena of life.

Gutman, D. (2001). *The Million Dollar Kick.* New York: Hyperion. **(I, M)**

character booktalk

> My name is Whisper, and don't even ask how I came to be chosen to try to win a million dollars kicking a goal against a professional goalie. It's not like I'm on a team or play a sport or anything. What you *can* ask me is how much I've learned since I've been preparing for the contest. First, I read up on the history of soccer. Did you know that in some tribal societies, the warriors' idea of fun was to kick the severed heads of their enemies back and forth? Okay, that knowledge wasn't going to increase my chances. But then Jess, the science geek in our seventh-grade class, came over with his laptop and showed me how he figured out that soccer is really all physics. He explained how high and wide a soccer goal is, what the circumference of the ball is, how tall the goalie I'll be going against is, etc., and then showed me the simulation game he created on his computer. He tells me, "I can make virtual Whisper kick the ball to any location and at any speed up to one hundred miles per hour. The computer will tell us if Virtual Carmen will be able to block the shot or not" (p. 97). Yikes. I've also learned about how an opponent tries to psyche you out, and how maybe the best way to prepare before a game is to relax with something you love, which in my case is modern art. Have I learned enough to become a millionaire? Read my story to see.

Have your students read this story for background knowledge before beginning a unit on soccer.

Howe, J. (2001). *The Misfits.* New York: Atheneum. **(M)**

If I were in charge of a character education program and could only use one text, this is the one I would

MUSIC

PE/HEALTH

select. Many middle schools impose well-intentioned rules such as "no put-downs" and "no name-calling," but in this story, a group of seventh graders form a political party and figure out a way to make their voices heard. Their motto becomes, "Sticks and stones may break our bones but names will break our spirit." This humorous novel with a very deep message could change the lives of your students who get picked on, and maybe just as important, the lives of those who do the bullying. Use this book in conjunction with a health or wellness curriculum as issues of self-esteem and mental health are raised. Bullying is good for no one and should never be tolerated. Empower your students, with this book's help, to stand up for their rights and to demand, with the help of school authorities, that everyone be treated with respect.

Johnson, A. (2003). *The First Part Last.* New York: Simon & Schuster. (M, H)

This book offers a tender look at a teenage father raising his baby girl alone. He's scared; he's insecure; he feels like a kid himself—too young for this responsibility. But he's sure it's the right thing to do, and his love for Feather is stronger than all competing emotions. Lots of lessons are there for our students to learn from visiting Bobby's life, though nothing about the book is preachy. Bobby is a powerful narrator. We grow to love him as he tells of his love for Feather. Chapters alternate between NOW, as he tells of his tiredness, his anxiety, his struggle to do what's right; and THEN, the time from his sixteenth birthday when his girlfriend told him she was pregnant, through the months of doctor's visits, decisions about whether to give the baby up for adoption, feelings of loss over the freedom and plans for the future he's had to give up, and his struggle to determine what's right.

Keep this short book handy when teaching about perspectives and family dynamics. There also are plenty of ethical issues to discuss. It fits perfectly into a unit about sexuality, pregnancy, and parenting.

When students hear this is a prequel to another Johnson book, they'll go running for *Heaven* (1998, New York: Simon & Schuster).

Lipsyte, R. (2003). *Warrior Angel.* New York: HarperCollins. (H)

This book about boxing and about life is the conclusion to the series that began in 1967 with *The Contender* and was followed by *The Brave* (1991) and *The Chief* (1993). Have students discuss things like character development, theme, and conflict, as well as debate issues relating to boxing, since it's a controversial sport about which there are many expert opinions. Where would Robert Lipsyte stand, based

on the values the stories convey? Are there interviews where he gives his thoughts?

Alongside these stories provide biographies of great boxers, and nonfiction books such as Don Wood's *A World-Class Boxer* (2005), which contains chapters on training and techniques for those interested in pursuing the sport for fun and/or fitness.

Moon, E. (2003). *The Speed of Dark.* New York: Ballantine Books. (H)

Imagine yourself living a few years into the future. Scientists have been able to find ways to prevent certain disorders from occurring, by treating babies in the womb, for example, and so there are virtually no young children with autism. Also, society has come a long way in how it serves and provides for adults with the disorder. So, a friend of yours who is autistic works in a company alongside other high-functioning colleagues, and they have a recreation room with special equipment to meet their special needs.

But, as you know, new medical advances occur every day. Now it's announced that there's a treatment that can reverse the effect of autism, even for adults. Your friend now has a chance to lead a life that would be considered much more "normal." You have an opportunity to give your opinion on whether he or she should be part of the experimental group to receive the treatment—cost free! Think about the pros and cons of this potential change, and form your opinion.

Now, read *The Speed of Dark* to meet Lou, who faces this decision that might affect his very identity. And meet his friends, who have formed opinions, as you have.

Physical education teachers could read excerpts from this book to introduce fencing as a sport that may be enjoyed long after students have left school. (Lou belongs to a fencing group, whose members are very supportive when he faces challenges and obstacles.) It will work in a health class to raise and discuss issues of difference and disability.

Murphy, C. R. (2002). *Free Radical.* New York: Clarion Books. (M, H)

I'm Luke. I'm a good baseball player, and baseball is what my mind was focused on when I was in eighth grade in Alaska. Then my whole world changed. Oh, this is hard to tell; I'm sweating. Uh, okay, let me start with an ethics question for you. What do you think should happen to someone who ran away from the law thirty years ago, but then led a great life of helping people all those years? Okay, now what if that person turned out to be your mom? My mother wanted to protest the violence of the Vietnam War, but—get ready for irony—her form of protest ended up killing someone. How do you think my baseball game fared

character booktalk

PE/HEALTH

after I found that out??? Read *Free Radical* to come along for the ride, but, I warn you, the results of the Vietnam War are still being felt.

As a physical education teacher, try building a library of stories featuring characters who reflect on sports. Mark or highlight quotes that might encourage students to think about their own abilities, strengths, and preferences. For example, after a game in which Luke had four RBIs, three hits, and an error-free night as catcher, he is asked what his favorite part of baseball is. He responds, "'Running the bases...when I do get a hit or even a walk, then I'm in control and can just go for it. Batting—you're under the gun. You hit it or you die. Fielding—you catch it or you die. But running...then I feel free'" (p. 22).

Park, B. (1995). *Mick Harte Was Here.* New York: Scholastic. (I, M, H)

Phoebe is a talented narrator—she has her readers laughing and crying at the same time. Her manner is straightforward: "Just let me say right off the bat, it was a bike accident....So this isn't the kind of book where you meet the main character and you get to like him real well and then he dies at the end. I hate those kind of books" (pp. 3–4). Phoebe doesn't hold back talking about the down sides of her relationship with her brother, as she tells of their squabbles along with the cool things about Mick. The book shows a family grieving, working through issues of guilt, responsibility, loss, and the necessity of facing the future. No lesson on bike safety could have more of an effect than Phoebe's memorial speech to her school, as she shows the never-used helmet Mick's parents had given him for his tenth birthday. "'He said it made him look like a dork'" (p. 81).

Ritter, J. H. (2003). *The Boy Who Saved Baseball.* New York: Philomel Books. (M, H)

Tom is a teen baseball player who keeps what some people might call a journal, though rather than writing about "What is," he prefers to think about "What if?" (p. 18). In his *Dreamsketcher*, he writes his plans, dreams, reflections; he sketches plays for the big baseball game that could save his hometown from the developers.

Lots of dialogue describes ways to improve hitting and the other skills of baseball. Is there a secret? Is there a scientific method to improve the ability to track the ball? Is there "'...clear scientific evidence that the neural pathways in our brains can be altered by repetitious action'" (p. 143)? Is there a way the kids can improve fast with the help of videos and computers? And is the David vs. Goliath game that will decide the fate of the town really "'...a metaphor for the entire game of baseball'" (p. 156)? Students who read this story will be able to think about the best ways to improve performance, prepare for a big event, and tackle their own fears.

Spinelli, J. (2000). *Stargirl.* New York: Scholastic. (M, H)

Exclusion. This is a terrible word for most teens. What they want and need more than anything else is to belong. Every person deals with issues of inclusion and exclusion in groups, whether connected with church, school, job, neighborhood, country. We negotiate our own belonging, and we make decisions regarding the inclusion or exclusion of others. *Stargirl* is an excellent book to get students thinking about this important concept that they'll deal with throughout life. Previously home-schooled, Stargirl is at first eagerly accepted at her new school, but events cause many students to turn against her, and the narrator must make some choices that affect not only Stargirl, but himself as well. I would pair this book with Spinelli's *Loser* (2002), which deals with another unique individual who will stay with readers long after his story is resolved.

Health and wellness teachers are often responsible for helping students deal with social issues, including conformity, belonging to groups, and personal relationships. This book will stimulate conversation, and may help students reflect on how they treat others who don't neatly fit into any social categories. **English** teachers may also use this book as they teach point-of-view; static and rounded characters; character development; theme; and imagery and symbolism. The book also lends itself to discussions of values, morality, peer pressure, and friendship. In short, it's a good read and makes an excellent selection for use with the three-level comprehension guide activity discussed in Part 2 of this chapter.

Trueman, T. (2003). *Inside Out.* New York: HarperTempest. (M, H)

Talk about an unreliable narrator—because Zach has schizophrenia, he can't even be sure as he tells us about being held as a hostage if what he's experiencing is true or part of his psychotic visits from imaginary enemies. What he does know is that he is going to be in bad trouble if he doesn't get his medicine soon. What he learns is that the teenagers who bungled in their attempt to rob the coffee shop are good kids who felt scared and desperate due to their mother's cancer. There will be lots for your students to discuss, both in terms of mental illness, and societal concerns such as health care.

Before the last chapter, ask students to decide what they think an appropriate punishment would

PE/HEALTH

be for this very serious crime. Have them respond to the verdict and people's reaction to it as reported in the newspaper three months after the fiasco:

> After months of mental evaluations and a firestorm of public controversy, Alan and Joseph Mender, 17 and 14, were sentenced today to nine months in juvenile detention and two years' probation after their attempted hold-up of Sunshine Expresso. . . .
>
> Defense attorneys insisted the brothers were driven to desperation by the burden of their mother's cancer diagnosis and costly treatment. Opponents lambasted the light sentence, insisting it sent a misleading message to other teens. (p. 116)

Trueman, T. (2000). *Stuck in Neutral.* New York: HarperCollins. **(M, H)**

Our 14-year-old narrator is a great health or biology teacher as he tells his personal story:

> The deal is, I have cerebral palsy (C.P.). C.P. is not a disease; it's a condition. When I was born I got brain damaged. A tiny blood vessel burst inside my head and, as luck would have it, this blood vessel was in exactly the 100 percent perfectly *wrong* spot. I don't know enough about the brain to be able to say where in my brain this injury happened (frontal lobe? cerebral cortex?), but whatever it was, it wiped out my muscle control. (p. 6)

Readers continue to learn more, and want to know more, as Shawn tells the story of how his father doesn't realize that he can actually think and hear and learn and feel pleasure, despite not being able to communicate that to others. Shawn is getting data indicating that his father might be planning to kill him, thinking he'd be doing his son a favor. After reading this book, students might research the debates about euthanasia and assisted suicide, and add their voices, or stories, to the mix.

SCIENCE

Anderson, L. H. (2002) *Catalyst.* New York: Penguin Group. **(H)**

This suspenseful story follows a girl's struggle with her identity and her future and her past. At the same time, it provides a review of chemistry vocabulary, principles, and safety tips, for the narrator has organized her telling of her senior-year experiences by using chemistry-related headings throughout the chapters. As they ponder the connections between Kate's actions and the terms, students might come to a deeper understanding of the principles and remember them longer, because Kate (both *Good*

Kate and *Bad Kate*, as she identifies herself) is certainly memorable. I'll outline Chapter 2 to give you an idea of the setup. The chapter title is "Delayed Reactions," and the subtitles are: 2.1 Acid, 2.2 Transition Element, 2.2.1 Base, 2.3 Caustic, 2.4, The Crucible, 2.5 Reactants, 2.5.1 Bonds, 2.6 Boron, 2.7 Solubility, 2.8 Reduction, 2.9 Surface Tension, 2.10 Elastic Collision, 2.11 Half-Life. This is a good book for chemistry classrooms, **English** classrooms, and even Guidance Offices, since the story involves seniors waiting to hear from the colleges they've applied to, with their futures hanging in the balance. I have no chemical formula to predict students' reactions to the story, but I can assure you they'll be strong.

Bear, G. (2003). *Darwin's Children.* New York: Ballantine Books. **(H)**

If evolution caused a change in human DNA that resulted in babies that were genetically enhanced, demonstrating advanced characteristics, that would be good, right? Wouldn't these children be blessed, and be at an advantage in terms of survival and well-being? Not if they are perceived as a threat to those without those traits! That's where this novel begins. The "virus children" have been isolated, and are in great danger from those who refuse to see them as human. Throughout the story, ethical dilemmas are weighed, as characters act and react according to their philosophies, their knowledge of science, their fears and other emotions. Ask your students to apply some of the same principles in this story to things that are happening in the field of genetics today, especially as they peruse articles representing breakthroughs, hypothesizing about the future, or reporting on procedures the medical field and/or scientific researchers are on the brink of being able to do.

After the novel, the author adds a section labeled "Caveats," where he takes responsibility for any misleading science concepts in the book, though ". . . all of the speculations found here are supported, to one degree or another, by research published in texts and in respected scientific journals" (p. 373). He discusses the novel's theological speculations and gives his views on the debate concerning evolution, as well as on religious belief. The next section is called "A Short Biological Primer," which is followed by a "Short Glossary of Scientific Terms." Finally, he adds "A Brief Reading List" for further exploration of the curricular topics relevant to his story.

Bloor, E. (1997). *Tangerine.* New York: Scholastic. **(M)**

> Hi. My name's Paul. Most people, including my parents, would say my defining characteristic is my poor vision.

Okay, so I'm legally blind, but there's a lot more to me than that. I think of myself as a soccer goalie. I think of myself as a seventh-grade scientist: Why is the Florida town I've moved to sinking? How can my cooperative learning group do a great research presentation on tangerines? I also think I'm the most perceptive person in the family—my parents are blind to the signs that my older brother, the football hero, is dangerously messed up and headed for trouble. Read *Tangerine*, and I'll tell you more about what's going on.

Use this book along with others dealing with teens fighting environmental battles (such as *Hoot* [2003] and *Flush* [2005], both by Carl Hiaasen) as a stimulus for students' action research into their neighborhood environments and the scientific connections inherent in the issues they investigate.

Carlson, R. (2003). *The Speed of Light.* New York: HarperTempest. (M, H)

This fits in the **physical education** and **health** category as well, since Larry, the narrator, is a baseball player, and the story deals with parent–child relationships. But a big part of it has to do with the scientific experiments Larry's friend Witt has been conducting ever since they were in first grade. Witt wants to understand the whole world, the big picture. As Larry says, ". . . in a basement overgrown with foul junk, we are trying to discover the laws that make the world work" (p. 33). Scientific and mathematical principles begin every chapter. But what laws can explain why Witt's father would murder Witt's pet alligator? And what explanation is there for Larry liking girls all of a sudden? And how is the world making any sense when Witt has to leave home after his father breaks his son's arm? This is a coming-of-age novel, but not a novel that provides nice neat scientific answers for the characters or the readers. Bring in real-life examples of scientists who grappled with difficult questions for their whole careers, and you will help students join in the continuing quest to find answers about the laws governing our world and universe.

Curtis, C. P. (2004). *Bucking the Sarge.* Random House. (M, H)

Students completing scientific investigations or competing in science fairs will enjoy following Luther's progress as he attempts to win his school's science fair for the third consecutive year. His research involves the consequences of the use of lead paint. Unfortunately, he does not win the adulation of his mother, who is abusing her position as landlord in a slum, and who has been knowingly using lead paint in her apartments for years. Readers will see the social, political, and personal consequences

of our actions. Luther is a young philosopher as well as scientist, so he thinks through some ethical issues and makes some tough choices. This is one of several novels (See Bloor, above) that can be used in connection with curricular material on environmental issues and on scientists as activists.

Dickerson, P. (1988). *Eva.* New York: Delacorte. (M, H)

If the only way your mind could stay alive was to have doctors place it in the body of a chimpanzee, what would you choose? Well, no one asked *me*. My parents made the decision after an accident, and now I (and they) have to live with the consequences. What's my identity now? Who are my kin? Mom wants me to still be the old me, to act totally human and not partake in any animal behavior. Guess again, Mom; you can't have it both ways. So, two-legged reader, come to the zoo (ha, ha) and join me by reading this book. I'll show you around.

It will be increasingly important for our students to understand issues of ethics related to scientific breakthroughs. Pair this book with Jonathan Marks's nonfiction book, *What It Means to Be 98% Chimpanzee: Apes, People, and their Genes* (2003, Berkeley: University of California Press) to stimulate some lively discussion.

Farmer, N. (2002). *The House of the Scorpion.* New York: Atheneum. (H)

If your students ever say to you that they don't think cloning is such a big ethical deal, and they don't understand what the fuss is about, give them this book and have them join Matt's journey. For Matt is a clone, and while he recognizes himself as an individual—a person—others don't. He was cloned from the DNA of the rich El Patrón, harvested rather than born, for the express purpose of helping El Patrón continue his life by replacing his worn-out organs with those of the young boy. Nothing like knowing what your future holds! The science is explained along the way in this story of Matt trying to escape his intended fate. And the ethical dilemma is clear.

Feinberg, A. (1999). *Borrowed Light.* New York: Delacorte. (M, H)

Callisto (named after one of Galileo's moons) is a teen astronomer who loves to read the sky; her understanding of science helps her to contemplate her life. She classifies people as stars or moons—those who make their own light or those who must borrow it from others. She values astronomical facts. "They enlarge the perimeter of your life, sweeping you away. . . . They signpost the way to other worlds you might want to live in" (p. 5). Science helps her put things in perspective. "... compared to the catastrophe that happened when I was sixteen, the sum of all the painful events of my childhood would be as microscopic as those first single-celled bacteria climbing up the lips of volcanoes" (p. 6).

Callisto finds help navigating problems in her own life by reading about comet discoverer Caroline Herschel, by thinking about black holes and dwarf stars. Might there be a down side to this? A boy once surmised, "I think you hide behind science. Do you?" (p. 184). Some readers might say yes, and others might see science as her way of illuminating thoughts about family and relationships, and a way to dream:

> I'll give my babies endless helpings of love, just as a mother should. And when they're old enough, they'll have all the fuel they need to make their own. Little rockets of energy they'll be. They'll have pockets of happiness inside them, like microchips of joy. (p. 278)

Read from this book before assigning a skywatching assignment; the book would make a good companion to a guide for amateur astronomers, also.

Fogelin, A. (2001). *Anna Casey's Place in the World.* Atlanta: Peachtree. (M, H)

Miss Johnette, the biology teacher, gets asked out on a date. A biologist has asked her to go to a bat watch with him. What else would you expect from a novelist who writes before the sun comes up and spends every fall tagging monarch butterflies? As readers join foster child Anna in her new neighborhood, they'll become intrigued with her explorer's notebook and scientific habits. They'll get lots of mini–biology lessons as children follow Miss Johnette to her home, where there are animal skulls placed where another house might have knick-knacks, to a thrift store where she buys used jeans to preserve the environment, on a rock hunting expedition, and to a field where they dig up trees to save them from a construction crew.

This book will motivate students to investigate their own neighborhoods for interesting species and examples of good or not so good ways that humans are interacting with nature. And who knows, that might lead to action that will be good for the environment surrounding your school.

Grunwell, J. M. (2003). *Mind Games.* Boston: Houghton Mifflin. (M)

Join the seventh-grade Mad Science Club as they test a hypothesis regarding the state lottery. Six characters set out individually to prove that ESP exists. They read research on paranormal experiences, they conduct experiments they've devised, they record data in charts and tables, they keep track of experimenter comments and subject comments. There are unexpected results, including some deep thinking about topics such as death and becoming able to see things through others' eyes. Think about reading this great story at science fair time in your school to provide your students with inspiration about their own projects.

Holman, S. (2002). *Sondak: Princess of the Moon and Stars: Korea, A.D. 595.* New York: Scholastic. (M, H)

What would your students like for their next birthday? Sondak wants an observatory, to be built at her favorite star-gazing spot, so that she can map the sky. She lives in a land where astronomers have been put to death for inaccurate predictions, but her passion cannot be subdued, even when she is told, "... astronomy is not the proper adornment for a young lady. A woman interested in the stars is like a fish interested in the treetops—it is a dangerous, unnatural place for her to be. A young lady should adorn herself with jewelry and children, and leave science to those whose minds are best equipped for it'" (p. 28). Despite the warning, Sondak sneaks out at night to chart constellations and gazes out her window reciting the planets "... like I would chant a Buddhist mantra" (p. 76). As future queen, she ponders hard questions, such as "How are we to wage wars against our enemies when our Buddha forbids us to kill?" (p. 112).

Readers of this book, part of the *Royal Diaries* series, will learn things such as how people in the sixth century protected their eyes when an eclipse occurred: "Our astronomers have prepared a deep basin of water, blackened with Chinese ink. It will serve to reflect an exact image of the eclipse. The other safe way of observing the eclipse is to view it through a lens of semitransparent jade" (p. 150).

Historical notes, charts, and photographs are included at the end. We discover that the real Queen Sondak built the oldest astronomical observatory in the Far East, which still stands!

Klass, D. (1994). *California Blue.* New York: Scholastic. (M, H)

I'm John. Glad to meet you. Have you ever felt between a rock and a hard place? I'm in a no-win situation at the moment. I've discovered a new species of butterfly. It's blue, and beautiful beyond beautiful. This is the most exciting thing that's ever happened to me. So why can't I enjoy it, you ask? Well, if I side with the environmentalists and fight to protect it at the cost of the lumber industry, my town suffers. My family suffers. I know what my father expects of me. But our relationship was strained way before this; our values are not the same. My decision isn't made any easier

SCIENCE

character booktalk

knowing he has cancer. A butterfly has made me realize that life and death issues are pretty complex. Why don't you think through the issues with me as you read *California Blue*? I can use all the help I can get!

Books such as *California Blue* help our students understand that decisions they make, and political action they take, will help save endangered species. Have your students read the nonfiction books *The Race to Save the Lord God Bird*, by Philip Hoose (2004), and *The Grail Bird*, by Tim Gallagher (2005), to learn about the ongoing fight to protect the environment of what might be the last ivory-billed woodpecker in existence. Then ask them to compare the situation with the one John faced in the novel.

L'Engle, M. (1994). *Troubling a Star.* New York: Farrar Straus Giroux. (M, H)

How many narrators tell their story while abandoned on an iceberg? Vicky Austin tells this romance/adventure story from Antarctica. There's much scientific information shared as she reads from a marine biologist's journal. For example:

> We are all awed by the proliferation of diatoms in these frigid waters, which is . . . to the rest of plankton like the Milky Way to the other visible stars in the sky . . . there are, in the sea, somewhere around ten billion billion diatoms, little particles of energy invisible to the naked eye, and each as individual as a maple leaf or a snowflake. Ten billion billion is about the same order of magnitude as all of the stars in the universe. (p. 47)

Students might want to go on to read some of the many other Madeleine L'Engle books; I know of no one who writes more beautifully about stars and other scientific topics than she.

Mass, W. (2003). *A Mango-Shaped Space.* New York: Little, Brown and Company. (M)

Mia is a synesthete; she processes information differently, experiencing letters, numbers, and sounds in color that comes in geometric shapes. This might sound exciting, and it definitely is. She listens to Mozart and tells the reader, "The colors immediately and gently flow over me, energizing me. . . . The glossy red-barnlike color of the violin, the silvery-bluish white of the flute, the school-bus yellow of the French horn. All of them layering on top of one another, changing, shifting . . ." (p. 17). But it also causes learning problems. Her synesthesia interferes with her ability to do school math, and reading is difficult. Would she better off if she were "normal"? Students may ponder the pluses and drawbacks of giftedness as they accompany Mia on her journey to

self-awareness. The Author's Note supplies resources for learning more about synesthesia. Have students investigate these to find out the biological basis of the condition, how it is diagnosed, and some famous people who had, or have, synesthesia.

Mills, C. (1998). *Standing Up to Mr. O.* New York: Farrar Straus Giroux. (I, M)

Maggie, in addition to refusing to dissect a worm, writes a persuasive essay on the topic of animal rights, which alludes to the Ten Commandments and the Declaration of Independence. She learns from her biology teacher the purpose of his planned *pithing*, cutting an animal's head off while it's still alive:

> The point of it was supposed to be to cut Froggles's central nervous cord so that they could see exactly how the nerves were connected to the muscles, and how the different muscles could be twitched by manipulating different nerves. (p. 139)

Readers of this book might be motivated to read articles on the benefits of scientific research using animals, as well as those written by credible scientists who are against sacrificing animals for the sake of knowledge and possible medicinal help for humans. Like Maggie, they'll come to appreciate the complexity of the arguments and issues.

Smith, G. L. (2003). *Ninjas, Piranhas, and Galileo.* New York: Little, Brown and Company. (I, M)

Three friends play various roles in both a science fair and a student court room. At the climax, Eli has been found guilty of vandalism, though nothing was destroyed. And he is practically failing science, though he knows his procedures were not flawed and his findings were valid. He faces a choice not unlike the one Galileo was given by the Inquisition: recant or face condemnation. Your students will delight in the knowledge connected with the events of this book. They'll find out if piranhas can be trained to eat a banana, they'll see examples of how classical music relates to science experiments, and they'll grapple with the ethics of science, strategies of courtroom defense, and the workings of friendship.

Wallace, R. (2003). *Restless: A Ghost's Story.* New York: Viking. (H)

The narrator of *Restless* has been dead for 10 years. Frank is watching his little brother Herbie, who's now 17, the age when cancer ended his own life, at least within his body. Herbie, in addition to being a good athlete, is interested in physics. In conversation with others in his favorite physics Internet chat room, he ponders issues relating to space, time, religion, and death. Several places in the story offer messages on an Internet physics board. Classes may

SCIENCE

participate in similar online chat rooms, realizing that there is great interest in the topics they are studying in high school physics.

Because Herbie is open to ideas, as scientists must be, Frank thinks he'll be receptive to connecting with the spirit of his brother. And he's right. To see how the brothers' relationship continues, your students will enter the space–time continuum as they read this book.

Werlin, N. (2004). *Double Helix.* New York: Penguin Putnam, Dial. (H)

As Eli is figuring out the mystery of who he is and his origins in a doctor's lab, he fills us in on his relevant knowledge of genetic engineering, as well as his musings about the morality of making decisions regarding gene swapping to eliminate disorders and enhance beauty and performance. Because his mother had asked a scientist for help, Eli was spared inheriting the gene that gave her Huntington's disease, but she had to pay a great price (I don't want to give it away, but it was something that could lead to deep discussion in a biology or ethics class about the use of donor eggs). Are some things inevitable? Eli figures:

> We humans are going to tinker with our genetic makeup. The human genome is a locked box that we are going to pry open. Any mistakes, missteps, problems, unanticipated difficulties—they will be the inevitable price of progress, the price of the good that will surely result as well. (p. 224)

And then he hears a story involving this quote from a man with Down syndrome at a genetics conference: "'I don't understand. We don't make any trouble. We don't steal things or kill people. We don't take the good jobs. Why do you want to kill us?'" (p. 244). The doctor telling this story reflects, "I got a glimpse of the world we really might create, with our high-flying ideas about the eradication of suffering. A world in which so many people are found lacking. Are considered unfit even to be born" (p. 245).

This book is a good companion to Martha Beck's *Expecting Adam* (1999) and might even lead students to go back to the original *The Double Helix*, by James Watson (1998 New York: Scribner).

SOCIAL STUDIES/HISTORY

Alexie, S. (1993). *The Lone Ranger and Tonto Fistfight in Heaven.* New York: The Atlantic Monthly Press. (H)

Several narrators interweave these short stories set on the Spokane Indian Reservation. Poverty, alcoholism, and despair exist here; however, hopes, dreams, ideals, visions, friendship, traditions, athlet-

ic accomplishments, and educational pursuits thrive as well. Here's a taste from one eleventh grader's account of his school experiences:

> Last night I missed two free throws which would have won the game against the best team in the state. The farm town high school I play for is nicknamed the "Indians," and I'm probably the only actual Indian ever to play for a team with such a mascot.
>
> This morning I pick up the sports page and read the headline: INDIANS LOSE AGAIN. Go ahead and tell me none of this is supposed to hurt very much. (p. 179)

We want our students to read original works by authors representing a diversity of cultures; if your curriculum includes learning about Native American cultures, then by all means include this book in your lessons.

Anderson, L. H. (2000). *Fever 1793.* New York: Scholastic. (M, H)

Philadelphia is the setting; a yellow fever epidemic is the antagonist. Mattie Cook, a 14-year-old with dreams and hopes, experiences loss and fear during this crucial adolescent year. After riding the highs and lows with one family during the months when 5,000 Philadelphians (10 percent of the population) died, readers will be ready to absorb the history lesson provided. The helpful Appendix educates in sections labeled "Battle of the Doctors," which talks about the controversy among medical practitioners about the best way to treat the disease; "Take Two Sponges and Call Me in the Morning," which talks about remedies people were willing to try; "Famous People Touched by the Fever"; and "Yellow Fever Today," among others. This book offers a great lesson in early American history. A play also is based on the novel.

Boling, K. (2004). *January 1905.* Harcourt. (M, H)

Pauline and Arlene are twins who each think the other has the better life. Actually, today's readers will realize that they both are working harder than children should have to work. Your students will learn about factory labor and farm labor. They'll also learn that siblings can come to appreciate each other and see things from others' points of view. In conjunction with this book, have your students research the child labor laws in our country, past and present.

Carmi, D. (2000). *Samir and Yonatan.* New York: Scholastic. (I, M, H)

There are good guys and bad guys. To Samir, a Palestinian whose beloved brother was killed by the enemy, this is clear. Until he winds up in an Israeli hospital, waiting for an operation. The boundaries begin to blur, the complexities mount, as he watches and then interacts with his Jewish roommate. This novel weaves in background information about trouble in the Middle East, and is a great resource to begin discussion about causes of conflict, and possible solutions.

Chotjewitz, D. (2004). *Daniel Half Human and the Good Nazi*. Trans. D. Orgel. New York: Atheneum. (M, H)

Sometimes a book title is a booktalk in itself; such is the case with this one, I think. I was enticed to read the book to find out both how someone could acquire the name "Half Human," and what exactly was meant by a "good Nazi." The story does answer my questions, while providing many opportunities for critical thinking. Readers can't help asking themselves what they would do if they suddenly found out during the 1930s in Germany that they were half Jewish. Would they try to hide that fact? Would they think about themselves differently than when they thought they were Aryan? And what would they do if they found out their best friend was half Jewish? Should it change the friendship? Would it? The concepts of loyalty, betrayal, patriotism, ethics, humanity, and courage await your students with this book.

Cofer, J. O. (1998). *The Year of Our Revolution: New and Selected Stories and Poems*. Houston, TX: Pinata Books. (I, M, H)

The year referred to in the title is 1968; Mary Ellen's mother refers to it as "the worst year in the history of parents and children" (p. 87), though many present-day readers will be experiencing their own "worst years" and revolutions just as the characters in these stories do. Adolescents are straddling two cultures, having been raised with the Puerto Rican or Cuban values of their parents, but being surrounded by new values in their American peer groups. They're throwing things out, like religion and customs. They're trying things on, like sex and revolutionary ideas about war and peace. Readers will be thinking and sorting things out with the characters as they come of age.

As with *The Lone Ranger and Tonto Fistfight in Heaven*, discussed above, this is a good selection to have in your collection of short stories written by members of diverse cultures. Students will learn about the cultures through authentic voices.

Danticat, E. (2002). *Behind the Mountains*. New York: Orchard. (M)

This novel could very well motivate students to learn more about current events. It's set in the early

2000s; Celiane writes entries in her journal that help her to reflect on, and readers to learn about, her life in turbulent Haiti, her coming to America, and her adjusting to home life and school life in New York City. Celiane listens to the farewell speech of President Clinton, and takes his words to heart: "'In our hearts and in our laws, we must treat all our people with fairness and dignity . . . regardless of when they arrived in our country'" (p. 119). After the story, the author tells of her personal journey from her beloved Haiti to New York two decades ago. This would make a good companion to Tracy Kidder's nonfiction work that goes back and forth between the United States and Haiti, *Mountains Beyond Mountains* (2003).

Gallo, D. R. (Ed.). (1999). *Time Capsule: Short Stories About Teenagers Throughout the Twentieth Century*. New York: Delacorte. (M, H)

In a few hours, your students will travel through a century of history as they read these stories organized by decade. Before each story, Gallo gives a one-to-two-page summary of major events and innovations of the decade. The stories themselves give readers a feel for the times, which will help them remember the historical facts and themes. After each story there's a short biography of the young adult author of the piece; authors include Chris Crutcher, Bruce Brooks, Richard Peck, and Jeanette Ingold. Have students add to the collection by writing a story of the present decade, or imagining a future decade, or traveling back to an earlier century. With a time capsule, anything is possible.

Hautman, P. (2004). *Godless*. New York: Simon & Schuster. (H)

This book starts off with a common theme, that of a teenager questioning, then resisting, the faith in which he was brought up. Jason goes a step further than drifting away from his parents' mainstream church, however. He begins a protest movement by claiming to worship a water tower in town. He finds himself with a growing following; he becomes unsure of where things are headed. This story will spark discussion about the role of religion in communities, countries, and the world. There are many curricular connections history teachers and students can make, such as how religious rebellions occur, how cult leaders gain followers, and how religious extremists can cause destruction.

Kurtz, J. (Ed.). (2004). *Memories of Sun: Stories of Africa and America*. New York: Greenwillow Books. (M, H)

What a fascinating concept and format. Kurtz divides these stories and poems by place. The stories and poems in Part One take place in Africa or are about Africa. The second section contains stories of Americans in Africa, and is followed by a section about Africans in America. The editor explains that she herself is what some would call a "'third-culture kid,' a person who doesn't fully belong in her parents' culture but doesn't fully belong in the culture around her, either" (p. 2). After reading this book, your students will understand more about the identity issues inherent in being displaced, while learning about two lands on opposite sides of the globe.

Meyer, C. (2002). *Doomed Queen Anne.* New York: Scholastic. (I, M, H)

Encourage students to read this story after Meyer's earlier work, *Mary, Bloody Mary* (2001). In the earlier work, Mary narrates her fall from her father's graces as Henry VIII casts off her mother, Catherine of Aragon; he marries Anne Boleyn, a member of her mother's court. Mary has nothing good to say about Anne, and describes Anne's behavior toward her as being horribly mean. Students now will be primed to hear Anne's side of the story. Even from Anne herself, we don't get a pretty picture about her conniving ways, nor her treatment of Mary. Awaiting execution in the Tower of London, she realizes that her greatest mistake, and sin, had been that of pride, "That I desired too much, reached too high" (p. 227). Henry VIII is presented as an object of Anne's hopes for most of the story, but as a cruel, selfish person at the end. The Epilogue gives a brief recounting of his next four marriages and his descendents. Readers will be ready to hear from Elizabeth, the daughter of Anne Boleyn and Henry VIII, next, in *Beware, Princess Elizabeth!* (2001).

All three books contain historical information about the reign of Henry VIII, as well as a timeline and chart to help readers place the people and events in context.

Rinaldi, A. (2003). *Or Give Me Death.* Orlando, FL: Harcourt. (M, H)

Ann Rinaldi, writer of dozens of historical novels, tells in her Author's Note that she had always wanted ". . . to create a book in which something terrible is going on within a household that makes what is going on in the outside world seem mild by comparison" (p. 223). Most novels set during the days leading up to the American Revolution concentrate on what the male leaders were doing, but Patrick Henry's home life gave Rinaldi the chance to create a story based on the inner lives of his wife and children. Told from a daughter's point of view, we get the sad story of Sarah, the wife and mother, locked in their basement due to mental illness. We get opportunities galore to explore personal dilemmas

such as the one the narrator faces, "'When do you tell the truth and when do you lie? Do you lie to protect someone? Is it wrong to keep a secret when, if you tell, someone gets hurt?'" (pp. 221–222). And we do get facts, such as those relating to slave uprisings, about the historical time period, contexted by a story resulting from a combination of research and imagination. Rinaldi explains that she put the story together from facts, but allowed the characters to lead her. "So, then all I had to do was connect the dots" (p. 222).

So often history is taught through the heroes, and the big events. But historians are also interested in the ordinary, the people whose names don't make it into textbooks. Your students will benefit from vicarious experiences with the lesser known people of our nation's history; their vision of what life was like in the past will be expanded and deepened. They might even become lifelong history buffs.

Stratton, A. (2004). *Chanda's Secrets.* New York: Annick Press. (M, H)

An awful lot of death is seen in this book. That's because it is set in present-day sub-Saharan Africa, where there is an epidemic of AIDS and not enough resources to care for those infected. The story begins as young Chanda is arranging a burial for her infant sister. There never comes a point in the story where she can properly mourn for any person she loses, because the deaths affecting her family and friends come too fast upon one another. She must care for younger siblings and handle responsibilities no child should be burdened with, along with worrying about her own health and trying to get the education she desperately wants. The truly amazing thing is that the story ends with Chanda still able to hope.

This book puts human faces to the statistics your students hear about; it helps readers understand how the disease is being so rapidly spread and what must be done to combat it. Chanda's mother has bequeathed her—and us—knowledge:

> Mama said I should save my anger to fight injustice. Well, I know what's unjust. The ignorance about AIDS. The shame. The stigma. The silence. The secrets that keep us hiding. . . . (p. 192)

Students in social studies classes are responsible for learning about current events; after reading this book, have them investigate national and world organizations that are trying to cope with the pandemic in Africa. Teach them how the social, economic, and medical problems are related; they'll begin to think about solutions to complex situations.

REFERENCES

Alvermann, D. E., Phelps, S. F., & Ridgeway, V. G., (2007). *Content area reading and literacy: Succeeding in today's diverse classrooms* (5th ed.). Boston: Pearson.

Beck, C., Nelson-Faulkner, S., & Pierce, K. M. (2000). Historical fiction: Teaching tool or literary experience? *Language Arts, 77* (6), 546–555.

Blasingame, J. (2003). An interview with Avi, 2003 Newbery Medal winner for *Crispin, The Cross of Lead. The ALAN Review, 30* (3), 38–39.

Bogstad, J. M. (2004). Editor's introduction I: Girls and science fiction. *The Lion and the Unicorn, 28* (2), v–vii.

Bucher, K. T., & Manning, M. L. (2001). Taming the alien genre: Bringing science fiction into the classroom. *The ALAN Review, 28*, 41–44.

Chandler-Olcott, K., & Mahar, D. (2003). Adolescents' *anime*-inspired "fanfictions": An exploration of multiliteracies. *Journal of Adolescent and Adult Literacy, 46* (7), 556–566.

Colman, P. (2007). A new way to look at literature: A visual model for analyzing fiction and nonfiction texts. *Language Arts, 84* (3), 257–268.

Crew, H. S. (2004). Not so brave a world: The representation of human cloning in science fiction for young adults. *The Lion and the Unicorn, 28* (2), 203–221.

Crutcher, C. (2005). What I wouldn't give to be that good. *Voices from the Middle, 12* (4), 6–7.

Erickson, B. (1996). Read-Alouds reluctant readers cherish. *Journal of Adolescent and Adult Literacy, 40* (3), 212–214.

Fadiman, A. (1998). *Ex libris: Confessions of a common reader.* New York: Farrar, Straus, & Giroux.

Gerstein, M. (2005). Picture Book Award winner (2004 Boston Globe–Horn Book Awards acceptance speech). *The Horn Book Magazine* (January/February), 19–22.

Haven, K., & Clark, D. (1999). *100 most popular scientists for young adults.* Englewood, CO: Libraries Unlimited.

Herber, H. L. (1978). *Teaching reading in content areas* (2nd ed.). Upper Saddle River, NJ: Prentice Hall.

Hesse, K. (1998). Newbery Medal acceptance. *The Horn Book Magazine, 64* (4), 422–427.

Kass, L. R. (2002). *Foreword. Human Cloning and Human Dignity: The Report on the President's Council on Bioethics.* New York: Public Affairs.

Lesesne, T. S. (2006). Reading aloud: A worthwhile investment? *Voices from the Middle, 13* (4), 50–54.

Nilsen, A. P., & Donelson, K. L. (2001). *Literature for today's young adults.* New York: Longman.

Paterson, K. (1989). *The spying heart: More thoughts on reading and writing for children.* New York: Lodestar Books.

Raham, G. (2004). *Teaching science fact with science fiction.* Portsmouth, NH: Teacher Ideas Press.

Ryan, L. (2005). Words to the rescue: Walter Dean Myers reaches out to teen readers. *Syracuse Post Standard, Stars Magazine* (Sunday, April 17), 4–5.

Say, A. (1994). Caldecott Medal acceptance. *The Horn Book Magazine, 70* (4), 427–431.

LITERATURE CITED

Ames, M. (1981). *Anna to the infinite power.* New York: Scribner.

Anderson, L. A. (2002). *Catalyst.* New York: Viking.

Avi. (2002). *Crispin: The cross of lead.* New York: Hyperion.

Bauer, J. (2005). *Best foot forward.* New York: G.P. Putnam's Sons.

Bauer, J. (1998). *Rules of the road.* New York: G.P. Putnam's Sons.

Beck, M. (1999). *Expecting Adam: A time of birth, rebirth, and everyday magic.* New York: Times Books.

Bloor, E. (1997). *Tangerine.* San Diego: Harcourt Brace.

Brown, D. (2000). *Angels and demons.* New York: Pocket Books.

Bryant, J. (2004). *The trial.* Illus. L. Wells. New York: Alfred A. Knopf.

Choldenko, J. (2004). *Al Capone does my shirts.* New York: G.P. Putnam's Sons.

Cormier, R. (2005). *I am the cheese.* Waterville, ME: Thorndike Press.

Cormier, R. (1977). *I am the cheese: A novel.* New York: Pantheon.

Creech, S. (1994). *Walk two moons.* New York: HarperCollins.

Demi. (1997). *One grain of rice: A mathematical folktale.* New York: Scholastic.

di Camillo, K. (2001). *The tiger rising.* Cambridge, MA: Candlewick Press.

Dreiser, T. (1978). *An American tragedy.* Illus. G. Reynard. Cambridge, MA: R. Bentley.

Dumas, A. (1996). *The Count of Monte Cristo.* New York: Modern Library.

Edwards, J., & Comport, S. W. (2003). *The Great Expedition of Lewis and Clark: by Private Reubin Field, member of the Corps of Discovery.* New York: Farrar, Straus and Giroux.

Ellis, D. (2004). *Three wishes: Palestinian and Israeli children speak.* Berkeley, CA: Douglas & McIntyre.

Farmer, N. (2002). *The house of the scorpion.* New York: Atheneum.

Feelings, T. (1995). *The Middle Passage: White ships/Black cargo.* New York: Dial Books.

French, J. (2003). *Hitler's daughter.* New York: HarperCollins.

Gallagher, T. (2005). *The grail bird: Hot on the trail of the ivory-billed woodpecker.* Boston: Houghton Mifflin.

Gardner, C., adapter. (2004). *The Beatles: Yellow submarine.* Book design F. Andreanelli, Artwork H. Edelmann. Cambridge, MA: Candlewick Press.

Griffin, A. (2002). *Hannah, divided.* New York: Hyperion.

Haddix, M. P. (1999). *Just Ella.* New York: Simon & Schuster/ Aladdin.

Haddon, M. (2003). *The curious incident of the dog in the night-time.* New York: Doubleday.

Hale, M. (2004). *The truth about sparrows.* New York: Henry Holt.

Hale, S. (2003). *Goose girl.* New York: Bloomsbury.

Hassinger, P. W. (2004). *Shakespeare's daughter.* New York: Laura Geringer Books.

Hautman, P. (2004). *Godless.* New York: Simon & Schuster.

Hemingway, E. (1987). *The old man and the sea.* New York: Macmillan.

Hesse, K. (1997). *Out of the dust.* New York: Scholastic.

Hiaasen, C. (2005). *Flush.* New York: Alfred A. Knopf.

Hiaasen, C. (2002). *Hoot.* New York: Alfred A. Knopf.

Hill, J. B. (2000). *The legacy of Luna: The story of a tree, a woman, and the struggle to save the redwoods.* San Francisco: Harper San Francisco.

Hoose, P. (2004). *The race to save the Lord God bird.* New York: Farrar, Straus and Giroux.

Hughes, T. (1998). *Birthday letters.* New York: Farrar, Straus, Giroux.

Juster, N. (2001).*The phantom tollbooth.* Illus. J. Feiffer. New York: Scholastic.

Kalish, G. (2001). *Rachel Rude Rowdy.* Tucson, AZ: Zephyr Press.

Kidder, T. (2003). *Mountains beyond mountains: The quest of Dr. Paul Farmer, a man who would cure the world.* New York: Random House.

Konigsburg, E. L. (2000). *Silent to the bone.* New York: Atheneum.

Kurzweil, R. (1999). *The age of spiritual machines: When computers exceed human intelligence.* New York: Viking.

Lasky, K. (2001). *Star split.* New York: Hyperion.

L'Engle, M. (1962). *A wrinkle in time.* New York: Ariel Books.

Lipsyte, R. (1993). *The chief.* New York: HarperCollins.

Lipsyte, R. (1991). *The brave.* New York: HarperCollins.

Lipsyte, R. (1967). *The contender.* Santa Barbara, CA: ABC-CLIO.

Lowry, L. (1993). *The giver.* Boston: Houghton Mifflin.

McClaren, C. (1996). *Inside the walls of Troy: A novel of the women who lived the Trojan War.* New York: Atheneum.

McLynn, F. (1993). *Famous letters: Messages and thoughts that shaped our world.* Pleasantville, NY: Reader's Digest.

Meyer, C. (2002). *Doomed Queen Anne.* San Diego: Harcourt.

Meyer, C. (2001). *Beware, Princess Elizabeth!* San Diego: Harcourt.

Meyer, C. (2001). *Mary, Bloody Mary.* San Diego: Harcourt.

Moon, E. (2003). *The speed of dark.* Del Ray/Ballantine Books.

Myers, W. D. (1999). *The journal of Joshua Loper: A Black cowboy: The Chisolm Trail.* New York: Scholastic.

Myers, W. D. (1998). *Angel to angel: A mother's gift of love.* New York: HarperCollins.

Myers, W. D. (1997). *Harlem: A poem.* Illus C. Myers. New York: Scholastic Press.

Myers, W. D. (1995). *Glorious angels: A celebration of children.* New York: HarperCollins.

Myers, W. D. (1993). *Brown angels: An album of pictures and verse.* New York: HarperCollins.

Myers, W. D. (1988). *Fallen angels.* New York: Scholastic.

Nafisi, A. (2003). *Reading Lolita in Tehran: A memoir in books.* New York: Random House.

Namioka, L. (1999). *Ties that bind, ties that break.* New York: Delacorte.

Nardo, D. (2005). *Cloning.* San Diego: Lucent Books.

Nolan, H. (1999). *Dancing on the edge.* New York: Puffin Books.

Orgel, D. (2003). *My mother's daughter: Four Greek goddesses speak.* Brookfield, CT: Roaring Brook Press.

Park, L. S. (2001). *A single shard.* New York: Clarion Books.

Paulsen, G. (2000). *The beet fields: Memories of a sixteenth summer.* New York: Delacorte.

Pullman, P. (2000). *The amber spyglass.* New York: Alfred A. Knopf.

Ridley, M. (1999). *Genome: The autobiography of a species in 23 chapters.* New York: HarperCollins.

Rowling, J. K. (2005). *Harry Potter and the half-blood prince.* New York: Arthur A. Levine.

Ryan, P. M. (2004). *Becoming Naomi Léon.* New York: Scholastic.

Ryan, P. M. (2000). *Esperanza rising.* New York: Scholastic.

Satrapi, M. (2003). *Persepolis: The story of a childhood.* New York: Pantheon.

Shah, S. (2003). *The storyteller's daughter: One woman's return to her lost homeland.* New York: Alfred A. Knopf.

Smith, A. D. (1993). *Fires in the mirror: Crown Heights, Brooklyn, and other identities.* KCET. Los Angeles. Produced by C. Fortis. Directed by G. C. Wolfe. PBS Video.

Sobel, D. (1999). *Galileo's daughter: A historical memoir of science, faith, and love.* New York: Walker & Co.

Spinelli, J. (2002). *Loser.* New York: Joanna Cotler Books.

Spinelli, J. (2000). *Stargirl.* New York: Alfred A. Knopf.

Springer, N. (2001). *I am Morgan Le Fay: A tale from Camelot.* New York: Philomel Books.

Steinbeck, J. (1939). *Grapes of wrath.* New York: Viking.

Tamplin, R. (1995). *Famous love letters.* Pleasantville, NY: Reader's Digest.

Taylor, M. (2001). *Roll of thunder, hear my cry.* New York: Dial Press.

Tripp, V. (2000). *Meet Kit, an American girl.* Illus W. Rane, vignettes S. McAliley. Middleton, WI: Pleasant Company Publications.

Vreeland, S. (2005). *Life studies: Stories.* New York: Viking.

Watson, J. (1998). *The double helix.* New York: Scribner.

Werlin, N. (2004). *Double helix.* New York: Dial Books.

Wharton, E. (1964). *House of mirth.* New York: New American Library.

White, E. E. (2002). *The journal of Patrick Seamus Flaherty.* New York: Scholastic.

White, E. E. (2002). *Where have all the flowers gone?: The diary of Molly Mackenzie Flaherty.* New York: Scholastic.

Wilmut, I., Campbell, K., & Tudge, C. (2000). *The second creation: Dolly and the age of biological control.* New York: Farrar, Straus and Giroux.

Wood, D. (2005). *A world-class boxer.* Chicago: Heinemann Library.

Biography, Autobiography, and Memoir

5

Through biography "... students and teachers alike gain insight into a life lived in a different time and place but involving emotions, hopes, needs, challenges, and frailties that make us human."

SHIRLEY A. LECKIE, 2006, P. 7

P A R T   1

the why and how
OF USING BIOGRAPHICAL BOOKS

People are social; middle school and high school students are perhaps especially characterized by their social behavior. Meeting and getting to know people is considered by most of them to be highly desirable. How perfect, then, is the genre of biography. Through the stories of people's lives, our students may become friends, acquaintances, or even critics or foes of people past and present from our chosen disciplines. As a teacher, you can help them view biographical reading as a way to eavesdrop; to hear and evaluate gossip and news; to join a circle of talented, dedicated, or notorious players in the fields they are studying.

Why, then, do some people consider biographies less interesting than fiction or other genres? True, some biographies are dull, or outdated, or just not at the right level for those we're teaching. Some students may have had negative academic experiences involving biographies. So we might face challenges in terms of convincing our students that biographies can open up a whole new, enjoyable world for them. One obstacle might be that the students learn about most important people in our subject areas in terms of their accomplishments as adults. They view the people they learn about as so much older, maybe even older than their parents or caretakers, who can be perceived as ancient enough! And the pictures in textbooks often reinforce this understanding.

In my own experience, I've tried to counteract this dilemma by having my students imagine famous people as teenagers. Picture Albert Einstein in eighth grade, Susan B. Anthony at age 17, Picasso in elementary school. I've had students research contributors to athletics, sciences, and arts in terms of their early years, to see whether we could have predicted that they'd be famous, that they were destined for great things. Sometimes what they find is surprising. I've also shared biographies of people who accomplished things at a young age, such as authors S. E. Hinton and Carson McCullers, artist Salvador Dali, and that epitome of a musical prodigy, Wolfgang Amadeus Mozart.

To help in this endeavor, a good place to start is the book *Heading Out: The Start of Some Splendid Careers*, edited by Gloria Kamen (2003). The 30 chapters highlight the childhoods of scientists, authors, artists, athletes, and others. Students will find it fascinating, and when they have researched the early years of other famous lives, they will want to create a class book that might be considered a sequel to Kamen's. Then there's Welden's *Girls Who Rocked the World: Heroines from Sacajawea to Sheryl Swoopes* (1999), which has 35 biographical entries of girls younger than 20 who changed history! I've found biographies of individuals, also, that focus on the early years of the book's subject. For example, *I See You I See Myself: The Young Life of Jacob Lawrence*, by Deba Foxley Leach (2001), has a wealth of information about the artist just from his birth to age 25, though he lived another 58 productive years!

Education literature is filled with examples showing how teachers capitalize on the easily accessible genre of biography, autobiography, and memoir. Daisey (1996/1997) offers ways of promoting literacy in content area classrooms with biography projects. In fact, she gives a list of 25 possible post-reading activities from which students can choose. She asks her pre-service teachers to choose and read a biography of a person of color, a woman or a man, in a nontraditional role in their content area; after completing a project, they make a presentation where they show a transparency of their biography character, show the book, read an excerpt, and explain their project. Certainly this would be appropriate for middle and secondary students as well. Daisey and her students gained insights about equity and about how to promote interest in content area instruction. She concludes:

> I find that the first challenge in my content area literacy course is to recover secondary preservice teachers' interest in reading and writing. To do this it is essential to model construction of knowledge rather than transmission of information. Thus, I encourage the use of biography projects to offer students a context for instruction and a reason to read, as well as a direction by which to live. (p. 277)

Watson (2002) discusses the value of using a particular type of biographical writing, the memoir, to help students learn history. She argues, "Reading memoir, coupled with primary sources, such as legal texts, newspapers, and others' scholarship, offers students a rich set of documents portraying a particular period of history" (p. 11). In contrast to textbooks, where, too often, ". . . the narrative voice is missing and omniscient; anonymous authors strive for little elaboration and much authority" (p. 10), in memoir, ". . . one reads of the author as protagonist or hero, engaged with an antagonist or critical incident and resolution" (p. 10). The author shows how the following three memoirs can help students examine the U. S. Civil Rights Movement: *Outside the Magic Circle,* by Virginia Durr (1985); *Warriors Don't Cry,* by Melba Patillo Beals (1994); and *Coming of Age in Mississippi,* by Anne Moody (1968). After discussing how each could benefit students of history, Watson concludes:

> The stories of Virginia Durr, white and privileged, from Alabama; of Melba Patillo Beals, a middle class, African American high school girl from Little Rock, Arkansas; and of Anne Moody, a rural Mississippi, poor African American young adult, illustrate particular and individual responses to their worlds. Each of these lives, richly chronicled in memoir, reveals a three dimensional human being making choices, celebrating and suffering as she makes her way in the world. . . .
>
> Reading or listening to memoir of experience during a particular period deepens students' understanding of the history. More than a chronology of events, memoir offers varying perspectives and attitudes of the historical complexities rather than the distilled simplicity represented in texts. . . . (p. 13)

Memoir has similar benefits beyond the history classroom. Memoirs written by scientists and mathematicians bring students into the worlds and minds of practitioners as they dream of what might be, struggle with obstacles, make life-changing decisions, and face moral dilemmas related to their work. Memoirs written by people who have moved from one country to another and met the challenges of a new culture and different language can help students and teachers in foreign language classes and ESL classes. Memoirs reflecting on the formative and/or crucial years of an athlete can be enjoyable and thought-provoking to students in physical education courses. Several memoirs are highlighted in Part 3 of this chapter, so consider this popular genre.

instructional
STRATEGIES AND ACTIVITIES

Involving Biographical Books

▶ ▶ ▶   **SCRAPBOOK BIOGRAPHY**

Standards Addressed

Art: Students understand and apply media, techniques, and processes.

History: Students draw upon visual, literary, and musical sources. All students should be able to read historical narratives imaginatively.

English/Language Arts: Students use spoken, written, and visual language to accomplish their own purpose (e.g., for learning, enjoyment, persuasion, and the exchange of information).

Context/Rationale

Several recently published biographies have a scrapbook format. For example, in *Anastasia's Album* (1996), which author Hugh Brewster has subtitled *The Last Tsar's Youngest Daughter Tells Her Own Story*, readers see the photographs that Anastasia and other family members took as well as the letters she wrote. Brewster's text about her life in the palace, and about the Russian Revolution, accompanies strategically placed photos of dolls, toys, period clothing, buildings—all bringing us into the real life of the time and place. By the time students reach the quote from Anastasia's last letter, "Though we know that the storm is coming nearer and nearer, our souls are at peace. Whatever happens will be through God's will" (p. 57), they will feel they know her well. They'll grieve while reading the Epilogue, telling of the 18-year-old being shot by soldiers in her home in 1918. They'll be ready to learn what the curriculum holds—and more—on the topic of the Russian Revolution.

Procedure

- For the activity, provide a variety of biographies that use the scrapbook format. Good examples include *Laura's Album: A Remembrance Scrapbook of Laura Ingalls Wilder* (Anderson, 1998), *Through My Eyes* (Ruby Bridges, 1999), *My Fellow Americans: A Family Album* (A. Provensen, 1995), *Charlotte in Giverny* (Knight, 2000), and *The World of William Joyce Scrapbook* (Joyce, 1997). (I have used all these with my students.)

- Tell students that the purpose of this activity is to tell a person's story in pictures.

- Divide students into small groups and have them discuss aspects of the lives and books with each other. They should decide on the key events in the person's life or key character traits. Give them the option of providing a theme for their scrapbook (e.g., the photos tell the story of the person's courage).

- Have them select photos they will use in the scrapbook. If applicable, they should select stories with their theme in mind.

- Have students decide if they will write captions or use quotes for captions, then prepare the needed captions.

- Ask them to decide on the pages' photo arrangements. Students may choose to organize photos by grouping those that relate to a particular theme or period in a person's life together. They may select them by size or by color combination.

- Suggest that they make two L-shaped figures with cardboard and masking tape to help them crop and size their photos.

- Additionally, instruct students to gather cheap materials, appropriate for the story they are telling; these will provide visual interest. Include fabric, buttons, sequins, yarn, glitter, and so forth.

- Have them arrange the photos, captions, and miscellaneous materials they have collected in an album-like format. They may use a three-ring binder or a spiral binder, or make a post-bound album with paper fasteners.

- Invite them to design a cover for the book, using a fabric and adding appropriate magazine pictures, greeting cards, photos, lettering, stickers, and stamping.

- Invite students to bring in scrapbooks of their own to share with their groups.

Additionally, you may have students research Internet sites, such as www.mycraftbook.com/scrapbooking.asp, that give tips for creating scrapbooks of many types. Visit www.alienteacher.com/digital_scrapbooking.htm for instructions for making digital scrapbooks.

A variation of scrapbooking involves a project where students collect or create artifacts representing a person's life after reading one or more biographical sources on that person, arranging them into a three-dimensional showcase to present to classmates or a community audience. For example, a bagful of peanuts would go into a showcase of George Washington Carver's biography; students might compose letters of congratulations about accomplishments, and so forth. Suggest a model or diorama of a setting in which a person worked, or have them fill a poster with a collage-like assembly of pictures and words representing the biographical subject.

Walk-Through

Picture five areas of a middle school social studies classroom. Students have been given the choice of reading the following picture book biographies by Demi: *Muhammad* (2003), *Ghandi* (2001), *Mother Teresa* (2005), *Buddha* (1995), and *The Dalai Lama* (1998). Groups of about five students have read each book, then discussed key points, thought of symbols or representative objects they'd like to gather, divided up responsibilities, and worked together on their scrapbook projects. They've brought in materials from home, imported documents and pictures from the Internet, and discussed the design and arrangement of the pages to tell their subject's life story. At the completion of the project, students visit other groups' corners or alcoves to view their scrapbooks and learn about other great spiritual thinkers.

BIOGRAPHY TALK SHOWS

Standards Addressed

History: Students identify the central question(s) the historical narrative addresses. Students differentiate between historical fact and historical interpretations. All students should be able to consider multiple perspectives.

Science: All students should understand historical perspectives of science and the nature of scientific knowledge.

English/Language Arts: Students use spoken, written, and visual language to accomplish their own purpose (e.g., for learning, enjoyment, persuasion, and the exchange of information).

Context/Rationale

In order for our knowledge to grow in any discipline, we must have opportunities to listen to experts in the field, whether current or historical. Ideas build upon others' ideas; progress is cumulative. Arranging for experts to come together as a panel may help your students think of ideas in relation to each other, make connections, and note contradictions and disagreements. Most students are familiar with the talk-show format from watching television, so should find participating as an audience member nonthreatening and enjoyable. They'll get to practice their critical-thinking and questioning skills, too. Playing the roles of the people they have read about may help them summarize points; dispute attacks against theories, research, or creative works; and ponder implications of actions and discoveries.

Procedure

- To prepare for this activity, give your students a number of books from which to select having a certain subject or theme. For example, in a lesson on oppression, students might read accounts of teens who grew up under oppression, such as *Zlata's Diary* (Filipovic, 1994), *Thura's Diary* (Al-Windawi, 2004), *Daniel's Story* (Matas, 1993), *Red Scarf Girl* (Jiang, 1998), *Persepolis* (Satrapi, 2003), and *The Diary of a Young Girl* (Frank, 1967).

- Have students who have selected the same book form literature circles. (See Chapter 2.)

- After they've had a chance to talk with others who have read the same choice, set up a TV talk show.

- Have each group select someone to represent the writer of the memoir read, and ask them to select another student to take on the role of talk-show host.

- Have the groups brainstorm questions about which they would like to ask the writer based on their reading.

- Ask the groups to research the answers to the questions in your class or school library or on the Internet.

- Schedule times for the talk show to take place.

- In front of the whole class, have the "talk-show host" introduce the writer or ask them to briefly introduce themselves. Then the talk show host should ask questions of the interviewee. Following are examples appropriate for the lesson on oppression:

  - Where did you grow up?
  - What were you frightened of?
  - Did your political beliefs change over time?
  - How did you cope with the bad things happening around you?
  - Was there something that gave you hope?
  - What are your future plans? etc.

Walk-Through

In a variation of a student talk show, Gallagher (1993) describes an activity she used in her class following the reading of *Anthony Burns: The Defeat and Triumph of a Fugitive Slave*, by Virginia Hamilton (1988). She invited the school principal and an attorney to play the roles of Anthony Burns and Richard Dana, the lawyer who offered to defend Burns without charge when he was captured after escaping to Boston in 1854. Gallagher set the time period for the talk show several years after the trial, when Burns, now free and educated, had become a minister. Students prepared to ask the two guests questions based on the book they had read and other background information their teacher had provided. Gallagher gives many sample questions for Anthony Burns, such as "Why didn't more slaves run away?" and "How did you finally become free?" (p. 32) and for Richard Dana, including, "Why did you volunteer to defend Anthony Burns?" "Did President Franklin Pierce have any influence on what happened to Anthony Burns?"(p. 52). At the end of the hour, the adults resumed their real identities so that students could discuss the experience with them.

Gallagher suggests using a timeline to help students understand the historical context and maps of the United States then and now to help students comprehend the location of the events involving Anthony Burns. She includes an annotated bibliography of other books that would work for classroom talk shows. It's obvious that the opportunities for learning and thinking are great with the talk show activity.

I have used this method of instruction using a variety of genres, usually having students themselves play the roles of characters in their books. Sometimes the characters are from a book the whole class has read, but often I have a panel of characters from different books individuals or groups have selected. For example, after the class has explored a number of picture books written from the perspectives of several members of the Corps of Discovery (See Chapter 2 for a list of books), you could form a panel consisting of Lewis, Clark, Sacagawea, York, Reubin Field, and the dog Seaman.

In a science class, ask several naturalists and biologists to step out of their biographies and into the classroom TV studio. John Muir, Rachel Carson, Charles Darwin, James Audubon, and Jane Goodall could discuss events and issues with each other and answer interview questions from the classroom audience. In an art class, reunite the Impressionist painters who worked and exhibited in real life, or have artists from different times meet each other with the help of your students who read their biographies. Imagine a panel of Michelangelo, Frida Kahlo, Mary Cassatt, Andy Warhol, Jacob Lawrence, Georgia O'Keeffe, and a previously anonymous early cave painter of Lascaux discussing what is beauty, what is art, what is the artist's role in society. You will find suggestions for books about these scientists and artists in Part 4 of this chapter.

THINK-ALOUD BIOGRAPHY READING

Standards Addressed

Science: All students should develop an understanding of biological evolution.

English/Language Arts: Students participate as knowledgeable, reflective, creative, and critical members of a variety of literacy communities.

Context/Rationale

You may model comprehension strategies for your classes by thinking aloud as you read new material on a subject they're studying. Students will see that reading is an active process, that good readers monitor their reading and make adjustments and decisions as they go along. Later, have them do a think-aloud to become aware of their own processes while tackling a new, and perhaps challenging, text. Listen to them as a means of assessment, and give suggestions at the end. Have them read and do a think-aloud with peers; pass out a text and have students work with a partner, taking turns reading and verbalizing the thinking during the process of making meaning as they interact with the text.

Walk-Through

Here's what my think-aloud sounded like as I read the beginning of Peter Sis's *The Tree of Life: A Book Depicting the Life of Charles Darwin: Naturalist, Geologist & Thinker* (2003) for the first time.

> *I'm looking at the cover of* The Tree of Life, *with a dark picture of an old man holding a tiny twig. I love Peter Sis's work, and I'm wondering if I'm going to like this book as much as I do* Starry Messenger, *his biography of Galileo. I'm thinking that I don't know as much about Charles Darwin as I should. I know he sailed on the* Beagle, *and kept a journal of his observations. I know his theory of evolution was controversial (and, amazingly, still is). I know he lived during the nineteenth century, though I can't pinpoint when* On the Origin of the Species *came out. I want to learn about how he reacted to pressure after the publication of his book. I'm also interested in his early life, because I love to think of what led important people on the paths they took. Okay, here goes. I'm opening the book.*
>
> *Wow, quite the end pages! They tell a story in pictures. The top panels are showing the six days of creation as depicted in Genesis. I see another panel with the famous segment of the Sistine Chapel where God's finger is about to touch Adam's to bring it to life. There are many more. I'll come back to them later.*
>
> *On the first page is a map of Britain, and the year of Darwin's birth: February 12, 1809. Okay, that date helps me already. Sis gives us six facts about Darwin's life that the infant does not yet know. A clever way to give a little overview to help me out.*
>
> *On the next page is a visual family tree. Charles, a little boy holding a bird in the yard, is in the center. Circles hold information about his grandfathers and parents. (Oh, dear, his mother dies when he is eight years old!). The text underneath the picture tells us that Dr. Darwin wants the best for his sons, including an education that will include the classics and the Greek and Latin languages. Then in tiny italics comes the line, "Charles sees things his own way." Uh-oh, I see conflict being foreshadowed. The next page reinforces this feeling. Charles is nine years old, and doesn't like his boarding school. He likes being outside, walking through the countryside collecting things, we're told. Ah, just what I would have suspected Darwin would be doing as a boy.*
>
> *Whoa, the next page is gruesome! Charles is at the University of Edinburgh, for his father wants him to be a doctor. There's a circular lecture hall with a doctor performing surgery on a child (without anesthesia, the text tells us). Charles is running away.*
>
> *The next page strikes me as funny, though I'm sure it wasn't to Charles. His father tries a second plan, sending Charles to be educated as a clergyman. Charles studies botany and ". . . is passionate about beetle-collecting" (unpaged). There's my favorite topic—passion for learning! The text says that Charles went on a geological walking trip through Wales and dreamed about an expedition to the Canary Islands. "He sees himself as a naturalist." Oh, I'm thinking I could ask students to stop here and write an entry in their journals with the sentence starter, "I see my future self as a . . ."*
>
> *The next pages give entries from several sources: the invitation to go on the voyage of the Beagle, an entry from Charles's journal, a list of his father's objections, a letter from Charles to his father. It's clear that parent–child conflict is not just a phenomenon of the twenty-first century.*
>
> *[Now I'm skimming.] From here on, every page is packed with intricate designs, little pictures, lots of text in different fonts and handwriting. The paintings are incredibly clever; I intend to savor them, and to read all the little bits of information that accompany them. I see by flipping through the book that I'll get lots of information about other people (like Gregor Mendel) and places (such as the Galapagos Islands) and historical events (such as a dinosaur skeleton exhibit) that will provide a context and help me understand Darwin better. My opinion at this point in my reading is that this is a book that I must have for myself; I see myself sharing it with colleagues and students most enthusiastically.*

TIME TRAVEL DIALOGUES

Standards Addressed

History: Students consider multiple perspectives. Students compare competing historical narratives. Students evaluate major debates among historians.

English/Language Arts: Students use spoken, written, and visual language to accomplish their own purpose (e.g., for learning, enjoyment, persuasion, and the exchange of information).

Context/Rationale

What advice might Galileo have for Charles Darwin? What would Charles Darwin and James Audubon have to say to each other? What would happen if Adolph Hitler read *The Diary of Anne Frank* and then talked with her? What would Thomas Jefferson say to Martin Luther King Jr.? How would Michelangelo and Picasso get along? If John Brown and Malcolm X shared a prison cell, what conversation would ensue? What would a conversation between Amelia Earhart and Christa McAuliffe be like?

Norton (2003) has found that "Children enjoy contemplating what historic personalities might say to each other if they had the opportunity to meet" (p. 573). Through the use of imaginative writing and talk, students may use the information from biographies they've read to compose meaningful, and maybe emotional, dialogue between biographical subjects.

Procedure

- Provide your students with a group of biographies in your subject area (see Part 4 of this chapter).

- Instruct students to work individually or in pairs to decide on which historical figures they would like to create the dialogue.

- Have the students research the persons thoroughly, using the information from the Internet, videos, magazine articles, and other resources as well as the biographies.

- From the research, ask the students to compose a list of questions they would like their historical figures to ask each other related to topics in your curriculum. For example, Cesar Chavez could ask Thomas Jefferson if discrimination should be allowed against any person or group.

- After the students have composed the dialogue, have them present it to the class orally.

- In a follow-up discussion, you and your students may clear up any inconsistencies between what they know about the biographical figures and statements in the dialogue, providing documented reasons for any objections to the statements.

Walk-Through

The following reflections by students show what can result from participation in this activity:

> I'm Cesar Chavez. When great minds get together, they are able to make connections, and perhaps see earlier influences, previously unknown. For example, Thomas Jefferson told me that he believed in the 1700s that all men should be treated as equals. Centuries later, I was still fighting for fair treatment of farmers. Did Jefferson pave the road for me and my crusade? If so, why did I still have to fight? Wasn't what he did enough? Why were people so ignorant for so long, to behave as if they were better than others?
>
> —Nichole Ince

I am Eratosthenes. I met Pablo Picasso today—finally, another man who is as smart as I! We discussed our latest research. He showed me his sketches for his upcoming self-portrait series. And I shared my sketches and drafts for how the earth could be measured to prove it is round.

—Leigh Ramage

My name is Marian Anderson, and I just had the most wonderful conversation with a real saint—Saint Patrick. I learned all about his life in Ireland and his strong belief in God. It is the same strong belief in God that helped me break the constrictive barriers that the United States has for Black singers. Patrick learned about my struggles to reach my goals in segregated America.

—Christina Piazza

▶ ▶ ▶ BIOGRAPHY WALLPAPER

Standards Addressed

Math: Students create and use representations to organize, record, and communicate mathematical ideas.

Science: All students should develop an understanding of the history and nature of science.

English/Language Arts: Students employ a wide range of strategies to comprehend, interpret, evaluate, and appreciate texts.

Context/Rationale

Consider this as an extension of word walls, which are used extensively in schools today to reinforce vocabulary and key concepts. Word walls may consist of lists, semantic webs, or a combination of words, definitions, and visuals. They may be initiated by teachers and/or created and expanded by students as they read and learn about a subject in more depth. Biography wallpaper is what its name implies; the wall gets covered with posters, or rolls of newsprint or wrapping paper, and students post information about the people whose lives they've visited through independent reading of biographies and memoirs. Information is categorized and charted so that peers can easily find key facts about those people whom they have not read about (at least not yet; they might be inspired by the wallpaper to seek out more biographies).

Procedure

- Instruct your students to read a biography of their choice that relates to a person or people in your subject area. Get suggestions for titles from this chapter, and look for those or other biographies in the school and/or public libraries.
- Ask them to write a free response in their learning logs after they have finished the biography. You will find that many express surprise at how interesting they find books about the lives of the people they have learned a bit about in their course of studies.
- On the day the assignment is due, group students with others who have read either the same biography or biographies about the same person and have literature circle time (see Chapter 2) so that they can share highlights, discoveries, and recommendations with their peers.
- Pass out sheets asking students to provide the information described in Figure 5.1. Have each group fill out one sheet.
- Allow a few minutes for students to fill out the chart using the biography they have read.

Using the categories listed below, create a chart for students to fill out. Arrange the items as column heads across the top of an 11 x 14 sheet of paper.

> Title, author, copyright date, and publisher
>
> Main characters' dates of birth and death; other important dates in life
>
> Important people—colleagues, relatives, contemporaries, adversaries, etc.
>
> Highlights, main events, accomplishments, obstacles overcome
>
> Stance of biographer, writing style, any biases
>
> Ways you might use this book in your studying
>
> Pictures, symbols, or quotes

When finished, your class will have a strip of related charts giving pertinent information about the major figures in your subject area. Your wall will not only be beautiful but also full of information for all who choose to explore it.

- Give each group a large sheet of colored paper taken from a roll and ask them to tape their charts to that background paper and hang it on one of your classroom walls.

Walk-Through

Figure 5.2 shows an example of what a piece of math/science biography "wallpaper" might contain; I'm using information from templates my students filled out.

"WHAT IS TRUTH?"

Standards Addressed

History: Students compare competing historical narratives. Students evaluate major debates among historians. Students differentiate between historical facts and historical interpretations.

English/Language Arts: Students participate as knowledgeable, reflective, creative, and critical members of a variety of literacy communities.

Context/Rationale

Since a biography is by definition the true story of a person's life, all biographies of an individual probably read pretty much the same, right? Wrong! See how far this is from the case when you compare biographies of chosen women and men in the fields you explore. Zarnowski (2003) notes, "When we show students how to use . . . questions as a means of considering different biographies of the same person, we are engaging them in the process of historical thinking in a rigorous and discipline-specific way" (p. 33). By looking for similarities and differences, we may come to realize that biographers sometimes use different sources, choose unique focuses, prioritize events and characteristics differently, and, through their writing, make value judgments about the worth of accomplishments, or moral behavior. Readers may determine main ideas and details. They might discover inaccuracies, or accuse the author of "lying by omission" if the biographer has failed to deal with flaws of the "hero" about whom he or she has written.

FIGURE 5.2 Biography wallpaper example for math/science.

Title, author, copyright date	Main characters' dates of birth and death; other dates	Highlights, main events, accomplishments, obstacles overcome	Stance of biographer; writing style; any biases	Ways you might use this book in your studying	Pictures, symbols, or quotes
Madame Curie, by Eve Curie, 1937 [synopsis by Rob Talamo]	Born 11/7/1867 Died 7/4/34	Came from poor family; very intelligent from early on; interested in physics & chemistry; did research in many area of those sciences; discovered radium; died from effects . . .	Biographer was Curie's daughter; claimed every part was verifiable fact; I got the impression that Eve was puffing up Marie's childhood as a way to gain sympathy from the reader; despite this, the biography seemed historically accurate.	Can be used when discussing radiation and radioactive elements; could be used to show diligence in research; example of the importance of women in science. —Rob Talamo	
My Brain Is Open: The Mathematical Journeys of Paul Erdős, by Bruce Scheckter, 1998 [synopsis by Amie Notareschi]	Born 1913? Died 9/20/96	Published over 1,500 papers with over 450 collaborators; discovered many proofs, some as a teenager; two sisters died of scarlet fever, parents had only him; lived during WW I in Hungary; father fought (was Jewish); worked on number theory	Very pro-Erdos; author used many examples and other math people to tie in ideas of Erdos	I'd use quotes to show how passionate Erdos was about math	"Mathematicians are finite, flawed beings who spend their lives trying to understand the infinite and perfect." (p. 47) —Amie Notareschi
Women & Numbers: Lives of Women Mathematicians Plus Discovery Activities, by Teri Perl, 1993 [synopsis by Steve Johnson]	Mary Somerville, 1780–1872; Ada Lovelace, 1815–1852; Sofia Kovalevsky, 1850–1891	M.S. Interested in math but turned to astronomy; wrote books used at Cambridge, e.g., "The mechanism of the Heavens." A.L. "Inventor of Computer Programming"; rewrote Babbage's information so everybody could read it. S.K. First American female professor.	The author was a feminist; she was very fair and depicted both the good and the bad of the women.	Between the biographies there are activities— e.g., coloring and puzzles. —Steve Johnson	

Zarnowski had her students create a data chart listing information from different biographies about Benjamin Franklin in multiple categories: accuracy, style, illustration, theme, selection of information, primary sources, author's note and end matter, and illustrator's note. See Figure 5.3 for example questions for students to consider when filling out each category in the chart and Figure 5.4 for an example of a completed chart.

After the students completed the data chart, they created a planning sheet for writing a compare/contrast essay (see Figure 5.5). You might ask students to make a Venn diagram showing overlapping circles, with facts in the center portion that both books include, with information that one or the other has given in the parts of the circle that are exclusive (see Figure 5.6).

Sample questions for students to consider when completing their data charts. FIGURE **5.3**

ACCURACY

- Is there evidence of the author's research?
- What sources did the author use?
- Did a fact-checker review the manuscript?

STYLE

- Did the author include vivid details and anecdotes?
- Is the writing imaginative, memorable, and thought provoking?
- Did the author use different types of sentences and interesting word choices?

ILLUSTRATION

- Do the illustrations extend the text by providing additional information and interesting details?
- Are captions included that provide additional information and focus the reader's attention on information and details?

THEME

- What is the big idea that is used to organize the facts?

SELECTION OF INFORMATION

- What information was included in all of the biographies?
- What information was included in one of the biographies, but not the others?

PRIMARY SOURCES

- Are primary sources used?
- Is the author convinced that they are reliable? Are we?

AUTHOR'S NOTE AND END MATTER

- Does the author discuss his or her personal interest in the topic?
- Does the author discuss the research process?
- What additional information is provided at the end of the book?

ILLUSTRATOR'S NOTE

- Does the illustrator discuss the process of creating the illustrations?
- Does the illustrator discuss the research involved?

FIGURE 5.4   Example data chart completed by a student.

DATA CHART: POWERFUL PAIRS

Book	Accuracy and Authenticity	Style	Illustration	Theme	Selection and Interpretation of Information	Primary Sources	Author's Note	Illustrator's Note
A Picture Book of Benjamin Franklin (Adler)	Author didn't list any sources.	Short and choppy sentences. "Ben wrote poetry. He loved books and reading." For beginning readers.	Pictures don't give extra information.	Ben Franklin was a great American.	Most information can be found in any textbook.	None.	Some historians are not sure about the kite-flying story.	None.
What's the Big Idea, Ben Franklin? (Fritz)	No sources listed.	Likes to list things: "Cow Lane, Flounder Lane . . ." Funny: Likes to take facts and point out funny parts.	Pictures give no extra information. Comical: Funny text with funny drawings. Go well together.	He had many ideas. He had big ideas about daily life, civics, and government.	Not included in any other books: seeing a lion, magic squares, list of street names, being a vegetarian, the electrical picnic.	None.	Notes with extra information, but no note from the author.	None.
The Amazing Life of Benjamin Franklin (Giblin)	Author did list sources. Author traveled to Philadelphia. Two fact-checkers.	Focuses on one topic and then moves on. It's not really funny, though a humorous song is included. Advanced vocabulary.	Pictures tell more than the words. They show people's feelings. Very realistic. Suitable for fifth graders.	Ben Franklin had an amazing life. Called the "wisest American." Tells more about his political life.	Not included in any other books: the arguments between Ben and his son William, falling in love with Madame Helvétius, ballooning, epitaph for his gravestone (B Franklin, printer).	Song Ben wrote. Quote from a letter to his sister.	Discusses primary sources, other books used, and historic sites.	Tells how he did research to make the pictures match Ben's life. Tells how he put in feelings.

Source: Reprinted with permission from *History Makers: A Questioning Approach to Reading and Writing Biographies,* by M. Zarnowski, p. 37. Copyright © 2003 by M. Zarnowski. Published by Heinemann, Portsmouth, NH. All rights reserved.

FIGURE   **5.5**

Sample planning sheet completed by a student on theme (compiled from Zarnowski, 2003, pp. 39 and 42).

COMPARING BENJAMIN FRANKLIN BIOGRAPHIES: PLANNING SHEET

TOPIC: Theme

Paragraph 1: What is your topic? What does it mean?

My topic is theme. Theme is the main idea of something. It tells you what the author based the book on and it is usually found at the end of a book. It is there because that is what you should remember about the book.

Paragraph 2: How are the books similar? (Only in terms of your topic)

The theme of all three books, A Picture Book of Benjamin Franklin (Adler), What's the Big Idea, Ben Franklin? (Fritz), and The Amazing Life of Benjamin Franklin (Giblin) was similar because they all thought Benjamin Franklin was an amazing American. They probably thought he was a good role model.

Paragraph 3: How are the books different?

The theme of all three books is different because, even though the authors thought Ben was great, they said it in their own way. The author of What's the Big Idea, Ben Franklin? thought he was a great inventor. The author of The Amazing Life of Benjamin Franklin thought he took an important part in the Revolutionary War and the writing of the Constitution. The author of A Picture Book of Benjamin Franklin just wrote that he was a good American.

Paragraph 4: Why is your topic important?

Theme is important because the main idea helps you understand the book. You should know what the author thinks about Ben Franklin and why the author wrote the book. This is why theme is important.

FIGURE   **5.6**

Sample Venn diagram for planning a comparison/contrast essay.

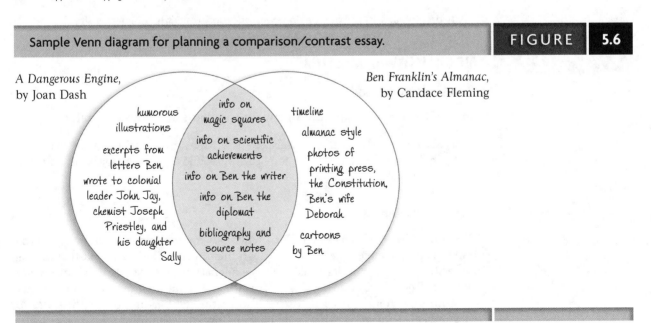

A Dangerous Engine, by Joan Dash

Ben Franklin's Almanac, by Candace Fleming

humorous illustrations

excerpts from letters Ben wrote to colonial leader John Jay, chemist Joseph Priestley, and his daughter Sally

info on magic squares

info on scientific achievements

info on Ben the writer

info on Ben the diplomat

bibliography and source notes

timeline

almanac style

photos of printing press, the Constitution, Ben's wife Deborah

cartoons by Ben

Walk-Through

Let's try to find out the "truth" about one of America's early heroes. I've used Benjamin Franklin, as Zarnowski did, but I've chosen different books about him to create my own guide.

READING AND THINKING GUIDE FOR BIOGRAPHIES OF BEN FRANKLIN

Directions: Our classroom library has several copies of the following five biographies of Ben Franklin:

Ben Franklin's Almanac: Being a True Account of the Good Gentleman's Life, by Candace Fleming (2003, New York: Atheneum)

Benjamin Franklin: An American Genius, by K. M. Olson (2006, illus. B. Schulz & G. Purcell, Graphic Biography Series. Mankato, MN: Capstone Press)

The Amazing Mr. Franklin: Or the Boy Who Read Everything, by Ruth Ashby (2004, Atlanta, GA: Peachtree)

Benjamin Franklin, by Tom Streissguth. Just the Facts Biographies Series (2005, Minneapolis, MN: Lerner Publications)

A Dangerous Engine: Benjamin Franklin, from Scientist to Diplomat, by Joan Dash (2006, illus. D. Petriéciâc, New York: Frances Foster Books)

Skim them to see how they're alike and different. You may work with a partner. The following questions may guide your analysis:

1. Are the books in agreement in terms of Ben's major accomplishments?
2. How do you think the authors feel about their subject? Do they all treat him as an unqualified hero? Do any point out any flaws, faults, or failures?
3. How do the styles of the books differ? Which do you find most appealing?
4. Did the authors list the same resources they used to learn about Ben Franklin? Did they use primary sources? Which do you consider the best account in terms of accuracy, depth, and richness?
5. Here's your chance to point out anything you wish about one or more of the books you've perused. You can share an interesting anecdote, point out errors and/or biases, compare the information in one or all to what is in our history textbook, or tell why you think one should win an award, for instance.

[Note: This activity can also be done with encyclopedia entries or Internet sites.]

▶ ▶ ▶   BIOGRAPHY WAX MUSEUM

Standards Addressed

Art: Students make connections between visual arts and other disciplines.

English/Language Arts: Students use spoken, written, and visual language to accomplish their own purpose (e.g., for learning, enjoyment, persuasion, and the exchange of information).

Context/Rationale

Wax museums are very popular. The lifelike but immobile figures allow visitors to bring the people represented to life through their imaginations. The text that accompanies the various exhibits usually gives explanations and details that can further observers' knowledge and thinking. When students plan their own version of a wax museum to demonstrate what they've learned through reading biographies and to teach others, many good things may happen, involving the community as well.

Procedure

- Ask your class to read a biography of their choice relating to your curriculum.
- Divide the students into groups who have read the same book. Then have students choose roles to play among the figures presented in their biography.
- Ask them to find or make appropriate costumes and have them create tableaux representing some key scene in the life of the biography's subject using simple props. Neither the costumes nor the props need be elaborate, but they should suggest the figures and event the students wish to re-create. For example, students may use a toy black cat and a picture of a raven to depict Edgar Allan Poe, have a microscope and a poster with the symbol for radium in their tableau for Marie Curie, or include nuts and bolts, ice skates, an artichoke heart, and box within boxes to represent Frank Gehry.
- Ask them to create signs displaying pertinent information about the scene depicted and select a "docent" who will provide historical data and answer questions.
- Schedule an opening night for the museum. Invite other teachers and students, parents, relatives, and other members of the community to attend the opening.
- On the night of the event, have your students stand immobile in their costumes in the midst of their tableaux. Visitors can be led through the museum, and by the end they will have received quite an education about the historical figures in your field!

Walk-Through

You and your students may adapt this idea; there are endless variations on this wax museum theme. For example, imagine your school halls turned into a Sports Hall of Fame, with student "statues" depicting heroes of basketball, wrestling, gymnastics, swimming, cycling, and mountain climbing. Or an art museum with student "statues" representing artists from various eras and movements, surrounded by information students have found in biographical materials at their disposal.

CREATIVE DRAMATIZATIONS OF BIOGRAPHIES

Standards Addressed

History: Students differentiate between historical fact and historical interpretations. Students read historical narratives imaginatively.

English/Language Arts: Students participate as knowledgeable, reflective, creative, and critical members of a variety of literacy communities.

Context/Rationale

Norton (2003) suggests having students act out scenes from biographies. Readers can choose the scenes they deem important and conducive to dramatizing. Or:

> These scenes may also be developed into a sequence game that involves careful observation by all players, who must interpret what someone else is doing and, according to directions written on their cue cards, stand and perform the next action at the correct time. (p. 572)

Procedure (Adapted from Norton, 2003)

- To begin the activity, select several biographies in your subject area. Allow students to select the biography they would like to read and divide them into groups of students who have chosen the same biography.

- As a group, have them choose scenes that they think are important and which they can dramatize.

- Have them prepare cards with cues or prompts in order to "act out" scenes in sequence according to the biography they've read (usually chronologically). Each card should include (1) A "cue," which describes the scene on the PREVIOUS card; this alerts the card holder as to which action PRECEDES the one on the card she is holding, so that students pay attention to sequence and know when to perform; and (2) Directions, which describe a scene to dramatize.

- Later, when the cards are redistributed, the person receiving the card will decide on an appropriate pantomime of the action for each scene. For your information, the sample cards below include suggestions for acting out the scene. Students should decide on these dramatizations themselves.

- At least one card should be created for each student in the groups, but more can be added if desired. Having students write the cues and directions in two different color inks is also helpful. Option: Quotes from the book can be added to the cards that students can speak while dramatizing the events.

- Collect the cards after they are created, keeping each group of cards together. Prepare a master sheet of the group's cues in sequential order to help if students become confused about the order of events.

- Distribute each group of cards to a group whose members did not create them. Give the master list of cues to a student in each group who can serve as a director for the scene. At this time students should be given time to decide on an appropriate dramatization for the scene described on their card.

- Have each group stage the scenes from their cards in sequential order in front of the class. Students must listen and observe carefully to recognize the cue that indicates which card should be performed next.

Walk-Through

Figure 5.7 provides an example of what cards would look like for the picture book biography *The Champ: The Story of Muhammad Ali*, by Tanya Bolden.

▶ ▶ ▶ TIMELINE AND MAP MARKING

Standards Addressed

Social Studies: All students must learn to create, interpret, use, and distinguish various representations of the earth, such as maps, globes, and photographs.

History: Students interpret data presented in timelines. Students establish temporal order in constructing historical narratives of their own.

English/Language Arts: Students apply a wide range of strategies to comprehend, interpret, evaluate, and appreciate texts.

Context/Rationale

After students explore the works of a biographer, instruct them to make a timeline on a classroom wall and mark the dates represented by the people about whom the biographer has written. For example, a timeline of Diane Stanley's biographical works (which are highlighted in Part 3 of this chapter) might look like the sample shown in Figure 5.8.

On the opposite wall, hang a world map and ask students to mark the places with pushpins where these same people lived. For example, have them mark Eng-

Sample cards for biography dramatizations. Note that these cards are numbered for purposes of the figure only; the actual cards should not be numbered; instead, students will rely on the cues to present in sequence.

FIGURE   **5.7**

1

Cue: You begin the game.

Directions: It's the 1950s. Pretend that you are young Cassius Clay, dodging the rocks your brother throws at you, then beginning boxing lessons.

[An appropriate dramatization of this scene might be to pretend to be dodging rocks while punching the air, then throwing some punches in a tentative manner.]

2

Cue: Someone pretends to be young Cassius Clay taking boxing lessons. [Cue is based on previous card's scene.] Now it's your turn.

Directions: It's 1960. You are the 18-year-old Cassius, returning home after winning a Gold Medal at the Rome Olympics. You are greeted with cheers from some, and taunts from others who are racist.

[An appropriate dramatization of this scene might be to pantomime boxing moves and throw punches. You can call out, "Float like a butterfly, sting like a bee!"]

3

Cue: Someone pretends to be Cassius Clay being turned away from a luncheonette in Louisville and being taunted by racists. Now it's your turn.

Directions: It's 1964. Pretend to be Cassius Clay during and after winning the heavyweight championship against Sonny Liston.

[An appropriate dramatization of this scene might be to hold your arms up in a victory clasp, bowing, then backing away and holding your hands up in a way that suggests creating distance.]

4

Cue: Someone pretends to be Cassius Clay in 1964, when he becomes the heavyweight champion. Now it's your turn.

Directions: It's 1967. Pretend that you are now that champion, with a new name, Muhammad Ali, having converted to the Nation of Islam. You have resisted being drafted. You have been stripped of your heavyweight crown and have been banned from boxing. You express your beliefs at lectures and on TV.

[An appropriate dramatization of this event might be folding your arms and shaking your head no, followed by lifting your head in a proud gesture. You can say the following words from Ali's address to college students while out on bail during a legal appeal: "'I would like to say to those of you who think I've lost so much, I have gained everything. I have peace of heart; I have a clear, free conscience. And I'm proud.'" (unpaged)]

The game continues. The student with the last card will re-enact Ali's lighting the Olympic torch in Atlanta in 1996, to the cheers of classmates who have become, through Tonya Bolden's biography, fans of *The Champ*.

| FIGURE | 5.8 | Sample timeline for Diane Stanley biographies. |

Cleopatra	Saladin	Joan of Arc	Leonardo da Vinci	Michelangelo	Elizabeth I	Shakespeare	Peter the Great	Charles Dickens
69–30 BCE	1138–1198	1412(?)–1431	1452–1519	1475–1564	1533–1603	1564–1616	1672–1725	1812–1870

land with student-made flags for Queen Elizabeth, Shakespeare, and Dickens, while Peter the Great would be over in Russia, and Michelangelo and Leonardo would be in Italy. Saladin and Cleopatra would be placed in the ancient Middle East. As students read more biographies by different authors, they may add flags to the map in different colors. The ongoing timeline/map activity will help students understand history and geography better by having a visual reminder of how people relate to each other in terms of time and place.

Walk-Through

To extend the activity, involve your students in creating a timeline of the particular people covered in your curriculum, based on information they find in biographies written by a variety of authors rather than by a single author, as exemplified above. Here's what such a timeline might look like in a middle school–integrated math/science/technology classroom, where all the students have read biographies of their choice. Students may ask each other about what they learned from the books they read, whether they'd recommend them, and so forth. Or, consider forming a human timeline by having students hold cards with the names and dates of their subjects. After properly arranging themselves, as shown below, students could announce whom they read about, show the book, and tell an interesting thing they learned.

Euclid: around 325 BCE–265 BCE. *Euclid: The Great Geometer* by C. Hayhurst (Kaitlin's choice)

Albucasis: 936–1013. *Albucasis: Renowned Muslim Surgeon of the Tenth Century* by F. Ramen (Aditi's choice)

Benjamin Banneker: 1731–1806. *Benjamin Banneker: Astronomer and Mathematician* by L. B. Litwin (Vishal's choice)

Charles Babbage: 1791–1871. *Charles Babbage and the Engines of Perfection* by | B. Collier and J. MacLachlan (Rahul's choice)

Lise Meitner: 1878–1968. *Lise Meitner: Pioneer of Nuclear Fission* by J. Hamilton (Carlianna's choice)

Rachel Carson: 1907–1964. *Rachel: The Story of Rachel Carson* by A. Ehrlich (Humma's choice)

Paul Erdös: 1913–1996. *My Brain Is Open* by B. Schechter (Shaan's choice)

Marjory Stoneman Douglas: 1890–1998. *Marjory Stoneman Douglas: Guardian of the 'Glades* by K. Doherty (Haleigh's choice)

Jane Goodall: 1934–. *Reason for Hope: A Spiritual Journey* by J. Goodall with P. Berman (Brody's choice)

Mae Jemison: 1956– . *Find Where the Wind Goes: Moments from My Life* by M. Jemison (Wanisha's choice)

IMAGINARY DIALOGUES WITH
WOMEN AND MEN IN BIOGRAPHIES

Standards Addressed

Visual Arts: Students reflect on and assess the characteristics and merits of their work and the work of others.

English/Language Arts: Students participate as knowledgeable, reflective, creative, and critical members of a variety of literacy communities.

Context/Rationale

Gelb (2003) encourages those who want to increase their own "genius thinking" to create imaginary dialogues with superior minds (p. 22). He tells of how one man with a great mind, Niccolo Machiavelli, did just that. He quotes Machiavelli's depiction of his process:

> ". . . I am not ashamed to speak with [men of antiquity] and ask them the reasons of their actions, and they, because of their humanity, answer me. Four hours can pass and I feel no weariness; my troubles forgotten, I neither fear poverty nor dread death. I give myself over entirely to them." (p. 23)

Consider modeling a conversation with a great mind in your discipline, then instruct your students to dialogue with a person whose biography they've explored.

Procedure

- Model an imaginary dialogue for your students with yourself taking both the part of the questioner/commenter and that of a historical subject in your discipline.
- Divide your students into pairs and ask them to select a biography of interest to them in your content area. (This may also be done as an individual activity.)
- Instruct each pair to decide on who will take the role of the biographical figure and who will be the questioner/commenter.
- After reading the biography, have them create a script for the dialogue. The dialogue for the questioner/commenter should reflect on the significance of life and work of the biographical subject to him. He should also ask questions of the subject. The subject should then respond to the questions and discuss her life and work, adding details and revealing the person's character as depicted in the biography. Option: Have students indicate page numbers from the book supporting their representation of the biographical figure.
- Have students rehearse the dialogue several times and then present it to the whole class.

Walk-Through

Here is a script from an English teacher who decided to speak to and listen to one of her heroes, Robert Frost, after reading Peggy Caravantes's (2006) biography of him.

Ms. Zhang (in her regular speaking voice): Hi, Robert. Hope you don't mind me addressing you by your first name, but I have felt for a long time that we are kindred spirits. I was introduced to you when I was in middle school and got a picture book out of the library: *Stopping by Woods on a Snowy Evening,* written by you, of course, and illustrated by Susan Jeffers. I read "The Road Not Taken" every time I need to make a big decision in my life. It's like you've been a spiritual guide to me. Now that I'm a teacher, I try to channel you when I use your work with my tenth graders. So, can you tell me anything about the relationship between lived experiences and the creation of poetry?

Robert Frost (in a slightly deeper voice): Oh, that's an easy one. Sure, there's a significant relationship between those two things. An example I can think of right away is that one of my favorite themes is the inevitability of change. Of course anyone who observes nature is aware of this. I wrote "Nothing Gold Can Stay" to illustrate this. I wanted to express my belief that instead of lamenting things that we can't control, we should enjoy each moment before it's gone. We have to accept that life's losses and gains bring a combination of sorrow and joy. (based on p. 94)

Ms. Zhang: Oh, my students love that poem. They encountered it when they read S. E. Hinton's *The Outsiders* (1967). Thanks for contexting it for me. Okay, I've been wondering about something else. What's the relationship between emotional states and the creation of art? My students notice that many of the great writers we study have had turbulent lives, often with tragic endings. And I read that you suffered from depression.

Robert Frost: I suffered from many emotional states. I feared loneliness, so I surrounded myself with people. After my dear wife Elinor died, I blamed myself, since I dragged her through so much for one as frail as she. I wandered around my farm and wished I could join her in death. At that point I couldn't write, and I didn't care if I ever came up with anything good again. (based on p. 116)

But, really, a poet needs to experience a range of emotions. When I put together my first collection of poetry, I spread out over a hundred poems on the floor and arranged them in a way that showed a spiral of moods, moving from withdrawal and discouragement to affirmation and hope. The collection showed a quest. So, it's possible to use the sorrow and turmoil of one's life to create art. (based on pp. 57–58)

Ms. Zhang: This is helping me so much. I need to know one more thing. How can I get my students to love and appreciate poetry, and to not be afraid to try to write in that genre?

Robert Frost: Well, you know I taught off and on throughout my life, at the high school and college levels. I used what some considered innovative teaching techniques, not always appreciated by my peers. I required my students to read poetry aloud and to memorize it. I encouraged my students to learn from life as well as from books and schooling, to think independently, to develop their own ideas. Discussion replaced lecture in my classes; I wanted my students to be active participants in their learning. (based on p. 54)

Ms. Zhang: I have dialogued with the great, and now feel energized to create a poetry learning center for my classroom, with Robert Frost as our guide. Thanks, Robert!

▶ ▶ ▶ USE OF TEACHER-CREATED READING GUIDES

Standards Addressed

History: Students consider multiple perspectives. Students challenge arguments of historical inevitability. Students interrogate historical data.

Math: Students analyze and evaluate the mathematical thinking and strategies of others.

English/Language Arts: Students apply a wide range of strategies to comprehend, interpret, evaluate, and appreciate texts.

Context/Rationale

As explained in earlier chapters, reading guides are a great aid to comprehension as students tackle challenging texts in the disciplines. Teachers may provide a structure to the reading process so that students know what to focus on, what patterns of organization to be cognizant of, and how to think critically about the issues raised and explained in the text.

Walk-Through

Figures 5.9 through 5.11 show several examples of how teachers created guides that would structure their students' learning and aid their comprehension and critical and creative thinking at every stage of their reading.

Reading guide for *Fiery Vision: The Life and Death of John Brown*, by Clinton Cox, created by Chelsea Besio.	FIGURE	5.9

Directions: We'll be reading an award-winning biography of a famous and controversial abolitionist. This guide will help you comprehend the issues and think critically about the man, his cause, and those opposed to him.

BEFORE READING

1. Write down anything you know about John Brown [leave space for students to write].

2. What do you think the United States was like during the first half of the nineteenth century?

3. Write A (agree) or D (disagree) for the following statements:

   _____ Slavery is unjust, any time and any place.

   _____ It is all right to kill in self-defense.

   _____ Murder can be justified is some select circumstances.

   _____ The end justifies the means.

   _____ Citizens must always follow the law.

   _____ Citizens must always support the president of the United States.

   _____ A government may make any law to keep the social order intact.

   _____ It is okay to risk the lives of others for a very good cause.

   _____ The Civil War was necessary.

Okay, now that you've committed your views to paper, you're ready to dig into this intriguing biography. Jot down notes or questions that come to mind as you read.

AFTER READING

Answer these questions on your own. When you are finished, get together with a group of four or five people and discuss your responses.

1. Was there a better way John Brown could have fought to free the slaves?

2. Do you think John Brown expected to be successful in his raid on Harper's Ferry, or did he purposely make himself a martyr for the cause?

3. Do you think John Brown acted fanatically and unreasonably, or do you think he was a sane man of strong convictions? Or is there yet another explanation for his actions?

4. Do you think John Brown's life and death sped up the fight to free the slaves?

5. Did John Brown have any influence on President Lincoln?

6. Could the Civil War have been avoided?

POST-READING PROJECT OPTIONS

Now that you have read the biography and discussed your reactions and thinking with others, complete one of the following assignments. If you'd like to initiate a project not listed, write up a one-paragraph proposal and bring it to me.

1. Write an obituary as you think it may have appeared in John Brown's hometown newspaper.

2. Write a poem about the life of John Brown.

3. Write an essay either defending or condemning John Brown's actions at Harper's Ferry.

4. Make an estimated ledger of all the money spent and received for the cause of freeing the slaves.

5. Visually represent John Brown's life; make a poster, collage, video, or comic strip.

6. Imagine you're a reporter, either pro-slavery or antislavery, and write an article on John Brown at any particular point in his life.

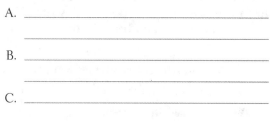

FIGURE   5.10   Anticipation guide for *The Random Walks of George Pólya,* created by Anthony Fisher.

1. Brainstorm to come up with words, phrases, people, and concepts you associate with the word *math* [leave space for students to write].

2. List any math-related works of literature you have read, or movies you've seen, or mathematicians you know of.

3. Respond Yes or No to the following statements:

    _____ Mathematics has no actual purpose in daily life outside of school.

    _____ Only a few unusual or odd people are good at math.

    _____ All the best mathematicians were born with a great mathematical ability.

    _____ Mathematics can be like a foreign language for a lot of people.

    _____ To be good at math, you have to study and practice for years and years.

    _____ Excelling in mathematics has no practical purpose or reward.

Now that you've begun thinking about mathematics as a topic, you're ready to read a biography of a fascinating person—an influential mathematician, George Pólya. List any surprises or discoveries in your learning log at the end of each chapter. We'll talk about him when you're finished.

FIGURE   5.11   Reading guide for *Cleopatra,* by Diane Stanley, created by Tim Nicholas.

This guide will help you understand the biography of an extremely influential woman. You'll complete part of it before reading the picture book, and part when you've finished.

BEFORE THE READING:

1. Write down three facts or ideas you can recall that pertain to Egypt, before or after Cleopatra's time.

    A. _____

    _____

    B. _____

    _____

    C. _____

    _____

2. Think about Julius Caesar and the Roman Empire around 70 BCE. Do you have any ideas about how Rome and Egypt were connected? If so, mention them. If not, write about the most interesting thing that might have happened. (**Hint:** Julius and Cleopatra fall in love!)

3. Discuss one or two other historical figures or important people of the present whose lives you think would make a good story, and think about

writing a creative piece about them later on. For now, just write down a few names and the most interesting things about them.

AFTER THE READING:

4. Now that you have finished the biography of Cleopatra, write down the three most interesting things you have learned.

    A. _____

    _____

    B. _____

    _____

    C. _____

    _____

5. Who do you think was a better husband for Cleopatra, Caesar or Antony? Think about the political reasons and the personal reasons why one marriage would have been more fulfilling.

6. Do you agree with Cleopatra's solution to the problem of her being captured by Octavian? If you were Cleopatra, what might you have done differently to avoid such conflict?

author STUDIES

JAN GREENBERG AND SANDRA JORDAN

Use these authors' books in **art, English, music, social studies,** *and other disciplines.*

Figure 5.12 contains a bibliography of selected works of Jan Greenberg and Sandra Jordan.

Jan Greenberg and Sandra Jordan have collaborated on a range of wonderful books on art-related topics. Sometimes they concentrate on a single artist. The picture book *Action Jackson* (2005) takes readers on a journey with Jackson Pollack during May and June of 1950, when Pollack painted *Lavender Mist*. They explain before the story begins that they have imagined some details, but that their story is based on firsthand reports of the artist's habits and mode of painting. The pages are more illustrations (by Robert Andrew Parker) than text. Both are exhilarating, capturing the motion of the artist in action. The authors tell us:

> An athlete with a paintbrush, he uses his whole body to make the painting. Layers build with each gesture, new colors emerging, blending, and disappearing into the wet surface. He swoops and leaps like a dancer, paint trailing from a brush that doesn't touch the canvas. (p. 11)

They use Pollack's own words to effectively describe his creative process: "'I want to make a longer and longer line. I want to keep it going'" (p. 11). "'I don't know where my pictures come from, they just come'" (p. 17). "'On the floor I am much more at ease. I can walk round it, work from the four sides, . . . be in the painting'" (p. 17). I'd love to have students experience this picture book after observing a print or slide of the painting itself, and before seeing a film clip of Jackson at work in his studio wearing his signature paint-splattered boots.

Chuck Close Up Close (2000) combines Greenberg's and Jordan's story of Close's life, obtained through interviews with the artist, with photographs of his art. Readers might be amazed at Close's recollection of report card comments calling him dumb, lazy, and a shirker. His severe learning disabilities were not diagnosed until he was an adult. He credits art with saving his life, and even describes his school ordeals as giving him the discipline and methods for his later creativity:

> Almost every decision I've made as an artist is an outcome of my particular learning disorders. I'm overwhelmed by the whole. How do you make a big head? How do you make a nose? I'm not sure! But by breaking the image down into small units, I make each decision into a bite-size decision. . . . The system liberates and allows for intuition. And eventually I have a painting. (p. 10)

Selected works by Jan Greenberg and Sandra Jordan.   FIGURE   **5.12**

Freedman, E. B., Greenberg, J., & Katz, K. A. (2003). *What does being Jewish mean?: Read-aloud responses to questions Jewish children ask about history, culture, and religion.* New York: Simon & Schuster.

Greenberg, J., Jordan, S., & Parker, R. A. (2005). *Action Jackson.* London: Frances Lincoln.

Greenberg, J., & Jordan, S. (2004). *Andy Warhol: Prince of pop.* New York: Delacorte Press.

Greenberg, J. (2003). *Hudson Valley harvest: A food lover's guide to farms, restaurants, and open-air markets.* Woodstock, VT: Countryman Press.

Greenberg, J. (2003). *Romare Bearden: Collage of memories.* New York: Harry N. Abrams.

Greenberg, J., & Jordan, S. (2003). *Runaway girl: The artist Louise Bourgeois.* New York: Harry N. Abrams.

Greenberg, J., & Jordan, S. (2003). *Vincent van Gogh: Portrait of an artist.* New York: Dell Yearling.

Greenberg, J. (2001). *Heart to heart: New poems inspired by twentieth-century American art.* New York: Harry N. Abrams.

Greenberg, J., & Jordan, S. (2000). *Chuck Close, up close.* New York: DK Ink.

Greenberg, J., & Jordan, S. (2000). *Frank O. Gehry: Outside in.* New York: DK Ink.

The pages of the biography take us through a progression of life events and works of art, until we're startled by an account of "the event" of 1988, when a spinal artery collapse caused Chuck Close to be paralyzed from the neck down. "Art and medical experts agreed on one point: His career was finished" (p. 36). Wrong! Close decided, "'I was trapped in a body that didn't work, but somehow I was going to get the paint on canvas'" (pp. 36–37). The rest of the book tells how he did this, along with Greenberg's and Jordan's interpretation of his later works. Both the artist and this book about him are truly inspiring.

Frank O. Gehry: Outside In (2000) introduces readers to an architect with a ". . . gift for changing the ordinary into the amazing" (p. 5). Greenberg and Jordan chronicle his life and work, including

- the childhood cities he made from scraps of wood
- his fascination as a teenager with everyday materials such as pipes, nuts and bolts, chains, and glass in his grandparents' hardware store
- his no-frills beginning as an architect with one client
- the outrage his hostile neighbors expressed when he remodeled his own house
- his lifelong philosophy of "You can turn junk into a virtue" (p. 21)

Photographs throughout the book showing his Binoculars Building in Venice, California; the National-Nederlanden (Fred and Ginger) in Prague; the Guggenheim Museum in Bilboa, Spain; as well as models for ongoing projects capture the reader's imagination. The authors include poetry; pictures of Gehry at work, at home, and in skates on a hockey rink; and other tidbits that add to the main story. One of my favorite additions is an inset titled "A Leap into Metaphor," where Greenberg and Jordan list some of the phrases journalists used to describe Gehry's Guggenheim: "a pile of improbably huge fish," "Marilyn Monroe's wind-assisted skirts," "an exploded artichoke heart," "a gigantic game of Chinese boxes within boxes," "an explosion in a sardine factory" (p. 44). Reading this book may stimulate a lively discussion about whether the metaphors aptly represent the buildings.

Vincent van Gogh: Portrait of an Artist (2003) has won multiple awards as an outstanding biography for children and young adults, deservedly so. It's not a picture book, though it does include inserts of reproductions of Van Gogh's works as well as family photographs. In this compassionate rendering of a complicated life, the authors do not gloss over the burdens the painter's family had to bear due to his emotional instability, personality quirks,

and inability to support himself. The biography intertwines talk of the events of van Gogh's passionate life with the development of his passionate art, as is fitting for this unusual man's story. Your students will learn of his changing techniques; his changing moods; his changing relationships; his changing values and views of life, of himself and his place in the world. A postscript following the last chapter telling of van Gogh's tragic death helps the book end on a bright note. For example, "The poster of Vincent's sunflowers is one of the most popular reproductions in the world, thus making Vincent's wish come true that it might 'brighten the rooms of working people'" (p. 106).

Runaway Girl: The Artist Louise Bourgeois (2003) is filled with interesting connections between Bourgeois's life and art. The book begins with a recounting of the authors' visit to the 90-year-old sculptor in order to interview her for their biography, but quickly moves back to the early 1900s when World War I was brewing and things were happening in the toddler Louise's home that would lead to lifelong memories and anger that inspired her art. In 1982, at a retrospective of her work (the first of a woman sculptor in New York City's Museum of Modern Art's history), Louise "shocked her audience by speaking out for the first time about her childhood. . . . For an artist to talk about the psychological roots of her creative process was highly unusual" (p. 54). Although Greenberg and Jordan note that Louise's autobiography became almost inseparable from people's view of her art, they add Louise's warning to her listeners to keep their attention on the art itself. "'An artist's words are always to be taken cautiously. . . . The sculpture speaks for itself and needs no explanation. . . . Not a word out of me is needed'" (p. 54). The photographs of her work throughout the decades as well as the text of this biography will help readers ponder the relationship of art to artist as well as a plethora of other rich topics.

Romare Bearden: Collages of Memories (Greenberg, 2003) is a combination of a biography, contexting the twentieth-century artist's life within the larger stories of life in the South, the Harlem Renaissance, and beyond; and a commentary on Bearden's way of making art, what he called "'putting something over something else'" (p. 46). Greenberg's words helped me pay attention to some details I might have missed in the depicted collages and photomontages. In the section "Studio Visit with Romie" I learned about his processes and could study his photograph while reading the words:

Dressed in workman's overalls, he stood at a table scattered with painted paper, pens, markers, brushes, scraps of fabric, and clippings from books and magazines. He began by pasting down rectangles of color, usually on a board. On top of that, he layered bits and pieces of photographic images—African masks, animal eyes, plants, or faces, all taken out of context and rearranged together. A master with scissors, he expertly cut paper, slicing it in quick, deft strokes. . . . (p. 44)

I imagined myself as an art teacher, allowing this book to inspire my students to stretch their imaginations as they prepare to create new collages the world has yet to see, drawing upon their memories as Romare Bearden did.

Jan Greenberg and Sandra Jordan also co-produced a trio of books about groups of artists and about how to understand and appreciate aspects of art. *The Painter's Eye: Learning to Look at Contemporary American Art* (1991), *The Sculptor's Eye: Looking at Contemporary American Art* (1993), and *The American Eye: Eleven Artists of the Twentieth Century* (1995) provide a crash course in modern American art. I learned a lot, both in terms of who's who and how-to, by reading the short biographies and commentaries provided in these texts.

KATHLEEN KRULL

*Use this author's books in **art, English, music, science, social studies,** and other disciplines.*

Figure 5.13 contains a selected bibliography of Kathleen Krull's work.

If I were an administrator or literacy coach in a middle school, I would encourage my faculty to conduct a school-wide author study of Kathleen Krull. Her books relate to most content areas, including **music, art,** **English, physical education, social studies,** and **science.** Students would find Krull books throughout the school, and would probably find teachers talking excitedly to each other and to their classes about them. They'd see connections among the disciplines, and their vocabulary and background knowledge would grow as they read the books themselves.

Krull has a popular series of biography collections students may peruse to find important information along with often funny details about people within the categories her books represent. I call them her Gossip Series. Even the titles beckon curious readers. Here they are, along with examples of the intrigue within:

Krull, K. (1993). *Lives of the Musicians: Good Times, Bad Times (And What the Neighbors Thought).* **Illus. K. Hewitt.** New York: Harcourt Brace Jovanovich.

Chapter titles give glimpses of what's to come in the biographies: "Traveling Troubadour" (Woody Guthrie), "The Entertainer" (Scott Joplin), "Tender Tyrant" (Nadia Boulanger). I love the chatty "Musical Notes" at the ends of the chapters, from which I learned things such as Chopin's "Minute Waltz" being written for his dog. Did you know that to play all of Mozart's music in a row would take 202 hours, or that Clara Schumann didn't learn to talk until she was eight years old, the same age at which point she was becoming a world-famous pianist? After reading this book, you'll be able to gossip in the best of music circles, and you'll be searching for more knowledge about these and other musicians.

Krull, K. (1994). *Lives of the Writers: Comedies, Tragedies (And What the Neighbors Thought).* **Illus. K. Hewitt.** New York: Harcourt Brace & Company.

Selected works by Kathleen Krull.   FIGURE **5.13**

Krull, K. (2006). *Isaac Newton.* Illus. B. Kulikov. New York: Viking.

Krull, K. (2006). *Sigmund Freud.* Illus. B. Kulikov. New York: Viking.

Krull, K. (2005). *Leonardo da Vinci.* Kulikov, Boris. New York: Viking.

Krull, K., & Velasquez, E. (2005). *Houdini: World's greatest mystery man and escape king.* New York: Walker & Co.

Krull, K. (2004). *A woman for president: The story of Victoria Woodhull.* New York: Walker.

Krull, K., Johnson, S., Fancher, L., et al. (2004). *The boy on Fairfield Street: How Ted Geisel grew up to become Dr. Seuss.* New York: Random House.

Krull, K. (2003). *The book of rock stars: 24 musical icons that shine through history.* Illus. S. Alcorn. New York: Hyperion Books for Children.

Krull, K. (2003). *Harvesting hope: The story of Cesar Chavez.* Illus. Y. Morales. New York: Scholastic.

Krull, K. (2003). *M is for music.* Illus. S. Innerst. Orlando, FL: Harcourt.

Krull, K., & Santoro, C. (2003). *What really happened in Roswell?: Just the facts (plus the rumors) about UFOs and aliens.* New York: HarperCollins.

Rector, A. E., with additional text by Krull, K. (2004). *Anne Elizabeth's Diary: A young artist's true story.* Boston: Little, Brown & Company.

Each chapter is titled descriptively. Edgar Allan Poe's chapter is called "Imp of the Perverse"; Mark Twain's is "Killingly Funny"; Isaac Bashevis Singer's is "Blintzes Stuffed with Cheese." After several pages of biographical information, the chapters end with "Bookmarks," which some readers will like best of all: tidbits of information that help explain the times, contexting each writer's life; and follow-ups on how the writer's works have influenced society or subsequent literature. For example, readers learn that Martin Luther King Jr. used Langston Hughes's poems in his speeches, and Zora Neale Hurston's *Their Eyes Were Watching God* was named the out-of-print book most in demand by the Modern Language Association (which may have helped bring it back into print!).

Krull, K. (1997). *Lives of the Athletes: Thrills, Spills (And What the Neighbors Thought). Illus K. Hewitt.* New York: Harcourt Brace & Company.

Again, the chapter titles are enticing; who could resist turning to "The Power of Pickled Eels" (Babe Ruth), "Dragons, Dragons, Dragons" (Bruce Lee), "Coffee, Boxer Shorts, and Pajamas" (Pelé), or "A Tigerbelle in the Fresh Air" (Wilma Rudolph)? The brief biographies end with "Athleticisms," anecdotes that reveal something about the subject's character. We learn that Arthur Ashe walked off the tennis court when his opponent's racial taunts became unbearable, "defaulting rather than responding in anger" (p. 77). Babe Didrikson Zaharias practiced golf for as long as 16 hours a day. "Sometimes she hit fifteen hundred balls in a row, bandaging her hands when they became bloody or blistered" (p. 41).

Krull, K. (1999). *They Saw the Future: Oracles, Psychics, Scientists, Great Thinkers, and Pretty Good Guessers. Illus. K. Brooker.* New York: Atheneum.

The Table of Contents contains fascinating quotes that help us immediately begin to know the subjects of the chapters: "I know the number of grains of sand, and all the measures of the sea" (The Oracle at Delphi), "What haven't you noticed lately?" (Marshall McLuhan), "I see and hear and understand at one and the same time" (Hildegard of Bingen), "Sometimes dreams are wiser than talking" (Nicholas Black Elk). This book takes a topic many students are fascinated with (and some parents are wary of) and brings in medical and scientific information to help us think about the subjects' skills and abilities. For example, we're told:

> Recently doctors have looked again at Hildegard's descriptions of her visions. Her physical symptoms correspond to what we now know to be signs of migraine attacks. These headaches of overwhelming intensity are usually followed by temporary paralysis and blindness—all reported by Hildegard: "I did not die, yet I did not altogether live." When they pass, there is a euphoria, also described by her: "Every sadness and pain vanishes from my memory, so that I am again as a simple maid and not as an old woman." (p. 40)

Krull, K. (2000). *Lives of Extraordinary Women: Rulers, Rebels (And What the Neighbors Thought). Illus. K. Hewitt.* New York: Harcourt.

This book's chapters include very different titles, such as "A Blazing Light" (Joan of Arc), "Strongman or Granny?" (Golda Meir), "Tiger Among Monkeys" (Indira Ghandi), "Hair Like a Halo" (Eva Perón), "Life at the Library" (Cleopatra), and "Dancing on the Roof" (Wilma Mankiller), but what these chapters have in common are depictions of extremely strong women. The "Ever After" sections at the conclusion of chapters give evidence of the person's legacy. For example, we learn that Eleanor Roosevelt, after noticing that only nine of JFK's first 240 appointments were women, sent him three pages of names of qualified candidates; after which, Kennedy established the Commission on the Status of Women. Hillary Clinton calls herself a die-hard Eleanor Roosevelt fan, and has spoken of imaginary talks with her. "When confronted with a particular situation, I might say to Mrs. Roosevelt, 'Oh, my goodness, what do I do now?'" (p. 69).

Krull's achievements don't end with this series. She wrote *Presenting Paula Danziger* (1995), part of the Twayne's *Young Adult Author* series. It's a combination biography and commentary on Danziger's books. I knew this was going to be an honest work when I read in Krull's Preface her reaction upon meeting Danziger and hearing her speak at a conference:

> . . . she also struck me as possibly in need of therapy, or maybe more therapy. Her anger was towering, almost out of control. She seemed a troubled soul, full of compassion for others but only unhappiness with herself. . . . She talked of Holden Caulfield (the narrator of *The Catcher in the Rye*) as her emancipator and of the healing power of writing and the written word . . . (p. xi)

Use this book along with some of the obituaries and tributes written by Danziger's fellow authors after her death in 2004.

Krull's *The Book of Rock Stars* (2003) provides mini-biographies of 24 musical icons. Numerous school-related references can be good-naturedly pointed out by teachers, such as Joni Mitchell's dedicating her first album to her seventh-grade English teacher, "'who taught me to love words,'" or the fact that Kurt Cobain excelled in art class in high school. Of course plenty of musical information is there, too, along with block print portraits of the musicians by Stephen Alcorn.

In 2003, Krull published *Harvesting Hope: The Story of Cesar Chavez.* Here Krull shows Chavez's happy boyhood on the Arizona family-owned farm; the move to California as migrant workers when drought destroyed all but hope; the gradual understanding of the violation of human rights he and others were experiencing, and also the power of nonviolence; and the courage and conviction of the young adult Chavez as he organized what was to be the first successful farm strike in the country.

Next, Krull came out with a book on a very different biographical subject. *The Boy on Fairfield Street: How Ted Geisel Grew Up to Become Dr. Seuss* (2004) chronicles the growing-up years of the great author and illustrator. But wait—not everyone found him great or even promising. When he took his one and only art class in high school, the teacher scolded him for breaking rules and warned him he would never be successful at art (p. 20). Dartmouth classmates voted him "'Least Likely to Succeed'" (p. 26). When he started publishing his cartoons, the response was also mixed. "A prisoner on death row wrote to say he didn't mind dying if Ted's work was the best publishers could do" (p. 34). In the four-page "On Beyond Fairfield Street" at the end of the book, Krull fast-forwards readers through the rest of Dr. Seuss's incredibly prolific and successful life.

Also in 2004, Krull published an adaptation of the diary of a 12-year-old who lived in New York City in 1912. Anne Elizabeth Rector was given art supplies and a diary by her parents for Christmas, and the journal that resulted was later found in her childhood home. *Anne Elizabeth's Diary: A Young Artist's True Story* gives us the child's words and pictures, and Krull's sidebars give us information both about the girl, who would go on to become an accomplished, recognized artist, and details about New York City at this point in history. Sidebars give facts, all related to Anne Elizabeth's diary entries, about school, the underwear of the day, girls in sports, dentistry, African Americans struggling for equal rights, movies, and more. Krull also adds sections called "What Happened Next?" (p. 56), "A Note from Anne Elizabeth's Granddaughter" (p. 59), and "Some Tips on Keeping a Diary" (p. 60).

Krull's 2004 picture book biography, *A Woman for President: The Story of Victoria Woodhull* (2004), will surprise students who do not realize that in the 1800s a woman actually ran for president of the United States. Krull brings readers back to the mid-1800s, when "Personal ambition in a woman was thought to be evil" (unpaged) then carries them

through the unusual life of Woodhull, fortune-teller and healer, friend of rich and influential people such as Cornelius Vanderbilt, founder of the first American stock-selling and -buying company that was female owned, suffragist, newspaper founder, and the Equal Rights Party's candidate for president in 1872. Quite a life, quite a book.

Krull has begun a new series of easy readers (appropriate for upper primary grades and beyond) that includes *The Night the Martians Landed: Just the Facts (Plus the Rumors) About Invaders from Mars* (2003) and *What Really Happened in Roswell?: Just the Facts (Plus the Rumors) About UFOs and Aliens* (2003). Both contain historical and scientific information, and direct curious readers to further resources. In addition, she has an entertaining "Giants of Science" Series appropriate for middle and high school students.

Go on Krull's website, www.kathleenkrull.com, for ideas about how to teach her *Lives of . . .* series, and also for general suggestions about teaching biographies.

DIANE STANLEY

Use this author's books in **art, English, math, science, social studies,** *and other disciplines.*

Figure 5.14 contains a selected bibliography of Diane Stanley's work.

I consider writer and illustrator Diane Stanley a co-teacher, since I use her books so often in lessons on teaching in the content areas. *Good Queen Bess: The Story of Elizabeth I of England* (1990) creates a perfect backdrop for students in **social studies** or **English** classes who need to understand that oft-heard phrase, "the Elizabethan Age." Stanley depicts through examples the monarch's intelligence, strength, and influence, such as in the area of theater (luckily for William Shakespeare) throughout her 45-year reign. Use this book along with *The Queen's Progress: An Elizabethan Alphabet*, by Celeste Davidson Mannis (2003). And of course it would make a great companion book to Stanley and Vennema's *Bard of Avon: The Story of William Shakespeare* (1992). The pictures in this one make the action at the Globe Theatre come alive.

Charles Dickens: The Man Who Had Great Expectations, co-written with Peter Vennema (1993), provides information that will help readers of Dickens's novels see how the stories and his life entwined, and gives great background about nineteenth-century London and the complexities of life during the Industrial Age. *Saladin: Noble Prince of Islam* (2002) brings us back all the way to the

| FIGURE | 5.14 | Selected works by Diane Stanley. |

Stanley, D., & Bagram, I. (2006). *Bella at midnight: The thimble, the ring, and the slippers of glass*. New York: HarperCollins.

Stanley, D. (2003). *Michelangelo*. New York: Harper-Collins.

Stanley, D. (2002). *Rumpelstiltskin's daughter*. New York: HarperCollins.

Stanley, D. (2002). *Saladin: Noble Prince of Islam*. New York: HarperCollins.

Stanley, D., & Holly, B. (2002). *Roughing it on the Oregon Trail*. New York: Scholastic.

Stanley, D. (1998). *Joan of Arc*. New York: Scholastic.

Stanley, D. (1996). *Leonardo da Vinci*. New York: Scholastic.

Stanley, D. (1994). *Cleopatra*. New York: Scholastic.

Stanley, D., & Vennema, P. (1993). *Charles Dickens: The man who had great expectations*. Illus. Diane Stanley. New York: Morrow.

Stanley, D., & Vennema, P. (1992). *Bard of Avon: The story of William Shakespeare*. Illus. Diane Stanley. New York: Morrow.

Stanley, D., & Vennema, P. (1990). *Good Queen Bess: The story of Elizabeth I of England*. Illus. D. Stanley. New York: Four Winds Press.

Stanley, D. (1986). *Peter the Great*. New York: Scholastic.

twelfth century and to another part of the world, where your students will read about war, morality, honor, religion, and leadership. They will see the dramatic changes Peter the Great, the epitome of the lifelong learner, brought to early eighteenth-century Russia in his 53 years.

Diane Stanley has given us superb illustrated life stories of contemporaries *Leonardo da Vinci* (1996) and *Michelangelo* (2003). In addition, she has brought to life the stories of two extremely strong women of different ages, *Cleopatra* (1994) and *Joan of Arc* (1998). **History** teachers could use the last page of the latter to teach about researching original documents, since Stanley explains that all of the quotes in her book were taken from the transcript of Joan's trial for heresy and the Trial of Rehabilitation. She explains the value of the primary sources, "Because of these two remarkable documents, we know more about Joan of Arc than about any other woman who lived before modern times" (unpaged). She also supplies what might be considered a "think-aloud" sharing her analysis of the data:

> But now that we have the story, what are we to make of it? How, in reading a historical account

that is based on hard facts and documentary evidence, are we supposed to make sense of miraculous visions and voices? Depending on our point of view, we can account for them in one of three ways. First, they were exactly what Joan said they were: divine revelations. Second, they were hallucinations produced by some illness of mind or body. And third, seeing the terrible state of her country and having heard the prophecy about the young girl who would save France, she began to wish, and then actually to believe, that she was the chosen one. To this day, however, no historian has been able to do more than spin the occasional theory. Sometimes, in studying history, we have to accept what we know and let the rest remain a mystery. (unpaged)

Diane Stanley's body of work can be a tremendous resource for teachers and students. She's a colleague in our goal to increase interest in and understanding of history. To find out more about her life, her thoughts, her current activities, and ways to use her books, visit www.dianestanley.com and www.harpercollins.com/authors/12765/Diane_Stanley/index.aspx.

P A R T   4

ANNOTATED **books and booktalks**

CODE: E = Elementary, **I** = Intermediate, **M** = Middle school, **H** = High School

The following annotations will vary in format. Most will be annotations I wrote directed at a teacher audience. Some will be character booktalks, which are brought to listeners via some character's point of view, and these will be labeled "Character Booktalk." Still others will be excerpts from my students' reader response logs. You may adapt any of them to make the booktalk just right for your audience and appropriately connected to your curricular topics.

ART

Bolden, T. (2004). *Wake Up Our Souls: A Celebration of Black American Artists.* New York: Harry N. Abrams. (M, H)

The lives of the artists presented here are fascinating, but what I like even better are the sidebars with explanations next to the works of art themselves. Students will experience such variety, from paintings by slave artists to Faith Ringgold's quilts that she still produces today. There are sculptures and murals, abstract paintings and photographs and folk art. The book is published in association with the Smithsonian American Art Museum, and I felt like I had just toured a great museum when I finished reading it. It's a great resource to use with the literary field trip strategy.

Cheng, C., & Low, A. (1991). *A Young Painter: The Life and Paintings of Wang Yani—China's Extraordinary Young Artist.* Photos Z. Zhensun. New York: Scholastic. (I, M, H)

A painter who was famous at an age younger than our students are presently? Yes. Yani is a self-taught artist who communicated her feelings and needs through painting pictures. By age 14, she was exhibiting her work at the Smithsonian. After responding to the works of art reproduced in this book and reading about this Chinese national treasure, students will want to find out what Yani is now doing as a young adult. This book offers a look at a non-Western style of art, so will work toward your curricular goal of helping students understand and appreciate diverse cultures.

Cohen, C. D. (2004). *The Seuss, the Whole Seuss, and Nothing but the Seuss: A Visual Biography of Theodor Seuss Geisel.* New York: Random House. (I, M, H)

Almost 400 pages of Seuss territory to explore—what a treat! The text is loaded with information about the artist's growing-up years, his various careers, his fertile imagination, his writing and drawing processes, his life philosophies, his personal relationships. Hundreds of marginal notes and Seuss illustrations accompany the main text. Fledgling artists will get inspiration and models if this book is part of a classroom library. A chapter on the misinterpretations of Dr. Seuss's work by scholars and others could be used in **English** classrooms as teachers and students discuss analysis of literature and the construction of meaning, especially in the area of symbolism. Could *The Cat in the Hat Comes Back really* be a warning about the spread of communism? Hmmm. . . .

de Bie, C. (2002). *My Brother Vincent van Gogh.* Los Angeles: Getty Publications. (I, M, H)

Written from the perspective of brother Theo, who loved and supported van Gogh, this picture book gives information about the siblings' childhood, the road to Vincent's becoming a painter, his interactions with fellow painters, and his fight to produce beauty in spite of increasingly poor mental health. Reproductions of paintings, including self-portraits, and photographs, such as the touching scene of the brothers' side-by-side headstones that ends the book, add to the eerie and exhilarating experience of immersing oneself in this book. Use this book to stimulate students' creative juices as they create fanfiction (see Part 2 of Chapter 4), telling a famous person's story from the perspective of a relative, colleague, or fan.

Duggleby, J. (1998). *Story Painter: The Life of Jacob Lawrence.* San Francisco: Chronicle. (I, M, H)

This biography tells of an artist who was himself a biographer and historian, who painted the legacies of Harriet Tubman, Frederick Douglass, General Toussaint L'Ouverture, and the Migration of the Negro in series of pictures. Lawrence's own paintings accompany Duggleby's text, and chapters open with quotes from Langston Hughes, Martin Luther King

ART

Jr., Jimmy Carter, and a traditional spiritual. After reading this book, you will no doubt want to explore more of Jacob Lawrence's art. Art students may experiment with painting in the style of Lawrence, or adapting his style as they create art to make political or social statements, or to convey a message or feeling about a historical figure. This book would also be appropriate for **history** class.

Frazier, N. (2001). *Georgia O'Keeffe.* North Dighton, MA: JG Press. (M, H)

This oversize book is the right size for the seemingly oversized flowers and other objects O'Keeffe immortalized in her paintings. A long, rich introduction is followed by chapters categorizing O'Keeffe's work into "Nature in Focus," "Places," and "Mindscapes," each with an introduction of its own that offers a way to interpret, or at least think about, the included paintings. Students could use the "Imaginary Dialogue" strategy (see Part 2 of this chapter) to tell O'Keeffe what they think of or feel as they read about her and look at her work, and to seek her advice and inspiration as they create art stimulated by nature.

Freedman, R. (1998). *Martha Graham: A Dancer's Life.* New York: Clarion Books. (M, H)

If I could travel through time and space, I would go to a performance of Martha Graham during every decade of her long career, partly because of being captivated by this biography. I see a picture of Helen Keller visiting Graham's studio in the 1940s, and I want to be there. I see her dancing as Emily Dickinson (The One Who Dances) in Letter to the World, and I want to be there. I look at pictures from her first independent concert in 1928, and I want to be there. I want to see her dance as Medusa, as Joan of Arc, as Heloise. A photo from 1990 of her with a former pupil, Madonna, is included. And the text is every bit as enticing. Since we can't go to Graham, we can bring Graham to students via Russell Freedman. It's powerful.

Gehrman, B. (2002). *Ansel Adams: America's Photographer.* Boston: Little, Brown and Company. (M, H)

The chapters read like vignettes, telling of the artist's experiences at different ages that help us get to know the person behind the camera and pictures. I loved the early portions showing his teen years—the hyperactivity that made it impossible for him to succeed in a school setting, the dedication to music and plans to become a pianist, the sicknesses that added to his powers of observation and sense of wonder. Adams recognized the factors leading to his vocation:

"How different my life would have been if it were not for those early hikes in the Sierra—if I had not experienced that memorable first trip to Yosemite—if I had not been raised by the ocean—if, if, if! Everything I have done or felt has been in some way influenced by the impact of the Natural Scene. . . . I *knew* my destiny when I first experienced Yosemite." (p. 24)

Have students use the "What-If?" strategy (see Part 2 of Chapter 4) to muse with Adams, and to imagine scenarios such as, "What if I were Ansel Adams's assistant and fellow traveler?" "What if I painted the same scenes he photographed?" "What if we tried color film?"

Hamanaka, S., & Ohmi, A. (1999). *In Search of the Spirit: The Living National Treasures of Japan.* New York: Morrow Junior Books. (I, M, H)

What a great official label for those artists recognized for their talent, dedication, and life's work: living national treasures. The authors introduce us to a potter, a cloth dyer and kimono-maker, a puppet master, a sword maker, a noh actor (who works with masks), and a bamboo weaver. Text, drawings, and photos teach us about the artists' lives, tools, processes, thinking, and values. Students will want to look further into some of these art forms. Natural questions arise from studying this book that students and teachers in art or **social studies** classes may want to explore, such as the following: If we were to choose six "national treasures" living in our country to write a book about, what forms of art would we look at? What criteria would we use to select the best at each art form? Who would likely be chosen? Teachers and students may want to extend their reading of this text by attempting to answer these questions.

Haskins, J. (1997). *Spike Lee: By Any Means Necessary.* New York: Walker and Company. (M, H)

Movie fans should enjoy reading about the life of this highly successful filmmaker. They'll be intrigued by the story of his childhood, the discussion of the controversy surrounding him and some of his films, his work habits, and beliefs. Ask your students to research what Lee has accomplished in the years since the publication of this book, and maybe review some of his films.

Rubin, S. G. (2006). *Andy Warhol: Pop Art Painter.* New York: Abrams Books for Young Readers. (I, M, H)

When Andy Warhol was nine years old, his art teacher at the Carnegie Museum of Art espoused the philosophy, "'Everything you look at has art'" (p. 7). As teachers, we want our students to take this stance, also, and Warhol is a good role model. He achieved fame for his various paintings of Campbell's soup cans, which he saw at lunch every day for 20 years. Andy struggled in school, even failing an art class because he did things his own way rather than follow directions; that could lead to a discussion about why (or whether) artists should follow rules at some times, and about originality and creativity. Rubin's biography is filled with Warhol's artwork in several genres, and includes critics' quotes, a timeline, source notes, and a list of resources for further investigation. Teachers may encourage students to do some Andy Warhol–like experimentation, perhaps with technology enhancement as they generate art using software tools available in the classroom. A celebration will be in order as the classes exhibit their Warhol-inspired artistic creations.

Schulke, F. (2002). *Witness to Our Times: My Life as a Photojournalist.* Chicago: Cricket Books. **(M, H)**

Can a photograph change the course of history? Schulke's words and pictures in this autobiography indicate an affirmative answer. Viewers were affected by his photos, as readers of this book will be. Above a picture taken at the funeral of slain civil rights leader Medgar Evers, who was killed on his front steps in Jackson, Mississippi, in 1963, Schulke writes:

> All people are affected by emotion, and I wanted the nation to see that this family had a father who had been cut down at a very young age. I wanted to show his widow's devastation. I got a picture with just one tear coming down her face. She didn't dissolve into crying, but to me that tear was even more devastating. Those pictures across the casket were the hardest pictures I ever took. (p. 30)

Schulke covered the funerals of Martin Luther King Jr. and John F. Kennedy as well. He recorded some triumphs, too. Photos include space launches, his daughter swimming with dolphins, Chi Shi the giant panda, the Berlin Wall, and iguanas on the Galapagos Islands. He tied himself to a utility pole to photograph Hurricane Betsy, but his most exciting assignment involved Namu, the killer whale. "I had a sense of doing something no one else had done before, of being alone with this wonderful creature that was like a big St. Bernard. . . . I can remember every minute when I was shooting. . . . this was something that was just a joy" (p. 97).

Students in a **photography** or **photojournalism** class may use this book as a stimulus to imagine their own future careers. Have them describe their dream jobs, perhaps involving covering the Olympics, accompanying world leaders at a summit,

or interviewing and photographing children from developing countries as well as our own. The book of photographs could also be used in a **social studies** class.

Sills, L. (1989). *Inspirations: Stories About Women Artists.* Niles, IL: Albert Whitman & Company. **(I, M)**

Meet Georgia O'Keeffe, Frida Kahlo, Alice Neel, and Faith Ringgold when they are little girls, experiencing their surroundings and learning from the influential people around them. Watch their personalities develop as teens and young adults. Be with them as the world recognizes their unique talents. Respond to the works of art accompanying their stories. You'll leave this book knowing some women who have left their mark.

Slaymaker, M. E. (2004). *Bottle Houses: The Creative World of Grandma Prisbrey.* **Illus. J. Paschkis.** New York: Henry Holt and Company. **(E, I, M, H)**

Would your students like to step inside ". . . a rainbow or a kaleidoscope or a jewel" (unpaged)? According to this book, that's the experience of entering one of folk artist Grandma Prisbrey's houses made of bottles. The illustrations also show examples of other bottle creations: a sidewalk, a birdbath, a chapel. Photographs of the Bottle Village, located in California, and of the artist herself, issue a further invitation. Finally, the text, after telling of the damage incurred in the 1994 earthquake, gives the website for yet another trip: http://echomatic.home.mindspring.com/bv. Your classroom artists may try out some of her mediums: pencils, vegetable dyes, buttons, shells, rocks. They'll gain confidence in their identities as artists as they take to heart Grandma Prisbrey's words, "'But I guess there are different kinds of art'" (unpaged).

ENGLISH/LANGUAGE ARTS

Brown, D. (2003). *American Boy: The Adventures of Mark Twain.* Boston: Houghton Mifflin. **(I, M, H)**

In the time students could read an encyclopedia entry on Samuel Clemens, they could finish this delightful illustrated account of his growing up and becoming a writer. Students will be able to see the childhood friends, settings, and experiences that would later be woven into his famous stories. My favorite line is, "'My literature attracted the town's attention, but not its admiration,' Sam said" (unpaged). A century and a half later, members of some schools and towns are reacting the same way. This could lead to a spirited discussion in the English classroom about censorship.

Caravantes, P. (2006). *Deep Woods: The Story of Robert Frost.* Greensboro, NC: Morgan Reynolds. **(M, H)**

Did you ever picture Robert Frost sitting in a high school English class learning poetry? An early chapter in this book helps us visualize the young Bobby, varsity football player, editor of the school paper, and budding poet. We also see Frost near the end of his life, reciting "A Gift Outright" at President Kennedy's inauguration. And we get to know many aspects of Frost during the decades between his start and his finish. This book would be a great supplement to anthologies and critical works that teachers might use during a poetry unit, for Caravantes includes inserts teaching various curricular material, such as "Major Types of Poetry," (p. 81), and "Metaphysical Poetry" (p. 94). Aspiring poets will appreciate the photo of Frost's "Stopping by Woods on a Snowy Evening" written in the poet's own handwriting. Part 2 of this chapter shows how a teacher could use and model the "Imaginary Dialogue" strategy with this biography.

Caravantes, P. (2006). *Writing Is My Business: The Story of O. Henry.* Greensboro, NC: Morgan Reynolds. **(M, H)**

How's this for an intriguing opening paragraph?:

> William Porter began to use the pen name "O. Henry" while he was in prison in the Ohio State Penitentiary. During his incarceration Porter began to write and tell stories to support his daughter. He needed a pseudonym because he did not want publishers to know he was a convict. (p. 11)

Students studying the short story genre will learn much from this book about O. Henry's life (including the reason for his serving time in prison) and about his writing processes. They'll even learn about "an O. Henry–esque surprise ending" (p. 127) that occurred at his funeral. Have the class read the ever-popular "The Gift of the Magi," then share the excerpt (pp. 111–112) about how that particular story came about. This might lead to a fruitful discussion about the writing processes of published writers and budding writers (i.e., the students themselves).

Carpenter, A. S. (2003). *Lewis Carroll: Through the Looking Glass.* Minneapolis, MN: Lerner Publications. **(M, H)**

Charles Dodson, aka Lewis Carroll, was many things during his lifetime: a mathematician, mathematics professor, and writer of mathematics books (in order to make math more interesting for reluctant students); a photographer; a letter writer (his letter register had 98, 721 entries, and that doesn't represent all of his letters). This book tells about many aspects of his life, but highlights the rela-

tionships and influences that led to *Alice in Wonderland* and *Through the Looking Glass and What Alice Found There.* My favorite chapter was the Epilogue, "Curiouser and Curiouser," documenting events from his death in 1898 to the present, including details such as Alice's handwritten, illustrated manuscript of her story being bought for 50,000 pounds. Readers get treated to a picture of the real Alice in New York in 1932 attending the centennial celebration of Carroll's birth. Scholars and psychiatrists are still debating the meanings of his works and his friendships. **Math** students might want to check out Carroll's math-related works and English students explore *The Annotated Alice* (Carroll, Tenniel, & Gardner, 2000) to think about connections and allusions.

Carpenter, H. (2000). *Tolkien: A Biography.* Boston: Houghton Mifflin. **(H)**

From the reader response journal of Brandon Moran:

> In relating to Tolkien's life, my mind is aghast. By the age of fifteen, young John Roald already knew three or more languages and hungered for more. He even invented a few of his own. As a student, I thirst for knowledge. The more I learn, the more I understand how much information exists and how much I will never know. This man's quest for knowledge dwarfs mine unspeakably. Although intimidating, I leave the book feeling inspired. Inspired to read, to learn, and to write. And most of all, I leave the book with a new appreciation for Tolkien's legendary works. . . .
>
> The author notes that Tolkien spoke in an interview about his [*Lord of the Rings*] not as if it were a work of fiction, but as if it was almost historical in nature, as if he was describing events that actually took place. In his mind, no doubt, these things did take place. I believe that in all good writers' minds, the stories they tell exist in their memories. The characters they describe are real people to them and that is why readers come to believe the story and love it, too.

Darrow, S. (2003). *Through the Tempests Dark and Wild: A Story of Mary Shelley, Creator of Frankenstein.* Illus. A. Barrett. Cambridge, MA: Candlewick Press. **(I, M, H)**

I found this in the Biography section of my public library, but the author explains that this story is a fictionalized account of researched events in Mary Shelley's life. It does contain an Introduction and an Afterword that are strictly biographical. Combine this with the recent *Mary Shelley* (Garrett, 2002) for a more complete biographical account.

It would be normal for your students to wonder how the 19-year-old Mary came to write what has been called the first science fiction book. Sharon Darrow offers two answers. Her own analysis follows:

Mary's deep emotional responses to her life experiences are sure to have influenced her fiction. Her mother's death in childbirth, the estrangement from her father, the need for someone to love her, and the death of her own baby were all elements that played into the shaping of the story of Frankenstein. (Afterword, unpaged)

The second answer is given in Mary Shelley's own words, explaining a dream she had after an evening reading ghost stories before a fire at Lord Byron's villa:

> "My imagination, unbidden, possessed and guided me. . . . I saw a pale student of unhallowed arts kneeling beside the thing he had put together. I saw the hideous phantasm of a man stretched out, and then, on the working of some powerful engine, show signs of life." (Afterword, unpaged)

Dommermuth-Costa, C. (1998). *Emily Dickinson: Singular Poet.* Minneapolis, MN: Lerner Publications. **(M, H)**

Many biographies are available on Emily Dickinson, and I'd love to have a classroom shelf full of them. The author of this version lets Emily's own words, through her letters and poems, tell the story of her development as a person and a writer. The photographs are especially intriguing—a silhouette of Emily in her teens, a page of her writing, the home she stayed within for so much of her life, and more. Use this along with Michael Bedard's picture book *Emily* (1992), told from the perspective of a little girl who lived across the street from the poet, to show how we can observe unique individuals using varying lenses, thereby often coming to varying conclusions.

Hart, J. (2003). *Native Son: The Story of Richard Wright.* Greensboro, NC: Morgan Reynolds. **(H)**

Part of the *World Writers* series, this biography begins with a chapter called "A Troubling Beginning," and the opening sentence, "When he was four years old, Richard Wright set his grandparents' house on fire" (p. 9). Trouble was a theme throughout his life; yet his accomplishments in the writing world were many and astonishing. The book gives some context for his novel *Native Son* (1998) and autobiography *Black Boy: A Record of Childhood and Youth* (1993), and photographs add to the world we are allowed into while reading about this extraordinary life of a rebel and an intellectual.

Haskins, J. (2002). *Toni Morrison: Telling a Tale Untold.* **Brookfield,** CT: Twenty-First Century Books. **(M, H)**

Sometimes a biographer's admiration for his or her subject shines through, and such is the case here. Haskins begins by describing Toni Morrison as the first African American woman to win the Nobel Prize

for Literature, telling in the Introduction of Morrison's love for and gifts involving language. The book chronicles her growing up amid racism, and then using her experiences in her crafting of a "Canon of Black Work" (p. 47). For students who want a shorter version of Haskins's take on Morrison's life, recommend *Toni Morrison: The Magic of Words* (2001, Brookfield, CT: The Millbrook Press).

Kenyon, K. S. (2003). *The Brontë Family: Passionate Literary Geniuses.* Minneapolis, MN: Lerner Publications. **(M, H)**

Jane Eyre, by Currer Bell. Hmmm? Many students will be surprised, perhaps appalled, at what they learn in the first chapter: Charlotte Bronte had to use a male pseudonym when her now famous book was first published. They'll go on to learn about the Bronte siblings' childhood, from rising each morning to the sound of their father's pistol firing a wake-up call, to experiencing the deaths of their mother and sisters Maria and Elizabeth. One chapter tells of the wooden soldiers the children played with; Branwell and Charlotte wrote stories about these soldiers for eight years, producing at least 22 volumes each. Readers will learn of early careers, writing processes, publishing adventures, Branwell's debilitating alcoholism, and too many tragic early deaths. Read excerpts aloud during a unit on the novels of the Bronte sisters or as mini-lessons in a writing workshop setting.

Kerley, B. (2004). *Walt Whitman: Words for America.* **Illus B. Selznick.** New York: Scholastic. **(I, M, H)**

"Even when he wasn't working, Walt surrounded himself with words" (unpaged). Readers see a literate, language-loving teen as they see a picture of him reading *Arabian Nights.* On other pages, readers see the future poet walking, running, always on the move and observing and exploring. In this book, students read of Whitman's encounters with Abraham Lincoln, as well as with Civil War soldiers; they encounter his letter to the parents of a dead soldier. They get to know the man. What a model for our fledgling writers: He made tiny notebooks—a few sheets of paper secured with a ribbon or pin—and carried one in his pocket at all times, so that at a moment's notice he could record what he saw and felt. Consider showing your own daybook, and invite students to share theirs, as well as later poems inspired by their seeds, similar to Whitman's composing process.

King, S. (2000). *On Writing: A Memoir of the Craft.* New York: Scribner. **(H)**

Imagine having young Stephen King in your class, completing writing assignments for you. As scary a thought as any in his novels, don't you think? In this book, King tells of his youth, his early writing career, his inspirations and fears, even his process of writing this book. He gives advice, but usually through story, which of course is his strength. Invite Stephen King into your class to be your co-teacher with this autobiographical work.

Kirk, C. A. (2003). *J. K. Rowling: A Biography.* Westport, CT: Greenwood Press. **(M, H)**

Readers who are fascinated by Harry Potter will be eager to find out about his creator. This book gives information about Rowling's childhood, where she gets her ideas, her writing process, her personal philosophy and values, and some hints about what her future holds. One chapter deals with controversies and criticism surrounding her work, and an appendix tells some of the books she has read herself. Have your students seek out other sources to get updated information on Rowling and life after the Harry Potter series. They may compare the information in this book with Harmin's *J. K. Rowling: Author of Harry Potter* (2006).

Lasky, K. (2003). *A Voice of Her Own: The Story of Phillis Wheatley, Slave Poet.* Illus. P. Lee. Cambridge, MA: Candlewick. **(E, I, M)**

The year is 1761. New Englander Susannah Wheatley wonders if it's possible to teach an African to read and write. Despite the unwritten rule that slaves should be kept illiterate, she begins to teach her nine-year-old slave Phillis, who surpasses all expectations as she reads the Bible, then learns Latin, Greek, math and geometry, and has a poem published by age 14. What is the future for such a gifted, but unfree, young woman? Encourage your classroom poets to join Phillis as she meets George Washington, secures her freedom, and composes poetry to bring her native Africa to life and memory.

Lazo, C. E. (2003). *F. Scott Fitzgerald: Voice of the Jazz Age.* Minneapolis, MN: Lerner Publications. **(M, H)**

This "photobiography" is filled with captivating pictures that can be read as one version of Fitzgerald's life story. The chapters on his childhood and school years are fascinating, as are the later ones detailing his climb to success; his wild behaviors; his relationships with wife Zelda, daughter Scottie, and fellow artists; his literary achievements; and his failing health, and death. Consider using this book as a companion to Fitzgerald's works that students read; it could work well as either an introduction or a follow-up.

McGinty, A. B. (2003). *Meet Jerry Spinelli.* New York: PowerKids Press. **(I, M)**

Millions of children have met author Jerry Spinelli's book characters, including Maniac Magee, Stargirl,

and Loser. Now they can meet the man who married into a family of six children, whom he credits for giving him many of his ideas for stories. In this biography the font is large, and the text simple, which makes for a quick read. The photos of Spinelli as a child and now with his family are intriguing. Use this book as a springboard to reading a more sophisticated book about the author or some of his speeches and interviews. It would work well as part of a learning center where students read fiction while simultaneously reading about the authors who created the tales.

McKissack, P. C., & McKissack, F. L. (1998). *Young, Black, and Determined: A Biography of Lorraine Hansberry.* New York: Holiday House. **(M, H)**

A Raisin in the Sun, Lorraine Hansberry's play that opened on Broadway in 1959, is still required reading in many high schools, with good reason. This biography gives lots of background about the play and its author, and includes photographs from the play. But what I liked best about this book was the way it contexted Hansberry's short life (she died at age 34) by telling about her relationship with other activists and writers; the timeline tells what she was doing during certain years and what other significant national events were happening in those same years. I'd surely want this book in my English or **social studies** classroom "Author Library."

Rosen, M. (2001). *Shakespeare: His Work & His World.* **Illus. R. Ingpen.** Cambridge, MA: Candlewick Press. **(I, M, H)**

It's pretty amazing to some students that so many movies and books continue to appear about a guy long dead. "What's So Special About Shakespeare?" is the title of the second chapter, and the answer comes partly from quotes in the bard's plays. This biography is filled with action, from the plays as well as from the playwright's life, in both the text and illustrations. In the final chapter, "The Legacy," readers learn the origins of common sayings our students might not realize came from Shakespeare. An excellent five-page illustrated timeline is included at the end of the book.

Thompson, S. L. (2003). *Robert Cormier.* New York: The Rosen Publishing Group. **(H)**

Readers find Cormier's novels pretty strange, eerie, and disturbing. His characters have included individuals with troubling mental illnesses, with major behavioral issues, or with a tendency to be a serial killer. Many of Cormier's titles have made it to a banned book list. What must the author be like—strange, eerie, disturbing? Readers find out that this is not the case; in fact, Cormier describes himself as an incurable optimist, though he is willing to discuss hard topics such as the creation of evil and the pull of the dark. Cormier says in an interview, after hearing an excerpt from *I Am the Cheese* (2005) read, along with the interviewer's commentary that the passage is "... probably the quintessential teenage cry for identity...." (p. 73):

> I think identity is so important to teenage people. And in this particular case, [Adam's] entire identity has been obliterated completely... poor Adam Farmer is completely isolated. And I think that isolation that adolescents feel is paramount in their lives. (p. 73)

This biography includes some selected reviews of Cormier's novels, as well as sources to find more information about this celebrated author of young adult literature. Consider bringing into class some of the obituaries that appeared in literary journals after Cormier's death in 2000; they show how beloved and respected he was among his peers. Many readers will want more and more of both Cormier's fiction and works about his life and the literature he created. (There's an entire book of essays devoted to *I Am the Cheese* [Keely, 2001]!) In many ways, Robert Cormier is still among us.

Walker, A. (2002). *Langston Hughes: American Poet.* Illus. C. Deeter. New York: HarperCollins. **(I, M, H)**

Students familiar with Alice Walker's fiction, essays, and poetry will be happy to know that she writes biography, too. After telling Hughes's fascinating life story, she adds a note talking about her own relationship with this best of mentors. Here's what she has to say about Langston the person:

> There are places in the world that emit so much magnetism, energy, and power that people who visit them call them holy. There are people who have this quality, too. Langston was one of them. He was a person who loved unconditionally. He seemed to gaze directly into the heart; gender and race, for instance, were not barriers for him. (p. 37)

After reading this book, teachers and students may want to discuss the similarities and differences between Alice Walker and Langston Hughes, as well as to investigate and celebrate texts both authors have given us.

Walker, R. (2001). *Black White and Jewish: Autobiography of a Shifting Self.* New York: Riverhead Books. **(H)**

Virtually all readers have shared the experience of sometimes not knowing where they belonged, what groups they were a part of. Walker's memoir focuses on a seemingly constant identity crisis. She lived with her mother on the West Coast and her father on the East Coast, alternating every two years between two disparate cultures. This book is so much her own story it took me a while to realize her mother is Alice Walker. I especially liked the stories she told of her life within school settings. She credits some teachers with saving her life.

Wilson, A. (2003). *S. E. Hinton.* New York: The Rosen Publishing Group. **(M, H)**

Part of *The Library of Author Biographies*, this book is one of several about the author who did something almost unheard of. How could a 16-year-old girl write *The Outsiders* (1967)? How could she know the human heart in such depth, how could she understand structure, symbolism, theme, setting, and character development while still a teen? Aren't teenagers supposed to be egocentric, unable to see beyond themselves and their narrow circle of family and friends? How could young Susan Eloise almost single-handedly start the now hugely popular genre we know as "Young Adult"? We may never understand completely, but S. E. Hinton shatters stereotypes that depict adolescents as limited, selfish, unable to generalize or care beyond an inner circle. This easy read also offers recommendations for further exploration for those who want even more.

LANGUAGES AND CULTURE

Davis, J. (Ed.). (2003). *Open Your Eyes: Extraordinary Experiences in Faraway Places.* New York: Viking. **(M, H)**

Readers join some of their favorite young adult authors in learning about different cultures through the memoirs in this book. Katherine Paterson shares excerpts of letters she wrote home as a college student traveling through Europe for a summer. Harry Mazer's piece is titled, "Join the Army and See the World," while Lois Lowry tells of her childhood adventures when her father's work led the family to live in Tokyo for a few years. Elizabeth Partridge recalls her family's cross-country trip in 1963, "looking for America" (p. 124). The underlying feeling of all the stories can be summed up by the quote by Mark Twain that precedes the editor's Introduction: "Travel is fatal to prejudice, bigotry, and narrow-mindedness."

Englar, M. (2006). *Le Ly Hayslip.* Chicago: Raintree. **(I, M, H)**

Sometimes the problems in the world can seem so overwhelming, we may begin to despair of finding a way to heal relationships and end animosity. Readers take heart as they read what one woman, who immigrated to the United States from Vietnam in 1970, has been able to accomplish in the attempt to bring East and West together. After losing two husbands to death, Le Ly worked many jobs and eventually started her own restaurant business to support herself and three sons. She became a successful author, telling her life story and writing of the people of Vietnam. She founded charitable organizations that have enhanced the medical care of her region of Vietnam, as well as provided schools and a home for orphans. Ask students who want to learn more about this remarkable entrepreneur to read her books, *When Heaven and Earth Changed Places: A Vietnamese Woman's Journey from War to Peace* (with Jay Wurtz, 1989) and *Child of War, Woman of Peace* (1993). Oliver Stone made of movie of Le Ly's life, *Heaven and Earth*, released in 1994.

Language teachers may encourage students to look for places in the book where language issues are at play (e.g., when Le Ly went on a book tour, ". . . she was shy about her accent, but the audiences welcomed her" (p. 45).

Hoffman, E. (1989). *Lost in Translation: A Life in a New Language.* New York: E. P. Dutton. **(H)**

When 13-year-old immigrant Ewa is brought to her first day of school in Canada, her name gets changed (without consultation) to Eva, to suit the needs of English speakers. Her sister's changes from Alina to Elaine. This mattered. "Our Polish names didn't refer to us; they were as surely us as our eyes or hands. These new appellations, which we ourselves can't yet pronounce, are not us. They are identification tags, disembodied signs pointing to objects happening to my sister and myself" (p. 105). Throughout this memoir, the author helps us understand the relationship of language to one's identity. She takes readers on her journey as she learns to speak and to think in English; it's a journey that involves losses along with the gains. Teachers may read excerpts as students are either learning English, or learning another language, to help them verbalize what speaking in another language is like at whatever stage or level of proficiency they are experiencing.

Kingston, M. H. (1989). *The Woman Warrior: Memoirs of a Girlhood Among Ghosts.* New York: Vintage Books. **(H)**

Early in this memoir, Maxine Hong Kingston ponders, "Chinese Americans, when you try to understand what things in you are Chinese, how do you separate what is peculiar to childhood, to poverty, insanities, one family, your mother who marked your growing with stories, from what is Chinese?" (p. 5). Readers may use the remainder of the book to figure out answers, if there indeed are answers. The unique style combining childhood stories and cultural myths invites your students into a world where they'll learn things about immigration, learning a new language, and cultural conflicts while enjoying an imaginative rendering of the coming-of-age theme.

Rodriguez, R. (1983). *Hunger of Memory: The Education of Richard Rodriguez: An Autobiography.* Boston: Godine. **(H)**

In the Prologue, Rodriguez introduces himself this way:

> Once upon a time, I was a socially disadvantaged child. An enchantedly happy child. Mine was a childhood of intense family closeness. And extreme public alienation.
>
> Thirty years later I write this book as a middle-class American man. Assimilated. (p. 1)

His story is a testimony to both the gains and losses he experienced as the son of Mexican immigrant parents who entered school knowing about 50 English words and ended up educated and successful, but at a tremendous cost. His eloquently told memoir will help English learners to express their own feelings of accomplishment as well as their frustrations and concerns. It might also help their peers and teachers to realize the emotional as well as academic struggles they may be encountering.

Santiago, E. (1993). *When I Was Puerto Rican.* New York: Vintage Books. **(M, H)**

You can't help but like a narrator who opens a chapter with, " I didn't mean to steal the nickels from the baby's glass piggy bank" (p. 173). The line announces that a master storyteller is about to explain. And Esmeralda Santiago does explain incidents of her childhood beautifully. I especially like her stories of school. Then, when she's 14, the family moves from Puerto Rico to Brooklyn. Scenery changes, language changes, people change. Does Esmeralda's identity change? Her new guidance counselor asks what she wants to be when she grows up. She says she doesn't know, though she does tell the reader that she had indeed given thought to her future over the years, wanting to be a cartographer, then a topographer. The book ends with Esmeralda's graduation from Performing Arts, and many readers will want to immediately pick up *Almost a Woman* (1998) to be her companion through the next stage of her life's journey.

MATH AND TECHNOLOGY

Abeel, S. (2003). *My Thirteenth Winter: A Memoir.* New York: Orchard Books. **(M, H)**

> I am twenty-five years old and I can't tell time. I struggle with dialing phone numbers, counting

money, balancing my checkbook, tipping at restaurants, following directions, understanding distances, and applying basic math to my everyday life. . . . I have been diagnosed with dyscalculia, a learning disability that affects my capacity to learn skills based on sequential processing, such as math, spelling, and grammar. (p. 1)

So begins Samantha's story, which is representative of an intriguing segment of the population: those who have both learning gifts and learning disabilities. As happens in so many cases, for years the giftedness masked the disability, and the disability masked the giftedness, so that she was seen as an average learner (whatever that means) and did not receive the educational services she needed. Samantha recounts in detail the panic attacks, stomachaches, and nightmares that finally led her parents to seek medical help, and the struggles and prejudices encountered as they fought for school services to help their daughter succeed. Many of our students may identify with Samantha's feelings of difference, low self-esteem, insecurity; they'll rejoice as they read about her publishing a book and going on author lectures before she's even in high school. She portrays aspects of her life beyond school walls, countering the too-common belief that learning disabilities only affect school performance.

Math teachers may read excerpts that demonstrate Samantha's thinking metacognitively about how she proceeds with math problems and processes. Invite your students to do the same, and to verbalize where and how their solving of math problems sometimes breaks down.

Alexanderson, G. L. (2000). *The Random Walks of George Pólya.* Washington, DC: Mathematical Association of America. (H)

From the reader response journal of Anthony Fisher:

> As a math major myself, I have experienced unbelievable admiration for the devotion that George Pólya expressed towards mathematics. Some of the subjects he researched throughout his career are not even conceivable to me, even after nearly two years of advanced mathematical studies. It is amazing to think that he collaborated with some of the names I hear about in my math courses, such as Einstein. It is funny to read through his proofs and realize how much of a role they play in the curriculum of nearly every math course I have ever taken. . . . Gaining perspective on how a mathematician is born and grows is a reassuring concept for a math major such as myself. . . . This book has created a desire in me to read more about those who have expanded the field in which I plan to make a living.

Collier, B., & MacLachlan, J. (1998). *Charles Babbage: And the Engines of Perfection.* New York: Oxford University Press. (M, H)

The year is 1821. Two sets of people have calculated values for the positions of a number of stars as seen at regular times through the year. You have to compare the results, and you find the number of errors in the data mounting. What must you do? Is there a better way than human counting? You might think of a computer, a calculator at least, but there is no such thing in 1821. Charles Babbage was actually one of the persons doing this counting, and complained, "I wish to God these calculations could be done by a steam engine" (p. 9). Thus started his life's work. You and your students may read this biography to learn about the invention of his "Difference Engine."

Flannery, S., with Flannery, D. (2001). *In Code.* New York: Workman Publishing. (M, H)

Can a teenager be considered a real mathematician? Sarah Flannery is an adolescent with an international reputation as a result of her discoveries in Internet cryptography and the creation of a new algorithm. This memoir will be thought provoking and inspiring for students in math classes.

Hayhurst, C. (2006). *Euclid: The Great Geometer.* New York: The Rosen Publishing Group. (I, M, H)

A secondary mathematics curriculum includes an introduction to the history of mathematics, and this book surely will help with that. Readers are invited to "Forget, if just for a while, the things that surround you, and instead submerse yourself in a world where life itself is a mystery. . . . Set your imagination free. . . . Welcome to ancient Greece" (p. 7). Before introducing Euclid, known as the Father of Geometry, Hayhurst provides a chapter on the origins of mathematics and provides a context for the information that is known about the author of *The Elements.* There's a section on Euclid's most famous student, Archimedes. As a math teacher, you may find the chapter on Euclid's work to be most helpful, since it includes definitions from *The Elements* of concepts such as point, line, obtuse angle, and plane figure, as well as postulates and axioms that your students will encounter in geometry class.

Consider also the companion book in *The Library of Greek Philosophers* series, *Pythagoras: Pioneering Mathematician and Musical Theorist of Ancient Greece,* by Dimitra Karamanides (2006). Its potential usefulness for giving students an appreciation of the early mathematicians will continue to build on the foundations of present-day mathematicians.

MATH

Keating, S., & Tartarotti, S. (2003). *Archimedes: Ancient Greek Mathematician.* Philadelphia: Mason Crest Publishers. **(E, I, M, H)**

The cartoon-like pictures, combined with the fictionalized format of the text (the story is narrated by the Roman statesman Cicero, who in 75 BCE traveled to Sicily, Archimedes' homeland), will cause elementary grade students, especially those who are fascinated by inventions, to enjoy this book. But the information is appropriate for math and science learners of any age, as I can attest. I learned how he built his geometric thinking on geniuses such as Euclid; I learned about his thinking processes through anecdotes about his figuring problems in the sand of the beach and his active thinking in the bathtub.

Follow up this book by sending your students into their schools, homes, and communities to find examples of the Archimedes screw, the lever, pulleys, catapults, and other machines connected to the principles worked out by Archimedes.

Litwin, L. B. (1999). *Benjamin Banneker: Astronomer and Mathematician.* Berkeley Heights, NJ: Enslow Publishers. **(M, H)**

There's a high school in Washington, D.C., named for Benjamin Banneker, which is appropriate, since this free Black man worked in the 1790s surveying the land that would become the nation's capital. He spent almost 60 years of his life in solitude on his Maryland farm, then began a much more public life. A self-taught astronomer, he invented many things and wrote a farmer's almanac, which publishers were at first reluctant to publish because he was Black. His correspondence with Thomas Jefferson about the evils of slavery helped the abolitionist cause. Even after his death he helped the cause, for a Baltimore newspaper's obituary pointed out that this mathematician and astronomer "'is a prominent instance to prove that a descendent of Africa is susceptible of as great mental improvement and deep knowledge into the mysteries of nature as that of any other nation'" (p. 92).

This biography belongs in our classrooms; Banneker can inspire students to learn about the applications of math and **science,** and to speak out against injustice. He is a great example of a passionate practitioner, even though he was a quiet and humble man.

Nasar, S. (1998). *A Beautiful Mind: The Life of Mathematical Genius and Nobel Laureate John Nash.* New York: Simon & Schuster. **(H)**

Your students may have seen the movie based on this book and sharing its title. You might be able to show two copies of the book, one with Russell Crowe on the cover, the other with the actual subject of the biography. Through reading this book, or parts of it, students will be able to appreciate the brilliance of Nash's work in mathematics and in game theory; they'll also get a picture of an actual mathematics community, which might make math more than just a school subject for them. The story of his life is fascinating and compelling, and the mathematical principles are woven into that story in an authentic way. Students who show talent in math and/or love the subject will be inspired by all aspects of this book, and students who are intrigued by computer games and mathematical puzzles will benefit from this book as well.

Petroski, H. (2002). *Paperboy: Confessions of a Future Engineer.* New York: Alfred A. Knopf. **(H)**

Before introducing this memoir, teachers might choose to read amusing anecdotes from Petroski's popular books about everyday things, such as *The Pencil* (1990) and *The Book on the Bookshelf* (2000). Then the students will be ready to learn about the boyhood of Henry Petroski, who shows in *Paperboy* that his mind and hands were always actively asking questions and seeking answers. He explains:

> As a poet can see a world in a grain of sand, so an engineer, even a budding one, can see a bicycle in a ball of steel. The movement of my fingers separating lock nuts from wheel nuts, spoke nipples from needle valves, and hubcaps from bearing cones became my mechanical mantra. An engineer before my time, and alone with the parts of the whole, I came to a new appreciation of the bicycle as the sum of its parts. (pp. 56–57)

Students are often more willing to learn our curricular material if they understand the concepts' real-world applications. This book is full of connections between theory and practice.

Reimer, L., & Reimer, W. (1990). *Mathematicians Are People, Too: Stories from the Lives of Great Mathematicians.* Palo Alto, CA: Dale Seymour Publications. **(M)**

The Table of Contents is enticing; chapters with titles such as "The Short Giant" (Isaac Newton), "Life on an Obstacle Course" (Emmy Noether), "The Man Who Concentrated Too Hard" (Archimedes), "Numbers Were His Greatest Treasure" (Ramanujan), and "Mathematics at Midnight" (Sophie Germain) invite readers into them, if only to find out the reason for the title! This book, as well as the following, will help students understand and appreciate the history of mathematics, and the authentic stories will help students realize that math gets used well beyond the schoolhouse.

Reimer, L., & Reimer, W. (1995). *Mathematicians Are People, Too: Stories from the Lives of Great Mathematicians. Volume Two.* Palo Alto, CA: Dale Seymour Publications. **(M)**

Chapters in this volume include "A Shy Sky Watcher" (Benjamin Banneker), "The Computer's Grandfather" (Charles Babbage), "The Mystery of X and Y" (Mary Somerville), "The Lessons on the Wall" (Sonya Kovalevsky), "The Overlooked Genius" (Neils Abel), "The Stay-in-Bed Scholar" (Rene Descartes), "The Conceited Hypochondriac" (Girolamo Cardano), and "Lean on the Blockhead" (Fibonacci). Need I say more?

Schechter, B. (1998). *My Brain Is Open: The Mathematical Journeys of Paul Erdös.* New York: Simon & Schuster. **(H)**

What is a mathematician? Surely that is an important question for high school math students to ponder. This book provides several answers. The author defines the term this way. "Mathematicians are finite, flawed human beings who spend their lives trying to understand the infinite and perfect" (p. 47). Maybe your students will like this definition, attributed to Erdös, better: "'A mathematician is a machine for turning coffee into theorums'" (p. 15).

The story of Erdös, the genius who spent his life thinking, performing, and publishing mathematical proofs, is thought provoking. His story may help our students see the value of collaboration; Erdös co-authored hundreds of papers. Schechter explains, "For Erdös, the mathematics that consumed most of his waking hours was not a solitary pursuit but a social activity, a movable feast" (p. 14).

This book is filled with explanations of concepts Erdös worked with, concepts that are now part of the high school curriculum, such as number theory, prime numbers, set theory, and formulas involving polygons. For your students who want further stories and discussion of the mathematical contributions of Erdös, lead them to another biography published the same year as Schechter's: *The Man Who Loved Only Numbers*, by Paul Hoffman. There's also a movie, *N Is a Number: A Portrait of Paul Erdös* (Csicsery & Locker, 2004).

Viegas, J. (2007). *Pierre Omidyar: The Founder of eBay.* New York: The Rosen Publishing Group. **(M, H)**

Many of our students are participating members of the eBay community. It's a community of millions. Perhaps they'd be interested in meeting the person responsible for eBay, a person whose net worth was estimated in 2005 to be around $10 billion. (There! You just got your students' attention!) Would people have predicted Pierre Omidyar's success? He tells us that during his four years at Tufts University, "'. . . my GPA improved every single semester, which gives you an idea of where I started. No, I was not a good student'" (p. 26). But he internal-

ized the college's values, including diversity and global orientation. And he put his creative ideas and his technical and fiscal skills to work. Students will enjoy the pictures and captions relating to some of the things sold on eBay, such as Beanie Babies, which sometimes went for thousands of dollars; and Muhammad Ali's boxing shoes, for which bids started at more than $100,000. Use this book as an initiating activity during a unit where teams of students design a new technology or use for an existing technology. Recommend other books in Rosen Publishing's *Internet Career Biographies* series during the unit or throughout a technology course, including

> *Jeff Bezos: The Founder of Amazon.com* (2007) by Ann Byers
>
> *Jerry Yang and David Filo: The Founders of Yahoo* (2007) by Michael R. Weston
>
> *Marc Andreessen and Jim Clark: The Founders of Netscape* (2007) by Simone Payment
>
> *Sergey Brin and Larry Page: The Founders of Google* (2007) by Casey White
>
> *Shawn Fanning: The Founder of Napster* (2007) by Renee Ambrosek

MUSIC

Bankston, J. (2004). *The Life and Times of Wolfgang Amadeus Mozart.* Bear, DE: Mitchell Lane Publishers. **(I, M, H)**

This book's format provides for the story of Mozart's childhood and career, while also providing their historical and social context. Separate pages provide information about Vienna, the Age of Reason, and smallpox (a disease prevalent in the eighteenth century), for example. There's also interesting information on child prodigies. Teachers may show photographs and read from this book as students are learning, practicing, and performing music composed by Mozart. Use this book along with Reich's *Clara Schumann: Piano Virtuoso* (see p. 197), asking students to compare and contrast these two young musical geniuses, both of whom were pushed by their fathers, who went on to lead very different adult lives. Ask your students to express their thinking about the role they expect music to play in their own adulthoods.

Chippendale, L. A. (2004). *Yo-Yo Ma: A Cello Superstar Brings Music to the World.* Berkeley Heights, NJ: Enslow Publishers. **(M, H)**

The author describes her subject not only as possibly the greatest cellist in the world, but as someone who ". . . is always interested in taking risks and exploring different kinds of music and ways of performing" (p.

6). Through photographs and text, readers will follow Yo-yo Ma's years at Harvard; his travels and performances around the world; his decisions involving balancing his life, such as refusing to play concerts on his children's birthdays and appearing as a guest on *Mr. Rogers' Neighborhood*; his exploration of connections between traditions and instruments throughout the world. The anecdotes are thought-provoking. Ma visited the Bushmen of Africa and was deeply affected by a trance dance that women told him they do because the ritual gives them meaning. He played Bach for the Bushmen, but:

> They were not very interested. They wanted to play their music for him instead. Ma listened carefully to the villagers' music. He was fascinated by their homemade instruments, and he asked them many questions about how they worked. (p. 56)

Because Yo-yo Ma is willing to continue to learn about others, he will use new experiences to inform and shape his own work, for he views music as being about communication. What a great role model for our students.

Dylan, B. (2004). *Chronicles, Volume One.* New York: Simon & Schuster. (H)

When you teach a unit on folk music, having lots of the songs to sing and listen to will be important. In addition, you may help students realize the social and political aspects of many of the singers' songs and lives. Bring legendary as well as living folk singers into your classroom via books to create a sort of Woodstock atmosphere as you teach. Provide composite biographies, and also individual biographies of icons like Pete Seeger, Woodie Guthrie, and Joan Baez. Students who want to hear artists' takes on their music and careers might delve into Bob Dylan's memoir. He tells of signing his first contract, at a time when ". . . folk music was considered junky, second-rate and only released on small labels." He tells of the way the media interpreted his songs and tried to control his image. He tells of life on the road, and of life at home with his family. One part that music teachers may use as they teach music composition is Dylan's explanation of his composing process. After a dry spell when he had lost interest in songwriting and thought he might never do it again, something changed one night:

> I wrote about twenty verses for a song called "Political World" and this was about the first of twenty songs I would write in the next month or so. They came from out of the blue. . . . They were easy to write, seemed to float downstream with the current. (p. 165)

After he tells of his individual experience, he generalizes:

> A song is like a dream, and you try to make it come true. They're like strange countries that you have to enter. You can write a song anywhere, in a railroad compartment, on a boat, on horseback—it helps to be moving. Sometimes people who have the greatest talent for writing songs never write any because they are not moving. (p. 166)

Consider having your students write a song while moving in some way. They might surprise you both with their products and with their stories of motion.

Freedman, R. (2004). *The Voice That Challenged a Nation: Marian Anderson and the Struggle for Equal Rights.* New York: Clarion. (M, H)

Imagine singing to 75,000 people. The first two photographs in this book (preceding p. 1, and p. 2) depict Marian Anderson on the steps of the Lincoln Memorial in 1939 doing just that. Students may be stunned to learn that this world-famous singer was denied the right to sing at Constitution Hall in Washington, D.C. Why? She was an African American.

I can think of no better introduction to the pre–civil rights era than this book, and thus the book would be appropriate for a **social studies** as well as a music class. It's one story, but will get the students ready for many more individual stories, group stories, and the big picture story of the Civil Rights Movement. Have available the picture book by Pam Muñoz Ryan, *When Marian Sang* (2002), as well as a CD with the voice of Marian Anderson for your music class to listen to. The power of music to change attitudes is evident; our students can discuss musicians who are currently breaking barriers and changing society.

Keogh, P. C. (2004). *Elvis Presley: The Man, the Life, the Legend.* New York: Atria Books. (M, H)

Why would music teachers want this book in their classroom libraries? Keogh offers one reason given by one of Elvis's friends, "'. . . today, when young kids hear his music, they don't know who he is, they just like it. When Elvis sings, you just feel better'" (p. 257). There might be some rolling of the eyes and some smart remarks about Elvis sightings, but students will have fun while listening to and singing his songs, and analyzing for themselves what makes his particular music so appealing to so many, and why his legend and legacy continue, even 30 years after his death.

Rappaport, D. (2004). *John's Secret Dreams: The Life of John Lennon.* Illus. B. Collier. New York: Hyperion. (E, I, M)

Teachers may use this book to show how the arts come together. The author juxtaposes facts about John Lennon's life with relevant lyrics from his songs. Illustrator Bryan Collier uses symbolism and imagery to allude to the text while telling a fresh story visually. He states, "John Lennon's life inspired me to create my art in a painterly way I never had used before. It forced me to consider structure, anatomy, and organic movement—the wind around a figure—to illustrate thoughts and dreams" (unpaged). Students will cross disciplines as they sing Lennon's songs, create new music and lyrics stimulated by those songs, and add a visual component as modeled by this book. Direct students who want to learn more about John Lennon's life and music to the photographic biography *John Lennon: All I Want Is the Truth*, by Elizabeth Partridge (2005).

Reich, S. (1999). *Clara Schumann: Piano Virtuoso.* New York: Clarion. **(M, H)**

I've mentioned earlier that I have an interest in people who accomplish things early in life. Readers will be amazed at the young Clara, who at age 12 embarked on a European concert tour. They may be further inspired when they read of her continuing career despite becoming the mother of eight! The book includes many examples of Clara's own words from diaries and letters, so it's easy to get to know her thoughts and feelings. The photographs, from the young eight-year-old just a year before her professional debut, through her young adult, middle, and later years, provide much for students to wonder about. Music teachers may include this valuable resource when they teach music history, and offer it to students who are serious about pursuing music as a career.

Slavicek, L. C. (2006). *Carlos Santana.* New York: Chelsea House. **(M, H)**

This biography does not just concentrate on Santana's music and music career, though the chapters give many details about how he evolved as a musician. The author puts the music aspects within a larger context: we also meet the man who had serious problems to overcome, and the man who is known for his humanitarian projects such as the Milagro Foundation to enhance art, education, and health for children around the world. Music teachers will find the shaded sections especially useful, since they give added information on topics such as "A Brief History of the Blues" (p. 28) and "Carlos Santana's Advice to Young Musicians and Songwriters" (p. 23) that address curricular areas.

Sting. (2003). *Broken Music.* New York: The Dial Press. **(M, H)**

The back cover features a photograph of the musician Sting as present fans would recognize him. A smiling young preteen boy graces the front cover. This memoir tells some of the incidents and relationships that were influential as the boy became the man. Readers find out about Sting's childhood, where music was always present, but so was the unhappiness of his parents' marriage. He tells what musicians he liked to listen to. (Hint: "I first heard the Beatles in my final year at junior school" [p. 80]; "I pour [sic] over Beatles albums with the same obsessive and forensic scrutiny that I'd applied to Rogers and Hammerstein, only now I have a guitar" [p. 81]). He reflects on other learning experiences, too, realizing they could have been better. Listen to this analysis:

> . . . I never had much of an affinity for maths. Numbers were cold and cruel abstractions whose only seeming function was to torture hapless souls like me with their strange, puzzling tricks and pointless adding and subtracting, multiplying, dividing and extrapolating to fearful infinities. I feared them instinctively the way wild animals fear sprung traps. No one in my entire school career so far had ever managed to demonstrate the beauty of an equation to me, or the elegance of a theorum, nor had anyone had the foresight to point out the clear parallel between numbers and my passion for music. (p. 75)

Both **math** and music teachers could read this passage to students and ask them to react in writing or in discussion. Use it as a starting point for making some great connections and life applications in your classes. Some students will want to hear more from this person who will explain why he chose to title his story *Broken Music*.

PHYSICAL EDUCATION, HEALTH, AND WELLNESS

Armstrong, L., with Jenkins, S. (2000). *It's Not About the Bike: My Journey Back to Life.* New York: G.P. Putnam's Sons. **(H)**

Your students probably know that one of the strongest motifs in literature is that of the journey. Lance Armstrong's account of his battle with cancer and his return to bike racing after it certainly fits the category. He doesn't offer easy answers. He recognizes that many strong, determined people have not been able to beat the odds, and he can only guess at why he is still alive. "I have a tough constitution, and my profession taught me how to compete against long odds and big obstacles. I like to train hard and I like to race hard. That helped, it was a good start, but it certainly wasn't the determining factor. I can't help feeling that my survival was more a matter of blind luck" (p. 3).

MUSIC

PE/HEALTH

Readers will learn much from Armstrong as he tells how his illness was ultimately the best thing that ever happened to him. When they research what Armstrong has been doing since the publication of his book, there will be lots of material to discuss in physical education classes about the training necessary to accomplish his later feats. Health teachers may use this book as a springboard to showing students how to research topics such as the relationship between exercise and cancer survival, and the effects of attitude and emotional health on cancer recovery.

Bruchac, J. (2004). *Jim Thorpe's Bright Path.* **Illus. S. D. Nelson.** New York: Lee & Low Books. **(E, I, M)**

What would it take to be voted "Athlete of the Century" by ABC's Wide World of Sports in 2000? Whatever it was, Jim Thorpe had it. Joseph Bruchac chronicles the athlete's youth in a log cabin in the Indian Territory that later became the State of Oklahoma, then at various boarding schools, where he struggled with academic subjects but shone at athletic endeavors. He grieved the deaths of his twin brother, his mother, then his father, but kept their memory alive and lived his life according to the ideals his family and culture had provided him. He ran track, he broke records for the high jump, he played football. The Author's Note at the conclusion fills in lots of information about the sports Jim played as an adult, becoming ". . . the world's best known American Indian as well as the world's most famous athlete" (unpaged).

Holdsclaw, C., with J. Frey. (2001). *Chamique Holdsclaw: My Story.* New York: Aladdin Paperbacks. **(M, H)**

Chamique is big—an Olympic athlete, winner of the Women's National Basketball Association's Rookie of the Year Award, named a Naismith Player of the Century! But she started out small, and this memoir tells of her growing up in Queens, being raised by her grandmother—surrounded by people in her neighborhood who were using and selling drugs—and getting shot. She wasn't always admired for her values and sense of purpose and direction. How did she react to peer pressure? She tells us:

> The girls used to taunt me when I was younger. They called me a tomboy and took away my basketball. It bothered me, but I never let it deter me. I knew what I wanted to do. . . . I'd talk back to them, stand up for myself. . . . But I wouldn't change who I was just to make them like me, or even leave me alone.

Colored photographs depict Chamique at different ages, and the book includes many stories of her journey to greatness. Readers will learn about basketball skills, about dedication, about living life well.

Jamison, K. R. (1995). *An Unquiet Mind: A Memoir of Moods and Madness.* New York: Alfred A. Knopf. **(H)**

This now-classic autobiography by a professor of psychiatry who herself has manic-depressive illness will cause readers to think deeply and caringly about issues relating to mental illness. Kay tells about the highs and the lows she has experienced, and ponders questions such as whether she'd be sacrificing too much if she could magically become "normal"; whether the world would be better off or not if some of the great geniuses had been able to control their manic and/or depressed states; who (if anyone) has the right to decide whether a person with a mental disability should be forbidden to have children; what new ethical concerns will arise as genetic discoveries and screening develop.

This book was first recommended to me by a teen who told me, "This will tell you better than I can how I feel." It did, and I trust it will for the students in your health classes as well.

Kingsbury, R. (2003). *Roberto Clemente.* New York: The Rosen Publishing Group. **(I, M, H)**

Part of the *Baseball Hall of Famers* series, this book gives fans all the records and statistics they'd like to know, and, perhaps more important, offers the story of a life rich with personal struggles and successes, from a boyhood in Puerto Rico, through life in the Big Leagues, to the contributions made to better the lives of others. Readers might ponder the legacy of this first Hispanic to join the 3,000 Hit Club, this humanitarian who died in a plane crash while bringing supplies to victims of an earthquake in Nicaragua. The book is easy reading enhanced by action-filled photographs. Physical education teachers and coaches may want to use it to motivate student athletes.

Krull, K. (1996). *Wilma Unlimited: How Wilma Rudolph Became the World's Fastest Woman.* **Illus. by D. Diaz.** New York: Voyager Books. **(I, M, H)**

If a novelist turned in a draft of a story like Wilma Rudolf's life, she'd be told it wasn't believable, it was too far-fetched. First of all, she had 21 siblings! Wilma contracted polio (on top of scarlet fever) at age four, and the prognosis was that she would never walk again. How she went from paralysis to walking with a brace to winning three gold medals in track at the 1960 Olympics is the subject of this short but powerful picture book about an amazing African American athlete and humanitarian.

PE/HEALTH

Mahaney, I. F. (2005). *Tony Hawk: Skateboarding Champion.* New York: The Rosen Publishing Group. **(I)**

As extreme sports have become more popular, many of your students may have heard of Tony Hawk. From this biography in Rosen Book's *Extreme Sports Biography* series, your students will learn how Hawk helped to make skateboarding a respectable, mainstream sport. In addition to well-researched biographical information about this champion athlete, this book provides a history of the sport, presents information about skateboarding safety and competitions, and contains dynamic photos showing skateboarding action. Use this book to introduce a unit on skateboarding in your physical education class. After reading about Tony Hawk, your students may become interested in other extreme sports champions and want to read other books in the series, which includes *Danny Harf: Wakeboarding Champion* (2005), *Dave Mirra: BMX Champion* (2005), *Kevin Jones: Snowboarding Champion* (2005), *Taïg Khris: In-Line Skating Champion* (2005), all by Ian F. Mahaney.

Mochizuki, K. (2006). *Be Water, My Friend: The Early Years of Bruce Lee.* **Illus.** D. Lee. New York: Lee Et Low Books. **(E, I, M)**

Some of our students will be able to identify with the nickname young Bruce Lee, future actor, was given by his family: Mo Si Tung, which translates to "never sits still" in English (unpaged). The one thing Bruce would stay still for was reading books about heroes who fought for the oppressed. Teachers may read aloud the story of how Bruce trained with a martial arts master, practicing moves and stances for up to six hours a day. This may motivate students to practice the skills of the physical education curriculum or of a sport they're pursuing. They'll also be inspired by the mental discipline Bruce learned that helped him to use his opponents' energy against them while expending less energy himself. Teachers of all subjects may use Bruce Lee's own words as they discuss character development and values, words such as "'In every passionate pursuit, the pursuit counts more than the object pursued'" (unpaged).

Petit, P. (2002). *To Reach the Clouds: My High Wire Walk Between the Twin Towers.* New York: North Point Press. **(M, H)**

Being afraid of heights, I found this book almost too scary to read. How could anyone walk on a cable tied between buildings a quarter of a mile above the ground? It's not that Philippe didn't have practice; his first illegal performance occurred in 1971, between the top towers of Notre Dame Cathedral; next he conquered the world's largest steel bridge in Sydney, Australia. Philippe ponders, "Without these first clandestine walks, would I have reached inside the red box for a more formidable opponent?" (p. 9).

I'd probably first introduce students to Mordicai Gerstein's Caldecott winner, *The Man Who Walked Between the Towers* (2003). Then they'd be ready for this more extensive autobiography. The first part of the book tells of Philippe's early life, and includes photographs of him climbing things as a very young child. The middle tells of his preparation for his 1976 walk across the Twin Towers, and the end tells of his present-day life. He explains how he wrote the book and describes his personal philosophy, talking directly to his reader. "The child of the trees I was, the skyscraper I became, still wants to *conquer* the world—*explore*, I should say—convinced that the world inside you, inside me, inside those around us is equally rich in marvels and mysteries" (p. 237). What does the future hold? Petit recommends rebuilding the twin towers, higher, and with a twist. And:

> When the towers again twin-tickle the clouds, I offer to walk again, to be the expression of the builders' collective voice. Together, we will rejoice in an aerial song of victory. I will carry my life across the wire, as your life, as all our lives, past, present, and future—the lives lost, the lives welcomed since, (p. 241)

Physical education teachers could read aloud from this book as they teach concepts and techniques relating to gymnastics and balance.

Robinson, S. (2004). *Promises to Keep: How Jackie Robinson Changed America.* New York: Scholastic Press. **(I, M, H)**

Written by the baseball hero's only daughter, Sharon, this photobiography tells of Jackie Robinson's feats not only in athletics, but also in politics, civil rights, business, and home life. He endured much as the first player to break baseball's color barrier, but left a lasting legacy. The author personalizes the story by telling family anecdotes and including letters he wrote home while he traveled during the season, and photos of father and babies. She remembers him as a man who kept his promises, and concludes that, after his 1972 death, ". . . Dad would have expected us to stay in the game of life and to meet each challenge with strength and compassion. That's been my promise to him" (p. 59).

Rodriguez, L. J. (1993). *Always Running: La Vida Loca: Gang Days in L.A.* Willimantic, CT: Curbstone Press. **(H)**

I heard the author speak at the NCTE Conference in San Francisco in 2003, where many teachers in the audience stood up and thanked Rodriguez for

PE/HEALTH

writing this memoir of his life as a gang member. He wrote *Always Running* when his own 15-year-old son joined a gang in Chicago, but the book has spoken to youths in many cities who needed to hear his story and to learn that he proved it is possible to get out of a gang. There are interesting sections about Louis's interactions with high school teachers and administrators. Health teachers may assign or read parts of this gripping memoir to stimulate discussions about peer pressure, the causes and effects of violence, lifestyle choices, and the phenomenon of gangs.

Street, P., with White, D. (2002). *Picabo: Nothing to Hide.* New York: Contemporary Books. (H)

In a sense, this memoir became dated soon after it was written, for, after telling her story of growing up, overcoming obstacles, and achievements, Picabo Street looks forward to the 2002 Olympics. Students may research to see if her dreams came true, and what life has brought since the Olympics to this intense, spirited woman. Physical education teachers and coaches may offer this book as they talk about the value of sports and exercise in living a health-conscious life.

Tallchief, M., with Wells, R. (1999). *Tallchief: America's Prima Ballerina.* Illus. G Kelley. New York: Viking. (I, M)

I learned from reading this book about early obstacles Maria Tallchief faced. On the Osage Indian Reservation in Oklahoma, her language and culture were against the law, for, "In those days it was illegal for Indians to live in any way but the white man's way" (p. 9). Fortunately, her grandmother took her to hidden ceremonies to watch forbidden dances. Maria recognized the gift she had been given, and later set off to make her contributions as a dancer. Our students will be inspired by her words:

All I had to offer was my ability to speak the language of music. I knew how it was sung by a voice or played by a flute or piano, and how it was spoken by the body itself. That language I knew in the way I knew how to breathe the air. (p. 26)

Your students may find the language of music in their own body movements after reading this book.

SCIENCE

Brown, D. (2004). *Odd Boy Out: Young Albert Einstein.* Boston: Houghton Mifflin. (E, I)

Readers of this picture book might be surprised to discover that the man whose name has become synonymous with genius was not always recognized for his brilliance. He learned to speak late, did not fit in with his peers at school, struggled with Latin and Greek. And:

When questioned in class, Albert lingers over his responses, frustrating his teachers, who prefer quick, snappy answers. And afterward the teachers see his lips move as he quietly repeats the answer to himself.

Is Albert dull-witted? the teachers wonder. (unpaged)

The author gives examples of the child's talent with **math** and **music,** but also explains that he was bored by methods of teaching that he considered mechanical or mindless. As teachers, we want to keep in mind Einstein's comment, "'I believe that love [of a subject] is a better teacher than a sense of duty—at least for me'" (unpaged). Together with our students, let's explore and discuss how Einstein's love of his subject resulted in his success as a scientist.

Burleigh, R. (2003). *Into the Woods: John James Audubon Lives His Dream.* Illus. W. Minor. New York: Atheneum. (I, M, H)

I'd want this book for my science classroom—or, for that matter, for my **art, social studies,** or **English** classroom. This account is a combination of a brief biography told in verse and excerpts from Audubon's journals. The biographical poem is narrated by Audubon and addressed to his father, who had wanted him to go into business. His passion for drawing and his love of nature are evident, and Wendell Minor's paintings make me want to climb the trees and crawl on the rocks with Audubon in order to see those baby birds and magnificent herons. I might ask students to keep a nature journal as Audubon did, recording their observations and feelings about what nature shows them.

Byman, J. (2001). *Carl Sagan: In Contact with the Cosmos.* Greensboro, NC: Morgan Reynolds. (M, H)

Young, gifted Carl Sagan was encouraged by his parents, who allowed him to skip several grades, and who brought him to libraries and planetariums. But they didn't think one could actually make money as a scientist; that notion was unfamiliar to them. This biography of the man who "... became the world's best known scientist" (back cover) details his career and contributions. The author states:

Carl's memories of his schooling are food for thought for teachers and students today: But none of his teachers ever put these facts and phenomena into context. Long division was nothing more than a set of rules; the teachers never explained how the right answer was produced.

Carl never found his excitement about science reflected in the classroom. Evolution was not even mentioned. "School was little more than a detention camp," Carl said later. (p. 14)

Do today's science classrooms offer a more nurturing and stimulating environment for our future Carl Sagans? Use this book to inspire your students to discover how Sagan was able to develop and nurture his passion for science outside of school.

Doherty, K. (2002). *Marjory Stoneman Douglas: Guardian of the 'Glades.* Brookfield, CT: Twentieth-First Century Books. (M)

There's so much wrong with our environment; humans have been very unkind to the planet. Can anything we do really make a difference now? Students find out when they read this book what one person is able to accomplish. In the 1920s, Marjory Stoneman Douglas, a journalist, joined a committee that had been established to save a part of the Everglades from development. In 1942, she began serious research, finding that politicians were doing a terrible job of managing the natural resources in the area, and becoming convinced that if the Everglades were drained, as some were proposing, South Florida would turn into a semitropical desert. Five years later, her book, *The Everglades: River of Grass* (1947), opened with the now famous sentence, "'There are no other Everglades in the world'" (p. 102 Doherty). For the rest of her long life, she worked as a speaker and activist to educate people on the importance of protecting the environment. Students using Douglas as a role model might pick an area in their little corner of the world to research and to protect.

Ehrlich, A. (2003). *Rachel: The Story of Rachel Carson.* Illus. W. Minor. New York: Silver Whistle/Harcourt. (E, I, M, H)

Imagine having a Rachel Carson in your science class! She had always had an affinity with nature, but had planned to be a writer until one day in a required college science class, her teacher, Miss Skinker, helped her focus her slide, and "A transparent, elongated paramecium drifted slowly across the microscope's field. . . . In that simple one-celled organism she saw the complexity of the universe" (unpaged). Rachel changed her major to biology, and in 1962 published *Silent Spring*, sounding a warning about the fate of nature in the face of threats from toxins in pesticides—the environmental movement began. This book is a great introduction to her now classic work, and is also an inspirational reminder that one life, even one cut short as Rachel's was by cancer, may have a tremendous impact on the planet. Science teachers may offer this biography, along with Carson's writing and later articles about it, as they teach a unit on the environment. Have your students write their own essays on local or global environmental issues.

Fox, R. (2001). *Shark Man.* Sydney, Australia: Scholastic. (I, M, H)

You know I believe we should be introducing our students to passionate practitioners through literature. Rodney Fox might win my PPP (passionate practitioner prize). He loved skindiving so much that he continued even after surviving a shark attack at age 23. Plenty of gory pictures and descriptions of his operations are included for the stouthearted. He couldn't give up exploring the sea, which he considered not a hobby, but rather a way of life. He became a defender of sharks, despite further close encounters as he filmed them and tried out various defense mechanisms such as a shark-resistant chain mail suit. "As my understanding of sharks and their behaviour grew I began to believe that neither fear nor fun was a good reason to kill sharks. It seemed to me that they had as much right to live as I did. . . . I was asked more frequently to participate in documentaries and scientific studies. Each expedition taught me more . . ." (p. 28). Each chapter in this excitement-filled book will teach readers much about how humans and animals can co-exist to the benefit of all. You may want to use this book to introduce a unit on sharks.

Fradin, D. B. (2003). *Nicolaus Copernicus: The Earth Is a Planet.* Illus. C. von Buhler. New York: Mondo. (E, I, M, H)

"High up in a cathedral tower, a man in a long robe gazes at the night sky" (p. 5). The stargazers in your class may join Copernicus in this sixteenth-century scene or follow his childhood as he first notices that "To a person moving fast, someone moving more slowly can appear to be going backward" (p. 8). Perhaps they'll want to accompany him in his university classes as he is taught wrongly that the earth is the center of the universe and doesn't move. They'll question with him as he wonders about the backward loops he observes Mars making, recalls his childhood observation about fast moving and slow moving objects, and asks, "Wouldn't the same thing be true of planets?" (p. 19). Readers will stand at the astronomer's deathbed in that same cathedral tower and ponder the consequences of Copernicus's writings in the work of great scientists like Galileo Galilei and Isaac Newton as well as twentieth-century astronauts. Maybe they'll foresee a future for themselves in this history of people who have "'stood upon the shoulders of giants'"(p. 29) such as Nicolaus Copernicus.

SCIENCE

Goodall, J., with Berman, P. (1999). *Reason for Hope: A Spiritual Journey.* New York: Warner Books. (H)

Jane Goodall is known as a champion for the chimpanzee. She has studied the primates extensively, and she has shared her knowledge and brought their cause before the world. After reading this memoir, your students will learn much biology, and much about the environmental threats to wildlife. In addition, they will learn what people can do to actively work for the good of the earth and all that dwell thereon. They'll also come to know a passionate practitioner who has endured many trials as well as triumphs during her long career, who has interesting writing processes, who reflected on how the many aspects of her life experiences relate to the whole of her being and to her beliefs. This is a good book to offer those students who might think that science and religion are mutually exclusive. Goodall has also written books aimed at a younger audience.

Hamilton, J. (2002). *Lise Meitner: Pioneer of Nuclear Fission.* Berkeley Heights, NJ: Enslow Publishers. (I, M, H)

In 1992, element 109 was named Meitnerium in honor of Lise Meitner, showing respect by the scientific community for her accomplishments. Readers of this biography will admire Meitner for many reasons. Despite graduating summa cum laude with a Ph.D. in physics, and having research published in scientific journals, she faced obstacles in her work life due to her gender, but overcame them. Other huge barriers to a peaceful, productive life arose—World War I, and then persecution of Jews in Nazi Germany, for example. Her life story is inspiring; it may teach our students much about physics and about courageous, determined living.

Hickam, H. H., Jr. (1998). *October Sky.* New York: Dell Publishing. (H)

Originally published as *Rocket Boys, October Sky*—a memoir—tells how a teenager and his friends made miracles happen through their passionate learning, experimenting, building, convincing, and launching. Listen to Homer explain a bit of his process in a chapter titled "We Do the Math":

> The book [on rocket design] called for us to make decisions we'd never made before: How high and fast was our rocket to go, and how heavy was our payload going to be? We understood that the questions were related. The first thing Quentin and I did was scratch any payload from consideration. We were committed to the glory of pure altitude. "Let's go for two miles," Quentin said.
>
> "Why not thirty?" I demanded.

> . . . I . . . pulled out a pad of notebook paper. The same equation we'd used to calculate altitude based on time was the one we needed first, good old S 5 1/2^2.
>
> I did the calculations, assuming our rocket reached maximum velocity immediately upon launch and rounding off the altitude to ten thousand feet. The result equaled a velocity of eight hundred feet per second, or 545.45 miles per hour. When I recalculated, I came up with the same result. (p. 339)

Your students will learn from Homer, a boy their age from a West Virginia coal mining town where football was big but college was not, who became a NASA engineer, fulfilling a dream. This book will provide an opportunity to discuss this equation as well as other equations and their practical applications.

Hoffman, R. (1997). *The Same and Not the Same.* New York: Columbia University Press. (H)

This Character Booktalk was presented by pre-service teacher Jennifer Bogert, wearing a white lab coat

> **character booktalk**
>
> Hello, class! My name is Roald Hoffman and I am here to tell you about the wonderful world of chemistry. Now, because I just won the Nobel Prize in Chemistry, I can do anything I want. [Turn off light.] Today, I'm going to take you into a pitch black room full of mannequin hands. You have five seconds to separate the left hands from the right hands or else something terrible will happen. Are you ready? GO! 5-4-3-2-1! Did you do it in time? I know I did. It was easy for me because I just took each hand in my right hand as if I were going to shake a person's hand. If it felt right, I tossed it to the pile on the right because I knew it was a right hand. If it felt wrong, I tossed it to the left into the left hand pile. Now, in chemistry we have these things called enantiomers, which are just like your right and left hands. [Put my hands in the air.] Just like your hands, enantiomers are made up of the same elements, yet they are mirror images of each other.
>
> Another example of these enantiomers can be found by taking a look at the carvone compound. Now, the carvone compound's "right hand" enantiomer would be what we call the caraway seed. We use it while cooking to spice up our breads and our meats. Its "left hand" enantiomer is spearmint. This is used to flavor many brands of gum. I see you [pointing to a girl chewing gum] over there chewing some gum. Maybe there's the carvone enantiomer in your mouth right now!
>
> These enantiomers are found throughout the entire universe. Actually, many things in our world are the same and not the same, and I will point them out to you and help you gain a better understanding of

SCIENCE

the similarities and differences in these molecules when you read my book *The Same and Not the Same.* Thank you!

Following a booktalk such as this one and reading the book, teachers and students may engage in a lively discussion of the similarities and differences between molecules.

Jemison, M. (2001). *Find Where the Wind Goes: Moments from My Life.* New York: Scholastic. **(M, H)**

Dr. Mae Jemison calls this a collection of moments from her growing up rather than an autobiography. The chapter titles all have to do with moving air, such as "Caught in the Eye of a Hurricane," "Wafts of Formaldehyde: *Medical School*," "Harnessing Explosive Winds." Her accomplishments are astounding: she's been an astronaut, an international traveler and speaker, a professor, the head of a technology consulting firm, director of an international science camp, an actress in *Star Trek: The Next Generation,* an M.D., and an author, as is evident from this highly readable memoir. Listen in as she reflects on how it felt to be in space:

> . . . I realized I would feel comfortable anywhere in the universe—because I belonged to and was part of it, as much as any star, planet, asteroid, comet, or nebula. Didn't my body and my mind contain the same atoms and energy as do the stars? (p. 193)

Science teachers may have this book on a classroom library shelf labeled "Passionate Practitioners." Readers will be inspired to pursue their multiple dreams.

Lasky, K. (2006). *John Muir: America's First Environmentalist.* Illus. S. Fellows. Cambridge, MA: Candlewick Press. **(I, M, H)**

How many of your students would predict that by the time they are 40, they will have walked tens of thousands of miles? John Muir could claim this. He walked in order to study nature, and he even walked from the United States to Canada when the Civil War broke out because he could not bear the thought of killing another human being. Much of this book focuses on John's growing-up years, which our young readers will appreciate. Once they get to know him as a curious youngster, always inventing things and eager to make discoveries outdoors, it will be easy for them to follow the adult Muir as he walks over mountains and on glaciers, and as he writes and becomes politically active in order to promote conservation of wilderness areas.

It's evident today that all of us, old and young alike, must learn how to protect our planet and conserve resources. Reading about John Muir's legacy will be an inspiration as this learning and action take place. Students might like to compare this book with another picture book by Thomas Locker: *John Muir, America's Naturalist* (2003, Golden, CO: Fulcrum Publishing). And they might decide to take up walking, with Muir as their mentor, for the good of their **health** and that of our environment.

Lewen, T. (2003). *Tooth and Claw: Animal Adventures in the Wild.* New York: HarperCollins. **(I, M, H)**

Ted Lewen's passion for interacting with animals began at an early age; he shared his childhood home not only with parents and siblings but also with an iguana, a chimpanzee, and a lion. The author recounts his travels and adventures as a nature photographer. Some of his haunts include the Galapagos Islands, where he photographed sea lions, Alaska (grizzlies), India (Bengal tigers and elephants), the arctic (polar bears), Canada (bison), Africa (rattlesnakes), the Great Barrier Reef (sharks). He tells of close encounters with dangerous animals. Photographs and sketches with the author's jotted notes are interspersed throughout the text, and extra Author's Notes at the chapters' ends give further details. Even the Glossary is fun to read. Students will feel they are researchers and companions as they travel through these chapters. You may want to assign this book to stimulate student interest before a unit on an ecosystem or species.

Macdonald, F. (2001). *Edwin Hubble.* Chicago: Heinemann Library. **(M, H)**

Part of the *Groundbreakers* series, this is visually appealing and a fast read, while loaded with information about the scientist who first produced evidence that the universe is expanding. Hubble's interest in astronomy began at age eight when he joined his grandfather in stargazing. The biography details his work with nebulae, his discovery of the mathematical concept that bears his name (the Hubble constant) as well as Hubble's Law, which proved that the more distant a galaxy is, the faster it is traveling away from the earth. The astronomy work is contexted by two world wars, Hubble's family life, travels, illness, political action to ban nuclear weapons and work for peace, and relationships with other scientists. As your students read this book, you may show recent pictures of distant space sent back to earth by the Hubble Space Telescope.

MacLeod, E. (2003). *Albert Einstein: A Life of Genius.* Toronto, ON: Kids Can Press. **(I, M, H)**

The chapters are but two pages long, yet filled with engaging text and super pictures. Your students will

SCIENCE

love seeing the old smiling Albert riding his bicycle, or sticking out his tongue at the camera on his 72nd birthday. They'll see the young Albert and the middle-aged Albert, too, always busy, always thinking. They may be encouraged by the highlighted quotes from him, such as "It's not that I'm so smart, it's just that I stay with problems longer" (p. 5), and "Anyone who has never made a mistake has never tried anything new" (p. 11). They'll meet the activist Albert, who campaigned for the end of atomic weapons and spoke out about the rights of minorities. This book is a great introduction to *Time* magazine's "Person of the Century." After reading this book, ask your students to research further and discuss his stance on atomic weapons.

Montgomery, S. (2004). *The Tarantula Scientist.* Photographs by N. Bishop. Boston: Houghton Mifflin. **(I, M, H)**

How does an arachnologist greet visitors to his indoor workspace? "'It's the only comparative tarantula lab in the world that's global in reach,' Sam says by way of a welcome" (p. 56). Your students will be given a tour through the lab and also into the natural habitats of the great hairy spiders. Part of the *Scientists in the Field* series, this book provides a sort of a crash course through text and stunning photographs as readers accompany Sam Marshall in his lab. Your students will learn lots of biology and get a feel for the career and passion of a person who has devoted his life to this area of study. The end sections supply some statistics on spiders, and a glossary explains the technical language arachnologists use ("Spider Speak," p. 77). The author provides details of how this book was researched and includes a selected bibliography. In addition, there are Internet addresses for readers who loved this literary field trip enough to want to visit the American Tarantula Society site, for instance, or want to follow Sam Marshall's students' current research.

Ramen, F. (2006). *Albucasis (Abu Al-Qasim Al-Zahrawi): Renowned Muslim Surgeon of the Tenth Century.* New York: The Rosen Publishing Group. **(M, H)**

Readers can't help but be impressed by the accomplishments of the subject of this book. These achievements include writing a comprehensive encyclopedia of medicine, training midwives so that their enhanced skills would ensure more safe deliveries, describing a method for repairing a dislocated shoulder (which the Western world didn't discover until the late nineteenth century), developing techniques to reimplant teeth, practicing reconstructive plastic surgery, perfecting surgical techniques for operating on bowels and on the urinary system,

treating breast cancer, and designing a host of surgical instruments, some of which are still used today in some form. He was a genius, and he was ethical and respectful of his patients.

Ramen notes, ". . . had [Albucasis] been a Christian of the fifteenth century instead of a Muslim of the tenth, he would be remembered today as a true Renaissance man" (p. 74). It's important that we help our students understand the history of science from a multicultural perspective, and this book will certainly help that goal. It is also appropriate for a **health** class. A lot of historical background is provided, and there are helpful and intriguing photographs as well.

Ross, M. E. (1997). *Bird Watching with Margaret Morse Nice.* Minneapolis, MN: Carolrhoda Books. **(I, M)**

Quick, who's the founder of ethology? I'll give you a hint; it's someone who had birdmania, according to the author of this book. Here's more information from the last page:

> In spite of prejudices against women becoming scientists, Margaret followed her desire to share her love of nature with the world. By the time she stopped writing in her eighties, she had published seven books, 250 journal and newspaper articles, and 3,133 reviews of other scientists' work . . . her autobiography, . . . *Research Is a Passion with Me* was published after her death, in 1979. (p. 44)

Pretty impressive resume for Margaret Morse Nice, wouldn't you say? Ethology is the study of animal behavior, and when Margaret was too busy raising daughters to study her beloved birds, she studied her daughters' speech and vocabulary, and then published papers on language development!

This book goes beyond the genre of biography. There are instructions in every chapter for readers who want to follow in the footsteps of this scientist and activist, from choosing and using a field guide, to hunting for nests and mapping territories.

Russell, C. A. (2000). *Michael Faraday: Physics and Faith.* New York: Oxford University Press. **(H)**

This reader-friendly text tells of Faraday's life in the context of his times. His values were formed early by his family, and his faith ". . . was to have profound effects in every area of his life" (p. 21). A huge influence was his bookbinding job as a teenager. The manipulative skills he developed binding the books helped later as he did scientific experiments. Also, his being surrounded by books made him long for knowledge, and supplied the means to acquire it. One book he read, *The Improvement of the Mind*, by

SCIENCE

Isaac Watts, recommended "...assiduous reading, attendance at lectures, correspondence with others of similar mind, formation of discussion groups, and the keeping of a 'commonplace book' in which to record facts and opinions which might otherwise be forgotten" (p. 27). Thus began Faraday's first commonplace book, "The Philosophical Miscellany." He was off and running in his very successful journey toward self-improvement. The world reaped rewards over the next several decades. This biography may introduce our intellectually curious youth to a tremendous role model.

Sacks, O. (2001). *Uncle Tungsten: Memories of a Chemical Boyhood.* New York: Alfred A. Knopf. **(H)**

I went to a lecture by Oliver Sacks once; unlike other famous lecturers I have been to hear, he wore a T-shirt with the Periodic Table of the Elements! How appropriate for the writer of this memoir, telling of a tiny child who pondered endlessly the mysteries of metals:

> Why were they shiny? Why smooth? Why cool? Why hard? Why did they bend, not break? Why did they ring? Why could two soft metals like zinc and copper, or tin and copper, combine to produce a harder metal? What gave gold its goldness, and why did it never tarnish? (p. 7)

All this before he was six years old, when, in 1939, his parents felt they had no choice but to send him to a boarding school away from London to protect him from the bombs of World War II. He chronicles the next several years, which were devastating for him; he explains how he took refuge in numbers, especially his love for primes. He returned to London at age ten, "...withdrawn and disturbed in some ways, but with a passion for metals, for plants, and for numbers" (p. 32). The rest of the book tells of how he explored his passions. After reading it, many students will no doubt want to explore Sacks's other works, detailing the continuing scientific passions of his adult life.

Senker, C. (2003). *Rosalind Franklin.* New York: Raintree Steck-Vaughn Company. **(I, M, H)**

She got the shaft! This view comes across clearly in Senker's telling of the crucial role of Franklin's work in the discovery of the structure of DNA. Many people can name Watson and Crick as the scientists responsible for our initial knowledge of the double helix shape of the DNA molecule. Not as many know that Watson attended a lecture by Franklin in 1951 where she hypothesized about the helix shape; not as many know that Franklin's colleague secretly gave her lab work to Watson and Crick shortly before they made their discovery. Senker purports, "Crick and Watson simply could not have built a correct DNA model without her data" (p. 42). Yet the pair did not credit her in their historic 1953 publication of their discovery. As teachers, you may use this book to help students understand the way scientists work—and sometimes compete with each other. Read to your students excerpts showing how difficult life was for scientists who were women, and others that demonstrate how "Whether a person makes history or not depends on who writes it" (p. 40).

Sis, P. (2003). *The Tree of Life: A Book Depicting the Life of Charles Darwin: Naturalist, Geologist & Thinker.* New York: Frances Foster Books. **(I, M, H)**

This sophisticated picture book has an unusual style and structure; there is a variety of fonts, and the text is often circular rather than linear. Readers learn about Darwin's public life through the text in bold print; his private life in a standard font, and his secret life in tiny font. He knew his theories would cause an uproar, so held off publishing them for some time. This book may be used as students study about natural selection, as well as about the importance of observation and recording data in science. They might be interested to know that "Darwin did not say that God had not created life on earth. What he said was that creation did not happen all at once" (unpaged). A teacher's modeling the think-aloud strategy using this book can be found in Part 2 of this chapter.

Swinburne, S. R. (2002). *The Wood Scientist.* Photos by S. C. Morse. New York: Houghton Mifflin. **(I, M)**

Part of the *Scientists in the Field* series, this book invites readers to join "forester, habitat ecologist, professional tracker, and passionate student of the woods" (p. 6) Sue Morse as she reads her environment. Lessons (such as carnivores dispersing plants by carrying in their colons the seeds eaten by the prey animals they ate, and then passing them on somewhere else, prepared for germination by their stomach acids) are interspersed throughout the naturalist's story. The text is also full of literary allusions; Sue has a bear skull named Yorick, for example, and one chapter is titled, "Don't Build and They Will Come." The photographs invite readers into Sue's world, and she offers challenging projects at the end for eager budding scientists and environmentalists.

Zannos, S. (2004). *Linus Pauling and the Chemical Bond.* Bear, DE: Mitchell Lane Publishers. **(I, M)**

Part of the *Unlocking the Secrets of Science* series, this small volume introduces a figure who is large

SCIENCE

in terms of his contributions to chemistry. In addition to his research, discoveries, and writing, he was known for his extraordinary teaching skills. His college teaching career began while still an undergraduate:

> He had little patience with teachers who were boring or were not well prepared for their classes. He felt that he had to prove to his own students that having someone their own age as an instructor did not shortchange them. Linus was well prepared to teach. Not only did he know a lot about chemistry, he had also studied public speaking. Linus was actually a better teacher than many of the professors. Word spread and students were enrolling early to get into his classes.

This book would serve as a good segue into the writings of Pauling himself, where students could put themselves in the hands of the master.

SOCIAL STUDIES/HISTORY

Al-Windawi, T. (2004). *Thura's Diary: My Life in Wartime Iraq.* **Trans. by Robin Bray.** New York: Viking. **(M, H)**

Your students will see from the colored photographs and Thura's words how similar this 19-year-old is to them, despite having to write practically daily of new fears and sorrows in Baghdad during 2003. Her writing is at times poetic. On March 23, just days after the United States attacked, she wrote about freak sandstorms occurring: "It's as though Mother Nature's showing us how angry and hurt she is about the war" (pp. 25–26). The details, such as the difficulty the family had securing insulin and needles for Thura's diabetic sister, hit home. And when Thura returned to her college, which had been interrupted by bombings, there was discussion about what they should change the college's name to. It had been called the Leader's College of Pharmacology, but "Leader" had referred to Saddam Hussein. Here's how Thura describes herself in her final entry:

> . . . a girl who has lived through war and fear and cruel sanctions on her country; a girl whose parents are always worried; a girl whose little sisters are terrified by the bombs and the looters, and come to her for comfort; a girl with American soldiers all around her neighborhood, every bit as scared as she is; a girl born in the wrong place at the wrong time—but a girl who still has hope. (120)

Thura concludes, "I believe that there is a book in every person's life . . ." (p. 126). Your students will

be glad Thura shared hers, and might feel inspired to entrust their experiences and thoughts to their own diaries as a result of getting to know Thura.

Ashby, R. (2004). *The Amazing Dr. Franklin: The Boy Who Read Everything.* Atlanta, GA: Peachtree. **(I, M)**

The organizational theme to all the chapters of this biography is reading. Franklin loved books as a boy, and his reading, book collecting, meeting with other readers, starting a library, and writing of his almanac are some of the many evidences of that love. Our students might love the details of the story. For example, in his *Poor Richard's Almanac*, the advice is given:

> If you would not be forgotten,
> As soon as you are dead and rotten,
> Either write things worth reading,
> Or do things worth the writing. (p. 66)

Readers may also visualize Franklin being carried in a sedan at age 81 to the State House by four inmates of the local jail. He was frail, but he was needed at the Constitutional Convention. He made the action come alive in 1787; he will do so again today, as your students learn the important curricular topics relating to the early days of our country.

Blumberg, R. (2004). *York's Adventures with Lewis and Clark: An African-American's Part in the Great Expedition.* New York: HarperCollins. **(I, M, H)**

You could use James J. Holberg's Introduction as an example of how history gets written. This introduction explains that, in 1988, some letters William Clark wrote to his brother were found in an attic, and Holberg edited and published the letters. Holberg tells of other documents that have helped historians piece together the story of York, Clark's slave, yet laments the gaps that still exist. Students will also be interested in discovering how the past connects with the present: York's story goes on, as evidenced by President Clinton making York an honorary sergeant in the U.S. Army in 2001.

This biography shows students how much one person can affect history, for Blumberg makes clear that:

> . . . without his presence the Corps of Discovery might have failed. York acted as a peaceful passport to the Indians . . . he became "Big Medicine" when Indians assumed his color indicated spiritual powers. His importance mounted when tribes praised him as "Black Indian" and "Brave Warrior," for to them his blackness marked him as a great person. (p. 80)

They were right. York was a great person. And this is a great book about him. I'd offer Pringle's *American Slave, American Hero: York of the Lewis & Clark Expedition* (2006) as a companion book. Students may compare and contrast the information and the visuals of the two picture book biographies.

Bolden, T. (2005). *Maritcha: A Nineteenth Century American Girl.* New York: Harry N. Abrams. (I, M, H)

There are two stories here. There's the retold memoir of Maritcha Rémond Lyons, an African American girl whose family fled from their Manhattan home during the 1863 Draft Riots, settling in Providence, Rhode Island. Later, Maritcha became the first black person to graduate from the previously segregated Providence High School, and she was an educator for the next half-century.

A second story evolves as Tanya Bolden also shares the story of her research, of being shown Maritcha's unpublished autobiography by the curator of the Manuscripts, Archives, and Rare Books division of the Schomburg Center for Research in Black culture. The author and her subject grew up in the same area of New York City, and:

> Maritcha, born over a century before me, allowed me insights into my city's history, and imaginings of what my life might have been like had I been a child when she was. Maritcha remained, to borrow from Toni Morrison, "a friend of mine" over the years. (p. 41)

Your students will meet this inimitable child and gain a new friend by entering this book. They'll gain insight into the centuries-long struggle for equality for African Americans.

Brown, D. (2000). *Uncommon Traveler: Mary Kingsley in Africa.* Boston: Houghton Mifflin. (E, I, M)

I am a timid traveler who loves to be led by someone who will not require any decisions of me. Mary Kingsley was the opposite: independent and bold. After 30 years of staying home, teaching herself, and caring for her ill mother, she set out for Africa, where she thrived as she explored and got to know the people. She became a popular writer and lecturer, and I can see why. Here's her description of what happened one night when she was out paddling her canoe alone: "'I felt the earth quiver under my feet, and heard a soft big soughing sound, and looking around saw I had dropped in on a hippo banquet . . . I made out five of the immense brutes round me, so I softly returned to the canoe and shoved off'" (unpaged).

Kingsley's writings added to her contemporaries' knowledge of West Africa in the late nineteenth century. She will be your students' guide as they embark on a literary field trip (see Part 2 in Chapter 3) through this picture book during your unit on Africa.

Brown, L., & Hort, L. (2006). *Nelson Mandela: A Photographic Story of a Life.* New York: DK Publishing. (M, H)

When and how did Nelson Mandela become involved in his country's struggle for freedom? He offers this answer. "'I cannot pinpoint a moment when I became politicized . . . but a steady accumulation of a thousand slights, a thousand indignities, a thousand unremembered moments, produced in me an anger, a rebelliousness, a desire to fight the system that imprisoned my people'" (pp. 21–22). The photographs of Mandela in prison, and of supporters around the world carrying signs demanding his release, may be a powerful aid as we teach the principles of political protest and working for social justice.

Bruchac, J. (1994). *A Boy Called Slow.* Illus. R. Baviera. New York: Philomel Books. (I, M)

It remains for other biographies to tell of the adult adventures and deeds of Lakota warrior Sitting Bull. This is a story of the child who wanted to exchange his given name for a more honorable one, such as his father's, "Returns Again to Strike the Enemy." He proved his worthiness during his fourteenth winter. "How?", your students might ask. Hand them this beautifully illustrated book as your answer and provide them with additional information about the Lakota culture during the mid-nineteenth century.

Carter, J. (2001). *An Hour Before Daylight: Memories of a Rural Boyhood.* New York: Simon & Schuster. (M, H)

From the reader response journal of Kathleen Coffta:

> Imagine growing up on a farm in rural Georgia during the Depression: No running water, no television, no in-house phone service, out of bed by 4:30 A.M. to start your day in the cotton fields, at the smokehouse, or in the barn. Imagine not being able to be seen with your best friend at a baseball game in town or to ride with him in the same car on the train because of his color. . . . These are just a few of the experiences I was treated to when I read *An Hour Before Daylight: Memories of a Rural Boyhood,* by former U. S. President Jimmy Carter. . . . The book, loaded with charming anecdotes from Carter's childhood, is also an excellent historical look at the South during the early to mid-1900s. . . .
>
> Reading this book brought back long-forgotten memories for me, but it also caused me to look at the man Carter eventually became and realize that his

SS/HIS

childhood greatly influenced his actions later in life. His father was an honest, hardworking man who believed, above all, in fairness. His mother was truly remarkable in her ability to be "color-blind" at a time when so much emphasis was placed on race. Most important, both of Carter's parents believed in giving back to society and to the world around you in small and large ways. Knowing this, it is easy for me to understand why Jimmy Carter [won] a Nobel Peace Prize, why he works tirelessly for so many organizations and causes, and why he is admired by so many people throughout the world.

Use Carter's memoir as a primary source when your students study our 39th president.

Cox, C. (2000). *Black Stars: African American Teachers.* New York: John Wiley & Sons. **(M, H)**

What a great book to have as part of a library representing possible careers for our students to explore. Some of the 25 chapters will be about people who have made it into our students' textbooks: Benjamin Banneker, Booker T. Washington, W. E. B. DuBois, Mary McLeod Bethune, Mae Jemison among them. But equally fascinating stories are told about less well-known heroes. Susie King Taylor, for example, was a slave girl who attended a secret school, under threat of whippings if caught, in order to learn to read and write. (This chapter would go well with Gary Paulsen's novel *Nightjohn* (1993), since its narrator undertook similar risks for the same purpose.) Susie started a school at age 14; she also spent the years of the Civil War teaching black Union soldiers (former slaves) to read and write. Stories of African American teachers from the 1700s through the 1900s offer inspiration and direction for readers.

Demi. (2003). *Muhammad.* New York: Simon & Schuster. **(I, M, H)**

Readers are immediately drawn to the art in this biography in picture book format. Demi uses a lot of gold, and, holding true to Islamic tradition, she does not depict Muhammad and his family; rather, they are shown as gold figures or outlines. The text holds a wealth of information about the origin and spread of the religion practiced today by almost a quarter of the world's population. Along with the historical information about Muhammad's life are quotes from the Koran; Muhammad's tenets known as the Five Pillars of Islam; an explanation of the Arabic words that translate as "There is no god but God"; a map of Muhammad's world; and a bibliography. Teachers might ask students to reflect in writing on present-day applications of Muhammad's words: "'When a person dies, his deeds come to an end, except in respect of three matters which he

leaves behind: a continuing charity, knowledge from which benefit can be derived, and righteous children who will pray for him'" (unpaged).

Demi. (1998). *The Dalai Lama: A Biography of the Tibetan Spiritual and Political Leader.* New York: Henry Holt and Company. **(E, I, M, H)**

My knowledge was broadened by this short, beautifully illustrated story of the 14th Dalai Lama, who grew up learning and exhibiting the virtues espoused by Buddhism, and continued to do so in exile when Tibet came under the rule of China. Social studies teachers may make good use of this resource, perhaps reading it aloud during a lesson on world religions and philosophies. The Foreword is written by His Holiness the Dalai Lama, and the last page gives a quote from his 1989 Nobel Peace Prize ceremony that is much needed today:

> "Because we all share this small planet earth, we have to learn to live in harmony and peace with each other and with nature.
>
> "Live simply and love humanity. For as long as space endures and for as long as living beings remain, until then may I, too, abide to dispel the misery of the world." (unpaged)

Fleming, C. (2003). *Ben Franklin's Almanac: Being a True Account of the Good Gentleman's Life.* New York: Atheneum. **(M, H)**

The format of this book is remarkable. The biography is modeled on Franklin's own *Poor Richard's Almanac*, and tells his life story topically rather than chronologically. The author explains this choice:

> . . . I hope you will see clearly each of the many, varied interests Ben pursued throughout his long life. You will watch specific events as they unfold, particular ideas develop, and relationships progress. . . . Like a scrapbook, the story of Ben's life has been centered around visuals—portraits, etchings, cartoons, and sketches. These images—most created long ago—will bring you face-to-face with history, and help you to connect with Ben the Person, rather than just a name and dates. . . . Together these bits and pieces shape the story of Ben's life and show us his many sides—his intense commitment, his wise reasonableness, his sense of social justice, and his unfailing good humor. Indeed, they show us both his "grand accomplishments" and his "smaller goods." (pp. iv–v)

Help your students see how Ben Franklin is an interdisciplinary figure; he doesn't belong just in the social studies classroom, as they might have thought. The section called "The Scientist's Scrapbook" talks of his first experiment (swimming and flying a kite simultaneously), his creation of mathematical puzzles called magic squares, his discoveries about the language of ants, the inventions of the Franklin stove and bifocals, etc. Another section, "The Writer's Journal," is filled with examples of genres ranging from fables to "Ben's Rules for Being a Better Writer."

Fradin, D. B., & Fradin, J. B. (2003). *Fight On! Mary Church Terrell's Battle for Integration.* New York: Clarion Books. (M, H)

In 1950, Mary Church Terrell phoned a Baptist minister in Washington, D.C., and invited him to go to lunch at Thompson's Cafeteria. He pointed out that they wouldn't be served by this all-white establishment. "'I know we won't be served, but let's go anyway,' Mrs. Terrell answered" (p. 1). Does this sound like a brave, determined woman? Will your students think so? What will they think when you add that she was 86 years old at the time?

This book takes readers back to 1863, when Mary was born the daughter of slaves, and brings them through the next nine decades, as she becomes the first African American woman on the Washington, D.C., Board of Education, as she works with Susan B. Anthony to fight for voting rights for women, and as she, when an old woman, leads organized sit-ins. This biography, containing thought-provoking photographs, will give your students new insights on what leadership can be and can do.

Giblin, J. C. (1997). *Charles A. Lindbergh: A Human Hero.* New York: Clarion Books. (M, H)

Your students could name several living people who have been hailed as heroes and then have fallen from grace: sports figures, politicians, actors, music stars, preachers. What do we do with people who have great talent, or have made important contributions, but whose personal lives or at least specific actions cause us to see them as less than admirable? James Cross Giblin tackles this subject through his biography of Charles Lindbergh, whose nonstop transatlantic flight in 1927 brought him fame and admiration, but who later angered people over his isolationist views during World War II, his acceptance of a medal from Adolf Hitler, and his anti-Semitic remarks in public speeches. Your students will be given a lot to think about, as well as a way to think about all heroes who, because they are human, are flawed.

Hatt, C. (2004). *Catherine the Great.* Milwaukee, WI: World Almanac Library. (H)

Included in the *Judge for Yourself* series, the first part of this book is straight biography. Students will be amazed at Catherine's teen years; the arranged engagement when she was 15 and the Russian Peter was 16 is told in great detail. When they met the year before, Catherine found him to be immature and showing poor judgment. Later, her memoirs show her thoughts, "'If you allow yourself to love that man, you will be the unhappiest creature on this Earth . . . this man scarcely looks at you, talks of nothing but dolls or such things, and pays attention to any other woman than yourself'" (p. 11). Predictably, things did not improve after the marriage. But the story of Catherine's rise to power and reign as empress continue throughout the chapters. The second part of the book is arranged by questions such as "Enlightenment Empress or Old-Fashioned Autocrat?" "The Serfs' Friend or the Serfs' Enemy?" "Catherine's Foreign Policy—A Cause for Pride or Shame?" Arguments for both sides are provided, along with marginal boxes of source notes, quotes, statistics, excerpts from letters and documents, etc. Students will be able to see how answers to historical questions are not always clear-cut. Have them use the information to form their own opinions, write persuasive and document-based essays, and compare issues in Catherine's era to those in our present day and other times.

Heiligman, D. (2003). *High Hopes: A Photobiography of John F. Kennedy.* Washington, DC: National Geographic. (I, M)

In the Foreword, Eunice Kennedy Shriver tells readers that if her brother were writing the foreword, he'd challenge young readers to not wait until they are older, but to look around to see what they could do now, today, to make things better. "He would make you laugh and think and work hard, all at the same time" (p. 7). The text and photos of this book chronicle the life of JFK in ways young people can relate to. Quotes from him are interspersed throughout, so that in a way he is still guiding our present generation of schoolchildren to ponder and act upon words such as he offered in his Pulitzer Prize–winning *Profiles in Courage*: "The stories of past courage . . . can teach, they can offer hope, they can provide inspiration, but they cannot supply courage itself. For this each man must look into his own soul" (p. 28). Quotes are included for school and community leaders to harken to as well, such as "The life of the arts, far from being an interruption, a distraction in the life of a nation, is very close to the center of a nation's purpose—and it is the test of the quality of a nation's civilization" (p. 51).

The book ends with a chronology and a list of further resources that can be used along with this biography as you teach about our 35th president.

McDonald, A. (1999). *Henry VIII and His Chopping Block.* New York: Scholastic. **(I, M)**

Part of the *Famous Dead People* series, this book has a lot of fun at Henry's expense, but is actually loaded with information. It's partly in comic book style. One example of the charts in this book is a report card, an "End of Term Report." Henry earned points for Art (A skillful hand. Thanks for the Holbeins!) and Languages (Deft. Being able to write Spanish, French, and Latin came in handy for secret letters to Anne Boleyn). He didn't fare well in Economics (Disastrous. If he'd paid as much attention to money as he did to fighting the country would be rich) or Architecture (Destructive. A sad waste of fine monasteries) or Religion (Devious. Prepared to do anything to win an argument. Even start his own church.) (p. 172). There are newspaper reports, secret diaries of Henry and his queens, and timelines, all done in a humorous way.

After reading this book, you and your students may enjoy a lively discussion about whether Henry's strengths as a ruler outweighed his weaknesses.

Rose, O. N. (2003). *Abraham Joshua Heschel: Man of Spirit, Man of Action.* Philadelphia: The Jewish Publication Society. **(I, M, H)**

In the Foreword, we read Heschel's daughter's memories of his tenderness and his hospitality shown the refugee scholars who would gather at their home. In the Introduction, Heschel is described as a man who looked like a prophet from the Bible and believed that "standing up for the rights of others was a religious obligation" (p. x). The chapters will engross readers in stories of his childhood in Poland, his writing of a series of articles, *Gates of Torah*, at the age of 14, his writing and speaking against the Nazi burning of Jewish holy books, his meetings with Catholic leaders during the Vatican II Council, his walking with Martin Luther King Jr. as they protested the Vietnam War and marched for civil rights. Students may ponder Heschel's quotes that begin every chapter, such as "Remember to build a life as if it were a work of art" (p. 61). Teachers may offer this book when issues of social justice and activism arise.

St. George, J. (2004). *You're on Your Way, Teddy Roosevelt.* **Illus. M. Faulkner.** New York: Philomel Books. **(I, M)**

The author focuses on the circumstances of Theodore Roosevelt's early years that impacted the adult person he became. She tells of his recurring asthma and other illnesses that could have defined him as an invalid and been treated as obstacles to success, but which he treated as challenges. He was small and weak, but as readers turn the pages they see him growing and learn of his determined efforts to gain strength and accomplish personal feats. St. George ends this biography in 1876 as the young man entered Harvard College, but listed the adventures that lay ahead: ". . . politics, writing, traveling, ranching, soldiering, mountain climbing, hunting, conservation, social reforms, exploration—even the presidency itself" (unpaged). Use this book as a starting point for teaching the highlights of a unique and well-remembered president.

Turnipseed, J. (2003). *Baghdad Express: A Gulf War Memoir.* **Illus. Brian Kelly.** St. Paul, MN: Borealis Books. **(H)**

Many of our students know more about the wars of past centuries than they do of the wars their parents and grandparents lived through. Joel Turnipseed's account and reflections of his time in the Middle East in the early 1990s brings a unique perspective. Not much older than our students' present ages, Joel was a philosophy major, so he did a lot of critical thinking while part of the Marine Corps's logistical operation, serving as a model for our students as they try to untangle present as well as past events. Cartoon illustrations are interspersed throughout his story, offering yet another path for students into the issues and historical facts and interpretations.

Winter, J. (2004). *The Librarian of Basra: A True Story from Iraq.* New York: Harcourt. **(E, I, M)**

What a perfect way to help your students understand the similarities of peoples everywhere. Afraid of impending war in Iraq in the spring of 2003, librarian Alia Muhammed Baker secretly takes books from the library and hides them in a restaurant and homes to protect them from the destruction of bombs. The library burns to the ground, but the 30,000 books are saved, thanks to this librarian who knows the value of reading and is willing to dream of a future home for the books. Readers will applaud her courage and cheer her victory. Use this book as a companion to *Faithful Elephants*, by Tsuchiya (1998). Both show the far-reaching consequences for innocent people—as well as animals and precious treasures—when bombs, no matter what country drops them, no matter how just the cause, fall.

SS/HIS

REFERENCES

Blasingame, J. (2003). An interview with Avi, 2003 Newbery Medal winner for *Crispin, The Cross of Lead. ALAN Review, 30* (3), 38–39.

Csicsery, G. P., & Locker, J. (2004). *N is a number: Portrait of Paul Erdös.* Oakland, CA: Zala Films.

Daisey, P. (1996–1997). Promoting equity in secondary science and mathematics classrooms with biography projects. *School Science and Mathematics, 97* (8), 413–418.

Gallagher, A. F. (1993). Talk shows and trade books. In M. Zarnowski & A. F. Gallagher (Eds.), *Children's literature and social studies: Selecting and using notable books in the classroom.* Dubuque, IA: Kendall/Hunt.

Gelb, M. J. (2003). *Discover your genius: How to think like history's ten most revolutionary minds.* New York: Quill.

Keely, J. (2001). *Understanding* I Am the Cheese. San Diego: Lucent Books.

Leckie, S. A. (2006). Why biographies matter in the classroom. *OAH Magazine of History, 20* (1), 7–10.

Norton, D. E. (2003). *Through the eyes of a child: An introduction to children's literature* (6th ed.). Upper Saddle River, NJ: Merrill.

Watson, J. S. (2002). Learning history through literary memoir. Interdisciplinary Connections Column, J. Brewbaker (Ed.). *The ALAN Review, 29* (3), 10–14.

Zarnowski, M. (2003). *History makers: A questioning approach to reading and writing biographies.* Portsmouth, NH: Heinemann.

LITERATURE CITED

If you don't find a book listed here, it is included in Part 4, Annotated Books and Booktalks.

Alexanderson, G. L. (2000). *The random walks of George Pólya.* Washington, DC: Mathematical Association of America.

Al-Eindawi, T. (2004). *Thura's diary: My life in wartime Iraq.* Trans. R. Bray. New York: Viking.

Anderson, W. (1998). *Laura's album: A remembrance scrapbook of Laura Ingalls Wilder.* New York: HarperCollins.

Beals, M. P. (1994). *Warriors don't cry: A searing memoir of the battle to integrate Little Rock's Central High.* New York: Pocket Books/Washington Square Press.

Bedard, M. (1997). *Emily.* Illus B. Cooney. Toronto: Stoddart Kids.

Boerst, W. J. (2004). *Isaac Newton: Organizing the universe.* Greensboro, NC: Morgan Reynolds.

Bolden, T. (2004). *The champ: The story of Muhammad Ali.* Illus. R. G. Christie. New York: Alfred A. Knopf.

Brewster, H. (1996). *Anastasia's album: The last tsar's youngest daughter tells her own story.* New York: Hyperion.

Bridges, R. (1999). *Through my eyes.* New York: Scholastic.

Caravantes, P. (2006). *Deep woods: The story of Robert Frost.* Greensboro, NC: Morgan Reynolds.

Carroll, L., Tenniel, J., & Gardner, M. (2000). *The annotated Alice: Alice's adventures in Wonderland & through the looking-glass.* New York: Norton.

Carson, R. (1962). *Silent Spring.* Boston: Houghton Mifflin.

Cormier, R. (2005). *I am the cheese.* Waterville, ME: Thorndike Press.

Cox, C. (1997). *Fiery vision: The life and death of John Brown.* New York: Scholastic.

Curie, E. (1937). *Madame Curie: A biography.* Trans. V. Sheean. New York: Doubleday & Co.

Demi. (2005). *Mother Teresa.* New York: Margaret K. McElderry Books.

Demi. (2003). *Muhammad.* New York: Margaret K. McElderry Books.

Demi. (2001). *Gandhi.* New York: Margaret K. McElderry Books.

Demi. (1998). *The Dalai Lama: A biography of the Tibetan spiritual and political leader.* New York: Henry Holt.

Demi. (1995). *Buddha.* New York: Henry Holt.

Douglas, M. S. (1947). *The Everglades: River of grass.* New York: Rinehart.

Durr, V. (1985). *Outside the magic circle: Autobiography: Virginia Foster Durr.* H. F. Bernard (Ed.). Tuscaloosa: University of Alabama Press.

Filipovic, Z. (1994). *Zlata's diary: A child's life in Sarajevo.* New York: Viking.

Frank, A. (1967). *The diary of a young girl.* New York: Doubleday.

Frazier, N. (2001). *Georgia O'Keeffe.* North Dighton, MA: JG Press.

Garrett, M. (2002). *Mary Shelley.* New York: Oxford University Press.

Gerstein, M. (2003). *The man who walked between the towers.* Brookfield, CT: Roaring Brook Press.

Greenberg, J., & Jordan, S. (1991). *The painter's eye: Learning to look at contemporary American art.* New York: Delacorte Press.

Greenberg, J., & Jordan, S. (1993). *The sculptor's eye: Looking at contemporary American art*. New York: Delacorte Press.

Greenberg, J., & Jordan, S. (1995). *The American eye: Eleven artists of the twentieth century*. New York: Delacorte Press.

Hamilton, V. (1988). *Anthony Burns: The defeat and triumph of a fugitive slave*. New York: Knopf.

Harmin, K. L. (2006). *J.K. Rowling: Author of* Harry Potter. Berkeley Heights, NJ: Enslow Publishers.

Hayslip, L. L., & Hayslip, J. (1993). *Child of war, woman of peace*. New York: Doubleday.

Hayslip, L. L., with Wurts, J. (1989). *When heaven and earth changed places: A Vietnamese woman's journey from war to peace*. New York: Doubleday.

Hinton, S. E. (1967). *The outsiders*. New York: Viking Press.

Hoffman, P. (1998). *The man who loved only numbers: The story of Paul Erdös and the search for mathematical truth*. New York: Hyperion.

Jiang, J. L. (1998). *Red scarf girl: A memoir of the Cultural Revolution*. New York: HarperTrophy.

Joyce, W. (1997). *The world of William Joyce scrapbook*. Photographs by P. Gould, designed by C. Ketter. New York: Laura Geringer.

Kamen, G. (Ed.). (2003). *Heading out: The start of some splendid careers*. New York: Bloomsbury.

Karamanides, D. (2006). *Pythagoras: Pioneering mathematician and musical theorist of ancient Greece*. New York: The Rosen Publishing Group.

Knight, J. M. (2000). *Charlotte in Giverny*. Illus. M. Sweet. San Francisco: Chronicle Books.

Leach, D. F. (2001). *I see you I see myself: The young life of Jacob Lawrence*. Washington, DC: Phillips Collection.

Leckie, S. A. (2006). Why biographies matter in the classroom. *OAH Magazine of History, 20* (1), 7–10.

Mahaney, I. (2005). *Danny Harf: Wakeboarding champion*. New York: Rosen Publishing Group.

Mahaney, I. (2005). *Dave Mirra: BMX champion*. New York: Rosen Publishing Group.

Mahaney, I. (2005). *Kevin Jones: Snowboarding champion*. New York: PowerKids Press.

Mahaney, I. (2005). *Taig Khris: In-line skating champion*. New York: PowerKids Press.

Mannis, C. (2003). *The queen's progress: An Elizabethan alphabet*. Illus. B. Ibatoulline. New York: Viking.

Matas, C. (1993). *Daniel's story*. New York: Scholastic.

Mattern, J. (2003). *Elizabeth Cady Stanton and Susan B. Anthony: Fighting together for women's rights*. New York: The Rosen Publishing Group.

McDonough, Y. Z. (2002). *Peaceful protest: The life of Nelson Mandela*. Illus. M. Zeldis. New York: Walker & Company.

Moody, A. (1968). *Coming of age in Mississippi*. New York: Dial Press.

Nelson, M. (2001). *Carver: A life in poems*. Asheville, NC: Front Street.

Partridge, E. (2005). *John Lennon: All I want is the truth*. New York: Viking.

Paulsen, G. (1993). *Nightjohn*. New York: Delacorte Press.

Perl, T. (1993). *Women & numbers: Lives of women mathematicians*. Illus. A. Nunan. San Carlos, CA: Wide World Publishing/Tetra.

Petroski, H. (2000). *The book on the bookshelf*. New York: Vintage Books.

Petroski, H. (1990). *The pencil: Its history and design*. New York: Knopf.

Pringle, L. (2006). *American slave, American hero: York of the Lewis & Clark expedition*. Illus. C. Van Wright and Y. Hu. Honesdale, PA: Calkins Creek Books.

Provensen, A. (1995). *My fellow Americans: A family album*. San Diego: Browndeer Press.

Ryan, P. M. (2002). *When Marian sang*. Illus. B. Selznick. New York: Scholastic.

Santiago, E. (1998). *Almost a woman*. Reading, MA: Perseus Books.

Satrapi, M. (2003). *Persepolis: The story of a childhood*. New York: Pantheon.

Sis, P. (2003). *The tree of life: A book depicting the life of Charles Darwin: Naturalist, geologist & thinker*. New York: Francis Foster Books.

Tsuchiya, Y. (1998). *Faithful elephants: A true story of animals, people, and war*. Illus. T. Lewin. Trans. T. T. Dyke. Boston: Houghton Mifflin.

Welden, A. (1999). *Girls who rocked the world: Heroines from Sacajawea to Sheryl Swoopes*. Illus. J. McCann. New York: Stevens.

Wright, R. (1998). *Native son*. New York: HarperCollins.

Wright, R. (1993). *Black boy: A record of childhood and youth*. New York: HarperPerennial.

Poetry

6

"There are many things we may come to know about poetry, but some of the initial essences stay the same: it's a portable, intimate genre, pocket-sized, which should make it quickly inviting in a classroom setting."

NAOMI SHIHAB NYE (2000)

P A R T   1

the why and how
OF USING POETRY

I've talked with teachers who give me many reasons why they don't use poetry in their classrooms. They don't have time for extras, since their curriculums are packed. Or, "I'm not confident with poetry; I don't read it myself; I don't write it myself; I don't know where to find poetry relating to my content area, if it even exists." This chapter is meant to assure teachers that poetry may be introduced and nurtured in classrooms in ways that take very little time. Poetry is well worth that time because it may lead to learning that lasts. I'll share methods that teachers have already used to their students' benefit, and I'll provide annotations in the form of booktalks for you and your students so that your search for relevant poetry will be well on its way.

There's a body of educational literature that demonstrates that many content area teachers find poetry useful to their teaching of concepts in their disciplines. For example, Meadows (1999) uses poetry to reveal complexities of historical moments through the capturing of powerful emotions. She teaches her students to explore poems as historical documents, discovering how their messages are rooted in a certain place and time. They read Gwendolyn Brooks's poem "We Real Cool," and then compare and contrast conditions of 1960, when the poem was written, and today. In other examples, Danks (1995) teaches the topic of the Holocaust partly through poetry because of the emotional power of its images, and Donaldson (2001) teaches geographic concepts through poetry, finding that it deepens high school students' learning of fundamental principles such as those relating to spatial phenomena and weather. His choices of poems include those by Shakespeare, Tennyson, Walt Whitman, and Robert Frost.

According to Chatton (1993), using poetry across the curriculum makes a lot of sense, since poets share characteristics with practitioners in other disciplines. She explains, "Science and poetry are closely allied. Both the scientist and the poet are close observers and chroniclers of the world around them. Scientists investigate and interpret events in the natural and physical environment. Poets investigate and interpret these same events with a slightly different eye" (p. 27). Because of this, she recommends using poetry about the physical world and nature to enhance lessons in the physical and the life sciences, and she includes dozens of titles in bibliographies that connect to curricular topics, such as flight, rocks and minerals, the senses, changes in nature, and scientific frames of reference. Moreover, she advises connecting the language of numbers with the language of letters by exploring poetry that has to do with patterns, logic, problem solving, classification, time, and mathematical processes. For example, the concept of zero is an important one for mathematicians and mathematics students, and teachers may utilize these three poems to enliven lessons: "Zero Makes Me Hungry" by Aliki, "Zero" by Eve Merriam, and "I Am Zero, Naught, One Cipher" by Carl Sandburg. She offers examples of poems, such as Walt Whitman's "When I Heard the Learn'd Astronomer," that have to do with attitudes toward mathematics. (There's a beautiful 2004 edition of this poem illustrated by L. Long.) Chatton makes similar connections to and suggestions for using poetry in social studies, art, music, physical education, and health, as well as demonstrating how to use poetry in interdisciplinary thematic units.

Abisdris and Casuga (2001) found that analyzing poetry about science concepts with students increases their understanding of the contributions of scientists and appreciation of scientific developments. They use poetry ranging from that written by Robert Frost to verse they've penned themselves. Alber (2001) uses his and his students' poetry writing in an advanced placement chemistry class. Walders (2000) recommends weaving poetry throughout the science curriculum, such as using Emily Dickinson to introduce a unit on the human body, noting that poems help clarify for students concepts that direct methods of teaching might not. Others, such as McGee (1995) and Szenher and Worsley (1998) make connections between poetry and the teaching and learning of math. Rule, Carnicelli, and Kane (2004) used poetry reading and writing to enhance the teaching and learning of earth science concepts in a high school course. Numerous articles are available that will help you visualize how teachers incorporate poetry into their teaching in ways that enhance, rather than detract from, the curricular material they and their students are responsible for.

I've known teachers who simply post a different poem on the bulletin board or overhead projector each day. They make no comment about them; they are simply there. But if you do this for a few weeks, and then go a day without changing the poem, students will be quick to alert you, asking, "Where is the new poem?" That might be the time to invite them to bring in poems to share, either related to the discipline you teach, or simply old and new favorites. Consider creating a new kind of wallpaper for the classroom, with texts and accompanying illustrations your students draw, paint, or find on the Internet or in magazines. The possibilities are endless.

Do you know any poems by heart? Do any of your students? Enabling students to build a repertoire of memorized poems may be a great contribution on our parts. Why, you might wonder? Poet Liz Rosenberg (1996) explains:

> The poet Galway Kennell says we should learn a poem, "by heart, by hand, and by mouth." That means that if you really want to get to know a poem, you'll want to memorize it, write it down in your own handwriting, and say it out loud in your own voice. This is true whether the poem is written by you or by somebody else. If I could give one piece of advice to teachers of young poets, it would be this: ask your students to memorize two poems a month, one poem that they have written, and one written by someone else. At the end of one year they would have twenty-four poems "by heart and by mouth." That is a lot of company to have, on walks, in hospital waiting rooms, on lonely nights. Memorization and recitation fell out of favor many years ago, and some people associate it with terrible flowery poems, and humiliating moments in front of other people. It doesn't have to be like that. Young people ought to be free to choose the poems they like. Simply keeping books of poetry around, and having the chance to look through them frequently, is one way of being more comfortable with poetry. Then, too, it doesn't really matter if you keep the poem in front of you when you recite it—the point is not whether you have memorized it perfectly, but to speak the poem from the heart and mouth, as best you can. It's not a test, but an exercise of affection and respect. (pp. 191–192)

Not only schools, but also whole cities are tuning in to the joys of group immersion in the poetry genre. To celebrate National Poetry Month, the New York City Department of Education teams up with the Department of Cultural Affairs, the

New York Times, the Office of the Mayor, City University of New York, and other agencies to sponsor an annual "Poetry in Your Pocket Day." The title comes from a poem written by Beatrice Schenk de Regniers. All New Yorkers are encouraged to carry a favorite or meaningful poem, ready to share with coworkers and friends. Poets visit schools, libraries, parks, and other venues; there are open mic opportunities at various social gathering places; bookstores give free bookmarks. For one day, and hopefully much longer, poetry rules. Other communities have found similar ways to celebrate National Poetry Month and to encourage readers to explore and embrace the genre. To find out more, visit www.nyc.gov/html/poem/html and www.poets.org/page.php/prmID/41.

One caveat about how you use poetry: Be careful not to ruin it in the teaching. Billy Collins (2003), a former U. S. poet laureate who is highlighted later in this chapter, warns:

> . . . the classroom emphasis on what a poem means can work effectively to kill the poetry spirit. Too often the hunt for Meaning becomes the only approach; literary devices form a field of barbed wire that students must crawl under to get to "what the poet is trying to say," a regrettable phrase which implies that every poem is a failed act of communication. (p. xix)

Collins offers alternatives to this traditional, potentially deadly explication of poetry:

> . . . there are other ways to increase a reader's intimacy with a poem. A reader can write the poem out, just as Keats or Frost did, or learn how to say a poem out loud, or even internalize a poem by memorizing it. The problem is that none of these activities requires the presence of a teacher. Ideally, interpretation should be one of the pleasures poetry offers. Unfortunately, too often it overshadows the other pleasures of meter, sound, metaphor, and imaginative travel, to name a few. (p. xix)

For our purposes, it's actually fortunate that the pleasures of poetry that Collins promotes do not need a teacher's time or expertise. We may enjoy the poems along with our students, and note the extra pleasure that poems that connect to our curriculum bring to different students, in different ways. We just have to give them the ticket to the imaginative travel Collins refers to; we do that by providing the poems and encouraging them to find more to share.

Lowery (2003) advocates using poetry to help students make personal connections, think about their future, and deepen their thinking processes, as well as appreciate the beauty of language. In a dropout prevention sixth-grade language arts class, she asked students about the dreams they had for their lives, then recited Langston Hughes's poem, "Dreams." After a follow-up discussion on the same topic, the class created a "dream wall," with the Hughes poem in the middle and their personal connections and dreams, which they wrote on index cards, connected by yarn to the poem. They could revisit and update their dream cards whenever they wished. Lowery notes, "Although poetry has the power to generate wonderful experiences in its readers, historically it has been the most neglected genre utilized in schools' curricula. Some teachers do not share poetry in their classrooms because they too had negative experiences in their early exposure to the genre" (p. 49). As teachers become more aware of the superb poetry related to curricular topics, and learn about project ideas such as the one Lowery describes, this scenario may change. Imagine science classrooms with these wall charts displaying students' connections with poems about space, ecology, chemistry, sports physics, minerals, or human growth. The index cards on art room posters will probably have lots of visual representations of students' reactions to the art-related poems, arranged however your art students have decided to place them.

It's important to understand that, as with other genres, we must give students instruction in comprehending poetry. What we do before introducing a poetic text, while the students read it, and after they read it is crucial. The activities and strategies in Part 2 should stimulate your thinking as you plan how to incorporate wonderful verse into your instruction.

instructional
STRATEGIES AND ACTIVITIES
Involving Poetry

INVESTIGATING INTERTEXTUALITY THROUGH POEMS

Standards Addressed

English/Language Arts: Students apply knowledge of language structure, language conventions (e.g., style, vocabulary) to communicate effectively with a variety of audiences for a variety of purposes.

Context/Rationale

Intertextuality refers to the concept of "one writer (or filmmaker or artist) elaborating upon or consciously paying homage to the works of another" (Abair & Cross, 1999, p. 85). An example of intertextuality that most teens and young adults are familiar with is the television episode of *The Simpsons* that is based on Edgar Allan Poe's classic poem "The Raven." Intertextuality is at play when a modern story mirrors a mythological tale or fairy tale, when book characters meet characters from other books, or when motifs or themes, such as from the Bible, are woven into new works. The concept is related to other literary terms, such as allusion and parody. Fanfiction, described in a previous chapter, involves intertextuality. Poetry offers wonderful examples of intertextuality, and you may teach your students how to look for and notice them, as well as create them in their own creative writing. The more background knowledge students gain, the more they'll recognize and appreciate intertextuality as they read and write.

Procedure

- Select two poems that you think students have likely encountered previously and which have an illustrated version (e.g., "The Red Wheel Barrow" and "Stopping by Woods").

- Show your class a copy of one of the poems on an overhead transparency, computer projector, or on large poster paper. Give them a chance to respond in any way they wish on paper, and then aloud.

- Say something like, "I think I can make a poem like that," and unveil a poem you've written out on chart paper using the same format.

- After sharing your poem, explain the concept of intertextuality, which involves an author alluding to or using ideas, phrasing, or the form from the work of another, as you did, borrowing the feel of the original poem you introduced.

- For homework that night, invite them to try writing a poem like the poem you have chosen. You might also show other examples of intertextuality, such as the poems found in *Science Verse* (Scieszka & Smith, 2004) and *Because I Could Not Stop My Bike* (Shapiro, 2003).

- The next day, ask students to share the poems they have written.
- Then, switch to another poem you think they've heard before.
- As a class, try to re-create the poem from memory. You may find that many remember at least being introduced to it. And someone might say he or she had to memorize it in sixth grade, and can recall quite a bit with help from classmates. In the Frost example, students may talk about learning about the symbolism of "miles to go before I sleep."
- Pass out the entire poem, and give the class time to reflect silently and then draw a picture on the paper next to the poem—just for themselves.
- Then pass out copies of the poem in illustrated book form. For the Frost example, I use the version illustrated by Susan Jeffers (Frost, 2001).
- Encourage your students to talk about whether the meaning or feeling of the poem changes for them after viewing the artist's visual interpretation.
- Have them try writing a poem similar to the Frost poem.

Walk-Through

When I introduce intertextuality to my class, I often obtain copies of the book *Love That Dog*, by Sharon Creech. The two poems I use ("The Red Wheelbarrow" and "Stopping by Woods") are contained in the back of this book. Figure 6.1 shows the poem I wrote based on Williams's poem.

After I have introduced students to both poems, I introduce the book *Love That Dog*, by Sharon Creech, by giving a booktalk or character booktalk such as the following:

> Hi, y'all, I'm Miss Stretchberry, a teacher who just LOVES poetry. Do you ever have a student you identify as a challenge, a pure challenge? Well, that's my Jack. For some reason, he thinks writing poetry is for girls. I can't imagine why. Look at all those poets he met in elementary school—Dr. Seuss, Jack Prelutsky, Shel Silverstein. And he'll meet plenty more in high school—Robert Frost, Langston Hughes, Edgar Allan Poe—nice guys, but, well, GUYS! Anyway, here's Jack in middle school, resisting my poetry lessons, thinking he's no good at composing, convinced he has nothing to write about. If you want to find out how I handle Jack, or maybe it's what poetry itself does to him, come into my classroom in *Love That Dog*.

I then have students read the book for homework. During the reading, they discover that the poems we've gone over in class are in the book, in Miss Stretchberry's class, and that Jack writes poems using the style of the poems he's been introduced to.

FIGURE	6.1	Example poem based on "The Red Wheelbarrow" illustrating intertextuality.

Literacy 505

So much depends

upon 26 people

gathered together

in Room 306

committed to learning

about literacy

RESPONDING IN VERSE TO NOVELS IN VERSE

Standards Addressed

History: Students identify ... the temporal structure a historical narrative or story. Students establish temporal order in constructing historical narratives of their own.

English/Language Arts: Students apply knowledge of language structure, language conventions (e.g., spelling and punctuation) media techniques, figurative language, and genre to create, critique, and discuss print and nonprint works.

Context/Rationale

Many novels in verse have been published in the past several years, and the genre is enjoying tremendous popularity. They're accessible; Amanda Hughes of the Children's Book Shop in Brookline, Massachusetts, notes that kids gravitate toward them, partly because "'they see the words down the center of the page and it's not as daunting as a traditional novel form" (Whitney, 2004). Whitney points out that novels in verse offer an immediacy of feelings in just a few lines, and that the images touch readers in a special way. Sonya Sones, author of the novel-in-verse *Stop Pretending!: What Happened When My Big Sister Went Crazy* (2001), believes:

> "Poetry takes you right to the feelings. And that's where teenagers live! ... I think telling the stories with so few words adds to their power because the people who read them are called upon to fill in the emotional blanks with their own personal experiences ... and this makes them feel like they can relate to them. This makes even the most reluctant readers want to read on—because they have found themselves in the pages of a book, at last." (Whitney, p. 4)

Procedure

The steps to this procedure are simple.

- Select a novel in verse that relates to a topic in your curriculum (see Figure 6.3).
- Have the students read the novel.
- Once readers get used to the novel in verse form, have them respond via their journal. It makes sense that their responses should also be in the form of a poem.

Walk-Through

I tried this in my class after reading Karen Hesse's Newbery winner *Out of the Dust* (1997), which takes place in America's Dust Bowl during the Great Depression, making it a good choice for history/social studies teachers. The poems are narrated by 14-year-old Billy Jo, during the year 1934. Billy Jo has lost her mother in a tragic accident that also resulted in her own hands being badly burned, so she and her father are dealing with grief as well as with economic crisis and crop failure. The first poem, however, looks back at the year of her birth, which prompted me to look ahead 14 years after the novel's end and imagine how Billy Jo's life might have evolved.

Attempting to take on her voice, I wrote the poem shown in Figure 6.2.

Figure 6.3 contains a bibliography of selected novels in verse form. They are all appropriate as part of an English curriculum. I have listed other subjects to which the books relate.

FIGURE 6.2 Poem inspired by *Out of the Dust.*

Comin' Ripe

Louise and Pa, they stayed put.
The ground wasn't any good for roots,
But they rooted there in spite.
Times of rain,
Times of no rain,
Together they flourished like a tree in Eden.

But I was still a tumbleweed.

Livie Killian, she stayed west.
Most of our neighbors went west over the years,
Lookin' to get out of the dust.
Or lookin', like folks did a hundred years ago,
for a place where the dust was gold.
Livie married a grape picker, *became* a grape picker—
And an onion picker, a beet picker, a melon picker.
Her five kids are pickers, too.

But I'd tried goin' west once,
And I'd returned.
So when I turned 20, I went East!
I came to a place called Binghamton, New York.
I settled where two rivers, Chenango and Susquehanna, cross,
Figurin' they should keep me well-watered!

I got me a job during the war,
in the Eureka Tent Company, sewin' window flaps.
My hands don't look too pretty, but they work good enough now.
And they play the piano somethin' fierce,
The piano my soldier, Jimmy, gave me when we got married,
Soon as he came home from the dust and ashes of Europe.

Soon I'll be playin' for our first-born,
due the first of April.
Pa writes he hopes it's a boy.
I write back sayin' "Give it up!
Ain't you learned yet that what you get is good enough?"

I'm out of the dust; I've made me a life.
And I hear Ma's voice sayin',
"Billy Jo, you do me proud. You keep playin', girl, all the while."

March, 1948

| Novels in verse. | FIGURE | 6.3 |

Bryant, J. (2006). *Pieces of Georgia*. New York: Knopf. (art)

Fullerton, A. (2007). *Walking on glass*. New York: Harper-Tempest. (health)

Hesse, K. (2005). *Witness*. Waterville, ME: Thorndike Press. (social studies)

High, L. O. (2004). *Sister Slam and the poetic motormouth roadtrip*. New York: Bloomsbury. (English)

Koertge, R. (2003). *Shakespeare bats cleanup*. Cambridge, MA: Candlewick Press. (physical education)

McCormick, P. (2006). *Sold*. New York: Hyperion. (social studies)

Myers, W. D. (2006). *Street love*. New York: Amistad. (English)

Patneaude, D. (2004). *Thin wood walls*. Boston: Houghton Mifflin. (social studies)

Roy, J. (2006). *Yellow star*. New York: Marshall Cavendish. (social studies)

Rylant, C. (2006). *Ludie's life*. New York: Harcourt. (social studies)

Sandell, L. A. (2006). *The weight of the sky*. New York: Viking Children's Books. (social studies)

Sones, S. (2007). *What my girlfriend doesn't know*. New York: Simon & Schuster Books for Young Readers. (art)

Testa, M. (2005). *Something about America*. Cambridge, MA: Candlewick Press. (languages and culture, social studies)

Turner, A. (2006). *Hard hit*. New York: Scholastic Press. (physical education, health)

Wolf, A. (2004). *New found land: A novel*. Cambridge, MA: Candlewick Press. (social studies)

Wong, J. L. (2005). *Seeing Emily*. New York: Amulet Books. (languages and culture)

Yeomans, E. (2007). *Rubber houses*. New York: Little, Brown and Company. (health, physical education)

Zimmer, T. V. (2007). *Reaching for sun*. New York: Bloomsbury Children's Books. (science)

USING OBJECTS TO STIMULATE POETRY WRITING

Standards Addressed

History: Students hypothesize the influence of the past. Students formulate historical questions. Students formulate a position or course of action on an issue.

Science: All students should develop an understanding of the structure and properties of matter. All students should develop an understanding of the abilities of technological design.

Math: Students organize and consolidate their mathematical thinking through communication. Students recognize and apply mathematics in contexts outside mathematics.

Art: Making connections between visual arts and other disciplines.

English/Language Arts: Students use spoken, written, and visual language to accomplish their own purpose (e.g., for learning, enjoyment, persuasion, and the exchange of information).

Context/Rationale

A very simple technique to get imaginations working and creativity happening is to use objects as jumping-off points for writing poetry about curricular topics. Poetry is highly descriptive, and poets generally observe objects in their surroundings carefully and employ original ways to talk about those objects, often using symbolism and connecting the objects to other aspects of life. These skills may benefit learning in whatever subject area you teach.

Procedure

- Select a short poem or novel in verse that describes an object related to a topic in your curriculum. See Part 4 of this chapter for suggestions.

- Provide objects, and/or invite students to bring in objects relating to the poem or book. For example, a social studies teacher could share the book *Who Was the Woman Who Wore the Hat?* (Patz, 2003). The author pondered the question that became the book's title as she observed a particular hat at the Holocaust Museum, and her questions became a book. Thinking about the hat, and then thinking about the woman who must have worn the hat, humanized the facts and figures about the genocide that occurred during World War II. A social studies, physical education, or language teacher could read Gary Soto's "Ode to Pablo's Tennis Shoes" (1992, p. 20) to help students see where a poet can go with something as simple as a dirty sneaker. A math teacher could read a poem from *Echoes for the Eye: Poems to Celebrate Patterns in Nature* (1996) by B. I. Esbensen and bring in a sunflower or other example of a geometric shape in nature while a science teacher could read from *Earthshake: Poems from the Ground Up* (2003) by L. W. Peters and bring in example rocks described in the poems.

- After your students have had time to peruse the pages and immerse themselves in the verbal images and illustrations (if any), ask them to create a poem based on the objects brought to class. You might also share your own attempt at capturing in verse your experience of responding to one of the objects. See my poetic reaction to the painting by Mary Cassatt, *Child in a Straw Hat* (Figure 6.5). You might also suggest that students provide an illustration to accompany their poem.

- Assemble the poems in a class book for all to enjoy.

- In addition, ask students to write a process note on an index card and tape it to the back of the page on which their pictures and poems reside. The note may include what they have learned regarding the product they have written about as well as what they have gleaned from the process of writing poetry.

Walk-Through

I have found Jan Greenberg's edited text, *Heart to Heart: New Poems Inspired by Twentieth-Century American Art* (2001) to be helpful in my own teaching using this activity. In her Introduction, Greenberg shares her discovery that there is a long tradition of poets, as far back as ancient Greece, writing on art. Her anthology is the result of ". . . connections between reader and viewer, writer and artist . . . celebrating the power of art to inspire language" (p. 4). She invited a group of distinguished American poets to choose an American artwork and write a poem it inspired. She has categorized their responses into chapters titled "Stories," "Voices," "Impressions," and "Expressions." She juxtaposes the new poems with photographs of the paintings the poets used as stimuli, and includes biographical sketches of both the painters and the poets. It's a rich text, begging to be used as a model. And so I have; I ask my students to create a poem based on a work of art of their choice depicted in the book.

The class book that results from our personal journeys from art to poetry is astonishing. The book shows students reflecting on the stages and phases they went through as they wrote, often expressing initial fear, ongoing struggle, a breakthrough, and then a feeling of exultation or pride over their art-inspired creations. *Heart to Heart* is a masterpiece filled with masterpieces that will lead to many more.

DRAMATIC MONOLOGUES IN POETRY FORM

Standards Addressed

History: Students read historical narratives imaginatively. Students draw upon visual, literary, and musical sources.

English/Language Arts: Students adjust their own use of spoken, written, and visual language (e.g., conventions, style, vocabulary) to communicate effectively with a variety of audiences for a variety of purposes.

Context/Rationale

You may encourage your students to perform poetry, their own and others, in various ways. Annie Thoms and Ann Frkovich have used a monologue project for creating vital poetic drama in high schools. They developed their method based on the work of Anna Deavere Smith's one-woman shows, in which she interviewed and performed in the character of people in the neighborhoods that experienced the Los Angeles riots of 1992 and of Crown Heights, Brooklyn, in 1991.

Procedure

Frkovich and Thoms (2004) give recommendations for using this method with students, including

- Provide students with examples of previous students' work.
- Watch Anna Deavere Smith's films *Fires in the Mirror* and *Twilight: Los Angeles 1992*, and/or previous students in taped performances, dramatically reciting their poems.
- Discuss and determine the critical issue or event on which to base the dramatic monologue.
- Choose relevant experts to interview.
- Develop strong interview questions.
- Practice note-taking skills.
- Record the interview on audiocassette.
- Transcribe and edit the interview, choosing appropriate places for line breaks so that it becomes a poem.
- Determine the performance venue (e.g., in-class, for the school, etc.).

The authors explain each of these recommendations and give examples of what might occur or how teachers might guide students in the process. You'll think of ways to adapt the process to fit current events or topics within your curriculum.

Walk-Through

As an example, one teacher has adapted Deavere's monologue project to fit her particular classroom and context. Thoms, who teaches at Stuyvesant High School in New York City, describes how the students with whom she worked interviewed people after the World Trade Center collapsed just four blocks away from the school; they then worked with the transcripts and performed them as poetic monologues for the community. Thoms explains:

> Our interviewees spoke eloquently, thoughtfully, as if they had been waiting to be listened to. Their words were vital, and their voices varied: students of different ages, teachers, a custodian, a security guard, a dining hall worker, two students from the special education satellite program within our building. The mono-

FIGURE 6.4 Monologue on September 11 from *With Their Eyes: September 11th—The View from a High School at Ground Zero.*

Once we came out we saw the big smoke . . .
I dunno,
when people started talking about this was a . . .
terrorist attack
I was completely,
uh,
I just couldn't accept that.
I dunno.
I was just coming into myself that
this wasn't the case, that
this was probably just an accident.
Yeah, well, when people say that, um,
when you're . . .
sometimes your rationality fails you during a time of crisis.
I never believed that until that day.
I just couldn't think correctly.
So, what can I say?
But,
but, uh,
the soot and the dust was so dense we couldn't see anything.
So,
I didn't know that both were,
you know,
down, already.

Source: A. Thoms (Ed). (2002). *With their eyes: September 11th—the view from a high school at Ground Zero,* p. 27. New York: HarperTempest. Used with permission.

logues took on personal reactions and political rhetoric; they delved into great pain but were sprinkled with hope and humor. When performed together, they formed an extraordinary tapestry. (p. 12)

The monologues were later compiled in the book *With Their Eyes: September 11th—The View from a High School at Ground Zero,* edited by Thoms (2002). Because the students carefully decided on line breaks, the monologues have the appearance of poems on the pages and can be read as poetry. See Figure 6.4 for a sample monologue from the book.

▶ ▶ ▶ POETRY SLAMS

Standards Addressed

History: Students read historical narratives imaginatively. Students draw upon visual, literary, and musical sources. Students interrogate historical data. Students formulate a position or course of action on an issue.

English/Language Arts: Students adjust their own use of spoken, written, and visual language (e.g., conventions, style, vocabulary) to communicate effectively with a variety of audiences for a variety of purposes.

Context/Rationale

In "'Out Loud': The Common Language of Poetry" (2003), Ellis, Gere, and Lamberton offer a way of breathing life into poetry instruction by holding slam competitions and workshops in the classroom. A slam competition is performance poetry that occurs in a competitive poetry event. During the event, people perform their original poems, which are judged on a numeric scale by members of an audience. Ellis, Gere, and Lamberton explain performance poems as those "presented to an audience with the whole body: in word, in voice, and in gesture" (p. 45). They point out that performance poetry may be a gateway for students to start thinking about language, and I would add that it serves to help students reflect on and appreciate content in our disciplines.

Procedure

- Explain the concepts of performance poetry and slam competitions.
- Demonstrate a performance poem you or another student has written for your students. You may or may not choose to use or allow your students to use props and music.
- Help students to choose a role in the competition. Roles include performers, timekeepers, scorekeepers, audience members, judges, and an emcee. Note: Not every student needs to perform a poem, but competition is livelier if there are at least six performers. Also, make sure that you have an odd number of judges, with about five judges preferred.
- Together with students decide on how the competition will be judged. Factors to consider include
  - adherence to topic/theme
  - originality/creativity of the poem
  - clarity and diction in speaking
  - facial expression
  - energy
  - overall impact of the performance
  - weight given to the poem's composition versus that of its performance
- Working individually or in small groups, have every student or group compose a poem for the slam competition. Allow them to choose a theme based on topics from your curriculum.
- Explain that each poetry performance will have a time limit of three minutes so they need to write a poem that can be performed in that time frame.
- In small groups, ask students to make decisions as to how to perform their individual poems. For example: If students are performing in groups, should students alternate stanzas? Should some lines be read in unison? How should dialogue be handled?
- In groups, have them practice their performance poems before the competition.
- To conduct the slam, schedule a class session for this purpose. Student judges will rate the poems from "0" to "10," the scoring used in the Olympic Games.
- Following the competition, publish all poems in a class book.

Walk-Through

Ellis, Gere, and Lamberton (2003) give an example of an Asian American high school student in their summer program who performed a poem about immigration and nationalism to his small-group workshop:

As the students discussed the performer's bodily movements, they unanimously identified shifts in the poet's figurative language—from race as internalized blood or behavioral pathway to race as externalized skin color . . . they also employed cross-textual symbolism to make meaning together. (p. 46)

The authors offer ideas for variations and adaptations of their workshop. If students are not writing original poems, they recommend giving students an online or physical library of poetry so they can read widely to select poems to explicate, memorize, and perform. They conclude, based on their experience, that the slam sessions actually lead to more and better reading on the part of students. "Performance poetry can, ultimately, lead students back to the page, though when they return to the page they return with a way of reading that allows them to hear and see and feel and do the poem differently" (p. 49).

Other good sources for this strategy are *Wham! It's a Poetry Jam* (Holbrook, 2002) and von Ziegesar's *SLAM* (2000). Teachers of American history might have students perform poems such as "Oh Captain, My Captain," by Walt Whitman, and "The Midnight Ride of Paul Revere" and "Hiawatha," by Longfellow. They could choose poems from Bobbi Katz's collection *We the People* (2000) and Walter Dean Myers's *Here in Harlem: Poems in Many Voices* (2004). English teachers may have students choose poems from Edgar Lee Masters's *Spoon River Anthology* (1992) for a Spoon River Poetry SLAM that will rouse the audience with the voices of the narrators speaking from their graveyards.

▶ ▶ ▶ ▶   ## ODES IN THE CONTENT AREAS

Standards Addressed

Visual Arts: Students reflect on and assess the characteristics and merits of their work and the work of others.

English/Language Arts: Students employ a wide range of strategies as they write and use different writing process elements appropriately to communicate effectively with a variety of audiences for a variety of purposes.

Context/Rationale

Nancie Atwell, writing teacher par excellence, offers a brief background note on odes. "Odes were invented long ago—around 500 BCE—by Pindar, a Greek poet. Back then odes followed a complicated pattern of stanzas. They were serious, dignified, choral songs, performed to celebrate victories, like in the Olympic games" (2002, p. 151). She then contrasts traditional odes with Pablo Neruda's *Odes to Common Things* (1994) in which he sings the praises of everyday objects and events. She guides her students as they create their own modern-day odes to whatever or whomever they wish.

Procedure

Atwell (2002) gives the following tips for writing odes in the style of Pablo Neruda:

- Choose a subject you have strong feelings about.
- Describe the subject inside and out.
- Exaggerate its admirable qualities, until it seems to become central to human existence.
- Tap all five senses.
- Use metaphors and similes.
- Perhaps directly address the subject of the ode.

- Tell your feelings about the subject *and* give exalted descriptions of its qualities: a balance.
- Keep the lines short.
- Choose strong words: language that's packed with meaning and cut to the bone. (p. 152)

Walk-Through

I was intrigued by this activity, so I tried it out with my pre-service teachers. After giving several examples of published odes, including several from Gary Soto's collection *Neighborhood Odes* (1992), I asked them to create an ode to a person, concept, or principle representative of their discipline. We brainstormed some titles, including *Ode to a Civil War Drummer Boy, Ode to the Microchip, Ode to Venus and Serena Williams, Ode to My Scientific Calculator, Ode to the Victims of Nagasaki, Ode to Vincent's Paint Box.* They played, they struggled, they reflected and talked, and eventually came up with original, memorable poetry. Figure 6.5 shows mine, based on my favorite painting.

Sample ode to a person representative of art.	FIGURE	6.5

Ode to Mary Cassatt's *Child in a Straw Hat*

I stand before you and I cry—
Every time.

How such power in eyes forlorn?
I try to reach in,
Lift you out,
Bring you home,
Make you mine,
The daughter I dreamed I'd have.

If I held you,
If you knew how much I love you,
Would you show the trace of a smile?
Would your laughter tug at me
The way your silent waif-look does?

Would you transform into another child
If we put a sunny party dress on you,
And a matching lace bow in new curls?
If so, then I need to let you
Stay as you are,
Where you are,
With your straw hair.
Therein lies your power.

So I stand before you,
And I sigh,
Every time.

▶ ▶ ▶   **IN-DEPTH EXPLORATION OF A POET**

Standards Addressed

History: Students read historical narratives imaginatively. Students draw upon visual, literary, and musical sources. Students interrogate historical data. Students formulate a position or course of action on an issue.

English/Language Arts: Students read a wide range of literature from many periods in many genres to build an understanding of the many dimensions (e.g., philosophical, ethical, aesthetic) of human experience.

Context/Rationale

Introduce your students to poets who relate to your content area, then as a class choose one or more to investigate. For example, social studies teachers may choose poets from the countries their students are studying. Adding Pablo Neruda's voice to a unit on South America will add a human dimension to the content material. If a history curriculum includes the study of the political turmoil in Ireland in the past century, Seamus Heaney's poems will help students feel the pain, understand the reasons for dissent and disagreement, and get a personal perspective about the violence and sorrow, as well as the pride and love, of the land. They'll also see that, while some poems are very political and refer to specific incidents and places, others express universal feelings and thoughts about family, love, relationships, and concerns about life that readers everywhere share. The Author Studies in Part 3 will give you ideas about which poets might work for you.

Procedure

- Introduce students to poets who relate to your content area, then as a class choose one or more to investigate.
- Build background knowledge about the poet by showing photographs, maps of the area about which he or she has written, and any pertinent historical/biographical background.
- Ask questions to determine what students know about the poet and his or her life.
- Ask students to investigate the poet's life and work on their own. They may look for articles, websites, books he or she has written, etc. Inform them that they may use the resources in your classroom or may ask the school librarian or public librarian for assistance.
- Have students choose one poem by the author and bring a copy of the poem to class.
- Ask them to memorize three to six lines and be prepared to recite them.
- Also have them bring in some kind of response to the poem. Some suggestions include
  - a personal reader's response
  - a summary about what you learned about the content area subject from the poem
  - an informal analysis of a literary convention used in the poem, such as symbolism, imagery, structure, rhyme scheme, theme
  - a letter to a figure in the poem or to someone else
  - a poem you've created stimulated by the ideas in the poem
  - a continuation of the poem
  - a teaching idea related to the poem (a mini-lesson plan)

- a response to a published review or criticism of the poem
- a slide show of photos that go along with the poem
- a visual response; artwork that you create stimulated by the poem
- a poster or collage
- a pairing of this poem with another, with an explanation for the choice
- a piece of music that goes along with the poem
- a dialogue with the poet, with another reader, with the narrator of the poem
- an original idea not mentioned here

- Ask them to be ready to give a three-to-five-minute presentation on the poem and their response to it.

Walk-Through

One semester, I asked my students what they knew about Seamus Heaney. Someone offered that he was Irish; a few said they had read poems by him in their English classes. But most admitted to having never heard of the Nobel Prize–winning poet. So we began a group exploration. The following week students brought in photographs, biographical information, critiques and reviews of his work. Most important, they brought in published collections of his poetry. We chose our favorites, and, using the suggestions above, we responded, shared, and created something new by combining our creative abilities with the results of Heaney's creative abilities. I showed them, as a sample response, a letter I had written to my newly engaged son after I had read Heaney's poem, "Mother of the Groom" (1998, p. 66). I read to them from Heaney's 1995 Nobel lecture, which they were now ready for. Finally, we went on a field trip; we attended a lecture given by Seamus Heaney in Syracuse, New York. The group exploration they had done prepared them for the event and aided their appreciation of what the poet offered that night.

BIOPOEMS

Standards Addressed

Math: Students organize and consolidate their mathematical thinking through communication.

English/Language Arts: Students adjust their own use of spoken, written, and visual language (e.g., conventions, style, vocabulary) to communicate effectively with a variety of audiences for a variety of purposes.

Context/Rationale

This simple strategy provides a structure for students as they reflect on main points of biographical texts and their reactions to what they learned from the text. They need to do some summarizing, synthesizing, and decision making as they create poems about people they've read about. They may also write biopoems about themselves and their friends. I've checked Internet sites and found that teachers have adapted the strategy in a variety of ways to fit their curricula and the needs of their students. Numerous student-generated examples of biopoems are included on these sites.

Procedure

- Ask students to choose and read a biography of a passionate practitioner, past or present, in your field of study. You may want to follow the reading by doing some of the post-reading activities described in Chapter 3.

FIGURE   6.6   Sample template for a biopoem.

Line 1:   First name _____

Line 2:   Four traits that describe person _____

Line 3:   Relative (brother, sister, daughter, etc.) of _____

Line 4:   Lover of _____   (list 3 things or people)

Line 5:   Who feels _____   (3 items)

Line 6:   Who needs _____   (3 items)

Line 7:   Who fears _____   (3 items)

Line 8:   Who gives _____   (3 items)

Line 9:   Who would like to see _____   (3 items)

Line 10:   Resident of _____

Line 11:   Last name _____

- Show students examples of published poems that are biographical, e.g., Jacob Lawrence's tribute to Harriet Tubman, *Harriet and the Promised Land* (1993) (social studies), Marilyn Nelson's *Carver: A Life in Poems* (2001) (science), or Margarita Engle's *The Poet Slave of Cuba: A Biography of Juan Francisco Manzano* (2006) (English/language arts, social studies).
- Give your students a template such as the one shown in Figure 6.6 for a biopoem.
- Ask students to compose a song or poem about or addressed to or narrated by a person in the biography they chose to read. They may use a variation of the biopoem structure, or they may choose another format. They might create a poem for several voices, or a sestina, limerick, or haiku. Some will prefer free verse, others rhyme.

Walk-Through

Figure 6.7 is an example of a biopoem inspired by Sylvia Nasar's *A Beautiful Mind* (1998).

FIGURE   6.7   Sample biopoem based on the life of John Forbes Nash.

A Life of Triumph over Adversity

JOHN

Brilliant, intense, prodigy, schizophrenic

Lover of numbers, formulas, codes

Husband of Alecia, who remained steadfast and supportive

JOHN

Who feels exhilarated, confused, alone

Who fears nothing—oh yes, something—insanity

Who gave us game theory, and look where others have taken it!

JOHN

Resident of Princeton University, and then of a psychiatric ward

Complex human being, caught between two worlds—which will win?

Winner of the Nobel Prize in Economics, 1994

JOHN FORBES NASH

FOUND POEMS

Standards Addressed

History: Students read historical narratives imaginatively. Students draw upon visual, literary, and musical sources.

English/Language Arts: Students read a wide range of print and nonprint texts to build an understanding of texts, of themselves, and of the cultures of the United States and the world; to acquire new information.

Geography: The geographically informed person knows and understands the physical and human characteristics of places.

Context/Rationale

Students may create what has come to be called a *found poem* by using and rearranging text from an expository or fictional text. They make decisions about where line breaks and stanza breaks need to occur, and what kind of font is appropriate. Seeing the material in a new configuration, perhaps combined with reading the found poems aloud, may lead to increased understanding, retention, and appreciation. As a variation, students can contribute a line from their original found poem to a class found poem.

Compulsive readers, those of us who read the cereal boxes in front of us at breakfast and the friendly messages in public restrooms about how hand dryers save trees and don't spread germs, can turn whatever text appears in front of us into found poetry. Naomi Shihab Nye wrote a poem titled "Having Forgotten to Bring a Book She Reads the Car Manual Aloud" (2005, p. 46) where she places each little instruction, such as "Do not place coins into the accessory pocket" on a separate line. Using italics, she inserts her own musings about the line "The cup holder should not be used while driving." Students will appreciate the humor, as well as the point that *anything* can become a found poem.

Walk-Through

Here's an example of a found poem for a geography class. I've chosen a passage from Kenneth C. Davis's informational book *Don't Know Much About Planet Earth* (2001). Figure 6.8 presents the excerpt with a found poem based on it. Note that the text

---

Excerpt from an informational book and a found poem based on the passage.	FIGURE	**6.8**

The Nile River in Africa stretches farther than any other river on the planet. Its 4,241 miles (6,825 km) would flow all the way across the United States and halfway back again. You don't have to worry about anyone taking you on a never-ending cruise on the Never-ending Nile, though. The river, like others in Africa, is so hard to travel that no one even went from one end to the other until 1864—even though people had lived along its shores for nearly 7,000 years. (p. 48)

The Nile River in Africa
s t r e t c h e s .... farther
than any other river on the PLANET.
Its 4,241 miles (6, 825 km)
would ......flow....... all the way
across the United States
And halfway back again.

You don't have to *worry*
About anyone taking you

On a .....never-ending...... cruise
On the...... Never-ending....... Nile, though.
The river, like others in Africa,
Is so *HARD* to travel that
No one even went from one end to the other
Until 1864—
Even though people had lived along its shores
nearly 7,000 years.

presents information about the Nile River in a straightforward manner whereas the poem, while presenting the same information, creates a more memorable image of the river for the reader.

Groups may perform their found poems, which will provide entertainment and added reinforcement of the material. Have them compare how different individuals or groups composed variations depending on their choices of presentation.

▶ ▶ ▶   USE OF VOCABULARY GUIDES

Standards Addressed

Math: Students use the language of mathematics to express mathematical ideas precisely.

Science: All students should develop an understanding of the structure of atoms. All students should develop an understanding of the interactions of energy and matter.

English/Language Arts: Students apply a wide range of strategies to comprehend, interpret, evaluate, and appreciate texts. They draw on their . . . knowledge of word meaning and other texts. . . .

Context/Rationale

There is technical and specialized vocabulary relating to every content area; comprehension of text often depends heavily on whether or not students know most of the vocabulary in it, and know how to deal with words they come across that they don't know. One of our jobs as teachers as we plan lessons is to determine how best to handle the vocabulary necessary for the lesson. When do we introduce the words and concepts and teach them directly? When do we show students how to figure out a word's meaning by its context? When do we ask them to look up the words they don't know? What kinds of reading guides can we construct as aids to vocabulary knowledge that will lead to comprehension? How do we encourage interest in the concepts and terms specific to our subject? The answers will vary lesson-to-lesson, text-to-text. We may explain to students our reasons for choosing one method of vocabulary development over another as we instruct and give assignments. In the activity, students use poetry as well as other resources to learn content-related vocabulary and concepts.

Procedure

- Have students select five poems that they particularly like from a book of poetry related to your content area, for example, *Verse and Universe: Poems About Science and Mathematics* (Brown, 1998). (See Part 4 of this chapter for additional suggestions.)

- Instruct them to create a form for each of the five poems with the following headings: Author/Title, Vocabulary, Definitions, and Related Concepts/ Information.

- On the form, ask students to write the titles and authors of the poems and then list the technical or specialized vocabulary that occurs in each poem. Show them a sample form in which you have filled in the first block as a model for students.

- To fill in the definitions and related concepts, tell students that they need to consult the resources they have been using to study the subject of the poem (for example, their textbook, Internet sites, trade books, original documents, and so forth). In the space provided, have them write the definitions they have found for the unknown vocabulary words. Finally, have them write content information related to the poem that is contained in or found in the other resources consulted.

- On the following day, form students in groups of three and have them read one of their poems with expression, telling what it means to them and/or how they feel about it, and teaching their peers the vocabulary and content-related concepts within the poem using their form.

- Have students in the groups take turns. Each person should select a different poem to read from their group of five so different concepts and vocabulary are presented.

Walk-Through

Figure 6.9 provides an example of a vocabulary guide that gives choice to the students, and expects them to go to resources and use both the poems and other texts, such as their textbooks, to complete the guide. Students will then be able to teach each other new words as they talk about why they picked the poems they did, and how they explored the unfamiliar vocabulary they encountered.

Sample vocabulary guide using poetry and other resources to learn content area vocabulary and concepts.	FIGURE	6.9

TITLE AND AUTHOR

"Robert Oppenheimer," 1945 by John Witte

Vocabulary	Definitions
plutonium	
point of criticality	
ionization chambers	
beryllium	
pelonium alphas	

RELATED CONCEPTS/INFORMATION

Oppenheimer was both afraid the atom bomb wouldn't work and afraid it would. Very conflicted.

Scientists had code names for the bomb (topic boat, baby).

The poet uses images of life (toads, rabbit, fetus) to contrast with the destruction of life due to the bomb.

RESOURCES FOR DEFINITIONS AND INFORMATION

[list resource matreials]

P A R T 3

author STUDIES

NAOMI SHIHAB NYE

Use this author's books in **social studies, art, English,** *and other disciplines.*

Figure 6.10 contains a selected bibliography of Naomi Shihab Nye's works.

Naomi Shihab Nye's poetry takes us both around the world and into the human heart. Her Palestinian background shines through in *19 Varieties of Gazelle: Poems of the Middle East* (2002). In her collection, *The Space Between Our Footsteps: Poems and Paintings from the Middle East* (1998), she offers more than 100 textual and visual works of art in an effort to counter what she laments as a woeful lack of knowledge and distorted perceptions based on news stories. "I can't stop believing human beings everywhere hunger for deeper-than-headline news about one another. Poetry and art are some of the best ways this heartfelt 'news' may be exchanged" (p. vii). She edited *Salting the Ocean: 100 Poems by Young Poets* (2000), selecting poems written by students in grades 1 through 12 from her experiences as a "writer-in-the-schools," where she convinced students that "Writing a poem was not separate from living, it was more like *Living Twice*" (p. xiii).

Nye is the compiler of *This Same Sky: A Collection of Poems from Around the World* (1992). In *What Have You Lost?* (1999), she offers poems that she collected over the years about losses of all kinds. She found the question "What have you lost?" to stimulate much writing from students, for "Everyone had lost so much already" (p. xii). (We could adapt that question to apply to practitioners in our disciplines. Think about it—Galileo lost his membership in the Catholic church as well as his freedom on account of his scientific discoveries; Linus Pauling lost the race to discover the structure of DNA. What have the protagonists of classic tragedies lost? And what have we lost as a society over the years and centuries?) *Come with Me: Poems for a Journey* (2000) is a picture book with poems exemplifying the journey motif that is so prevalent in our literature and our lives. *I Feel a Little Jumpy Around You: A Book of Her Poems and His Poems Collected in Pairs* (1996) was co-authored with a poet highlighted later in this chapter, Paul B. Janeczko. It invites readers to reflect on gender issues, among a thousand other things.

Nye is the selector and the author of the introduction of *Is This Forever, or What?: Poems & Paintings from Texas* (2004). One hundred forty Texans contributed; there's Lee Robinson's poem narrated

---

FIGURE 6.10   Selected works by Naomi Shihab Nye.

Nye, N. S. (2005). *Going going.* New York: Greenwillow Books.

Nye, N. S. (2005). *You and yours: Poems.* Rochester, NY: BOA Editions.

Nye, N. S., & Maher, T. (2005). *A maze me: Poems for girls.* New York: Greenwillow Books.

Nye, N. S. (2004). *Air fare: Stories, poems & essays on flight.* Louisville, KY: Sarabande Books.

Nye, N. S. (2004). *Is this forever, or what?: Poems & paintings from Texas.* New York: Greenwillow Books.

Nye, N. S. (2004). *Just one gazelle would be fine with me: Reading and writing in our current world.* Madison, WI: Friends of the CCBC.

Nye, N. S. (2003). *Kindness.* Eugene, OR: Knight Library Press.

Nye, N. S. (2002). *The flag of childhood: Poems from the Middle East.* New York: Aladdin Paperbacks.

Nye, N. S. (2002). *19 varieties of gazelle: Poems of the Middle East.* New York: HarperTempest.

Nye, N. S. (2000). *Come with me: Poems for a journey.* Illus. D. Yaccarino. New York: Greenwillow Books.

Nye, N. S. (2000). *Salting the ocean: 100 poems by young poets.* Illus. A. Bryan. New York: Greenwillow Books.

Nye, N. S. (Selector). (1999). *What have you lost?* Photographs by Michael Nye. New York: Greenwillow Books.

Nye, N. S. (Selector). (1998). *The space between our footsteps: Poems and paintings from the Middle East.* New York: Simon & Schuster.

Nye, N. S., & Janeczko, P. B. (Eds.). (1996). *I feel a little jumpy around you: A book of her poems & his poems collected in pairs.* New York: Simon & Schuster.

Nye, N. S. (1997). *Habibi.* New York: Simon & Schuster.

in the voice of Georgia O'Keeffe; there's Sandra Cisneros's poem addressed to a cloud; there is incredible beauty throughout. She wrote *A Maze Me: Poems for Girls* (2005) remembering her own transition from childhood to adolescence and adulthood. About her middle school years, she recalls:

> *What* do you want to be? people always ask. They don't ask *who* or *how* do you want to be?
>
> I might have said, *amazed forever*. I wanted to be curious interested, interesting, hopeful—and a little bit odd was ok, too. I did *not* know if I wanted to run a bakery, be a postal worker, play a violin or the timpani drum in an orchestra. That part was unknown. (p. 4)

Find more information on Naomi Shihab Nye by visiting www.harperchildrens.com/authorintro. Teaching ideas and lesson plans related to her work can be found at www.pbs.org/now/classroom/poet.html and www.supportlibrary.com/nl/users/keene/web/NaomiShihabNye.html.

PAUL B. JANECZKO

Use this author's books in **science, social studies, art, English**, *and other disciplines.*

Figure 6.11 contains a selected bibliography of Paul B. Janeczko's works.

The word that comes to mind when I think of Paul Janeczko is *versatility*. We content area teachers can use him in so many ways. His *Dirty Laundry Pile: Poems in Different Voices* (2001) includes only poems that have an object or animal as a narrator. He explains in his introduction:

> In these persona or mask poems, as they are called, the poets let their imaginations fly and feel what it might be like to be a mosquito, a crayon, a kite, a turtle. . . . As you read these poems, if you find yourself wondering what it would feel like to be a caterpillar, a soccer ball, or a honeybee, grab a pencil and let your imagination fly in a poem. (unpaged)

This book could be a stepping stone to Diane Siebert's geography poems, or Paul Fleischman's insect and bird poems, where objects and animals are also the narrators.

Janeczko's works may enhance our curricular units. For example, *Home on the Range: Cowboy Poetry* (1997) is an anthology that offers an aesthetic experience to anyone studying the American Westward Movement. Text and pictures featuring buffalo, coyote, barn cats, bear, awesome weather, tough and talented women, trails with memories, and campfire meals make the western adventure come alive. Use *That Sweet Diamond* (1998) to introduce a physical education unit on baseball. In *Seeing the Blue Between: Advice and Inspiration for Young Poets* (2002),

---

Selected works by Paul B. Janeczko.   FIGURE | 6.11

Janeczko, P. B. (Ed.). (2007). *Hey, you!* New York: HarperCollins.

Janeczko, P. B., & Lewis, J. P. (2007). *Birds on a wire, or a jewel tray of stars.* Illus. G. Lippincott. Honesdale, PA: Wordsong.

Janeczko, P. B. (2005). *A kick in the head: An everyday guide to poetic forms.* Illus. C. Raschka. Cambridge, MA: Candlewood Press.

Janeczko, P. B. (2004). *How to write haiku and other short poems.* New York: Scholastic.

Janeczko, P. B. (2004). *Worlds afire.* Cambridge, MA: Candlewick Press.

Janeczko, P. B., & LaReau, J. (2004). *Top secret: A handbook of codes, ciphers, and secret writing.* Cambridge, MA: Candlewick Press.

Janeczko, P. B. (2003). *Blushing: Expressions of love in poems and letters.* New York: Orchard/Scholastic.

Janeczko, P. B. (2003). *Good for a laugh: A guide to writing amusing, clever, and downright funny poems.* New York: Scholastic.

Janeczko, P. B. (2003). *Opening a door: Reading poetry in the middle school classroom.* New York: Scholastic.

Janeczko, P. B. (2002). *Seeing the blue between: Advice and inspiration for young poets.* Cambridge, MA: Candlewick Press.

Janeczko, P. B. (Selector). (2001). *Dirty laundry pile: Poems in different voices.* Illus. M. Sweet. New York: HarperCollins.

Janeczko, P. B. (Selector). (2001). *A poke in the I: A collection of concrete poems.* Illus. C. Raschka. Cambridge, MA: Candlewick Press.

Janeczko, P. B. (2001). *Writing funny bone poems.* Jefferson City, MO: Scholastic.

Janeczko, P. B. (Compiler). (1997). *Home on the range: Cowboy poetry.* Illus. B. Fuchs. New York: Dial Books.

Janeczko, P. B. (Selector). (1983). *Poetspeak: In their work, about their work.* Scarsdale, NY: Bradbury Press.

Lewis, J. P., Janeczko, P. B., & Tusa, T. (2006). *Wing nuts: Screwy haiku.* New York: Little, Brown and Company.

he has compiled letters to readers along with examples of poetry from more than 30 contemporary poets. His earlier work, *Poetspeak: In Their Work, About Their Work* (1983), combines poems with comments reflecting on them by 62 active artists. Students will truly get expert instruction about how to create poetry from these two books.

Then there's *A Poke in the I: A Collection of Concrete Poems* (2001). Although most poetry is meant to be read aloud, concrete poetry can be understood only when the visual aspects are comprehended. Janeczko explains in his introductory note, "The arrangement of letters or words on the page, the typefaces chosen, and the way space is used, add meaning to the poem beyond that contained in the actual words" (p. 1). He calls the poems playful, and indeed they are. They're especially good to use with our visual and spatial learners. And, in *Blushing: Expressions of Love in Poems & Letters* (2003), he uses love letters of famous people (which he says feel like the first drafts of poems) to introduce his sections of poems that are grouped by the themes from beginning love, to lost and remembered loves.

Janeczko explores new territory in his novel in verse, *Worlds Afire* (2004). It tells the story of a Hartford, Connecticut, circus fire in 1944 that claimed the lives of 167 people. Each poem is narrated by a person, such as the gorilla attendant, a detective, a sideshow fan, a child, a firefighter, the man accused of starting the fire, a nurse.

Janeczko shares his poetry-writing skills and advice with fledgling poets. In *How to Write Haiku and Other Short Poems* (2004), he first warns new writers not to think that writing short poems is easy. "Writing a good short poem is challenging because it uses only a handful of words" (p. 2). But he gives lots of tips and examples and encouragement throughout the rest of the chapters. *A Kick in the Head: An Everyday Guide to Poetic Forms* (2005)

contains examples and explanations of many types of poetry, including the couplet, ballad, limerick, sonnet, ode, elegy, epitaph, and cinquain.

Paul B. Janeczko's work transcends discipline boundaries and age ranges. He truly has something for everybody.

Visit Janeczko's website, www.pauljaneczko.com, to find out about what he's writing now, what he has to say about the writing process, where he's traveling, and more. The links to other sites provide lesson plans and instructional suggestions dealing with his work. There is also much information at www.harpercollins.com/authors/17103/Paul_B_Janeczko/index.aspx.

BILLY COLLINS

*Use this author's books in **English** and other disciplines.*

Figure 6.12 contains a selected bibliography of Billy Collins's works.

One might think that a poet laureate of the United States would be a person from whom poetry flowed easily, who showed early talent and brilliance. Billy Collins, who held that esteemed position from 2001 to 2003, would say that was not always so. He admitted in a speech at his alma mater, the College of the Holy Cross, that his freshman year had come to an appalling end, with a D and an F among his grades. "You could have gotten very good odds on me as a future commencement speaker" (Collins, 2002). But he persisted, and eventually succeeded. He uses the metaphor of TV cartoon character Lisa Simpson's saxophone to represent finding one's passion and persisting with it, despite all odds and obstacles:

> My saxophone was poetry. I began playing it in high school, and I'm still playing it. For years,

---

| FIGURE | 6.12 | Selected works by Billy Collins. |

Collins, B. (Ed.). (2006). *The best American poetry: 2006.* Series editor D. Lehman. New York: Scribner Poetry.

Collins, B. (2005). *180 more: Extraordinary poems for every day.* New York: Random House Trade Paperbacks.

Collins, B. (2005). *The trouble with poetry and other poems.* New York: Random House.

Collins, B., & Kneen, M. (2004). *Daddy's little boy.* New York: HarperCollins.

Collins, B. (2003). *Nine horses: Poems.* New York: Random House.

Collins, B. (2003). *Picnic, lightning.* Pittsburgh: University of Pittsburgh Press.

Collins, B. (Ed.). (2003). *Poetry 180: A turning back to poetry.* New York: Random House Trade Paperbacks.

Collins, B. (2003). *Voyage.* Washington, DC: Center for the Book.

Collins, B. (2001). *Sailing alone around the room: New and selected poems.* New York: Random House.

Collins, B. (1995). *The art of drowning.* Pittsburgh: University of Pittsburgh Press.

people would cover their ears when they heard me—and for good reason. My poetry was shamelessly imitative, heartless, humorless, merely clever at best. Why I continued to write as I stood in a driving blizzard of rejection slips I don't know. But I did. . . . So, I stand before you here— a model of grim persistence.

So, our students, perhaps especially those who haven't met with much academic success lately, have been given two good role models: Lisa Simpson and Billy Collins himself.

Billy Collins has given high school teachers and students a gift in his Poetry 180 website (www.loc.gov/poetry/180) and the book by the same title (2003). He explains, "High school is the focus of my program because all too often it is the place where poetry goes to die" (2003, p. xvii). To counteract this, he has chosen enough poems for every day of a school year, poems that are clear enough to be understood without being formally studied. He is convinced that ". . . for every nonreader of poetry there is a poem waiting to reconnect them to poetry. If a student hears a poem every day, the odds of he or she encountering the right poem increases dramatically" (p. xxii).

Once students have gotten in the habit of reading a poem or two a day, "Like pills, for the head and the heart" (p. xxiii), they'll probably want to read more poetry by Collins himself. He has several collections to oblige, including *Nine Horses* (2003), *Sailing Alone Around the Room* (2002), and *The Art of Drowning* (1995).

Readers can get to all the poems in Poetry 180, as well as Collins's recommendations for how to read poetry, by going to www.loc.gov/poetry/180. More information on the poet can be found at www.poets.org/poet/php/prmPID/278 and at www.poemhunter.com/billy-collins/poems/. Teaching ideas relating to his poetry are offered at www.randomhouse.com/highschool/catalog/display.pperl?9780812968873&view=tg.

JOSEPH BRUCHAC

Use this author's books in **physical education, social studies, science, English,** *and other disciplines.*

Figure 6.13 contains a selected bibliography of Joseph Bruchac's works.

Imagine a teacher in September greeting her new students with "In this season when leaves begin to turn color . . ." and the rest of the poem "Moose Calling Moon" (unpaged) from Joseph Bruchac and Jonathan London's collection *Thirteen Moons on a Turtle's Back* (1992). During the next lunar cycle, she recites the poem from the 10th moon, "Moon of

Selected works by Joseph Bruchac.   FIGURE 6.13

Bruchac, J. (2006). *Code Talker: A novel about the Navajo marines of World War II.* New York: Dial Books.

Bruchac, J. (2006). *Geronimo.* New York: Scholastic.

Bruchac, J. (2006). *Jim Thorpe: Original all-American.* New York: Dial Books.

Bruchac, J. (2003). *Above the line: New poems.* Albuquerque, NM: West End Press.

Bruchac, J. (2003). *Pocahontas.* New York: Harcourt.

Bruchac, J. (2002). *Navajo long walk: The tragic story of a proud people's forced march from their home.* Illus. S. Begay. Washington, DC: National Geographic Society.

Bruchac, J. (2000). *Pushing up the sky: Seven Native American plays for children.* New York: Dial Books for Young Readers.

Bruchac, J. (2000). *Sacajawea.* New York: Scholastic.

Bruchac, J. (1999). *No borders: New poems.* Duluth, MN: Holy Cow! Press.

Bruchac, J. (1998). *Earth under Sky Bear's feet: Native American poems from the land.* Illus. T. Locker. New York: Putnam & Grosset Group.

Bruchac, J. (1997). *Lasting echoes: An oral history of Native American people.* Illus. P. Morin. New York: Silver Whistle/Harcourt Brace.

Bruchac, J. (1997). *Tell me a tale: A book about storytelling.* New York: Harcourt Brace.

Bruchac, J. (1996). *The circle of thanks: Native American poems and songs of thanksgiving.* Illus. M. Jacob. Mahwah, NJ: BridgeWater Books.

Bruchac, J. (1996). *Four ancestors: Stories, songs, and poems from Native North America.* Illus. S. S. Burrus et al. Mahwah, NJ: BridgeWater Books.

Bruchac, J., & London, J. (1992). *Thirteen moons on a turtle's back: A Native American book of moons.* Illus. T. Locker. New York: Philomel.

Caduto, M. J., & Bruchac, J. (1997). *Keepers of the earth: Native American stories and environmental activities for children.* Illus. J. K. Fadden. Golden, CO: Fulcrum.

Caduto, M. J., & Bruchac, J. (1994). *Native American stories and nocturnal activities for children.* Illus. D. K. Fadden. Golden, CO: Fulcrum.

Falling Leaves." Students are eager to see what's coming next, so she offers a sign-up sheet for students who want to participate in the poetry reading for the rest of the year. The children study the illustrations by Thomas Locker, and they want to learn more about the tribes whose legends the poems are based on. **Science, art, social studies,** and **language arts** have come together for this class.

Joseph Bruchac is of Abenaki and Slovak descent, and his poetry appeals to all ages and offers opportunity for many curricular connections. *Earth Under Sky Bear's Feet: Native American Poems from the Land* (1998) is a collection of poems about the Big Dipper, based on various Native American cultures. Bruchac tells about the geographic regions of the tribes where the folktales originated. *The Circle of Thanks: Native American Poems and Songs of Thanksgiving* (1996) contains 14 original poems based on Native American prayers and songs, showing their gratitude for the beauty of creation and the natural resources they enjoy. *Four Ancestors: Stories, Songs, and Poems from Native North America* (1996) celebrates the elements of fire, air, earth, and water. As usual, Bruchac bases his artistic creations on traditions from numerous tribes. He has several other collections (listed in Figure 6.13) and his poems can be found in anthologies collected by others, as well.

Joseph Bruchac could have been highlighted in any chapter of this book, since his work represents many genres. If you're looking for biography, his *Jim Thorpe: Original All-American* (2006) is a good place to begin. He bases several novels on the lives of real people, such as *Geronimo* (2006), *Sacajawea* (2000), and *Pocahontas* (2003). He provides historical fiction, as in *Code Talker: A Novel About the Navajo Marines of World War II* (2006). Bruchac is known as a storyteller, and many of his works are collections of Native American tales (see Figure 6.13). He also has books in the "how-to" category, co-written with M. Caduto, including *Keepers of the Earth: Native American Stories and Environmental Activities for Children* (1997), and *Native American Stories and Nocturnal Activities for Children* (1994). These books are filled with ideas **science** teachers could use. **English** teachers will appreciate the advice he gives in *Tell Me a Tale: A Book About Storytelling* (1997), while **social studies** teachers may teach about constructing oral histories through Bruchac's *Lasting Echoes: An Oral History of Native American People* (1997). Bruchac has numerous nonfiction books about various aspects of Native American **history.**

Joseph Bruchac's homepage, www.joseph-bruchac.com, offers biographical material on the author as well as suggestions for using his books and links to other resources. Lesson plans relating to his texts can be found at www.abbemuseum.org/teacher_resources.html and www.fulcrum-books.com/contributorinfo.cfm?contribID=4590.

P A R T   4

A N N O T A T E D **books and booktalks**

CODE: E = Elementary, **I** = Intermediate, **M** = Middle school, **H** = High School

The following annotations will vary in format. Most will be annotations I wrote directed at a teacher audience. Others will be excerpts from my students' reader response logs. You may adapt any of the annotations to make the booktalk just right for your audience and appropriately connected to your curricular topics.

ART

Angelou, M. (1993). *Life Doesn't Frighten Me.* **Paintings by Jean-Michel Basquiat, edited by Sara Jane Boyers.** New York: Stewart, Tabori & Chang. **(E, I, M, H)**

Such a simple idea, but a powerful one. The editor has combined the lines of Maya Angelou's poem, "Life Doesn't Frighten Me," with paintings by Basquiat. Every page, which uses a repetitive format listing the many things that cannot frighten her, offers much to ponder. Biographies of the poet and the artist follow the poem. After discussing their responses to this newly arranged creation, students could use this book as a model, as they choose a favorite or personally meaningful poem and search for appropriate artwork to match it. Or they could supply their own artistic interpretations of the lines in a new book. (See Sandburg & Rand entry in math section below for another model.) Consider using small groups to design different layouts for the pages of the same poem, and have them use different artwork to show how new meanings of the text can be evoked or constructed stimulated by the varied illustrations.

Brenner, B. (Selector). (2000). *Voices: Poetry and Art from Around the World.* New York: National Geographic. (M, H)

As I read this book, I felt like I was taking a voyage around the world. So I was not surprised when I read the "Note from the Author, where Barbara Brenner described her process of selecting material for the book as a "real voyage of discovery for me" (p. 7). She extends the metaphor by speaking of a treasure map, a direction for her travels, surprises, new appreciations. The book is divided into sections categorized by the continents, so students get a sense of **geography** as well as contrasts in artistic styles of the visuals and the poems from around the world. Students may consider the similarities and differences between the artistic styles of the different cultures, countries, or regions as they explore this book.

Rochelle, B. (Selector). (2001). *Words with Wings: A Treasury of African-American Poetry and Art.* (I, M, H)

I like the poetic definition of poetry that Belinda Rochelle offers: "Poems are word wings, wings made out of words." She follows it with instructions and an invitation I'd like our students to hear: "But we must help give the poems and art their wings by bringing to them our own experiences and histories, and our willingness to let them take us somewhere new" (Introduction, unpaged). There's no better starting place to do that than with the paired poems and paintings in this awesome book. As mentioned in connection with the previous book, students may pair a favorite poem with artwork of their choice.

ENGLISH/LANGUAGE ARTS

Aquado, B., & Newirth, R. (2003). *Paint Me Like I Am: Teen Poems from WritersCorps.* New York: HarperTempest. (M, H)

The organization WritersCorps has flourished for over a decade, offering teenagers space, instruction, and encouragement to express themselves through creative writing. This collection of poems might inspire your own students, or give them an opportunity to respond to, perhaps critique, work by their peers that expresses personal struggles and longings, reflections on identity and on writing, emotions and questions. There's a foreword by Nikki Giovanni, written, appropriately, in verse. You might use this book to encourage your students before a class slam poetry competition (see Part 2 of this chapter).

Bowman, C. (Ed.). (2003). *Word of Mouth: Poems Featured on NPR's All Things Considered.* New York: Random House, Vintage. (M, H)

Since 1995, Catherine Bowman has featured and introduced poets to million of listeners on the title show. Why has this segment been so popular? Bowman uses data collected from responders to answer: "Listeners of NPR have told me over and over that hearing poems read out loud offered a way into poetry they had not discovered through simply reading; they discovered new ways to experience the poem. To take the poem off the page and into the airwaves gives us a way to participate in the physicality of the poem" (p. xiv). Though this book represents the poems' return to the page, we need not keep them there. Students can choose their favorites (mine is "Wedding Cake," by Naomi Shihab Nye, p. 85) and perform them at an open mic lunchtime activity, or even in class during a slam competition as discussed in Part 2 of this chapter.

Bryan, A. (1997). *Ashley Bryan's ABC of African American Poetry.* New York: Atheneum. (E, I, M, H)

This book could be the start of an ambitious research project for your class. Bryan explains in his Foreword that he decided to use only lines from poems that inspired images for his artwork, rather than include entire poems. But he sets forth a challenge:

> You may find African American poets you know in this collection and others you might like to get to know. The acknowledgments list sources for all of the poems. Some poems are complete, others are fragments. I hope you will seek out the whole poems and go on to discover more work of these African American artists. (p. x)

Since there are 26 excerpts from 26 poets' work, each student could pick one person to follow up, or teams of two could research two poets together. When the research and new favorite poems are shared, the overall knowledge of the whole class will increase tremendously. Maybe the newly found treasure could be shared with the whole school as well as with families and the community.

Fields, T. (2002). *After the Death of Anna Gonzales.* New York: Henry Holt and Company. (M, H)

This book is easy to read in some ways—quick, not many words on a page, not hard to comprehend. But emotionally, it's difficult, because the poems are narrated by people in a school the day after a young girl's suicide—teachers, students, the principal, and the custodian. They wonder why; they wonder if there was something they could have done differently; they find it, as will readers, hard to comprehend. English teachers may use these poems to teach perspective, as well as to help students reflect on values, and **health** teachers could include this book in a unit on suicide.

Fletcher, R. (2005). *A Writing Kind of Day: Poems for Young Poets.* Illus. A. Ward. Honesdale, PA: Wordsong. **(E, I, M, H)**

There's no Introduction, no Author's Note at the end. Nor does there need to be; the poems take the reader through a day in the life of a poet-narrator, who writes about his three-month-old bald sister using the earth as a metaphor (for the most interesting parts of the face you have to look at the equator) and portrays his little brother as a human wrecking ball; he gives advice about writer's block and provides a poetry recipe; he ends with "A Writing Kind of Night" (p. 32). Your students might compose their way through a day in their lives; Ralph Fletcher has taught them how. See the Intertextuality strategy in Part 2 of this chapter for ideas about how to get your students started with their own day-in-the-life poem.

Fletcher, R. (2002). *Poetry Matters: Writing a Poem from the Inside Out.* New York: HarperCollins. (I, M)

The poet shares his own passion for the genre as well as a lot of advice to help your students gain skill and confidence in reading and writing poetry. There are several interviews with popular poets, and an Annotated Bibliography of recommended poetry books to use as inspiration and models. In Fletcher's words, "In these books you'll find plenty of poems you can apprentice yourself to" (p. 135). Fletcher himself is a good master to apprentice ourselves to.

Frost, H. (2003). *Keesha's House.* New York: Frances Foster Books. (M, H)

This is an English teacher's dream—a modern-day, engaging, realistic story of homeless teens (or at least they would have been if they hadn't found the house of the title), written in sestinas and sonnets. The poetry types are explained briefly and clearly by the author at the end. I'd let students explore the story that unfolds as the multiple narrators have their say, then ask them to investigate the form of the poems and maybe try some additions of their own. Afterward, this book could be a bridge to reading some of the classic sonnets and sestinas that

have been written through the ages. I can hear a teacher as students read Shakespeare's poetry saying, "Remember *Keesha's House?*" This would be a good book to use with the Odes strategy described in Part 2. Students could write an ode to one of the characters, or to the house itself, or to the principles and values embodied in the story.

Goldstein, B. S. (Selector). (1992). *Inner Chimes: Poems on Poetry.* Illus. J. B. Zalben. Honesdale, PA: Boyds Mill/Wordsong. **(E, I, M)**

Sit back and let the poets teach your students about creating poetry when you offer this book. Within the poems, advice is given on how to get ideas, how to think of images and metaphors, how to express feelings, all without sounding a bit preachy! Readers will experience the ultimate in authentic learning as they read these poems celebrating poetry in all its richness and variation.

Harley, A. (2000). *Fly with Poetry: An ABC of Poetry.* Honesdale, PA: Boyds Mills. **(I, M, H)**

I accepted the title's invitation to fly, and traveled through a world of vocabulary, where familiar terms including *cinquain, haiku, quatrain, villanelle,* and *internal rhyme* were defined, along with less familiar ones like *kyrielle, rhopalic verse, uta, triolet,* and *ghazal* to make the flight more challenging. A poem exemplifying each highlighted technique or form is provided. The author gives advice on how to use this book:

> An ideal way to use this book is to savor the playfulness of the poems, encourage children to interact with the ideas, and discuss how the forms shape the reader's experience. Each poem is full of carefully-made choices which begin with the poem and continue with the reader. . . . It is best not to "back into" a poem by discussing a form before reading the poem. The delight is in the discovery. . . . (Introduction, unpaged)

Heller, R. (1989). *Many Luscious Lollipops: A Book About Adjectives.* New York: Scholastic. (E, I, M, H)

Do you remember having to learn the parts of speech? You might recall worksheets, tests, sentences constructed for the sole purpose of having you diagram them. Students taught this way often don't appreciate the beauty of the structure of language, of the infinite possibilities in terms of sentence construction. An antidote to the lessons of drudgery may be found in Ruth Heller's series of poems celebrating the parts of speech. Learning about adjectives through *Many Luscious Lollipops* is painless as rhythm, pictures, and examples combine on the colorfully illustrated pages. The book is filled with vocabulary terms, all used in context. Other titles in the series, all published by Scholastic, follow:

Fantastic! Wow! And Unreal!: A book About Interjections and Conjunctions (1998)

Mine, All Mine: A Book About Pronouns (1997)

Behind the Mask: A Book About Prepositions (1995)

Up, Up and Away: A Book About Adverbs (1991)

Merry-Go-Round: A Book About Nouns (1990)

A Cache of Jewels: And Other Collective Nouns (1989)

Kites Sail High: A Book About Verbs (1988)

Housden, R. (2004). *Ten Poems to Last a Lifetime.* New York: Harmony Books. **(M, H)**

Most people who say they don't like poetry will give a reason somehow connected to fear. They're afraid it's too hard; they might get laughed at if they don't understand the hidden meanings; they never could get those test questions on symbolism and metaphor and simile right. Something seems to happen to readers in school, particularly English class, that takes away self-confidence and replaces it with an aversion to the poetic form. What I love about this book is that Housden presents a poem he thinks is worth keeping for your whole life, then spends a chapter talking about it in a relaxed manner. It isn't preachy, telling the reader what the poem is supposed to be saying. Rather, Housden muses, and asks his own questions. After Billy Collins's "My Life," he wonders:

> How does he do this? I mean, write about trifles, the little moments of any ordinary day, a wry, half-smile flickering all the way through the poem, and yet at the same time manage to address something so wonderful? (p. 21)

Housden doesn't hammer us with lessons, or expect any critical analysis from us. Instead, he takes us along the journey of his reading and response:

> This poem, "My Life," winds me effortlessly between its banks like a river from beginning to end, no hard knocks, no rapids, all flow and ease; yet by the time I come out at the other end something has happened; I feel different, and I don't quite know why. (p. 22)

Now that I've read the poems and Housden's reflections, I'm eager to share what happened to me as I brought my life experiences to each poem. I don't feel scared to tell, because his modeling has assured me that there is no teacher's edition waiting to tell

me that I am wrong. I want my students to feel like that, too.

Hovey, K. (2000). *Arachne Speaks.* Illus. B. Drawson. New York: Margaret K. McElderry Books. **(I, M, H)**

A spider narrator speaking to a spider audience, exhorting them to unravel their web of dreams, and weave a tapestry that will cover the earth—hmm, that's different. I was lured into this spider's web, entranced by the mythological tale of Arachne and her challenge to proud Athena. The poem becomes a dialogue, with Athena's words in brown. There's plenty of suspense, violence, imagination, and beauty for all. This great resource may be read aloud as you teach a mythology unit, or weave mythological stories throughout your school year.

Livingston, M. C. (1991). *Poem-Making: Ways to Begin Writing Poetry.* New York: HarperCollins. **(I, M, H)**

The teacher voice in this handbook has credibility because it is combined with the poet voice. Myra Cohn Livingston uses examples from her own and others' poetry to exemplify the points she makes and advice she gives about sound and rhyme, rhythm and metrics, figures of speech, and various forms of poetry. She offers snippets from her own experiences to show where she gets ideas, how she lives the life of a writer.

Medina, T. (2002). *Love to Langston.* Illus. R. G. Christie. New York: Lee & Low Books. **(I, M, H)**

Why would the author title his biography of Langston Hughes *Love to Langston*? Maybe because when Tony Medina was a boy, he encountered Hughes's *Selected Poems*, and reacted to the cover photo of Hughes sitting in front of his typewriter. "It was the first brown face I had ever seen looking out at me from the cover of a book—a face that reminded me of *my* face and the faces of my family" (Introduction, unpaged). The poems inside also reminded him of his neighborhood, his people, his music. Now he wants to pass his love along: "This is the Langston I wish for you to meet in this book, which represents one Harlem poet's homage to another" (Introduction, unpaged).

Though I know Langston Hughes from my own reading of his poems and other biographies, I did meet Tony Medina's Langston through these biographical poems. It's a unique interpretation of a life. The Notes at the end give further information about the events memorialized in each poem. Students may enjoy matching these poems with some of Hughes's own. Maybe they'll add their own voice as further harmony to the jazz. This poem would be good to use with the Biopoem strategy described in Part 2 of this chapter.

ENG/LA

Nelson, M. (2005). *A Wreath for Emmett Till.* Illus. P. Lardy. Boston: Houghton Mifflin. **(M, H)**

This certainly could also be used to advantage in **social studies** classes, since the lynching of Emmett Till at age 14 and the subsequent trial that freed his killers was one of the sparks that ignited the Civil Rights Movement. But I've given it here to English teachers, because it's written as a crown of sonnets, ". . . a sequence of interlinked sonnets in which the last line of one becomes the first line, sometimes slightly altered, of the next" (unpaged). Nelson adds a 15th sonnet made up of the opening lines of the 14 others, making it a *heroic crown of sonnets.* She chose this tight form deliberately:

> The strict form became a kind of insulation, a way of protecting myself from the intense pain of the subject matter, and a way to allow the Muse to determine what the poem would say. I wrote this poem with my heart in my mouth and tears in my eyes, breathless with anticipation and surprise. (unpaged)

At the end is a summary of the Emmett Till trial, followed by notes on each sonnet, and finally the Artist's Note, which is very informative about the use of color, shape, and images. I'll provide just a taste:

> I call the second part "the mourning." In this section, I used earthy mineral colors for loss. The brown background represents earth and death, but also transformation into new life, new meaning.
>
> In contrast to the other parts, the rectangle was used throughout this second section: it is a coffin when placed horizontally, an evocation of the World Trade Center when tilted vertically. Flowers are placed in these dark settings, for hope and transcendence. The double-page spread depicts a number of coffins, one of which holds the image of Emmett Till. This stands as an icon of all anonymous victims. (unpaged)

I'd use this book as my class studies Shakespeare's sonnets, to help the students see that the sonnet form is alive and well in the twenty-first century.

Niven, P. (2003). *Carl Sandburg: Adventures of a Poet.* (with Poems and Prose by Carl Sandburg). Illus. M. Nadel. New York: Harcourt. **(I, M, H)**

This book combines genres. It is a biography of the Poet of the People, yet includes samples of Sandburg's works to exemplify the categories Niven has employed, so we get poems, a letter written to President Harry Truman, an excerpt from a piece of journalism, a story. A little bit of everything, and a lot of enjoyment and learning. This book would be

appropriate for use with the In-Depth Exploration of a Poet strategy described in Part 2 of this chapter.

Paschen, E., & Mosby, R. P. (2001). *Poetry Speaks.* Naperville, IL: Sourcebooks MediaFusion. **(H)**

This is a heavy book, in many ways. It includes biographical information on dozens of modern poets as well as commentary written by poets practicing the craft today. For example, we find out what Sonia Sanchez has to say about Gwendolyn Brooks, and read Robert Pinsky's reflections on William Carlos Williams, Seamus Heaney on William Butler Yeats, Billy Collins on Ogden Nash, Anne Stevenson on Sylvia Plath. There are three audio CD-ROMs that provide poems read by their creators. Our students will better understand that the poems they read in anthologies had or have real voices behind them, real lives with a context and with riches that they transformed by using words.

Shapiro, K. J. (2003). *Because I Could Not Stop My Bike: And Other Poems.* Illus. M. Faulkner. Watertown, MA: Charlesbridge. **(I, M, H)**

You may teach students the term *intertextuality,* or you may call it "Steal a Structure," as your classes play with classic poems on their way to creating their own (see Part 2 of this chapter). Shapiro has transformed Joyce Kilmer's "Trees," Andrew Marvell's "To His Coy Mistress," William Blake's "A Poison Tree," Elizabeth Barrett Browning's "How Do I Love Thee?" and several poems of Shakespeare into humorous rhymes about everyday relationships. In order to do this trick, students will need to really hear the rhythm, rhyme, and structure of the original verse. They'll be searching through collections of Emily Dickinson, Edgar Allan Poe, and others Shapiro spun off of, so that they'll be able to laugh as they borrow structures to provide future volumes of poetry like this.

Shakespeare, W. (2001). *To Sleep: Perchance to Dream: A Child's Book of Rhymes.* Illus. J. Mayhew. New York: Scholastic. **(E, I, M, H)**

I like to show high school and college students this illustrated version with its small quotes from *Hamlet, As You Like It, The Tempest, A Midsummer Night's Dream, The Merchant of Venice,* and other plays to demystify what too many think are works that are just too hard, too frightening, meant for students more advanced or sophisticated than they. Then I ask them to choose other quotes from Shakespeare's works that friends might enjoy and understand, or that would lend themselves to illustration. They pay close attention to the language and look at the texts in a new light when they become editors, making decisions for new purposes.

Shakespeare, W. (1998). *Shakespeare in Love: The Love Poetry of William Shakespeare.* Compilation. New York: Miramax Books/Hyperion. **(H)**

You can go to the movies with this book. The compilers have arranged selected sonnets, poetic excerpts from several plays, lines from the hit movie *Shakespeare in Love*, and photos from the movie in a pleasing way. I found myself reading out loud. I have a shelf of my classroom library devoted to resources relating to Shakespeare, and this book is among them. Students may use it as a model as they create their own syntheses of their favorite quotes and poems from the Bard.

von Ziegesar, C. (2000). *SLAM.* **Foreword by Tori Amos.** New York: Alloy Books. **(M, H)**

This book is hard to classify, hard to describe. It seems to be shouting at me, from the open mouth depicted on the cover to the chapter titles in huge font to the varied visuals alongside, or running through, the poetry. The Introduction gives a brief history of the genre, from the bards of ancient Greece to the Beat poets of the 1950s ranting, to dancing to poetry in the '60s and '70s. Performance poetry has been strong ever since. In addition to many poems, there's advice in this book about how to conduct a slam that you can use in conjunction with the strategy described in Part 2 of this chapter. Your classroom can be converted to a very active, engaging stage.

Willard, N. (1981). *A Visit to William Blake's Inn: Poems for Innocent and Experienced Travelers.* **Illus. A. and M. Provensen.** New York: Harcourt Brace. **(I, M, H)**

Winner of the Newbery Medal and a Caldecott Honor. Not a bad combination. Nancy Willard tells about her own introduction to the poetry of William Blake when she was seven and asked for a story about tigers, to which her babysitter recited "Tyger, Tyger, burning bright...." This book may introduce and enhance our lessons on Blake and his poetry. The more your students learn about the poet and his works, the more connections they'll make and allusions they'll catch.

Woodson, J. (2003). *Locomotion.* New York: G. P. Putnam's Sons. **(I, M)**

Do you hope that what and how you teach will make a difference in the life of a child? Foster child Lonnie uses the poetry forms his teacher introduces, such as haiku, sonnet, occasional poem, and epistle poem, to work out his grief over the death of his parents and his separation from his little sister. His teacher gives him the gift of encouragement,

telling him "You have a poet's heart" (p. 87). After your students read this book, consider asking them to choose important events from their lives and express their responses to them using one of the poetic forms.

LANGUAGES AND CULTURE

Adedjouma, D. (Ed.). (1996). *The Palm of My Heart: Poetry by African American Children.* **Illus. G. Christie.** New York: Lee & Low Books. **(E, I, M, H)**

Why put together a book of children's writing? The editor explains that these poems came from a series of writing workshops with children from the Inner City Youth League and the African-American Academy for Accelerated Learning. As a student herself, she experienced memorable visits from writers, storytellers, and performers. "Each taught me that art was not just a luxury for the very few, but a tool of survival for many. Each taught me that creativity could and **should** be applied equally to math and science, English and social studies" (Editor's Note, unpaged). That's a good reason for us to put together a book of our students' writing relating to their own backgrounds and cultures, and they'll gain inspiration and confidence by first exploring the texts by students and the very cool paintings by Gregory Christie in this book. **Social studies** teachers may also use this book as they raise social justice issues and teach concepts related to perceptions of and celebrations of cultures. In the Introduction, poet Lucille Clifton explains that when she was growing up, "Black" was fighting language, and associated by the world around her with everything negative. She rejoices in this treasury of poems, starting with the word *Black*, for "Here dark is equated with wonderful and Black with Joy!" (unpaged).

Agard, J., & Nichols, G. (Eds.). (2003). *Under the Moon and Over the Sea: A Collection of Caribbean Poems.* Cambridge, MA: Candlewick Press. **(E, I, M)**

This book offers not a flavor of *the* Caribbean culture, but rather the flavor of many aspects of life in the Caribbean in the past and present. This is accomplished partly by the division of the 50-plus poems into five sections, each illustrated by a different artist: Cathie Felsted, Jane Ray, Christopher Corr, Satoshi Kitamura, and Sara Fanelli. Reading the poems, I learned of various folktales, natural phenomena, games, songs, and Caribbean proverbs. I felt like I had visited a very beautiful place and learned about the people, animals, and island life of the Caribbean.

Begay, S. (1995). *Navajo: Visions and Voices Across the Mesa.* New York: Scholastic. **(I, M, H)**

The Introduction tells about the author's childhood in the 1950s and '60s; he was forced to go to government boarding schools, where his mouth was washed out with soap if he spoke his native language and he was not allowed to see his parents; then the social movements occurred that allowed him to live in his own culture again. His book is an attempt to "... reach out to people in the mainstream of society who have no idea what it means to be an Indian, a Navajo, a *Dinéh* child" (p. 6). The poems can be used in **social studies** because they give a historical perspective, and the feel for the spiritual and nature-filled life of the families. The paintings drew me right in, making me feel like I could get to know these people and places.

Brodsky, B. (2003). *Buffalo.* New York: Marshall Cavendish. **(M, H)**

The author has selected Native American Song-poems to go with her text and her original paintings. She explains how early images were made in the Paleolithic period, and tells of Native Americans' relationship to the buffalo as far back as 4,000 years ago. Much information is given about the spiritual lives of various tribes, as well as details about how the buffalo were hunted and used to sustain life. Native American **art** is also explored, and the book ends with an original poem by Brodsky.

Carlson, L. M. (2005). *Red Hot Salsa: Bilingual Poems on Being Young and Latino in the United States.* New York: Henry Holt and Company. **(M, H)**

This book will help students tremendously in seeing the value of being bilingual. Readers who know just one language (Spanish or English) will be able to see they're missing something in these poems that combine the two languages in many ways. They will be inspired to get every word, every image, every bit of dialogue and emotion. The poems are grouped in categories having to do with identity, love, neighborhoods, family, and finally, victory.

Carlson, L. M. (Ed.). (1994). *Cool Salsa: Bilingual Poems on Growing Up Latino in the United States.* New York: Ballantine Books. **(M, H)**

Some poems are translated from English to Spanish, some from Spanish to English. Some are a combination of both languages—Spanglish—in one poem. All are full of emotion and packed with rich meanings. They express struggle, celebration, wonder, relationships. English learners will be able to identify with the stories; those whose first language is English will vicariously experience what it's like to belong to more than one culture. Students in a

Spanish class may go back and forth between the translated poems, learning vocabulary while marveling at the structure of language.

DeDonato, C. (Ed.). (2004). *City of One: Young Writers Speak to the World.* San Francisco: Aunt Lute Books. **(M, H)**

This anthology of poems about peace written by youth from many cultures celebrates the 10th anniversary of WritersCorps, an organization that involves adult writers teaching children in low-income families and neighborhoods. In the Foreword, novelist and activist Isabel Allende speaks of being born into a time of violence—during the Holocaust, and just before the dropping of the first atomic bombs:

> I have seen military occupation, revolutions, and civil wars. I had to leave my country, Chile, after a brutal military coup in 1973, and I lived in exile with my family for thirteen years. I have good reason to wish for peace.... (p. 17)

Allende is uplifted by the poems in this collection. Despite the anger and sadness expressed:

> ... there is hope and light in these pages. The written word has miraculous healing power; it cleans the wounds, eases the pain, leaves proud scars. The written word sorts out the confusion of life, gives us a voice, makes us strong, and connects it to other human beings. And when we are connected we are invincible! (p. 19)

That's Isabel Allende's response to this book. Your students will make their own valuable connections to their fellow writers represented in these pages. Teachers may choose particular poems as they teach about various places, languages, and cultures. The young poets are from China, Iran, Mexico, the United States, Haiti, Ukraine, and other countries; yet, as the title of Chapter 3 expresses, "Our Words Are Universal" (p. 93).

If students want more poems written by members of their generation, offer them *Shooting the Rat: Outstanding Poems and Stories by High School Writers* (Pawlak et al., 2003).

Demi. (Ed.). (1992). *In the Eyes of the Cat: Japanese Poetry for All Seasons.* Illus. by Demi, trans. by Tze-si Huang. New York: Henry Holt and Company. **(E, I, M, H)**

Many students like poetry if it's really, really short. Well, here are some really, really short, but really good poems about nature, organized by seasons and accompanied by colorful paintings. Japanese masters of the **art** are represented; students might be curious to find out more about Issa, Basho, Buson, and others. Class poets and artists can collaborate to compose more of this type of creation. Your poetry collection might grow wild when students take off with "In the Eyes of the Horse," "In the Eyes of the Class Gerbil," "In the Eyes of Our Custodian," etc.

Engle, M. (2006). *The Poet Slave of Cuba: A Biography of Juan Francisco Manzano.* **Illus. S. Qualls.** New York: Henry Holt and Company. **(M, H)**

The author does homage to the poet slave by writing his biography in verse. Most poems are narrated by Juan himself as a child and adult during the nineteenth century, but some are told in the voice of his mother (the slave, the real one), his owner, who treats him as her child (or pet, really), his father, and other key figures in his life, up until the night he escapes. The Historical Note at the end gives further detail of his smuggled poems, his censored work, his imprisonment as a rebel. There are excerpts from his poetry, first in the original Spanish, followed by Engle's English translation. Students in Spanish classes will be able to learn from these bilingual examples, and will perhaps write their responses both in Spanish and in verse form!

Gollub, M. (1998). *Cool Melons—Turn to Frogs!: The Life and Poems of Issa.* **Illus. K. G. Stone.** New York: Lee & Low Books. **(E, I, M, H)**

What a gentle book this is. Gollub tells the life story of Japanese haiku master Issa and complements the text with Issa's poems he has translated. The pictures are appealing. When I read these poems, I get the feeling I could practice the art of haiku writing, also. I feel invited into a magical culture where words and nature meet.

Liu, S., & Protopopescu, O. (2002). *A Thousand Peaks: Poems from China.* **Illus. S. Liu.** Berkeley, CA: Pacific View Press. **(I, M, H)**

There's much Chinese history and much beauty in this book, making it an ideal instructional resource. The poems are presented in their original Chinese characters along with the translations, and the authors comment on the poems and how they relate to the country and the people. Siyu Liu tells us in the Afterword that she had grown up within the constraints of China's Cultural Revolution; she was two years old when it began in 1966. She explains, "My schoolbooks were filled with quotes and poetry from the writings of China's leader, Mao Zedong. Children were given so few books that I had read everything available by the time I was ten" (p. 49). At age 13, desperate for something else to read, she dared open some books hidden in her parents' closet and discovered some of the poems presented in this collection. The book includes a pronunciation and translation guide, and further resources on Chinese poetry, history, and philosophy for young readers and for teachers.

Occhoa, A. P., Franco, B., & Gourdine, T. L. (Eds.). (2003). *Night Is Gone, Day Is Still Coming: Stories and Poems by American Indian Teens and Young Adults.* Cambridge, MA: Candlewick Press. **(M, H)**

As a teenager, I would have loved an outlet for my writing. This book has 58 entries from Native American Indians ranging from 11 to 22 years old. What a gift, for everyone, both readers and writers. The poems, stories, and memoirs are exemplars of many perspectives. Your students may explore the different perspectives after reading "My Indian Pooh Bear" by 16-year-old Beth Yana J. Pease (p. 45), "Red Girls" by 16-year-old Mary Redhouse (p. 18), or "Tough Style Rez" by 18-year-old Sharla Florez (p. 115). Some poems are written in a native language, and the jacket art pays homage to the four basic elements of earth, air, water, and sky.

Soto, G. (1995). *New and Selected Poems.* San Francisco: Chronicle Books. **(H)**

In the Preface, Gary Soto gives some of the details of his becoming a Chicano poet, telling of his early poverty, lack of books, working in the San Joaquin Valley as a fruit picker, sharing experiences with other local poets. He introduces the poems in this collection, written between the 1970s and 1990s. Students reading this book will get to know a person, a culture, a way of life, and a way that words can combine beautifully to tell a story.

Wong, J. S. (1996). *A Suitcase of Seaweed and Other Poems.* New York: Margaret K. McElderry Books. **(E, I, M, H)**

The poems in this collection are divided into three categories: Korean Poems, Chinese Poems, and American Poems. The author, via introductions to the sections, talks about her Korean heritage (her mother is Korean), her Chinese heritage (her father is Chinese), and her American identity (she was born in Los Angeles). She shows respect for all her cultures even as she has fun with them. I especially like the last poem, as she uses a quilt metaphor to describe her family, and brings out the warmth that both quilt and family provide. Teachers may use this book to stimulate student writing about the particular combinations of cultures represented in their families and communities.

MATH AND TECHNOLOGY

Brown, K. (Ed.). (1998). *Verse and Universe: Poems About Science and Mathematics.* Minneapolis, MN: Milkweed. **(H)**

In case you have any students who think that math and poetry don't mix, here's a book to open their minds. Chapter 10, "Number," is a good place to start, with "Boolean Algebra: $X^2 = X$" by William

Bronk, "Fractals" by Eiana Der-Hovanessian, "Geometry" by Rita Dove, "Pure Mathematics" by Rodney Jones, "Integrals" by Jonathan Holden, and many more. Teachers may read relevant poems when teaching concepts related to zero, integrals, fractals, geometric patterns, pure mathematics, and more. In Chapter 11, "Biography," students will read poems inspired by the lives of Copernicus, Isaac Newton, Ludwig Boltzmann, Ramanujan. They'll be intrigued by "The Fall of Pythagoras" by Jonathan Holden, "The Mathematician's Disclaimer" by Ira Sadoff, "Fibonacci Time Lines" by Michael L. Johnson, and "Einstein Thinks About the Daughter He Put Up for Adoption and Then Could Never Find" by Jennifer Clement. "Poems Overheard at a Conference on Relativity Theory" by Emily Grosholz may serve as a model for student and teacher-created poetry; for example, as an inspiration before engaging in the Biopoem strategy described in Part 2 of this chapter.

Esbensen, B. I. (1996). *Echoes for the Eye: Poems to Celebrate Patterns in Nature.* Illus. H. K. Davie. New York: HarperCollins. (E, I, M, H)

What looks like a simple picture book is actually a poetic lesson on the Fibonacci series. Your students will learn to count clockwise and counterclockwise to understand the arithmetic inherent in the rows of seeds in a sunflower. They will be helped to notice spirals, polygons, and other geometric shapes within nature. The book jacket warns that once you know how to look for the repetition of patterns in living things, you'll see them everywhere. If so, the learning from this book offers its own kind of repetitive pattern! Challenge your students to find geometric shapes in their environment. The book is also an excellent choice for the Using Objects to Stimulate Poetry Writing activity in Part 2 of this chapter.

Hopkins, L. B. (Selector). *Marvelous Math: A Book of Poems.* Illus. K. Barbour. New York: Aladdin Paperbacks. (E, I, M)

This book, I think, should be one that sits on the teacher's desk. Students will want to pick it up, if only to see what Lee Bennett Hopkins thinks is so great about math. Those who find math anxiety-producing might find solace in Betsy Franco's "Math Makes Me Feel Safe" (p. 13). Those who prefer **history** will realize upon reading Madeleine Comora's "Pythagoras" (p. 24) that math is part of history and indeed has a history of its own. Students who like **science** will enjoy "Nature Knows Its Math," by Joan Bransfield Graham (p. 23). A marvelous collection of marvelous poems about a marvelous subject.

Morrison, L. (1981). *Overheard in a Bubble Chamber: And Other Science Poems.* Illus. E. de Lanux. New York: Lothrop, Lee & Shepard. (M, H)

This book, also booktalked in the **science** category, has a whole section of poems inspired by math. Students learn about number theory, contemplate the locus of a point as well as the concept of infinity, and reflect on the author's perceived connection between poets and mathematicians. This book could serve well as a model for student writing about the principles they're learning to work, and play, with. It serves well as a model for the Found Poems strategy in Part 2 of this chapter.

Sandburg, C., & Rand, T. (1993). *Arithmetic.* New York: Harcourt Brace. (I, M, H)

The cover tells us that this book is Carl Sandburg's *Arithmetic,* "Illustrated as an anamorphic adventure by Ted Rand." The inside jacket description provides a definition, "An anamorphic image is a picture that has been precisely stretched or condensed so it looks distorted until you view it in just the right way." A Mylar sheet (with mirror properties) is provided so that the reader can resolve the puzzles. A mini-lesson on drawing anamorphic pictures is included at the end of the book. The text and artwork invite interaction from the reader. After sharing this poem, invite your students to think about what "arithmetic" means to them, and have them compose a poem about applications of numbers and arithmetic to their lives both inside and outside of school.

Tang, G. (2003). *Math Appeal: Mind-Stretching Math Riddles.* Illus. H. Briggs. New York: Scholastic. (E, I)

The author's goal is to make math as engaging and appealing to children as **science** that is taught through hands-on experiments, and to lay a foundation for both higher math skills and an enduring love of the subject. He states, "I use poems and pictures to encourage clever, creative thinking, and I provide an answer key that teaches four important concepts: thinking out-of-the-box, finding strategic sums, using subtraction to add, and simplifying through patterns and symmetries" (unpaged).

Tang, G. (2002). *Math for All Seasons: Mind-Stretching Math Riddles.* Illus. H. Briggs. New York: Scholastic. (E, I)

This book introduces intuitive methods with which to group and add numbers. The author states that he encourages kids to think strategically and to simplify problems by looking for symmetries and patterns. The poems contain clues to problem solving. Students could also make up their own poems and problems based on the illustrations.

MATH

Tang, G. (2001). *The Grapes of Math: Mind-Stretching Math Riddles.* **Illus. H. Briggs.** New York: Scholastic. **(I, M)**

Tang does not believe that math is something that you're just good at or not, so he allows for no excuses. But his poems do teach how to do math efficiently; he shows how to group items and numbers in order to make them easier to manipulate. Students will be able to take a different stance toward new problems when they realize they can transfer what they get told to do here through clues to new situations involving problem solving. Math will seem less formidable and more enjoyable.

MUSIC

Bates, K. L. (2003). *America the Beautiful.* **Illus. W. Minor.** New York: G. P. Putnam's Sons. **(I, M, H)**

Wendell Minor understands that each person who has sung the title song has had a unique vision based on individual images and memories. He paints his version, his images, his sense of history and perceptions of our country's beauty in this book. He offers a wish and a challenge at the end of his Introduction:

> It is my sincerest wish that Katherine Lee Bates's words and my paintings will serve as a reminder, to children and parents, of America's gifts. May you always enjoy her natural beauty and help preserve it. May you feel her pride of spirit, and may you make your own contributions to keep America great! (unpaged)

Biographical information is given on Bates and on Samuel Augustus Ward, who wrote the melody. The music is there, a page of a sample of the text in Bates's handwriting is there, and notes on the places pictured on each page are provided by the illustrator. Have your students read the music as they sing the song, perhaps in preparation for a concert or celebration of a national holiday. The book might also inspire them to research how some of their favorite songs came into being.

Bowdish, L. (2002). *Francis Scott Key and "The Star-Spangled Banner."* **Illus. H. Burman.** New York: MONDO Publishing. **(I, M, H)**

How does a poem get written? What provides the impetus and inspiration? Many times we never know the answer, but once in a while an interesting story comes along that makes us appreciate the poem in a new way. This book, also appropriate for **language arts,** has the text to both verses of the poem Francis Scott Key wrote at sea early in the morning on September 14, 1814, after a British attack on Fort McHenry. Readers are given historical background leading up to that night, as well as the results of the poem's publication in a Baltimore newspaper. The music by John Stafford Smith is also provided. Ask your students to compose words and music to create a song based on something dramatic or meaningful they have witnessed, to record a response to an event that can educate or inspire others.

Guthrie, W. (1998). *This Land Is Your Land.* **With a Tribute by Pete Seeger. Illus. K. Jakobsen.** Boston: Little, Brown and Company. **(E, I, M, H)**

Your class will rolick to this folk music as the words by Guthrie and the paintings by Kathy Jakobsen take them on a cross-country trip. They'll appreciate all aspects of weather and land forms and nature, and take in some scenes of Americans at the rodeo, on the farm, fishing off the coast of the Gulf of Mexico, playing volleyball on a California beach, camping out under a bridge when there is no home to go to. They'll peek at activities in San Francisco, Niagara Falls, New York City, New Orleans. Landmarks such as the Golden Gate Bridge, the Gateway Arch of St. Louis, the Statue of Liberty can be found. Biographical information about Woody Guthrie is included at the end. A very full book—full of fun, full of meaning, full of history, full of the features of our country. But at the heart of it is the song itself, which your students may remember for the rest of their lives after performing it in your class, your school.

Jewel. (1998). *A Night Without Armor.* New York: HarperCollins. **(H)**

Is a songwriter always a poet? Can all poems be sung? Your students will find answers in this collection, and they'll be able to compare themes and images in the poems here and the songs on Jewel's CDs. In the Preface, Jewel shares the poets she loved as a child, the poetic lyricists who influence her present work, and information about her own journal writing. "For me poetry allowed word to be given to the things that otherwise had no voice, and I discovered the strength and soul of poetry—through it we come to know; we are led to feel, sense, and to expand our understanding beyond words" (p. xv). I consider that a better mini-lesson on the value and purpose of poetry than any words I could give my students.

Be sure to look through this volume before you put it on your classroom bookshelf, so you'll know whether it's appropriate for your audience. Some of the poems contain sexual content, others religious content.

Johnson, J. W. (1995). *Lift Ev'ry Voice and Sing.* **Illus. J. S. Gilchrist.** New York: Scholastic. **(E, I, M, H)**

The text to this hymn that is considered the African American National Anthem is presented one line per page, along with entrancing illustrations by Jan

Spivey Gilchrist. The music, written by J. Rosamond Johnson, the lyrics writer's brother, is provided. This book is a great introduction to *Lift Every Voice and Sing* (Johnson, 2000).

Johnson, J. W. (2000). *Lift Every Voice and Sing: A Pictorial Tribute to the Negro National Anthem.* New York: Hyperion Books for Children. **(E, I, M, H)**

This version is accompanied by black-and-white photos depicting scenes from African American history. It begins with a short history, by Henrietta M. Smith, of the song itself. The photographs are powerful, yet very different from the paintings in the previous work. Together the books offer a great opportunity for comparison and contrast as different readers voice their responses, as well as a wonderful aesthetic experience as the song is sung and the visuals are studied.

McGill, A. (Collector and singer). (2000). *In the Hollow of Your Hand: Slave Lullabies.* Illus. M. Cummings. Boston: Houghton Mifflin. **(E, I, M)**

Music teachers and **social studies** teachers will have to share this one. Professional storyteller Alice McGill writes of how these songs were sung by the slaves to their babies and passed down as a record of their history and philosophy. The main part of the book consists of the text to the lullabies, accompanied by commentary by the author and quilt paintings by Michael Cummings. The music to each is provided in the back, and there is a CD included with these 13 songs from African American history.

Myers, W. D. (2003). *Blues Journey.* Illus. C. Myers. New York: Holiday House. **(E, I, M, H)**

Myers includes **history** lessons both before and after his lyrical tribute to the beloved music genre known as the blues. At the beginning, he explains the African origins of the structure of blues songs (a call and response format, plus a five-tone, or pentatonic, scale rather than the seven-tone scale our children often learn in school). At the end, a timeline from 1865 through the 1960s is included, with relevant information about blues singers and the spread of the genre. The helpful Glossary will aid in students' vocabulary development and comprehension of the story Myers tells through poetry.

Rogers, S. (1998). *Earthsong.* Illus. M. B. Mathis. New York: Dutton Children's Books. **(E, I, M)**

This book is based on folksinger Sally Rogers's song, "Over in the Endangered Meadow." Through it students will meet whales in the North Atlantic, pandas in China, Bengal tigers in the Bangladeshi jungles, Gila monsters in Arizona, crocodiles in the Florida Keys, and more endangered species around the world. Endnotes on the animals are provided. It's a good song to have students sing during a lesson on how folk music reflects a culture and sometimes affects it.

Seeger, P. (2003). *Turn! Turn! Turn!* Illus. W. A. Halperin. New York: Simon & Schuster. **(I, M, H)**

Words from the book of *Ecclesiastes* from the Hebrew Scriptures begin this book. The rest of the pages take lines from the song Pete Seeger composed by adapting those words, and show in a circle multiple pictures by Wendy Anderson Halperin. A CD of the song "Turn! Turn! Turn!" is enclosed, and the music, also by Seeger, completes the book. In his suggestions at the end for using this book, Seeger exhorts:

> My longtime aim has been to put songs on people's lips, not just in their ears. Let's encourage people to be participants, not just spectators, not just listeners, or even just readers. Ideally, books can help us be participants in trying to save this world from selfishness and shortsightedness.
>
> And perhaps if more of us participate in trying to put together a world of some kind of peace and justice, then a century from now, there will still be a human race here. Competing, yes, but cooperating, too. Speaking out at times, but at other times keeping silent.

Teachers, let's do our part. We can participate in Seeger's grand vision, beginning with making this book and Seeger's music accessible to our students.

PHYSICAL EDUCATION, HEALTH, AND WELLNESS

Adoff, A. (2000). *The Basket Counts.* Illus. M. Weaver. New York: Simon & Schuster. **(I, M)**

Here's a book whose pages are filled with passion for basketball. The first narrator starts playing as he gets ready for the school bus, with "My shot is sweet as jelly on the toast." The last poem is titled, "Before My Mother Yells Her Dinner Invitation." The day is filled with basketball, in the mind if not always on the court. Consider having your students make companion books based on their favorite sports and activities. They'll have lots to share as their favorite memories and visions of stardom are elicited by reading these poems.

Blaustein, N. (Ed.). (2001). *Motion: American Sports Poems.* Iowa City: University of Iowa Press. **(M, H)**

This book is aptly named—there's a lot of fast action in the dozens of poems about a great variety of sports. Some students will be drawn to "Skateboard" by Thom Gunn (p. 99), others to "400-Meter Freestyle" by Maxine Kumin (p. 152), or "The Death of the Race Car Driver" by Norman Dubie (p. 59). Do you have any nocturnal students? Perhaps they'd enjoy "The Midnight Tennis Match" by Thomas Lux (p. 166), or "Run Before Dawn" by William Stafford (p. 207). Do some of your students love the outdoors? Maybe they'll be drawn to "To Kill a Deer" by Carol Frost (p. 88), "Fishing the Dream" by Mike Delp (p. 53), or "Horseback" by Carolyn Kizer (p. 147). There are poems for those who pump iron, shoot free throws, pole vault, golf; belong to the soccer club; or take karate lessons. Better have more than one copy of this one. We want our students to stay active and physically fit, and these poems send the right message.

Burleigh, R. (2001). *Goal*. Illus. S. T. Johnson. New York: Harcourt Brace. **(I, M, H)**

A great companion to *Hoops* (below), this poem takes you to the soccer field. It celebrates winning, but not just any winning, rather winning as a result of teamwork. Again, very few words, but they become champion words in this text. Students might want to take this form and run with it—to the track, to the pool, anywhere they can combine the poetry of a game with the poetry of their words. The instructional implications for *Hoops* are applicable to this book, also.

Burleigh, R. (1997). *Hoops*. Illus. S. T. Johnson. New York: Harcourt Brace. **(I, M, H)**

Just a few words per page, otherwise filled with action on the court. How is this poetry? You and your students will answer that together as you discover the metaphors and similes, the alliteration, the condensed, compact language, the line breaks, the imagery. Coaches will find this quick read a motivating tool before a practice or game. Physical education teachers will want to have it as part of their classroom lending library.

Chambers, V. (2002). *Double Dutch: A Celebration of Jump Rope, Rhyme, and Sisterhood*. New York: Hyperion/Jump. **(I, M, H)**

I placed this book in the Poetry chapter because it's filled with rich rhymes girls (and sometimes boys) have used in the past and are still using as they participate in the style of jumping rope known as double Dutch. Yet the book has more text, including a history of the sport and information about current competitions and tournament circuits. The chants, combined with photographs of children and adults exercising their jumping skills in some sophisticated ways, might inspire students in your classes to take up this great form of cardiovascular activity. I envision clubs and teams forming as a result of this

piece of literature. Use the book as you teach about teamwork and cooperation, for as Tonya Lewis Lee says in the Introduction, "No one can get good at double Dutch working alone" (p. 6).

Knudson, R. R., & Swenson, M. (Eds.). (1988). *American Sports Poems*. New York: Orchard Books. **(M, H)**

A classic. Students can gravitate to whatever activities they want—running, volleyball, swimming, shadowboxing, karate, skiing, riding, bowling, hockey, golf. They can have fun with "Casey's Daughter at the Bat" by Al Graham or "To Kate, Skating Better Than Her Date" by David Daiches. Or they can visit some greats, including Cassius Clay, Patrick Ewing, Babe Didrikson, Jackie Robinson, Vince Lombardi, and Joan Benoit. They'll meet winners and losers, experience fear and thrills, and maybe be inspired to try a new sport and/or a new form of poetry! Use this book to promote interdisciplinary connections between **language arts** and physical education.

Smith, C. R., Jr. (2004). *Diamond Life: Baseball Sights, Sounds, and Swings*. New York: Orchard Books. **(E, I, M)**

Numerous examples of onomatopoeia in this book will help readers and listeners recall the sounds of a baseball park during an action-filled game. Smith makes use of color, font changes, and words that seem to move on the page to accelerate the pace and emotion. One poem, "Excuses, Excuses" (unpaged) consists of just what the title warns us of: "I didn't strike out, I just didn't see a pitch I liked"; "I let the ball go between my legs so the outfield could get it," etc. You'll feel like getting autographs at the end! Use this book to stimulate discussion about the emotions involved in playing a sport or experiencing other types of physical activities. This will be very motivating as students verbalize specifics about mind-body connections.

Smith, C. R., Jr. (2003). *Hoop Queens*. Cambridge, MA: Candlewick Press. **(I, M, H)**

Each poem is a tribute to a female basketball star, and is accompanied by photographs of the player in action. I especially like Smith's Poem Notes at the end, where he tells what characteristics of the players led to the metaphors he uses. For example, he explains "The Chef" this way:

> Ticha Penicheiro's poem was easy to write because she has a very flashy game. But instead of taking shots, she sets her teammates up for them. I call her the chef because she uses a variety of skills to move the ball around and "feed" her teammates. I followed this image all the way through the poem by drawing on the techniques a chef would use to create a meal. (p. 33)

PE/HEALTH

Teachers may use this book as a lead-in to a lesson on Title IX and the resulting flourishing of women's sports in schools and beyond.

Smith, C. R., Jr. (2001). *Short Takes: Fast-Break Basketball Poetry.* New York: Dutton Children's Books. (I, M, H)

When I experienced the photos and haikus and poems such as "Trash on the Court," "The Predator," and "Afterburner," I heard **music.** I understood this more when I read the author's process notes in the final section he calls "Inspirations." Smith explains the challenge he faced as he attempted to make the images ". . . look dynamic and be 'visual jazz' for the words. I wanted to have the images move like a rap song and have different beats" (unpaged). He succeeded! And where did the poetry come from? He explains:

> For the poetry, I immersed myself in music. I listened to lots of jazz to get a feel for rhythm. From Miles Davis, I learned how to use space and silence. . . . From John Coltrane, I learned how to improvise. . . . I learned how to paint a picture with words by listening to hip-hop artists Jay-Z, A Tribe Called Quest, The Notorious B.I.G., and The Roots.

After reading this section and performing (e.g., doing dramatic readings before an audience of peers) and/or studying *Short Takes*, teachers in **English** and **art** as well as physical education and their students will be able to construct their own movement/musical/visual creation celebrating their favorite sports or activities, as well as verbalize the sources of their inspiration and the processes they went through.

Thayer, E. L. (2006). *Casey at the Bat.* Illus. J. Morse. Tonawanda, NY: Kids Can Press. (I, M, H)

Consider this terrific book when teaching narrative poetry and for eliciting emotions about winning and losing competitions; it will create an interdisciplinary bridge between **language arts** and physical education. Students may or may not know the poem that has been part of American culture for more than 100 years, but it will seem very current as they hear it while experiencing the full-page, sometimes double-spread, images. I'll quote from the publisher's information about the illustrator:

> Reinventing this American classic for a new generation, Morse portrays the cool, swaggering Casey (a.k.a. KC) and his Mudville 9 as a group of multiracial inner-city kids playing ball in an urban jungle of concrete buildings, chain-link fences and graffiti-covered walls. It is a particularly relevant approach in an era where kids dream of escaping their present-day realities by following in the footsteps of the sports figures they idolize. (unpaged)

English teachers might also show students other versions of *Casey at the Bat*, including those illustrated by Christopher Bing (2000) and C. F. Payne (2003), and invite comparisons and contrasts in terms of style, mood, and tone. I'd also offer the sequel, Gutman's *Casey Back at the Bat* (2007), after having students consider "What if Casey had another chance?" and make predictions of the outcome.

SCIENCE

Asch, F. (1996). *Sawgrass Poems: A View of the Everglades.* Photographs by T. Levin. New York: Harcourt Brace. (I, M, H)

After reading this book, I felt like I had been to the Everglades; well, not exactly, because I also feel I must now get there in person and actually touch what I've experienced vicariously through the poems. The Introduction gives a history of this wetland wilderness, starting 5,000 years ago as Ice Age sea levels began to recede. The poems introduced me to baby snail kites, manatees, vultures, water moccasins, mangrove trees, strangler figs, mosquitoes, and trees recovering from a hurricane. The book ends with Notes and Photo Captions that add a wealth of information. It's a great resource for a unit on the protection and preservation of environments and habitats.

Brown, K. (Ed.). (1998). *Verse and Universe: Poems About Science and Mathematics.* Minneapolis, MN: Milkweed Editions. (H)

The chapter titles offer topical categories relating to space, time, matter, heavenly bodies, earth, animals, humans, and more. There's a section of poems relating to theory and speculation, and one of biographical poems. The initial poem is "Poet to Physicist in His Laboratory" by David Ignatow; later comes "The Poet Studies Physics" by Carol Jane Bangs. Readers may contemplate Pattiann Rogers's "Life in an Expanding Universe," Alane Rollings's "Tomorrow Is a Difficult Idea," and Carter Revard's "This Is Your Geode Talking." Teachers may introduce lessons on curricular vocabulary relating to the limbic system, cybernetics, intelligence, particle physics, chaos theory, dark matter, sound, lunar eclipses, and the expanding universe by utilizing selected poems. Knowledge and aesthetics are combined superbly in this collection.

George, K. O. (2004). *Hummingbird Nest: A Journal of Poems.* Illus. B. Moser. San Diego: Harcourt. (E, I, M, H)

The author explains that the poems in this collection evolved from a journal she kept over eight weeks of observing a hummingbird family outside her home. The sequence is evident from the titles of the poems, including "Nest Construction," "Expectant," "Just Hatched," "Helpless," "Feed Me! Feed Me!", "Flight Practice," and "Empty Nest." This book could be a model as your students do observation projects, recording changes over time.

Hopkins, L. B. (Selector). (1999). *Spectacular Science: A Book of Poems.* Illus. V. Halstead. New York: Simon & Schuster. **(E, I, M)**

The text and pictures in this book exude enthusiasm for and wonder about magnets, crystals, microscopes, snowflakes, rocks, wind, stars, and many other aspects of science. My favorite is the opener, "What Is Science?" by Rebecca Kai Dotlich. She gives several answers to the title question, and gently invites readers to question along with scientists ". . . the how the where when and why" (p. 10). Students may compile their answers to "What Is Science?" as they conduct lab experiments and explore the outdoors studying curricular topics.

Morrison, L. (1981). *Overheard in a Bubble Chamber: And Other Science Poems.* New York: Lothrop, Lee & Shepard. **(M, H)**

These poems, from "Plate Tectonics on Waking" to "Some Quarks Have a Strange Flavor," are loaded with information. The Glossary gives the specialized meanings of words that also have a generic meaning, such as *flavor* and *strange*, as well as technical terms like *antiquark* and *interferometer*. It would be a great book to use with the Vocabulary Guide strategy in Part 2 of this chapter. If your students wonder what happens "When Two Protons Meet," a poem with this title will tell them and will build background for reading about this same topic in their textbook.

Moss, J. (1997). *Bone Poems.* Illus. T. Leigh. New York: American Museum of Natural History/Scholastic. **(I, M)**

The author thanks the paleontologists at the American Museum of Natural History (home of millions of dinosaur bones) for helping him make his poems scientifically accurate. There are many terms and concepts in this book that will relate to science topics. For example, there's "A Poem to Help You Figure Out What Bone the Patella Is" (p. 64), there's a poem and illustration comparing the 206 human bones with the 206 Tyrannosaurus Rex bones, and a poem that will no doubt help students begin to realize what a comparatively short time humans have existed.

Nelson, M. (2004). *Fortune's Bones: The Manumission Requiem.* Notes and annotations by P. Espeland. Asheville, NC: Front Street. **(M, H)**

This poetic tribute to a slave will help bring both science and **history** to life in our classrooms. Readers learn about the skeleton that is displayed in a Connecticut museum. Though more than 200 years old, it wasn't until the late 1990s that citizens researched and found out about the man (a slave who was owned

by a doctor, a slave who had a wife and children) whose bones they were. Students can join the debate about whether Fortune's bones should be buried:

> [Members of the Fortune Project committee] are divided on this issue, as are visitors to the museum's exhibit "Fortune's Story/Larry's Legacy." Fortune's bones were preserved by Dr. Porter to teach human anatomy. Many members of the African American History Project committee believe that Fortune has more to teach us still. Others feel strongly that it is time to rest his bones in consecrated ground. (p. 31)

Students representing both sides of the argument can check the latest developments on the website www.Fortune.org.

Nelson, M. (2001). *Carver: A Life in Poems.* New York: Scholastic. **(M, H)**

A blurring of genres: Is this a poetry book or a biography? It's the best of both and would be great to use in the Biopoem strategy in Part 2 of this chapter. Each poem gives a glimpse of George Washington Carver's life, and together they tell the story of his boyhood as a foster child in the home where his mother was a slave; his fight for an education that so many would try to deny him due to his race; and his life as a scientist, the most passionate of practitioners. Changing narrators offer a variety of perspectives from people who knew this great, good, faith-filled man. There are many science concepts that are integral to the poems that tell Carver's story, including cross-breeding, hybridization, the use of soil-replenishing crops, Halley's Comet, and conservation.

Peters, L. W. (2003). *Earthshake: Poems from the Ground Up.* Illus. C. Felstead. New York: Greenwillow Books. **(E, I, M)**

There will be some rock lovers in your classes. Treat them to these playful geology-based poems, including "Continental Promises," "Living with Lava," "Pumice Stone Seeks Work," "Obituary for a Clam," "Wyoming Layer Cake," and "Earth Charged in Meteor's Fiery Death." Endnotes give a clear paragraph explaining the scientific principles relating to each poem. For example, the Endnote connected to the poem "River Meets Crack in the Earth" offers the following knowledge and vocabulary:

> The earth's plates are in constant motion, like the pieces of a restless jigsaw puzzle, because of the earth's inner heat. The plate containing Western California is sliding north past the North American plate along the San Andreas fault. The fault is very active, and its movement—a few centimeters per year—is marked by earthquakes. Many things, such as landforms, rivers, and roads, are disrupted by the fault. (p. 31)

SCIENCE

Scieszka, J., & Smith, L. (2004). *Science Verse.* New York: Viking. **(E, I, M, H)**

This is a follow-up to the authors' popular *Math Curse* (1995, New York: Viking). Each poem is about a scientific topic (e.g., evolution, the water cycle, matter, the earth's origin), but borrows the format and rhythm from famous poems by others. Thus, we're treated to "'Twas the Night Before Any Thing . . .," "Astronaut Stopping by a Planet on a Snowy Evening," and "Scientific Method at the Bat" (unpaged). The accompanying CD will help your classroom become a lively place, as your students join in the rolicking fun:

> Glory, glory evolution.
> Darwin found us a solution . . . (unpaged)

Shields, C. D. (2003). *Brain Juice Science: Fresh Squeezed.* New York: Handprint Books. **(I, M)**

The poet explains in her dedication to her former science teacher that, due to the wonderful teaching of Miss Fullerton, she had wanted to grow up to be a scientist, and even wrote a poem about astronomers, botanists, entomologists, meteorologists, chemists, etc., to help her decide. What she did instead was write this collection of 41 "thirst-for-knowledge-quenching poems" to replace the 25-pound textbooks children have been expected to lug around. Students can learn while chorusing the "Song of the Cell," entering "The Clone Zone," sitting at "The Periodic Table," and joining the itsy-bitsy spider as it ponders the water cycle. Involve your students in squeezing out some new poems on science concepts they are learning to add to the juice.

Siebert, D. (1991). *Sierra.* **Illus. W. Minor.** New York: HarperCollins. **(I, M, H)**

From the voice of a mountain, readers learn about and appreciate how the Sierra Nevada mountain range came into being millions of years ago, how glaciers affected it, how it sustains life and is an integral part of the environment, and how it is presently threatened, not by weather or water, but by a force that is human. The accompanying paintings can be savored by your classroom naturalists.

Siebert, D. (1988). *Mohave.* **Illus. W. Minor.** New York: Thomas Y. Crowell. **(I, M, H)**

Would you accept an invitation to go on a desert vacation? What if the invitation was in poetry form? What if the invitation came from the desert itself? Such is the case in *Mohave.* The desert narrator gives enticing details of the animals, including hawks, lizards, snakes, tortoises, hedgehogs, wild mustangs, burros, and butterflies; plants, such as various cacti, joshua trees, creosote bushes, tumbleweeds; and natural formations like limestone cliffs, sandstone canyons, and white salt flats. Weather patterns offer further pictures of the shifting scenery. Let's answer "Yes" to the cordial "Come walk the sweeping face of me" (unpaged). We'll learn about animal habitats in an authentic way; we'll appreciate the delicate balance of nature, and want to do our part to preserve it. We'll then be anxious to travel with Siebert to other parts of the United States in *Sierra* (1991) and *Heartland* (1989).

Simon, S. (Ed.). (1995). *Star Walk.* New York: Morrow. **(I, M, H)**

Astronomy-related poems by famous poets, such as William Blake, Sara Teasdale, May Swenson, and Walt Whitman, are included here. There are also words written by an Inuit poet and a Sioux poet. The words used in authentic contexts will reinforce curricular vocabulary: heliocentric universe, nebulae, Sea of Tranquility, friction, gravitation; and the book would be an excellent choice for the Vocabulary Guide strategy in Part 2. The editor, Seymour Simon, has written my booktalk for me, giving both a description of this collection of photographs and poetry and suggestions for how to use it. I'll turn it over to him:

> I have selected each poem and each photograph because it says or shows something dramatic or thoughtful about the subject . . . the photographs are not intended to illustrate the poems, nor are the poems intended to explain the photographs. Each is a different way of looking at the same thing, but I hope they go together and enrich each other.
>
> Try reading each poem slowly and looking at the accompanying photograph for a long while. Allow the words of the poem and the shapes and colors of the photograph to swirl together in your mind. Then read the words again after looking at the photograph to help you broaden your appreciation of both. I hope you will write your own poetry and make your own photographs or drawings to create a new and personal connection of words and images about space. (unpaged)

Interestingly, Simon at one point chose some prose by Thoreau and set it as poetry. This is an example of "found poetry," explained earlier in this chapter.

Singer, M. (2003). *How to Cross a Pond: Poems About Water.* **Illus. M. So.** New York: Alfred A. Knopf. **(E, I, M)**

Would you like your students to appreciate the value and beauty and many facets of water as they learn about its properties and uses and the need for conservation? The simple poems along with the minimalist illustrations by Meilo So will evoke awe, wonder, and a desire to protect this resource. Use it alongside companion books by the same illustrator and author, *Footprints on the Roof: Poems About the Earth* (2002) and *Central Heating: Poems About Fire and Warmth* (2005). Have students add their own nature poetry collections to your classroom library as they study about other natural phenomena.

Whitman, W. (2004). *When I Heard the Learn'd Astronomer.* Illus. L. Long. New York: Simon & Schuster. **(I, M)**

No page holds more than one line of Walt Whitman's famous poem, and there are many double-page spreads of just pictures. This book will provide inspiration for your student stargazers; their imaginations will be called forth, which is good, since the last page includes the quote by Albert Einstein, "'Imagination is more important than knowledge. Knowledge is limited. Imagination encircles the world'" (unpaged). Teachers may use this book to foster a discussion about the importance of the combinations of book learning and personal experience, of schooling and self-education through observation, thinking, and wonder.

Wolf, A. (2003). *The Blood-Hungry Spleen: And Other Poems About Body Parts.* Illus. G. Clarke. Cambridge, MA: Candlewick. **(E, I, M)**

The title says it all. Your students and those in **health** classes might say these poems are corny, but they won't be able to resist checking out the illustrations, and they're apt to learn vocabulary and concepts from poems such as "Consider the Anus," "Your Navel Is No Mystery," "You Cannot Rankle the Sturdy Ankle," "Your Hormones Are Exciting," and the simple "Spit." I love to have my students perform "Kidney Trouble," a poem written for two voices, representing the two kidneys with personality, Kendra and Kenneth.

Yolen, J. (2003). *Least Things: Poems About Small Things.* Photographs by J. Stemple. Honesdale, PA: Wordsong/Boyds Mills Press. **(E, I, M, H)**

Might you have students who would like to read a little book of little poems about little things? These haiku celebrate the tiny things in nature, including the spider, dragonfly, hummingbird, snail, and human baby. Details about the miniature creatures are on opposite pages. The photographs tell a story in themselves. This would be a great opening to a lesson on science's growing knowledge of the minuscule in biology, chemistry, physics, and the earth sciences.

SOCIAL STUDIES/HISTORY

Adoff, A. (Ed.). (1997). *I Am the Darker Brother: An Anthology of Modern Poems by African Americans.* New York: Simon & Schuster. **(M, H)**

Even the Foreword by Nikki Giovanni is in verse form. The poems convey meaning and evoke emotion for readers in general, but in social studies and **English** classes this collection can be invaluable, since, as Rudine Sims Bishop explains in the Introduction:

> If these poems illuminate the Black experience in America, they also place that experience in the context of American literature and social history. They are reminders, in this era of controversies over multiculturalism and affirmative action, that the song of America, which invariably includes some dissonance, requires a multi-voiced chorus; and that, as Langston Hughes notes in the title poem, the 'darker brother' (and, I would like to add, the darker sister) sings America, too. (p. 15)

Bolden, T. (2001). *Rock of Ages.* Illus. R. G. Christie. New York: Alfred A. Knopf. **(I, M, H)**

In the Author's Note, Bolden makes a thought-provoking claim: "To be sure, regardless of your religion, if you have any interest in American history, you cannot overlook the role that the Black Church has played in black survival and triumphs" (unpaged). The celebratory poem goes a long way in helping us understand this role in communities, in times "When we were the **not-alloweds** and **go-to-the-back-door** people" (unpaged); and this role in individual lives, such as that of Aretha, Martin, Brother Baldwin, etc. The historical notes at the back are very helpful.

Clinton, C. (Ed.). (2003). *A Poem of Her Own: Voices of American Women Yesterday and Today.* Illus. S. Alcorn. New York: Henry N. Abrams. **(M, H)**

This is a perfect companion to an American history textbook, and a good choice for the Biopoem strategy in Part 2. Read Anne Bradstreet when you study the Colonial period, along with slave poet Phillis Wheatley; introduce Julia Ward Howe when you study the Civil War; help students discover where and how Emily Dickinson fits into America's story; present various cultural perspectives of modern times by Julia Alvarez, Sylvia Plath, Nikki Giovanni, Sandra Cisneros, and Lucille Clifton. The poet biographies at the end are fascinating and help to create a big picture of history. Your classes could create a timeline and place the poets and their major works on it. As Catherine Clinton states in her

Introduction, "These brief sketches of women poets reveal not only individuals, but, together, comprise a particularly intriguing story of America, a story of courage in the face of hardship, a story which traces varieties of creative expression unfolding over three centuries" (p. 5).

Clinton, C. (1998). *I, Too, Sing America: Three Centuries of African American Poetry*. Illus. S. Alcorn. Boston: Houghton Mifflin. (M, H)

Three centuries is a long time span for our students to imagine, but these poems help them journey with slaves, school children, free farmers, civil rights activists, a Pulitzer Prize winner, a poet laureate. The accompanying paintings by Stephen Alcorn evoke emotion and will prompt discussion about topics involving discrimination, leaders such as Malcolm X and Martin Luther King Jr., Jim Crow laws, and various roles of African American women throughout the centuries. Your students will benefit from the information given about the poets themselves. Here's one bit worth pondering:

> Born a slave on a tobacco farm in rural North Carolina, George Moses Horton began to compose verses in his head while still an illiterate teenager. Though denied an education, he was allowed by his master to visit the University of North Carolina nearby. He would recite his poems to students, who eagerly wrote them down and paid for his compositions. His fame spread, and a collection of poems was published under the title *The Hope of Liberty* (1829). . . . Horton's master permitted him to support himself by his writing, but he refused to allow Horton's patrons to purchase his freedom. (p. 21)

After reading the historical information, students will be able to hear the voice of this poet they've come to know when they read Horton's poem, "On Liberty and Slavery" (p. 22).

Granfield, L. (1995). *In Flanders Fields: The Story of the Poem by John McCrae*. Illus. J. Wilson. New York: Doubleday. (M, H)

On the first page we're spoken to by the dead soldiers from World War I buried in Flanders Field. The poem is re-created in McCrae's handwriting and is bordered by a black-and-white drawing of poppies. When we turn the page, a beautiful painting of poppies in full color greets us, with the first line of the poem below, and the beginning of the poem's—and the war's—history is on the opposite page. We learn, and feel, more and more as the pages progress. This is a great resource for teaching the topic of World War I, or for exploring and appreciating poetry.

Grimes, N. (2004). *Tai Chi Morning: Snapshots of China.* Illus. E. Young. Chicago: Cricket Books. (I, M, H)

This book is a good model for a travel journal. Poet Nikki Grimes toured parts of China in 1988, then crafted this memory album containing prose, poetry, snapshots, a map, and an itinerary. It's combined with sketches by Caldecott Medal–winner Ed Young, who was born in China and visited there around the same time as Nikki Grimes. The issues range from the lighthearted accounting of Nikki's having to settle for green tea–flavored ice cream when she was craving butter pecan or chocolate chunk, to her pondering about how her pleasant memories of enjoying the huge panda sculpted from greenery in Tiananmen Square have been forever altered by the violence that happened soon after her visit. After experiencing this poet's reflections, students will be ready to pick up pen and camera to begin their own artistic travel journals based on their virtual travels through their social studies curriculum (see the Reading and Writing Travel Journals strategy in Chapter 3, Part 2).

hooks, b. (2004). *Skin Again*. Illus. C. Raschka. New York: Hyperion. (E, I, M)

If you are looking for ways to promote social justice, tolerance, and understanding in your classroom, I recommend this book. Using very few words, bell hooks's poem recognizes that skin color offers ". . . one small way to trace my identity" (unpaged), then celebrates the fact that on the inside, we are all "made up of real history . . ." and offers a way for people of all races to come together.

Hopkins, L. B. (Selector). (2000). *My America: A Poetry Atlas of the United States*. Illus. S. Alcorn. New York: Scholastic. (I, M, H)

The poems are categorized by geography; there are sections celebrating the Northeast States, the Capital, the Plains States, the Mountain States, the Great Lakes States, etc. Maps and facts for all the states are included, as well as poems that deliver the flavor of the unique areas. You and your students will enjoy a "Sioux Lullaby" by Prince Redcloud (p. 46); experience "Wisconsin in Feb-b-rr-uary" by Lee Bennett Hopkins (p. 34); hear "Alabama Earth," the poem Langston Hughes subtitled "At Booker Washington's Grave" (p. 26); and reflect on "California Missions" by Ann Whitford Paul (p. 72). Your class will travel the country with poetic flair.

Hopkins, L. B. (Selector). (1999). *Lives: Poems About Famous Americans*. Illus. L. Staub. New York: HarperCollins. (E, I, M)

Hopkins includes poems about people he calls icons, influential people from various fields: Paul

Revere, Sacajawea, Walt Whitman, Eleanor Roosevelt, Langston Hughes, Neil Armstrong and Buzz Aldrin Jr., Anne Sullivan Macy and Helen Keller, among other greats. I'll let the last paragraph of Hopkins' Introduction serve as my booktalk:

> The power of poetry! Power that makes us appreciate the magnitude of lives filled with courage, enthusiasm, inspiration—lives that have sparked hope and will provide role models for generations to come. (p. 1)

The subjects of the poems here are the subjects in our American history curriculum, making this book a wonderful supplement to a textbook.

Katz, B. (2000). *We the People.* **Illus. N. Crews.** New York: HarperCollins. **(I, M, H)**

I can picture students arriving for the first day of a history class to find "The First Americans" (p. iii) posted on the wall. The next day there is a poster beside it with "Arriving in Virginia" (p. 1). On successive days throughout the year the poetic wallpaper grows, as "For the Love of William Penn (p. 10), "Poor Richard's Almanac" (p. 11), "The Trail of Tears" (p. 27), "A Bird's-Eye View of the Civil War" (p. 35), "A Song for Suffrage" (p. 58), "Vietnam: Are We Winning?" (p. 82), and dozens more panels are added. Many of the poems, such as the double-narrative "Thoughts After the Great War" (p. 62) and "The First Airplane" (p. 52) are perfect for performance in the classroom (see the Poetry Slam strategy in Part 2 of this chapter) or beyond.

Katz, B. (1998). *American History Poems.* New York: Scholastic Professional Books. **(I, M, H)**

This helpful resource contains 30 poems that can be reproduced for classroom use. Each has an accompanying page of information on the topic, along with a box with vocabulary defined, and a discussion question, a writing prompt, and an extension activity. Various perspectives are offered by narrators such as a tea-merchant's daughter at the time of the Boston Tea Party, the people who were here before the first European settlers, a pioneer woman, a gold-miner, an immigrant awaiting processing at Ellis Island, an assembly-line worker. Your students could create additional pages using new voices and new thoughts on current events as well as historical eras and events.

McCormick, P. (2006). *Sold.* New York: Hyperion. **(M, H)**

This powerful sequence of poems tells the story of a 13-year-old girl sold into prostitution in India. It's set in the present, and the system works so that the girls are rendered powerless, economically and otherwise. They are slaves. Teachers may recommend it as they teach about current social justice issues and ways that people, even (maybe especially) youth, are going about fighting to end injustices such as child bondage and sex trade trafficking, which affect up to half a million children according to the Author's Note. Ask students to read individual poems that convey the pain, the courage, and the hope of children like Lakshmi; they will be immersed in an education of caring.

Meltzer, M. (Compiler). (2003). *Hour of Freedom: American History in Poetry.* Honesdale, PA: Boyds Mills Press. **(I, M, H)**

Imagine Nancy Hanks coming back from the dead. The mother of Abraham Lincoln, she died when he was nine years old. How will she remember her child? What will she want to know about the man he became after she could no longer see or guide him? Rosemary Carr Benét's poem titled "Nancy Hanks" (p. 41) takes on these questions. Milton Meltzer places the poem on the page opposite the classic poem mourning Lincoln, "O Captain! My Captain!" by Walt Whitman (p. 40). The poems he has selected take us from the colonial era through the struggle for independence and beyond, the journey from slavery to freedom, the expansion of the country, wars, and the face of changing America, even into the present. An example of the latter is "Elena," by Pat Mora, which is narrated by a Spanish-speaking mother lamenting that her children are leaving her behind because she can't master the English language into which they have grown.

Milton introduces each poem with a historical note and commentary. For example, before the powerful poem "Learning to Read," by Frances Ellen Watkins Harper (p. 38), he explains:

> This African American poet captures the excitement of the freed people who, for the first time, were given a chance on schooling when Northern teachers came to the South to help during Reconstruction. (p. 38)

Myers, W. D. (2004). *Here in Harlem: Poems in Many Voices.* New York: Holiday House. **(M, H)**

Inspired by Edgar Lee Masters's *Spoon River Anthology* (1992), this book gives us the voices of a multitude of Harlem residents. We learn the age and occupation of each narrator; there's a 42-year-old jazz artist, 12-year-old students, a 24-year-old furniture mover, a 67-year-old mechanic, octogenarian veterans, a 14-year-old evangelist, a 32-year-old hairdresser, a 33-year-old English teacher, and many more. Use this along with Myers's earlier picture book poem, *Harlem* (1997, New York: Scholastic) and his book of short stories set in the neighborhood, *145th Street*

SS/HIS

(2000, New York: Delacorte Press) to help students understand the depth, vibrancy, and complexity of Harlem and its place in American history. They no doubt will be inspired to look at their own cities and neighborhoods with new eyes, and you might even compile a class anthology of poems relating to the region in which you live.

Philip, N. (Ed.). (1998). *War and the Pity of War.* New York: Clarion. **(H)**

This book naturally encourages critical thinking. It's not pro-war or anti-war, though individual poems certainly express strong opinions. Rather, as the title so aptly expresses, it gives a big picture of the existence of war throughout history, complete with feelings of pride and glory and victory, alongside the ravages, the grief, the destruction that are the inevitable consequences of war. Many countries are represented; there's the German Bertolt Brecht's "To My Countrymen" (p. 70), written after World War II, entreating mothers, children, and men to stand against future war, to choose the spade over the knife, and life over ruins and death. There are several perspectives on the Vietnam War, such as

"Manuel Is Quiet Sometimes" by Martin Espada (p. 76)

"Central Highlands, Viet Nam (sic), 1968" (p. 75)

"Vapor Trail Reflected in the Frog Pond" by Galway Kinnell (p. 78)

"For a Friend Who Was Killed in the War" by Mazisi Kunene (p. 82)

"Hell No! I Ain't Gonna Go!" by Matthew Jones & Elaine Lavon (p. 72)

There are poems to go along with units on the Civil War and ancient wars, for as Wilfred Owen wrote at the time of World War I:

My subject is War, and the pity of War.
The poetry is in the pity. (p. 8)

Provensen, A. (1997). *The Buck Stops Here: The Presidents of the United States.* **(E, I, M, H)**

I tagged this as suitable for all ages because the two-lined verses about each president are easy enough for elementary school children. Yet my college students love the book and assure me they learn from exploring it. The Endnotes contain further information about the tenures of the presidents, and the illustrations contain many symbols and lots of text in various forms (posters, quilts, stamps, quotes, timelines, graffiti, documents, maps). Your students will learn something new every time they pick up this book.

Siebert, D. (2003). *Rhyolite: The True Story of a Ghost Town.* **Illus. D. Frampton. New York: Clarion Books. (I, M, H)**

I'm not usually enticed by ghost towns, but I love Diane Siebert's work, so this rhyming historical tale intrigued me. I learned about the town's birth in 1904, when two prospectors discovered gold. I, along with the coyotes watching from a distance, saw the dreams and the population grow larger, with the addition of a school, an ice cream parlor, a railroad, churches, restaurants—in a word, prosperity. The ever-present laughing coyotes foreshadowed Rhyolite's demise within six short years. Investors backed out, the mines shut down, water ceased to flow, streetlights dimmed—ah, but I'm telling too much. Please visit yourself to see if anyone but the ghosts are about. This book would certainly enhance a unit on Western expansion.

Silken, J. (Ed.). (1996). *The Penguin Book of First World War Poetry, 2nd Edition.* New York: Penguin Books. **(H)**

My students have asked me why there are so many more trade books available relating to World War II than World War I. I'm glad to have this resource to offer them. The poets are from the various combatant countries, representing many perspectives. Students will find themselves in the trenches, in the homes of those who are grieving the loss of loved ones, on the battlefield with soldiers from opposing armies. They can compare Herbert Read's "Meditation of a Dying German Officer' (p. 162) with his "Meditation of the Waking English Officer" (p. 171). Edna St. Vincent Millay offers "Conscientious Objector" (p. 236) and Archibald MacLeish "The Silent Slain" (p. 234). By reading this text, students will get a big picture view of this big war.

Vecchione, P. (2004). *Revenge and Forgiveness: An Anthology of Poems.* New York: Henry Holt. **(H)**

Inspired by the events of September 11, this is a compilation of about 50 poems with themes involving betrayal, both personal and cultural. The poets represent various cultures and times; they include Shakespeare, Robert Frost, Louise Glück, Ted Hughes, Sandra Cisneros, and Naomi Shihab Nye.

The Introduction is invaluable for teachers. Did you know there was such a thing as writing-revenge? Vecchione gives examples of poets taking revenge through writing, using anecdotes involving D. H. Lawrence, Ezra Pound, and Walt Whitman. She tells of bringing in some of these poems to high school classes, and includes some of the student-written work she got as responses to the texts. Use the poems as writing prompts, and/or introduce them to get students thinking about answers to some big questions, such as those asked in the Introduction:

"How do we live with what overwhelms and frightens us? . . . How can beauty be made out of ugliness and fear? Can it rise from ash?" (p. 4), "And the response of our country [to the September 11 attacks], is that justice or revenge?" (p. 4), and "Ultimately isn't that where cruelty begins—when we see ourselves as not lovable?" (p. 8).

Weatherford, C. B. (2002). *Remember the Bridge: Poems of a People.* **Designed by S. Megged.** New York: Philomel Books. **(M, H)**

Over 400 years of African American history—told in about 50 pages of original poems combined with photos and historic engravings. The author explains her process in an Endnote. The project began with a pilgrimage into her past, fueled by a photo-essay assignment when she was a graduate student. Her research might inspire our fledgling researchers: "Like a detective, I pored over hundreds of prints and photographs at libraries, museums, historical societies and state archives. . . . After a while, I was no longer looking for photos to illustrate poems, but writing poems inspired by pictures that begged for words. . . . Sometimes I felt as if I'd entered a museum where the pictures talked" (p. 52). The people depicted ordered her to never forget, and her poems in this book are a fulfillment of their command to remember. The courage of a people is documented from a beginning poem about Africans being captured, through poems about slaves' work, the auction block, the Underground Railroad. We read about "Bronze Cowboys" (p. 27), we celebrate the achievements of Madam C. J. Walker, Bessie Smith, Marian Anderson, Rosa Parks, Joe Louis, Mae Jemison. The pictures and words in this book will help readers to remember the bridge, and to understand that:

> The bridge is men and women,
> famous and unknown,
> leaving paths of memories,
> timeless stepping stones. (p. 50)

Yolen, J. (1996). *O Jerusalem.* **Illus. J. Thompson.** New York: Scholastic. **(M, H)**

Before her poems, Yolen tells us a bit about the location and history of the city of Jerusalem. "Every day, people in Jerusalem—Jews, Christian, and Muslims—pray to God. All three groups believe that Jerusalem should belong to them. And that is Jerusalem's weakness—and its strength" (unpaged). After the poems, which are written from multiple perspectives, the author adds a bit of helpful commentary. The final poem, "Jerusalem 3000," hopes for a future reign of peace, and she ends her Afterword with the thought that perhaps by the next millennium, ". . . the spilling of blood in the name of the City of

Peace will—at last—be at an end" (unpaged). The illustrations add to the powerful text, leading to the appreciation of the significance and awesomeness of Jerusalem. This book will enhance students' affective and cognitive understanding of this part of the Middle East.

Yu, C. (2005). *Little Green: Growing Up During the Chinese Cultural Revolution.* New York: Simon & Schuster. **(M, H)**

This memoir told in verse is a powerful portrait of a family's situation during a time of severe political oppression. Chun Yu's first 10 years of life, from 1966 to 1976, were lived under the watchful eyes of the Red Guards, and with a loudspeaker in every house broadcasting commune news; it was all she knew, though it was certainly not all her parents had known. She tells of her father being sent to be reeducated by living the life of a peasant in the fields, and of her mother, a teacher who had to bring her children to live with 11 other teachers' families, where she was once awakened and ordered to march to another town and participate in a parade in the middle of the night, shouting the slogan, "Ten Thousand Years Chairman Mao. . . . Ten Thousand, Ten Thousand, and Ten Ten Thousand!" (p. 14). The poems end with the death of Chairman Mao, and the mourning that took place in the child's school. In the Epilogue, Chun Yu concludes with a reflection:

> As a child, I grew up half blind to and half aware of the glory and cruelty of such a revolution. It took me many years to learn some of the facts but perhaps never the total truth of an event that brought a nation such suffering. (p. 107)

Knowledge of the Cultural Revolution is an important part of a world history or global studies curriculum. This book provides an authentic way to teach about it.

INTERDISCIPLINARY

Feelings, T. (1993). *Soul Looks Back in Wonder.* New York: Dial Books. **(I, M, H)**

Which comes first, the pictures or the text? In most cases, a written text is given to an illustrator to work with. In this case, Tom Feelings's artwork was given to poets, including Maya Angelou, Lucille Clifton, Walter Dean Myers, and Langston Hughes. The result is both a celebration of African American heritage and inspiration for future creativity and literacy to all readers. I believe this book will touch each person who holds it and savors it in a unique way. **Art** teachers may ask students to respond to and/or imitate Feelings's work. **English** teachers may connect this book with other works by the authors represented. **Social studies** teachers may use the book as they teach aspects of the African American experience throughout our country's history.

George, C. O. (2002). *Swimming Upstream: Middle School Poems.* Illus. D. Tilley. New York: Clarion. **(M)**

There are some things that are true of middle schools, and middle schoolers, everywhere, and these poems capture those universals. After enjoying them, kids could take the titles and write poems that would include the particulars of their subjects, their insecurities, their friendships, their teachers. There should be many versions worth comparing of "My Locker," "Which Lunch Table?" "Math," "Gossip," "School Librarian," "Pop Quiz," "Passing Notes," etc.

Ghigna, C. (2003). *A Fury of Motion: Poems for Boys.* Honesdale, PA: Boyds Mills Press. **(I, M)**

I wouldn't have titled this book in a way that seems to preclude girls. The poems are short, about topics ranging from fireflies to chess, from the air force to the beach. The author explains in his Introduction that when he was the age of his intended audience, he thought poetry was for sissies and grandmothers, but learned differently when a poem he wrote for a girl he liked had good results. In the Foreword, renowned poet X. J. Kennedy addresses the gender issue this way:

> . . . to any girls who might have wandered into this all-boy party: There isn't any law against your reading these poems. Some of them, I think, could appeal to anybody. Reading certain ones will be like looking at the world through a boy's glasses. Who knows what secrets you might find out? (p. x)

Used before a unit on poetry, this book would make a good companion to Sharon Creech's *Love That Dog* (2001), since Jack, the narrator of that novel in verse, also thinks poetry is for girls only.

Haas, J. (2004). *Hoofprints: Horse Poems.* New York: Greenwillow Books. **(M, H)**

Would you ever think to write a poem as a Power-Point presentation by Miohippus 30 million years ago? Jessie Haas did. This collection of poetry contains curricular concepts spanning **history, science, English, physical education,** and more. The poems address evolution, the great wall of China, today's global warming, gender issues, and the Trojan War myths. The equine narrators speak from such places as Mesopotamia, North America, Greece, Egypt, China, Saudi Arabia, northern Europe, and India. The book includes a Glossary and an Afterword explaining how horses have been used through history, significantly affecting wars, the Industrial Revo-

lution, sports, travel. It's a very full book, which some of your horse-loving students will gallop through.

Heard, G. (Selector). (2002). *This Place I Know: Poems of Comfort.* Cambridge, MA: Candlewick Press. **(E, I, M, H)**

This book represents a truly cooperative venture. Georgia Heard was asked by a superintendent in New York City to gather poems of comfort to read to the children who had watched the events of September 11, 2001, from their classroom windows. She did, bringing poems together for a purpose, choosing poems by Emily Dickinson, Langston Hughes, Walt Whitman, and many more classic and living poets. Eighteen renowned artists contributed a picture to accompany a poem. Include this book in your classroom to be brought out whenever an individual or a group needs comforting. It may also serve as a model for classes or groups within classes to gather poems relating to a theme. Decisions about artwork, about collaboration, about criteria for selection will all have to be made within the groups, offering the opportunity for creative thinking and problem solving.

Lyne, S. (Compiler). (2004). *Soft Hay Will Catch You: Poems by Young People.* Illus. J. Monks. New York: Simon & Schuster. **(I, M, H)**

Do you have visiting poets in your schools? Sanford Lyne is such a poet-teacher, and the poems in this collection show what students can produce under his tutelage and encouragement. How does he do it? In his Introduction, he explains how he was able to convince rural students that they lived in paradise:

> . . . I had learned a long time ago to look beneath the surface of things and to believe in the treasures and lessons hidden in each life, to believe in the history of each smile and tear. As a poet myself, I knew that my own world of images and metaphors was grown in the deep topsoil and in the seed experiences of my childhood. . . . (p. xii)

Through this book, many young poets can visit your school, helping you to teach your students to turn their wanderings and wonderings into verses to share.

Morrison, L. (Compiler). (2001). *More Spice Than Sugar: Poems About Feisty Females.* Illus. A. Boyajian. Boston: Houghton Mifflin. **(I, M, H)**

Your students will learn details about the feats of women in many professions and fields: poet Emily Dickinson, aviator Amelia Earhart, physician Elizabeth Blackwell, soldier Jeanne d'Arc, artist Georgia O'Keeffe, athlete Wilma Rudolph, abolitionist Sojourner Truth, and others, making the book appropriate for **art, history, English, health, science, physical education,** and other curriculums.

They can imagine what it was like to be "A Pioneer Girl Driving West" by Ann Turner (p. 12) or a colonial "Girl with Sampler" by Stanley Kunitz (p. 19). At the same time they will enjoy the varied formats, such as concrete poetry, rhymed poetry, free verse, epistolary poetry; and the imagery and metaphors and voices the various poets chose. The most powerful poem, to me, was the one by Marjorie Agosin that begins, "Anne Frank, where are you?" (p. 51).

Rosenberg, L. (Ed.). (1996). *The Invisible Ladder: An Anthology of Contemporary American Poems for Young Readers.* New York: Henry Holt and Company. **(M, H)**

The editor tells us, "There is no wrong way to use this book" (p. 191). My own reading confirmed this, for I have read it a number of ways. In each section are photographs of a poet in her youth and at the time of the book's publication. There is commentary, where the poets talk to readers about their lives, their inspirations, their fears, their writing habits and processes. Then there are the poems themselves. I go back and forth, I jump around, I savor poems and study pictures. I, of course, note the poems that I can collect for my **math** and **English** colleagues, such as

> "In Praise of Zigsags: For a Girl Failing Geometry" by Jane O. Wayne (p. 181)
>
> "The Mystery of Emily Dickinson" by Marvin Bell (p. 12)
>
> "Barbie Says Math Is Hard" by Kyoko Mori (p. 124)

Check out this book to see how you and your students can use it.

Wong, J. S. (1999). *Behind the Wheel: Poems About Driving.* New York: Margaret K. McElderry Books. **(I, M, H)**

I challenge you—write a poem about what driving means to you, or makes you feel. Or write a poem about your car, or maybe *to* your car. The ideas will flow as you read Wong's collection of driving poems that also manage to say something about how parents worry and care for us, how we observe others, how to live life joyously and responsibly.

REFERENCES

Abair, J. M., & Cross, A. (1999). Patterns in American literature. *English Journal*, 88 (6), 83–87.

Abisdris, G., & Casuga, A. (2001). Atomic poetry: Using poetry to teach Rutherford's discovery of the nucleus. *Science Teacher*, 68 (6), 58–62.

Alber, M. (2001). Creative writing and chemistry. *Journal of Chemical Education*, 78 (4), 478–480.

Angel, A. M. (2004). Striking pensively, beating playfully: The power of poetic novels. In Bold books for innovative teaching, D. Gallo, (Ed.). *English Journal*, 93 (3), 101–104.

Atwell, N. (2002). *Lessons that change writers.* Portsmouth, NH: Heinemann.

Chatton, B. (1993). *Using poetry across the curriculum: A whole language approach.* Phoenix, AZ: Oryx Press.

Collins, B. (2003). *Poetry 180: A turning back to poetry.* New York: Random House.

Collins, B. (2002). Commencement Speech at the College of the Holy Cross. www.holycross.edu/departments/publicaffairs/website/features/collins_address.htm, retrieved 7/11/02.

Danks, C. (1995). Using Holocaust short stories and poetry in the social studies class. *Social Education*, 59 (6), 358–361.

Donaldson, D. P. (2001). Teaching geography's four traditions with poetry. *Journal of Geography*, 100 (1) 24–31.

Ellis, L., Gere, A. R., & Lamberton, L. J. (2003). "Out loud." The common language of poetry. *English Journal*, 93 (1), 44–49.

Frkovich, A., & Thoms, A. (2004). The monologue project for creating vital drama in secondary schools. *English Journal*, 94 (2), 76–84.

Lowery, R. M. (2003). Dreams of possibilities: Linking poetry to our lives. *The ALAN Review*, 30 (2), 49–51.

Longfellow, H. W. (2001). *The midnight ride of Paul Revere.* Illus. C. Bing. Brooklyn, New York: Handprint Books.

Longfellow, H. W. (2006). *The song of Hiawatha.* Dover Publications.

Meadows, D. (1999). African-American poetry and history: Making connections. *Magazine of History*, 13 (2), 36–37.

McGee, L. (1995). Widening the circle: Poetry, math and beginning adult students. *Quarterly of the National Writing Project and the Center for the Study of Writing and Literacy*, 17 (4), 20–23.

Nye, N. S. (2000). *Salting the ocean: 100 poems by young poets.* Illus. A. Bryan. New York: Greenwillow Books, p. xii.

Rosenberg, L. (Ed.). (1996). *The invisible ladder: An anthology of contemporary American poems for young readers.* New York: Henry Holt and Company.

Rule, A. C., Carnicelli, L. A., & Kane, S. (2004). Using poetry to teach about minerals in earth science class. *Journal of Geoscience Education*, 52 (1), 10–14.

Szenher, M., & Worsley, D. (1998). The probability of poetry: From math to literature. *Teachers & Writers, 30* (2), 8–12.

Walders, D. (2000). *Poetry and science education.* ERIC Digest. (ED 463946)

Whitney, K. A. (2004). The Novel novel: A look at alternative formats in today's YA literature. *KLIATT, 38* (1), 3–5.

LITERATURE CITED

If you don't find a book listed here, it is included in Part 4, Annotated Books and Booktalks.

Aliki. (1976). Zero makes me hungry. In E. Lueders & P. St. John (Compilers), *Zero makes me hungry.* Glenview, IL: Scott Foresman.

Brown, K. (Ed.). (1998). *Verse & universe: Poems about science and mathematics.* Minneapolis, MN: Milkweed Editions.

Creech, S. (2001). *Love that dog.* New York: HarperCollins.

Davis, K. (2001). *Don't know much about planet earth.* Illus. T. Bloom. New York: HarperCollins.

Frost, R. (2001). *Stopping by woods on a snowy evening.* Illus. S. Jeffers. New York: Dutton Children's Books.

Greenberg, J. (Ed.). (2001). *Heart to heart: New poems inspired by twentieth-century American art.* New York: Harry N. Abrams.

Gutman, D. (2007). *Casey back at the bat.* Illus S. Johnson & L. Fancher. New York: HarperCollins.

Heaney, S. (1998). *Opened ground: Selected poems 1966–1996.* New York: Farrar, Straus, and Giroux.

Hesse, K. (1997). *Out of the dust.* New York: Scholastic.

Holbrook, S. (2002). *Wham! It's a poetry jam: Discovering performance poetry.* Honesdale, PA: Wordsong/Boyds Mills Press.

Katz, B. (2000). *We the people.* Illus. N. Crews. New York: Greenwillow Books.

Lawrence, J. (1993). *Harriet and the promised land.* New York: Simon & Schuster.

Masters, E. L. (1992). *Spoon River anthology.* Edited and introduction and annotations by J. E. Hallwas. Urbana, IL: University of Illinois Press.

Merriam, E. (1987). Zero. In *Halloween ABC.* Illus. L. Smith. New York: Macmillan.

Myers, W. D. (2004). *Here in Harlem: Poems in many voices.* New York: Holiday House.

Nasar, S. (1998). *A beautiful mind: A biography of John Forbes Nash, Jr., winner of the Nobel Prize in Economics, 1994.* New York: Simon & Schuster.

Nelson, M. (2001). *Carver: A life in poems.* Asheville, NC: Front Street.

Neruda, P., Cook, F., & Krabbenhoft, K. (1994). *Odes to common things.* New York: Bullfinch Press.

Nye, N. S. (2005). *A maze me: Poems for girls.* Illus. T. Maher. New York: Greenwillow Books.

Patz, N. (2003). *Who was the woman who wore the hat?* New York: Dutton Books.

Pawlak, M., Lourie, D., Hershon, R. M., & Schreiber, R. (2003). *Shooting the rat: Outstanding poems and stories by high school writers.* New York: Hanging Loose Press.

Sandburg, C. (1990). I am zero, naught, one cipher. In *The people, yes.* Orlando, FL: Harcourt.

Scieszka, J., & Smith, L. (2004). *Science verse.* Illus. L. Smith. New York: Viking.

Shapiro, K. J. (2003). *Because I could not stop my bike: And other poems.* Illus. M. Faulkner. Watertown, MA: Whispering Coyote.

Singer, M. (2002). *Footprints on the roof: Poems about the earth.* Illus. M. So. New York: Alfred A. Knopf.

Sones, S. (2001). *Stop pretending!: What happened when my big sister went crazy.* New York: HarperTempest.

Singer, M. (2005). *Central heating: Poems about fire and warmth.* Illus. M. So. New York: Alfred A. Knopf.

Soto, G. (1992). *Neighborhood odes.* Illus. D. Diaz. Orlando, FL: Harcourt.

Thayer, E. L. (2000). *Casey at the bat: A ballad of the republic sung in the year 1888.* Illus. C. Bing. Brooklyn, NY: Handprint Books.

Thayer, E. L. (2003). *Casey at the bat: A ballad of the republic sung in the year 1888.* Illus. C.F. Payne. New York: Simon & Schuster Books for Young Readers.

Thoms, A. (Ed.). (2002). *With their eyes: September 11th—The view from a high school at Ground Zero.* New York: HarperTempest.

von Ziegesar, C. (Ed.). (2000). *SLAM!* New York: Alloy Books.

Whitman, W. (2004). *When I heard the learn'd astronomer.* Illus. L. Long. New York: Simon & Schuster.

Williams, W. C. (2004). The red wheelbarrow. In C. MacGowan (Ed.), *Poetry for young people: William Carlos Williams* (p. 27). Illus. R. Crockett. New York: Scholastic.

How-To and Hands-On Books

"'Hands-on' and 'problem-based' are words that . . . have more important meanings to children. When attached to activities, they may spark learning. When implemented by committed teachers, these activities may become the heartbeat for future careers."

SUSAN JOHNSEN (1997)

P A R T   1

the why and how
OF USING HOW-TO AND HANDS-ON BOOKS

O ur own experience tells us that numerous skills and topics are best learned by doing, and scholars help us reflect on this maxim. Flannery (2001), a science educator with expertise in the area of the relationship between biology and art, discusses how vital and varied hands-on experiences are by turning to the topic of the hand itself. She shows how students can explore hands not only in terms of biology, but also in terms of their social significance and their importance to artists. She draws on research regarding hand–brain connections:

> Maybe hands-on activities nurture the mind in more basic ways by extending, broadening and deepening the links between the brain and the hand. The phenomenon of awakening to hidden talents that occurs with some students when doing crafts can also occur in science courses and helps to explain why some students find lab work the most satisfying part of a science course. (p. 285)

Classroom teachers in every discipline may find many ways to provide students with hands-on experiences. Social studies teachers can introduce students to both knowledge of diverse cultures and to the principles of anthropology by bringing in artifacts to accompany, or as an integral part of, their lessons. Art classes are often taught as studio courses. Eggleton (2001) recognized that we teachers can't just give knowledge to students. "Far too often, . . . educators attempt to put the knowledge into the student. If anything, students will 'rent' this knowledge for a short period of time, but it is not 'owned' until they create the knowledge for themselves" (p. 537). He wanted a way to help his students learn the way the students of Pythagoras learned, by making observations from real experiences and then translating them into mathematical principles and concepts. He taught his students triangle-congruence theorems using several sizes of fettuccine he had spray-painted different colors. One student gave this feedback:

> "This activity was more hands-on than anything usually done in math class and more interesting because you can actually see for yourself why different things did or did not work. It was definitely more fun than sitting and listening to someone talk about how triangles relate to dead guys. I think I'll remember the postulates better now, as well. It's like a pasta proof." (p. 537)

Using hands-on exploration will no doubt help students with various learning styles. Strutchens, Harris, and Martin (2001) point to the lack of such investigation as the reason why students often show little understanding of measurement and of geometry concepts. "More often than not, students are asked to memorize geometric properties rather than experience geometry through nature walks or worthwhile tasks that involve hands-on explorations" (p. 402). Smith and Reese (2003) point out that "Difficult concepts that are hard to master on paper can often be easily understood kinesthetically by touching, feeling, manipulating, and thinking" (p. 35). They suggest the use of computer programs that offer virtual experiences.

Moyer, Bolyard, and Spikell (2002) also espouse the use of virtual manipulatives. They point out potential disadvantages of actual manipulatives. There may be a shortage of blocks; it's time consuming to distribute manipulatives and clean up afterward; and manipulatives can be viewed negatively by older students who might think blocks are for little kids. The authors define virtual manipulatives as dynamic visual representations that ". . . can be manipulated in the same ways that a concrete manipulative can. . . . [A student] can use a computer mouse to actually . . . flip, and turn the dynamic visual representation as if it were a three-dimensional object" (pp. 372–373).

Where do books come in during this discussion of hands-on learning? Can books be used as manipulatives? Some can. Reading certain books can be a kinesthetic experience. Kurkjian et al. (2005) contend that "Hands-on participation books can add, extend, and develop the theme of the book and enhance dramatic response in dramatic ways" (p. 481). They recommend books that ". . . evoke personal response; reader participation; and life-to-text, text-to-life connections" (p. 480). Huber and Moore (2001) note that hands-on activities do not necessarily guarantee that true inquiry takes place on the part of the student participants. This is often because ". . . hands-on science activities, as traditionally implemented, fail to support inquiry-based science instruction, because the activities direct teachers to terminate lessons prematurely" (p. 32). They offer several suggestions for extending the activities, such as teachers introducing discrepant events to direct the focus of the inquiry, and providing writing assignments that add structure and support. I would add that the addition of trade books to the materials at hand would provide resources to add explanations for the phenomena students are observing and wondering about as they complete their investigations. Friedrichson (2001) describes a hands-on biology education course focusing on both teaching methods and biology content, which is based on the National Science Education Standards. An innovative part of the course is the incorporation of children's literature connecting to the science content.

Since the advent of the Internet and computers with hypertext, researchers have found that children read differently (Dresang, 1999; Tapscott, 1997). Books have changed in recent years, reflecting the nonlinear aspects of the digital age. Many are more interactive, calling for decisions and participation from the reader. For example, many books are set up to act as a gateway to further exploration. *The Usborne Internet-Linked Complete Book of the Microscope* (Rogers, 2001) has wonderful visuals and explanations relating to robots, germs, fibers and fabrics, nanotechnology, and food science; in addition, every page also suggests an Internet site with much, much more to explore.

Dresang has categorized such books for youth as exhibiting one type of what she terms *radical change*:

> Type One Radical Change books convey information in a bold, graphic manner and in exciting new forms and formats. They incorporate one or more of the following characteristics:
>
> - graphics in new forms and formats
> - words and pictures reaching new levels of synergy
> - nonlinear organization and format
> - nonsequential organization and format
> - multiple layers of meaning
> - interactive formats (p. 19)

Dresang says books that reflect the characteristics of CD-ROMs could be called "handheld hypertext," and the arrangement of information "digital design" (p. 105). These books "demand a high level of cognitive interaction from the reader"

(p. 119). Many of the books described in this chapter will exhibit radical change, and the strategies will help students negotiate texts that call for much more from the reader than mere absorption of information.

Smolkin and Donovan's (2003) research provides support for using interactive information book read-alouds with both emerging and older, nonfluent readers. The adjective *interactive* in their instructional approach actually modifies a *context* "... in which a teacher genuinely shares, not abandons, authority with the children during the reading of a book," rather than books themselves, but they do use books with what they call "dual-purpose text" (p. 27); these books by nature call for active engagement on the part of readers. They recommend:

> ... access to the ideas, vocabulary, syntax, and text structures of informational texts. ... We believe that this exposure is as important for nonreaders (children identified with learning disabilities and receiving special education services) as it is for emerging readers. ... This belief proves particularly important if we accept that context (including book type) is important in developing reasoning abilities. (p. 27)

The researchers give examples of discussions showing how teachers use students' spontaneous remarks and questions to make decisions regarding modeling, instruction, and experimenting. They include a conversation taking place during the reading of a book where "... student comments, a key in the interactive aspect, result in an adult's making visible what we are to do when acts of comprehension go awry" (p. 35).

We subject area teachers can make great use of this practice of active reading and talking about interactive books. The books and strategies addressed in this chapter call for reader participation in a variety of ways. Both teaching and learning will be stimulating and rewarding when our discipline-based classrooms are filled with resources that call for manipulation of materials (including the books themselves), hands-on experimentation, performance and dramatization, and grappling with authentic problems posed by practitioners in the fields we are teaching.

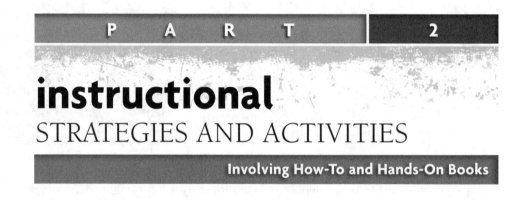

PART 2

instructional
STRATEGIES AND ACTIVITIES

Involving How-To and Hands-On Books

▶ ▶ ▶ **DISCOVER YOUR GENIUS IN THE SUBJECTS YOU STUDY**

Standards Addressed

History: Students consider multiple perspectives. Students evaluate alternative courses of action. Students hypothesize the influence of the past.

English/Language Arts: Students read a wide range of literature from many periods in many genres to build an understanding of the many dimensions (e.g., philosophical, ethical, aesthetic) of human experience.

Context/Rationale

No matter what you teach, you can use *Discover Your Genius: How to Think Like History's Ten Most Revolutionary Minds* (2002) to help your students discover their "genius" in your subject matter. I consider this book, by Michael J. Gelb, to be the ultimate how-to book. Gelb applied certain criteria to come up with his Genius Dream Team: Plato, Brunelleschi, Columbus, Copernicus, Elizabeth I, Shakespeare, Jefferson, Darwin, Gandhi, and Einstein. (In case you're wondering why there's only one person of color and one woman, or if you've thought of others you would include, such as Jesus Christ, Mozart, or Leonardo da Vinci, Gelb has anticipated your questions. You could ask your students to hypothesize and then send them to pages 17–18 for answers.)

The chapters are structured in a consistent manner. I'll use the one on Elizabeth I as an example. After an opening quote, Gelb gives a brief biography, concentrating on traits that set Elizabeth's thinking apart from the ordinary; subtitles of this section include "Entitlement and Empowerment," "Body of a Woman, Heart of a King," "Tolerance and Ruthlessness," "Majesty and Mildness." There's a chart summarizing her achievements, then a section called "Elizabeth and the Liberation of Women's Power," and, finally, "Elizabeth and You." Then comes the most interactive part. A self-assessment in the area of "Wielding Your Power with Balance and Effectiveness" is included, followed by exercises that will help your students think like Elizabeth and connect what they've learned about her to our work and other areas of life today.

Of course, if your class is not interdisciplinary, you may want to have your students focus only on the featured people appropriate for your discipline.

Procedure

Gelb gives instructions for how to use his book effectively. He advises readers to

- overview the whole book;
- contemplate the illustrations;
- reflect on the self-assessments;
- explore and enjoy the exercises;
- form a group to go over answers;
- keep a Genius Notebook; and
- take part in imaginative dialogues with the masters. (pp. 19–22)

Walk-Through

If I were a principal, I'd recommend this book to my entire faculty (after assuring them that I've read it and am trying to implement some of its valuable lessons into my own style of leadership), and provide avenues for using the book with students and parents. It's interdisciplinary, and the author himself suggests that readers should skip around and start with the people and the exercises that are most fun or meaningful for them. Think of the Dream Team you could have in your school of thinkers.

JOB "TRY-OUTS" THROUGH HOW-TO/HANDS-ON BOOKS

Standards Addressed

Science: All students should develop an understanding of abilities necessary to do scientific inquiry. All students should develop an understanding of chemical reactions.

English/Language Arts: Students read a wide range of print and nonprint texts to build an understanding of texts, of themselves . . . to respond to the needs and demands of society and the workplace; and for personal fulfillment.

Context/Rationale

The practice of having students shadow people, following them around at their jobs, is a popular one. Through how-to/hands-on books, your students are able to take job "shadowing" one step further and "try out" jobs in your subject area, both of the routine type and more radical, extreme forms of "doing" science, math, art, music, business, and so forth.

Procedure

- Select either one book or a number of how-to/hands-on books that provide information about practitioners working in your field. For example:

  So, You Wanna Be a Comic Book Artist?: How to Break into Comics! by P. Amara (2001) (art)

  Camera Crafts by C. Finkle (1997) (art)

  Attack of the Killer Video Book: Tips & Tricks for Young Directors by M. Schulman and H. Krog (2004) (art)

  The Complete Audition Book for Young Actors: A Comprehensive Guide to Winning by Enhancing Acting Skills by R. Ellis (2001) (English/language arts)

  So, You Wanna Be a Writer? by V. Hambleton and C. Greenwood (2001) (English/language arts)

  The DC Comics Guide to WRITING Comics by D. O'Neil (2001) (English/language arts)

  Career Ideas for Kids Who Like Writing by D. L. Reeves (1998) (English/language arts)

  So, You Wanna Be a Rock Star?: How to Create Music, Get Gigs, and Maybe Even Make It BIG! by S. Anderson (1999) (music)

  Show Time!: Music, Dance and Drama Activities for Kids by L. Bany-Winters (2000) (music)

  The Art of Mixing: A Visual Guide to Recording, Engineering and Production by D. Gibson (2005) (music)

  Inside Songwriting: Getting to the Heart of Creativity by J. Blume (2003) (music)

  The Ultimate Girls' Guide to Science: From Backyard Experiments to Winning the Nobel Prize! by B. C. Hoyt and E. Ritter (2003) (science)

  Archaeology for Kids: Uncovering the Mysteries of our Past: 25 Activities by R. Panchyk (2001) (social studies/history)

  See Part 4 of this chapter for additional suggestions.

- If you have selected multiple books, allow students to choose a book to read based on their interests.

- Introduce students to the book(s) providing some background and indicating the profession involved.

- Divide students into small groups. If using multiple books, divide the students into groups based on the book they have chosen.

- Have students choose one of the projects/activities mentioned in the book and complete it in order to "try out" the job.

- Schedule a career day to bring all the groups together. Have them share the information they learned about the job, and the project they created to "try out" the job.

Walk-Through

The following scenario shows how this activity might play out in a chemistry class whose students have been "shadowing" Anita Brandolini through active engagement with her book *Fizz, Bubble & Flash: Element Explorations & Atom Adventures* (2003). Listen in as students report.

> *Olivia:* I followed Dr. Brandolini as she explained the most prevalent element: helium. She gave me a history lesson about the disaster of the passenger airship Hindenburg in 1937 to help me remember that by itself, helium is extremely explosive. Then I followed her instructions to break the compound water (H_2O) molecules apart. Finally, we looked into the future. If we future scientists can figure out an inexpensive way to use hydrogen rather than gasoline to fuel our cars, we'll be lessening pollution problems.

> *Alexandra:* I shadowed Dr. Brandolini, our mentor, to learn about lead. This element has a long history, since humans could melt lead and make things from it about six thousand years ago. Ancient Rome had lead pipes; in the American Revolution (okay, I've jumped a few thousand years there—wanted to see if you were paying attention) the colonists used lead balls in their muskets. Dr. B. led (Did you catch the word play?) me through an experiment using eight lead crystal wineglasses. By putting different amounts of water in each and then rubbing the rims, I can play the musical scale!

Other students follow with reports from the chapters they used for the Job Try-Out strategy. The whole class benefited from hearing about individual experiments and interesting lessons involving phosphorus, carbon, iron, silicon, calcium, magnesium, and other elements, which no longer existed for these students simply as symbols residing in the periodic table for the purpose of stumping them on quizzes. Through authentic learning, the students saw the chemical elements as being real and having an impact on their lives; they also obtained an idea about the activities of a chemist.

ROLE PLAYING

Standards Addressed

History: Students marshal evidence of antecedent circumstances and contemporary factors contributing to problems and alternative courses of action. Students formulate a position or course of action on an issue. Students evaluate the implementation of a decision.

English/Language Arts: Students participate as knowledgeable, reflective, creative, and critical members of a variety of literacy communities.

Context/Rationale

Role playing is a time-honored method that allows people to understand and explain their own beliefs, positions, or stances on issues, as well as analyze and appreciate perspectives other than their own. No matter what the subject area and topic, many skills are involved in role playing as students develop and enact their roles, as well as listen and react to others' roles. They'll gain confidence and understanding as they read texts and present position statements in the roles of mathematicians, sociologists, psychologists, historians, government leaders, scientists, teachers, immigration officials, war protesters, patent officers, law enforcers, poets, parents, computer experts, painters, musicians, accountants, school administrators, doctors, tourist agents, language mavens, and countless others.

Unlike in readers theatre, there are no scripts in role playing other than those the students create themselves. Many law schools, colleges, and high schools sponsor moot court competitions, often requiring participants to argue from both sides of a case, or from the position they least favor. Using the books in this chapter, among others, you may teach and facilitate role-playing activities that will help students think critically and express viewpoints relative to concepts in your social studies, science, biology, or art curriculum. Imagine students taking on the roles of scientists and leaders who had to decide whether to use the atomic bomb against Japan in 1945; environmentalists, business leaders, and politicians arguing the pros and cons of legislation affecting regions where species of plants and wildlife are in danger; art historians debating which works of which artists are worthy of displaying in a museum. We can help our students research background information to support the side they represent and discredit the side they will argue against, and organize their presentations in a way that will persuade an audience.

Procedure

- Select a book that contains different perspectives on a controversial issue in your discipline or court cases or case studies. Possible examples include:

  Art Against the Odds: From Slave Quilts to Prison Paintings (2004, see Chapter 3) (art)

  The History of Rap Music (2001, see Chapter 3) (music)

  Marjory Stoneman Douglas: Guardian of the 'Glades (2002, see Chapter 5) (science)

  They Broke the Law—You Be the Judge: True Cases of Teen Crime (2003, see Part 4 of this chapter) (English and social studies)

  You Be the Jury: Courtroom Collection (2005, see Part 4 of this chapter) (English and social studies)

- Preview the book and ask students to select the roles they would like to play (e.g., a panel of scientists, a group of environmentalists appearing before a government group, museum curators making a case for a special exhibit to the museum director or board, or figures in a court case such as judge, jury, prosecutor, defense attorney, witnesses, and so on).

- Instruct students to read the book paying special attention to the arguments/ responses of the character whose role they will assume.

- Recommend that they take notes about important points in the reading.

- Suggest that students prepare exhibits as needed to reinforce their arguments.

- Provide simple props and arrange the classroom appropriately to simulate a courtroom, legislative body, etc.

- Instruct students that when it's their turn to present to be sure to speak clearly, make eye contact, and present a persuasive argument. Recommend that they use their notes from the reading, and provide a pointer they can use as they explain their exhibits.

- After the arguments have been presented, have the listening audience (e.g., judge, jury, congressional committee) decide on the effectiveness of the arguments.

- Repeat this activity using different books and with different students playing the role of presenters and deciding audience.

Walk-Through

As an example, the book *They Broke the Law—You Be the Judge: True Cases of Teen Crime* by Thomas A. Jacobs (2003) could be used profitably in an English or a government course. The author, a judge who really had to decide consequences for the juveniles found guilty in the cases presented in this book, describes the role-playing experience:

Sample role-playing guide.   FIGURE   7.1

CLASSROOM COURTROOM GUIDE FOR USING *YOU BE THE JURY* BY MARVIN MILLER

Directions: You'll notice that there's a gavel on the teacher's desk and a witness chair set up beside the desk. For the next week, our classroom is going to be a courtroom, and you are going to get the chance to take on the roles of defense attorney, lawyer for the plaintiff, and jury. The book by Marvin Miller has been taken apart, and the 40 cases are arranged in plastic sleeves. You are to choose two cases and study them thoroughly. For one, you will present the case for the plaintiff to a jury of your peers (classmates). Someone else will plead the defendant's case. For the second, you will be the defense lawyer, and someone else will be the prosecutor. When other cases are presented, you will be a juror, examining the evidence the lawyers present in Exhibits A, B, and C, listening to the arguments, and talking with others to reach a verdict.

When it's your turn to be an attorney, be sure to speak clearly, make eye contact with the jury, and pre-sent a persuasive argument. You may take notes up with you that you have prepared from the evidence you've been given, and you'll have a pointer to use as you explain the exhibits to the jury.

These exercises will help your listening and speaking skills, and will give you practice making inferences and drawing conclusions as you critically think about the evidence others provide. These are all valuable skills both in the classroom and in the real world. Most likely, some day you will be called for jury duty. And you might decide to pursue a career in the legal field or some other field where you must advocate for others or make a strong case for a product or policy.

We'll hear the first cases on next Monday. I'll draw numbers from a hat, so be prepared to present at any time.

This book puts you in the role of answering . . . hard questions. You'll see these cases unfold, as they did before me. You'll be asked to step into my shoes—to become a juvenile court judge and determine how a teenager should be held responsible for her crime. . . . You will have all the information that was available to me at the time of sentencing. (p. ix)

The book gives the actual sentence ordered by Jacobs in each of the 21 cases, so that students, after they've played and argued the role of judge, are able to compare their decisions with the real ones, perhaps concluding that they did a better job than Jacobs. Turn your classroom into a virtual courtroom, as students prepare and act out the roles of defendant, defense attorney, judge, court reporter, prosecutor, and witnesses.

A second example of how a teacher can guide students as they role-play using a book can be seen in the guide shown in Figure 7.1.

MODELING PREVIEWING: GETTING AN OVERVIEW OF A BOOK

Standards Addressed

History: Students evaluate alternative courses of action.

English/Language Arts: Students apply a wide range of strategies to comprehend, interpret, evaluate, and appreciate texts.

Context/Rationale

Sometimes we don't realize how little practice students have had with browsing through books and perusing their contents. Students who have had little book experience outside of the school setting often think that a book is supposed to be read because it is assigned, and that a book should be read from cover to cover. They might not realize that mature readers, good readers, often turn to the back to see how many pages there are, skim something from the middle to get an idea of a writer's style, check out the table of contents, pictures and captions, read selected parts that serve particular purposes, and abandon books that they don't enjoy or are not finding useful. These students might also be unaware of how very differently we need to read different genres, or how many books use a format that invites perusing and does not require chapters to be read sequentially. We teachers need to model the practices of successful readers in order to give our students tools for reading and confidence when they open a new book.

Procedure

- Have the students begin by examining the text features designed to serve as aids for the reader.

- Suggest that they begin with the table of contents and predict what they think the various chapters will be about. They should also consider if they have prior knowledge about any of the chapter topics.

- Have them select a chapter in which they are most interested.

- Instruct them to review Chapter 1 and then review their selected chapter. Suggest that they look at the illustrations and read the captions, heads, and subheads with the chapters, and any special features in the text (numbered or bulleted lists, excerpts, quotes, and so forth).

- Have the students look for any other reader aids that the book may offer (index, glossary, resource lists).

- After following the above steps, students should now be ready to read their selected chapter.

Walk-Through

The following scenario shows a teacher of a government course that has a service learning component talking through her processes as she reads a "how-to" book.

Ms. Sanchez: Next week you'll be signing up for the kind of service learning you'd like to participate in. To help you as you make your choices, Mr. Mazza, the librarian, and I have gathered a couple dozen books on the topic. They'll be on this cart in our classroom for the next two weeks. You'll be given some time in class to explore them, and you'll also be allowed to borrow them overnight.

Now, obviously, most of you do not have the time to read all these books in their entirety. I'm going to do a think-aloud as I investigate the book *Volunteering: The Ultimate Teen Guide* by Kathlyn Gay (2004). This will remind you of some of the techniques you can use when you find a book and need to find out whether it will help you for your particular purposes. Ready? Here goes:

I see on the cover a boy and a girl, both smiling as they work with food. I wonder if the whole book is going to be about working in a soup kitchen, and other ways to work in neighborhoods with poverty. Turning to the Table of Contents, I can see that it's going to cover a much broader range of volunteer opportunities. Chapter Five is about "Helping the Homeless, Feeding the Hungry," but I see that Chapter Four deals with health care, Chapter Six is about protecting the environment and animals, Chapter Seven is "Preserving the Past," and Chapter Eight is called "Counseling, Teaching, and Tutoring." The titles of Chapters Nine and Ten are "Reducing Bigotry, Prejudice, and Racism," and "Campaigning, Communicating, and Collecting," respectively. I'm stopping for a minute to think. I realize that, if I want to, I can eliminate some chapters altogether, and so can you. Some of you are politically and socially active already (maybe partially because of this government course you're in), so Chapters Nine and Ten might be what you turn to first. Kyoko wants to be a doctor, so I'd suggest she start with Chapter Four; Laurene and

Tyler want to be teachers, so the chapter involving tutoring should be of special interest to them. I know several of you are vegetarians, and many of you have pets, so why not check out Chapter Six. You get the idea.

Okay, I've decided that before I go to the chapter that intrigues me the most, the one on preserving the past, I want to see what the introductory chapter has to offer. Chapter One, "Being a Volunteer," starts with some real-life examples of teens volunteering. There's a whole page (three) on one girl's experience, but I look at the photo of her and the caption underneath, "Volunteer Christina Mahous in Ohio packs supplies for a summer 'Project ARISE' to help immigrant children in South Texas." I already know a lot; if I'm interested, I can come back and read the whole thing. Now I notice a bulleted list on page two of characteristics that make a successful volunteer. They include empathy and compassion, reliability, enthusiasm, willingness to collaborate, and other qualities. I could stop here to reflect on how I think I measure up in these categories, or I can go on. I turn to Chapter Two, "Building and Repairing," look at the picture of a volunteer for "Habitat for Humanity" posing on top of a house that's under construction. I realize it's time for me to choose which chapters to read more thoroughly, based on my own interests, rather than read every chapter in order. But first, I'm flipping to the end to see what's there for me. Ah, there's a list of resource organizations. They might come in handy by next week.

I've just modeled for you how I conduct an overview of a book that's a guide to hands-on experiences. You won't do it exactly the same way, and that's okay. The other books on the shelf here will use different formats and offer a variety of types of information. So try it out, and if you seem to get bogged down, call me over, and I'll give you advice on how to skim and make decisions about how, and whether, you'll continue with the book you've picked up. I predict that by the end of the week, you all will have found at least one book you want to pursue in more depth. Tomorrow I'll give a mini-lesson on taking notes as you read this kind of book. But for the rest of this class period, choose a book to bring back to your seat to explore, and feel free to come up and exchange one book for another at any point.

K-W-L-S

Standards Addressed

Art: Students apply subjects, symbols, and ideas in their artworks and use the skills gained to solve problems in daily life. Students select media, techniques, and processes; analyze what makes them effective or not effective in communicating ideas; and reflect upon the effectiveness of their choices.

History: Students draw upon visual, literary, and musical sources.

English/Language Arts: Students use spoken, written, and visual language to accomplish their own purpose.

Context/Rationale

K-W-L-S (Sippola, 1995) works well with how-to books because of the assumed purposeful activity it will lead to. Using K-W-L-S, teachers can assess what students already know about a curricular topic as well as stimulate thinking to remind students of what they know. As students share what they already *know* during the **"K"** part to the activity, students are learning from each other and getting an overview as well as details about the subject that will be read about. In the **"W"** phase, teachers will help students to wonder about the topic and think of *what* they would like to learn and of questions that they might, or at least hope to, find answers to as they read. They now have a purpose for reading; readers truly want to comprehend the text, since it will result in a meaningful product. During the **"L"** phase, they jot down things they've *learned* from a text. This may help them remember the key points. Finally, in the **"S"** phase, students work together to determine what they would *still* like to learn and to ask new questions and to decide where to look next for further information that will deepen their understanding and satisfy their curiosity.

Walk-Through

The following scenario exemplifies how a teacher could help facilitate the strategy near the beginning of an interdisciplinary art/social studies project.

> *Mr. Trey:* We've looked at several books about famous people and events that use a scrapbook format, such as *Our Eleanor: A Scrapbook Look at Eleanor Roosevelt's Remarkable Life* by Candace Fleming (2005) and *For Home and Country: A Civil War Scrapbook* by Norman Bolotin and Angela Herb (1995). Over the course of the next month, you will be producing two scrapbooks. The first will focus on you, in the context of your family and/or friends and of your community. I'll want you to think of an audience for your work. Who might it be a gift for? Or how might you put it to use later in your life? Who will be viewing it in order to better understand you? The second scrapbook will be done with two or three of your classmates, and it will be a scrapbook of a particular person and/or social or artistic movement you have learned about in social studies or art this year. Before we begin the actual hands-on work, we're going to read this book: *The Kids' Guide to Making Scrapbooks and Photo Albums!: How to Collect, Design, Assemble, Decorate* by Laura Check (2002). I've posted a K-W-L-S chart on our bulletin board, and I invite you to choose a recorder and begin calling out some things you already know about scrapbooks.

After brainstorming and discussion, the first column of the class K-W-L-S chart contains the information shown in Figure 7.2.

> *Mr. Trey:* Okay, I know you're anxious to get into the book and into the project itself, but I want you to think about things you *need* to know, or *want* to know, about scrapbooking, keeping in mind the two real scrapbooks you'll be producing. Let's pick a new recorder and begin questioning.

The chart now has the information shown in Figure 7.3 in the **W** column.

FIGURE **7.2**   The K column of a K-W-L-S chart on creating a scrapbook.

What We Know About Creating a Scrapbook

— need to ask self or others what are some key events or traits about the person

— need to find inexpensive materials to work with

— need to go through photographs we own, and then ask others for permission to use theirs (try to use only ones we can keep)

— need to make a commitment to spending a lot of time in order to make it look good

— it should tell a story in pictures; there might be a theme; we need to make decisions about sequence

— the text can vary—we could have just captions under the pictures, or quotes from the person or others

| The W column of a K-W-L-S chart on creating a scrapbook. | FIGURE | 7.3 |

What We Want or Need to Know About Creating a Scrapbook

— Where can we get cheap materials like fabric, buttons, blank albums, sequins, yarn, glitter, etc.?

— Can we use digital pictures and text? What are the advantages and/or disadvantages of using technology for this project?

— Once we've got our pictures chosen and organized and on pages, how do we actually put the book together?

— How can we convince people to give us some photos for our project?

— How can we best get across a theme or make our message powerful? How can we make sure our scrapbook really captures ourselves or the focus person we've chosen?

Students are now ready and eager to see what the book has to offer. After they've read it and had further discussion with Mr. Trey, they list things they've learned, so that the **L** column looks as shown in Figure 7.4.

> *Mr. Trey:* All right, I think we'll be ready to start our projects tomorrow. We'll make a list of things we can ask family members and neighbors for to help us decorate the scrapbooks. But first, are there things you still want to know after reading the book? Any unanswered questions, or new questions that have popped into your minds?

| The L column of a K-W-L-S chart on creating a scrapbook. | FIGURE | 7.4 |

What We've Learned About Creating a Scrapbook

— We should have several types of pens available, including fine-point for outlining and wide tips for broad strokes. If we're using colored paper, gel-ink pens will show up well.

— How we arrange pictures on a page is referred to as the composition. We can put a large photo in the center and surround it with smaller photos, and we should put pictures together that relate thematically or that represent good color combinations.

— We can overlap photos to give our page the look of a collage.

— We can make 2 L-shaped figures with cardboard and masking tape to help us when we need to crop pictures to make them smaller or to change the shape or cut out a part we don't want. Measuring is important.

— There are all kinds of ways to bind our scrapbook. We can use a 3-ring binder or a spiral binder, or make a post-bound album with paper fasteners.

— We can design a cover using fabric like denim or lace; we can decoupage the cover using magazine pictures, greeting cards, and/or photos. We'll need a clear finish to coat the cover with if we decide on the decoupage design. We can also add stickers, stamping, and lettering to suit our needs. The cover, like the rest of the scrapbook, should represent us, so we make the final decisions.

FIGURE	7.5	The S column of a K-W-L-S chart on creating a scrapbook.

What Do We Still Want to Know About Creating a Scrapbook?

— How much do gel-ink pens cost? How about spiral binders and 3-ring binders?

— What's the best sealer for a decoupage cover? (Barry will check the office supply store tonight.)

— This book says it's a guide for kids. What do adult-level books about scrapbooking have to add? (Lucy will go to the public library this evening.)

— Where can we see more examples of real scrapbooks? (Mr. Trey will ask the faculty at a meeting tomorrow. Marcy and Rodney will ask their mothers to lend theirs. Chauncey is going to bring in a scrapbook he made of his favorite football team last season.)

Figure 7.5 shows the final column on the K-W-L-S chart. Students, of course, can add to it as the project gets under way, and Mr. Trey has provided a new resource, Susan Pickering Rothamel's *The Encyclopedia of Scrapbooking: Tools & Techniques* (2005) to the classroom library to help students advance in their skills and search for answers to their new questions.

The K-W-L-S chart can be revisited after the students make their first scrapbook. There will be new questions and sources of information to deal with as they proceed to the social studies–related version.

▶ ▶ ▶ INSIDE–OUTSIDE CIRCLE

Standards Addressed

English/Language Arts: Students adjust their use of spoken, written, and visual language (e.g., conventions, style, vocabulary) to communicate effectively with a variety of audiences and for different purposes.

Students apply knowledge of language structure, language conventions . . . figurative language, and genre to create, critique, and discuss print and nonprint texts.

Context/Rationale

As the name suggests, the inside–outside circle strategy (Kagan, 1989) involves students forming two circles; those on the inside face partners on the outside, and a conversation ensues about a text they've read or a curricular topic the teacher has suggested. Everyone talks at once, but those in pairs are focused on talking and listening to each other, so they're actively involved at all times. After a few moments, the teacher or other facilitator gives a signal that indicates students should move to a new position. Perhaps the teacher instructs the inside circle participants to move counterclockwise past two people, and then to start conversing again with a different partner, using the same prompt or a new one.

Depending on your subject area, there are many variations an inside–outside circle involving interactive books can take. For example, after learning new signs from a book such as Grayson's *Talking with Your Hands Listening with Your Eyes* (2003; see Part 4), *Signing Illustrated* (Flodin, 2004), or *The American Sign Language Puzzle Book* (Segal, 2003; see Part 4), students in a sign language class could participate in a circle where communication must be done through signing and other visual forms of communication. A circle in a physical education class where the students have read Cooper's *Um, Like ***OM: A Girl Goddess's Guide to Yoga* (2005; see Part 4) could involve a lot of movement as students show each other yoga positions and exercises they have learned by following instructions in the book. Science students who have worked with *Ecology Crafts for Kids: 50 Great Ways to Make Friends with Planet Earth* (Needham, 1998; see Part 4) can use the inside-outside circle strategy to share the individual projects they've completed with their classmates and learn about the principles behind the creations their peers have produced.

Walk-Through

Mr. Keating has been helping his seventh-grade English students increase their vocabularies by teaching prefixes, suffixes, and roots throughout the school year. The students have thoroughly enjoyed teleporting with the Kryptokids through the interactive *Cryptomania!* by Edith Hope Fine (see Part 4). In the spring, he tells his students that the sixth-grade teacher, Ms. Delduchetto, has invited them to teleport across the hall to teach her students some affixes that will help them in all of their subject areas. The class is familiar with the inside–outside circle strategy, and decides that is the most efficient way to give every seventh grader a chance to teach and to give every sixth grader a chance to interact with a person who can answer questions and give examples.

Let's teleport ourselves to the sixth-grade classroom, where a lot of vocabulary lessons are being taught simultaneously. If we position ourselves near one speaker–listener pair, we hear this bit of conversation:

Molly: I remember last year we spent a lot of time learning about science. What are you studying in that subject?

Lourdes: We studied about the ocean, and we've just started a unit on astronomy.

Molly: Guess what! You just used a word that is built from parts. I learned in this book, *Cryptomania!* that astro = star. Can you think of other words that might be built from the same part?

Lourdes: Umm, astronaut?

Molly: For sure! And think about what an asterisk is—a little star! The book also taught me that naut = sailor, so think how those two parts together would make sense. An astronaut can sail through the sky!

As we travel through space to a different part of the circle, we can eavesdrop on another pair of learners:

Esperanza: Lots of words that have to do with technology come from Latin and Greek roots. On this page you can see a little bird telling a squirrel that ". . . cursor is Latin for 'runner.'" The squirrel answers, "And deletus is Latin for 'destroyed' or 'erased.' Delete—get it?" (p. 19)

Rory: I use those words when I'm at the computer. I never thought about where they came from. Are there more?

Esperanza: Oh, yeah. Look at this part. The kids explain two different systems of coding numbers. We usually use a decimal system. *Decem* = ten. But computers use a binary system. Can you guess what *bin* or *bi* means?

Rory: Uh, not really.

Esperanza: That's okay. Let's think of other words that start with bi: bicycle, bisect, bilateral . . .

Rory: Bifocals, binoculars— It must mean *two.*

Esperanza: Exactly! Look, it tells us here that computers use a sort of machine code that uses just zeroes and ones. That's a binary code.

Rory: I know other number prefixes. Tri means three, and quad means four.

Esperanza: Hey, you're good! We can teleport to the Mathopolis page; look, it gives other number prefixes. I'll bet you know *octo*. But do you know *hex*?

The teaching and learning continue, with various combinations of sixth- and seventh-graders, until the teachers give a signal to conclude. They might give students a few moments to write out the prefixes and suffixes they've learned.

▶ ▶ ▶ USING TEACHER-CONSTRUCTED READING GUIDES

Standards Addressed

Math: Students specify locations and describe spatial relationships using coordinate geometry and other representational systems. Students use visualization, spatial reasoning, and geometric modeling to solve problems.

English/Language Arts: Students adjust their use of spoken, written, and visual language (e.g., conventions, style, vocabulary) to communicate effectively with a variety of audiences for different purposes.

Context/Rationale

The benefit of using reading guides created by teachers who know their students' needs and interests as well as their school's or state's curriculum has been discussed in previous chapters. Some hands-on and how-to books will need no other instruction, but others may be structured in a way that would be more accessible if reading guides accompanied them. There are dozens of types of guides from which teachers may select. With certain books, teachers might decide to create a vocabulary guide; with others, graphic organizers making clear the patterns of organization would be more appropriate.

Walk-Through

The two examples of reading guides shown in Figures 7.6 and 7.7 made by teachers exemplify how this strategy can help students. One is a guide to be completed before reading; the other is intended to be completed after reading the book.

FIGURE 7.6   Anticipation guide and reading guide for *Groovy Geometry,* by Lynette Long.

Part A: Before we begin this new book, there are questions I'd like you to answer to get your minds ready for what the text will offer.

1. Parallel lines are lines that never intersect. A rectangle has two pairs of parallel lines. The yellow lines on the sides of roads are parallel. Can you name or draw another example of parallel lines?

2. You have all used the famous Pythagorean theorem, $a^2 + b^2 = c^2$. Draw a picture showing what this could look like.

3. Quadrilaterals are four-sided figures such as a kite $\diamondsuit$ or a square $\square$. Please name and draw two more. (You may look in your textbook or a dictionary for help.)

4. You have all seen cubes, such as ice cubes and a Rubik's Cube. How many sides does a cube have?

(continued)

Anticipation guide and reading guide, continued.   FIGURE   **7.6**

Part B: We are going to explore a fun interactive book. From the desk at the front of the room you will need to get a ruler, graph paper, tape, scissors, and four colored pencils. You will work with a partner so you can share materials.

1. You are going to draw two parallel lines with a transversal (a line going through both parallel lines). You are then going to color in the different angles formed. You may use your own paper or the graph paper. Read and follow the instructions on page 15 of *Groovy Geometry*, "Color by Angles."

2. Using graph paper and a ruler, you are going to draw a right triangle and its squared sides. This will give you a better understanding of the Pythagorean Theorem. Read and follow the instructions on page 49, "Pythagorean Proof."

3. You and your partner are going to construct and play a game using quadrilaterals. Follow the instructions on page 55, "Crazy About Quadrilaterals."

4. At right, you have been provided with a cube pattern. You need to cut it out and form a cube. I would also like to know from you the volume of the cube. If you need help, see page 97, "Cube Construction."

Post-reading activity guide for *Because of Winn Dixie: The Official Movie Scrapbook*, by Jean K. Kwon and Suzanne Tenner, created by Chrystal Bailey.   FIGURE   **7.7**

Directions: We have read *Because of Winn Dixie*, by Kate di Camillo, and watched excerpts of the movie with the same title. After reading *Because of Winn Dixie: The Official Movie Scrapbook*, by Jean K. Kwon and Suzanne Tenner, notice the format of the book, the layout of the photographs, and the features it contains. Note that the information is narrated by the dog himself, and told from his point of view.

Now, with your base groups, decide on another novel we've read this year. Using the scrapbook you've just read as a model, create one for the book you've chosen. Decide on a narrator, key lists, and pictures you'll include, appropriate recipes or songs or poems to add. Talk about which character should narrate the key points of your scrapbook. (Choose one other than the narrator in the novel itself.) Be sure to describe and/or picture the setting for your readers. Divide responsibilities among you. One person might be the artist, another the lead writer, another the data organizer. When we're done, we'll have six scrapbooks to add to our classroom library. Your group will get a chance to present your creation one week from today.

PART 3

author STUDIES

JANICE VANCLEAVE

Use this author's books in **English, science,** *and other disciplines.*

Figure 7.8 is a selected bibliography of Janice VanCleave's works.

Want literally thousands of ideas and instructions for science projects at many levels of difficulty? Janice VanCleave is at your service as fast as you can get to the library catalog. She even understands that sometimes you might be in a rush, as her title *Help! My Science Project Is Due Tomorrow!* (2001) shows. Or you might like surprises and challenges, which you can find in *Janice VanCleave's The Solar System: Mind-Boggling Experiments You Can Turn into Science Fair Projects* (2000). Do your middle and high school students like to receive grades of A+? Direct them to *A+ Science Fair Projects* (2003). She gives research hints, hypothesis hints, and experimentation hints in the first chapter. The next chapter helps readers learn how to choose topics. Part 2 incorporates all the projects, categorized by the branches of science. Helpful appendices are included, also.

If you're a **physics** teacher, you probably know that the words *physics* and *difficult* seem to go hand in hand for many people. VanCleave, in her *A+ Projects in Physics* (2003), helps the principles of the subject become accessible to those willing to participate in the projects she presents. She explains the scientific method and encourages readers to try new approaches, keep a journal, assemble a display. The 30 topics cover areas from rotational inertia to magnetic fields, from thermal conduction to longitudinal sound waves. There are projects dealing with light, heat, measurement, sound, fluids, force and motion, and electricity and magnetism. It's a science lab in book form.

Perhaps your curriculum deals with the life sciences. *Janice VanCleave's Insects and Spiders* (1998) has 20 chapters with a consistent organizational pattern. I'll use Chapter 3, "Jointed" (pp. 12–15), as an example. The problem is stated as a question: "What are the main external identifying features of adult insects?" (p. 12). Then the materials you'll need are listed, followed by the steps of the procedure you'll want to follow for the guaranteed results, which are followed by a scientific explanation. The "Let's Explore" section suggests further activities that could become a science fair project, and then "Show Time!" tells how to prepare diagrams or display other insects to demonstrate what you've learned. Finally, a "Check It Out!" section is included for

---

FIGURE 7.8 Selected works by Janice VanCleave.

VanCleave, J. P. (2006). *Hands-on Bible explorations: 52 fun activities for Christian learning.* Hoboken, NJ: John Wiley & Sons.

VanCleave, J. P. (2005). *Janice VanCleave's A+ projects in biology: Winning experiments for science fairs and extra credit.* Princeton, NJ: Recording for the Blind & Dyslexic. Sound Recording: Non-music: Secondary (senior high) school: Compact disc.

VanCleave, J. P. (2005). *Janice VanCleave's energy for every kid.* Hoboken, NJ: John Wiley & Sons.

VanCleave, J. P. (2005). *Janice VanCleave's teaching the fun of math.* Hoboken, NJ: John Wiley & Sons.

VanCleave, J. P. (2004). *Janice VanCleave's science around the world: Activities on biomes from pole to pole.* Hoboken, NJ: John Wiley & Sons.

VanCleave, J. P. (2004). *Janice VanCleave's scientists through the ages.* Hoboken, NJ: John Wiley & Sons.

VanCleave, J. P. (2004). *Janice VanCleave's super science models.* Hoboken, NJ: John Wiley & Sons.

VanCleave, J. P., & Wauters, A. (2004). *Janice VanCleave's food and nutrition for every kid: Easy activities that make learning science fun.* Washington, DC: National Library Service for the Blind and Physically Handicapped, Library of Congress. Sound Recording: Non-music. Cassette tape.

VanCleave, J. P. (2003). *Janice VanCleave's A+ projects in physics: Winning experiments for science fairs and extra credit.* Hoboken, NJ: John Wiley & Sons.

VanCleave, J. (2003). *A+ science fair projects.* Hoboken, NJ: John Wiley & Sons.

VanCleave, J. P. (2003). *Janice VanCleave's A+ science fair workbook and project journal. Grades 7–12.* Hoboken, NJ: John Wiley & Sons.

advanced exploration. The chapter layouts are conducive to differentiated instruction, since teachers and/or students can determine how far they want to go to investigate the problems.

A historical perspective is present in *Janice VanCleave's Scientists Through the Ages* (2004). After five introductory chapters explaining types of scientists, along with activities for readers to try out, there are chapters on individuals in the context of their times, including Mary Anning, Maria Mitchell, Rachel Carson, Archimedes, and Caroline and William Herschel. Here, too, are "Fun Time!" experiments so that the reader can not merely imagine, but replicate, some of the observing and thinking of these great people. For example, after reading of Rosalyn Sussman Yalow, the first American woman to receive the Nobel Prize in Medicine, students can follow the directions to build a model of a biochemical locator. After playing with the pipe cleaners and magnets involved, they'll understand some scientific principles better; equally important, they'll have an appreciation for the woman who researched the use of radioisotopes, and who encourages women to pursue science careers. "She is known for saying the world cannot afford the loss of the talents of half its people if it is to solve its many problems" (p. 109).

The website http://school.discovery.com/science-faircentral/jvc/ provides a wealth of resources related to Janice VanCleave. There's a biography detailing some of her scientific travels and adventures, a database of more than 300 questions about science fairs, a treasury of science facts and experiments, and help for teachers wishing to organize a science fair.

ROBERT SABUDA

*Use this author's books in **art, English, math, science,** and other disciplines.*

Figure 7.9 is a selected bibliography of Robert Sabuda's works.

Who doesn't like pop-up books? Not very many hands would be raised in your class in response to this question. So the works of master pop-up artist Robert Sabuda should be an easy sell. At first glance, it might not be readily apparent how many curricular connections we can make from them. But, to start with, there are the topics themselves. He's designed and illustrated versions of classic works of literature: L. Frank Baum's *The Wizard of Oz* (2000), Lewis Carroll's *Alice's Adventures in Wonderland* (2003), Clement Moore's *The Night Before Christmas* (2002), *The Twelve Days of Christmas* (1996), *The Moveable Mother Goose* (1999). **Social studies** and **music** teachers can proudly display *America the Beautiful* (2004). Everyone can learn from his *Kwaanza Celebration: A Pop-Up Book* (1995). **Art** and **English** students might model their own alphabet books after his *Christmas Alphabet: Deluxe Anniversary Pop-Up* (2004). Home and Careers students will enjoy *Cookie Count: A Tasty Pop-Up* (1997). Students interested in ancient **history** will want to explore *Tutankhamen's Gift* (1994) and *Encyclopedia Prehistorica: Dinosaurs* (2005). **Biology** teachers can introduce students to *Young Naturalist's Pop-Up Handbook: Beetles*, and *Young Naturalist's Pop-Up Handbook: Butterflies*, both produced in 2001 with Matthew Reinhart.

Selected works by Robert Sabuda.   **FIGURE 7.9**

Findlay, J. A., Kubasta, V., Sabuda, R., et al. (2004). *Paper engineering: The pop-up book structures of Vojtech Kubasta, Robert Sabuda, and Andrew Binder.* Ft. Lauderdale, FL: Bienes Center for the Literary Arts, the Dianne and Michael Bienes Special Collections and Rare Book Library, Broward County.

Sabuda, R., & Reinhart, M. (2006). *Sharks and other sea monsters: Encyclopedia prehistorica.* Cambridge, MA: Candlewick Press.

Sabuda, R., & Reinhart, M. (2005). *Dinosaurs: Encyclopedia prehistorica.* Cambridge, MA: Candlewick Press.

Sabuda, R. (2004). *The Christmas alphabet: Deluxe anniversary pop-up.* New York: Orchard Books.

Sabuda, R., & K. L. Bates. (2004). *America the beautiful.* New York: Simon & Schuster.

Sabuda, R. (2003). *Robert Sabuda travels in time and space.* Videorecording: VHS tape.

Sabuda, R., & Carroll, L. (2003). *Alice's adventures in Wonderland.* New York: Little Simon.

Sabuda, R. (2002). *The adventures of Providence traveler, 1503: Uh-oh, Leonardo!* New York: Atheneum Books for Young Readers.

Sabuda, R. (2002). *Popping up in Ecuador: How a pop-up book is made.* Videorecording: VHS tape.

Sabuda, R., & Reinhart, M. (2001). *Young naturalist's pop-up handbook: Butterflies.* New York: Hyperion Books for Children.

Sabuda, R., & Reinhart, M. (2001). *Young naturalist's pop-up handbook: Beetles.* New York: Hyperion Books for Children.

Sabuda, R., & Baum, F. (2000). *The wonderful wizard of Oz.* London: Simon & Schuster.

Science, math, technology, and **art** come together in Sabuda's creations. What does it take to create the elaborate and fine-tuned motions that occur when the pages of his books are opened? Teachers, have your students ponder the scientific and mathematical principles involved as they study the paper sculptures and examine what makes them work. Then ask them to research books, articles, and websites that explain paper engineering, and try out some creations of their own. *The Elements of Pop-Up: A Pop-Up Book for Aspiring Paper Engineers*, by David A. Carter and James Diaz (1999) and their follow-up, *Let's Make It Pop-Up* (2004) are good places to start. Also, Sabuda's website (www.robertsabuda.com) has directions and patterns for making a pop-up book, as well as a monthly poll in which kids can give input, dozens of answers to frequently asked questions, highlights of other pop-up artists, and suggestions of books that teach the art of paper engineering.

Robert Sabuda is a great role model to turn to when you speak to your students about passionate learners and practitioners. He recalls that his career and training started early. "With the ability to hold a crayon, came the discovery that I was an artist" (www.robertsabuda.com/bio.asp). He spent his childhood school days making bulletin boards with cut paper collages, composing stories and pictures for the books he made from folded paper. He studied the pop-up books he got as gifts and practiced making his own from file folders.

Sabuda spends up to two years designing and engineering a book. He shares details of the time-consuming process. Of *Alice's Adventures in Wonderland*, he says:

> All those cards on the last page took *forever* to work out. And since I'm so detail oriented I wanted to make sure that I didn't repeat a card's face the wrong number of times, so there are exactly two full decks of playing cards (minus jokers) on that spread. Who knew a deck of cards could cause so much trouble! (www.kidsreads.com/authors/au-sabuda-robert.asp)

Students should find this self-taught artist an inspiration. I love his metacognitive reflections on his own growth:

> For many years I illustrated flat, traditional picture books but at the back of my mind was always a little voice whispering, "How about a little bit more?"
>
> So I pulled out my old pop-up books and began the laborious process of learning how to create pop-ups for the rest of the world. The task was daunting and took me many years. I can still remember looking at some of my failed pop-ups and saying to them, "Why don't you work?" (Kurkjian et al., 2005, p. 482)

WILL SHORTZ

Use this author's books in **English, math,** *and other disciplines.*

Figure 7.10 is a selected bibliography of Will Shortz's works.

I went to a lecture by enigmatologist Will Shortz, and when I saw how he engaged an audience of close to 2,000 people in a game of word puzzles, I pictured him as a teacher with a very large class. I wanted to learn from this master how to find and create fascinating questions involving plays on words, and how to facilitate a group investigation of language issues in a lively and stimulating manner.

Perhaps you paused at the word *enigmatologist*; students who are pondering future careers and college majors might be interested to know that Shortz created his own major in college to explore the study of puzzles, labeling it *enigmatology*. Already we have an example of problem solving; we can infer that he was not satisfied with any existing major, so thought creatively to meet his needs. Then he had to figure out a way to make a living with his degree and skills. He was an editor of *Games Magazine* for a while, then became crossword editor of the *New York Times*.

Introducing our students to this word lover can lead to their completing crossword puzzles, either those supplied daily by the *New York Times* or others; creating crossword puzzles of their own, maybe using the curricular content of the course you teach; and listening to National Public Radio to participate along with people from around the country in solving weekly puzzles presented over the air by Shortz. Fans may also do research to find out how Shortz thinks about his job, what process he uses to publish daily crossword puzzles, some of the ways he talks about his love of language, and tips he has for puzzle solvers.

In your classroom library, you will want to have books such as *Games Magazine Presents Will Shortz's Brain Busters* (1991) as well as other puzzle books that represent a range in difficulty, thus making them ideal for differentiated instruction. Instruct your students to start out with easy puzzles, get teacher guidance as needed, and work their way up to the more challenging versions. **Math** teachers will be especially pleased when students eagerly interact with numbers to solve Shortz's many Sudoku puzzles.

Shortz is co-editor of *World-Class Puzzles from the World Puzzle Championships, Volume 3* (2002). In the Foreword, he and Nick Baxter give some background on the annual competition, showing how puzzling has even become a spectator sport, and then they

Selected works by Will Shortz.   FIGURE   **7.10**

Longo, F., & Shortz, W. (2002). *The New York Times on the Web crosswords for teens.* New York: New York Times Digital: St. Martin's Griffin.

Shortz, W. (2006). *Sudoku to boost your brainpower: 100 wordless crossword puzzles.* New York: St. Martin's Griffin.

Shortz, W. (2005). *The new puzzle classics: Ingenious twists on timeless favorites.* New York: Sterling Publishing.

Shortz, W. (2005). *The New York Times large-print Will Shortz's favorite crossword puzzles: From the pages of the New York Times.* New York: St. Martin's Griffin.

Shortz, W. (2005). *The New York Times quicker & easier crossword puzzles.* New York: St. Martin's Paperbacks.

Shortz, W. (2004). *Baseball crosswords.* New York: Sterling Publishing.

Shortz, W. (2004). *A cup of tea and crosswords: 75 light and easy puzzles.* New York: St. Martin's Griffin.

Shortz, W. (2004). *The New York Times Will Shortz's favorite Sunday crossword puzzles.* New York: St. Martin's Griffin.

Shortz, W. (2003). *The New York Times ultimate crossword omnibus.* New York: St. Martin's Griffin.

Shortz, W. (2003). *The puzzlemaster presents Will Shortz's best puzzles from NPR. Vol. 2.* New York: Random House Puzzles & Games.

Shortz, W., & Baxter, N. (2003). *World-class puzzles from the world puzzle championships. Vol. 4.* New York: Random House Puzzles & Games.

Shortz, W. (2002). *The New York Times Monday through Friday easy to tough crossword puzzles.* New York: St. Martin's Griffin.

Shortz, W. (1991). *Games Magazine presents Will Shortz's brain busters.* New York: Times Books.

invite readers to think about trying out for a future competition, offering helpful websites. The remainder of the book consists of the actual puzzles that were used for the United States and Canada qualifying test and for the actual championship. There are mazes, equations, dice puzzles, word search grids, visual puzzles, and more. This could keep a club, or a class, or a whole school busy for a long time.

There's a 2006 documentary, *Wordplay*, about Will Shortz and some famous people who love puzzles. You could show the film and also have *Wordplay: The Official Companion Book* (2006) available in your lending library. There are numerous websites inviting visitors to participate in solving all levels of crossword puzzles, Sudoku, and other forms of mind-stretching games.

PART 4

ANNOTATED books and booktalks

CODE: E = Elementary, **I** = Intermediate, **M** = Middle school, **H** = High School

The following annotations will vary in format. Most will be annotations I wrote directed at a teacher audience. Some will be character booktalks, which are brought to listeners via some character's point of view, and these will be labeled as such. Still others will be excerpts from my students' reader response logs. You may adapt any of them to make the booktalk just right for your audi-

ence and appropriately connected to your curricular topics.

ART

Amara, P. (2001). *So, You Wanna Be a Comic Book Artist?: How to Break into Comics!* Illus. P. Mehan. Hillsboro, OR: Beyond Words Publishing. **(M, H)**

Aspiring comic book artists are treated with respect and given much encouragement and

ART

instruction in the chapters of this book, whose topics range from starting a studio and procuring appropriate tools to submitting a portfolio to a publisher; from creating superheroes and villains to designing video games. Vocabulary of the trade is defined, and examples from real comics fill the pages. Established comics creators are profiled, showing readers that this is indeed a potentially rewarding career path. Art teachers and **English** teachers can mentor students as they follow the instructions for writing scripts, creating characters from villains to superheroes, sketching and inking the panels, and creating a portfolio in preparation for submitting work to publishers.

Brazelto, B. (2004). *Altered Books Workshop.* Cincinnati, OH: North Light Books. **(M, H)**

Palimpsest, a very old method of recycling paper, has been in the news recently. Scientists are working with X-rays to recover the words of Archimedes that were covered over by a monk's writing several centuries later. Beverly Brazelton explains that altered book artists of today transform existing books into new forms of art by removing pages, then adding new writing, photographs, painting, stitching, calligraphy, whatever works for a particular theme or inspiration. She gives instructions in basic techniques and variations; she shows how to cut shadow boxes, how to layer glaze over pages, how to make collage covers. The illustrations are helpful and inviting. Following the directions in this book, every student in your art class can make his or her own altered book—a signature creation, representing a unique individual.

Burleigh, R. (2004). *Seurat and La Grande Jatte.* New York: Harry. N. Abrams. Published in association with the Art Institute of Chicago. **(I, M, H)**

I think Seurat, who did such close, painstaking work, would be happy with this book that demonstrates how to look closely at a work of art to unlock its mystery and ponder its stories. The author collaborates with the reader, asking, "What do we notice first?" (p. 3). There's no preaching, no lecturing, just informed investigating. There's a sense of excitement even in the directions given. "Look at the surface of the painting. Do you see how the paint has been put on? Do you see them—the many hundreds of them? Yes, the dots!" (p. 12). Burleigh becomes a mentor, requiring readers to take on the role of art appreciator as they participate by following the instructions on the pages; he does not allow them to be passive learners.

Surely your students will want to go to the website of the Art Institute of Chicago to view and learn more; maybe they'll look for reproductions; maybe

some day they will sit before the masterpiece and remember this book that first invited them into the park on a Sunday in 1884.

Dean, I. S. (2003). *Polymer Clay: 30 Terrific Projects to Roll, Mold & Squish.* New York: Lark Books. **(I, M, H)**

Have your aspiring sculptors start here, learning about tools, textures, materials, baking tips, and design possibilities. They'll learn what polymer clay is and what forms it can take, how to condition the clay, how to mix and marble colors, and final decorating ideas. The instructions for projects will not only exemplify the concepts of your curriculum; they will lead to products such as spirit dolls, space mobiles, picture frames, clocks, locker mirrors, jewelry, and vases. Templates are provided.

d'Harcourt, C. (2003). *Art Up Close: From Ancient to Modern.* **Trans. S. Kirk-Jegousse.** San Francisco: Chronicle Books. **(E, I, M, H)**

This oversized, interactive book holds 23 masterpieces, each surrounded by circles containing enlarged details from the pictures. Readers are invited to observe very closely, and find where in the paintings the details are located. There are keys under flaps at the end of the book to help with the tough ones. Many cultures are represented by the works of art, which include an Egyptian papyrus painting from around 1300 BCE, a Byzantine mosaic from the sixth century BCE, an Arabic manuscript from the fifteenth century, an Aztec manuscript, and works from the European masters. There's information on the art types and the artists at the end, as well as information on where the paintings are now located. Your students, having actively engaged with the activities on these pages, will be begging to go to real museums to look—up close—at original works of art.

Ellis, M. (2002). *Ceramics for Kids: Creative Clay Projects to Pinch, Roll, Coil, Slam and Twist.* New York: Sterling/Lark. **(I, M, H)**

The author encourages readers to check out pottery in museums, galleries of modern-day potters, and their own homes. The basics of pottery involve using ". . . clay from the earth to make more objects than you can imagine—some useful, some beautiful, some weird" (p. 6). The projects in this book help student artists create totem poles, Egyptian canopic jars, wind chimes, teapots, Appalachian face jugs, and nature vases. Your students will learn techniques involving glazes and paints, as well as history related to ancient African clay portraits and Japanese haniwa sculptures. The photographs of children's ceramic masterpieces are inviting; they seem to call out, "You try, too!"

Finkle, C. (1997). *Camera Crafts*. Illus. J. McDonald. Los Angeles: Lowell House Juvenile. **(I, M)**

This is a good introduction to the art form, since the author covers tips on many types of photography, including, "nature, sports, travel, scenic, documentary, art, portrait, and special effects" (p. 5). For each activity, she gives preparatory advice, and explicit directions. I particularly liked the chapter on the photo essay, since I could think of so many cross-curricular connections, for example, to **English.** Readers are advised to look through issues of magazines that tell stories largely through pictures, and they learn bits about the career of photojournalism:

> A *National Geographic* photographer shoots approximately 200 rolls of film (that's over 7000 pictures!) per assignment. The final story will usually be a selection of 5 to 13 photos that best represent the subject. (p. 30)

Freeman, M. (2003). *Digital Photography: Special Effects.* New York: Amphoto Books. **(H)**

This book could be considered a course in itself; the author is a teacher who expects his readers to try things out, solve problems, apply strategies. The chapters are organized into sections dealing with tools, techniques, and application. The text is loaded with various kinds of information. For example, the chapter on surrealism gives a short history of the surrealist movement, shows photographs of a step-by-step process of creating a CD cover, and gives computer directions for distorting images based on Dali's famous *Persistence of Memory*, and other artists' work. The author uses a conversational tone as he guides readers through the process and helps them reflect. "Taking irreverence a stage further, let's now tackle a true Surrealist icon with some of the techniques and strategies we've gathered" (p. 130). "Combining familiar objects in unfamiliar ways creates 'revolutionary objects,' but it also makes us think about the original objects' meaning" (p. 134). After they read this book, have your students experiment with creating the projects using the digital techniques discussed. For example, they could create a personal CD cover using a surrealistic style.

Hosking, W. (2005). *Asian Kites: Asian Arts & Crafts for Creative Kids.* Boston: Tuttle Publishing. **(I, M)**

After a fascinating introduction about the history of the kite (dating back to 196 BCE) and a discussion of some of the military, religious, and cultural purposes of kites, this book goes into its instructional portion. Readers can complete 15 projects relating to kites from Malaysia, China, Korea, Thailand, and Japan. The book lends itself to an interdisciplinary study, since it includes science lessons on the sub-ject of winds, and plenty of historical anecdotes. **Math** concepts relating to measurements and patterns are inherent in the instructions, and the results of following the directions will be creations that are artistically beautiful.

Nguyen, D. (2003). *Jungle Animal Origami.* New York: Sterling Publishing. **(I, M)**

I can picture parents and community members visiting a school that has been decorated with hundreds of figures made from the origami patterns in this book. Students will learn math principles as they follow the explicit folding directions and illustrations; they'll re-create jungle scenes from geography texts with giraffes, gorillas, hyenas, water buffalo, wildebeest, ostriches, vultures, lions, and hippopotomi set around the classrooms and halls. Naomi Shihab Nye's collection of poetry, *19 Varieties of Gazelle* (2005), could be on display, surrounded by students' paper gazelles. This could be the beginning of something big, as teachers across the curriculum help students actively apply and combine curricular concepts related to **math, culture,** structure, engineering, and art.

Nilsen, A. (2003). *The Great Art Scandal.* Boston: Kingfisher. **(I, M, H)**

Your amateur detectives will get engrossed in this interactive book, for the narrator, City Gallery curator Molly Adams, enlists the help of her readers to put together clues to solve a crime and save her art show from ruin. The pages are cut so that readers can examine the gallery paintings on the top of the pages along with the famous works and biographical information on artists presented on the bottoms. You can learn a lot as you take on the sleuth role and attempt to be the hero who saves the day. You can connect what students are doing to solve the mystery to other types of critical thinking you have modeled and encouraged in your class.

Raczka, B. (2003). *More Than Meets the Eye: Seeing Art with All Five Senses.* Brookfield, CT: The Millbrook Press. **(E, I, M, H)**

Enter this book and respond to the invitation to taste, smell, hear, and touch famous paintings. You'll find yourself experiencing art differently as you focus on various senses. Under each painting is the title, artist, date, and present museum location. Students, after being taught skills related to art appreciation through this text, could use the book as a springboard to explore the websites of those museums to try out their senses on different paintings. In addition, you could have them cut pictures from old calendars and make individual or class books modeled after this one. Very stimulating!

Sabbeth, C. (2002). *Monet and the Impressionists for Kids (21 Activities)*. Chicago: Chicago Review Press. **(I, M, H)**

The Introduction, appropriately, welcomes readers to Claude Monet's garden, made famous by his numerous paintings from all angles and at varying times of day and seasons of the year. In Part I, we meet his friends: Pierre Auguste Renoir, Edgar Degas, and Mary Cassatt. Part II brings us into the world of some post-impressionists; we enter their lives and their paintings, and we try our hand at creating a still life à la Cezanne, imitate Gauguin's pottery techniques, and follow the recipe provided to bake Seurat sugar cookies. Art teachers will want to use the hands-on activities of this book to engage students in trying out a medium, or a style, or a persona of the artist in this book whose life, talent, philosophy, or perseverance impresses them the most. The author has also published *Frida Kahlo and Diego Rivera: Their Lives and Ideas* (2005), which has instructions for 24 hands-on activities as well as a wealth of information about these Mexican artists.

Schwarz, R. (2000). *Papier-Mâché: Kids Can Do It*. Niagara Falls, NY: Kids Can Press. **(I, M)**

The author gives a definition: . . . papier-mâché objects are layers of paper and paste—that's all" (p. 4); a bit of history, recounting that everything from delicate jewelry to houses have been made from paper-mache; a list of materials that crafters will need; a recipe for making papier-mâché goo; and tips for constructing, painting, and decorating the objects. Subsequent chapters give step-by-step instructions for making bookends, a vase, a bowl, a magazine holder, and many other animal-shaped objects. Teachers can set up the studio, provide the materials and the choices of projects that fit their curricular goals, and work alongside students, modeling and guiding as needed.

Withrow, S. (2003). *Toon Art: The Graphic Art of Digital Cartooning*. New York: Watson-Guptill Publications. **(I, M, H)**

This impressive book is divided into four major parts. After a history of cartooning that includes definitions and a timeline, there are chapters on "The Creative Process," where readers learn how to create characters, write a storyline, sketch, use color and special effects to advantage, and edit. Experts in the various subfields give tips on digital and pixel-based painting, 3D graphics and animation, making word balloons, and so on. After showcasing "toon hilarities" (p. 62), "toon personas" (p. 126), and "toon thrills" (p. 82), the final part predicts what the future holds for cartoons and cartoonists. A reference section leads readers to other "how-to" books as well as to extensive websites. Art as well as **English** teachers can guide students through the step-by-step

creative process the book uses for structure; the nine steps are as follows:

1. Choose form, format, and formula;
2. create characters;
3. write a storyline;
4. sketch backgrounds and composition;
5. draw characters;
6. color;
7. letter;
8. alter digitally; and
9. edit and post. (p. 22, paraphrased)

I predict this book will not stay on the shelves of a classroom library; classroom cartoonists will need the resource at hand.

Wolfe, G. (2002). *Look!: Zoom in on Art!* New York: Oxford University Press. **(E, I, M)**

Each chapter focuses on a certain way of looking at a painting, using examples of famous works. Readers are directed to look up, down, inside, outside, close up, and inward, among other ways. After the instruction on viewing, the author invites the reader to try out a technique. For example, after discussing the brush strokes in a self-portrait by Vincent van Gogh, there's this suggestion:

> Try this: Lightly sketch a face, then mix some beautiful, clear paint colors. Paint the face using a thin brush for the features to help you control the paint, and broader brushes for the rest. Don't be afraid to use narrow strips of bright color right next to each other. Keep your eye on this picture of Vincent van Gogh all the time, to give you an idea of how to mold the face with your brush strokes. (p. 26)

Ask your students to compare the advice and direction they receive from this book with what they have been taught from other sources in the course, letting them know there will be many voices of guides and mentors for them as they pursue art. They'll need to learn to listen carefully, recognize which ones intersect with or contradict others, and follow the ones that help them attain the goals they have set for themselves and hone their talents.

ENGLISH/LANGUAGE ARTS

Aagesen, C., & Blumberg, M. (1999). *Shakespeare for Kids: His Life and Times: 21 Activities*. Chicago: Chicago Review Press. **(M, H)**

This could have been placed in the biography or informational chapter, but the suggested projects prompted me to put it here. While reading of Will's early years, students will learn to juggle, decorate gloves, build a birdfeeder, and coin new words just as the Bard did. Another section tells of Shakespeare's career as a playwright in London, and provides instructions for designing a coat of arms, creating sound effects, making costumes, and staging a sword fight. Students can use this book as they produce a scene from *Julius Caesar*, or paint one from *A Midsummer Night's Dream*. This book could carry a class through a school year, resulting in students who have replaced fear and anxiety over the difficulty of Shakespeare with a willingness to experiment and play in his world.

Chinn, M. (2004). *Writing and Illustrating the Graphic Novel: Everything You Need to Know to Create Great Graphic Books.* Hauppauge, NY: Barron's. **(M, H)**

Fans of graphic novels will be enticed by the panels and speech bubbles on the cover, and will enjoy the many examples of graphic novel pages within. After reading about the techniques for getting inspiration, observing and recording, framing panels, writing realistic characters, drawing from a script, lighting, lettering, conveying body language, and getting a publisher, readers might be eager to try their hand at becoming a graphic novelist. A list of print resources, organizations, and websites about graphic novels is included for those who want to study the art form further and/or join the community of writers and artists in the field.

Ellis, R. (2001). *The Complete Audition Book for Young Actors: A Comprehensive Guide to Winning by Enhancing Acting Skills.* Colorado Springs, CO: Meriwether Publishing. **(M, H)**

I found the words *complete* and *comprehensive* in the title to be apt. Readers will be well prepared for both auditioning and acting if they follow the recommendations and practice the exercises supplied here. The author deals with the aspiring actor's voice, self-image, physical condition, and script-reading skills. He teaches how to prepare for a cold reading, how to develop an acting resume and supporting materials, and how to network with others in the field. Scenes and monologues are provided, as well as resources about jobs and scholarships.

Use this book before a readers theatre or more formal theater presentation. It is also an excellent choice to use with the Job Try-Out strategy described in Part 2 of this chapter.

Fine, E. H. (2004). *Cryptomania: Teleporting into Greek and Latin with the Kryptokids.* **Illus. K. Doner.** Berkeley, CA: Tricycle Press. **(I, M, H)**

Lots of books are interactive, but not many involve the reader in teleporting, as this one does! This very busy book invites readers to solve riddles and find keys to decipher vocabulary based on Greek and Latin roots. They'll visit Mathopolis, where cartoon figures using speech bubbles will teach words such as *radius, obtuse, acute, plane,* and *parallelogram,* along with prefixes and roots including *dia-, sesqui-, ped-, centi-, hex-, -gon, poly-, -polis,* and *octo-.* Dialogue between a squirrel and a bird goes like this: "Eschew sesquipedalianism!" "Right! I'll avoid using words that are a foot-and-a-half long!" (p. 27). The visual story also takes readers to the classical world, the worlds of the skies and seas, terra firma, and back to Alphasaurus Academy. It ends with a Greek and Latin Glossary and Index as well as an English Glossary and Index. Some students will want to go on the whole journey with the Kryptokids, figuring out clues with them, while others will prefer to skip right to the back and use the book as a reference tool or an efficient way to reach their goal of increasing their vocabulary.

Frank, S. (2003). *The Pen Commandments: A Guide for the Beginning Writer.* New York: Random House. **(M, H)**

As rule books go, this is a fun read. The chapters' commandments are sometimes stated negatively: "Though Shalt Not Waste Words," "Thou Shalt Not Take Essay Tests in Pain"; and sometimes positively: "Thou Shalt Overcome Writer's Block," "Thou Shalt Honor Thy Reader." One chapter says it both ways: "Thou Shalt Not Covet Thy Neighbor's Prose*," "*or how to write in a voice all your own" (p. 273). The author is encouraging and affirming throughout, and gives lots of practical examples and explanations to develop his points. Writing teachers may guide students as they follow the directions in this book on how to write well for tests, other school assignments, and self-initiated projects.

Hambleton, V., & Greenwood, C. (2001). *So, You Wanna Be a Writer?* Hillsboro, OR: Beyond Words Publishing. **(M, H)**

This book is a pep talk; the cover enticingly claims its purpose: "How to Write, Get Published, and Maybe Even Make it BIG!" Who could resist? There are interviews with published writers, such as Michael Crichton and Todd Strasser, as well as with 10 kids who have been published. A list of famous authors who published while in their teens includes Louisa May Alcott, Langston Hughes, Sylvia Plath, Stephen King, Edgar Allan Poe, F. Scott Fitzgerald, and James Joyce. The book is loaded with lists of dos and don'ts, tips, suggestions for topics, and guidelines for writing to publishers. This book might be saying what we teachers have been saying all along, but it's in a form our students are likely to listen to.

Heiligman, D. (with the cooperation of the New York Public Library). (1998). *The Kids' Guide to Research.* New York: Scholastic. **(I, M)**

I'd start with the 13th, and final chapter, "Hands-On Research," because I like my students to understand that research is a real-life activity, not something limited to finding things out for the purpose of writing an academic paper, which seems to be the definition in too many of our students' minds. This chapter recommends observing, experimenting, cooking and eating, making and doing things, all through the lens of the researcher. I'd work backward through the chapters giving advice on taking trips, interviewing people, conducting surveys. Then, I think, students will have a good broad context for interacting with the rest of the chapters, which focus on learning from reference books, the Internet, newspapers and magazines, books, visual resources. There's a good chapter on evaluating the reliability of sources.

Holbrook, S. (2002). *Wham! It's a Poetry Jam: Discovering Performance Poetry.* Honesdale, PA: Wordsong/Boyds Mills Press. **(I, M, H)**

After a rousing Introduction given in poetry form, the author provides a historical perspective on the topic of performance poetry with a quote:

> Do not commit your poems to pages alone.
> Sing them, I pray you.
>
> —Vergil*

At the bottom of the page comes the footnote:

> *Who in the name of holey sweat socks is Vergil? He's a Roman poet who performed his poems to audiences more than two thousand years ago. And folks are still talking about him. That's some kind of poet performer. (p. 10)

Holbrook has set the standard high, but the book gives great advice and even greater sample poetry. Readers will find the Call and Response format, which has been used throughout history in Africa, exemplified in a poem for today entitled "All My Fault?" (p. 13). There's advice about memorizing, attending to rhythm, voicing a point of view, composing poems for multiple voices, merging poems, and coordinating a poetry jam.

Janeczko, P. B. (2003). *Writing Winning Reports and Essays.* **Scholastic Guides Series.** New York: Scholastic. **(I, M, H)**

The writer of this guide, who is highlighted in Chapter 6 of this book, has a lot of credibility, since he makes his living writing and teaching writing. However, our students might also appreciate his confession that he was not a good writer in his school days:

> The words *torture* and *agony* come to mind. I remember spending countless hours . . . staring at the blank page, pencil clenched firmly in my fist, as if I could squeeze the words onto the page. . . . Part of the problem was the way I was taught writing. I wasn't. I was taught grammar and spelling. But that's not writing. (p. 6)

Janeczko encourages his readers to keep a writer's notebook, which he promises ". . . can turn out to be one of your best friends. . . ." (p. 5). He gives research tips and pointers about the craft in each section as well as sample essays representing various genres, such as writing about a person in **history,** writing a **science** report, writing a persuasive essay, and writing a problem–solution essay.

Leedy, L. (2004). *Look at My Book: How Kids Can Write and Illustrate Terrific Books.* New York: Holiday House. **(I, M)**

The author addresses her audience directly and respectfully as "Young Authors and Artists" (p. 3), then gives advice through various chapters on how to brainstorm, research, do rough sketches, revise and edit, design a layout, binding, and more. Cartoon writers with speech and thought bubbles allow readers to follow some fledgling writers through their composing processes. A list of further resources is at the end, including some on how to get published.

O'Neil, D. (2001). *The DC Comics Guide to WRITING Comics.* New York: Watson-Guptill Publications. **(M, H)**

This very practical guide is accompanied by graphic (no pun intended) illustrations from real comic books that help readers get the points. The author does not just give a simple formula; rather, he discusses topics such as story structure, subplots, characterization, and ways to create drama and humor, explaining and using comic book terminology when appropriate. He lists the advantages of writing a full script, and those of adopting a plot-first approach. By the time readers reach the Denouement (p. 118) of this book, they'll be thinking in terms of mega-series!

Reeves, D. L. (1998). *Career Ideas for Kids Who Like Writing.* New York: Checkmark Books. **(I, M)**

The very first page is interactive, set up like a "Choose Your Own Adventure" book, calling for readers to select either Choice A: "Wait until you're in college to start figuring out what you want to do" (p. 1), or Choice B: "Start now figuring out your options and thinking about the things that are most important in your life's work. . . ." (p. 2). The subsequent chapters lead the reader on a tour of working places of a journalist, a librarian, a paralegal, a talk-show producer, an author, an advertising copywriter, and other types of writers. The "Literary Agent" chapter exemplifies the format used in all of them. It first explains what a literary agent is and does, gives hints, book titles and website addresses on how to try out the job, suggests reading literary reviews in the newspaper by book critics who ". . . express their brutally honest opinions . . ." (p. 106), and invites the reader to assume the role of a critic with some best sellers or award winners. Then the picture and story of a literary agent are presented, along with his advice to young people thinking about joining the business.

Later sections give information about where to go for further investigation once a reader has narrowed her choices, and give steps for shadowing a professional. Recommended resources include some that target audiences who do not wish to go to college.

Rhatigan, J. (2003). *In Print!: 40 Cool Publishing Projects for Kids.* New York: Lark Books. (I, M, H)

The author talks directly to young aspiring writers, offering advice about the writing process; creative ways to get your messages seen, such as painting poetry on umbrellas and T-shirts; and resources and directions for actually sending work to publishers. Consider decorating your classroom by hanging your students' mood mobiles, or by making a doorway curtain by putting your students' writing in plastic photograph negative sleeves and attaching them to a curtain rod. Rhatigan encourages readers to start a writers' group, to play around with design possibilities, and to avoid the "Curse of the First Draft. That's when you write your first draft and fall instantly in love with it. . . . It's perfect . . . done" (p. 11). He counters with good tips for revision.

Schulman, M., & Krog, H. (2004). *Attack of the Killer Video Book: Tips & Tricks for Young Directors.* Art by M. Newbigging. New York: Annick Press. (M, H)

I could have put this in the **art** or **technology** section, but settled on here because much of this book had to do with composing as well as producing. First, the authors offer a little inspirational advice to be followed before making a movie:

> Try this simple exercise. Look in the mirror and ask yourself, "Am I a brilliant video master with 'Hollywood Legend' written all over my face?" Now move that face up and down. The answer is "Yes." (p. 6)

The book continues with advice in a multitude of areas: planning, technology, technique, special effects, leadership. It offers rules of visual storytelling; tips for choosing locations, props, and costumes; ways to work within a low budget; and a directing checklist. It ends with a sample script and a Glossary.

As the field of English language arts moves more toward involving multi-modality learning, books like this can bridge the textual and visual aspects of a middle school or high school English curriculum. For example, you might guide your students through the lesson on making a storyboard (pp. 17–18), just as movie directors and crews do in real life. Or draw attention to the lesson on editing (pp. 46–50) and compare it to other mini-lessons on editing you've given when students were writing essays, stories, or research papers.

Snicket, L. (2004). *A Series of Unfortunate Events: The Puzzling Puzzles: Bothersome Games That Will Bother Some People.* New York: HarperCollins. (I, M, H)

I don't think teachers will be among those bothered by the book series, which has delighted many readers, or by these puzzles, which can provide our students with vocabulary and with thinking opportunities in the name of fun. There are Muddling Math Tasks, Terminal Trivia, Laborious Language Games, Convoluted Grafts, Perplexing Pictures, and Enigmatic Enigmas. In other words—something for everyone! Readers will want to have their own copies so they can write in the book as they complete the many interactive activities in the form of word searches, mazes, crossword puzzles, and matching games.

Van Allsburg, C. (1996). *The Mysteries of Harris Burdick: Portfolio Edition.* Boston: Houghton Mifflin. (I, M, H)

Fifteen drawings are included in this set, but very little information is given about them by the author. The drawings are clues to some larger mystery; there will be as many interpretations and hypotheses as there are students in your class. Readers are invited to visit the website, www.hmco.com/vanallsburg, to share their own interpretations of these drawings and stories they create using the book's drawings as a stimulus. The posters, which come in the portfolio edition, displayed around your room will be a great start to transforming the classroom into a creative writing studio. There are hundreds of ways students can interact with the posters; it's a great way to show how a visual can stimulate the creation of new text.

LANGUAGES AND CULTURE

Farber, B. (1991). *How to Learn Any Language: Quickly, Easily, Inexpensively, Enjoyably, and On Your Own.* New York: Carol Publishing Group. (H)

I find this concept intriguing; while most language instructional books focus on a particular language, this one cuts across languages by introducing general principles. Teachers may ask students to see if the advice offered in chapters such as "The Multiple-Track Attack," "Harry Lorayne's Magic Memory Aid," "Gathering Your Tools," "Hidden Moments," and "Motivations" match the methods used so far in the courses they are teaching. Readers will want to try out the suggestions and then talk back to the author, in their chosen target language, of course!

Grayson, G. (2003). *Talking with Your Hands Listening with Your Eyes: A Complete Photographic Guide to American Sign Language.* Garden City Park, NY: Square One Publishers. **(M, H)**

I loved this book from its first sentence invitation: Welcome to the world of silent music and visual poetry that is the beautiful and expressive art of sign language!" (p. xiii). As well as fitting this description, ASL (American Sign Language) is a recognized language that fulfills schools' language requirements and is offered in increasing numbers of high schools and colleges. The lessons in this book are accompanied by photos of live models (Orchid, Alaina, Gabriel, and Monique, to whom we're introduced early on) communicating through hand signs and facial expressions. For each of the hundreds of signs included, the author gives a description of and position of the hand shape; instructions for the movement and direction of the hands; and instructions for the reader to visualize something connected to the meaning of the sign that will aid memory and understanding (e.g., holding on to a baseball bat, or a rabbit's ears twitching). Teachers and students together can follow the step-by-step instructions as they learn this language to communicate with each other.

McCulloch, J. (2001). *Mexico: A World of Recipes.* Chicago: Heinemann Library. **(I, M, H)**

Wouldn't you love to be known as the teacher in whose class students get to make Mexican hot chocolate, caramel custard, and cinnamon oranges? There are clear instructions for making salsa, nachos, guacamole, cheese-filled enchiladas, and many more delicious foods. But there's also information on geography, the history of farming in Mexico, cultural traditions surrounding mealtime and eating. A section on healthy eating is included, as well as resources for further exploration on both the country and the cooking.

Pirz, T. S. (2002). *Kids Stuff Inglés.* Shoreham, NY: Chou Chou Press. **(I, M, H)**

This book is filled with hundreds of English phrases for Spanish speakers. Each phrase is accompanied by a phonetic translation and a Spanish translation. The phrases are grouped by categories, such as shop-ping, school and home, mealtime, weather, time, seasons and holidays, animals, and clothes. The book includes a vocabulary list, a pronunciation guide, and an index. It's a helpful reference tool. Other books in the series by the same author will help readers who wish to be able to say phrases in Russian, French, German, and Italian.

Segal, J. (2003). *The American Sign Language Puzzle Book: The Fun Way to Learn to Sign.* New York: Contemporary Books. **(M, H)**

The author explains the various types of puzzles supplied at different levels of difficulty. There are alphabet puzzles, definition puzzles, pyramid puzzles, crossword puzzles, and so forth—in other words, something for everyone. He gives instructions for how to read the signs, explaining the aids such as arrows for showing the direction of the hand movement, the angle of the pictures, and the facial expressions used. In addition, the manual alphabet is provided. Teachers will want to model for students the signs provided to help communicate such topics as health, food, civics, religion, weather, family, sports, and money. The puzzles can be completed by individuals or by groups of students cooperating to figure out answers. Use this book in conjunction with another instructional text such as Mickey Flodin's *Signing Illustrated: The Complete Learning Guide* (2004).

Stacey, M., & Hevia, A. G. (2001). *Teach Yourself Beginner's Spanish.* Blacklick, OH: McGraw-Hill. **(M, H)**

This could be used as the primary text in an introductory course or a supplement to provide independent practice at home. Readers are told up front how to study sequentially the first 11 units, which are based on language functions, "uses of language that can apply to a wide variety of situations" (p. 2). The exercise sections engage the learner; the authors recommend solving the problems by going back to the Spanish passages and dialogues, using the key at the back of the book only when other strategies have failed. The final nine units are based on topics and can be studied in any order depending on needs and interests, as well as curricular demands. There are other books in this series introducing different languages students might like to investigate or pursue as they learn one language from their co-teachers: you and the authors of this book.

Stein, G. (2004). *Countdown to French: Learn to Communicate in 24 Hours.* New York: McGraw-Hill. **(H)**

Talk about a crash course! Challenge your students to see how much they can learn in a day (perhaps using the Job Try-Out strategy described in Part 2 of this chapter) with this book. The author gives numerous tips on pronunciation and grammar as well as the vocabulary needed to handle conversation in various places such as stores, hair salons, post offices, tourist attractions, medical establishments, airports, banks, train stations, and schools. The interactive exercises at the end of each chapter provide practice and self-assessment. Readers are instructed to fill in the blanks of passages, performing tasks such as asking for today's date, telling the time, handling getting film developed, and ordering a dessert. Readers or teachers can prioritize lessons based on their interests or needs. I recently used this book to prepare for a trip to Benin, and decided the first three sentences I would master in French would be, "I adore chocolate," "I have understood nothing," and "Help; I'm lost."

MATH AND TECHNOLOGY

Benjamin, A., & Shermer, M. (1993). *Mathemagics: How to Look Like a Genius Without Really Trying.* Los Angeles: Lowell House. **(M, H)**

Know immediately how much to tip the waiter? Multiply and divide faster than someone with a calculator? Look inside my shopping basket and know how much my grocery bill will be? That would take magic! Well, Dr. Arthur Benjamin is a mathematician and a magician. This book gives methods anyone can use to greatly improve their ability to calculate and problem-solve, and have fun and impress people besides. It promises to reduce the fear of math and replace it with awe. There are also sidebars with stories of mathematical geniuses, along with explanations for their extraordinary feats.

Teachers could put some of the pencil-and-paper mathematics examples on the board so that students will rush to class to see who can solve them first. Impress your students with your ability to do mental division and advanced multiplication; then share the secrets provided in the book.

Berg, B. (2000). *Opening Moves.* Photographs by D. Hautzig. Boston: Little, Brown and Company. **(E, I, M, H)**

Well, I never knew I could learn so much from a six-year-old! This book explains how Michael Thaler became a chess champion while in kindergarten and includes tips from the child himself regarding preparation, patience, respecting opponents, focusing, winning and losing, and keeping chess in perspective in the larger game of life. Pages are included that chart out the moves of some of his tournament games, through which teachers can guide students using a real chess set in the room or a virtual one

on the computer. The Afterword gives advice from Michael's parents on being a chess mom or dad.

After sharing this book in class, help your students investigate connections between math and chess, including the relationship between chess and improved math test scores, through exploring Internet sites. Teachers might also want to check out Todd Bardwick's *Teaching Chess in the 21st Century: Strategies and Connections to a Standards-Based World* (2004), which shows how to incorporate chess into the curriculum in ways that address the NCTM (National Council of Teachers of Mathematics) standards. It includes lesson plans on teaching chess that highlight math concepts.

Blum, R. (2002). *Mathamazing.* Illus. J. Sinclair. New York: Sterling Publishing. **(I, M)**

Readers of this book will learn math skills through card games, calculator riddles, brainteasers, jokes, and visual puzzles. The author provides clear instructions, and sometimes clues are upside down in boxes in case the reader gets stuck. Readers learn a bit of history, too. For example, the author introduces one game this way: "Go-Moku is a board game from the Far East that has been played for thousands of years. . . ." (p. 37).

Teachers will want to use Chapter 9, "Calculator Conjuring," to introduce a lesson on calculator use; they can impress a class with a magic trick from Chapter 5, "Arithmetricks," that will help students practice prediction skills as they tackle math problems.

Farmer, L. S. J. (1999). *Go Figure! Mathematics Through Sports.* Englewood, CO: Teacher Ideas Press. **(M, H)**

This book is directed at teachers, providing units that investigate mathematical concepts through the motivating context of sports, and providing a structure for lessons through the "Teacher Play Book" sections; teachers may choose appropriate examples to share with students as they teach their curricular content. But the "Warm-Ups" and "Student Game Plan" sections could also be explored and put into action independently by students. Many topics, including measurement, functions, geometry, statistics, and economics, are covered. Students will be fighting to be the first to get this math book off your shelf. Go figure!

Graham, A. (2001). *Teach Yourself Basic Mathematics.* Chicago: McGraw-Hill. **(M, H)**

For students who enjoy independent learning and like to go at their own pace, this is a wonderful book. Teachers can offer it both to students who need a challenge and to students who need extra practice with concepts taught in class. One useful

LANG/CUL

MATH

thing I liked is how it explains why certain math topics and procedures are useful. Anticipating the question "Why bother with percentages?" the author answers:

> The main advantages of percentages is that they are much easier to compare than fractions. . . . Which do you think is bigger, 3/4 or 7/10? Written like this, you can't really say, because the slices of the whole "cake" (quarters and tenths, respectively) are not the same size. In order to make a proper comparison, the fractions need to be broken down to the same size of slice, and hundredths are very convenient. So here goes. . . . (p. 76)

Hart-Davis, A. (1998). *Amazing Math Puzzles.* **Illus. J. Sinclair.** New York: Scholastic. **(M, H)**

After his Dedication "To my dear old dad," the author thanks those people who inspired his interest in math; the name of his first math teacher, Mr. Turner, sits right alongside Aristotle, Eratosthenes, Diophantus, Ian Stewart, and David Wells. The Table of Contents itself in intriguing: readers turn to puzzles named "Slippery Slopes," "Chewed Calculator," "Oddwins," "Sesquipedalian Farm," "The Rolling Quarter," "Crate Expectations," "The Pizza and the Sword," and dozens more. Solutions and explanations are provided, along with pictures and questions in the middle of puzzles that call for thinking while providing clues. Readers will build skills and confidence, as well as challenge family members, peers, and even teachers. Label the puzzles according to which curricular concepts they exemplify, and use them accordingly throughout the year. For example, use the "Puzzle of the Sphinx" (p. 78) and "Magic Hexagon" (p. 59) during a geometry unit.

Hemme, H. (1998). *Math Mind Games.* New York: Sterling Publishing. **(M, H)**

Heinrich Hemme is so passionate about creating mathematical puzzles he has written more than 400 articles and eight books full of them. This particular selection has 45 stories that show readers how they can think about everyday situations through a math lens. He muses about coins, people's ages, jigsaw puzzle pieces, calendars, speeds of bicycles, sizes of fences, bowling alleys. One story involves converting temperature measurements from Celsius to Fahrenheit; another involves a number generator spitting out random numbers. Math teachers will be able to find a puzzling story that will liven up lessons involving mathematical terms and concepts, including radius, divisibility, hypotenuse, estimate, minimal overlap, tetrahedron, quadratic equation, and frame of reference.

King, D. (2000). *Chess: From First Moves to Checkmate.* New York: Scholastic. **(I, M, H)**

The opening chapters give a lively history of this "game of war" (p. 6) and there are brilliant accompanying photographs throughout. Grandmaster Daniel King explains the basics and offers quiz questions that invite readers to think through some moves. The later chapters share fascinating stories involving the shortest and longest chess games, heroes of the genre, and information about computers that play chess. Teachers may provide the chess boards and playing pieces, explain the mathematical principles as students try various strategies, and then give a booktalk for King's *Games: Learn to Play, Play to Win* (2003) when students are ready for further mathematical challenges.

Long, L. (2003). *Groovy Geometry.* Hoboken, NJ: John Wiley & Sons. **(I, M, H)**

To some students, math is so foreign it seems like something outside the bounds of reality. The first chapter introduces readers to "The Magic of Geometry" and assures them that geometry can be learned experimenting with everyday objects. It introduces key terms, readying us for subsequent chapters on angles, quadrilaterals, solids, and more. Here's an example of a typical chapter: "Pythagorean Proof" starts with a problem (or puzzle activity), a question to think about, a list of materials needed (in this case graph paper, pencil, ruler, scissors, and glue), and directions for the procedure to solve the problem. The hands-on approach will demystify theorems and proofs for your students.

The Math Forum. (2003). *Dr. Math Gets You Ready for Algebra.* **Cartoons by J. Wolk-Stanley.** Hoboken, NJ: John Wiley & Sons. **(M, H)**

Even the concept of this book is interesting. "Math Doctors," who are ". . . trained volunteers drawn from a pool of college students, mathematicians, teachers, and professionals from the mathematical community" (p. 1) answer questions from letters written by real students having trouble with algebraic principles and problems. For instance, Carissa writes, "How would you solve a problem using scientific notation? I know it's used to multiply large numbers to get a correct answer, but I don't understand how to do it. Here's what I've tried. . . ." (p. 19). The good doctor replies with an introduction to the laws of exponents, along with an example. There's a Glossary, too.

This book could be used as a model for a program in your school, where anyone can write in with questions, and volunteers from the student body, staff, and community could reply, perhaps on a website for the benefit of all.

Miller, B. (2000). *Bob Miller's Geometry for the Clueless.* New York: McGraw-Hill. **(M, H)**

The title alone attracts readers, and some of your students will identify with the target audience, knowing the author is speaking of them, to them. And they'll figure they're not alone if there's a book with this name! Miller begins with basic definitions of words, along with some postulates and axioms. The chapters are filled with teaching, examples, and explanations of solutions. Finally, Chapter 18 has questions consisting of sentences with blanks to be filled in by readers with "always," "sometimes," or "never," allowing the reader to actively participate in the problems. The following chapter has the answers—no need to sweat and wait to find out how you did. It's a reassuring book.

Müller, R. (2001). *The Great Book of Math Teasers.* New York: Scholastic. **(I, M)**

The blurb on the back cover promises that some of the tough puzzles in this book ". . . will stretch your brain cells," which is exactly what we want for our students. There are problems embedded within little stories, puzzles connected with pictures of such common objects as matchsticks and chess boards, problems relating to probability. In the answer section in the back, the author talks readers through the steps needed to solve a problem, and sometimes offers more than one way to think about the scenario. For instance, for the problem called "Tournament," he begins, "First let's try a mathematical solution . . ." but follows this with a short example of reasoning through applying logic skills that arrives at the same answer. Teachers can connect certain problems to particular curricular standards or lessons, or just let students loose with the book!

Peterson, I., & Henderson, N. (2000). *Math Trek: Adventures in the Math Zone.* New York: John Wiley & Sons. **(M, H)**

This book invites readers to have fun the way mathematicians have fun. The authors explain in the Preface that mathematicians:

> . . . start with the math that you study in school. They use numbers, arithmetic, geometry, algebra, and calculus. Then mathematicians also wander far afield. They tackle tricky logic problems, explore mind-boggling mental mysteries, and investigate hidden patterns in the universe. Along the way, they often amuse themselves with mathematical puzzles and games. (p. vii)

The chapters in this book consist of categories of conundrums involving knots, maps, fractals, codes, cards, and more. After the solutions come interesting facts and explanations. For example, at the end of a chapter on billiard balls and pool hall games, the authors instruct:

> We now know that when physical laws involve the phenomenon called chaos, it is hard to separate skill from luck. The flippers in modern pinball machines add an element of skill to a game that is otherwise mostly random. (p. 90)

Teachers can provide the dice, explain the mathematics, and model strategies for playing the various games introduced in this challenging book.

Pickover, C. A. (2003). *Calculus and Pizza: A Cookbook for the Hungry Mind.* Hoboken, NJ: John Wiley & Sons. **(H)**

> I hope that Calculus and Pizza will stimulate creative thinking, get some students interested in computer programming, and suggest the usefulness of simple mathematics for solving curious, practical, and even mind-shattering problems. (p. x)

So states the author. What math teacher could ask for anything more? The narrator is Luigi, a New York City pizza shop owner, who tells us, "I love calculus because it is an intellectual triumph and, like pizza, can be appreciated by devouring a small slice at a time" (p. 1). He goes on to explain the function of time using the example of throwing pizza dough in the air. The end-of-chapter exercises involve pizza or other practical things readers can visualize.

Pickover, C. A. (2002). *The Mathematics of Oz: Mental Gymnastics from Beyond the Edge.* Cambridge, MA: Cambridge University Press. **(H)**

In this book, which contains numerous allusions to Baum's *The Wonderful Wizard of Oz* (2001, see Part 3 of this chapter), Dorothy is not transported by a tornado; rather, she's been abducted by mathematically obsessed aliens. (If your students have ever accused you of being obsessed with math or of being an alien, you might as well play along with texts like this one.) There are puzzles galore, involving geometry, sequences, sets, probability, number theory, and arithmetic. Once your students' minds are opened and imaginations activated, they'll be motivated to solve the problems you give them as you lead them down the yellow brick road of your curriculum.

Romanek, T. (2001). *The Technology Book for Girls: And Other Advanced Beings.* Illus. P. Cupples. Tonawanda, NY: Kids Can Press. **(I, M, H)**

This book sets out to demystify technology. For example, for the chapter on light, there's an explanation of how a car's instrument panel illuminates when headlights are turned on, a phenomenon a reader could observe in almost any car. Fiber-optic

MATH

cables are responsible for carrying the light; the term is defined, and then instructions for an experiment are included so that readers can "Try this activity to see how a stream of water reflects light the way an optical fiber does" (p. 35). An analogy helps readers think of a bundle of fiber optics as telescopes that bend in all directions. There are visuals, and then there's information on Janet Borman, a plant physiologist who uses optical fibers in her job. Each chapter contains these elements.

Winkler, P. (2004). *Mathematical Puzzles: A Connoisseur's Collection.* Natick, MA: A. K. Peters. (H)

Try reverse psychology to booktalk this one; read the first sentence of the Preface: "These puzzles are not for everyone" (p. ix). The author tells us his intended audience consists of amateur mathematicians, bright high school and college students, and teachers, among others. He's a professional mathematician, with 14 years in industry and an equal number in academia. He collects puzzles by word of mouth ("Among mathematicians, puzzles like these spread the way jokes spread" [p. ix]), and he keeps them if they meet his criteria in terms of amusement, universality, difficulty, and solvability. The topics of the conundrums presented here include algorithms, geometry, geography, combinatorics, games, and probability. At the end, he offers some unsolved (as of yet) puzzles. Your students might be the ones to unlock the mysteries within them and represented by them.

Zaslavsky, C. (2003). *More Math Games & Activities from Around the World.* Chicago: Chicago Review Press. (I, M)

Readers will enjoy the challenges of the games as they learn how people from many cultures use numbers, measure objects, think about designs and patterns. There are number games from Ghana, Sudan, Spain, South Africa, Germany, Ancient Egypt, India, and many other places. Students will see how math relates to Navajo weaving and embroidery from Japan. A chart is included that shows how the activities align with the National Council of Teachers of Mathematics standards as well as standards in other subjects, such as **language arts, art, science,** and **social studies.**

MUSIC

Anderson, S. (1999). *So, You Wanna Be a Rock Star?: How to Create Music, Get Gigs, and Maybe Even Make it BIG!* New York: Scholastic. (M, H)

The title is a question; so are many of the chapter titles (What's It Like to be a Rock Star?", "Will Anyone Come See Us?", "Will We Be Rich?") and so are many of the section titles within chapters. It's a great organizing format, for after the questions come good discussions, suggestions, and even answers. For example, after the question, "What about music lessons?" come tips on finding the right instructor, along with advice about supplementing lessons with "how-to" instrument videos and books (p. 39). You'll find biographical sketches and photos of real young rock stars and bands, as well as personal stories and quotes from these credible young musicians. Your students will learn how to do demos, work from a budget, find or create a name, start up a band, attract attention, and become better at the skills needed to be a star.

Baldwin, D. (2006). *Play Guitar by Ear: An Innovative Guide to Listening and Learning.* Milwaukee, WI: Hal Leonard Corporation. (H)

You could begin by surveying students about whether they think it's better to learn to play an instrument by reading music or by developing listening skills. Chances are answers will vary, based on students' own experiences and learning preferences. Then you could read the opening sentences from the Introduction:

> Any musician who claims not to play by ear is lying, unless he or she is deaf. It is common sense that you've got to have a good ear to play music well, and a musician with a good ear and little else is often more successful than one with good technical skills and encyclopedic knowledge, but little else. . . . Most well-schooled musicians study and practice the skills of listening to music and figuring it out quickly in addition to reading from notated music and following an instructor's direction.

Chapters include lessons on tuning a guitar by ear, feeling rhythms, figuring out chord progressions, song structure, riffs, and scales. Exercises are provided, as is a CD filled with examples and demonstrations.

Bany-Winters, L. (2000). *Show Time!: Music, Dance and Drama Activities for Kids.* Chicago: Chicago Review Press. (I, M)

I was impressed to find out that the author founded a theater company and began directing plays at age 15. She gives an overview of the history of musical theater, discusses pervasive themes of musicals, and gives instruction in the areas of drama, dance, and music so that readers can become performers known as *triple threats* (p. xiii). She gives suggestions for creating a modern-day Shakespeare musical, a musical based on a favorite book, and a puppet musical. Students learn about auditioning, using musical instruments, memorizing scripts, doing a story dance. Team-building activities are also included.

Borg, B. (2003). *The Musician's Handbook: A Practical Guide to Understanding the Music Business.* New York: Billboard Books. **(H)**

Bobby Borg, who wrote this book from his own experience and much research for the purpose of helping aspiring musicians who need business advice in layperson's language, has written my book-talk for me:

> **Why should you read this book?** Most musicians spend years developing their musical talent only to learn about the music business the hard way—one mistake at a time. Focused on their creative passions and the dream of an exciting career, musicians often leave business matters entirely in the hands of others. . . . If you want music to be your livelihood, you must treat it as a business or the business will take advantage of you. You must . . . learn how to manage the professional relationships you will encounter. . . . You will thereby earn the respect of your employers, your fellow band members, and others within the music industry. (p. 13)

Teachers may use this comprehensive book to help students understand a number of aspects of a musical career, including setting goals and maintaining a good attitude; preventing mental and physical burnout; negotiating employment contracts; dealing with attorneys, personal managers, business managers, and agents; understanding sources of revenue for musicians; copyright laws; touring; and merchandising. Readers of this book will likely be motivated to practice their music diligently, knowing they are becoming prepared to live their dream of making a living with the music they love to make. This valuable book would be great to have in your classroom library.

Chapman, R. (2005). *Eyewitness Companions: Guitar.* New York: Dorling Kindersley. **(H)**

After informative and interesting chapters on great guitarists and classic guitars, the book concentrates on skills and techniques, for beginners and more advanced players. Text and photographs work together to explain hand positions, tuning the guitar, playing positions, scales and timing, chords, and song sequences, as well as finger style, alternative picking, playing riffs, and much more. There's a Chord Dictionary and a Glossary, and addresses of many resources. Offer this book as a way of reinforcing the terms, concepts, and skills that are taught through your curriculum.

Gibson, D. (2005). *The Art of Mixing: A Visual Guide to Recording, Engineering and Production.* **2nd edition.** Boston: Thompson. **(H)**

Many of your students are already motivated to record music, so use their interest to teach numerous music principles and connect them to the use of equipment. For example, Gibson explains that one section:

> . . . covers the mathematical harmonic structure of the individual frequencies that make up all sounds, or timbres. These harmonics are the basic building blocks of sounds. Understanding the harmonic structure is critical to understanding why an equalizer works differently on different sounds. (p. xxiv)

This book talks to readers in a way that assumes they are actively creating mixes, not just learning about how to do it in some vague future time. The 249 visuals will help students as they apply the instructions and create mixes they can be proud of as they meet the standards of your curriculum.

Mattingly, R. (2006). *All About Drums: A Fun and Simple Guide to Playing Drums.* Milwaukee, WI: Hal Leonard. **(H)**

Can one earn a living playing drums? Based on the 15 jokes in the beginning of this book, many people (perhaps especially parents) would say no. But the text handles the topic in a respectful and serious way. The book is part "how-to": how to hold the sticks, play by ear, warm up, tune drums, repair cymbals, read music, create special effects. It also includes information on famous drummers; song transcriptions; and explanations of styles, including early rock 'n' roll, Jazz, Latin, blues, progressive rock, and funk. A CD is included, containing play-along songs and demonstrations of exercises. Teachers will want to offer this book to all students interested in pursuing drum playing for profit or for pleasure.

Melton, W., & Weinstein, R. (2006). *The Complete Idiot's Guide to Playing the Harmonica.* **2nd edition.** Indianapolis, IN: Alpha Books. **(M, H)**

A group of students could explore and apply the instructions in this book as other literature circles discuss what they learn from similar how-to books about the piano, drums, violin, flute, and other instruments. The book gives a history of harmonica playing and offers advice about how to purchase the harmonica that's right for the reader's purposes (and budget), how to play notes and chords, how to use body language while playing, how to read music, how to tune and repair harmonicas, and even how to get a job using the skills they've learned here. A CD containing over 80 riffs and songs comes with the book.

MUSIC

Moylan, W. (2007). *Understanding and Crafting the Mix: The Art of Recording.* **2nd edition.** New York: Elsevier. **(H)**

Students learn about a variety of ways to publish their writing in **English** class, and are helped to present the **art** they create in art class in venues around the school or community. They appreciate practical applications of the academic material they encounter throughout their school days and years. This book teaches numerous principles relating to the aesthetic and artistic elements of sound, as well as what a musician needs to understand about the expression of musical ideas, text as song lyrics, needs of listeners, and musical forms and structure. It includes accompanying exercises to develop evaluation, listening, and production skills. This book will help your students realize how much goes into good music recording, and it provides the tools to develop a unique creative style and to produce quality recordings.

Watson, C. J. (2003). *The Everything Songwriting Book: All You Need to Create and Market Hit Songs.* Avon, MA: Adams Media Corporation. **(H)**

The title promises a lot, and the book delivers. I couldn't think of anything that was left out of this informative and helpful text. Almost any music teacher's curriculum involves having students exercise their creativity, and many of our students already write poems and songs in the privacy of their homes or as part of an Internet community of aspiring artists. Chapters include a history of songwriting, advice about thinking like a songwriter, information about elements of lyrics and melody, song structure, a crash course in music theory, and tips about playing instruments. Other chapters get into the legal and business aspects of songwriting. Some readers will use this book as a springboard to start a career or enrich a hobby.

PHYSICAL EDUCATION, HEALTH, AND WELLNESS

Carter, R., with S. K. Golant. (1998). *Helping Someone with Mental Illness: A Compassionate Guide for Family, Friends, and Caregivers.* New York: Times Books. **(M, H)**

Rosalynn Carter begins her book with examples from the media that show the stigma of mental illnesses was still present at the time of the book's publication. She offers much in this book to dispel myths and help readers know how to be alert to jokes and stereotypes, and how to replace them with accurate facts and helpful advice. She explains symptoms of and treatments for schizophrenia, anxiety disorders, manic-depression (bipolar disorder), and several other illnesses. Chapters deal with pre-

vention, caregiving, and advocating. Students can follow up by researching newer medicines and scientific findings.

Cooper, E. (2005). *Um, Like ***OM: A Girl Goddess's Guide to Yoga.* Boston: Little, Brown and Company. **(M, H)**

The author talks directly to her audience both about how to read and how to actively use this book:

> You can read it from start to finish, but who are we kidding? You're going to skip around, check out some chapters before others, and look at the pictures. . . . I will show you how exercises as simple as breathing will keep you sane when everything in your world seems insane, and how twisting yourself into a knot can help straighten things out. . . . The series of exercises I am about to teach you is devised to lead you into a deep sense of calm and confidence. . . . (pp. 5–6)

Physical education and health teachers may join students in poses to help them feel energetic and stimulated as they approach the rest of their classes and beyond.

Duden, J. (2001). *Vegetarianism for Teens.* Mankato, MN: Capstone Press. **(M, H)**

Many of our students are choosing to be vegetarians, and often their families don't have a lot of information about how to make sure these adolescents are meeting all their nutritional needs. Books like this one, therefore, can be very helpful to have in your classroom. Different types of vegetarians are described, and a brief history of vegetarianism around the world is presented. Reasons for being vegetarian, including world hunger, concern for animals, the environment, spiritual beliefs, and health are discussed. The remaining pages deal with ways to buy food and cook so that vegetarians can achieve a balanced diet that addresses all of the food groups. There are quotes from teens and questions for discussion.

Garofalo, R., Jr. (2004). *A Winner by Any Standard: A Personal Growth Journey for Every American Teen.* Berlin, CT: Teen Winners Publishing. **(M, H)**

The challenges set forth in this manual are accompanied by empowering suggestions, stories, and information. Its chapters are divided into goals that are set forth as weekly ones; a reader would reflect and work on "Watching What You Eat" in Week 32, "Getting Involved with the Arts" by Week 36, "Handling Life's Pressures" during Week 38, and so on. But you could also divide the sections among your students, so that one student or team might choose to study and then teach their classmates about "Resisting the Body-Image Takeover" (Week 40) and "Searching Out

Heroes" (Week 46), while others are investigating pages relating to patriotism, economics, alcohol use, valuing mistakes, and being less judgmental. Life applications are boxed at the end of each chapter, making this an interactive book. For example, during Week 16, "Seeing the Wonder of It All," readers are instructed, "This week, find books in a local library or bookstore that list the natural wonders in your state or region, including guide books that describe state parks and other hiking areas. Also, check your state's tourism websites for places you can visit to enjoy the wonder of it all" (p. 74). Readers can record how they've participated in the weekly projects, add personal life goals to the ones already listed, and come back to the book later in the year to see what progress they've made.

Haduch, B. (2004). *Go Fly a Bike!: The Ultimate Book About Bicycle Fun, Freedom & Science.* Illus. C. Murphy. New York: Dutton Children's Books. (M, H)

In addition to being chock full of information about bikes and their history, this is a guide to bicycle safety, maintenance, and biking that is so much fun readers hardly recognize they're being given rules to follow. Its tone is humorous rather than preachy, with chapters such as "Getting Squished Can Really Ruin Your Day: Staying Safe on your Bike," "Take a Ride: You'll Feel Better: What Riding Does for your Body and Brain," "Show Your Bike You Care: Easy Bike Maintenance," and "Gadgets and Gizmos: Cool Accessories/Dumb Accessories." Exercises such as "Testing Your Slickness" and "An Important Cycle-Logical Test" make the book interactive. Reading this book caused me to bring my cool pink bike out of the cellar and pump up the tires. Teachers can connect the information in this book with other texts that discuss the health benefits of bicycling, and opportunities to join cycling clubs and participate in group cycling tours.

SCIENCE

Art, H. W., & Robbins, M. W. (2003). *Woods Walk.* North Adams, MA: Storey Books. (I, M, H)

Spectacular photographs will lure even the most sedentary among us into these woods. This book is a field guide, supplying loads of information about wooded areas in the East and West in all four seasons, and offering advice about how to be safe and smart while exploring the aspects of nature with all our senses. Readers are invited to go on night walks, find treasure underfoot, identify poisonous snakes, taste berries, watch for signs of changing weather, listen to birds and insects. So walk into this book, breathe deeply, and enjoy. Use this book to prepare

your students for nature walks on school grounds or beyond, or use it to provide a "literary field trip" as described in Part 2 of Chapter 3 that will entice students to later explore a forest setting near them.

Brandolini, A. (2003). *Fizz, Bubble & Flash: Element Explorations & Atom Adventures.* Charlotte, VT: Williamson Publishing Company. (I, M, H)

An entire chemistry course, labs included, is found in this multi-genre book that contains poetry, jokes, instructions for experiments, biographical blurbs on chemists, cartoons, predictions of the future, some kitchen chemistry, and explanations of the makeup and uses of the elements. This book will keep your classroom chemists amused, busy, and curious. Help them learn about and remember details of the periodic table, displayed on page 10, by having them recite "A Periodic Poem," on page 11.

Diehn, G., Krautwurst, T., Anderson, A., Rhatigan, J., & Smith, H. (2003). *Nature Smart.* New York: Main Street. (M, H)

Dozens of suggested projects are here, connected with scientific information. Students learn to make a wind chime and discover what seashells are made of and where they come from; make a seed mosaic as they learn about various seeds and who eats them; create a nocturne night dial to find the North Star and Cassiopeia; read about John Muir and the Sierra Club as they make papier-mâché birds. The illustrations of the steps of the projects and of wildlife are colorful and helpful.

Eugene, T., & Fisher, R. (2003). *Hiking America's Geology.* Washington, DC: National Geographic. (M, H)

The book jacket promises satisfaction for both serious hikers and armchair travelers. My first walk through this book consisted of looking at the pictures, amazed at the bright colors in the photographs. It's hard to believe these formations are real, and that people can actually be there along with them. Earth science teachers can lead students on a "literary field trip" in preparation for a final exam or Internet exploration of the parks and regions described in the text. Introduce the book to stimulate the desire in your students to explore their own regions and travel beyond to put into practice the lessons learned in *Hiking America's Geology*.

Hoyt, B. C., & Ritter, E. (2003). *The Ultimate Girls' Guide to Science: From Backyard Experiments to Winning the Nobel Prize!* Hillsboro, OR: Beyond Words Publishing. (I, M, H)

"Ever since the moment my seventh grade biology class stepped into our classroom to find trays of gelatinous cow eyeballs on our lab tables, my career

PE/HEALTH

SCIENCE

field was set" (p. 41). So speaks 17-year-old Victoria Shum, one of many children and teens who respond in this book to the question "Why do you love science?" asked intermittently. Also included are biographical sketches showing famous women's (including Mary Leakey, Mae Jemison, Dian Fossey, and Rachel Carson) love of science. The various quizzes are meant to assess a reader's interest in environmental science, the earth sciences, chemistry, space sciences, and physics and engineering. There are descriptions of the types of work involved in scientific careers, as well as advice and resources relating to how to pursue those tracks. Every aspect of this book is appealing.

Encourage your students to take the quizzes, and perhaps respond in letter form to the scientists, living and dead, featured in the book. This book would be ideal for the Job Try-Out strategy described in Part 2. Readers could also place the scientists along a timeline displayed in the classroom or hall.

Lawson, K. (2003). *Darwin and Evolution for Kids, with 21 Activities.* Chicago: Chicago Review Press. (M, H)

This book has everything—Darwin's biography, an explanation of various theories related to evolution, a history of how people thought about human origins and our relationships with other species before Darwin's time and after, and the story of the Scopes trial. The 21 activities are easy to do and are thought-provoking. Your students will be encouraged to bring an observation journal to a zoo in order to record monkey behavior, noting ways they are similar to humans and ways they are different. Suggested plant experiments will help active readers understand concepts such as acquired characteristics and the migration of plants. Your students will learn how to make fossils, and will enjoy a game with coins that teaches how sexual selection works. Finally, your students will be asked to combine their knowledge and their imaginations to predict how humans might evolve to survive in future environments, such as under water or outer space.

Levine, S., & Johnstone, L. (2001). *The Incredible Secret Formula Book.* Illus. J. Manders. New York: Scholastic. (E, I, M)

Almost 60 activities can keep your young scientists reading and learning while trying formulas for products like invisible ink, shrunken heads, electric slime, and face paint. They'll discover the structure of crystals as they cook hard rock candy; they're introduced to Monet as they create watercolors; they'll appreciate the value of following directions carefully as they make multi-color foam, fizzy bubble bath balls, and swirling lava. They'll amaze

friends and family with a mouth volcano! Include this good book in your lending library; let students take it home so parents and siblings can glimpse the fun in your science class.

Needham, B. (1998). *Ecology Crafts for Kids: 50 Great Ways to Make Friends with Planet Earth.* New York: Scholastic. (I, M, H)

Along with learning how to make the projects described and shown here, your students will learn about why it's so important to work from recycled and renewable materials in order to reduce waste and protect animal habitats. As they decorate birdhouses made from gourds, they can read about how early Native American Indians did the same. When they make bat houses from old barn wood, they'll have the satisfaction of knowing they're counteracting the destruction of natural bat homes. As they make crafts from discarded plastic containers, they can read the chapter explaining how scientists have found ways to recycle plastic by shredding and melting it, then turning it into clothes, carpets, bikes, and sandals. The students who are making ecology crafts today might be the scientists and engineers of the future, inventing new ways to save the earth they came to value through projects in your class.

Norman, P. (2004). *DNA Wizard.* Artwork A. Huff. El Sobrante, CA: Norman & Globus. (I, M, H)

The book in this book/kit combination begins with a chapter explaining cells, nuclei, and DNA; there are many diagrams. The next chapter invites readers to extract DNA from fruit cells, giving a list of necessary tools and ingredients along with step-by-step instructions. After the experiment is an explanation as to why it worked, and more information about the code of DNA. In addition, biographical information about Rosalind Franklin, a key scientist involved with DNA research, is included. Also provided are a chromosome puzzle, an experiment to figure out the gender of a baby, and lots more to entertain and stretch youngsters' minds. Teachers may match the activities with certain areas of their curriculum, encouraging students to be aware of their role as scientists as they perform the experiments.

Norman, P., & Norman, K. (2001). *Energy Wizard.* El Sobrante, CA: Norman & Globus. (I, M, H)

Before readers even open the book or explore the contents of the kit, they're invited to "Join the Race to Save the Planet!" (cover). Once inside, there's lots to do. The authors explain kinetic energy and potential energy, and they include an energy game. Later chapters give instructions for making a flywheel generator, a solar race car, and hydrogen. Students will learn through both reading and experimentation how solar cells and batteries work, and will acquire much-needed information on renewable sources of energy. Consequently, they'll become wise consumers and teachers of others in the interest of helping our wonderful, but vulnerable, planet.

Panchyk, R. (2005). *Galileo for Kids: His Life and Ideas: 25 Activities.* Chicago: Chicago Review Press. **(M, H)**

The author uses quotes from primary sources to bring us into the life and times of the genius Galileo. The experiments are interspersed throughout, so as your students learn about Galileo's increasing knowledge, they can increase their own insights and discoveries in terms of gravity, light and shadow, motion, projectiles, the moon, the pendulum. For example, your students will read, "As a mathematician, Galileo was fascinated by the many unique mathematical relationships of geometric shapes" (p. 151). Then they will be instructed to explore the concept of a cycloid curve, which occurs when a point on a wheel is followed as the wheel is rolled on a straight line for a complete revolution. The materials needed are readily attainable and include a Frisbee or other flying disc, adhesive tape, crayon, a piece of foam board, and a friend! (p. 151).

Ring, S. (2002). *Gross Anatomy.* Illus. A. Snow. Norwalk, CT: Innovative KIDS. **(I, M, H)**

Labeled interactive-reference, this book combines a reference guide, games, and experiments relating to anatomy. Its six chapters correspond to body systems, and can be read in any order. Vocabulary and concepts are taught painlessly as readers unfold pages to create charts, place stickers on a body, and compete in games such as "Brain Gain," "Bag o' Bones," "Down the Hatch," and "Sicko." The back cover advertises the book as "TOTALLY GROSS"; I consider it a totally awesome hands-on learning experience for biology students learning about the structure and functions of the organs of the human body.

Sobey, E. (2002). *How to Build Your Own Prize-Winning Robot.* Berkeley Heights, NJ: Enslow. **(M, H)**

This book provides directions for 15 projects, all leading to a machine the reader can control by designing and implementing a computer program. Readers will learn much from the explanations of various sorts of motors, batteries, gears, and circuit boards. They'll learn technical vocabulary such as *servo, capacitor, potentiometer,* and *voltmeter.* Teachers will want to connect particular steps in the process and examples of applications to concepts studied as part of the regular curriculum. This book could be used in an extracurricular robotics club. Resources are listed that will help students connect to others who have participated in robotics competitions and organizations. There is even information about an Internet robot contest.

Turner, M. (2004). *e.guides: Earth.* New York: Dorling Kindersley. **(I, M, H)**

Interactive from the start, *e.guides: Earth* will grab readers' attention as the author explains how to access and use the website created just for this book by DK and Google. The many chapters give loads of information about the sun and moon, magnetism, the age of the earth, landslides, erosion, earthquakes, tsunamis, glaciers, weather forecasting, and more. But for every topic, readers are just a click away from key words linking them to extended information and many more ideas for interactive learning. There's also a timeline of discoveries made about the earth, which you can re-create in your classroom. Students will want to follow up with *e.guides: Rocks and Minerals* (2005, New York: Dorling Kindersley), which is set up the same way and includes text and Internet resources for curricular topics including plate tectonics, metamorphic rock, fossils, gemstones, volcanoes, and space rock. The "Geology in the Field" section, along with connected websites, would be a good text to use for the Job-Shadowing strategy described in Chapter 3, Part 2.

Vecchione, G. (2001). *100 Award-Winning Science Fair Projects.* New York: Scholastic. **(I, M, H)**

All branches of science are covered by this guide, and each chapter follows a formula telling students what materials they'll need, step-by-step procedures, what results to expect from the experiment, and an explanation of the science principles involved. Some of your students might want to simulate Mars dust storms, while others will sample the soil around the school for microorganisms. I decided to try the experiment involving triboluminesence in wintergreen Life Saver candies. Now I'm a scientist!

Walker, R. (2002). *Human Body Lab: The Ultimate Human Body Pack.* Illus. S. Hill & J. Cameron. San Diego: Silver Dolphin Books. **(I, M)**

The book part of the pack is a lab manual, giving explicit instructions for more than 40 experiments relating to vision, aromas, the circulatory system, muscles, hearing, touch, bones, digestion—almost anything having to do with the workings of our marvelous bodies. The activities are hands-on for the most part, but the final chapter calls for involvement of the imagination as it deals with future bodies. It tells of amazing developments in terms of replaceable parts; robotic limbs that respond to signals from muscles and nerves; and nanorobots that will be able to travel along blood vessels, find dam-

SCIENCE

age, repair it, send messages to doctors. Teachers can guide students through the lab experiments and connect them to the work scientists do in a number of laboratories representing medical research, industrial research, etc. Maybe some of your students will someday take this a chapter further into the realm of possibilities.

Wiese, J. (2004). *Weird Science: 40 Strange-Acting, Bizarre-Sounding, and Barely Believable Activities for Kids!* Hoboken, NJ: John Wiley & Sons. **(I, M)**

This book will invite your students into the world of physics, meteorology, biology, geology, and chemistry with some simple experiments and explanations of principles. They will learn how to make a geyser, quicksand, and lava, as well as how time travel is theoretically possible. The book will enable them to understand the origins of mirages, the aurora borealis, and optical illusions. Your students will even discover the secrets of naked mole rats! Included are tips on being a good scientist, and some history of inventors and discoverers along with the projects.

Readers who want more can read Jim Weise's earlier book, *Movie Science: 40 Mind-Expanding, Reality-Bending, Starstruck Activities for Kids* (2001), also published by Wiley & Sons.

SOCIAL STUDIES/HISTORY

Braman, A. N. (2003). *The Maya: Activities and Crafts from a Mysterious Land.* **Illus. M. Nidenoff.** Hoboken, NJ: John Wiley & Sons. **(I, M, H)**

This book provides a hands-on, interdisciplinary approach to learning about the curricular topic of ancient Mayan civilization. Readers learn about daily life, food, the society, **architecture,** writing, **math,** and **science** in various chapters as they participate in projects ranging from following recipes for chili chocolate drink and corn cakes to solving Maya math problems; from making a mosaic mask to weaving a wall hanging; from communicating via personal glyph rubbing to engineering a wheeled toy. It would work well in a unit on ancient civilizations.

Glicksman, J. (1998). *Cool Geography.* **Illus. R. Daugavietis.** New York: Scholastic. **(I, M)**

A very busy book! Contained in its pages are definitions and explanations of geographical concepts; interesting historical information about maps, explorers, and geographers; and "Far Out Factoids," on topics ranging from sailors relying on birds to help them navigate to the many homes of the prime meridian. Readers will enjoy the Geography Hall of Fame, celebrating people from long ago, such as Eratosthenes (approximately 276–194 BCE), Thales (625–547 BCE), and Ptolemy (second century CE). "Brain Busters" call for high-level thinking skills, and resources such as website addresses for further study are included.

The factual information and activities are combined, so learning is seamless. Your students will discover how to make a grapefruit globe while learning latitude and longitude, and enjoy reading about the historical efforts at solving the longitude problem, one by Galileo using a special navigation helmet, the other called the Wounded Dog Theory. Your students will be able to experiment with finding their latitude from the North Star, as well as finding the longitude and latitude opposite their location. (They'll be able to supply a retort to those adults who tell them that if they dig a deep enough hole, they'll find China.)

The title is right—this **geography** is very cool.

Jacobs, T. (2003). *They Broke the Law—You Be the Judge: True Cases of Teen Crime.* Minneapolis, MN: Free Spirit Publishing. **(M, H)**

character booktalk

Sixteen-year-old Ronald was caught with beer and wine in a car; a breath test showed he had been drinking (though he wasn't the driver). What should be the consequence? Adam, age 15, threatened to kill some of his peers at school. What should the authorities do? Tanya, 14, was caught shoplifting a pregnancy test kit. How should she be punished?

The author of this book was the judge who sentenced these youths and 18 others whose cases he describes. In each situation, readers are given background information on the convicted children and teens, along with information about the laws they broke and questions to consider before deciding what the sentence should be. Jacobs even provides questions to help readers react to the actual sentences he pronounced. He asks if readers are surprised, if they disagree, and what they predict will happen to the youths in the future. He includes a personal letter written by 15-year-old Ashley from jail before her sentencing, pleading for compassion. "'I now know that doing drugs and being away from home was slowly but surely killing me. . . . I would be so grateful to have just one final chance to prove that I can be trusted'" (p. 51). This is followed by a letter written several months later, expressing thanks and telling about how much she learned from the experience. "Not to sound rude, but I don't ever want to see you again!! In court, of course!" (p. 53).

Teachers can use this book to promote critical-thinking skills, debating strategies, and writing skills

Klee, S. (2000). *Volunteering for a Political Campaign.*
Danbury, CT: Children's Press. **(I, M, H)**

The font is large, the text is easy, yet the book will give your students what they need to get started on this form of service learning. Photos and captions help readers see volunteers in action, stuffing envelopes, making posters, talking with others to learn about candidates and government campaign procedures. Teachers could help students apply concepts and information from this book as they design and participate in in-school election campaigns or mock elections during election years.

Merrill, Y. Y. (2002). *Hands-on Ancient People, Vol. 1: Art Activities About Mesopotamia, Egypt and Islam.*
Salt Lake City, UT: Kits Publishing. **(I, M, H)**

Your students will learn about ancient cultures and religions when they interact with this book, because all of the activities come with great explanations about the cultures and religions. As they make Babylonian mosaics, your students will apply **math** and **science,** as well as learn the history of the Ishtar Gate that was covered with animal mosaics. They may write secret messages using Arabic calligraphy, hieroglyphics, and cuneiform on clay tablets; replicate toys from Egyptian tombs; make prayer rugs; and design fabric pictures using characteristics of Islamic art such as tesselations, star polygons, and arabesques. The book contains patterns for the projects.

Miller, M. (2005). *You Be the Jury: Courtroom Collection.*
Illus. B. Roper. New York: Scholastic. **(M, H)**

For each of the 40 courtroom mysteries, both the plaintiffs' and the defendants' cases are presented, along with three pieces of evidence. After readers decide on a verdict, they can turn the page and turn the book upside down to read an explanation of the clues that lead to the conclusion of the defendant's guilt or innocence. Students could choose cases from the book to compose readers theatre activities or practice role playing in an **English** course or a course dealing with law. An example of a teacher-created guide for using this book is included in Part 2.

Panchyk, R. (2001). *Archaeology for Kids: Uncovering the Mysteries of Our Past: 25 Activities.* Chicago: Chicago Review Press. **(M, H)**

A compilation of fascinating information about archaeologists and their discoveries, this book also includes projects that involve students in various stages of the processes involved in archaeology. Your students can play a game that simulates underwater archaeology, learn how to preserve artifacts, make a historical map and a time capsule, and date objects using patent numbers. They'll feel comfortable with this occupation when they finish interacting with this text, so this book would be a good choice for use with the Job Try-Out strategy described in Part 2 of this chapter.

REFERENCES

Alvarado, A. E., & Herr, P. R. (2003). *Inquiry-based learning using everyday objects: Hands-on instructional strategies that promote active learning in grades 3–8.* Thousand Oaks, CA: Corwin Press.

Bryant, R. J. (2003). Toothpick chromosomes: Simple manipulatives to help students understand genetics. *Science Scope, 26* (7), 10–15.

Carr, E., & Ogle, D. (1987). K-W-L Plus: A strategy for comprehension and summarization. *Journal of Reading, 30,* 626–631.

Carter, C. S, Cohen, S., Keyes, M., et al. (2000). *UnCommon knowledge: Projects that help middle-school-age youth discover the science and mathematics in everyday life. Volume Two: Hands-on math projects.* Charleston, WV: AEL.

Carter, C. S., Keyes, M., Kusimo, P. S., et al. (2000). *UnCommon knowledge: Projects that help middle-school-age youth discover the science and mathematics in everyday life. Volume One: Hands-on science projects.* Charleston, WV: AEL.

Carter, D. A., & Diaz, J. (2004). *Let's make it pop-up.* New York: Little Simon.

Dresang, E. T. (1999). *Radical change: Books for youth in a digital age.* New York: H. W. Wilson.

Eggleton, P. (2001). Triangles á la Fettuccine: A hands-on approach to triangle-congruence theorems. *Mathematics Teacher, 94* (7), 534–537.

Flannery, M. C. (2001). Hands-on—In many different ways. *American Biology Teacher, 63* (4), 282–285.

Friedrichson, P. M. (2001). Moving from hands-on to inquiry-based: A biology course for prospective elementary teachers. *American Biology Teacher, 63* (8), 562–568.

Gay, K. (2004). *Volunteering: The ultimate teen guide.* Lanham, MD: Scarecrow Press.

Heard, P. S., Divall, S. A., & Johnson, S. D. (2000). Can 'ears-on' help hands-on science learning—for girls and boys? *International Journal of Science Education, 22* (11), 1133–1146.

Huber, R. A., & Moore, C. J. (2001). A model for extending hands-on science to be inquiry-based. *School Science and Mathematics, 101* (1), 32–42.

Johnsen, S. (1997). Hands-on learning. *Gifted Child Today, 20* (2), p. 5.

Johnston, T. (2002). Hands-on high. *Teacher Magazine, 13* (5), 24–29.

Kurkjian, C., Livingston, N., Henkes, K., Sabuda, R., & Yee, L. (2005). Evocative books: Books that inspire personal response and engagement. *The Reading Teacher 58* (3), 480–488.

Moch, P. L. (2001). Manipulatives work! *Educational Forum, 66* (1), 81–87.

Moore, D. A., & Cortes-Figueroa, J. E. (2001). Hands-on discovery of mirror planes. *Journal of Chemical Education, 78* (1), 49.

Moyer, P. S., Bolyard, J. J., & Spikell, M. A. (2002). What are virtual manipulatives? *Teaching Children Mathematics, 8* (6), 372–377.

Ogle, D. (1986). KWL: A teaching model that develops active reading of expository text. *The Reading Teacher, 39* (6), 564–570.

Palladino, M. A., & Cosentino, E. (2001). A DNA fingerprinting simulation laboratory for biology students: Hands-on experimentation to solve a mock forensic problem. *American Biology Teacher, 63* (8), 562–568.

Sippola, A. E. (1995). K-W-L-S. *The Reading Teacher, 48* (6), 542–543.

Smith, S., & Reese, S. (2003). Vital virtual hands-on learning. *Techniques: Connecting Education and Careers, 78* (6), 35–37.

Smolkin, L. B., & Donovan, C. S. (2003). Supporting comprehension acquisition for emerging and struggling readers: The interactive information book read-aloud. *Exceptionality, 11* (1), 25–38.

Stein, M. K., & Bovalino, J. W. (2001). Manipulatives: One piece of the puzzle. *Mathematics Teaching in the Middle School, 6* (6), 356–359.

Strutchens, M. E., Harris, K. A., & Martin, W. G. (2001). Assessing geometric and measurement understanding using manipulatives. *Mathematics Teaching in the Middle School, 6* (7), 402–405.

Tapscott, D. (1997). *Growing up digital: The rise of the net generation.* New York: McGraw-Hill.

Teshome, Y., Maushak, N., & Athreya, K. (2001). Attitude toward informal science and math: A survey of boys and girls participating in hands-on science and math (Funtivities). *Journal of Women and Minorities in Science and Engineering, 7* (1), 59–74.

VanCleave, J. (2004). *Janice VanCleave's scientists through the ages.* Hoboken, NJ: John Wiley & Sons.

Weiss, J., & Kahn, R. (2004). *145 things to be when you grow up: Planning a successful career while you're still in high school.* New York: Random House.

Welton, E. N., Smith, W. S., & Owens, K. D. (2000). Hands-on science as a motivator for children with emotional/behavioral disabilities. *Journal of Elementary Science Education, 12* (2), 33–37.

Zollman, D. A., Rebello, N. S., & Hogg, K. (2002). Quantum mechanics for everyone: Hands-on activities integrated with technology. *American Journal of Physics, 70* (3), 252–259.

LITERATURE CITED

If you don't find a book listed here, it is included in Part 4, Annotated Books and Booktalks.

Barchers, S. I. (2000). *Multicultural folktales: Readers Theatre for elementary students.* Englewood, CO: Teacher Ideas Press.

Bardwick, T. (2004). *Teaching chess in the 21st century: Strategies and connections to a standards-based world.* Englewood, CO: Chess Detective Press.

Bolotin, N., & Herb, A. M. (1995). *For home and country: A Civil War scrapbook.* New York: Lodestar Books/ Dutton.

Carter, D. A., & Diaz, J. (1999). *The elements of pop-up.* New York: Simon & Schuster.

Check, L. (2002). *The kids' guide to making scrapbooks and photo albums!: How to collect, design, assemble, decorate.* Illus. B. Day. Charlotte, VT: Williamson.

Fleming, C. (2005). *Our Eleanor: A scrapbook look at Eleanor Roosevelt's remarkable life.* New York: Atheneum Books for Young Readers.

Flodin, M. (2004). *Signing illustrated: The complete learning guide.* New York: Perigee.

Gelb, M. (2002). *Discover your genius: How to think like history's ten most revolutionary minds.* New York: HarperCollins.

King, D. (2003). *Games: Learn to play, play to win.* Boston: Kingfisher.

Kwon, J. K., & Tenner, S. (2005). *Because of Winn-Dixie: The official movie scrapbook.* Cambridge, MA: Candlewick Press.

Nye, N S. (2005). *19 varieties of gazelle: Poems of the Middle East.* New York: HarperTempest.

Rogers, K. (2001). *The Usborne Internet-linked complete book of the microscope.* New York: Scholastic.

Rothamel, S. P. (2005). *The encyclopedia of scrapbooking: Tools & techniques.* New York: Sterling Publishing.

Sabbeth, C. (2005). *Frida Kahlo and Diego Rivera—Their lives and ideas: 24 activities.* Chicago: Chicago Review Press.

Concluding Thoughts

"Nothing is impossible if we have the courage to turn our dreams into reality."

ASTRONAUT BUZZ ALDRIN, 2005

A Final Scenario

I n Chapter 2, I asked you to imagine a middle school where the faculty had devoted a week to an interdisciplinary exploration of the Lewis and Clark Expedition. Now I invite you to peek in at a high school/community reading event:

Each year, a committee consisting of a librarian, an administrator, a local bookstore manager, teachers, students, and other interested people choose a book that everyone in the community will be invited to read over the summer. The selections usually offer interdisciplinary opportunities, but the main criteria are that the book must be interesting; have wide appeal; and have the power to evoke and provoke thought and discussion. This year, the selected book is Mark Haddon's *The Curious Incident of the Dog in the Night-time* (2003). (You were introduced to this book in Chapter 4.) It's a mystery, narrated by a 15-year-old boy, very bright and likeable, who exhibits characteristics of autism spectrum disorders. It offers humor, intrigue, surprise, and a great plot.

Graduating eighth graders are given paperback copies of the book as a welcoming gift from the high school they'll be attending. Parents have been sent letters suggesting that they obtain the audio version to listen to in the car on a family trip, or find other ways to discuss the story and their reactions to it. During the summer, the book is readily available throughout the town at libraries and bookstores. Signs in restaurant windows and in mall stores, including sporting good stores, department stores, and music stores, say, "We've read *Curious Incident*. Come in and talk to us about it!" In one mall, a huge wall has been devoted to drawings and comments related to the book that readers want to post there. A community Internet blog offers another opportunity for sharing opinions and responses.

Once school starts in the fall, conversations about the book and its themes continue in the hallways and cafeteria. Math teachers have books, websites, and games available dealing with prime numbers and other mathematical principles that protagonist Christopher Boone loves. English teachers offer students in all grade levels other fiction books with characters who have autism, Asperger's syndrome, or similar conditions; the choices include *Al Capone Does My Shirts,* by Gennifer Choldenko (2004), Lois Lowry's *The Silent Boy* (2003), and *The Speed of Dark,* by Elizabeth Moon (2003). They also provide biographical and autobiographical accounts of people who have various differences and disabilities. Science teachers have informational books, such as *Unstrange Minds: Remapping the World of Autism,* by Roy Richard Grinker (2007) along with recent articles about autism and current research being done in the field. Classroom libraries contain other texts by Mark Haddon. Students, teachers, and administrators are learning together.

Throughout the year, there are featured presentations that relate to the topics in *The Curious Incident.* The documentary "Autism Is a World" (Rubin & Margulies, 2004) is shown one Friday night. An assembly features a panel consisting of two current students who have autism (who initiated the event) and two former students with autism who are now attending college in the area. An art show highlights the work of people who have autism or other differences. There's a guest speaker from the state Autism Society, who gives students pins representing "Autism Awareness." There are math club meetings featuring puzzles, games, and contests.

The possibilities are endless when a community decides to read a book in common and see where it leads. Many cities and colleges are doing just that, so there are resources available to get such a project started. You could begin by asking a librarian to find examples and to suggest books to consider as a common text. The climate of a school can change when everyone reads.

If you've made it this far, you probably have a very long book list for imminent and future reading. Isn't that a good feeling? I'd like to end by reviewing the reasons for using trade books in our content area courses. First, there's the benefit for you, the teacher. Reading widely and deeply makes you even more knowledgeable and passionate about your subject area, and teaching with passion is good for students, as Moorman et al. (2007) show in an article titled "Teaching with Passion, Learning by Choice." The introduction promises the story of teachers who "dared to dream of teaching their passions and found a way to make their dreams come true" (p. 33). Since "teachers are the single most important factor that determines students' level of achievement" (Parris & Block, 2007, p. 583), you'll want to continue to grow in ways that will impact the academic growth as well as the passion of your students. Reading trade books can help toward this goal, for, as Parris and Block (and researchers before them whom they cite) found, a characteristic of highly effective secondary teachers is that "they implement intellectually challenging and widely varied reading and writing activities" (p. 584).

On the other hand, Azar Nafisi, whose *Reading Lolita in Tehran: A Memoir in Books* (2003) chronicles the secret, subversive book club she led in the repressive political climate of the Islamic Republic of Iran, puts personal enjoyment at the top of her reasons why we should read:

> You know, because books should be read for no benefit in mind. They should be read because of the joy and the pleasure of reading, and that joy and pleasure should always be shared. . . . Nabokov used to say, "Readers are born free, and they ought to remain free." We always talk about the freedom of writers. We forget that readers should also be free. (Ryan, 2007, p. 5)

Another reason to share our love of reading with our students and introduce them to books that engage their interest is that our influence on them will go far beyond the year or two that we have them in class. Lesesne (2007) points out that schools may do a good job of developing "school-time readers" (p. 53), but our goal is to develop lifelong readers. You can be the teacher who is remembered for initiating what Lesesne calls *unconscious delight.* "During this stage, we become lost in a book. Reality slips away and we fall into the story to such an extent that we lose touch with the world around us" (p. 53).

But I don't want to get too far away from reality here; we content area teachers have to remain firmly rooted in reality. The good news is that most of the trade books promoted in these chapters are indeed based on the real stuff of our disciplines. They introduce real practitioners, real present-day and historical dilemmas, real questions posed for real readers. Reading a variety of books can help our students become real participants in the pursuit of learning. Harste and Leland (2007) note that with virtually all commercial education programs:

> Students rarely, if ever, are expected to make real contributions to the existing knowledge base. Even in the more innovative programs, they are expected only to "discover" what is already known. Instead of taking their place on the front line of knowledge construction, they find themselves on the sideline. Under these conditions, it's little wonder that so many students see their school experiences as irrelevant and respond with perfunctory efforts. (p. 7)

When students read content-related trade books that interest them, and then share what they learn with peers who have read different materials, that's active engagement. That's real learning.

Let's look at a specific example. Sting is a code name used by a 14-year-old who was failing his English course. He hated reading the anthology used in class; he resisted reading it, and often argued with his teacher about it, and consequently was sent to the office. However, he was drawn into a trade book:

> I didn't mind the Anne Frank one,
> The way it was put,
> It just caught my attention
> Made me read.
> In the beginning I didn't really want to read it . . .
> I thought it was kind of sad . . .

Because of everything that was goin' on,
And they had to be locked up.

When I'm pretendin' all this stuff in my head
I'm usually in it, too.
I pictured her—
I pictured me as one of the characters
I just put me in the picture,
And then it felt like I was in the story already. (Reeves, 2004, p. 46)

A final example is that of Roy Daniels, a professor of biochemistry and genetics at Stanford University who has written over 175 articles about his research on muscular dystrophy and cystic fibrosis, among other topics. Daniels struggled throughout his school years due to a severe reading problem, and still has difficulty with decoding and visual-graphic skills. Yet he had a passionate interest in science; so, in addition to conducting science experiments at home, he read avidly from advanced science books to satisfy his desire to know how things worked. In grade school he loved to learn about airplanes; by eighth grade he was fascinated by propellant systems; in ninth he was reading complex texts in nitrogen chemistry. Fink (2006) reports that Daniels benefited ". . . when traveling library vans carried enticing science books to his neighborhood" and ". . . from teachers who mentored him, directing him to advanced books and magazines about chemistry, engineering, and calculus" (p. 73).

Let's make books available in every content classroom, at every grade level, in every school. Let's dream big. The Roy Daniels and the Stings and all the other "specific individual human beings" (Wilhelm, 2007) in our classrooms need us to do this, and they deserve nothing less.

REFERENCES

Fink, R. (2006). *Why Jane and John couldn't read—And how they learned: A new look at striving readers*. Newark, DE: International Reading Association.

Harste, J. C., & Leland, C. (2007). On getting lost, finding one's direction, and teacher research. *Voices from the Middle, 14* (3), 7–11.

Lesesne, T. (Ed.). (2007). Getting lost in a book: Unconscious delight and lifelong readers. *Voices from the Middle, 14* (3), 53–56.

Moorman, H., with DeHart, B., Flieger, R., Gregory, N., Ozuna, L., Perret, L., Reed, D., Stengel, A., & Valdés, L. M. (2007). Teaching with passion, learning by choice. *English Journal, 96* (4), 33–38.

Parris, S. R., & Block, C. C. (2007). The expertise of adolescent literacy teachers. *Journal of Adolescent and Adult Literacy, 50* (7), 582–596.

Reeves, A. R. (2004). *Adolescents talk about reading: Exploring resistance to and engagement with text*. Newark, DE: International Reading Association.

Rubin, S., & Margulies, J. (2004). *Autism is a world*. CNN.

Ryan, L. T. (2007). Azar Nafisi. *The Post-Standard/Stars Magazine*, April 8, 3–5.

Wilhelm, J. D. (2007). Personalizing our teaching: No specific human being left behind. *Voices from the Middle, 14* (4), 40–41.

LITERATURE CITED

Choldenko, G. (2004). *Al Capone does my shirts*. New York: G. P. Putnam's Sons.

Grinker, R. R. (2007). *Unstrange minds: Remapping the world of autism*. New York: Basic Books.

Haddon, M. (2003). *The curious incident of the dog in the night-time*. New York: Doubleday.

Lowry, L. (2003). *The silent boy*. Boston: Houghton Mifflin.

Moon, E. (2003). *The speed of dark*. New York: Ballantine Books.

Nafisi, A. (2003). *Reading Lolita in Tehran: A memoir in books*. New York: Random House.

Author and Title Index

Motion: American Sports Poems, 248

Mountain Solo, 142

Mountains Beyond Mountains: The Quest of Dr. Paul Farmer, a Man Who Would Cure the World, 151

Moveable Mother Goose, The, 279

Moyer, P. S., 262

Moylan, W., 294

Mozart Season, 142

Mufaro's Beautiful Daughters: An African Tale, 6

Muhammad, 159, 208

Mullen, C. A., 2

Müller, R., 291

Murphy, C. R., 144

Murphy, J., 25, 44, 133

Musical Prodigies: Perilous Journeys, Remarkable Lives, 142

Musician's Handbook: A Practical Guide to Understanding the Music Business, The, 50, 293

My America: A Poetry Atlas of the United States, 254

My Brain Is Open: The Mathematical Journeys of Paul Erdos, 174, 195

My Brother Vincent van Gogh, 185

My Contract with Henry, 133

My Diary from Here to There/Mi Diario de Aqui hasta Allá, 73

My Father Had a Daughter: Judith Shakepeare's Tale, 133

My Fellow Americans: A Family Album, 158

My Mother's Daughter: Four Greek Goddesses Speak, 131

My Name Is Sus5an Smith, the 5 Is Silent, 128

My Thirteenth Winter: A Memoir, 192

Myers, W. D., 90, 109, 111, 123, 124, 132, 226, 248, 255

Mysteries of Harris Burdick: Portfolio Edition, The, 287

Na, A., 136

Naden, C. J., 39

Nafisi, A., 96, 102, 135, 303

Namioka, L., 136

Napoleon's Buttons: How 17 Molecules Changed History, 83

Nardo, D., 98

Nasar, S., 75, 194, 230

National Center for Educational Statistics, 2

Native American Stories and Nocturnal Activities for Children, 238

Native Son, 189

Native Son: The Story of Richard Wright, 189

Nature Smart, 295

Navajo: Visions and Voices Across the Mesa, 244

NCTM, 75

Needham, B., 275, 296

Neighborhood Odes, 222, 227

Nelson, M., 25, 198, 230, 242, 251

Nelson Mandela: A Photographic Story of a Life, 207

Nelson, T., 132

Neruda, P., 226, 228

Neville, K., 140

New and Selected Poems, 245

Newmann, F., 3

Nguyen, D., 283

Nicolaus Copernicus: The Earth Is a Planet, 201

Night Before Christmas, The, 279

Night Is Gone, Day Is Still Coming: Stories and Poems by American Indian Teens and Young Adults, 245

Night the Martians Landed: Just the Facts (Plus the Rumors) About Invaders from Mars, The, 183

Night Without Armor, A, 247

Nightjohn, 208

Nilsen, A. P., 36, 98, 100, 283

Nine Horses, 237

1968: The Year That Rocked the World, 89

19 Varieties of Gazelle: Poems of the Middle East, 234, 283

Ninjas, Piranhas, and Galileo, 149

Niven, P., 242

Nolan, H., 107

No More!: Stories and Songs of Slave Resistance, 79

Norman, P., 296

Northern Light, A, 129

Norton, D. E., 36, 163, 171

Nothing But the Truth, 129

Nuclear Disaster, 48

Number Devil, The, 139

Nye, N. S., 231, 234, 235, 239, 283

Oaxaca journal, 53

Occhoa, A. P., 245

Ocean Apart, a World Away, An, 136

O'Connor, P. T., 72

October Sky, 202

Odd Boy Out: Young Albert Einstein, 200

O'Dell, S., 27

Odes to Common Things, 226

"Ode to Pablo's Tennis Shoes," 222

Odifreddi, P., 76

Of Sound Mind, 135

Oh Rats: The Story Of Rats And People, 81

O Jerusalem, 257

Oldfather, P., 9

Old Man and the Sea, The, 132

Olive's Ocean, 130

Olson, K. M., 170

One Grain of Rice: A Mathematical Folktale, 106

100 Award-Winning Science Fair Projects, 297

O'Neil, D., 266, 286

1,000 Places To See Before You Die: A Traveler's Life List, 54, 91

On Writing: A Memoir of the Craft, 189

O'Reilly, G., 72

Open Your Eyes: Extraordinary Experiences in Faraway Places, 191

Opened Ground: Selected Poems 1966–1996, 228–229

Opening Moves, 289

Opportunities in Visual Arts Careers, 50

Orgel, D., 131

Or Give Me Death, 152

Orphans of Normandy: A True Story, The, 73

Osa, N., 136

Our Documents: 100 Milestone Documents from the National Archives, 52, 60, 87

Our Eleanor: A Scrapbook Look at Eleanor Roosevelt's Remarkable Life, 272

Out of the Dust, 100, 101, 104, 219–220

Outcasts of 19 Schuyler Place, The, 128

Outsiders, The, 156, 191

Outside the Magic Circle: Autobiography: Virginia Foster Durr, 157

Overheard in a Bubble Chamber: And Other Science Poems, 246, 251

Owl Moon, 6

Painter's Eye: Learning to Look at Contemporary American Art, The, 181

Paint Me Like I Am: Teen Poems from WritersCorps, 239

Palincsar, A. S., 48

Palmer, R. G., 37

Palm of My Heart: Poetry by African American Children, 243

Panchyk, R., 266, 297, 299

Paperboy: Confessions of a Future Engineer, 194

Papier-Mache (Kids Can Do It), 284

Pappas, C. C., 17

Pardo, L., 27

Park, B., 145

Park, L. S., 99, 128

Parker, B., 83

Parris, S. R., 303

Parrot in the Oven: Mi vida, 135

Partners, 84

Partridge, E., 63, 64, 197

Paschen, E., 242

Paterson, K., 96

Patz, N., 222

Paulsen, G., 128, 132, 137, 138, 208

Pawlak, M., 244

Payment, S., 195

Payne, C. F., 250

Pencil: Its History and Design, The, 194